Dedication

Dedicated to the fine faculty at my alma mater, Northeast Missouri State University. In particular, I would like to thank: Dr. Monica Barron, Dr. Dennis Leavens, Dr. Ed Tyler, and Dr. Cole Woodcox, whom I also have the pleasure of calling my friend. I would not be who I am as a writer, as a student, as a teacher, or as a person if it were not for the magnanimous, affecting, and brilliant instruction I received from these educators.

Special Thanks to:

My heartfelt thanks to everyone at Peachpit Press, as always.

My gratitude to editor extraordinaire Rebecca Gulick, who makes my job so much easier. And thanks to Patricia Pane for her hard work, helpful suggestions, and impressive attention to detail. Thanks also to Valerie Haynes-Perry for indexing and Myrna Vladic and Deb Roberti for laying out the book, and thanks to Anselm Bradford for his technical review.

Kudos to the good people working on PHP, MySQL, Apache, phpMyAdmin, MAMP, and XAMPP, among other great projects. And a hearty "cheers" to the denizens of the various newsgroups, mailing lists, support forums, etc., who offer assistance and advice to those in need.

Thanks, as always, to the readers, whose support gives my job relevance. An extra helping of thanks to those who provided the translations in Chapter 17, "Example—Message Board," and who offered up recommendations as to what they'd like to see in this edition.

Thanks to Karnesha and Sarah for entertaining and taking care of the kids so that I could get some work done.

Finally, I would not be able to get through a single book if it weren't for the love and support of my wife, Jessica. And a special shout-out to Zoe and Sam, who give me reasons to, and not to, write books!

Table of Contents

PHP and MySQL

for Dynamic Web Sites

Fourth Edition

LARRY ULLMAN

 Peachpit Press

Visual QuickPro Guide
PHP and MySQL for Dynamic Web Sites, Fourth Edition
Larry Ullman

Peachpit Press
1249 Eighth Street
Berkeley, CA 94710
510/524-2178
510/524-2221 (fax)

Find us on the Web at: www.peachpit.com
To report errors, please send a note to: errata@peachpit.com
Peachpit Press is a division of Pearson Education.

Editor: Rebecca Gulick
Copy Editor: Patricia Pane
Technical Reviewer: Anselm Bradford
Production Coordinator: Myrna Vladic
Compositor: Debbie Roberti
Proofreader: Bethany Stough
Indexer: Valerie Haynes-Perry
Cover Design: RHDG / Riezebos Holzbaur Design Group, Peachpit Press
Interior Design: Peachpit Press
Logo Design: MINE™ www.minesf.com

COLEG SIR GAR
GRAIG CAMPUS

BBfS

ISBN-13: 978-0-321-78407-0
ISBN-10:   0-321-78407-3

9 8 7 6 5 4 3 2

Printed and bound in the United States of America

Introduction

Today's Web users expect exciting pages that are updated frequently and provide a customized experience. For them, Web sites are more like communities, to which they'll return time and again. At the same time, Web-site administrators want sites that are easier to update and maintain, understanding that's the only reasonable way to keep up with visitors' expectations. For these reasons and more, PHP and MySQL have become the de facto standards for creating dynamic, database-driven Web sites.

This book represents the culmination of my many years of Web development experience coupled with the value of having written several previous books on the technologies discussed herein. The focus of this book is on covering the most important knowledge in the most efficient manner. It will teach you how to begin developing dynamic Web sites and give you plenty of example code to get you started. All you need to provide is an eagerness to learn.

Well, that and a computer.

What Are Dynamic Web Sites?

Dynamic Web sites are flexible and potent creatures, more accurately described as *applications* than merely sites. Dynamic Web sites

- Respond to different parameters (for example, the time of day or the version of the visitor's Web browser)

- Have a "memory," allowing for user registration and login, e-commerce, and similar processes

- Almost always integrate HTML forms, allowing visitors to perform searches, provide feedback, and so forth

- Often have interfaces where administrators can manage the site's content

- Are easier to maintain, upgrade, and build upon than statically made sites

There are many technologies available for creating dynamic Web sites. The most common are ASP.NET (Active Server Pages, a Microsoft construct), JSP (Java Server Pages), ColdFusion, Ruby on Rails (a Web development framework for the Ruby programming language), and PHP. Dynamic Web sites don't always rely on a database, but more and more of them do, particularly as excellent database applications like MySQL are available at little to no cost.

What is PHP?

PHP originally stood for "Personal Home Page" as it was created in 1994 by Rasmus Lerdorf to track the visitors to his online résumé. As its usefulness and capabilities grew (and as it started being used in more professional situations), it came to mean "PHP: Hypertext Preprocessor."

According to the official PHP Web site, found at **www.php.net** Ⓐ, PHP is a "widely used general-purpose scripting language that is especially suited for Web development and can be embedded into HTML." It's a long but descriptive definition, whose meaning I'll explain.

Starting at the end of that statement, to say that PHP *can be embedded into HTML* means that you can take a standard HTML page, drop in some PHP wherever you need it, and end up with a dynamic result. This attribute makes PHP very approachable for anyone that's done even a little bit of HTML work.

Also, PHP is a *scripting* language, as opposed to a *compiled* language: PHP was designed to write Web scripts, not stand-alone applications (although, with some extra effort, you can now create applications in PHP). PHP scripts run only after an event occurs—for example, when a user submits a form or goes to a URL (Uniform Resource Locator, the technical term for a Web address).

I should add to this definition that PHP is a server-side, cross-platform technology, both descriptions being important. *Server-side* refers to the fact that everything PHP does occurs on the server. A Web server application, like Apache or Microsoft's IIS (Internet Information Services), is required and all PHP scripts must be accessed through a URL (**http://***something*). Its

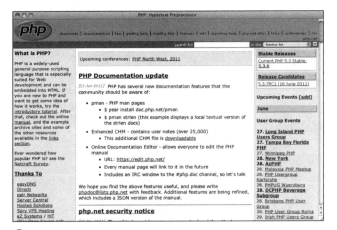

Ⓐ The home page for PHP.

What Happened to PHP 6?

When I wrote the previous version of this book, *PHP 6 and MySQL 5 for Dynamic Web Sites: Visual QuickPro Guide*, the next major release of PHP—PHP 6—was approximately 50 percent complete. Thinking that PHP 6 would therefore be released sometime after the book was published, I relied upon a beta version of PHP 6 for a bit of that edition's material. And then...
PHP 6 died.

One of the key features planned for PHP 6 was support for Unicode, meaning that PHP 6 would be able to work natively with any language. This would be a great addition to an already popular programming tool. Unfortunately, implementing Unicode support went from being complicated to quite difficult, and the developers behind the language tabled development of PHP 6. Not all was lost, however: Some of the other features planned for PHP 6, such as support for *namespaces* (an Object-Oriented Programming concept), were added to PHP 5.3.

At the time of this writing, it's not clear when Unicode support might be completed or what will happen with PHP 6. My hunch is that PHP will be making incremental developments along the version 5 trunk for some time to come.

cross-platform nature means that PHP runs on most operating systems, including Windows, Unix (and its many variants), and Macintosh. More important, the PHP scripts written on one server will normally work on another with little or no modification.

At the time this book was written, PHP was at version 5.3.6 and this book does assume you're using at least version 5.0. Some functions and features covered will require more specific or current versions, like PHP 5.2 or greater. In those cases, I will make it clear when the functionality was added to PHP, and provide alternative solutions if you have a slightly older version of the language.

If you're still using version 4 of PHP, you really should upgrade. If that's not in your plans, then please grab the second edition of this book instead.

More information about PHP can always be found at PHP.net or at Zend (**www.zend.com**), the minds behind the core of PHP.

Why use PHP?

Put simply, when it comes to developing dynamic Web sites, PHP is better, faster, and easier to learn than the alternatives. What you get with PHP is excellent performance, a tight integration with nearly every database available, stability, portability, and a nearly limitless feature set due to its extendibility. All of this comes at no cost (PHP is open source) and with a very manageable learning curve. PHP is one of the best marriages I've ever seen between the ease with which beginning programmers can start using it and the ability for more advanced programmers to do everything they require.

Finally, the proof is in the pudding: PHP has seen an exponential growth in use since its inception, and is the server-side technology of choice on over 76 percent of all Web sites B. In terms of all programming languages, PHP is the fifth most popular C.

Of course, you might assume that I, as the author of a book on PHP (several, actually), have a biased opinion. Although not nearly to the same extent as PHP, I've also developed sites using Java Server Pages (JSP), Ruby on Rails (RoR), and ASP.NET. Each has its pluses and minuses, but PHP is the technology I always return to. You might hear that it doesn't perform or scale as well as other technologies, but Yahoo!, Wikipedia, and Facebook all use PHP, and you can't find many sites more visited or demanding than those.

You might also wonder how secure PHP is. But *security isn't in the language*; it's in how that language is used. Rest assured that a complete and up-to-date discussion of all the relevant security concerns is provided by this book.

How PHP works

As previously stated, PHP is a server-side language. This means that the code you write in PHP sits on a host computer called a *server*. The server sends Web pages to the requesting visitors (you, the client, with your Web browser).

When a visitor goes to a Web site written in PHP, the server reads the PHP code and then processes it according to its scripted directions. In the example shown in D, the PHP code tells the server to send the appropriate data—HTML code—to the Web browser, which treats the received code as it would a standard HTML page.

This differs from a static HTML site where, when a request is made, the server merely sends the HTML data to the Web browser and there is no server-side interpretation

PHP	▰▰▰▰▰ 76.4%
ASP.NET	▰▰ 22.4%
Java	▰ 3.9%
ColdFusion	▎1.3%
Perl	▎1.1%
Ruby	▎0.6%
Python	▎0.2%

W3Techs.com, 27 June 2011

Percentages of websites using various server-side programming languages
Note: a website may use more than one server-side programming language

B The Web Technology Surveys site provides this graphic regarding server-side technologies (**www.w3techs.com/technologies/overview/ programming_language/all**).

Position Jun 2011	Position Jun 2010	Delta in Position	Programming Language	Ratings Jun 2011	Delta Jun 2010	Status
1	2	↑	Java	18.580%	+0.62%	A
2	1	↓	C	16.278%	-1.91%	A
3	3	=	C++	9.830%	-0.55%	A
4	6	↑↑	C#	6.844%	+2.08%	A
5	4	↓	PHP	6.602%	-2.47%	A
6	5	↓	(Visual) Basic	4.727%	-0.93%	A

C The Tiobe Index (**http://www.tiobe.com/ index.php/content/paperinfo/tpci/index.html**) uses a combination of factors to rank the popularity of programming languages.

D How PHP fits into the client/server model when a user requests a Web page.

occurring 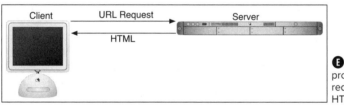. Because no server-side action is required, you can run HTML pages in your Web browser without using a server at all.

To the end user and the Web browser there is no perceptible difference between what **home.html** and **home.php** may look like, but how that page's content was created will be significantly different.

What is MySQL?

MySQL (**www.mysql.com**) ❶ is the world's most popular open-source database. In fact, today MySQL is a viable competitor to the pricey goliaths such as Oracle and Microsoft's SQL Server (and, ironically, MySQL is owned by Oracle). Like PHP, MySQL offers excellent performance, portability, and reliability, with a moderate learning curve and little to no cost.

MySQL is a database management system (DBMS) for relational databases (therefore, MySQL is an RDBMS). A database, in the simplest terms, is a collection of data, be it text, numbers, or binary files, stored and kept organized by the DBMS.

There are many types of databases, from the simple flat-file to relational and object-oriented. A relational database uses multiple tables to store information in its most discernible parts. While relational databases may involve more thought in the design and programming stages, they offer improved reliability and data integrity that more than makes up for the extra effort required. Further, relational databases are more searchable and allow for concurrent users.

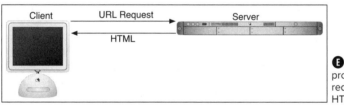

❶ The client/server process when a request for a static HTML page is made.

❶ The home page for the MySQL database application.

By incorporating a database into a Web application, some of the data generated by PHP can be retrieved from MySQL . This further moves the site's content from a static (hard-coded) basis to a flexible one, flexibility being the key to a dynamic Web site.

MySQL is an open-source application, like PHP, meaning that it is free to use or even modify (the source code itself is downloadable). There are occasions in which you should pay for a MySQL license, especially if you are making money from the sales or incorporation of the MySQL product. Check MySQL's licensing policy for more information on this.

The MySQL software consists of several pieces, including the MySQL server (*mysqld*, which runs and manages the databases), the MySQL client (*mysql*, which gives you an interface to the server), and numerous utilities for maintenance and other purposes. PHP has always had good support for MySQL, and that is even more true in the most recent versions of the language.

MySQL has been known to handle databases as large as 60,000 tables with more than 5 billion rows. MySQL can work with tables as large as 8 million terabytes on some operating systems, generally a healthy 4 GB otherwise. MySQL is used by NASA and the United States Census Bureau, among many others.

At the time of this writing, MySQL is on version 5.5.13, with versions 5.6 and 6.0 in development. The version of MySQL you have affects what features you can use, so it's important that you know what you're working with. For this book, MySQL 5.1.44 and 5.5.8 were used, although you should be able to do everything in this book as long as you're using a version of MySQL greater than 5.0.

Pronunciation Guide

Trivial as it may be, I should clarify up front that MySQL is technically pronounced "My Ess Que Ell," just as SQL should be said "Ess Que Ell." This is a question many people have when first working with these technologies. While not a critical issue, it's always best to pronounce acronyms correctly.

 How most of the dynamic Web applications in this book will work, using both PHP and MySQL.

What You'll Need

To follow the examples in this book, you'll need the following tools:

- A Web server application (for example, Apache, Abyss, or IIS)
- PHP
- MySQL
- A Web browser (Microsoft's Internet Explorer, Mozilla's Firefox, Apple's Safari, Google's Chrome, etc.)
- A text editor, PHP-capable WYSIWYG application (Adobe's Dreamweaver qualifies), or IDE (integrated development environment)
- An FTP application, if using a remote server

One of the great things about developing dynamic Web sites with PHP and MySQL is that all of the requirements can be met at no cost whatsoever, regardless of your operating system! Apache, PHP, and MySQL are each free; Web browsers can be had without cost; and many good text editors are available for nothing.

The appendix, which you can download from http://www.peachpit.com, discusses the installation process on the Windows and Mac OS X operating systems. If you have a computer, you are only a couple of downloads away from being able to create dynamic Web sites (in that case, your computer would represent both the client and the server in **D** and **E**). Conversely, you could purchase Web hosting for only dollars per month that will provide you with a PHP- and MySQL-enabled environment already online.

TIP To download this book's appendix from peachpit.com, create a free account at http://peachpit.com, and then register this book using ISBN number 0321784073. Once registered, you'll have access to the bonus content.

About This Book

This book teaches how to develop dynamic Web sites with PHP and MySQL, covering the knowledge that most developers might require. In keeping with the format of the Visual QuickPro series, the information is discussed using a step-by-step approach with corresponding images. The focus has been kept on real-world, practical examples, avoiding "here's something you could do but never would" scenarios. As a practicing Web developer myself, I wrote about the information that I use and avoided those topics immaterial to the task at hand. As a practicing writer, I made certain to include topics and techniques that I know readers are asking about.

The structure of the book is linear, and the intention is that you'll read it in order. It begins with three chapters covering the fundamentals of PHP (by the second chapter, you will have already developed your first dynamic Web page). After that, there are four chapters on SQL (Structured Query Language, which is used to interact with all databases) and MySQL. Those chapters teach the basics of SQL, database design, and the MySQL application in particular. Then there's one chapter on debugging and error management, information everyone needs. This is followed by a chapter introducing how to use PHP and MySQL together, a remarkably easy thing to do.

The following five chapters teach more application techniques to round out your knowledge. Security, in particular, is repeatedly addressed in those pages. Two new chapters, to be discussed momentarily, expand your newfound knowledge. Finally, I've included three example chapters, in which the heart of different Web applications are developed, with instructions.

Is this book for you?

This book was written for a wide range of people within the beginner-to-intermediate range. The book makes use of XHTML, so solid experience with XHTML or HTML is a must. Although this book covers many things, it does not formally teach HTML or Web-page design. Some CSS is sprinkled about these pages but also not taught.

Second, this book expects that you have one of the following:

- The drive and ability to learn without much hand holding, or...

- Familiarity with another programming language (even solid JavaScript skills would qualify), or...

- A cursory knowledge of PHP

Make no mistake: This book covers PHP and MySQL from A to Z, teaching everything you'll need to know to develop real-world Web sites, but particularly the early chapters cover PHP at a quick pace. For this reason I recommend either some programming experience or a curious and independent spirit when it comes to learning new things. If you find that the material goes too quickly, you should probably start off with the latest edition of my book *PHP for the World Wide Web: Visual QuickStart Guide*, which goes at a much more tempered pace.

No database experience is required, since SQL and MySQL are discussed starting at a more basic level.

What's new in this edition

The first three editions of this book have been very popular, and I've received a lot of positive feedback on them (thanks!). In writing this new edition, I wanted to do more than just update the material for the latest versions of PHP and MySQL, although that is an overriding consideration throughout the book. Other new features you'll find are:

- New examples demonstrating techniques frequently requested by readers

- Even more advanced MySQL and SQL instruction and examples

- A tutorial on using the jQuery JavaScript framework

- An introduction to the fundamentals and basic usage of Object-Oriented Programming

- Even more information and examples for improving the security of your scripts and sites

- Expanded and updated installation and configuration instructions

- Removal of outdated content (e.g., things used in older versions of PHP or no longer applicable)

- A "Review and Pursue" section at the end of each chapter, with review questions and prompts for ways in which you can further expand your knowledge based upon the information just covered

For those of you that also own a previous edition (thanks, thanks, thanks!), I believe that these new features will also make this edition a required fixture on your desk or bookshelf.

How this book compares to my other books

This is my fourth PHP and/or MySQL title, after (in order)

- *PHP for the World Wide Web: Visual QuickStart Guide*
- *PHP 5 Advanced for the World Wide Web: Visual QuickPro Guide*
- *MySQL: Visual QuickStart Guide*

I hope this résumé implies a certain level of qualification to write this book, but how do you, as a reader standing in a bookstore, decide which title is for you? Of course, you are more than welcome to splurge and buy the whole set, earning my eternal gratitude, but...

The *PHP for the World Wide Web: Visual QuickStart Guide* book is very much a beginner's guide to PHP. This title overlaps it some, mostly in the first three chapters, but uses new examples so as not to be redundant. For novices, this book acts as a follow-up to that one. The advanced book is really a sequel to this one, as it assumes a fair amount of knowledge and builds upon many things taught here. The MySQL book focuses almost exclusively on MySQL (there are but two chapters that use PHP).

With that in mind, read the section "Is this book for you?" and see if the requirements apply. If you have no programming experience at all and would prefer to be taught PHP more gingerly, my first book would be better. If you are already very comfortable with PHP and want to learn more of its advanced capabilities, pick up the second. If you are most interested in MySQL and are not concerned with learning much about PHP, check out the third.

That being said, if you want to learn everything you need to know to begin developing dynamic Web sites with PHP and MySQL today, then this is the book for you! It references the most current versions of both technologies, uses techniques not previously discussed in other books, and contains its own unique examples.

And whatever book you do choose, make sure you're getting the most recent edition or, barring that, the edition that best matches the versions of the technologies you'll be using.

Companion Web Site

I have developed a companion Web site specifically for this book, which you may reach at **www.LarryUllman.com**. There you will find every script from this book, a text file containing lengthy SQL commands, and a list of errata that occurred during publication. (If you have problems with a command or script, and you are following the book exactly, check the errata to ensure there is not a printing error before driving yourself absolutely mad.) At this Web site you will also find useful Web links, a popular forum where readers can ask and answer each other's questions (I answer many of them myself), and more!

Questions, comments, or suggestions?

If you have any questions on PHP or MySQL, you can turn to one of the many Web sites, mailing lists, newsgroups, and FAQ repositories already in existence. A quick search online will turn up virtually unlimited resources. For that matter, if you need an immediate answer, those sources or a quick Web search will most assuredly serve your needs (in all likelihood, someone else has already seen and solved your exact problem).

You can also direct your questions, comments, and suggestions to me. You'll get the fastest reply using the book's corresponding forum (I always answer those questions first). If you'd rather email me, my contact information is available on the Web site. I do try to answer every email I receive, although I cannot guarantee a quick reply.

Publisher's Tip: Check Out the Accompanying Video Training from Author Larry Ullman!

Visual QuickStart Guides are now even more visual: Building on the success of the top-selling Visual QuickStart Guide books, Peachpit now offers Video QuickStarts. As a companion to this book, Peachpit offers more than an hour of short, task-based videos that will help you master key features and techniques; instead of just reading about how to write PHP and MySQL scripts, you can watch it in action. It's a great way to learn all the basics and some of the newer or more complex features of the languages. Log on to the Peachpit site at www.peachpit.com/register to register your book, and you'll find a free streaming sample; purchasing the rest of the material is quick and easy.

Introduction
to PHP

Although this book focuses on using MySQL and PHP in combination, you'll do a vast majority of your legwork using PHP alone. In this and the following chapter, you'll learn its basics, from syntax to variables, operators, and language constructs (conditionals, loops, and whatnot). At the same time you are picking up these fundamentals, you'll also begin developing usable code that you'll integrate into larger applications later in the book.

This introductory chapter will cruise through most of the basics of the PHP language. You'll learn the syntax for coding PHP, how to send data to the Web browser, and how to use two kinds of variables (strings and numbers) plus constants. Some of the examples may seem inconsequential, but they'll demonstrate ideas you'll have to master in order to write more advanced scripts further down the line. The chapter concludes with some quick debugging tips...you know...just in case!

In This Chapter

Basic Syntax

As stated in the book's introduction, PHP is an *HTML-embedded* scripting language, meaning that you can intermingle PHP and HTML code within the same file. So to begin programming with PHP, start with a simple Web page. **Script 1.1** is an example of a no-frills, no-content XHTML Transitional document, which will be used as the foundation for most Web pages in the book (this book does not formally discuss [X]HTML; see a resource dedicated to the topic for more information). Please also note that the template uses UTF-8 encoding, a topic discussed in the sidebar.

To add PHP code to a page, place it within PHP tags:

```php
<?php
?>
```

Script 1.1 A basic XHTML 1.0 Transitional Web page.

```
1   <!DOCTYPE html PUBLIC "-//W3C//DTD XHTML
    1.0 Transitional//EN" "http://www.w3.org/
    TR/xhtml1/DTD/xhtml1-transitional.dtd">
2   <html xmlns="http://www.w3.org/1999/
    xhtml" xml:lang="en" lang="en">
3   <head>
4       <meta http-equiv="Content-Type"
        content="text/html; charset=utf-8" />
5       <title>Page Title</title>
6   </head>
7   <body>
8       <!-- Script 1.1 - template.html -->
9   </body>
10  </html>
```

Understanding Encoding

Encoding is a huge subject, but what you most need to understand is this: *the encoding you use in a file dictates what characters can be represented* (and therefore, what languages can be used). To select an encoding, you must first confirm that your text editor or Integrated Development Environment (IDE)—whatever application you're using to create the HTML and PHP scripts—can save documents using that encoding. Some applications let you set the encoding in the preferences or options area; others set the encoding when you save the file.

To indicate the encoding to the Web browser, there's the corresponding **meta** tag:

```
<meta http-equiv="content-type" content="text/html; charset=utf-8" />
```

The *charset=utf-8* part says that UTF-8 encoding is being used, short for *8-bit Unicode Transformation Format*. Unicode is a way of reliably representing every symbol in every alphabet. Version 6 of Unicode—the current version at the time of this writing—supports over 99,000 characters!

If you want to create a multilingual Web page, UTF-8 is the way to go, and I'll be using it in this book's examples. You don't have to, of course. But whatever encoding you do use, make sure that the encoding indicated by the XHTML page matches the actual encoding set in your text editor or IDE. If you don't, you'll likely see odd characters when you view the page in a Web browser.

Script 1.2 This first PHP script doesn't do anything, but does demonstrate how a PHP script is written. It'll also be used as a test script, prior to getting into elaborate PHP code.

```
1   <!DOCTYPE html PUBLIC "-//W3C//DTD XHTML
    1.0 Transitional//EN" "http://www.w3.org/
    TR/xhtml1/DTD/xhtml1-transitional.dtd">
2   <html xmlns="http://www.w3.org/1999/
    xhtml" xml:lang="en" lang="en">
3   <head>
4       <meta http-equiv="Content-Type"
        content="text/html; charset=utf-8" />
5       <title>Basic PHP Page</title>
6   </head>
7   <body>
8       <!-- Script 1.2 - first.php -->
9       <p>This is standard HTML.</p>
10  <?php
11  ?>
12  </body>
13  </html>
```

HTML5

At the time of this writing, the next major release of HTML—HTML5—is being actively developed and discussed, but is not production ready, which is why I chose not to use it in the book. In fact, I wouldn't be surprised if HTML5 is still not released by the time I start the fifth edition of this book, and it will take even longer for broad browser adoption of the language. Still, as HTML5 is an exciting future development, this book will occasionally mention features you can expect to see introduced and supported over time.

Anything written within these tags will be treated by the Web server as PHP, meaning the PHP interpreter will process the code. Any text outside of the PHP tags is immediately sent to the Web browser as regular HTML. (Because PHP is most often used to create content displayed in the Web browser, the PHP tags are normally put somewhere within the page's body.)

Along with placing PHP code within PHP tags, your PHP files must have a proper *extension*. The extension tells the server to treat the script in a special way, namely, as a PHP page. Most Web servers use **.html** for standard HTML pages and **.php** for PHP files.

Before getting into the steps, understand that *you must already have a working PHP installation*! This could be on a hosted site or your own computer, after following the instructions in Appendix A, "Installation," which is a free download from peachpit.com.

To make a basic PHP script:

1. Create a new document in your text editor or IDE, to be named **first.php** (**Script 1.2**).

   It generally does not matter what application you use, be it Adobe Dreamweaver (a fancy IDE), TextMate (a great and popular Macintosh plain-text editor), or vi (a plain-text Unix editor, lacking a graphical interface). Still, some text editors and IDEs make typing and debugging HTML and PHP easier (conversely, Notepad on Windows does some things that makes coding harder: *don't use Notepad*!). If you don't already have an application you're attached to, search the Web or use the book's corresponding forum (**www.LarryUllman.com/forums/**) to find one.

continues on next page

2. Create a basic HTML document:

```
<!DOCTYPE html PUBLIC "-//W3C//
→ DTD XHTML 1.0 Transitional//EN"
→ "http://www.w3.org/TR/xhtml1/DTD/
→ xhtml1-transitional.dtd">
<html xmlns="http://www.w3.org/
→ 1999/xhtml" xml:lang="en"
→ lang="en">
<head>
  <meta http-equiv="Content-Type"
  → content="text/html;
  → charset=utf-8" />
  <title>Basic PHP Page</title>
</head>
<body>
  <!-- Script 1.2 - first.php -->
<p>This is standard HTML.</p>
</body>
</html>
```

Although this is the syntax being used throughout the book, you can change the HTML to match whichever standard you intend to use (e.g., HTML 4.0 Strict). Again, see a dedicated (X)HTML resource if you're unfamiliar with any of this HTML code.

3. Before the closing **body** tag, insert the PHP tags:

```
<?php
?>
```

These are the *formal* PHP tags, also known as *XML-style* tags. Although PHP supports other tag types, I recommend that you use the formal type, and I will do so throughout this book.

4. Save the file as **first.php.**

Remember that if you don't save the file using an appropriate PHP extension, the script will not execute properly. (Just one of the reasons not to use Notepad is that it will secretly add the **.txt** extension to PHP files, thereby causing many headaches.)

5. Place the file in the proper directory of your Web server.

If you are running PHP on your own computer (presumably after following the installation directions in Appendix A), you just need to move, copy, or save the file to a specific folder on your computer. Check Appendix A or the documentation for your particular Web server to identify the correct directory, if you don't already know what it is.

If you are running PHP on a hosted server (i.e., on a remote computer), you'll need to use a File Transfer Protocol (FTP) application to upload the file to the proper directory. Your hosting company will provide you with access and the other necessary information.

6. Run **first.php** in your Web browser **A**.

Because PHP scripts need to be parsed by the server, you *absolutely must* access them via a URL (i.e., the address in the browser must begin with **http://**). You cannot simply open them in your Web browser as you would a file in other applications (in which case the address would start with **file://** or **C:** or the like).

A While it seems like any other (simple) HTML page, this is in fact a PHP script and the basis for the rest of the examples in the book.

If you are running PHP on your own computer, you'll need to use a URL like **http://localhost/first.php, http://127.0.0.1/first.php**, or **http://localhost/~<user>/first.php** (on Mac OS X, using your actual username for **<user>**). If you are using a Web host, you'll need to use **http://*your-domain-name*/first.php** (e. g., **http://www.example.com/first.php).**

7. If you don't see results like those in 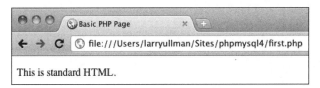, start debugging!

   Part of learning any programming language is mastering debugging. It's a sometimes-painful but absolutely necessary process. With this first example, if you don't see a simple, but perfectly valid, Web page, follow these steps:

1. Confirm that you have a working PHP installation (see Appendix A for testing instructions).

2. Make sure that you are running the script through a URL. The address in the Web browser must begin with **http://**. If it starts with **file://**, that's a problem **B**.

3. If you get a file not found (or similar) error, you've likely put the file in the wrong directory or mistyped the file's name (either when saving it or in your Web browser).

   If you've gone through all this and are still having problems, turn to the book's corresponding forum **(www.LarryUllman.com/forums/)**.

TIP To find more information about HTML and XHTML, check out Elizabeth Castro's excellent book *HTML, XHTML, and CSS, Sixth Edition: Visual QuickStart Guide,* (Peachpit Press, 2006) or search the Web.

TIP You can embed multiple sections of PHP code within a single HTML document (i.e., you can go in and out of the two languages). You'll see examples of this throughout the book.

TIP Prior to UTF-8, ISO-8859-1 was one of the more commonly used encodings. It represents most Western European languages. It's still the default encoding for many Web browsers and other applications.

TIP You can declare the encoding of an external CSS file by adding @charset "utf-8"; as the first line in the file. If you're not using UTF-8, change the line accordingly.

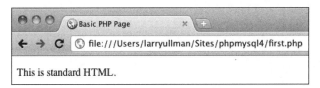

| ⊗ ⊗ ⊗ | Basic PHP Page | × | + |

← → C 🌐 file:///Users/larryullman/Sites/phpmysql4/first.php

This is standard HTML.

B PHP code will only be executed when run through *http://* (not that this particular script is affected either way).

Sending Data to the Web Browser

To create dynamic Web sites with PHP, you must know how to send data to the Web browser. PHP has a number of built-in functions for this purpose, the most common being **echo** and **print.** I personally tend to favor **echo**:

```
echo 'Hello, world!';
echo "What's new?";
```

You could use **print** instead, if you prefer (the name more obviously indicates what it does):

```
print 'Hello, world!';
print "What's new?";
```

As you can see from these examples, you can use either single or double quotation marks (but there is a distinction between the two types of quotation marks, which will be made clear by the chapter's end). The first quotation mark after the function name indicates the start of the message to be printed. The next matching quotation mark (i.e., the next quotation mark of the same kind as the opening mark) indicates the end of the message to be printed.

Along with learning how to send data to the Web browser, you should also notice that in PHP all statements—a line of executed code, in layman's terms—must end with a semicolon. Also, PHP is *case-insensitive* when it comes to function names, so **ECHO**, **echo**, **eCHo**, and so forth will all work. The all-lowercase version is easiest to type, of course.

Needing an Escape

As you might discover, one of the complications with sending data to the Web involves printing single and double quotation marks. Either of the following will cause errors:

```
echo "She said, "How are you?"";
echo 'I'm just ducky.';
```

There are two solutions to this problem. First, use single quotation marks when printing a double quotation mark and vice versa:

```
echo 'She said, "How are you?"';
echo "I'm just ducky.";
```

Or, you can *escape* the problematic character by preceding it with a backslash:

```
echo "She said, \"How are you?\"";
echo 'I\'m just ducky.';
```

An escaped quotation mark will merely be printed like any other character. Understanding how to use the backslash to escape a character is an important concept, and one that will be covered in more depth at the end of the chapter.

Script 1.3 Using **print** or **echo**, PHP can send data to the Web browser.

```
1    <!DOCTYPE html PUBLIC "-//W3C//DTD XHTML
     1.0 Transitional//EN" "http://www.w3.org/
     TR/xhtml1/DTD/xhtml1-transitional.dtd">
2    <html xmlns="http://www.w3.org/1999/
     xhtml" xml:lang="en" lang="en">
3    <head>
4        <meta http-equiv="Content-Type"
         content="text/html; charset=utf-8" />
5        <title>Using Echo</title>
6    </head>
7    <body>
8        <!-- Script 1.3 - second.php -->
9        <p>This is standard HTML.</p>
10   <?php
11   echo 'This was generated using PHP!';
12   ?>
13   </body>
14   </html>
```

```
Using Echo
+  http://localhost/second.php   ⟳

This is standard HTML.

This was generated using PHP!
```

Ⓐ The results still aren't glamorous, but this page was in part dynamically generated by PHP.

To send data to the Web browser:

1. Open **first.php** (refer to Script 1.2) in your text editor or IDE.

2. Between the PHP tags (lines 10 and 11), add a simple message (**Script 1.3**):

   **echo 'This was generated using
   ⇢ PHP!';**

   It truly doesn't matter what message you type here, which function you use (**echo** or **print**), or which quotation marks, for that matter—just be careful if you are printing a single or double quotation mark as part of your message (see the sidebar "Needing an Escape").

3. If you want, change the page title to better describe this script (line 5):

   <title>Using Echo</title>

   This change only affects the browser window's title bar.

4. Save the file as **second.php**, place it in your Web directory, and test it in your Web browser **Ⓐ**.

   Remember that all PHP scripts must be run through a URL (**http://something**)!

continues on next page

5. If necessary, debug the script.

If you see a parse error instead of your message **B**, check that you have both opened and closed your quotation marks and escaped any problematic characters (see the sidebar). Also be certain to conclude each statement with a semicolon.

If you see an entirely blank page, this is probably for one of two reasons:

▸ There is a problem with your HTML. Test this by viewing the source of your page and looking for HTML problems there **C**.

▸ An error occurred, but *display_errors* is turned off in your PHP configuration, so nothing is shown. In this case, see the section in Appendix A on how to configure PHP so that you can turn *display_errors* back on.

> **TIP** Technically, echo and `print` are *language constructs*, not functions. That being said, don't be flummoxed as I continue to call them "functions" for convenience. Also, as you'll see later in the book, I include the parentheses when referring to functions—say `number_format( )`, not just `number_format`—to help distinguish them from variables and other parts of PHP. This is just my own little convention.

> **TIP** You can, and often will, use echo and `print` to send HTML code to the Web browser, like so **D**:

```
echo '<p>Hello, <b>world</b>!</p>';
```

B This may be the first of many parse errors you see as a PHP programmer (this one is caused by the omission of the terminating quotation mark).

C One possible cause of a blank PHP page is a simple HTML error, like the closing **title** tag here (it's missing the slash).

D PHP can send HTML code (like the formatting here) as well as simple text **A** to the Web browser.

E Printing text and HTML over multiple PHP lines will generate HTML source code that also extends over multiple lines. Note that extraneous white spacing in the HTML source will not affect the look of a page **F** but can make the source easier to review.

F The return in the HTML source **E** has no effect on the rendered result. The only way to alter the spacing of a displayed Web page is to use HTML tags (like **
** and **<p></p>**).

TIP Echo and `print` can both be used over multiple lines:

```
echo 'This sentence is
printed over two lines.';
```

TIP What happens in this case is that the return (created by pressing Enter or Return) becomes part of the printed message, which isn't terminated until the closing quotation mark. The net result will be the "printing" of the return in the HTML source code **E**. This will not have an effect on the generated page **F**. For more on this, see the sidebar "Understanding White Space."

Understanding White Space

With PHP you send data (like HTML tags and text) to the Web browser, which will, in turn, render that data as the Web page the end user sees. Thus, what you are often doing with PHP is creating the *HTML source* of a Web page. With this in mind, there are three areas of notable *white space* (extra spaces, tabs, and blank lines): in your PHP scripts, in your HTML source, and in the rendered Web page.

PHP is generally white space insensitive, meaning that you can space out your code however you want to make your scripts more legible. HTML is also generally white space insensitive. Specifically, the only white space in HTML that affects the rendered page is a single space (multiple spaces still get rendered as one). If your HTML source has text on multiple lines, that doesn't mean it'll appear on multiple lines in the rendered page (**E** and **F**).

To alter the spacing in a rendered Web page, use the HTML tags **
** (line break, **
** in older HTML standards) and **<p></p>** (paragraph). To alter the spacing of the HTML *source* created with PHP, you can

- Use **echo** or **print** over the course of several lines.

  or

- Print the newline character (**\n**) within double quotation marks, which is equivalent to Enter or Return.

Writing Comments

Creating executable PHP code is only a part of the programming process (admittedly, it's the most important part). A secondary but still crucial aspect to any programming endeavor involves documenting your code. In fact, when I'm asked what qualities distinguish the beginning programmer from the more experienced one, a good and thorough use of comments is my unwavering response.

In HTML you can add comments using special tags:

```
<!-- Comment goes here. -->
```

HTML comments are viewable in the source but do not appear in the rendered page (see **E** and **F** in the previous section).

PHP comments are different in that they aren't sent to the Web browser at all, meaning they won't be viewable to the end user, even when looking at the HTML source.

PHP supports three comment syntaxes. The first uses the pound or number symbol (**#**):

```
# This is a comment.
```

The second uses two slashes:

```
// This is also a comment.
```

Both of these cause PHP to ignore everything that follows until the end of the line (when you press Return or Enter). Thus, these two comments are for single lines only. They are also often used to place a comment on the same line as some PHP code:

```
print 'Hello!'; // Say hello.
```

A third style allows comments to run over multiple lines:

```
/* This is a longer comment
that spans two lines. */
```

Script 1.4 These basic comments demonstrate the three comment syntaxes you can use in PHP.

```
1    <!DOCTYPE html PUBLIC "-//W3C//DTD XHTML
     1.0 Transitional//EN" "http://www.w3.org/
     TR/xhtml1/DTD/xhtml1-transitional.dtd">
2    <html xmlns="http://www.w3.org/1999/
     xhtml" xml:lang="en" lang="en">
3    <head>
4       <meta http-equiv="Content-Type"
        content="text/html; charset=utf-8" />
5       <title>Comments</title>
6    </head>
7    <body>
8    <?php
9
10   # Script 1.4 - comments.php
11   # Created March 16, 2011
12   # Created by Larry E. Ullman
13   # This script does nothing much.
14
15   echo '<p>This is a line of text.<br />
     This is another line of text.</p>';
16
17   /*
18   echo 'This line will not be
     executed.';
19   */
20
21   echo "<p>Now I'm done.</p>";
     // End of PHP code.
22
23   ?>
24   </body>
25   </html>
```

To comment your scripts:

1. Begin a new PHP document in your text editor or IDE, to be named **comments.php**, starting with the initial HTML (**Script 1.4**):

```
<!DOCTYPE html PUBLIC "-//W3C//
→ DTD XHTML 1.0 Transitional//EN"
→ "http://www.w3.org/TR/xhtml1/DTD/
→ xhtml1-transitional.dtd">
<html xmlns="http://www.w3.org/
→ 1999/xhtml" xml:lang="en"
→ lang="en">
<head>
  <meta http-equiv="Content-Type"
  → content="text/html;
  → charset=utf-8" />
  <title>Comments</title>
</head>
<body>
```

2. Add the initial PHP tag and write your first comments:

```
<?php
# Script 1.4 - comments.php
# Created March 16, 2011
# Created by Larry E. Ullman
# This script does nothing much.
```

One of the first comments each script should contain is an introductory block that lists creation date, modification date, creator, creator's contact information, purpose of the script, and so on. Some people suggest that the shell-style comments (**#**) stand out more in a script and are therefore best for this kind of notation.

continues on next page

3. Send some HTML to the Web browser:

```
echo '<p>This is a line of
→text.<br />This is another line
→of text.</p>';
```

It doesn't matter what you do here, just make something for the Web browser to display. For the sake of variety, the **echo** statement will print some HTML tags, including a line break (**
**) to add some spacing to the generated HTML page.

4. Use the multiline comments to comment out a second **echo** statement:

```
/*
echo 'This line will not be
→executed.';
*/
```

By surrounding any block of PHP code with **/*** and ***/**, you can render that code inert without having to delete it from your script. By later removing the comment tags, you can reactivate that section of PHP code.

5. Add a final comment after a third **echo** statement:

```
echo "<p>Now I'm done.</p>";
→// End of PHP code.
```

This last (superfluous) comment shows how to place a comment at the end of a line, a common practice. Note that double quotation marks surround this message, as single quotation marks would conflict with the apostrophe (see the "Needing an Escape" sidebar, earlier in the chapter).

6. Close the PHP section and complete the HTML page:

```
?>
</body>
</html>
```

7. Save the file as **comments.php**, place it in your Web directory, and test it in your Web browser **Ⓐ**.

Ⓐ The PHP comments in Script 1.4 don't appear in the Web page or the HTML source **Ⓑ**.

8. If you're the curious type, check the source code in your Web browser to confirm that the PHP comments do not appear there **B**.

TIP You shouldn't nest (place one inside another) multiline comments (/* */). Doing so will cause problems.

TIP Any of the PHP comments can be used at the end of a line (say, after a function call):

```
echo 'Howdy'; /* Say 'Howdy' */
```

Although this is allowed, it's far less common.

TIP It's nearly impossible to over-comment your scripts. Always err on the side of writing too many comments as you code. That being said, in the interest of saving space, the scripts in this book will not be as well documented as I would suggest they should be.

TIP It's also important that as you change a script you keep the comments up-to-date and accurate. There's nothing more confusing than a comment that says one thing when the code really does something else.

B The PHP comments from Script 1.4 are nowhere to be seen in the client's browser.

What Are Variables?

Variables are containers used to temporarily store values. These values can be numbers, text, or much more complex data. PHP supports eight types of variables. These include four scalar (single-valued) types—*Boolean* (**TRUE** or **FALSE**), *integer*, *floating point* (decimals), and *strings* (characters); two nonscalar (multivalued)—*arrays* and *objects*; plus *resources* (which you'll see when interacting with databases) and *NULL* (which is a special type that has no value).

Regardless of what type you are creating, all variable names in PHP follow certain syntactical rules:

- A variable's name must start with a dollar sign (**$**), for example, **$name**.

- The variable's name can contain a combination of letters, numbers, and the underscore, for example, **$my_report1**.

- The first character after the dollar sign must be either a letter or an underscore (it cannot be a number).

- *Variable names in PHP are case-sensitive!* This is a very important rule. It means that **$name** and **$Name** are entirely different variables.

To begin working with variables, this next script will print out the value of three *predefined variables*. Whereas a standard variable is assigned a value during the execution of a script, a predefined variable will already have a value when the script begins its execution. Most of these predefined variables reflect properties of the server as a whole, such as the operating system in use.

Before getting into this script, there are two more things you should know. First, variables can be assigned values using the equals sign (=), also called the *assignment operator*. Second, to display the value of a variable, you can print the variable without quotation marks:

```
print $some_var;
```

Or variables can be printed within *double* quotation marks:

```
print "Hello, $name";
```

You cannot print variables within single quotation marks:

```
print 'Hello, $name'; // Won't work!
```

Script 1.5 This script prints three of PHP's many predefined variables.

```
1   <!DOCTYPE html PUBLIC "-//W3C//DTD XHTML
    1.0 Transitional//EN" "http://www.w3.org/
    TR/xhtml1/DTD/xhtml1-transitional.dtd">
2   <html xmlns="http://www.w3.org/1999/
    xhtml" xml:lang="en" lang="en">
3   <head>
4       <meta http-equiv="Content-Type"
        content="text/html; charset=utf-8" />
5       <title>Predefined Variables</title>
6   </head>
7   <body>
8   <?php # Script 1.5 - predefined.php
9
10  // Create a shorthand version of the
    variable names:
11  $file = $_SERVER['SCRIPT_FILENAME'];
12  $user = $_SERVER['HTTP_USER_AGENT'];
13  $server = $_SERVER['SERVER_SOFTWARE'];
14
15  // Print the name of this script:
16  echo "<p>You are running the
    file:<br /><b>$file</b>.</p>\n";
17
18  // Print the user's information:
19  echo "<p>You are viewing this page
    using:<br /><b>$user</b></p>\n";
20
21  // Print the server's information:
22  echo "<p>This server is running:
    <br /><b>$server</b>.</p>\n";
23
24  ?>
25  </body>
26  </html>
```

To use variables:

1. Begin a new PHP document in your text editor or IDE, to be named **predefined.php**, starting with the initial HTML (**Script 1.5**):

```
<!DOCTYPE html PUBLIC "-//W3C//
→ DTD XHTML 1.0 Transitional//EN"
→ "http://www.w3.org/TR/xhtml1/DTD/
→ xhtml1-transitional.dtd">
<html xmlns="http://www.w3.org/
→ 1999/xhtml" xml:lang="en"
→ lang="en">
<head>
    <meta http-equiv="Content-Type"
    → content="text/html;
    → charset=utf-8" />
    <title>Predefined Variables
    → </title>
</head>
<body>
```

2. Add the opening PHP tag and the first comment:

```
<?php # Script 1.5 - predefined.php
```

From here on out, scripts will no longer comment on the creator, creation date, and so forth, although you should continue to document your scripts thoroughly. Scripts will, however, make a comment indicating the script's number and filename for ease of cross-referencing (both in the book and when you download them from the book's supporting Web site, **www.LarryUllman.com**).

continues on next page

3. Create a shorthand version of the first variable to be used in this script:

```
$file = $_SERVER['SCRIPT_FILENAME'];
```

This script will use three variables, each of which comes from the larger predefined **$_SERVER** variable. **$_SERVER** refers to a mass of server-related information. The first variable the script uses is **$_SERVER['SCRIPT_FILENAME']**. This variable stores the full path and name of the script being run (for example, **C:\Program Files\Apache\ htdocs\predefined.php**).

The value stored in **$_SERVER['SCRIPT_FILENAME']** will be assigned to the new variable **$file**. Creating new variables with shorter names and then assigning them values from **$_SERVER** will make it easier to refer to the variables when printing them. (It also gets around another issue you'll learn about in due time.)

4. Create a shorthand version of two more variables:

```
$user = $_SERVER['HTTP_USER_AGENT'];
$server = $_SERVER
→ ['SERVER_SOFTWARE'];
```

$_SERVER['HTTP_USER_AGENT'] represents the Web browser and operating system of the user accessing the script. This value is assigned to **$user**.

$_SERVER['SERVER_SOFTWARE'] represents the Web application on the server that's running PHP (e.g., Apache, Abyss, Xitami, IIS). This is the program that must be installed (see Appendix A) in order to run PHP scripts on that computer.

5. Print out the name of the script being run:

```
echo "<p>You are running the
→ file:<br /><b>$file</b>.</p>\n";
```

The first variable to be printed is **$file**. Notice that this variable must be used within double quotation marks and that the statement also makes use of the PHP newline character (**\n**), which will add a line break in the generated HTML source. Some basic HTML tags— paragraph and bold—are added to give the generated page a bit of flair.

6. Print out the information of the user accessing the script:

```
echo "<p>You are viewing this page
→ using:<br /><b>$user</b></p>\n";
```

This line prints the second variable, **$user**. To repeat what's said in the fourth step, **$user** correlates to **$_SERVER['HTTP_USER_AGENT']** and refers to the operating system, browser type, and browser version being used to access the Web page.

7. Print out the server information:

```
echo "<p>This server is running:
→ <br /><b>$server</b>.</p>\n";
```

8. Complete the PHP block and the HTML page:

```
?>
</body>
</html>
```

9. Save the file as **predefined.php**, place it in your Web directory, and test it in your Web browser **A**.

> **TIP** If you have problems with this, or any other script, turn to the book's corresponding Web forum (**www.LarryUllman.com/forums/**) for assistance.

> **TIP** If possible, run this script using a different Web browser and/or on another server **B**.

> **TIP** Variable names cannot contain spaces. The underscore is commonly used in lieu of a space.

> **TIP** The most important consideration when creating variables is to use a consistent naming scheme. In this book you'll see that I use all-lowercase letters for my variable names, with underscores separating words (**$first_name**). Some programmers prefer to use capitalization instead: **$FirstName** (known as "camel-case" style).

> **TIP** PHP is very casual in how it treats variables, meaning that you don't need to initialize them (set an immediate value) or declare them (set a specific type), and you can convert a variable among the many types without problem.

You are running the file:
~~[blurred]~~ **predefined.php**.

You are viewing this page using:
Mozilla/4.0 (compatible; MSIE 8.0; Windows NT 6.1; WOW64; Trident/4.0; SLCC2; .NET CLR 2.0.50727; .NET CLR 3.5.30729; .NET CLR 3.0.30729; Media Center PC 6.0; .NET4.0C)

This server is running:
Apache/2.0.63 (CentOS).

A The **predefined.php** script reports back to the viewer information about the script, the Web browser being used to view it, and the server itself.

```
● ● ●              Predefined Variables
◀ ▶   1P   +  🌐 http://localhost/predefined.php   ⟳   Q▾ Google
```

You are running the file:
/Users/larryullman/Sites/phpmysql4/predefined.php.

You are viewing this page using:
Mozilla/5.0 (Macintosh; U; Intel Mac OS X 10_6_6; en-us) AppleWebKit/533.20.25 (KHTML, like Gecko) Version/5.0.4 Safari/533.20.27

This server is running:
Apache.

B This is the book's first truly dynamic script, in that the Web page changes depending upon the server running it and the Web browser viewing it (compare with **A**).

Introducing Strings

Now that you've been introduced to the general concept of variables, let's look at variables in detail. The first variable type to delve into is the *string*. A string is merely a quoted chunk of characters: letters, numbers, spaces, punctuation, and so forth. These are all strings:

- 'Tobias'
- "In watermelon sugar"
- '100'
- 'August 2, 2011'

To make a string variable, assign a string value to a valid variable name:

```
$first_name = 'Tobias';
$today = 'August 2, 2011';
```

When creating strings, you can use either single or double quotation marks to encapsulate the characters, just as you would when printing text. Likewise, you must use the same type of quotation mark for the beginning and the end of the string. If that same mark appears within the string, it must be escaped:

```
$var = "Define \"platitude\", please.";
```

Or you can also use the other quotation mark type:

```
$var = 'Define "platitude", please.';
```

To print out the value of a string, use either **echo** or **print**:

```
echo $first_name;
```

To print the value of string within a context, you must use double quotation marks:

```
echo "Hello, $first_name";
```

You've already worked with strings once—when using the predefined variables in the preceding section (the values of those variables happened to be strings). In this next example, you'll create and use your own strings.

```
1    <!DOCTYPE html PUBLIC "-//W3C//DTD XHTML
     1.0 Transitional//EN" "http://www.w3.org/
     TR/xhtml1/DTD/xhtml1-transitional.dtd">
2    <html xmlns="http://www.w3.org/1999/
     xhtml" xml:lang="en" lang="en">
3    <head>
4        <meta http-equiv="Content-Type"
         content="text/html; charset=utf-8" />
5        <title>Strings</title>
6    </head>
7    <body>
8    <?php # Script 1.6 - strings.php
9
10   // Create the variables:
11   $first_name = 'Haruki';
12   $last_name = 'Murakami';
13   $book = 'Kafka on the Shore';
14
15   // Print the values:
16   echo "<p>The book <em>$book</em>
     was written by $first_name
     $last_name.</p>";
17
18   ?>
19   </body>
20   </html>
```

To use strings:

1. Begin a new PHP document in your text editor or IDE, to be named **strings.php**, starting with the initial HTML and including the opening PHP tag (**Script 1.6**):

```
<!DOCTYPE html PUBLIC "-//W3C//
→ DTD XHTML 1.0 Transitional//EN"
→ "http://www.w3.org/TR/xhtml1/DTD/
→ xhtml1-transitional.dtd">
<html xmlns="http://www.w3.org/
→ 1999/xhtml" xml:lang="en"
→ lang="en">
<head>
  <meta http-equiv="Content-Type"
  → content="text/html;
  → charset=utf-8" />
  <title>Strings</title>
</head>
<body>
<?php # Script 1.6 - strings.php
```

2. Within the PHP tags, create three variables:

```
$first_name = 'Haruki';
$last_name = 'Murakami';
$book = 'Kafka on the Shore';
```

This rudimentary example creates **$first_name**, **$last_name**, and **$book** variables that will then be printed out in a message.

continues on next page

3. Add an **echo** statement:

```
echo "<p>The book <em>$book</em>
→ was written by $first_name
→ $last_name.</p>";
```

All this script does is print a statement of authorship based upon three established variables. A little HTML formatting (the emphasis on the book's title) is thrown in to make it more attractive. Remember to use double quotation marks here for the variable values to be printed out appropriately (more on the importance of double quotation marks at the chapter's end).

4. Complete the PHP block and the HTML page:

```
?>
</body>
</html>
```

5. Save the file as **strings.php**, place it in your Web directory, and test it in your Web browser Ⓐ.

6. If desired, change the values of the three variables, save the file, and run the script again Ⓑ.

TIP If you assign another value to an existing variable (say $book), the new value will overwrite the old one. For example:

```
$book = 'High Fidelity';
$book = 'The Corrections';
/* $book now has a value of
'The Corrections'. */
```

TIP PHP has no set limits on how big a string can be. It's theoretically possible that you'll be limited by the resources of the server, but it's doubtful that you'll ever encounter such a problem.

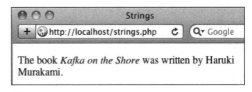

Ⓐ The resulting Web page is based upon printing out the values of three variables.

Ⓑ The output of the script is changed by altering the variables in it.

Script 1.7 Concatenation gives you the ability to append more characters onto a string.

```
1   <!DOCTYPE html PUBLIC "-//W3C//DTD XHTML
    1.0 Transitional//EN" "http://www.w3.org/
    TR/xhtml1/DTD/xhtml1-transitional.dtd">
2   <html xmlns="http://www.w3.org/1999/
    xhtml" xml:lang="en" lang="en">
3   <head>
4       <meta http-equiv="Content-Type"
        content="text/html; charset=utf-8" />
5       <title>Concatenation</title>
6   </head>
7   <body>
8   <?php # Script 1.7 - concat.php
9
10  // Create the variables:
11  $first_name = 'Melissa';
12  $last_name = 'Bank';
13  $author = $first_name . ' ' .
    $last_name;
14
15  $book = 'The Girls\' Guide to Hunting
    and Fishing';
16
17  //Print the values:
18  echo "<p>The book <em>$book</em>
    was written by $author.</p>";
19
20  ?>
21  </body>
22  </html>
```

Concatenating Strings

Concatenation is like addition for strings, whereby characters are added to the end of the string. It is performed using the *concatenation operator*, which is the period (**.**):

```
$city= 'Seattle';
$state = 'Washington';
$address = $city . $state;
```

The **$address** variable now has the value *SeattleWashington*, which almost achieves the desired result (*Seattle, Washington*). To improve upon this, you could write

```
$address = $city . ', ' . $state;
```

so that a comma and a space are concatenated to the variables as well.

Because of how liberally PHP treats variables, concatenation is possible with strings and numbers. Either of these statements will produce the same result (*Seattle, Washington 98101*):

```
$address = $city . ', ' . $state .
 ' 98101';
$address = $city . ', ' . $state .
 ' ' . 98101;
```

Let's modify **strings.php** to use this new operator.

To use concatenation:

1. Open **strings.php** (refer to Script 1.6) in your text editor or IDE.

2. After you've established the **$first_name** and **$last_name** variables (lines 11 and 12), add this line (**Script 1.7**):

   ```
   $author = $first_name . ' ' .
   → $last_name;
   ```

   As a demonstration of concatenation, a new variable—**$author**—will be created as the concatenation of two existing strings and a space in between.

continues on next page

3. Change the **echo** statement to use this new variable:

```
echo "<p>The book <em>$book</em>
→ was written by $author.</p>";
```

Since the two variables have been turned into one, the **echo** statement should be altered accordingly.

4. If desired, change the HTML page title and the values of the first name, last name, and book variables.

5. Save the file as **concat.php**, place it in your Web directory, and test it in your Web browser **Ⓐ**.

Ⓐ In this revised script, the end result of concatenation is not apparent to the user.

TIP PHP has a slew of useful string-specific functions, which you'll see over the course of this book. For example, to calculate how long a string is (how many characters it contains), use `strlen( )`:

```
$num = strlen('some string'); // 11
```

TIP You can have PHP convert the case of strings with: `strtolower( )`, which makes it entirely lowercase; `strtoupper( )`, which makes it entirely uppercase; `ucfirst( )`, which capitalizes the first character; and `ucwords( )`, which capitalizes the first character of every word.

TIP If you are merely concatenating one value to another, you can use the concatenation assignment operator (`.=`). The following are equivalent:

```
$title = $title . $subtitle;
$title .= $subtitle;
```

TIP The initial example in this section could be rewritten using either

```
$address = "$city, $state";
```

or

```
$address = $city;
$address .= ', ';
$address .= $state;
```

Using the PHP Manual

The PHP manual—accessible online at **www.php.net/manual**—lists every function and feature of the language. The manual is organized with general concepts (installation, syntax, variables) discussed first and ends with the functions by topic (MySQL, string functions, and so on).

To quickly look up any function in the PHP manual, go to **www.php.net/ functionname** in your Web browser (for example, **www.php.net/print**). For each function, the manual indicates:

- The versions of PHP the function is available in.

- How many and what types of arguments the function takes (optional arguments are wrapped in square brackets).

- What type of value the function returns.

The manual also contains a description of the function.

You should be in the habit of checking out the PHP manual whenever you're confused by a function, how it's properly used, or need to learn more about any feature of the language. It's also critically important that you know what version of PHP you're running, as functions and other particulars of PHP do change over time.

Introducing Numbers

In introducing variables, I stated that PHP has both integer and floating-point (decimal) number types. In my experience, though, these two types can be classified under the generic title *numbers* without losing any valuable distinction (for the most part). Valid number-type variables in PHP can be anything like

- 8
- 3.14
- 10980843985
- -4.2398508
- 4.4e2

Notice that these values are never quoted—quoted numbers are strings with numeric values—nor do they include commas to indicate thousands. Also, a number is assumed to be positive unless it is preceded by the minus sign (-).

Along with the standard arithmetic operators you can use on numbers (**Table 1.1**), there are dozens of functions built into PHP. Two common ones are `round( )` and `number_format( )`. The former rounds a decimal to the nearest integer:

```
$n = 3.14;
$n = round ($n); // 3
```

It can also round to a specified number of decimal places:

```
$n = 3.142857;
$n = round ($n, 3); // 3.143
```

The `number_format( )` function turns a number into the more commonly written version, grouped into thousands using commas:

```
$n = 20943;
$n = number_format ($n); // 20,943
```

This function can also set a specified number of decimal points:

```
$n = 20943;
$n = number_format ($n, 2); //
20,943.00
```

To practice with numbers, let's write a mock-up script that performs the calculations one might use in an e-commerce shopping cart.

TABLE 1.1 Arithmetic Operators

Operator	Meaning
+	Addition
-	Subtraction
*	Multiplication
/	Division
%	Modulus
++	Increment
--	Decrement

To use numbers:

1. Begin a new PHP document in your text editor or IDE, to be named **numbers.php** (Script 1.8):

```
<!DOCTYPE html PUBLIC "-//W3C//
→ DTD XHTML 1.0 Transitional//EN"
→ "http://www.w3.org/TR/xhtml1/DTD/
→ xhtml1-transitional.dtd">
<html xmlns="http://www.w3.org/
→ 1999/xhtml" xml:lang="en"
→ lang="en">
<head>
  <meta http-equiv="Content-Type"
  → content="text/html;
  → charset=utf-8" />
  <title>Numbers</title>
</head>
<body>
<?php # Script 1.8 - numbers.php
```

2. Establish the requisite variables:

```
$quantity = 30;
$price = 119.95;
$taxrate = .05;
```

This script will use three hard-coded variables upon which calculations will be made. Later in the book, you'll see how these values can be dynamically determined (i.e., by user interaction with an HTML form).

3. Perform the calculations:

```
$total = $quantity * $price;
$total = $total + ($total *
→ $taxrate);
```

The first line establishes the order total as the number of widgets purchased multiplied by the price of each widget. The second line then adds the amount of tax to the total (calculated by multiplying the tax rate by the total).

Script 1.8 The **numbers.php** script performs basic mathematical calculations, like those used in an e-commerce application.

```
1   <!DOCTYPE html PUBLIC "-//W3C//DTD XHTML
    1.0 Transitional//EN" "http://www.w3.org/
    TR/xhtml1/DTD/xhtml1-transitional.dtd">
2   <html xmlns="http://www.w3.org/1999/
    xhtml" xml:lang="en" lang="en">
3   <head>
4       <meta http-equiv="Content-Type"
        content="text/html; charset=utf-8" />
5       <title>Numbers</title>
6   </head>
7   <body>
8   <?php # Script 1.8 - numbers.php
9
10  // Set the variables:
11  $quantity = 30; // Buying 30 widgets.
12  $price = 119.95;
13  $taxrate = .05; // 5% sales tax.
14
15  // Calculate the total:
16  $total = $quantity * $price;
17  $total = $total + ($total * $taxrate);
    // Calculate and add the tax.
18
19  // Format the total:
20  $total = number_format ($total, 2);
21
22  // Print the results:
23  echo '<p>You are purchasing <b>' .
    $quantity . '</b> widget(s) at a cost
    of <b>$' . $price . '</b> each. With
    tax, the total comes to <b>$' .
    $total . '</b>.</p>';
24
25  ?>
26  </body>
27  </html>
```

4. Format the total:

```
$total = number_format ($total, 2);
```

The **number_format( )** function will group the total into thousands and round it to two decimal places. Applying this function will properly format the calculated value.

5. Print the results:

```
echo '<p>You are purchasing <b>' .
→ $quantity . '</b> widget(s) at
→ a cost of <b>$' . $price . '</b>
→ each. With tax, the total comes
→ to <b>$' . $total . '</b>.</p>';
```

The last step in the script is to print out the results. The **echo** statement uses both single-quoted text and concatenated variables in order to print out the full combination of HTML, dollar signs, and variable values. You'll see an alternative approach in the last example of this chapter.

6. Complete the PHP code and the HTML page:

```
?>
</body>
</html>
```

7. Save the file as **numbers.php**, place it in your Web directory, and test it in your Web browser **A**.

8. If desired, change the initial three variables and rerun the script **B**.

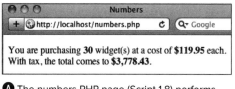

A The numbers PHP page (Script 1.8) performs calculations based upon set values.

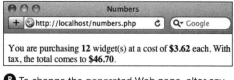

B To change the generated Web page, alter any or all of the three variables (compare with **A**).

Introducing Constants

Constants, like variables, are used to temporarily store a value, but otherwise, constants and variables differ in many ways. For starters, to create a constant, you use the **define( )** function instead of the assignment operator (=):

```
define ('NAME', value);
```

Notice that, as a rule of thumb, constants are named using all capitals, although this is not required. Most importantly, constants do not use the initial dollar sign as variables do (because constants are not variables).

A constant can only be assigned a *scalar* value, like a string or a number:

```
define ('USERNAME', 'troutocity');
define ('PI', 3.14);
```

And unlike variables, a constant's value cannot be changed.

To access a constant's value, like when you want to print it, you cannot put the constant within quotation marks:

```
echo "Hello, USERNAME"; // Won't work!
```

With that code, PHP literally prints *Hello, USERNAME* 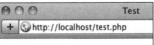 and not the value of the **USERNAME** constant (because there's no indication that **USERNAME** is anything other than literal text). Instead, either print the constant by itself:

```
echo 'Hello, ';
echo USERNAME;
```

or use the concatenation operator:

```
echo 'Hello, ' . USERNAME;
```

PHP runs with several predefined constants, much like the predefined variables used earlier in the chapter. These include **PHP_VERSION** (the version of PHP running) and **PHP_OS** (the operating system of the server). This next script will print those two values, along with the value of a user-defined constant.

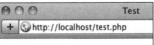

Hello, USERNAME

A Constants cannot be placed within quoted strings.

Script 1.9 Constants are another temporary storage tool you can use in PHP, distinct from variables.

```
1   <!DOCTYPE html PUBLIC "-//W3C//DTD XHTML
    1.0 Transitional//EN" "http://www.w3.org/
    TR/xhtml1/DTD/xhtml1-transitional.dtd">
2   <html xmlns="http://www.w3.org/1999/
    xhtml" xml:lang="en" lang="en">
3   <head>
4      <meta http-equiv="Content-Type"
       content="text/html; charset=utf-8" />
5      <title>Constants</title>
6   </head>
7   <body>
8   <?php # Script 1.9 - constants.php
9
10  // Set today's date as a constant:
11  define ('TODAY', 'March 16, 2011');
12
13  // Print a message, using predefined
    constants and the TODAY constant:
14  echo '<p>Today is ' . TODAY . '.<br />
    This server is running version <b>' .
    PHP_VERSION . '</b> of PHP on the <b>' .
    PHP_OS . '</b> operating system.</p>';
15
16  ?>
17  </body>
18  </html>
```

To use constants:

1. Begin a new PHP document in your text editor or IDE, to be named **constants.php** (Script 1.9).

   ```
   <!DOCTYPE html PUBLIC "-//W3C//
   → DTD XHTML 1.0 Transitional//EN"
   → "http://www.w3.org/TR/xhtml1/DTD/
   → xhtml1-transitional.dtd">
   <html xmlns="http://www.w3.org/
   → 1999/xhtml" xml:lang="en"
   → lang="en">
   <head>
      <meta http-equiv="Content-Type"
      → content="text/html;
      → charset=utf-8" />
      <title>Constants</title>
   </head>
   <body>
   <?php # Script 1.9 - constants.php
   ```

2. Create a new date constant:

   ```
   define ('TODAY', 'March 16, 2011');
   ```

   An admittedly trivial use of constants, but this example will illustrate the point. In Chapter 9, "Using PHP with MySQL," you'll see how to use constants to store your database access information.

3. Print out the date, the PHP version, and operating system information:

   ```
   echo '<p>Today is ' . TODAY .
   → '.<br />This server is running
   → version <b>' . PHP_VERSION .
   → '</b> of PHP on the <b>' . PHP_OS .
   → '</b> operating system.</p>';
   ```

   Since constants cannot be printed within quotation marks, use the concatenation operator in the **echo** statement.

   continues on next page

4. Complete the PHP code and the HTML page:

```
?>
</body>
</html>
```

5. Save the file as **constants.php**, place it in your Web directory, and test it in your Web browser 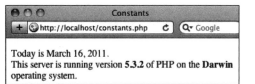.

> **TIP** If possible, run this script on another PHP-enabled server **C**.

> **TIP** The operating system called *Darwin* **B** is the technical term for Mac OS X.

> **TIP** In Chapter 12, "Cookies and Sessions," you'll learn about another constant, SID (which stands for *session ID*).

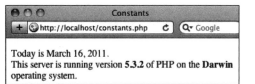

Today is March 16, 2011.
This server is running version **5.3.2** of PHP on the **Darwin** operating system.

B By making use of PHP's constants, you can learn more about your PHP setup.

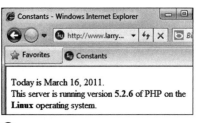

Today is March 16, 2011.
This server is running version **5.2.6** of PHP on the **Linux** operating system.

C Running the same script (refer to Script 1.9) on different servers garners different results.

Single vs. Double Quotation Marks

In PHP it's important to understand how single quotation marks differ from double quotation marks. With **echo** and **print**, or when assigning values to strings, you can use either, as in the examples used so far. But there is a key difference between the two types of quotation marks and when you should use which. You've seen this difference already, but it's an important enough concept to merit more discussion.

In PHP, *values enclosed within single quotation marks will be treated literally*, whereas *those within double quotation marks will be interpreted*. In other words, placing variables and special characters (**Table 1.2**) within double quotes will result in their represented values printed, not their literal values. For example, assume that you have

```
$var = 'test';
```

The code **echo "var is equal to $var";** will print out *var is equal to test*, but the code **echo 'var is equal to $var';** will print out *var is equal to $var*. Using an escaped dollar sign, the code **echo "\$var is equal to $var";** will print out *$var is equal to test*, whereas the code **echo '\$var is equal to $var';** will print out *\$var is equal to $var* **Ⓐ**.

As these examples should illustrate, double quotation marks will replace a variable's name (**$var**) with its value (*test*) and a special character's code (**\$**) with its represented value (*$*). Single quotes will always display exactly what you type, except for the escaped single quote (**\'**) and the escaped backslash (****), which are printed as a single quotation mark and a single backslash, respectively.

As another example of how the two quotation marks differ, let's modify the **numbers.php** script as an experiment.

TABLE 1.2 Escape Sequences

Code	Meaning
\"	Double quotation mark
\'	Single quotation mark
\\	Backslash
\n	Newline
\r	Carriage return
\t	Tab
\$	Dollar sign

Ⓐ How single and double quotation marks affect what gets printed by PHP.

To use single and double quotation marks:

1. Open **numbers.php** (refer to Script 1.8) in your text editor or IDE.

2. Delete the existing **echo** statement (**Script 1.10**).

3. Print a caption and then rewrite the original **echo** statement using double quotation marks:

   ```
   echo "<h3>Using double quotation
   → marks:</h3>";
   echo "<p>You are purchasing
   → <b>$quantity</b> widget(s) at
   → a cost of <b>\$$price</b> each.
   → With tax, the total comes to
   → <b>\$$total</b>.</p>\n";
   ```

   In the original script, the results were printed using single quotation marks and concatenation. The same result can be achieved using double quotation marks. When using double quotation marks, the variables can be placed within the string.

   There is one catch, though: trying to print a dollar amount as $12.34 (where 12.34 comes from a variable) would suggest that you would code **$$var**. That will not work (for complicated reasons). Instead, escape the initial dollar sign, resulting in **\$$var**, as you see twice in this code. The first dollar sign will be printed, and the second becomes the start of the variable name.

Script 1.10 This, the final script in the chapter, demonstrates the differences between using single and double quotation marks.

```
1   <!DOCTYPE html PUBLIC "-//W3C//DTD XHTML
    1.0 Transitional//EN" "http://www.w3.org/
    TR/xhtml1/DTD/xhtml1-transitional.dtd">
2   <html xmlns="http://www.w3.org/1999/
    xhtml" xml:lang="en" lang="en">
3   <head>
4       <meta http-equiv="Content-Type"
        content="text/html; charset=utf-8" />
5       <title>Quotation Marks</title>
6   </head>
7   <body>
8   <?php # Script 1.10 - quotes.php
9
10  // Set the variables:
11  $quantity = 30; // Buying 30 widgets.
12  $price = 119.95;
13  $taxrate = .05; // 5% sales tax.
14
15  // Calculate the total.
16  $total = $quantity * $price;
17  $total = $total + ($total * $taxrate);
    // Calculate and add the tax.
18
19  // Format the total:
20  $total = number_format ($total, 2);
21
22  // Print the results using double
    quotation marks:
23  echo "<h3>Using double quotation
    marks:</h3>";
24  echo "<p>You are purchasing
    <b>$quantity</b> widget(s) at a cost
    of <b>\$$price</b> each. With tax,
    the total comes to <b>\$$total</b>.
    </p>\n";
25
26  // Print the results using single
    quotation marks:
27  echo '<h3>Using single quotation
    marks:</h3>';
28  echo '<p>You are purchasing
    <b>$quantity</b> widget(s) at a cost
    of <b>\$$price</b> each. With tax,
    the total comes to <b>\$$total</b>.
    </p>\n';
29
30  ?>
31  </body>
32  </html>
```

4. Repeat the **echo** statements, this time using single quotation marks:

```
echo '<h3>Using single quotation
→ marks:</h3>';
echo '<p>You are purchasing
→ <b>$quantity</b> widget(s) at
→ a cost of <b>\$$price</b> each.
→ With tax, the total comes to
→ <b>\$$total</b>.</p>\n';
```

This **echo** statement is used to highlight the difference between using single or double quotation marks. It will not work as desired, and the resulting page will show you exactly what does happen instead.

5. If you want, change the page's title.

6. Save the file as **quotes.php**, place it in your Web directory, and test it in your Web browser **B**.

7. View the source of the Web page to see how using the newline character (**\n**) within each quotation mark type also differs.

You should see that when you place the newline character within double quotation marks it creates a newline in the HTML source. When placed within single quotation marks, the literal characters **** and **n** are printed instead.

TIP Because PHP will attempt to find variables within double quotation marks, using single quotation marks is theoretically faster. If you need to print the value of a variable, though, you must use double quotation marks.

TIP As valid HTML often includes a lot of double-quoted attributes, it's often easiest to use single quotation marks when printing HTML with PHP:

```
echo '<table width="80%" border="0"
→ cellspacing="2" cellpadding="3"
→ align="center">';
```

If you were to print out this HTML using double quotation marks, you would have to escape all of the double quotation marks in the string:

```
echo "<table width=\"80%\" border=
→ \"0\" cellspacing=\"2\" cellpadding=
→ \"3\" align=\"center\">";
```

TIP In newer versions of PHP, you can actually use $$price and $$total without preceding them with a backslash (thanks to some internal magic). In older versions of PHP, you cannot. To guarantee reliable results, regardless of PHP version, I recommend using the \$$var syntax when you need to print a dollar sign immediately followed by the value of a variable.

TIP If you're still unclear as to the difference between the types, use double quotation marks and you're less likely to have problems.

B These results demonstrate when and how you'd use one type of quotation mark as opposed to the other.

Basic Debugging Steps

Debugging is by no means a simple concept to grasp, and unfortunately, it's one that is only truly mastered by doing. The next 50 pages could be dedicated to the subject and you'd still only be able to pick up a fraction of the debugging skills that you'll eventually acquire and need.

The reason I introduce debugging in this somewhat harrowing way is that it's important not to enter into programming with delusions. Sometimes code won't work as expected, you'll inevitably create careless errors, and some days you'll want to pull your hair out, even when using a comparatively user-friendly language such as PHP. In short, prepare to be perplexed and frustrated at times. I've been coding in PHP since 1999, and occasionally I still get stuck in the programming muck. But debugging is a very important skill to have, and one that you will eventually pick up out of necessity and experience. As you begin your PHP programming adventure, I can offer the following basic but concrete debugging tips.

Note that these are just some general debugging techniques, specifically tailored to the beginning PHP programmer. Chapter 8, "Error Handling and Debugging," goes into other techniques in more detail.

To debug a PHP script:

- **Make sure you're always running PHP scripts through a URL!**

  This is perhaps the most common beginner's mistake. PHP code must be run through the Web server application, which means it must be requested via `http://something`. When you see actual PHP code instead of the result of that code's execution, most likely you're not running the PHP script through a URL.

- **Know what version of PHP you're running.**

  Some problems will arise from the version of PHP in use. Before you ever use any PHP-enabled server, run a `phpinfo.php` script (see Appendix A) or reference the `PHP_VERSION` constant to confirm the version of PHP in use.

- **Make sure `display_errors` is on.**

  This is a basic PHP configuration setting (also discussed in Appendix A). You can confirm this setting by executing the `phpinfo()` function (just use your browser to search for *display_errors* in the resulting page). For security reasons, PHP may not be set to display the errors that occur. If that's the case, you'll end up seeing blank pages when problems occur. To debug most problems, you'll need to see the errors, so turn this setting on while you're learning. You'll find instructions for doing so in Appendix A.

- **Check the HTML source code.**

  Sometimes the problem is hidden in the HTML source of the page. In fact, sometimes the PHP error message can be hidden there!

- **Trust the error message.**

  Another very common beginner's mistake is to not fully read or trust the error that PHP reports. Although an error message can often be cryptic and may seem meaningless, it can't be ignored. At the very least, PHP is normally correct as to the line on which the problem can be found. And if you need to relay that error message to someone else (like when you're asking me for help), do include the entire error message!

- **Take a break!**

  So many of the programming problems I've encountered over the years, and the vast majority of the toughest ones, have been solved by stepping away from the computer for a while. It's easy to get frustrated and confused, and in such situations, any further steps you take are likely to only make matters worse.

Review and Pursue

New in this edition of the book, each chapter ends with a "Review and Pursue" section. In these sections you'll find questions regarding the material just covered and prompts for ways to expand your knowledge and experience on your own. If you have any problems with these sections, either in answering the questions or pursuing your own endeavors, turn to the book's supporting forum (**www.LarryUllman.com/forums/**).

Review

- What tags are used to surround PHP code?

- What extension should a PHP file have?

- What does a page's *encoding* refer to? What impact does the encoding have on the page?

- What PHP functions, or language constructs, can you use to send data to the Web browser?

- How does using single versus double quotation marks differ in creating or printing strings?

- What does it mean to *escape* a character in a string?

- What are the three comment syntaxes in PHP? Which one can be used over multiple lines?

- What character do all variable names begin with? What characters can come next? What other characters can be used in a variable's name?

- Are variable names case-sensitive or case-insensitive?

- What is the assignment operator?

- How do you create a string variable?

- What is the concatenation operator? What is the concatenation assignment operator?

- How are constants defined and used?

Pursue

- If you don't already know—*for certain*—what version of PHP you're running, check now.

- Look up one of the mentioned string functions in the PHP manual. Then check out some of the other available string functions listed therein.

- Look up one of the mentioned number functions in the PHP manual. Then check out some of the other available number functions listed therein.

- Search the PHP manual for the **$_SERVER** variable to see what other information it contains.

- Create a new script, from scratch, that defines and displays the values of some string variables. Use double quotation marks in the **echo** or **print** statement that outputs the values. For added complexity include some HTML in the output. Then rewrite the script so that it uses single quotation marks and concatenation instead of double quotation marks.

- Create a new script, from scratch, that defines, manipulates, and displays the values of some numeric variables.

Programming with PHP

Now that you have the fundamentals of the PHP scripting language down, it's time to build on those basics and start truly programming. In this chapter you'll begin creating more elaborate scripts while still learning some of the standard constructs, functions, and syntax of the language.

You'll start by creating an HTML form, and then learn how you can use PHP to handle the submitted values. From there, the chapter covers conditionals and the remaining operators (Chapter 1, "Introduction to PHP," presented the assignment, concatenation, and mathematical operators), arrays (another variable type), and one last language construct, loops.

Creating an HTML Form

Handling an HTML form with PHP is perhaps the most important process in any dynamic Web site. Two steps are involved: first you create the HTML form itself, and then you create the corresponding PHP script that will receive and process the form data.

It is outside the realm of this book to go into HTML forms in any detail, but I will lead you through one quick example so that it may be used throughout the chapter. If you're unfamiliar with the basics of an HTML form, including the various types of elements, see an HTML resource for more information.

An HTML form is created using the `form` tags and various elements for taking input. The `form` tags look like

```
<form action="script.php"
→ method="post">
</form>
```

In terms of PHP, the most important attribute of your `form` tag is `action`, which dictates to which page the form data will be sent. The second attribute—`method`—has its own issues (see the "Choosing a Method" sidebar), but *post* is the value you'll use most frequently.

The different inputs—be they text boxes, radio buttons, select menus, check boxes, etc.—are placed within the opening and closing `form` tags. As you'll see in the next section, what kinds of inputs your form has makes little difference to the PHP script handling it. You should, however, pay attention to the names you give your form inputs, as they'll be of critical importance when it comes to your PHP code.

Choosing a Method

The **method** attribute of a form dictates how the data is sent to the handling page. The two options—*get* and *post*—refer to the HTTP (HyperText Transfer Protocol) method to be used. The **GET** method sends the submitted data to the receiving page as a series of name-value pairs appended to the URL. For example,

```
http://www.example.com/script.php?
→ name=Homer&gender=M&age=35
```

The benefit of using the **GET** method is that the resulting page can be bookmarked in the user's Web browser (since it's a complete URL). For that matter, you can also click Back in your Web browser to return to a **GET** page, or reload it without problems (none of which is true for **POST**). But there is a limit in how much data can be transmitted via **GET**, and this method is less secure (since the data is visible).

Generally speaking, *GET is used for requesting information*, like a particular record from a database or the results of a search (searches almost always use **GET**). *The POST method is used when an action is expected*: the updating of a database record or the sending of an email. For these reasons I will primarily use **POST** throughout this book, with noted exceptions.

```
1    <!DOCTYPE html PUBLIC "-//W3C//DTD
     XHTML 1.0 Transitional//EN"
     "http://www.w3.org/TR/xhtml1/DTD/
     xhtml1-transitional.dtd">
2    <html xmlns="http://www.w3.org/1999/
     xhtml" xml:lang="en" lang="en">
3    <head>
4       <meta http-equiv="Content-Type"
        content="text/html; charset=utf-8" />
5       <title>Simple HTML Form</title>
6       <style type="text/css" title="text/
        css" media="all">
7       label {
8          font-weight: bold;
9          color: #300ACC;
10      }
11      </style>
12   </head>
13   <body>
14   <!-- Script 2.1 - form.html -->
15
16   <form action="handle_form.php"
     method="post">
17
18      <fieldset><legend>Enter your
        information in the form below:
        </legend>
19
20      <p><label>Name: <input type="text"
        name="name" size="20" maxlength=
        "40" /></label></p>
21
22      <p><label>Email Address: <input
        type="text" name="email" size="40"
        maxlength="60" /></label></p>
23
24      <p><label for="gender">Gender:
        </label><input type="radio"
        name="gender" value="M" /> Male
        <input type="radio" name="gender"
        value="F" /> Female</p>
25
26      <p><label>Age:
27      <select name="age">
28         <option value="0-29">Under 30
           </option>
29         <option value="30-60">Between 30
           and 60</option>
```

code continues on next page

To create an HTML form:

1. Begin a new HTML document in your text editor or IDE, to be named **form.html** (Script 2.1):

```
<!DOCTYPE html PUBLIC "-//W3C//
→ DTD XHTML 1.0 Transitional//EN"
→ "http://www.w3.org/TR/xhtml1/DTD/
→ xhtml1-transitional.dtd">
<html xmlns="http://www.w3.org/
→ 1999/xhtml" xml:lang="en"
→ lang="en">
<head>
   <meta http-equiv="Content-Type"
   → content="text/html;
   → charset=utf-8" />
   <title>Simple HTML Form</title>
   <style type="text/css"
   → title="text/css" media="all">
   label {
      font-weight: bold;
      color: #300ACC;
   }
   </style>
</head>
<body>
<!-- Script 2.1 - form.html -->
```

The document uses the same basic syntax for an HTML page as in the previous chapter. I have added some inline CSS (Cascading Style Sheets) in order to style the form slightly (specifically, making **label** elements bold and blue).

CSS is the preferred way to handle many formatting and layout issues in an HTML page. You'll see a little bit of CSS here and there in this book; if you're not familiar with the subject, check out a dedicated CSS reference.

Finally, an HTML comment indicates the file's name and number.

continues on next page

2. Add the initial **form** tag:

```
<form action="handle_form.php"
→ method="post">
```

Since the **action** attribute dictates to which script the form data will go, you should give it an appropriate name (*handle_form* to correspond with this page: **form.html**) and the **.php** extension (since a PHP script will handle this form's data).

3. Begin the HTML form:

```
<fieldset><legend>Enter your
→ information in the form below:
→ </legend>
```

I'm using the **fieldset** and **legend** HTML tags because I like the way they make the HTML form look (they add a box around the form with a title at the top). This isn't pertinent to the form itself, though.

4. Add two text inputs:

```
<p><label>Name: <input type=
→ "text" name="name" size="20"
→ maxlength="40" /></label></p>
<p><label>Email Address: <input
→ type="text" name="email"
→ size="40" maxlength="60" />
→ </label></p>
```

These are just simple text inputs, allowing the user to enter their name and email address **Ⓐ**. In case you are wondering, the extra space and slash at the end of each input's tag are required for valid XHTML. With standard HTML, these tags would conclude with **maxlength="40">** instead. The **label** tags just tie each textual label to the associated element.

Script 2.1 *continued*

```
30        <option value="60+">Over 60
          </option>
31    </select></label></p>
32
33    <p><label>Comments: <textarea
      name="comments" rows="3" cols="40"></
      textarea></label></p>
34
35    </fieldset>
36
37    <p align="center"><input type=
      "submit" name="submit" value=
      "Submit My Information" /></p>
38
39  </form>
40
41  </body>
42  </html>
```

Name: [Larry Ullman]

Email Address: [Larry@LarryUllman.com]

Ⓐ Two text inputs.

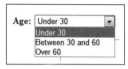

Gender: ● Male ○ Female

B If multiple radio buttons have the same **name** value, only one can be selected by the user.

Age:	Under 30	▼
	Under 30	
	Between 30 and 60	
	Over 60	

C The pull-down menu offers three options, of which only one can be selected (in this example).

	The textarea form element allows for lots and lots of text to be entered. The textarea form element allows for lots	▲ ▼
Comments:	and lots of text to be entered. The	

D The textarea form element type allows for lots and lots of text.

5. Add a pair of radio buttons:

```
<p><label for="gender">Gender:
→ </label><input type="radio"
→ name="gender" value="M" /> Male
→ <input type="radio" name=
→ "gender" value="F" /> Female</p>
```

The radio buttons **B** both have the same name, meaning that only one of the two can be selected. They have different values, though.

6. Add a pull-down menu:

```
<p><label>Age:
<select name="age">
    <option value="0-29">Under 30
    → </option>
    <option value="30-60">Between
    → 30 and 60</option>
    <option value="60+">Over 60
    → </option>
</select></label></p>
```

The **select** tag starts the pull-down menu, and then each **option** tag will create another line in the list of choices **C**.

7. Add a text box for comments:

```
<p><label>Comments: <textarea
→ name="comments" rows="3"
→ cols="40"></textarea></label></p>
```

Textareas are different from text inputs; they are presented as a box **D**, not as a single line. They allow for much more information to be typed and are useful for taking user comments.

continues on next page

8. Complete the form:

```
</fieldset>
<p align="center"><input type=
→"submit" name="submit" value=
→"Submit My Information" /></p>
</form>
```

The first tag closes the **fieldset** that was opened in Step 3. Then a submit button is created and centered using a **p** tag. Finally, the form is closed.

9. Complete the HTML page:

```
</body>
</html>
```

10. Save the file as **form.html**, place it in your Web directory, and view it in your Web browser **ⓔ**.

TIP Since this page contains just HTML, it uses an .html extension. It could instead use a .php extension without harm (since code outside of the PHP tags is treated as HTML).

TIP You can specify the encoding to accept in an HTML form tag, too:

```
<form accept-charset="utf-8">
```

By default, a Web page will use the same encoding as the page itself for any submitted data.

ⓔ The complete form, which requests some basic information from the user.

Handling an HTML Form

Now that the HTML form has been created, it's time to write a bare-bones PHP script to handle it. To say that this script will be *handling* the form means that the PHP page will do something with the data it receives (which is the data the user entered into the form). In this chapter, the scripts will simply print the data back to the Web browser. In later examples, form data will be stored in a MySQL database, compared against previously stored values, sent in emails, and more.

The beauty of PHP—and what makes it so easy to learn and use—is how well it interacts with HTML forms. PHP scripts store the received information in special variables. For example, say you have a form with an input defined like so:

```
<input type="text" name="city" />
```

Whatever the user types into that input will be accessible via a PHP variable named **$_REQUEST['city']**. It is very important that the spelling and capitalization match *exactly*! PHP is case-sensitive when it comes to variable names, so **$_REQUEST['city']** will work, but **$_Request['city']** and **$_REQUEST['City']** will have no value.

This next example will be a PHP script that handles the already-created HTML form (Script 2.1). This script will assign the form data to new variables (to be used as shorthand, just like in Script 1.5, **predefined.php**). The script will then print the received values.

To handle an HTML form:

1. Begin a new PHP document in your text editor or IDE, to be named **handle_form.php** starting with the HTML (**Script 2.2**):

```
<!DOCTYPE html PUBLIC "-//W3C//
→ DTD XHTML 1.0 Transitional//EN"
→ "http://www.w3.org/TR/xhtml1/DTD/
→ xhtml1-transitional.dtd">
<html xmlns="http://www.w3.org/
→ 1999/xhtml" xml:lang="en"
→ lang="en">
<head>
  <meta http-equiv="Content-Type"
  → content="text/html;
  → charset=utf-8" />
  <title>Form Feedback</title>
</head>
<body>
```

2. Add the opening PHP tag and create a shorthand version of the form data variables:

```
<?php # Script 2.2 -
→ handle_form.php
$name = $_REQUEST['name'];
$email = $_REQUEST['email'];
$comments = $_REQUEST['comments'];
```

Following the rules outlined before, the data entered into the first form input, which is called *name*, will be accessible through the variable **$_REQUEST['name']** (**Table 2.1**). The data entered into the email form input, which has a **name** value of *email*, will be accessible through **$_REQUEST['email']**. The same applies to the comments data. Again, the spelling and capitalization of your variables here must exactly match the corresponding **name** values in the HTML form.

Script 2.2 This script receives and prints out the information entered into an HTML form (Script 2.1).

```
1   <!DOCTYPE html PUBLIC "-//W3C//DTD
    XHTML 1.0 Transitional//EN"
    "http://www.w3.org/TR/xhtml1/DTD/
    xhtml1-transitional.dtd">
2   <html xmlns="http://www.w3.org/1999/
    xhtml" xml:lang="en" lang="en">
3   <head>
4       <meta http-equiv="Content-Type"
        content="text/html; charset=utf-8" />
5       <title>Form Feedback</title>
6   </head>
7   <body>
8   <?php # Script 2.2 - handle_form.php
9
10  // Create a shorthand for the form data:
11  $name = $_REQUEST['name'];
12  $email = $_REQUEST['email'];
13  $comments = $_REQUEST['comments'];
14  /* Not used:
15  $_REQUEST['age']
16  $_REQUEST['gender']
17  $_REQUEST['submit']
18  */
19
20  // Print the submitted information:
21  echo "<p>Thank you, <b>$name</b>,
        for the following comments:<br />
22  <tt>$comments</tt></p>
23  <p>We will reply to you at
        <i>$email</i>.</p>\n";
24
25  ?>
26  </body>
27  </html>
```

TABLE 2.1 Form Elements to PHP Variables

Element Name	Variable Name
name	$_REQUEST['name']
email	$_REQUEST['email']
comments	$_REQUEST['comments']
age	$_REQUEST['age']
gender	$_REQUEST['gender']
submit	$_REQUEST['submit']

At this point, you won't make use of the age, gender, and submit form elements.

3. Print out the received name, email, and comments values:

```
echo "<p>Thank you, <b>$name</b>,
→ for the following comments:<br />
<tt>$comments</tt></p>
<p>We will reply to you at
→ <i>$email</i>.</p>\n";
```

The submitted values are simply printed out using the **echo** statement, double quotation marks, and a wee bit of HTML formatting.

4. Complete the page:

```
?>
</body>
</html>
```

5. Save the file as **handle_form.php** and place it in the same Web directory as **form.html**.

6. Test both documents in your Web browser by loading **form.html** through a URL (**http://something**) and then filling out Ⓐ and submitting the form Ⓑ.

Because the PHP script must be run through a URL (see Chapter 1), the form must also be run through a URL. Otherwise, when you go to submit the form, you'll see PHP code Ⓒ instead of the proper result Ⓑ.

Ⓐ To test **handle_form.php**, you must load the form through a URL, then fill it out and submit it.

Ⓑ The script should display results like this.

Ⓒ If you see the PHP code after submitting the form, the problem is likely that you did not access the form through a URL.

TIP $_REQUEST is a special variable type, known as a *superglobal*. It stores all of the data sent to a PHP page through either the GET or POST method, as well as data accessible in cookies. Superglobals will be discussed later in the chapter.

TIP If you have any problems with this script, apply the debugging techniques suggested in Chapter 1. If you still can't solve the problem, check out the extended debugging techniques listed in Chapter 8, "Error Handling and Debugging." If you're still stymied, turn to the book's supporting forum for assistance (www.LarryUllman.com/forums/).

TIP If the PHP script shows blank spaces where a variable's value should have been printed, it means that the variable has no value. The two most likely causes are: you failed to enter a value in the form; or you mis-spelled or mis-capitalized the variable's name.

TIP If you see any *Undefined variable: variablename* errors, this is because the variables you refer to have no value and PHP is set on the highest level of error reporting. The previous tip provides suggestions as to why a variable wouldn't have a value. Chapter 8 discusses error reporting in detail.

TIP To see how PHP handles the different form input types, print out the $_REQUEST['age'] and $_REQUEST['gender'] values .

D The values of gender and age correspond to those defined in the form's HTML.

Magic Quotes

Earlier versions of PHP had a feature called *Magic Quotes*, which has since been deprecated and will eventually be removed entirely. Magic Quotes—when enabled—automatically escapes single and double quotation marks found in submitted form data (there were actually three kinds of Magic Quotes, but this one kind is most important here). As an example, Magic Quotes would turn the string *I'm going out* into *I\'m going out*.

The escaping of potentially problematic characters can be useful and even necessary in some situations. But if Magic Quotes are enabled on your PHP installation, you'll see these backslashes when the PHP script prints out the form data. You can undo the effect of Magic Quotes using the **stripslashes( )** function:

$var = stripslashes($var);

This function will remove any backslashes found in **$var**. This will have the result of turning an escaped submitted string back to its original, non-escaped value.

To use this in **handle_form.php** (Script 2.2), you would write:

$name = stripslashes($_REQUEST
⇢['name']);

If you're not seeing backslashes added to your form data, then you don't need to worry about Magic Quotes.

Conditionals and Operators

PHP's three primary terms for creating conditionals are **if**, **else**, and **elseif** (which can also be written as two words, **else if**).

Every conditional begins with an **if** clause:

```
if (condition) {
        // Do something!
}
```

An **if** can also have an **else** clause:

```
if (condition) {
        // Do something!
} else {
        // Do something else!
}
```

An **elseif** clause allows you to add more conditions:

```
if (condition1) {
        // Do something!
} elseif (condition2) {
        // Do something else!
} else {
        // Do something different!
}
```

If a condition is true, the code in the following curly braces (**{ }**) will be executed. If not, PHP will continue on. If there is a second condition (after an **elseif**), that will be checked for truth. The process will continue—you can use as many **elseif** clauses as you want—until PHP hits an **else**, which will be automatically executed at that point, or until the conditional terminates without an **else**. For this reason, it's important that the **else** always come last and be treated as the default action unless specific criteria—the conditions—are met.

A condition can be true in PHP for any number of reasons. To start, these are true conditions:

- **$var**, if **$var** has a value other than 0, an empty string, **FALSE**, or **NULL**

- **isset($var)**, if **$var** has any value other than **NULL**, including 0, **FALSE**, or an empty string

- **TRUE**, **true**, **True**, etc.

In the second example, a new function, **isset( )**, is introduced. This function checks if a variable is "set," meaning that it has a value other than **NULL** (as a reminder, **NULL** is a special type in PHP, representing no set value). You can also use the comparative and logical operators (**Table 2.2**) in conjunction with parentheses to make more complicated expressions.

TABLE 2.2 Comparative and Logical Operators

Symbol	Meaning	Type	Example
==	is equal to	comparison	$x == $y
!=	is not equal to	comparison	$x != $y
<	less than	comparison	$x < $y
>	greater than	comparison	$x > $y
<=	less than or equal to	comparison	$x <= $y
>=	greater than or equal to	comparison	$x >= $y
!	not	logical	!$x
&&	and	logical	$x && $y
AND	and	logical	$x and $y
||	or	logical	$x || $y
OR	or	logical	$x or $y
XOR	and not	logical	$x XOR $y

To use conditionals:

1. Open **handle_form.php** (refer to Script 2.2) in your text editor or IDE, if it is not already.

2. Before the **echo** statement, add a conditional that creates a **$gender** variable (**Script 2.3**):

```
if (isset($_REQUEST['gender'])) {
  $gender = $_REQUEST['gender'];
} else {
  $gender = NULL;
}
```

This is a simple and effective way to validate a form input (particularly a radio button, check box, or select). If the user checks either gender radio button, then **$_REQUEST['gender']** will have a value, meaning that the condition **isset($_REQUEST['gender'])** is true. In such a case, the shorthand version of this variable—**$gender**—is assigned the value of **$_REQUEST['gender']**, repeating the technique used with **$name**, **$email**, and **$comments**. If the user does not click one of the radio buttons, then this condition is not true, and **$gender** is assigned the value of **NULL**, indicating that it has no value. Notice that **NULL** is not in quotes.

Script 2.3 In this remade version of **handle_form. php**, two conditionals are used to validate the gender radio buttons.

```
1   <!DOCTYPE html PUBLIC "-//W3C//DTD
    XHTML 1.0 Transitional//EN"
        "http://www.w3.org/TR/xhtml1/DTD/
        xhtml1-transitional.dtd">
2   <html xmlns="http://www.w3.org/1999/
    xhtml" xml:lang="en" lang="en">
3   <head>
4       <meta http-equiv="Content-Type"
        content="text/html; charset=utf-8" />
5       <title>Form Feedback</title>
6   </head>
7   <body>
8   <?php # Script 2.3 - handle_form.php #2
9
10  // Create a shorthand for the form data:
11  $name = $_REQUEST['name'];
12  $email = $_REQUEST['email'];
13  $comments = $_REQUEST['comments'];
14
15  // Create the $gender variable:
16  if (isset($_REQUEST['gender'])) {
17      $gender = $_REQUEST['gender'];
18  } else {
19      $gender = NULL;
20  }
21
22  // Print the submitted information:
23  echo "<p>Thank you, <b>$name</b>,
    for the following comments:<br />
24  <tt>$comments</tt></p>
25  <p>We will reply to you at
    <i>$email</i>.</p>\n";
26
27  // Print a message based upon the
    gender value:
28  if ($gender == 'M') {
29      echo '<p><b>Good day, Sir!</b>
        </p>';
30  } elseif ($gender == 'F') {
31      echo '<p><b>Good day, Madam!
        </b></p>';
32  } else { // No gender selected.
33      echo '<p><b>You forgot to enter
        your gender!</b></p>';
34  }
35
36  ?>
37  </body>
38  </html>
```

Ⓐ The gender-based conditional prints a different message for each choice in the form.

Ⓑ The same script will produce different salutations (compare with Ⓐ) when the gender value changes.

Ⓒ If no gender was selected, a message is printed indicating the oversight to the user.

3. After the **echo** statement, add another conditional that prints a message based upon **$gender**'s value:

```
if ($gender == 'M') {
    echo '<p><b>Good day, Sir!</b>
    → </p>';
} elseif ($gender == 'F') {
    echo '<p><b>Good day, Madam!
    → </b></p>';
} else {
    echo '<p><b>You forgot to enter
    → your gender!</b></p>';
}
```

This **if-elseif-else** conditional looks at the value of the **$gender** variable and prints a different message for each possibility. It's very important to remember that the double equals sign (= =) means equals, whereas a single equals sign (=) assigns a value. The distinction is important because the condition **$gender == 'M'** may or may not be true, but **$gender = 'M'** will always be true.

Also, the values used here—*M* and *F*—must be exactly the same as those in the HTML form (the values for each radio button). Equality is a case-sensitive comparison with strings, so *m* will not equal *M*.

4. Save the file, place it in your Web directory, and test it in your Web browser Ⓐ, Ⓑ, and Ⓒ.

TIP Although PHP has no strict formatting rules, it's standard procedure and good programming form to make it clear when one block of code is a subset of a conditional. Indenting the block is the norm.

TIP You can—and frequently will—nest conditionals (place one inside another).

TIP The first conditional in this script (the isset( )) is a perfect example of how to use a default value. The assumption (the else) is that $gender has a NULL value unless the one condition is met: that $_REQUEST['gender'] is set.

TIP The curly braces used to indicate the beginning and end of a conditional are not required if you are executing only one statement. I would recommend that you almost always use them, though, as a matter of clarity.

TIP Both *and* and *or* have two representative operators, with slight, technical differences between them. For no particular reason, I tend to use && and || instead of AND and OR.

TIP XOR is called the *exclusive or* operator. The conditional $x XOR $y is true if $x is true or if $y is true, but not both.

Switch

PHP has another type of conditional, called the **switch**, best used in place of a long **if-elseif-else** conditional. The syntax of **switch** is

```
switch ($variable) {
    case 'value1':
        // Do this.
        break;
    case 'value2':
        // Do this instead.
        break;
default:
    // Do this then.
    break;
}
```

The **switch** conditional compares the value of **$variable** to the different cases. When it finds a match, the following code is executed, up until the **break**. If no match is found, the **default** is executed, assuming it exists (it's optional). The **switch** conditional is limited in its usage in that it can only check a variable's value for equality against certain cases; more complex conditions cannot be easily checked.

Validating Form Data

A critical concept related to handling HTML forms is that of validating form data. In terms of both error management and security, you should absolutely never trust the data being submitted by an HTML form. Whether erroneous data is purposefully malicious or just unintentionally inappropriate, it's up to you—the Web architect—to test it against expectations.

Validating form data requires the use of conditionals and any number of functions, operators, and expressions. One standard function to be used is **isset( )**, which tests if a variable has a value (including 0, **FALSE**, or an empty string, but not **NULL**). You saw an example of this in the preceding script.

One issue with the **isset( )** function is that an empty string tests as true, meaning that **isset( )** is not an effective way to validate text inputs and text boxes from an HTML form. To check that a user typed something into textual elements, you can use the **empty( )** function. It checks if a variable has an *empty* value: an empty string, 0, **NULL**, or **FALSE**.

The first aim of form validation is seeing if *something* was entered or selected in form elements. The second goal is to ensure that submitted data is of the right type (numeric, string, etc.), of the right format (like an email address), or a specific acceptable value (like **$gender** being equal to either *M* or *F*).

As handling forms is a main use of PHP, validating form data is a point that will be re-emphasized time and again in subsequent chapters. But first, let's create a new **handle_form.php** to make sure variables have values before they're referenced (there will be enough changes in this version that simply updating Script 2.3 doesn't make sense).

To validate your forms:

1. Begin a new PHP script in your text editor or IDE, to be named **handle_form.php** starting with the initial HTML (**Script 2.4**):

   ```
   <!DOCTYPE html PUBLIC "-//W3C//
   → DTD XHTML 1.0 Transitional//EN"
   → "http://www.w3.org/TR/xhtml1/DTD/
   xhtml1-transitional.dtd">
   ```

   continues on page 50

Script 2.4 Validating HTML form data before you use it is critical to Web security and achieving professional results. Here, conditionals check that every referenced form element has a value.

```
1    <!DOCTYPE html PUBLIC "-//W3C//DTD XHTML 1.0 Transitional//EN" "http://www.w3.org/TR/xhtml1/
     DTD/xhtml1-transitional.dtd">
2    <html xmlns="http://www.w3.org/1999/xhtml" xml:lang="en" lang="en">
3    <head>
4       <meta http-equiv="Content-Type" content="text/html; charset=utf-8" />
5       <title>Form Feedback</title>
6       <style type="text/css" title="text/css" media="all">
7       .error {
8          font-weight: bold;
9          color: #C00;
10      }
11      </style>
12   </head>
13   <body>
14   <?php # Script 2.4 - handle_form.php #3
15
```

code continues on next page

```
16    // Validate the name:
17    if (!empty($_REQUEST['name'])) {
18        $name = $_REQUEST['name'];
19    } else {
20        $name = NULL;
21        echo '<p class="error">You forgot to enter your name!</p>';
22    }
23
24    // Validate the email:
25    if (!empty($_REQUEST['email'])) {
26        $email = $_REQUEST['email'];
27    } else {
28        $email = NULL;
29        echo '<p class="error">You forgot to enter your email address!</p>';
30    }
31
32    // Validate the comments:
33    if (!empty($_REQUEST['comments'])) {
34        $comments = $_REQUEST['comments'];
35    } else {
36        $comments = NULL;
37        echo '<p class="error">You forgot to enter your comments!</p>';
38    }
39
40    // Validate the gender:
41    if (isset($_REQUEST['gender'])) {
42
43        $gender = $_REQUEST['gender'];
44
45        if ($gender == 'M') {
46            echo '<p><b>Good day, Sir!</b></p>';
47        } elseif ($gender == 'F') {
48            echo '<p><b>Good day, Madam!</b></p>';
49        } else { // Unacceptable value.
50            $gender = NULL;
51            echo '<p class="error">Gender should be either "M" or "F"!</p>';
52        }
53
54    } else { // $_REQUEST['gender'] is not set.
55        $gender = NULL;
56        echo '<p class="error">You forgot to select your gender!</p>';
57    }
58
59    // If everything is OK, print the message:
60    if ($name && $email && $gender && $comments) {
61
62        echo "<p>Thank you, <b>$name</b>, for the following comments:<br />
63        <tt>$comments</tt></p>
64        <p>We will reply to you at <i>$email</i>.</p>\n";
65
66    } else { // Missing form value.
67        echo '<p class="error">Please go back and fill out the form again.</p>';
68    }
69
70    ?>
71    </body>
72    </html>
```

```html
<html xmlns="http://www.w3.org/
→ 1999/xhtml" xml:lang="en"
→ lang="en">
<head>
  <meta http-equiv="Content-Type"
  → content="text/html;
  → charset=utf-8" />
  <title>Form Feedback</title>
</head>
<body>
```

2. Within the HTML **head**, add some CSS code:

```css
<style type="text/css"
→ title="text/css" media="all">
.error {
  font-weight: bold;
  color: #C00;
}
</style>
```

This code defines one CSS class, called *error*. Any HTML element that has this class name will be formatted in a bold, red color (which will be more apparent in your Web browser than in this black-and-white book).

3. In PHP block, check if the name was entered:

```php
if (!empty($_REQUEST['name'])) {
  $name = $_REQUEST['name'];
} else {
  $name = NULL;
  echo '<p class="error">You
  → forgot to enter your name!</p>';
}
```

A simple way to check that a form text input was filled out is to use the **empty( )** function. If **$_REQUEST['name']** has a

value other than an empty string, 0, **NULL**, or **FALSE**, assume that their name was entered and a shorthand variable is assigned that value. If **$_REQUEST['name']** is empty, the **$name** variable is set to **NULL** and an error message is printed. This error message uses the CSS class.

4. Repeat the same process for the email address and comments:

```php
if (!empty($_REQUEST['email'])) {
  $email = $_REQUEST['email'];
} else {
  $email = NULL;
  echo '<p class="error">You
  → forgot to enter your email
  → address!</p>';
}
if (!empty($_REQUEST['comments'])) {
  $comments = $_REQUEST['comments'];
} else {
  $comments = NULL;
  echo '<p class="error">You
  → forgot to enter your
  → comments!</p>';
}
```

Both variables receive the same treatment as **$_REQUEST['name']** in Step 3.

5. Begin validating the gender variable:

```php
if (isset($_REQUEST['gender'])) {
  $gender = $_REQUEST['gender'];
```

The validation of the gender is a two-step process. First, check if it has a value or not, using **isset( )**. This starts the main **if-else** conditional, which otherwise behaves like those for the name, email address, and comments.

continues on next page

6. Check **$gender** against specific values:

```
if ($gender == 'M') {
    $greeting = '<p><b>Good day,
    → Sir!</b></p>';
} elseif ($gender == 'F') {
    $greeting = '<p><b>Good day,
    → Madam!</b></p>';
} else {
    $gender = NULL;
    echo '<p class="error">Gender
    → should be either "M" or
    → "F"!</p>';
}
```

Within the gender **if** clause is a nested **if-elseif-else** conditional that tests the variable's value against what's acceptable. This is the second part of the two-step gender validation.

The conditions themselves are the same as those in the last script. If gender does not end up being equal to either *M* or *F*, a problem occurred and an error message is printed. The **$gender** variable is also set to **NULL** in such cases, because it has an unacceptable value.

If **$gender** does have a valid value, a gender-specific message is assigned to a new variable, so that the message can be printed later in the script.

7. Complete the main gender **if-else** conditional:

```
} else {
    $gender = NULL;
    echo '<p class="error">You
    forgot to select your
    → gender!</p>';
}
```

This **else** clause applies if **$_REQUEST ['gender']** is not set. The complete, nested conditionals (see lines 41–57 of Script 2.4) successfully check every possibility:

- ▸ **$_REQUEST['gender']** is not set
- ▸ **$_REQUEST['gender']** has a value of *M*
- ▸ **$_REQUEST['gender']** has a value of *F*
- ▸ **$_REQUEST['gender']** has some other value

You may wonder how this last case may be possible, considering the values are set in the HTML form. If a malicious user creates their own form that gets submitted to your **handle_form.php** script (which is very easy to do), they could give **$_REQUEST['gender']** any value they want.

8. Print messages indicating the validation results:

```
if ($name && $email && $gender
→ && $comments) {
    echo "<p>Thank you, <b>$name
    → </b>, for the following
    → comments:<br />
    <tt>$comments</tt></p>
    <p>We will reply to you at
    → <i>$email</i>.</p>\n";
    echo $greeting;
} else {
    echo '<p class="error">Please
    → go back and fill out the form
    → again.</p>';
}
```

A The script now checks that every form element was filled out (except the age) and reports on those that weren't.

B If even one or two fields were skipped, the *Thank you* message is not printed.

The main condition is true if every listed variable has a true value. Each variable will have a value if it passed its test but have a value of **NULL** if it didn't. If every variable has a value, the form was completed, so the *Thank you* message will be printed, as will the gender-specific greeting. If any of the variables are **NULL**, the second message will be printed (**A** and **B**).

9. Close the PHP section and complete the HTML page:

```
?>
</body>
</html>
```

10. Save the file as **handle_form.php**, place it in the same Web directory as **form.html**, and test it in your Web browser.

Fill out the form to different levels of completeness to test the new script **C**.

> **TIP** To test if a submitted value is a number, use the **is_numeric( )** function.

> **TIP** In Chapter 14, "Perl-Compatible Regular Expressions," you'll see how to validate form data using regular expressions.

> **TIP** It's considered good form (pun intended) to let a user know which fields are required when they're filling out the form, and where applicable, the format of that field (like a date or a phone number).

C If the form was completed properly, the script behaves as it previously had.

Introducing Arrays

Chapter 1 introduced two *scalar* (single valued) variable types: strings and numbers. Now it's time to learn about another type, the *array*. Unlike strings and numbers, an *array* can hold multiple, separate pieces of information. An array is therefore like a list of values, each value being a string or a number or even another array.

Arrays are structured as a series of *key-value* pairs, where one pair is an item or *element* of that array. For each item in the list, there is a *key* (or *index*) associated with it (**Table 2.3**).

PHP supports two kinds of arrays: *indexed*, which use numbers as the keys (as in Table 2.3), and *associative*, which use strings as keys (**Table 2.4**). As in most programming languages, with indexed arrays, arrays will begin with the first index at 0, unless you specify the keys explicitly.

An array follows the same naming rules as any other variable. This means that, offhand, you might not be able to tell that **$var** is an array as opposed to a string or number. The important syntactical difference arises when accessing individual array elements.

To refer to a specific value in an array, start with the array variable name, followed by the key within square brackets:

```
$band = $artists[0]; // The Mynabirds
echo $states['MD']; // Maryland
```

You can see that the array keys are used like other values in PHP: numbers (e.g., 0) are never quoted, whereas strings (*MD*) must be.

TABLE 2.3 Array Example 1: `$artists`

Key	Value
0	The Mynabirds
1	Jeremy Messersmith
2	The Shins
3	Iron and Wine
4	Alexi Murdoch

TABLE 2.4 Array Example 2: `$states`

Key	Value
MD	Maryland
PA	Pennsylvania
IL	Illinois
MO	Missouri
IA	Iowa

Because arrays use a different syntax than other variables, and can contain multiple values, printing them can be trickier. This will not work 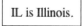:

```
echo "My list of states: $states";
```

However, printing an individual element's value is simple if it uses indexed (numeric) keys:

```
echo "The first artist is
→ $artists[0].";
```

But if the array uses strings for the keys, the quotes used to surround the key will muddle the syntax. The following code will cause a parse error:

```
echo "IL is $states['IL'].";  // BAD!
```

To fix this, wrap the array name and key in curly braces when an array uses strings for its keys:

```
echo "IL is {$states['IL']}.";
```

If arrays seem slightly familiar to you already, that's because you've already worked with two: **$_SERVER** (in Chapter 1) and **$_REQUEST** (in this chapter). To acquaint you with another array and to practice printing array values directly, one final, but basic, version of the **handle_form.php** page will be created using the more specific **$_POST** array (see the sidebar on "Superglobal Arrays").

My list of states: Array

A Attempting to print an array using only the variable's name results in the word *Array* being printed.

Parse error: syntax error, unexpected T_ENCAPSED_AND_WHITESPACE, expecting T_STRING or T_VARIABLE or T_NUM_STRING in /Users/larryullman/Sites/phpmysql4/test.php on line **13**

B Attempting to print an element in an associative array *without* using curly braces results in a parse error.

IL is Illinois.

C Attempting to print an element in an associative array *while* using curly braces works as desired.

To use arrays:

1. Begin a new PHP script in your text editor or IDE, to be named **handle_form.php** starting with the initial HTML (**Script 2.5**):

```
<!DOCTYPE html PUBLIC "-//W3C//
→ DTD XHTML 1.0 Transitional//EN"
→ "http://www.w3.org/TR/xhtml1/DTD/
→ xhtml1-transitional.dtd">
<html xmlns="http://www.w3.org/
→ 1999/xhtml" xml:lang="en" lang="en">
<head>
   <meta http-equiv="Content-Type"
   → content="text/html;
   → charset=utf-8" />
   <title>Form Feedback</title>
</head>
<body>
<?php # Script 2.5 -
→ handle_form.php #4
```

2. Perform some basic form validation:

```
if ( !empty($_POST['name']) &&
→ !empty($_POST['comments']) &&
→ !empty($_POST['email']) ) {
```

In the previous version of this script, the values are accessed by referring to the **$_REQUEST** array. But since these variables come from a form that uses the POST method (see Script 2.1), **$_POST** would be a more exact, and therefore more secure, reference.

This conditional checks that these three text inputs are all not empty. Using the *and* operator (**&&**), the entire conditional is only true if each of the three subconditionals is true.

3. Print the message:

```
echo "<p>Thank you, <b>{$_POST
→ ['name']}</b>, for the following
→ comments:<br />
<tt>{$_POST['comments']}</tt></p>
<p>We will reply to you at
→ <i>{$_POST['email']}</i>.</p>\n";
```

After you comprehend the concept of an array, you still need to master the syntax involved in printing one. When printing an array element that uses a

Script 2.5 The superglobal variables, like **$_POST** here, are just one type of array you'll use in PHP.

```
1    <!DOCTYPE html PUBLIC "-//W3C//DTD XHTML 1.0 Transitional//EN" "http://www.w3.org/TR/xhtml1/
     DTD/xhtml1-transitional.dtd">
2    <html xmlns="http://www.w3.org/1999/xhtml" xml:lang="en" lang="en">
3    <head>
4       <meta http-equiv="Content-Type" content="text/html; charset=utf-8" />
5       <title>Form Feedback</title>
6    </head>
7    <body>
8    <?php # Script 2.5 - handle_form.php #4
9
10   // Print the submitted information:
11   if ( !empty($_POST['name']) && !empty($_POST['comments']) && !empty($_POST['email']) ) {
12      echo "<p>Thank you, <b>{$_POST['name']}</b>, for the following comments:<br />
13   <tt>{$_POST['comments']}</tt></p>
14   <p>We will reply to you at <i>{$_POST['email']}</i>.</p>\n";
15   } else { // Missing form value.
16      echo '<p>Please go back and fill out the form again.</p>';
17   }
18   ?>
19   </body>
20   </html>
```

string for its key, use the curly braces (as in `{$_POST['name']}` here) to avoid parse errors.

4. Complete the conditional begun in Step 2:

```
} else {
  echo '<p>Please go back and
  → fill out the form again.</p>';
}
```

If any of the three subconditionals in Step 2 is not true (which is to say, if any of the variables has an empty value), then this **else** clause applies and an error message is printed .

5. Complete the PHP and HTML code:

```
?>
</body>
</html>
```

6. Save the file as **handle_form.php**, place it in the same Web directory as **form.html**, and test it in your Web browser **E**.

TIP Because PHP is lax with its variable structures, an array can even use a combination of numbers and strings as its keys. The only important rule is that the keys of an array must each be unique.

TIP If you find the syntax of accessing superglobal arrays directly to be confusing (e.g., `$_POST['name']`), you can continue to use the shorthand technique at the top of your scripts as you have been:

```
$name = $_POST['name'];
```

In this script, you would then need to change the conditional and the `echo` statement to refer to $name et al.

TIP You only need to use the curly brackets to surround an associated array used within quotation marks. All of these array references are fine:

```
echo $_POST['name'];
echo "The first item is $item[0].";
$total = number_format($cart['total']);
```

D If any of the three tested form inputs is empty, this generic error message is printed.

E The fact that the script now uses the **$_POST** array has no effect on the visible result.

Creating arrays

The preceding example uses a PHP-generated array, but there will frequently be times when you want to create your own. There are two primary ways to define your own array. First, you could add an element at a time to build one:

```
$band[] = 'Jemaine';
$band[] = 'Bret';
$band[] = 'Murray';
```

As arrays are indexed starting at 0, **$band[0]** has a value of *Jemaine*; **$band[1]**, *Bret*, and **$band[2]**, *Murray*.

Alternatively, you can specify the key when adding an element. But it's important to understand that if you specify a key and a value already exists indexed with that same key, the new value will overwrite the existing one:

```
$band['fan'] = 'Mel';
$band['fan'] = 'Dave'; // New value
$fruit[2] = 'apple';
$fruit[2] = 'orange'; // New value
```

Instead of adding one element at a time, you can use the **array()** function to build an entire array in one step:

```
$states = array (
'IA' => 'Iowa',
'MD' => 'Maryland'
);
```

(As PHP is generally insensitive to white space, you can use this function over multiple lines for added clarity.)

The **array()** function can be used whether or not you explicitly set the key:

```
$artists = array ('Clem Snide',
 'Shins', 'Eels');
```

Or, if you set the first numeric key value, the added values will be keyed incrementally thereafter:

```
$days = array (1 => 'Sun', 'Mon',
 'Tue');
echo $days[3]; // Tue
```

The **array()** function is also used to initialize an array, prior to referencing it:

```
$tv = array();
$tv[] = 'Flight of the Conchords';
```

Initializing an array (or any variable) in PHP isn't required, but it makes for clearer code and can help avoid errors.

Finally, if you want to create an array of sequential numbers, you can use the **range()** function:

```
$ten = range (1, 10);
```

Accessing entire arrays

You've already seen how to access individual array elements using its keys (e.g., **$_POST['email']**). This works when you know exactly what the keys are or if you want to refer to only a single element. To access every array element, use the **foreach** loop:

```
foreach ($array as $value) {
        // Do something with $value.
}
```

The **foreach** loop will iterate through every element in **$array**, assigning each element's value to the **$value** variable. To access both the keys and values, use

```
foreach ($array as $key => $value) {
        echo "The value at $key is
         $value.";
}
```

F These pull-down menus will be created using arrays and the **foreach** loop.

Script 2.6 This form uses arrays to dynamically create three pull-down menus.

```
1    <!DOCTYPE html PUBLIC "-//W3C//DTD
     XHTML 1.0 Transitional//EN"
     "http://www.w3.org/TR/xhtml1/DTD/
     xhtml1-transitional.dtd">
2    <html xmlns="http://www.w3.org/1999/
     xhtml" xml:lang="en" lang="en">
3    <head>
4       <meta http-equiv="Content-Type"
        content="text/html; charset=utf-8" />
5       <title>Calendar</title>
6    </head>
7    <body>
8    <form action="calendar.php"
     method="post">
9    <?php # Script 2.6 - calendar.php
10
11   // This script makes three pull-down
     menus
12   // for an HTML form: months, days,
     years.
13
14   // Make the months array:
15   $months = array (1 => 'January',
     'February', 'March', 'April', 'May',
     'June', 'July', 'August', 'September',
     'October', 'November', 'December');
16
17   // Make the days and years arrays:
18   $days = range (1, 31);
19   $years = range (2011, 2021);
```

code continues on next page

(You can use any valid variable name in place of **$key** and **$value**, like just **$k** and **$v**, if you'd prefer.)

Using arrays, this next script will demonstrate how easy it is to make a set of form pull-down menus for selecting a date **F**.

To create and access arrays:

1. Begin a new PHP document in your text editor or IDE, to be named **calendar.php** starting with the initial HTML (**Script 2.6**):

```
<!DOCTYPE html PUBLIC "-//W3C//
→ DTD XHTML 1.0 Transitional//EN"
→ "http://www.w3.org/TR/xhtml1/DTD/
→ xhtml1-transitional.dtd">
<html xmlns="http://www.w3.org/
→ 1999/xhtml" xml:lang="en"
→ lang="en">
<head>
  <meta http-equiv="Content-Type"
  → content="text/html;
  → charset=utf-8" />
  <title>Calendar</title>
</head>
<body>
<form action="calendar.php"
→ method="post">
<?php # Script 2.6 - calendar.php
```

One thing to note here is that even though the page won't contain a complete HTML form, the form tags are still required to create the pull-down menus.

continues on next page

2. Create an array for the months:

```
$months = array (1 => 'January',
→ 'February', 'March', 'April',
→ 'May', 'June', 'July', 'August',
→ 'September', 'October',
→ 'November', 'December');
```

This first array will use numbers for the keys, from 1 to 12. Since the value of the first key is specified, the following values will be indexed incrementally (in other words, the `1 =>` code creates an array indexed from 1 to 12, instead of from 0 to 11).

3. Create the arrays for the days of the month and the years:

```
$days = range (1, 31);
$years = range (2011, 2021);
```

Using the **range( )** function, you can easily make an array of numbers.

4. Generate the month pull-down menu:

```
echo '<select name="month">';
foreach ($months as $key =>
→ $value) {
  echo "<option value=\"$key\">
  → $value</option>\n";
}
echo '</select>';
```

The **foreach** loop can quickly generate all of the HTML code for the month pull-down menu. Each execution of the loop will create a line of code like **<option value="1">January</option>** **G**.

5. Generate the day and year pull-down menus:

```
echo '<select name="day">';
foreach ($days as $value) {
  echo "<option value=\"$value\">
  → $value</option>\n";
}
```

Script 2.6 *continued*

```
20
21   // Make the months pull-down menu:
22   echo '<select name="month">';
23   foreach ($months as $key =>
     $value) {
24       echo "<option value=\"$key\">
         $value</option>\n";
25   }
26   echo '</select>';
27
28   // Make the days pull-down menu:
29   echo '<select name="day">';
30   foreach ($days as $value) {
31       echo "<option value=\"$value\">
         $value</option>\n";
32   }
33   echo '</select>';
34
35   // Make the years pull-down menu:
36   echo '<select name="year">';
37   foreach ($years as $value) {
38       echo "<option value=\"$value\">
         $value</option>\n";
39   }
40   echo '</select>';
41
42   ?>
43   </form>
44   </body>
45   </html>
```

```
8   <form action="calendar.php" method="post">
9   <select name="month"><option value="1">January</option>
10  <option value="2">February</option>
11  <option value="3">March</option>
12  <option value="4">April</option>
13  <option value="5">May</option>
14  <option value="6">June</option>
15  <option value="7">July</option>
16  <option value="8">August</option>
17  <option value="9">September</option>
18  <option value="10">October</option>
19  <option value="11">November</option>
20  <option value="12">December</option>
21  </select><select name="day"><option value="1">1</option>
22  <option value="2">2</option>
23  <option value="3">3</option>
24  <option value="4">4</option>
25  <option value="5">5</option>
26  <option value="6">6</option>
27  <option value="7">7</option>
```

G Most of the HTML source was generated by just a few lines of PHP.

```
echo '</select>';
echo '<select name="year">';
foreach ($years as $value) {
  echo "<option value=\"$value\">
  ➝ $value</option>\n";
}
echo '</select>';
```

Unlike the month example, both the day and year pull-down menus will use the same data for the option's value and label (a number, Ⓖ). For that reason, there's no need to also fetch the array's key with each loop iteration.

6. Close the PHP, the form tag, and the HTML page:

```
?>
</form>
</body>
</html>
```

7. Save the file as **calendar.php**, place it in your Web directory, and test it in your Web browser.

TIP To determine the number of elements in an array, use count( ):

```
$num = count($array);
```

TIP The range( ) function can also create an array of sequential letters:

```
$alphabet = range ('a', 'z');
```

TIP An array's key can be multiple-worded strings, such as *first name* or *phone number*.

TIP The is_array( ) function confirms that a variable is of the array type.

TIP If you see an *Invalid argument supplied for foreach()* error message, that means you are trying to use a foreach loop on a variable that is not an array.

Multidimensional arrays

When introducing arrays, I mentioned that an array's values could be any combination of numbers, strings, and even other arrays. This last option—an array consisting of other arrays—creates a *multidimensional array*.

Multidimensional arrays are much more common than you might expect but remarkably easy to work with. As an example, start with an array of prime numbers:

```
$primes = array(2, 3, 5, 7, …);
```

Then create an array of *sphenic* numbers (don't worry: I had no idea what a sphenic number was either; I had to look it up):

```
$sphenic = array(30, 42, 66, 70, …);
```

These two arrays could be combined into one multidimensional array like so:

```
$numbers = array ('Primes' =>
➝ $primes, 'Sphenic' => $sphenic);
```

Now, **$numbers** is a multidimensional array. To access the prime numbers sub-array, refer to **$numbers['Primes']**. To access the prime number 5, use **$numbers['Primes'][2]** (it's the third element in the array, but the array starts indexing at 0). To print out one of these values, surround the whole construct in curly braces:

```
echo "The first sphenic number is
➝ {$numbers['Sphenic'][0]}.";
```

Of course, you can also access multi-dimensional arrays using the **foreach** loop, nesting one inside another if necessary. This next example will do just that.

To use multidimensional arrays:

1. Begin a new PHP document in your text editor or IDE, to be named **multi.php** beginning with the initial HTML (**Script 2.7**):

```
<!DOCTYPE html PUBLIC "-//W3C//
→ DTD XHTML 1.0 Transitional//EN"
→ "http://www.w3.org/TR/xhtml1/DTD/
→ xhtml1-transitional.dtd">
<html xmlns="http://www.w3.org/
→ 1999/xhtml" xml:lang="en"
→ lang="en">
<head>
  <meta http-equiv="Content-Type"
  → content="text/html;
  → charset=utf-8" />
  <title>Multidimensional
  → Arrays</title>
</head>
<body>
<p>Some North American States,
→ Provinces, and Territories:</p>
<?php # Script 2.7 - multi.php
```

This PHP page will print out some of the states, provinces, and territories found in the three North American countries (Mexico, the United States, and Canada).

2. Create an array of Mexican states:

```
$mexico = array(
'YU' => 'Yucatan',
'BC' => 'Baja California',
'OA' => 'Oaxaca'
);
```

This is an associative array, using the state's postal abbreviation as its key. The state's full name is the element's value. This is obviously an incomplete list, just used to demonstrate the concept.

Script 2.7 The multidimensional array is created by using other arrays for its values. Two **foreach** loops, one nested inside of the other, can access every array element.

```
1   <!DOCTYPE html PUBLIC "-//W3C//DTD
    XHTML 1.0 Transitional//EN"
    "http://www.w3.org/TR/xhtml1/DTD/
    xhtml1-transitional.dtd">
2   <html xmlns="http://www.w3.org/1999/
    xhtml" xml:lang="en" lang="en">
3   <head>
4     <meta http-equiv="Content-Type"
      content="text/html; charset=utf-8" />
5     <title>Multidimensional Arrays</
      title>
6   </head>
7   <body>
8   <p>Some North American States,
    Provinces, and Territories:</p>
9   <?php # Script 2.7 - multi.php
10
```

code continues on next page

 The end result of running this PHP page (Script 2.7), where each country is printed, followed by an abbreviated list of its states, provinces, and territories.

```
11   // Create one array:
12   $mexico = array(
13   'YU' => 'Yucatan',
14   'BC' => 'Baja California',
15   'OA' => 'Oaxaca'
16   );
17
18   // Create another array:
19   $us = array (
20   'MD' => 'Maryland',
21   'IL' => 'Illinois',
22   'PA' => 'Pennsylvania',
23   'IA' => 'Iowa'
24   );
25
26   // Create a third array:
27   $canada = array (
28   'QC' => 'Quebec',
29   'AB' => 'Alberta',
30   'NT' => 'Northwest Territories',
31   'YT' => 'Yukon',
32   'PE' => 'Prince Edward Island'
33   );
34
35   // Combine the arrays:
36   $n_america = array(
37   'Mexico' => $mexico,
38   'United States' => $us,
39   'Canada' => $canada
40   );
41
42   // Loop through the countries:
43   foreach ($n_america as $country =>
     $list) {
44
45       // Print a heading:
46       echo "<h2>$country</h2><ul>";
47
48       // Print each state, province, or
         territory:
49       foreach ($list as $k => $v) {
50           echo "<li>$k - $v</li>\n";
51       }
52
53       // Close the list:
54       echo '</ul>';
55
56   } // End of main FOREACH.
57
58   ?>
59   </body>
60   </html>
```

3. Create the second and third arrays:

```
$us = array (
'MD' => 'Maryland',
'IL' => 'Illinois',
'PA' => 'Pennsylvania',
'IA' => 'Iowa'
);
$canada = array (
'QC' => 'Quebec',
'AB' => 'Alberta',
'NT' => 'Northwest Territories',
'YT' => 'Yukon',
'PE' => 'Prince Edward Island'
);
```

4. Combine all of the arrays into one:

```
$n_america = array(
'Mexico' => $mexico,
'United States' => $us,
'Canada' => $canada
);
```

You don't have to create three arrays and then assign them to a fourth in order to make the desired multidimensional array, but I think it's easier to read and understand this way (defining a multidimensional array in one step makes for some ugly code).

The **$n_america** array now contains three elements. The key for each element is a string, which is the country's name. The value for each element is the array of states, provinces, and territories found within that country.

5. Begin the primary **foreach** loop:

```
foreach ($n_america as $country
→ => $list) {
    echo "<h2>$country</h2><ul>";
```

continues on next page

Following the syntax outlined earlier, this loop will access every element of **$n_america**. This means that this loop will run three times. Within each iteration of the loop, the **$country** variable will store the **$n_america** array's key (*Mexico*, *Canada*, or *United States*). Also within each iteration of the loop, the **$list** variable will store the element's value (the equivalent of **$mexico**, **$us**, and **$canada**).

To print out the results, the loop begins by printing the country's name within **H2** tags. Because the states and so forth should be displayed as an HTML list, the initial unordered list tag (**<ul>**) is printed as well.

6. Create a second **foreach** loop:

```
foreach ($list as $k => $v) {
   echo "<li>$k - $v</li>\n";
}
```

This loop will run through each sub-array (first **$mexico**, then **$us**, and then **$canada**). With each iteration of this loop, **$k** will store the abbreviation and **$v** the full name. Both are printed out within HTML list tags. The newline character is also used, to better format the HTML source code.

7. Complete the outer **foreach** loop:

```
   echo '</ul>';
} // End of main FOREACH.
```

After the inner **foreach** loop is done, the outer **foreach** loop has to close the unordered list begun in Step 5.

8. Complete the PHP and HTML:

```
?>
</body>
</html>
```

9. Save the file as **multi.php**, place it in your Web directory, and test it in your Web browser **🄗**.

10. If you want, check out the HTML source code to see what PHP created.

TIP Multidimensional arrays can also come from an HTML form. For example, if a form has a series of checkboxes with the name *interests[]*—

```
<input type="checkbox" name=
→ "interests[]" value="Music" /> Music
<input type="checkbox" name=
→ "interests[]" value="Movies" /> Movies
<input type="checkbox" name=
→ "interests[]" value="Books" /> Books
```

—the $_POST variable in the receiving PHP page will be multidimensional. $_POST['interests'] will be an array, with $_POST['interests'][0] storing the value of the first checked box (e.g., Movies), $_POST['interests'][1] storing the second (Books), etc. Note that only the checked boxes will get passed to the PHP page.

TIP You can also end up with a multidimensional array if an HTML form's select menu allows for multiple selections:

```
<select name="interests[]"
→ multiple="multiple">
   <option value="Music">Music
   → </option>
   <option value="Movies">Movies
   → </option>
   <option value="Books">Books
   → </option>
   <option value="Napping">Napping
   → </option>
</select>
```

Again, only the selected values will be passed to the PHP page.

Arrays and Strings

Because arrays and strings are so commonly used together, PHP has two functions for converting between them:

```
$array = explode (separator,
→$string);
$string = implode (glue, $array);
```

The key to using and understanding these two functions is the *separator* and *glue* relationships. When turning an array into a string, you establish the glue—the characters or code that will be inserted between the array values in the generated string. Conversely, when turning a string into an array, you specify the separator, which is the token that marks what should become separate array elements. For example, start with a string:

```
$s1 = 'Mon-Tue-Wed-Thu-Fri';
$days_array = explode ('-', $s1);
```

The **$days_array** variable is now a five-element array, with *Mon* indexed at **0**, *Tue* indexed at **1**, etc.

```
$s2 = implode (', ', $days_array);
```

The **$s2** variable is now a comma-separated list of days: *Mon, Tue, Wed, Thu, Fri.*

Sorting arrays

One of the many advantages arrays have over the other variable types is the ability to sort them. PHP includes several functions you can use for sorting arrays, all simple in syntax:

```
$names = array ('Moe', 'Larry',
→'Curly');
sort($names);
```

The sorting functions perform three kinds of sorts. First, you can sort an array by value, discarding the original keys, using **sort( )**. It's important to understand that the array's keys will be reset after the sorting process, so *if the key-value relationship is important, you should not use* **sort( )**.

Second, you can sort an array by value *while maintaining the keys*, using **asort( )**. Third, you can sort an array by key, using **ksort( )**. Each of these can sort in reverse order if you change them to **rsort( )**, **arsort( )**, and **krsort( )** respectively.

To demonstrate the effect sorting arrays will have, this next script will create an array of movie titles and ratings (how much I liked them on a scale of 1 to 10) and then display this list in different ways.

To sort arrays:

1. Begin a new PHP document in your text editor or IDE, to be named **sorting.php** starting with the initial HTML (**Script 2.8**):

```
<!DOCTYPE html PUBLIC "-//W3C//
→ DTD XHTML 1.0 Transitional//EN"
→ "http://www.w3.org/TR/xhtml1/DTD/
→ xhtml1-transitional.dtd">
<html xmlns="http://www.w3.org/
→ 1999/xhtml" xml:lang="en"
→ lang="en">
<head>
  <meta http-equiv="Content-Type"
  → content="text/html;
  → charset=utf-8" />
  <title>Sorting Arrays</title>
</head>
<body>
```

2. Create an HTML table:

```
<table border="0" cellspacing="3"
→ cellpadding="3" align="center">
  <tr>
    <td><h2>Rating</h2></td>
    <td><h2>Title</h2></td>
  </tr>
```

To make the ordered list easier to read, it'll be printed within an HTML table. The table is begun here.

3. Add the opening PHP tag and create a new array:

```
<?php # Script 2.8 - sorting.php
$movies = array (
'Casablanca' => 10,
'To Kill a Mockingbird' => 10,
'The English Patient' => 2,
'Stranger Than Fiction' => 9,
'Story of the Weeping Camel' => 5,
'Donnie Darko' => 7
);
```

Script 2.8 An array is defined, then sorted in two different ways: first by key, then by value (in reverse order).

```
1   <!DOCTYPE html PUBLIC "-//W3C//DTD
    XHTML 1.0 Transitional//EN"
    "http://www.w3.org/TR/xhtml1/DTD/
    xhtml1-transitional.dtd">
2   <html xmlns="http://www.w3.org/1999/
    xhtml" xml:lang="en" lang="en">
3   <head>
4       <meta http-equiv="Content-Type"
        content="text/html; charset=utf-8" />
5       <title>Sorting Arrays</title>
6   </head>
7   <body>
8   <table border="0" cellspacing="3"
    cellpadding="3" align="center">
9       <tr>
10          <td><h2>Rating</h2></td>
11          <td><h2>Title</h2></td>
12      </tr>
13  <?php # Script 2.8 - sorting.php
14
15  // Create the array:
16  $movies = array (
17  'Casablanca' => 10,
18  'To Kill a Mockingbird' => 10,
19  'The English Patient' => 2,
20  'Stranger Than Fiction' => 9,
21  'Story of the Weeping Camel' => 5,
22  'Donnie Darko' => 7
23  );
24
25  // Display the movies in their
    original order:
26  echo '<tr><td colspan="2"><b>In
    their original order:</b></td></tr>';
27  foreach ($movies as $title =>
    $rating) {
28      echo "<tr><td>$rating</td>
29      <td>$title</td></tr>\n";
30  }
31
32  // Display the movies sorted by title:
33  ksort($movies);
34  echo '<tr><td colspan="2"><b>Sorted by
    title:</b></td></tr>';
```

code continues on next page

```
35   foreach ($movies as $title =>
     $rating) {
36       echo "<tr><td>$rating</td>
37       <td>$title</td></tr>\n";
38   }
39
40   // Display the movies sorted by
     rating:
41   arsort($movies);
42   echo '<tr><td colspan="2"><b>Sorted by
     rating:</b></td></tr>';
43   foreach ($movies as $title =>
     $rating) {
44       echo "<tr><td>$rating</td>
45       <td>$title</td></tr>\n";
46   }
47
48   ?>
49   </table>
50   </body>
51   </html>
```

This array uses movie titles as the keys and their respective ratings as their values. This structure will open up several possibilities for sorting the whole list. Feel free to change the movie listings and rankings as you see fit (just don't chastise me for my taste in films).

4. Print out the array as is:

```
echo '<tr><td colspan="2"><b>In
→ their original order:</b>
→ </td></tr>';
foreach ($movies as $title =>
→ $rating) {
  echo "<tr><td>$rating</td>
  <td>$title</td></tr>\n";
}
```

At this point in the script, the array is in the same order as it was defined. To verify this, print it out. A caption is first printed across both table columns. Then, within the **foreach** loop, the key is printed in the first column and the value in the second. A newline is also printed to improve the readability of the HTML source code.

5. Sort the array alphabetically by title and print it again:

```
ksort($movies);
echo '<tr><td colspan="2"><b>
→ Sorted by title:</b></td></tr>';
foreach ($movies as $title =>
→ $rating) {
  echo "<tr><td>$rating</td>
  <td>$title</td></tr>\n";
}
```

The **ksort( )** function will sort an array by key, in ascending order, while maintaining the key-value relationship. The rest of the code is a repetition of Step 4.

continues on next page

6. Sort the array numerically by descending rating and print again:

```php
arsort($movies);
echo '<tr><td colspan="2"><b>
→ Sorted by rating:</b></td></tr>';
foreach ($movies as $title =>
→ $rating) {
  echo "<tr><td>$rating</td>
  <td>$title</td></tr>\n";
}
```

To sort by values (the ratings), while maintaining the keys, one would use the **asort( )** function. But since the highest-ranking films should be listed first, the order must be reversed, using **arsort( )**.

7. Complete the PHP, the table, and the HTML:

```php
?>
</table>
</body>
</html>
```

8. Save the file as **sorting.php**, place it in your Web directory, and test it in your Web browser **❶**.

TIP To randomize the order of an array, use **shuffle( )**.

TIP PHP's **natsort( )** function can be used to sort arrays in a more natural order (primarily handling numbers in strings better).

TIP Multidimensional arrays can be sorted in PHP with a little effort. See the PHP manual for more information on the **usort( )** function or check out my *PHP 5 Advanced: Visual QuickPro Guide* book.

Rating Title

In their original order:

10	Casablanca
10	To Kill a Mockingbird
2	The English Patient
9	Stranger Than Fiction
5	Story of the Weeping Camel
7	Donnie Darko

Sorted by title:

10	Casablanca
7	Donnie Darko
5	Story of the Weeping Camel
9	Stranger Than Fiction
2	The English Patient
10	To Kill a Mockingbird

Sorted by rating:

10	Casablanca
10	To Kill a Mockingbird
9	Stranger Than Fiction

❶ This page demonstrates different ways arrays can be sorted.

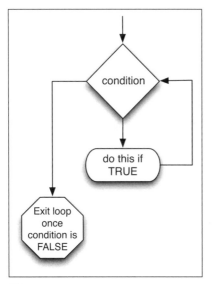

A A flowchart representation of how PHP handles a **while** loop.

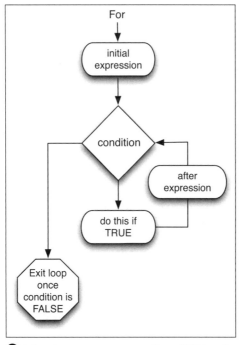

B A flowchart representation of how PHP handles the more complex **for** loop.

For and While Loops

The last language construct to discuss in this chapter is the loop. You've already used one, **foreach**, to access every element in an array. The other two types of loops you'll use are **for** and **while**.

The **while** loop looks like this:

```
while (condition) {
        // Do something.
}
```

As long as the *condition* part of the loop is true, the loop will be executed. Once it becomes false, the loop is stopped **A**. If the condition is never true, the loop will never be executed. The **while** loop will most frequently be used when retrieving results from a database, as you'll see in Chapter 9, "Using PHP with MySQL."

The **for** loop has a more complicated syntax:

```
for (initial expression; condition;
closing expression) {
        // Do something.
}
```

Upon first executing the loop, the initial expression is run. Then the condition is checked and, if true, the contents of the loop are executed. After execution, the closing expression is run and the condition is checked again. This process continues until the condition is false **B**. As an example,

```
for ($i = 1; $i <= 10; $i++) {
        echo $i;
}
```

The first time this loop is run, the **$i** variable is set to the value of 1. Then the condition is checked (*is 1 less than or equal to 10?*). Since this is true, 1 is printed out (**echo $i**). Then, **$i** is incremented to 2 (**$i++**), the condition is checked, and so forth. The result of this script will be the numbers 1 through 10 printed out.

continues on next page

The functionality of both loops is similar enough that **for** and **while** can often be used interchangeably. Still, experience will reveal that the **for** loop is a better choice for doing something *a known number of times*, whereas **while** is used when a condition will be true an *unknown number of times*.

In this chapter's last example, the calendar script created earlier will be rewritten using **for** loops in place of two of the **foreach** loops.

To use loops:

1. Open **calendar.php** (refer to Script 2.6) in your text editor or IDE.

2. Delete the creation of the **$days** and **$years** arrays (lines 18–19).

   Using loops, the same result of the two pull-down menus can be achieved without the extra code and memory overhead involved with creating actual arrays. So these two arrays should be deleted, while still keeping the **$months** array.

3. Rewrite the **$days foreach** loop as a **for** loop (Script 2.9):

   ```
   for ($day = 1; $day <= 31;
   → $day++) {
     echo "<option value=\"$day\">$day
     → </option>\n";
   }
   ```

   This standard **for** loop begins by initializing the **$day** variable as 1. It will continue the loop until **$day** is greater than 31, and upon each iteration, **$day** will be incremented by 1. The content of the loop itself (which is executed 31 times) is an **echo** statement.

Script 2.9 Loops are often used in conjunction with or in lieu of an array. Here, two **for** loops replace the arrays and **foreach** loops used in the script previously.

```
1    <!DOCTYPE html PUBLIC "-//W3C//DTD
     XHTML 1.0 Transitional//EN"
         "http://www.w3.org/TR/xhtml1/DTD/
         xhtml1-transitional.dtd">
2    <html xmlns="http://www.w3.org/1999/
     xhtml" xml:lang="en" lang="en">
3    <head>
4        <meta http-equiv="Content-Type"
         content="text/html; charset=utf-8" />
5        <title>Calendar</title>
6    </head>
7    <body>
8    <form action="calendar.php"
     method="post">
9    <?php # Script 2.9 - calendar.php #2
10
11   // This script makes three pull-down
     menus
12   // for an HTML form: months, days, years.
13
14   // Make the months array:
15   $months = array (1 => 'January',
     'February', 'March', 'April', 'May',
     'June', 'July', 'August', 'September',
     'October', 'November', 'December');
16
17   // Make the months pull-down menu:
18   echo '<select name="month">';
19   foreach ($months as $key => $value) {
20       echo "<option value=\"$key\">$value
         </option>\n";
21   }
22   echo '</select>';
23
24   // Make the days pull-down menu:
25   echo '<select name="day">';
26   for ($day = 1; $day <= 31; $day++) {
27       echo "<option value=\"$day\">
         $day</option>\n";
28   }
29   echo '</select>';
30
```

code continues on next page

Script 2.9 *continued*

```
31    // Make the years pull-down menu:
32    echo '<select name="year">';
33    for ($year = 2011; $year <= 2021;
      $year++) {
34        echo "<option value=\"$year\">
          $year</option>\n";
35    }
36    echo '</select>';
37
38    ?>
39    </form>
40    </body>
41    </html>
```

C This calendar form looks the same as it had previously but was created with two fewer arrays (compare Script 2.9 with Script 2.6).

4. Rewrite the **$years foreach** loop as a **for** loop:

   ```
   for ($year = 2011; $year <= 2021;
   → $year++) {
       echo "<option value=\"$year\">
       → $year</option>\n";
   }
   ```

   The structure of this loop is fundamentally the same as the **$day** **for** loop, but the **$year** variable is initially set to 2011 instead of 1. As long as **$year** is less than or equal to 2021, the loop will be executed. Within the loop, the **echo** statement is run.

5. Save the file, place it in your Web directory, and test it in your Web browser **C**.

TIP PHP also has a do...while loop with a slightly different syntax (check the manual). This loop will always be executed at least once.

TIP When using loops, watch your parameters and conditions to avoid the dreaded infinite loop, which occurs when a loop's condition is never going to be false.

Review and Pursue

If you have any problems with the review questions or the pursue prompts, turn to the book's supporting forum (**www. LarryUllman.com/forums/**).

Note: Some of these questions and prompts rehash information covered in Chapter 1, in order to reinforce some of the most important points.

Review

- What is the significance of a form's **method** attribute? Of its **action** attribute?

- Why must an HTML form that gets submitted to a PHP script be loaded through a URL? What would happen upon submitting the form if it were not loaded through a URL?

- What are the differences between using single and double quotation marks to delineate strings?

- What control structures were introduced in this chapter?

- What new variable type was introduced in this chapter?

- What operator tests for equality? What is the assignment operator?

- Why are textual form elements validated using **empty( )** but other form elements are validated using **isset( )**?

- What is the difference between an *indexed* array and an *associative* array?

- With what value do indexed arrays begin (by default)? If an indexed array has ten elements in it, what would the expected index be of the last element in the array?

- What are the *superglobal arrays*? From where do the following superglobals get their values?

  ▸ **$_GET**

  ▸ **$_POST**

  ▸ **$_COOKIE**

  ▸ **$_REQUEST**

  ▸ **$_SESSION**

  ▸ **$_SERVER**

  ▸ **$_ENV**

- How can you print an individual *indexed* array item? How can you print an individual *associative* array item? Note: there is more than one answer to both questions.

- What does the **count( )** function do?

- What impact does printing **\n** have on the Web browser?

- Generally speaking, when would you use a **while** loop? When would you use a **for** loop? When would you use a **foreach** loop? What is the syntax of each loop type?

- What is the **++** operator? What does it do?

Pursue

- What version of PHP are you using? If you don't know, find out now!

- Create a new form that takes some input from the user (perhaps base it on a form you know you'll need for one of your projects). Then create the PHP script that validates the form data and reports upon the results.

- Rewrite the gender conditional in **handle_form.php** (Script 2.4) as one conditional instead of two nested ones. Hint: You'll need to use the **AND** operator.

- Rewrite **handle_form.php** (Script 2.4) to use **$_POST** instead of **$_REQUEST**.

- Rewrite **handle_form.php** (Script 2.4) so that it validates the age element. Hint: Use the **$gender** validation as a template, this time checking against the corresponding pull-down option values (*0-29, 30-60, 60+*).

- Rewrite the **echo** statement in the final version of **handle_form.php** (Script 2.5) so that it uses single quotation marks and concatenation instead of double quotation marks.

- Look up in the PHP manual one of the array functions introduced in this book. Then check out some of the other array-related functions built into the language.

- Create a new array and then display its elements. Sort the array in different ways and then display the array's contents again.

- Create a form that contains a select menu or series of check boxes that allow for multiple sections. Then, in the handling PHP script, display the selected items along with a count of how many the user selected.

- For added complexity, take the suggested PHP script you just created (that handles multiple selections), and have it display the selections in alphabetical order.

Creating Dynamic Web Sites

With the fundamentals of PHP under your belt, it's time to begin building truly dynamic Web sites. *Dynamic* Web sites, as opposed to the static ones on which the Web was first built, are easier to maintain, are more responsive to users, and can alter their content in response to differing situations. This chapter introduces three new ideas, all commonly used to create more sophisticated Web applications (Chapter 11, "Web Application Development," covers another handful of topics along these same lines).

The first subject involves using external files. This is an important concept, as more complex sites often demand compartmentalizing some HTML or PHP code. Then the chapter returns to the subject of handling HTML forms. You'll learn some new variations on this important and standard feature of dynamic Web sites. Finally, you'll learn how to define and use your own functions.

Including Multiple Files

To this point, every script in the book has consisted of a single file that contains all of the required HTML and PHP code. But as you develop more complex Web sites, you'll see that this approach is not often practical. A better way to create dynamic Web applications is to divide your scripts and Web sites into distinct parts, each part being stored in its own file. Frequently, you will use multiple files to extract the HTML from the PHP or to separate out commonly used processes.

PHP has four functions for incorporating external files: `include( )`, `include_once( )`, `require( )`, and `require_once( )`. To use them, your PHP script would have a line like

```
include_once('filename.php');
require('/path/to/filename.html');
```

Using any one of these functions has the end result of taking all the content of the included file and dropping it in the parent script (the one calling the function) at that juncture. An important consideration with included files is that PHP will treat the included code as HTML (i.e., send it directly to the browser) unless the file contains code within the PHP tags.

In terms of functionality, it also doesn't matter what extension the included file uses, be it `.php` or `.html`. However, giving the file a symbolic name and extension helps to convey its purpose (e.g., an included file of HTML might use `.inc.html`). Also note that you can use either *absolute* or *relative* paths to the included file (see the sidebar for more).

Absolute vs. Relative Paths

When referencing any external item, be it an included file in PHP, a CSS document in HTML, or an image, you have the choice of using either an *absolute* or a *relative* path. An absolute path references a file starting from the root directory of the computer:

```
include ('C:/php/includes/
 file.php');
include('/usr/xyz/includes/
 file.php');
```

Assuming **file.php** exists in the named location, the inclusion will work, no matter the location of the referencing (parent) file (barring any permissions issues). The second example, in case you're not familiar with the syntax, would be a Unix (and Mac OS X) absolute path. Absolute paths always start with something like **C:/** or **/**.

A relative path uses the referencing (parent) file as the starting point. To move up one folder, use two periods together. To move into a folder, use its name followed by a slash. So assuming the current script is in the **www/ex1** folder and you want to include something in **www/ex2**, the code would be:

```
include('../ex2/file.php');
```

A relative path will remain accurate, even if the site is moved to another server, as long as the files maintain their current relationship to each other.

The **include( )** and **require( )** functions are exactly the same when working properly but behave differently when they fail. If an **include( )** function doesn't work (it cannot include the file for some reason), a warning will be printed to the Web browser **Ⓐ**, but the script will continue to run. If **require( )** fails, an error is printed and the script is halted **Ⓑ**.

Both functions also have a ***_once( )** version, which guarantees that the file in question is included only once regardless of how many times a script may (presumably inadvertently) attempt to include it.

```
require_once('filename.php');
include_once('filename.php');
```

Because **require_once( )** and **include_once( )** require extra work from the PHP module (i.e., PHP must first check that the file has not already been included), it's best

not to use these two functions unless a redundant include is likely to occur (which can happen on complex sites).

In this next example, included files will separate the primary HTML formatting from any PHP code. Then, the rest of the examples in this chapter will be able to have the same appearance—as if they are all part of the same Web site—without the need to rewrite the common HTML every time. This technique creates a *template system*, an easy way to make large applications consistent and manageable. The focus in these examples is on the PHP code itself; you should also read the "Site Structure" sidebar so that you understand the organizational scheme on the server. If you have any questions about the CSS (Cascading Style Sheets) or (X)HTML used in the example, see a dedicated resource on those topics.

Warning: include(includes/header.html) [function.include]: failed to open stream: No such file or directory in **/Users/larryullman/Sites/phpmysql4/index.php** on line **3**

Warning: include() [function.include]: Failed opening 'includes/header.html' for inclusion (include_path='.:/Applications/MAMP/bin/php5.3/lib/php') in **/Users/larryullman/Sites/phpmysql4/index.php** on line **3**

Content Header

This is where the page-specific content goes. This section, and the corresponding header, will change from one page to the next.

Ⓐ One failed **include( )** call generates these two error messages (assuming that PHP is configured to display errors), but the rest of the page continues to execute.

Warning: require(includes/header.html) [function.require]: failed to open stream: No such file or directory in **/Users/larryullman/Sites/phpmysql4/index.php** on line **3**

Fatal error: require() [function.require]: Failed opening required 'includes/header.html' (include_path='.:/Applications/MAMP/bin/php5.3/lib/php') in **/Users/larryullman/Sites/phpmysql4/index.php** on line **3**

Ⓑ The failure of a **require( )** function call will print an error and terminate the execution of the script. If PHP is not configured to display errors, then the script will terminate without printing the problem first (i.e., it'd be a blank page).

To include multiple files:

1. Design an HTML page in your text or WYSIWYG editor (**Script 3.1** and **C**).

   To start creating a template for a Web site, design the layout like a standard HTML page, independent of any PHP code. For this chapter's example, I'm using a slightly modified version of the "Plain and Simple" template created by Christopher Robinson (**www.edg3.co.uk**) and used with his kind permission.

2. Mark where any page-specific content goes.

   Almost every Web site has several common elements on each page—header, navigation, advertising, footer, etc.—and one or more page-specific sections. In the HTML page (Script 3.1), enclose the section of the layout that will change from page to page within HTML comments to indicate its status.

Site Structure

When you begin using multiple files in your Web applications, the overall site structure becomes more important. When laying out your site, there are two primary considerations:

- Ease of maintenance
- Security

Using external files for holding standard procedures (i.e., PHP code), CSS, JavaScript, and the HTML design will greatly improve the ease of maintaining your site because commonly edited code is placed in one central location. I'll frequently make an **includes** or **templates** directory to store these files apart from the main scripts (the ones that are accessed directly in the Web browser).

I recommend using the **.inc** or **.html** file extension for documents where security is not an issue (such as HTML templates) and **.php** for files that contain more sensitive data (such as database access information). You can also use both **.inc** and **.html** or **.php** so that a file is clearly indicated as an include of a certain type: **db.inc.php** or **header.inc.html**.

C The HTML and CSS design as it appears in the Web browser (without using any PHP).

Script 3.1 The HTML template for this chapter's Web pages. Download the **style.css** file it uses from the book's supporting Web site (**www.LarryUllman.com**).

```
1    <!DOCTYPE html PUBLIC "-//W3C//DTD XHTML 1.0 Strict//EN" "http://www.w3.org/TR/xhtml1/DTD/
     xhtml1-strict.dtd">
2    <html xmlns="http://www.w3.org/1999/xhtml">
3    <head>
4      <title>Page Title</title>
5      <link rel="stylesheet" href="includes/style.css" type="text/css" media="screen" />
6      <meta http-equiv="content-type" content="text/html; charset=utf-8" />
7    </head>
8    <body>
9      <div id="header">
10        <h1>Your Website</h1>
11        <h2>catchy slogan...</h2>
12     </div>
13     <div id="navigation">
14        <ul>
15           <li><a href="index.php">Home Page</a></li>
16           <li><a href="calculator.php">Calculator</a></li>
17           <li><a href="#">link three</a></li>
18           <li><a href="#">link four</a></li>
19           <li><a href="#">link five</a></li>
20        </ul>
21     </div>
22     <div id="content"><!-- Start of the page-specific content. -->
23        <h1>Content Header</h1>
24
25        <p>This is where the page-specific content goes. This section, and the
           corresponding header, will change from one page to the next.</p>
26
27        <p>Volutpat at varius sed sollicitudin et, arcu. Vivamus viverra. Nullam turpis.
           Vestibulum sed etiam. Lorem ipsum sit amet dolore. Nulla facilisi. Sed tortor. Aenean felis.
           Quisque eros. Cras lobortis commodo metus. Vestibulum vel purus. In eget odio in sapien
           adipiscing blandit. Quisque augue tortor, facilisis sit amet, aliquam, suscipit vitae, cursus
           sed, arcu lorem ipsum dolor sit amet.</p>
28
29     <!-- End of the page-specific content. --></div>
30
31     <div id="footer">
32        <p>Copyright &copy; <a href="#">Plain and Simple</a> 2007 | Designed by
           <a href="http://www.edg3.co.uk/">edg3.co.uk</a> | Sponsored by <a href="http://
           www.opendesigns.org/">Open Designs</a> | Valid <a href="http://jigsaw.w3.org/
           css-validator/">CSS</a> &amp; <a href="http://validator.w3.org/">XHTML</a></p>
33     </div>
34   </body>
35   </html>
```

3. Copy everything from the first line of the layout's HTML source to just before the page-specific content and paste it in a new document, to be named header.html (Script 3.2):

```
<!DOCTYPE html PUBLIC "-//W3C//
→ DTD XHTML 1.0 Strict//EN"
→ "http://www.w3.org/TR/xhtml1/
→ DTD/xhtml1-strict.dtd">
<html xmlns="http://www.w3.org/
→ 1999/xhtml">
<head>
  <title>Page Title</title>
  <link rel="stylesheet" href=
  → "includes/style.css" type=
  → "text/css" media="screen" />
  <meta http-equiv="content-type"
  → content="text/html;
  → charset=utf-8" />
</head>
<body>
<div id="header">
  <h1>Your Website</h1>
  <h2>catchy slogan...</h2>
</div>
<div id="navigation">
  <ul>
    <li><a href="index.php">
    → Home Page</a></li>
    <li><a href="calculator.
    → php">Calculator</a></li>
    <li><a href="#">link three
    → </a></li>
    <li><a href="#">link four
    → </a></li>
    <li><a href="#">link five
    → </a></li>
  </ul>
</div>
<div id="content"><!-- Start of
→ the page-specific content. -->
<!-- Script 3.2 - header.html -->
```

Script 3.2 The initial HTML for each Web page is stored in a header file.

```
1   <!DOCTYPE html PUBLIC "-//W3C//DTD XHTML 1.0 Strict//EN" "http://www.w3.org/TR/xhtml1/DTD/
    xhtml1-strict.dtd">
2   <html xmlns="http://www.w3.org/1999/xhtml">
3   <head>
4       <title><?php echo $page_title; ?></title>
5       <link rel="stylesheet" href="includes/style.css" type="text/css" media="screen" />
6       <meta http-equiv="content-type" content="text/html; charset=utf-8" />
7   </head>
8   <body>
9       <div id="header">
10          <h1>Your Website</h1>
11          <h2>catchy slogan...</h2>
12      </div>
13      <div id="navigation">
14          <ul>
15          <li><a href="index.php">Home Page</a></li>
16          <li><a href="calculator.php">Calculator</a></li>
17          <li><a href="#">link three</a></li>
18          <li><a href="#">link four</a></li>
19          <li><a href="#">link five</a></li>
20          </ul>
21      </div>
22      <div id="content"><!-- Start of the page-specific content. -->
23  <!-- Script 3.2 - header.html -->
```

This first file will contain the initial HTML tags (from **DOCTYPE** through the head and into the beginning of the page body). It also has the code that makes the Web site name and slogan, plus the horizontal bar of links across the top ○. Finally, as each page's content goes within a **DIV** whose **id** value is *content*, this file includes that code as well.

4. Change the page's title line to read:

```
<?php echo $page_title; ?>
```

The page title (which appears at the top of the Web browser ○) should be changeable on a page-by-page basis. For that to be possible, this value will be based upon a PHP variable, which will then be printed out. You'll see how this plays out shortly.

5. Save the file as **header.html**.

As stated already, included files can use just about any extension for the filename. This file is called **header. html**, indicating that it is the template's header file and that it contains (primarily) HTML.

6. Copy everything in the original template from the end of the page-specific content to the end of the page and paste it

in a new file, to be named **footer.html** (**Script 3.3**):

```
<!-- Script 3.3 - footer.html -->
  <!-- End of the page-specific
  → content. --></div>
  <div id="footer">
    <p>Copyright &copy; <a
    → href="#">Plain and Simple
    → </a> 2007 | Designed
    → by <a href="http://www.edg3.
    → co.uk/">edg3.co.uk</a> |
    → Sponsored by <a href=
    → "http://www.opendesigns.
    → org/">Open Designs</a> |
    → Valid <a href="http://
    → jigsaw.w3.org/css-validator/">
    → CSS</a> &amp; <a href=
    → "http://validator.w3.org/">
    → XHTML</a></p>
  </div>
</body>
</html>
```

The footer file starts by closing the *content* **DIV** opened in the header file (see Step 3). Then the footer is added, which will be the same for every page on the site, and the HTML document itself is completed.

continues on next page

Script 3.3 The concluding HTML for each Web page is stored in this footer file.

```
1   <!-- Script 3.3 - footer.html -->
2     <!-- End of the page-specific content. --></div>
3
4     <div id="footer">
5       <p>Copyright &copy; <a href="#">Plain and Simple</a> 2007 | Designed by <a href=
        "http://www.edg3.co.uk/">edg3.co.uk</a> | Sponsored by <a href="http://www.opendesigns.
        org/">Open Designs</a> | Valid <a href="http://jigsaw.w3.org/css-validator/">CSS</a>
        &amp; <a href="http://validator.w3.org/">XHTML</a></p>
6     </div>
7   </body>
8   </html>
```

7. Save the file as **footer.html**.

8. Begin a new PHP document in your text editor or IDE, to be named **index.php** (**Script 3.4**):

   ```
   <?php # Script 3.4 - index.php
   ```

   Since this script will use the included files for most of its HTML, it can begin and end with the PHP tags.

9. Set the **$page_title** variable and include the HTML header:

   ```
   $page_title = 'Welcome to this
   → Site!';
   include ('includes/header.html');
   ```

   The **$page_title** variable will store the value that appears in the top of the browser window (and therefore, is also the default value when a person bookmarks the page). This variable is printed in **header.html** (see Script 3.2). By defining the variable prior to including the header file, the header file will have access to that variable. Remember that this **include( )** line has the effect of dropping the contents of the included file into this page at this spot.

The **include( )** function call uses a *relative* path to **header.html** (see the sidebar, "Absolute vs. Relative Paths"). The syntax states that in the same folder as this file is a folder called **includes** and in that folder is a file named **header.html**.

10. Close the PHP tags and add the page-specific content:

    ```
    ?>
    <h1>Content Header</h1>
      <p>This is where the page-
      → specific content goes. This
      → section, and the corresponding
      → header, will change from one
      → page to the next.</p>
    ```

    For most pages, PHP will generate this content, instead of having static text. This information could be sent to the browser using **echo**, but since there's no dynamic content here, it's easier and more efficient to exit the PHP tags temporarily. (The script and the images have a bit of extra Latin than is shown here, just to fatten up the page.)

Script 3.4 This script generates a complete Web page by including a template stored in two external files.

```
1    <?php # Script 3.4 - index.php
2    $page_title = 'Welcome to this Site!';
3    include ('includes/header.html');
4    ?>
5
6    <h1>Content Header</h1>
7
8        <p>This is where the page-specific content goes. This section, and the
         corresponding header, will change from one page to the next.</p>
9
10       <p>Volutpat at varius sed sollicitudin et, arcu. Vivamus viverra. Nullam turpis.
         Vestibulum sed etiam. Lorem ipsum sit amet dolore. Nulla facilisi. Sed tortor.
         Aenean felis. Quisque eros. Cras lobortis commodo metus. Vestibulum vel purus.
         In eget odio in sapien adipiscing blandit. Quisque augue tortor, facilisis sit
         amet, aliquam, suscipit vitae, cursus sed, arcu lorem ipsum dolor sit amet.</p>
11
12   <?php
13   include ('includes/footer.html');
14   ?>
```

11. Create a final PHP section and include the footer file:

```php
<?php
include ('includes/footer.html');
?>
```

12. Save the file as **index.php,** and place it in your Web directory.

13. Create an **includes** directory in the same folder as **index.php**. Then place **header.html**, **footer.html**, and **style.css** (part of the downloadable code at **www.LarryUllman.com**), into this **includes** directory.

Note: In order to save space, the CSS file for this example (which controls the layout) is not included in the book. You can download the file through the book's supporting Web site or do without it (the template will still work, it just won't look as nice).

14. Test the template system by going to the **index.php** page in your Web browser **D**.

The **index.php** page is the key script in the template system. You do not need to access any of the included files directly, as **index.php** will take care of incorporating their contents. As this is a PHP page, you still need to access it through a URL.

continues on next page

Welcome to this Site!

http://localhost/index.php

Your Website
catchy slogan...

| Home Page | Calculator | link three | link four | link five |

Content Header

This is where the page-specific content goes. This section, and the corresponding header, will change from one page to the next.

Volutpat at varius sed sollicitudin et, arcu. Vivamus viverra. Nullam turpis. Vestibulum sed etiam. Lorem ipsum sit amet dolore. Nulla facilisi. Sed tortor. Aenean felis. Quisque eros. Cras lobortis commodo metus. Vestibulum vel purus. In eget odio in sapien adipiscing blandit. Quisque augue tortor, facilisis sit amet, aliquam, suscipit vitae, cursus sed, arcu lorem ipsum dolor sit amet.

Copyright © Plain and Simple 2007 | Designed by edg3.co.uk | Sponsored by Open Designs | Valid CSS & XHTML

D Now the same layout **C** has been created using external files in PHP.

15. If desired, view the HTML source of the page **E**.

> **TIP** In the `php.ini` configuration file, you can adjust the `include_path` setting, which dictates where PHP is and is not allowed to retrieve included files.

> **TIP** As you'll see in Chapter 9, "Using PHP with MySQL," any included file that contains sensitive information (like database access) should ideally be stored outside of the Web directory so it can't be viewed within a Web browser.

> **TIP** Since `require( )` has more impact on a script when it fails, it's recommended for mission-critical includes (like those that connect to a database). The `include( )` function would be used for less important inclusions.

> **TIP** If a block of PHP code contains only a single executable, it's common to place both it and the PHP tags on a single line:
>
> `<?php include ('filename.html'); ?>`

> **TIP** Because of the way CSS works, if you don't use the CSS file or if the browser doesn't read the CSS, the generated result is still functional, just not aesthetically as pleasing.

```
○ ○ ○              Source of http://localhost/index.php

<!DOCTYPE html PUBLIC "-//W3C//DTD XHTML 1.0 Strict//EN" "http://www.w3.org/TR/xhtml1/DTD/xhtml1-strict.dtd">
<html xmlns="http://www.w3.org/1999/xhtml">
<head>
        <title>Welcome to this Site!</title>
        <link rel="stylesheet" href="includes/style.css" type="text/css" media="screen" />
        <meta http-equiv="content-type" content="text/html; charset=utf-8" />
</head>
<body>
        <div id="header">
                <h1>Your Website</h1>
                <h2>catchy slogan...</h2>
        </div>
        <div id="navigation">
                <ul>
                        <li><a href="index.php">Home Page</a></li>
                        <li><a href="calculator.php">Calculator</a></li>
                        <li><a href="#">link three</a></li>
                        <li><a href="#">link four</a></li>
                        <li><a href="#">link five</a></li>
                </ul>
        </div>
        <div id="content"><!-- Start of the page-specific content. -->
<!-- Script 3.2 - header.html -->
<h1>Content Header</h1>

        <p>This is where the page-specific content goes. This section, and the corresponding header, will
change from one page to the next.</p>

        <p>Volutpat at varius sed sollicitudin et, arcu. Vivamus viverra. Nullam turpis. Vestibulum sed
etiam. Lorem ipsum sit amet dolore. Nulla facilisi. Sed tortor. Aenean felis. Quisque eros. Cras lobortis
commodo metus. Vestibulum vel purus. In eget odio in sapien adipiscing blandit. Quisque augue tortor,
facilisis sit amet, aliquam, suscipit vitae, cursus sed, arcu lorem ipsum dolor sit amet.</p>

<!-- Script 3.3 - footer.html -->
        <!-- End of the page-specific content. --></div>

        <div id="footer">
                <p>Copyright &copy; <a href="#">Plain and Simple</a> 2007 | Designed by <a
href="http://www.edg3.co.uk/">edg3.co.uk</a> | Sponsored by <a href="http://www.opendesigns.org/">Open
Designs</a> | Valid <a href="http://jigsaw.w3.org/css-validator/">CSS</a> &amp; <a
href="http://validator.w3.org/">XHTML</a></p>
        </div>
</body>
</html>
```

E The generated HTML source of the Web page should replicate the code in the original template (refer to Script 3.1).

Handling HTML Forms, Revisited

A good portion of Chapter 2, "Programming with PHP," involves handling HTML forms with PHP (which makes sense, as a good portion of Web programming with PHP is exactly that). All of those examples use two separate files: one that displays the form and another that receives its submitted data. While there's certainly nothing wrong with this approach, there are advantages to putting the entire process into one script.

To have one page both display and handle a form, a conditional must check which action (*display* or *handle*) should be taken:

```
if (/* form has been submitted */) {
    // Handle the form.
} else {
    // Display the form.
}
```

The question, then, is how to determine if the form has been submitted. The answer is simple, after a bit of explanation.

When you have a form that uses the POST method and gets submitted back to the same page, two different types of requests will be made of that script **A**. The first request, which loads the form, will be a GET request. This is the standard request made of most Web pages. When the form is submitted, a second request of the script will be made, this time a POST request (so long as the form uses the POST method). With this in mind, you can test for a form's submission by checking the request method, found in the **$_SERVER** array:

```
if ($_SERVER['REQUEST_METHOD'] ==
→ 'POST') {
    // Handle the form.
} else {
    // Display the form.
}
```

continues on next page

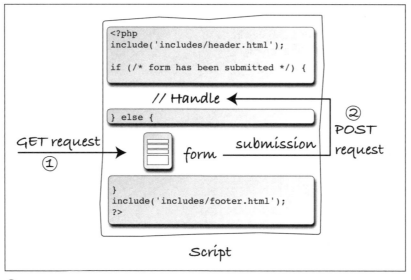

A The interactions between the user and this PHP script on the server involves the user making two requests of this script.

If you want a page to handle a form and then display it again (e.g., to add a record to a database and then give an option to add another), drop the **else** clause:

```
if ($_SERVER['REQUEST_METHOD'] ==
→'POST') {
       // Handle the form.
}
// Display the form.
```

Using that code, a script will handle a form if it has been submitted and display the form every time the page is loaded.

To demonstrate this important technique (of having the same page both display and handle a form), let's create a calculator that estimates the cost and time required to take a car trip, based upon user-entered values **B**.

To handle HTML forms:

1. Begin a new PHP document in your text editor or IDE, to be named **calculator.php** (Script 3.5):

   ```
   <?php # Script 3.5 - calculator.php
   $page_title = 'Trip Cost Calculator';
   include ('includes/header.html');
   ```

   This, and all the remaining examples in the chapter, will use the same template system as **index.php** (Script 3.4). The beginning syntax of each page will therefore be the same, but the page titles will differ.

2. Write the conditional that checks for a form submission:

   ```
   if ($_SERVER['REQUEST_METHOD'] ==
   →'POST') {
   ```

   As suggested already, checking if the page is being requested via the POST method is a good test for a form submission (so long as the form uses POST).

continues on page 88

Trip Cost Calculator

Distance (in miles): **225**

Ave. Price Per Gallon: ◯ **3.00** ⦿ **3.50** ◯ **4.00**

Fuel Efficiency: **Decent** ▲▼

Calculate!

B The HTML form, completed by the user.

Script 3.5 The `calculator.php` script both displays a simple form and handles the form data: performing some calculations and reporting upon the results.

```php
1   <?php # Script 3.5 - calculator.php
2
3   $page_title = 'Trip Cost Calculator';
4   include ('includes/header.html');
5
6   // Check for form submission:
7   if ($_SERVER['REQUEST_METHOD'] == 'POST') {
8
9       // Minimal form validation:
10      if (isset($_POST['distance'], $_POST['gallon_price'], $_POST['efficiency']) &&
11      is_numeric($_POST['distance']) && is_numeric($_POST['gallon_price'])
        && is_numeric($_POST['efficiency']) ) {
12
13          // Calculate the results:
14          $gallons = $_POST['distance'] / $_POST['efficiency'];
15          $dollars = $gallons * $_POST['gallon_price'];
16          $hours = $_POST['distance']/65;
17
18          // Print the results:
19          echo '<h1>Total Estimated Cost</h1>
20      <p>The total cost of driving ' . $_POST['distance'] . ' miles, averaging ' . $_POST
        ['efficiency'] . ' miles per gallon, and paying an average of $' . $_POST['gallon_price'] . '
        per gallon, is $' . number_format ($dollars, 2) . '. If you drive at an average of 65 miles
        per hour, the trip will take approximately ' . number_format($hours, 2) . ' hours.</p>';
21
22      } else { // Invalid submitted values.
23          echo '<h1>Error!</h1>
24      <p class="error">Please enter a valid distance, price per gallon, and fuel efficiency.</p>';
25      }
26
27  } // End of main submission IF.
28
29  // Leave the PHP section and create the HTML form:
30  ?>
31
32  <h1>Trip Cost Calculator</h1>
33  <form action="calculator.php" method="post">
34      <p>Distance (in miles): <input type="text" name="distance" /></p>
35      <p>Ave. Price Per Gallon: <span class="input">
36          <input type="radio" name="gallon_price" value="3.00" /> 3.00
37          <input type="radio" name="gallon_price" value="3.50" /> 3.50
38          <input type="radio" name="gallon_price" value="4.00" /> 4.00
39      </span></p>
40      <p>Fuel Efficiency: <select name="efficiency">
41          <option value="10">Terrible</option>
42          <option value="20">Decent</option>
43          <option value="30">Very Good</option>
44          <option value="50">Outstanding</option>
45      </select></p>
46      <p><input type="submit" name="submit" value="Calculate!" /></p>
47  </form>
48
49  <?php include ('includes/footer.html'); ?>
```

3. Validate the form:

```
if (isset($_POST['distance'],
→$_POST['gallon_price'],
→$_POST['efficiency']) &&
  is_numeric($_POST['distance'])
  →&& is_numeric($_POST['gallon_
  →price']) && is_numeric($_POST
  →['efficiency']) ) {
```

The validation here is very simple: it merely checks that three submitted variables are set and are all numeric types. You can certainly elaborate on this, perhaps checking that all values are positive (in fact, Chapter 13, "Security Methods," has a variation on this script that does just that).

If the validation passes all of the tests, the calculations will be made; otherwise, the user will be asked to try again.

4. Perform the calculations:

```
$gallons = $_POST['distance'] /
→$_POST['efficiency'];
$dollars = $gallons *
→$_POST['gallon_price'];
$hours = $_POST['distance']/65;
```

The first line calculates the number of gallons of gasoline the trip will take, determined by dividing the distance by the fuel efficiency. The second line calculates the cost of the fuel for the trip, determined by multiplying the number of gallons times the average price per gallon. The third line calculates how long the trip will take, determined by dividing the distance by 65 (representing 65 miles per hour).

5. Print the results:

```
echo '<h1>Total Estimated Cost</h1>
  <p>The total cost of driving '
  →. $_POST['distance'] . ' miles,
  →averaging ' . $_POST
  →['efficiency'] . ' miles per
  →gallon, and paying an average
  →of $' . $_POST['gallon_price']
  →. ' per gallon, is $' .
  →number_format ($dollars, 2) .
  →'. If you drive at an average
  →of 65 miles per hour, the
  →trip will take approximately
  →' . number_format($hours, 2)
  →. ' hours.</p>';
```

All of the values are printed out, while formatting the cost and hours with the **number_format( )** function. Using the concatenation operator (the period) allows the formatted numeric values to be appended to the printed message.

6. Complete the conditionals and close the PHP tag:

```
} else { // Invalid submitted
→values.
    echo '<h1>Error!</h1>
    <p class="error">Please enter
    →a valid distance, price
    →per gallon, and fuel
    →efficiency.</p>';
}
} // End of main submission IF.
?>
```

The **else** clause completes the validation conditional (Step 3), printing an error if the three submitted values aren't all set and numeric **C**. The final closing curly brace closes the **isset($_SERVER['REQUEST_METHOD'] == 'POST')** conditional. Finally, the PHP section is closed so that the form can be created without using **echo** (see Step 7).

7. Begin the HTML form:

```
<h1>Trip Cost Calculator</h1>
<form action="calculator.php"
→ method="post">
  <p>Distance (in miles): <input
  → type="text" name="distance" />
  → </p>
```

The form itself is fairly obvious, containing only one new trick: the **action** attribute uses this script's name, so that the form submits back to this page instead of to another. The first element within the form is a text input, where the user can enter the distance of the trip.

8. Complete the form:

```
  <p>Ave. Price Per Gallon: <span
  → class="input">
<input type="radio" name="gallon_
→ price" value="3.00" /> 3.00
<input type="radio" name="gallon_
→ price" value="3.50" /> 3.50
<input type="radio" name="gallon_
→ price" value="4.00" /> 4.00
</span></p>
  <p>Fuel Efficiency: <select
  → name="efficiency">
    <option value="10">Terrible
    → </option>
    <option value="20">Decent
    → </option>
    <option value="30">Very
    → Good</option>
    <option value="50">
    → Outstanding</option>
  </select></p>
  <p><input type="submit"
  → name="submit" value=
  → "Calculate!" /></p>
</form>
```

continues on next page

Error!

- -

Please enter a valid distance, price per gallon, and fuel efficiency.

Trip Cost Calculator

- -

Distance (in miles): [   ]

Ave. Price Per Gallon: ◯ 3.00 ◯ 3.50 ◯ 4.00

C If any of the submitted values is not both set and numeric, an error message is displayed.

The form uses radio buttons as a way to select the average price per gallon (the buttons are wrapped within **span** tags in order to format them similarly to the other form elements). For the fuel efficiency, the user can select from a drop-down menu of four options. A submit button completes the form.

9. Include the footer file:

```
<?php include ('includes/
→footer.html'); ?>
```

10. Save the file as **calculator.php**, place it in your Web directory, and test it in your Web browser **D**.

TIP You can also have a form submit back to itself by using no value for the **action** attribute:

```
<form action="" method="post">
```

By doing so, the form will always submit back to this same page, even if you later change the name of the script.

Total Estimated Cost

The total cost of driving 225 miles, averaging 20 miles per gallon, and paying an average of $3.50 per gallon, is $39.38. If you drive at an average of 65 miles per hour, the trip will take approximately 3.46 hours.

Trip Cost Calculator

Distance (in miles): [   ]

Ave. Price Per Gallon: ○ **3.00** ○ **3.50** ○ **4.00**

D The page performs the calculations, reports on the results, and then redisplays the form.

Making Sticky Forms

A *sticky form* is simply a standard HTML form that remembers how you filled it out. This is a particularly nice feature for end users, especially if you are requiring them to resubmit a form after filling it out incorrectly in the first place (as in ⓒ in the previous section).

To preset what's entered in a text input, use its **value** attribute:

```
<input type="text" name="city"
→ value="Innsbruck" />
```

To have PHP preset that value, print the appropriate variable (this assumes that the referenced variable exists):

```
<input type="text" name="city"
→ value="<?php echo $city; ?>" />
```

(This is also a nice example of the benefit of PHP's HTML-embedded nature: you can place PHP code anywhere, including within HTML tags.)

To preset the status of radio buttons or check boxes (i.e., to pre-check them), add the code **checked="checked"** to their **input** tags. Using PHP, you might write:

```
<input type="radio" name="gender"
→ value="F" <?php if ($gender == 'F') {
        echo 'checked="checked"';
} ?>/>
```

(As you can see, the syntax can quickly get complicated; you may find it easiest to create the form element and then add the PHP code as a second step.)

To preset the value of a textarea, print the value between the **textarea** tags:

```
<textarea name="comments" rows="10"
→ cols="50"><?php echo $comments;
→ ?></textarea>
```

Note that the **textarea** tag does not have a **value** attribute like the standard **text** input.

To preselect a pull-down menu, add **selected="selected"** to the appropriate option. This is really easy if you also use PHP to generate the menu:

```
echo '<select name="year">';
for ($y = 2011; $y <= 2021; $y++) {
        echo "<option value=\"$y\"";
        if ($year == $y) {
                echo ' selected=
                → "selected"';
        }
        echo ">$y</option>\n";
}
echo '</select>';
```

With this new information in mind, let's rewrite **calculator.php** so that it's sticky. Unlike the above examples, the existing values will be present in **$_POST** variables. Also, since it's best not to refer to variables unless they exist, conditionals will check that a variable is set before printing its value.

To make a sticky form:

1. Open **calculator.php** (refer to Script 3.5) in your text editor or IDE, if it is not already.

2. Change the distance input to read (Script 3.6):

   ```
   <input type="text" name="distance"
   ⇥ value="<?php if (isset($_POST
   ⇥ ['distance'])) echo $_POST
   ⇥ ['distance']; ?>" />
   ```

   The first change is to add the **value** attribute to the input. Then, print out the value of the submitted distance variable (**$_POST['distance']**). Since the first time the page is loaded, **$_POST['distance']**

has no value, a conditional ensures that the variable is set before attempting to print it. The end result for setting the input's value is the PHP code

```php
<?php
if (isset($_POST['distance'])) {
    echo $_POST['distance'];
}
?>
```

This can be condensed to the more minimal form used in the script (you can omit the curly braces if you have only one statement within a conditional block, although I very rarely recommend that you do so).

Script 3.6 The calculator's form now recalls the previously entered and selected values (creating a sticky form).

```
1    <?php # Script 3.6 - calculator.php #2
2
3    $page_title = 'Trip Cost Calculator';
4    include ('includes/header.html');
5
6    // Check for form submission:
7    if ($_SERVER['REQUEST_METHOD'] == 'POST') {
8
9        // Minimal form validation:
10       if (isset($_POST['distance'], $_POST['gallon_price'], $_POST['efficiency']) &&
11       is_numeric($_POST['distance']) && is_numeric($_POST['gallon_price'])
         && is_numeric($_POST['efficiency']) ) {
12
13           // Calculate the results:
14           $gallons = $_POST['distance'] / $_POST['efficiency'];
15           $dollars = $gallons * $_POST['gallon_price'];
16           $hours = $_POST['distance']/65;
17
18           // Print the results:
19           echo '<h1>Total Estimated Cost</h1>
20    <p>The total cost of driving ' . $_POST['distance'] . ' miles, averaging ' . $_POST
         ['efficiency'] . ' miles per gallon, and paying an average of $' . $_POST['gallon_price'] . '
         per gallon, is $' . number_format ($dollars, 2) . '. If you drive at an average of 65 miles
         per hour, the trip will take approximately ' . number_format($hours, 2) . ' hours.</p>';
21
22       } else { // Invalid submitted values.
23           echo '<h1>Error!</h1>
24    <p class="error">Please enter a valid distance, price per gallon, and fuel efficiency.</p>';
25       }
26
27    } // End of main submission IF.
```

code continues on next page

3. Change the radio buttons to:

```
<input type="radio" name="gallon_
→ price" value="3.00" <?php if
→ (isset($_POST['gallon_price'])
→ && ($_POST['gallon_price'] ==
→ '3.00')) echo 'checked="checked"
→ '; ?>/> 3.00 <input type="radio"
→ name="gallon_price" value="3.50"
→ <?php if (isset($_POST['gallon_
→ price']) && ($_POST['gallon_
→ price'] == '3.50')) echo 'checked=
→ "checked" '; ?>/> 3.50 <input
→ type="radio" name="gallon_price"
→ value="4.00" <?php if (isset
→ ($_POST['gallon_price']) &&
→ ($_POST['gallon_price'] ==
→ '4.00')) echo 'checked="checked"
→ '; ?>/> 4.00
```

For each of the three radio buttons, the following code must be added within the **input** tag:

```
<?php if (isset($_POST['gallon_
→ price']) && ($_POST['gallon_
→ price'] == 'XXX')) echo
→ 'checked="checked" '; ?>
```

For each button, the comparison value (*XXX*) gets changed accordingly.

continues on next page

Script **3.6** *continued*

```
28
29   // Leave the PHP section and create the HTML form:
30   ?>
31
32   <h1>Trip Cost Calculator</h1>
33   <form action="calculator.php" method="post">
34      <p>Distance (in miles): <input type="text" name="distance" value="<?php if
        (isset($_POST['distance'])) echo $_POST['distance']; ?>" /></p>
35      <p>Ave. Price Per Gallon: <span class="input">
36         <input type="radio" name="gallon_price" value="3.00" <?php if (isset($_POST
           ['gallon_price']) && ($_POST['gallon_price'] == '3.00')) echo 'checked="checked"
           '; ?>/> 3.00
37         <input type="radio" name="gallon_price" value="3.50" <?php if (isset($_POST
           ['gallon_price']) && ($_POST['gallon_price'] == '3.50')) echo 'checked="checked"
           '; ?>/> 3.50
38         <input type="radio" name="gallon_price" value="4.00" <?php if (isset($_POST
           ['gallon_price']) && ($_POST['gallon_price'] == '4.00')) echo 'checked="checked"
           '; ?>/> 4.00
39      </span></p>
40      <p>Fuel Efficiency: <select name="efficiency">
41         <option value="10"<?php if (isset($_POST['efficiency']) && ($_POST['efficiency']
           == '10')) echo ' selected="selected"'; ?>>Terrible</option>
42         <option value="20"<?php if (isset($_POST['efficiency']) && ($_POST['efficiency']
           == '20')) echo ' selected="selected"'; ?>>Decent</option>
43         <option value="30"<?php if (isset($_POST['efficiency']) && ($_POST['efficiency']
           == '30')) echo ' selected="selected"'; ?>>Very Good</option>
44         <option value="50"<?php if (isset($_POST['efficiency']) && ($_POST['efficiency']
           == '50')) echo ' selected="selected"'; ?>>Outstanding</option>
45      </select></p>
46      <p><input type="submit" name="submit" value="Calculate!" /></p>
47   </form>
48
49   <?php include ('includes/footer.html'); ?>
```

4. Change the select menu options to:

```
<option value="10"<?php if
→(isset($_POST['efficiency']) &&
→($_POST['efficiency'] == '10'))
→echo ' selected="selected"';
→?>>Terrible</option>
<option value="20"<?php if
→(isset($_POST['efficiency']) &&
→($_POST['efficiency'] == '20'))
→echo ' selected="selected"';
→?>>Decent</option>
<option value="30"<?php if
→(isset($_POST['efficiency']) &&
→($_POST['efficiency'] == '30'))
→echo ' selected="selected"';
→?>>Very Good</option>
<option value="50"<?php if
→(isset($_POST['efficiency']) &&
→($_POST['efficiency'] == '50'))
→echo ' selected="selected"';
→?>>Outstanding</option>
```

For each option, within the opening **option** tag, the following code is added:

```
<?php if (isset($_POST
→['efficiency']) && ($_POST
→['efficiency'] == 'XX')) echo '
→selected="selected"'; ?>
```

Again, just the specific comparison value (*XX*) must be changed to match each option.

5. Save the file as **calculator.php**, place it in your Web directory, and test it in your Web browser **A** and **B**.

TIP Because the price per gallon and fuel efficiency values are numeric, you can quote or not quote the comparison values within the added conditionals. I choose to quote them, because they're technically strings with numeric values.

TIP Because the added PHP code in this example exists inside of the HTML form element tags, error messages may not be obvious. If problems occur, check the HTML source of the page to see if PHP errors are printed within the value attributes and the tags themselves.

TIP You should always double-quote HTML attributes, particularly the value attribute of a text input. If you don't, multiword values like *Elliott Smith* will appear as just *Elliott* in the Web browser.

TIP Some Web browsers will also remember values entered into forms for you; this is a separate but potentially overlapping issue from using PHP to accomplish this.

Total Estimated Cost

The total cost of driving 425 miles, averaging 30 miles per gallon, and paying an average of $3.50 per gallon, is $49.58. If you drive at an average of 65 miles per hour, the trip will take approximately 6.54 hours.

Trip Cost Calculator

Distance (in miles): `425`

Ave. Price Per Gallon: ☐ 3.00 ⦿ 3.50 ☐ 4.00

Fuel Efficiency: `Very Good ▾`

A The form now recalls the previously submitted values…

Error!

Please enter a valid distance, price per gallon, and fuel efficiency.

Trip Cost Calculator

Distance (in miles): `garbage`

Ave. Price Per Gallon: ☐ 3.00 ☐ 3.50 ☐ 4.00

Fuel Efficiency: `Terrible ▾`

B …whether or not the form was completely filled out.

Creating Your Own Functions

PHP has a lot of built-in functions, addressing almost every need you might have. More importantly, though, PHP has the capability for you to define and use your own functions for whatever purpose. The syntax for making your own function is

```
function function_name () {
    // Function code.
}
```

The name of your function can be any combination of letters, numbers, and the underscore, but it must begin with either a letter or the underscore. You also cannot use an existing function name for your function (*print*, *echo*, *isset*, and so on). One perfectly valid function definition is

```
function do_nothing() {
    // Do nothing.
}
```

In PHP, as mentioned in the first chapter, function names are case-insensitive (unlike variable names), so you could call that function using **do_Nothing( )** or **DO_NOTHING( )** or **Do_Nothing( )**, etc., but not **donothing( )** or **DoNothing( )**.

The code within the function can do nearly anything, from generating HTML to performing calculations to calling other functions.

The most common reasons to create your own functions are:

- To associate repeated code with one function call.

- To separate out sensitive or complicated processes from other code.

- To make common code bits easier to reuse.

This chapter runs through a couple of examples and you'll see some others throughout the rest of the book. For this first example, a function will be defined that outputs the HTML code for generating theoretical ads. This function will then be called twice on the home page **Ⓐ**.

Home Page	Calculator	link three	link four	link five

This is an annoying ad! This is an annoying ad! This is an annoying ad! This is an annoying ad!

Content Header

This is where the page-specific content goes. This section, and the corresponding header, will change from one page to the next.

Volutpat at varius sed sollicitudin et, arcu. Vivamus viverra. Nullam turpis. Vestibulum sed etiam. Lorem ipsum sit amet dolore. Nulla facilisi. Sed tortor. Aenean felis. Quisque eros. Cras lobortis commodo metus. Vestibulum vel purus. In eget odio in sapien adipiscing blandit. Quisque augue tortor, facilisis sit amet, aliquam, suscipit vitae, cursus sed, arcu lorem ipsum dolor sit amet.

This is an annoying ad! This is an annoying ad! This is an annoying ad! This is an annoying ad!

Copyright © Plain and Simple 2007 | Designed by edg3.co.uk | Sponsored by Open Designs | Valid CSS & XHTML

Ⓐ The two "ads" are generated by calling the same user-defined function.

To create your own function:

1. Open **index.php** (Script 3.4) in your text editor or IDE.

2. After the opening PHP tag, begin defining a new function (**Script 3.7**):

   ```
   function create_ad( ) {
   ```

   The function to be written here would, in theory, generate the HTML required to add ads to a Web page. The function's name clearly states its purpose.

Although not required, it's conventional to place a function definition near the very top of a script or in a separate file.

3. Generate the HTML:

   ```
   echo '<p class="ad">This is an
    annoying ad! This is an annoying
    ad! This is an annoying ad! This
    is an annoying ad!</p>';
   ```

   In a real function, the code would output actual HTML instead of a paragraph of text. (The actual HTML would be

Script 3.7 This version of the home page has a user-defined function that outputs a theoretical ad. The function is called twice in the script, creating two ads.

```
1   <?php # Script 3.7 - index.php #2
2
3   // This function outputs theoretical HTML
4   // for adding ads to a Web page.
5   function create_ad( ) {
6       echo '<p class="ad">This is an annoying ad! This is an annoying ad! This is an
        annoying ad! This is an annoying ad!</p>';
7   } // End of the function definition.
8
9   $page_title = 'Welcome to this Site!';
10  include ('includes/header.html');
11
12  // Call the function:
13  create_ad( );
14  ?>
15
16  <h1>Content Header</h1>
17
18      <p>This is where the page-specific content goes. This section, and the
        corresponding header, will change from one page to the next.</p>
19
20      <p>Volutpat at varius sed sollicitudin et, arcu. Vivamus viverra. Nullam turpis.
        Vestibulum sed etiam. Lorem ipsum sit amet dolore. Nulla facilisi. Sed tortor.
        Aenean felis. Quisque eros. Cras lobortis commodo metus. Vestibulum vel purus.
        In eget odio in sapien adipiscing blandit. Quisque augue tortor, facilisis sit
        amet, aliquam, suscipit vitae, cursus sed, arcu lorem ipsum dolor sit amet.</p>
21
22  <?php
23
24  // Call the function again:
25  create_ad( );
26
27  include ('includes/footer.html');
28  ?>
```

provided by the service you're using to generate and tracks ads.)

4. Close the function definition:

`} // End of the function definition.`

It's helpful to place a comment at the end of a function definition so that you know where a definition starts and stops (it's helpful on longer function definitions, at least).

5. After including the header and before exiting the PHP block, call the function:

`create_ad( );`

The call to the `create_ad( )` function will have the end result of inserting the function's output at this point in the script.

6. Just before including the footer, call the function again:

`create_ad( );`

7. Save the file and test it in your Web browser **A**.

TIP If you ever see a *call to undefined function function_name* error, this means that you are calling a function that hasn't been defined. This can happen if you misspell the function's name (either when defining or calling it) or if you fail to include the file where the function is defined.

TIP Because a user-defined function takes up some memory, you should be prudent about when to use one. As a general rule, functions are best used for chunks of code that may be executed in several places in a script or Web site.

Creating a function that takes arguments

Just like PHP's built-in functions, those you write can take *arguments* (also called *parameters*). For example, the `strlen( )` function takes as an argument the string whose character length will be determined.

A function can take any number of arguments, but the order in which you list them is critical. To allow for arguments, add variables to a function's definition:

```
function print_hello ($first, $last) {
        // Function code.
}
```

The variable names you use for your arguments are irrelevant to the rest of the script (more on this in the "Variable Scope" sidebar toward the end of this chapter), but try to use valid, meaningful names.

Once the function is defined, you can then call it as you would any other function in PHP, sending literal values or variables to it:

```
print_hello ('Jimmy', 'Stewart');
$surname = 'Stewart';
print_hello ('Jimmy', $surname);
```

As with any function in PHP, failure to send the right number of arguments results in an error **B**.

To demonstrate this concept, let's rewrite the calculator form so that a user-defined function creates the price-per-gallon radio buttons. Doing so will help to clean up the messy form code.

Ave. Price Per Gallon:
Warning: Missing argument 1 for create_gallon_radio(), called in /Users/larryullman/Sites/phpmysql4/calculator.php on line 55 and defined in **/Users/larryullman/Sites/phpmysql4/calculator.php** on line **6**

B Failure to send a function the proper number (and sometimes type) of arguments creates an error.

To define functions that take arguments:

1. Open **calculator.php** (Script 3.6) in your text editor or IDE.

2. After the initial PHP tag, start defining the **create_gallon_radio( )** function (**Script 3.8**):

```
function create_gallon_radio
→ ($value) {
```

The function will create code like this:

```
<input type="radio" name=
→ "gallon_price" value="XXX"
→ checked="checked" /> XXX
```

or:

```
<input type="radio" name=
→ "gallon_price" value="XXX" /> XXX
```

In order to be able to dynamically set the value of each radio button, that value must be passed to the function with each call. Therefore, that's the one argument the function takes.

Notice that the variable used as an argument is not **$_POST['gallon_price']**. The function's argument variable is particular to this function and has its own name.

continues on page 100

Script 3.8 The **calculator.php** form now uses a function to create the radio buttons. Unlike the **create_ad( )** user-defined function, this one takes an argument.

```
1    <?php # Script 3.8 - calculator.php #3
2
3    // This function creates a radio button.
4    // The function takes one argument: the value.
5    // The function also makes the button "sticky".
6    function create_gallon_radio($value) {
7
8        // Start the element:
9        echo '<input type="radio" name="gallon_price" value="' . $value . '"';
10
11       // Check for stickiness:
12       if (isset($_POST['gallon_price']) && ($_POST['gallon_price'] == $value)) {
13           echo ' checked="checked"';
14       }
15
16       // Complete the element:
17       echo " /> $value ";
18
19   } // End of create_gallon_radio() function.
20
21   $page_title = 'Trip Cost Calculator';
22   include ('includes/header.html');
23
24   // Check for form submission:
25   if ($_SERVER['REQUEST_METHOD'] == 'POST') {
26
27       // Minimal form validation:
28       if (isset($_POST['distance'], $_POST['gallon_price'], $_POST['efficiency'])) &&
```

code continues on next page

```
29      is_numeric($_POST['distance']) && is_numeric($_POST['gallon_price']) &&
        is_numeric($_POST['efficiency']) ) {
30
31          // Calculate the results:
32          $gallons = $_POST['distance'] / $_POST['efficiency'];
33          $dollars = $gallons * $_POST['gallon_price'];
34          $hours = $_POST['distance']/65;
35
36          // Print the results:
37          echo '<h1>Total Estimated Cost</h1>
38      <p>The total cost of driving ' . $_POST['distance'] . ' miles, averaging
        ' . $_POST['efficiency'] . ' miles per gallon, and paying an average of $' .
        $_POST['gallon_price'] . ' per gallon, is $' . number_format ($dollars, 2) . '.
        If you drive at an average of 65 miles per hour, the trip will take
        approximately ' . number_format($hours, 2) . ' hours.</p>';
39
40      } else { // Invalid submitted values.
41          echo '<h1>Error!</h1>
42          <p class="error">Please enter a valid distance, price per gallon, and fuel
            efficiency.</p>';
43      }
44
45  } // End of main submission IF.
46
47  // Leave the PHP section and create the HTML form:
48  ?>
49
50  <h1>Trip Cost Calculator</h1>
51  <form action="calculator.php" method="post">
52      <p>Distance (in miles): <input type="text" name="distance" value="<?php if
        (isset($_POST['distance'])) echo $_POST['distance']; ?>" /></p>
53      <p>Ave. Price Per Gallon: <span class="input">
54      <?php
55      create_gallon_radio('3.00');
56      create_gallon_radio('3.50');
57      create_gallon_radio('4.00');
58      ?>
59      </span></p>
60      <p>Fuel Efficiency:
61      <select name="efficiency">
62          <option value="10"<?php if (isset($_POST['efficiency']) && ($_POST['efficiency']
            == '10')) echo ' selected="selected"'; ?>>Terrible</option>
63          <option value="20"<?php if (isset($_POST['efficiency']) && ($_POST['efficiency']
            == '20')) echo ' selected="selected"'; ?>>Decent</option>
64          <option value="30"<?php if (isset($_POST['efficiency']) && ($_POST['efficiency']
            == '30')) echo ' selected="selected"'; ?>>Very Good</option>
65          <option value="50"<?php if (isset($_POST['efficiency']) && ($_POST['efficiency']
            == '50')) echo ' selected="selected"'; ?>>Outstanding</option>
66      </select></p>
67      <p><input type="submit" name="submit" value="Calculate!" /></p>
68  </form>
69
70  <?php include ('includes/footer.html'); ?>
```

3. Begin creating the radio button element:

```
echo '<input type="radio" name=
→ "gallon_price" value="' .
→ $value . '"';
```

This code starts the HTML for the radio button, including its **value** attribute, but does not complete the radio button so that "stickiness" can be addressed next. The value for the input comes from the function argument.

4. Make the input "sticky", if appropriate:

```
if (isset($_POST['gallon_price'])
→ && ($_POST['gallon_price'] ==
→ $value)) {
  echo ' checked="checked"';
}
```

This code is similar to that in the original form, except now the comparison value comes from the function's argument.

5. Complete the form element and the function:

```
  echo " /> $value ";
} // End of create_gallon_radio()
→ function.
```

Finally, the **input** tag is closed and the value is displayed afterwards, with a space on either side.

6. Replace the hard-coded radio buttons in the form with three function calls:

```
<?php
create_gallon_radio('3.00');
create_gallon_radio('3.50');
create_gallon_radio('4.00');
?>
```

To create the three buttons, just call the function three times, passing different values for each. The numeric values are quoted here or else PHP would drop the trailing zeros.

7. Save the file as **calculator.php**, place it in your Web directory, and test it in your Web browser **C**.

Total Estimated Cost

The total cost of driving 685 miles, averaging 20 miles per gallon, and paying an average of $3.00 per gallon, is $102.75. If you drive at an average of 65 miles per hour, the trip will take approximately 10.54 hours.

Trip Cost Calculator

Distance (in miles): 685

Ave. Price Per Gallon: ⦿ 3.00 ○ 3.50 ○ 4.00

Fuel Efficiency: Decent ▾

Calculate!

C Although a user-defined function is used to create the radio buttons (see Script 3.8), the end result is no different to the user.

Setting default argument values

Another variant on defining your own functions is to preset an argument's value. To do so, assign the argument a value in the function's definition:

```
function greet ($name, $msg =
→'Hello') {
        echo "$msg, $name!";
}
```

The end result of setting a default argument value is that that particular argument becomes optional when calling the function. If a value is passed to it, the passed value is used; otherwise, the default value is used.

You can set default values for as many of the arguments as you want, as long as those arguments come last in the function definition. In other words, the required arguments must always be listed first.

With the example function just defined, any of these will work:

```
greet ($surname, $message);
greet ('Zoe');
greet ('Sam', 'Good evening');
```

However, just **greet( )** will not work. Also, there's no way to pass **$msg** a value without passing one to **$name** as well (argument values must be passed in order, and you can't skip a required argument).

To take advantage of default argument values, let's make a better version of the **create_gallon_radio( )** function. As originally written, the function only creates radio buttons with a name of *gallon_price*. It'd be better if the function could be used multiple times in a form, for multiple radio button groupings (although the function won't be used like that in this script).

To set default argument values:

1. Open **calculator.php** (refer to Script 3.8) in your text editor or IDE, if it is not already.

2. Change the function definition line (line 6) so that it takes a second, optional argument (**Script 3.9**):

   ```
   function create_radio($value,
   →$name = 'gallon_price') {
   ```

   continues on page 103

Script 3.9 The redefined function now assumes a set radio button name unless one is specified when the function is called.

```
1    <?php # Script 3.9 - calculator.php #4
2
3    // This function creates a radio button.
4    // The function takes two arguments: the value and the name.
5    // The function also makes the button "sticky".
6    function create_radio($value, $name = 'gallon_price') {
7
8        // Start the element:
9        echo '<input type="radio" name="' . $name .'" value="' . $value . '"';
10
11       // Check for stickiness:
12       if (isset($_POST[$name]) && ($_POST[$name] == $value)) {
13           echo ' checked="checked"';
14       }
```

code continues on next page

```
15
16      // Complete the element:
17      echo " /> $value ";
18
19   } // End of create_radio() function.
20
21   $page_title = 'Trip Cost Calculator';
22   include ('includes/header.html');
23
24   // Check for form submission:
25   if ($_SERVER['REQUEST_METHOD'] == 'POST') {
26
27      // Minimal form validation:
28      if (isset($_POST['distance'], $_POST['gallon_price'], $_POST['efficiency']) &&
29      is_numeric($_POST['distance']) && is_numeric($_POST['gallon_price'])
         && is_numeric($_POST['efficiency']) ) {
30
31         // Calculate the results:
32         $gallons = $_POST['distance'] / $_POST['efficiency'];
33         $dollars = $gallons * $_POST['gallon_price'];
34         $hours = $_POST['distance']/65;
35
36         // Print the results:
37         echo '<h1>Total Estimated Cost</h1>
38   <p>The total cost of driving ' . $_POST['distance'] . ' miles, averaging ' . $_POST
         ['efficiency'] . ' miles per gallon, and paying an average of $' . $_POST['gallon_price']
         . ' per gallon, is $' . number_format ($dollars, 2) . '. If you drive at an average of
         65 miles per hour, the trip will take approximately ' . number_format($hours, 2) . '
         hours.</p>';
39
40      } else { // Invalid submitted values.
41         echo '<h1>Error!</h1>
42         <p class="error">Please enter a valid distance, price per gallon, and fuel
            efficiency.</p>';
43      }
44
45   } // End of main submission IF.
46
47   // Leave the PHP section and create the HTML form:
48   ?>
49
50   <h1>Trip Cost Calculator</h1>
51   <form action="calculator.php" method="post">
52      <p>Distance (in miles): <input type="text" name="distance" value="<?php if (isset($_POST
         ['distance'])) echo $_POST['distance']; ?>" /></p>
53      <p>Ave. Price Per Gallon: <span class="input">
54      <?php
55      create_radio('3.00');
56      create_radio('3.50');
57      create_radio('4.00');
```

code continues on next page

There are two changes here. First, the name of the function is changed to be reflective of its more generic nature. Second, the function now takes a second argument, **$name**, although that argument has a default value, which makes that argument optional when the function is called.

3. Change the function definition so that it uses the **$name** argument in lieu of *gallon_price*:

```
echo '<input type="radio" name="'
. $name .'" value="' . $value .
'"';
if (isset($_POST[$name]) && ($_
POST[$name] == $value)) {
   echo ' checked="checked"';
}
```

Three changes are necessary. First, **$name** is used for the **name** attribute of the element. Second, the conditional that checks for "stickiness" now uses **$_POST[$name]** twice instead of **$_POST['gallon_price']**.

continues on next page

Script 3.9 *continued*

```
58      ?>
59      </span></p>
60      <p>Fuel Efficiency: <select name="efficiency">
61          <option value="10"<?php if (isset($_POST['efficiency']) && ($_POST['efficiency'] == '10'))
            echo ' selected="selected"'; ?>>Terrible</option>
62          <option value="20"<?php if (isset($_POST['efficiency']) && ($_POST['efficiency'] == '20'))
            echo ' selected="selected"'; ?>>Decent</option>
63          <option value="30"<?php if (isset($_POST['efficiency']) && ($_POST['efficiency'] == '30'))
            echo ' selected="selected"'; ?>>Very Good</option>
64          <option value="50"<?php if (isset($_POST['efficiency']) && ($_POST['efficiency'] == '50'))
            echo ' selected="selected"'; ?>>Outstanding</option>
65      </select></p>
66      <p><input type="submit" name="submit" value="Calculate!" /></p>
67  </form>
68
69  <?php include ('includes/footer.html'); ?>
```

4. Change the function call lines:

```
create_radio('3.00');
create_radio('3.50');
create_radio('4.00');
```

The function calls must be changed to use the new function name. But because the second argument has a default value, it can be omitted in these calls. The end result is the same as executing this call—

```
create_radio('4.00', 'gallon_price');
```

—but now the function could be used to create other radio buttons as well.

5. Save the file, place it in your Web directory, and test it in your Web browser **D**.

TIP To pass a function no value for an argument, use either an empty string (''), NULL, or FALSE.

TIP In the PHP manual, square brackets ([]) are used to indicate a function's optional parameters **E**.

Total Estimated Cost

The total cost of driving 141 miles, averaging 50 miles per gallon, and paying an average of $3.50 per gallon, is $9.87. If you drive at an average of 65 miles per hour, the trip will take approximately 2.17 hours.

Trip Cost Calculator

Distance (in miles): [141]

Ave. Price Per Gallon: ○ 3.00 ● 3.50 ○ 4.00

Fuel Efficiency: [Outstanding ▲▼]

[Calculate!]

D The addition of the second, optional argument, has not affected the functionality of the function.

---

number_format

(PHP 4, PHP 5)

number_format — Format a number with grouped thousands

⊟ **Description**

string **number_format** (float *$number* [, int *$decimals* = 0])

E The PHP manual's description of the **number_format( )** function shows that only the first argument is required.

Returning values from a function

The final attribute of a user-defined function to discuss is that of returning values. Some, but not all, functions do this. For example, **print** will return either a 1 or a 0 indicating its success, whereas **echo** will not. As another example, the **number_format( )** function returns a string, which is the formatted version of a number (see **E** in the previous section).

To have a function return a value, use the **return** statement. This function might return the astrological sign for a given birth month and day:

```
function find_sign ($month, $day) {
    // Function code.
    return $sign;
}
```

A function can return a literal value (say a string or a number) or the value of a variable that has been determined within the function.

When calling a function that returns a value, you can assign the function result to a variable:

```
$my_sign = find_sign ('October', 23);
```

or use it as an argument when calling another function:

```
echo find_sign ('October', 23);
```

Let's update the **calculator.php** script so that it uses a function to determine the cost of the trip.

To have a function return a value:

1. Open **calculator.php** (refer to Script 3.9) in your text editor or IDE, if it is not already.

2. After the first function definition, begin defining a second function (**Script 3.10**):

   ```
   function calculate_trip_cost
   ➝ ($miles, $mpg, $ppg) {
   ```

   The **calculate_trip_cost( )** function takes three arguments: the distance to be travelled, the average miles per gallon, and the average price per gallon.

continues on page 107

Script 3.10 Another user-defined function is added to the script. It performs the main calculation and returns the result.

```
1   <?php # Script 3.10 - calculator.php #5
2
3   // This function creates a radio button.
4   // The function takes two arguments: the value and the name.
5   // The function also makes the button "sticky".
6   function create_radio($value, $name = 'gallon_price') {
7
8       // Start the element:
9       echo '<input type="radio" name="' . $name ."' value="' . $value . '"';
10
11      // Check for stickiness:
12      if (isset($_POST[$name]) && ($_POST[$name] == $value)) {
13          echo ' checked="checked"';
14      }
```

code continues on next page

```
15
16      // Complete the element:
17      echo " /> $value ";
18
19   } // End of create_radio() function.
20
21   // This function calculates the cost of the trip.
22   // The function takes three arguments: the distance, the fuel efficiency, and the price
     per gallon.
23   // The function returns the total cost.
24   function calculate_trip_cost($miles, $mpg, $ppg) {
25
26      // Get the number of gallons:
27      $gallons = $miles/$mpg;
28
29      // Get the cost of those gallons:
30      $dollars = $gallons/$ppg;
31
32      // Return the formatted cost:
33      return number_format($dollars, 2);
34
35   } // End of calculate_trip_cost() function.
36
37   $page_title = 'Trip Cost Calculator';
38   include ('includes/header.html');
39
40   // Check for form submission:
41   if ($_SERVER['REQUEST_METHOD'] == 'POST') {
42
43      // Minimal form validation:
44      if (isset($_POST['distance'], $_POST['gallon_price'], $_POST['efficiency']) &&
45      is_numeric($_POST['distance']) && is_numeric($_POST['gallon_price'])
         && is_numeric($_POST['efficiency']) ) {
46
47         // Calculate the results:
48         $cost = calculate_trip_cost($_POST['distance'], $_POST['efficiency'],
            $_POST['gallon_price']);
49         $hours = $_POST['distance']/65;
50
51         // Print the results:
52         echo '<h1>Total Estimated Cost</h1>
53         <p>The total cost of driving ' . $_POST['distance'] . ' miles, averaging ' .
            $_POST['efficiency'] . ' miles per gallon, and paying an average of $' . $_POST
            ['gallon_price'] . ' per gallon, is $' . $cost . '. If you drive at an average of
            65 miles per hour, the trip will take approximately ' . number_format($hours, 2)
            . ' hours.</p>';
54
55      } else { // Invalid submitted values.
56         echo '<h1>Error!</h1>
57         <p class="error">Please enter a valid distance, price per gallon, and fuel
            efficiency.</p>';
58      }
```

code continues on next page

3. Perform the calculations and return the formatted cost:

```
$gallons = $miles/$mpg;
$dollars = $gallons/$ppg;
return number_format($dollars, 2);
} // End of calculate_trip_cost()
→ function.
```

The first two lines are the same calculations as the script used before, but now they use function variables. The last thing the function does is return a formatted version of the calculated cost.

4. Replace the two lines that calculate the cost (lines 32-33 of Script 3.9) with a function call:

```
$cost = calculate_trip_cost
→ ($_POST['distance'],
→ $_POST['efficiency'],
→ $_POST['gallon_price']);
```

Invoking the function, while passing it the three required values, will perform the calculation. Since the function returns a value, the results of the function call—the returned value—can be assigned to a variable.

continues on next page

Script 3.10 *continued*

```
59
60   } // End of main submission IF.
61
62   // Leave the PHP section and create the HTML form:
63   ?>
64
65   <h1>Trip Cost Calculator</h1>
66   <form action="calculator.php" method="post">
67       <p>Distance (in miles): <input type="text" name="distance" value="<?php if (isset($_POST
         ['distance'])) echo $_POST['distance']; ?>" /></p>
68       <p>Ave. Price Per Gallon: <span class="input">
69       <?php
70       create_radio('3.00');
71       create_radio('3.50');
72       create_radio('4.00');
73       ?>
74       </span></p>
75       <p>Fuel Efficiency: <select name="efficiency">
76           <option value="10"<?php if (isset($_POST['efficiency']) && ($_POST['efficiency'] ==
             '10')) echo ' selected="selected"'; ?>>Terrible</option>
77           <option value="20"<?php if (isset($_POST['efficiency']) && ($_POST['efficiency'] ==
             '20')) echo ' selected="selected"'; ?>>Decent</option>
78           <option value="30"<?php if (isset($_POST['efficiency']) && ($_POST['efficiency'] ==
             '30')) echo ' selected="selected"'; ?>>Very Good</option>
79           <option value="50"<?php if (isset($_POST['efficiency']) && ($_POST['efficiency'] ==
             '50')) echo ' selected="selected"'; ?>>Outstanding</option>
80       </select></p>
81       <p><input type="submit" name="submit" value="Calculate!" /></p>
82   </form>
83
84   <?php include ('includes/footer.html'); ?>
```

5. Change the **echo** statement to use the new variable:

```
echo '<h1>Total Estimated Cost</h1>
  <p>The total cost of driving
  ' . $_POST['distance'] .
  ' miles, averaging ' .
  $_POST['efficiency'] . ' miles
  per gallon, and paying an
  average of $' . $_POST
  ['gallon_price'] . ' per
  gallon, is $' . $cost . '.
  If you drive at an average of
  65 miles per hour, the trip
  will take approximately '
  . number_format($hours, 2) . '
  hours.</p>';
```

The **echo** statement uses the **$cost** variable here, instead of **$dollars** (as in the previous version of the script). Also, since the **$cost** variable is formatted within the function, the **number_format()** function does not need to be applied within the **echo** statement to this variable.

6. Save the file, place it in your Web directory, and test it in your Web browser **F**.

TIP The **return** statement terminates the code execution at that point, so any code within a function after an executed **return** will never run.

TIP A function can have multiple **return** statements (e.g., in a **switch** statement or conditional) but only one, at most, will ever be invoked. For example, functions commonly do something like this:

```
function some_function () {
    if (/* condition */) {
        return TRUE;
    } else {
        return FALSE;
    }
}
```

TIP To have a function return multiple values, use the **array()** function to return an array of values:

```
return array ($var1, $var2);
```

TIP When calling a function that returns an array, use the **list()** function to assign the array elements to individual variables:

```
list($v1, $v2) = some_function();
```

Total Estimated Cost

The total cost of driving 29837429 miles, averaging 10 miles per gallon, and paying an average of $4.00 per gallon, is $745,935.73. If you drive at an average of 65 miles per hour, the trip will take approximately 459,037.37 hours.

Trip Cost Calculator

Distance (in miles): 29837429

Ave. Price Per Gallon: ○ 3.00 ○ 3.50 ⦿ 4.00

Fuel Efficiency: Terrible ▾

F The calculator now uses a user-defined function to calculate and return the trip's cost. But this change has no impact on what the user sees.

Variable Scope

Every variable in PHP has a *scope* to it, which is to say a realm in which the variable (and therefore its value) can be accessed. For starters, variables have the scope of the page in which they reside. If you define $var, the rest of the page can access $var, but other pages generally cannot (unless you use special variables).

Since included files act as if they were part of the original (including) script, variables defined before an include( ) line are available to the included file (as you've already seen with $page_title and header.html). Further, variables defined within the included file are available to the parent (including) script *after* the include( ) line.

User-defined functions have their own scope: variables defined within a function are not available outside of it, and variables defined outside of a function are not available within it. For this reason, a variable inside of a function can have the same name as one outside of it but still be an entirely different variable with a different value. This is a confusing concept for many beginning programmers.

To alter the variable scope within a function, you can use the global statement.

```
function function_name( ) {
        global $var;
}
$var = 20;
function_name( ); // Function call.
```

In this example, $var inside of the function is now the same as $var outside of it. This means that the function $var already has a value of 20, and if that value changes inside of the function, the external $var's value will also change.

Another option for circumventing variable scope is to make use of the superglobals: $_GET, $_POST, $_REQUEST, etc. These variables are automatically accessible within your functions (hence, they are *super*global). You can also add elements to the $GLOBALS array to make them available within a function.

All of that being said, it's almost always best not to use global variables within a function. Functions should be designed so that they receive every value they need as arguments and return whatever value (or values) need to be returned. Relying upon global variables within a function makes them more context-dependent, and consequently less useful.

Review and Pursue

If you have any problems with the review questions or the pursue prompts, turn to the book's supporting forum (**www.LarryUllman.com/forums/**).

Review

- What is an *absolute* path? What is a *relative* path?

- What is the difference between **include( )** and **require( )**?

- What is the difference between **include( )** and **include_once( )**? Which function should you generally avoid using and why?

- Why does it *not* matter what extension is used for an included file?

- What is the significance of the **$_SERVER['REQUEST_METHOD']** value?

- How do you make the following form elements sticky?
  - ▸ Text input
  - ▸ Select menu
  - ▸ Radio button
  - ▸ Check box
  - ▸ Textarea

- If you have a PHP error caused by code placed within an HTML tag, where must you look to find the error message?

- What is the syntax for defining your own function?

- What is the syntax for defining a function that takes arguments?

- What is the syntax for defining a function that takes arguments with default values? How do default values impact how the function can be called?

- How do you define and call a function that returns a value?

Pursue

- Create a new HTML template for the pages in this chapter. Use that new template as the basis for new header and footer files. By doing so, you should be able to change the look of the entire site without modifying any of the PHP scripts.

- Create a new form and give it the ability to be "sticky". Have the form use a textarea and a check box (neither of which is demonstrated in this chapter).

- Change **calculator.php** so that it uses a constant in lieu of the hard-coded average speed of 65. (As written, the average speed is a "magic number": a value used in a script without explanation.)

- Better yet, modify **calculator.php** so that the user can enter the average speed or select it from a list of options.

- Update the output of **calculator.php** so that it displays the number of days and hours the trip will take, when the number of hours is greater than 24.

- As a more advanced trick, rewrite **calculator.php** so that the **create_radio( )** function call is only in the script once, but still creates three radio buttons. Hint: Use a loop.

Introduction
to MySQL

Because this book discusses how to integrate several technologies (primarily PHP, SQL, and MySQL), a solid understanding of each individually is important before you begin writing PHP scripts that use SQL to interact with MySQL. This chapter is a departure from its predecessors in that it temporarily leaves PHP behind to delve into MySQL.

MySQL is the world's most popular open-source database application (according to MySQL's Web site, **www.mysql.com**) and is commonly used with PHP. The MySQL software comes with the database server (which stores the actual data), different client applications (for interacting with the database server), and several utilities. In this chapter you'll see how to define a simple table using MySQL's allowed data types and other properties. Then you'll learn how to interact with the MySQL server using two different client applications. All of this information will be the foundation for the SQL taught in the next chapter.

Naming Database Elements

Before you start working with databases, you have to identify your needs. The purpose of the application (or Web site, in this case) dictates how the database should be designed. With that in mind, the examples in this chapter and the next will use a database that stores some user registration information.

When creating databases and tables, you should come up with names (formally called *identifiers*) that are clear, meaningful, and easy to type. Also, identifiers

- Should only contain letters, numbers, and the underscore (no spaces)

- Should not be the same as an existing keyword (like an SQL term or a function name)

- Should be treated as case-sensitive

- Cannot be longer than 64 characters (approximately)

- Must be unique within its realm

This last rule means that a table cannot have two columns with the same name and a database cannot have two tables with the same name. You can, however, use the same column name in two different tables in the same database (in fact, you often will do this). As for the first three rules, I use the word *should*, as these are good policies more than exact requirements. Exceptions can be made to these rules, but the syntax for doing so can be complicated. Abiding by these suggestions is a reasonable limitation and will help avoid complications.

To name a database's elements:

1. Determine the database's name.

   This is the easiest and, arguably, least important step. Just make sure that the database name is unique for that MySQL server. If you're using a hosted server, your Web host will likely provide a database name that may or may not include your account or domain name.

   For this first example, the database will be called *sitename*, as the information and techniques could apply to any generic site.

2. Determine the table names.

   The table names just need to be unique within this database, which shouldn't be a problem. For this example, which stores user registration information, the only table will be called *users*.

TABLE 4.1 users Table

Column Name	Example
user_id	834
first_name	Larry
last_name	David
email	ld@example.com
pass	emily07
registration_date	2011-03-31 19:21:03

3. Determine the column names for each table.

The *users* table will have columns to store a user ID, a first name, a last name, an email address, a password, and the registration date. **Table 4.1** shows these columns, with sample data, using proper identifiers. As MySQL has a function called *password*, I've changed the name of that column to just *pass*. This isn't strictly necessary but is really a good idea.

TIP Chapter 6, "Database Design," discusses database design in more detail, using more complex examples.

TIP To be precise, the length limit for the names of databases, tables, and columns is actually **64** *bytes*, not characters. While most characters in many languages require 1 byte apiece, it's possible to use a multibyte character in an identifier. But 64 bytes is still a lot of space, so this probably won't be an issue for you.

TIP Whether or not an identifier in MySQL is case-sensitive actually depends upon many things (because each database is actually a folder on the server and each table is actually one or more files). On Windows and normally on Mac OS X, database and table names are generally case-insensitive. On Unix and some Mac OS X setups, they are case-sensitive. Column names are always case-insensitive. It's really best, in my opinion, to always use all lowercase letters and work as if case-sensitivity applied.

Choosing Your Column Types

Once you have identified all of the tables and columns that the database will need, you should determine each column's data type. When creating a table, MySQL requires that you explicitly state what sort of information each column will contain. There are three primary types, which is true for almost every database application:

- Text (aka *strings*)
- Numbers
- Dates and times

Within each of these, there are many variants—some of which are MySQLspecific—you can use. Choosing your column types correctly not only dictates what information can be stored and how but also affects the database's overall performance. **Table 4.2** lists most of the available types for MySQL, how much space they take up, and brief descriptions of each type. Note that some of these limits may change in different versions of MySQL, and the character set (to be discussed in Chapter 6) may also impact the size of the text types.

Many of the types can take an optional *Length* attribute, limiting their size. (The square brackets, [ ], indicate an optional parameter to be put in parentheses.) For performance purposes, you should place some restrictions on how much data can be stored in any column. But understand that attempting to insert a string five characters long into a **CHAR(2)** column will result in truncation of the final three characters (only the first two characters would be stored; the rest would be lost forever). This is true for any field in which the size is set (**CHAR**, **VARCHAR**, **INT**, etc.). Thus, your length should always correspond to the maximum possible value (as a number) or longest possible string (as text) that might be stored.

The various date types have all sorts of unique behaviors, the most important of which you'll learn in this book (all of the behaviors are documented in the MySQL manual). You'll use the **DATE** and **TIME** fields primarily without modification, so you need not worry too much about their intricacies.

There are also two special types—**ENUM** and **SET**—that allow you to define a series of acceptable values for that column. An **ENUM** column can store only one value of a possible several thousand, while **SET** allows for several of up to 64 possible values. These are available in MySQL but aren't present in every database application.

TABLE 4.2 MySQL Data Types

Type	Size	Description
CHAR[Length]	Length bytes	A fixed-length field from 0 to 255 characters long
VARCHAR[Length]	String length + 1 or 2 bytes	A variable-length field from 0 to 65,535 characters long
TINYTEXT	String length + 1 bytes	A string with a maximum length of 255 characters
TEXT	String length + 2 bytes	A string with a maximum length of 65,535 characters
MEDIUMTEXT	String length + 3 bytes	A string with a maximum length of 16,777,215 characters
LONGTEXT	String length + 4 bytes	A string with a maximum length of 4,294,967,295 characters
TINYINT[Length]	1 byte	Range of –128 to 127 or 0 to 255 unsigned
SMALLINT[Length]	2 bytes	Range of –32,768 to 32,767 or 0 to 65,535 unsigned
MEDIUMINT[Length]	3 bytes	Range of –8,388,608 to 8,388,607 or 0 to 16,777,215 unsigned
INT[Length]	4 bytes	Range of –2,147,483,648 to 2,147,483,647 or 0 to 4,294,967,295
BIGINT[Length]	8 bytes	Range of –9,223,372,036,854,775,808 to 9,223,372,036,854,775,807 or 0 to 18,446,744,073,709,551,615 unsigned
FLOAT[Length, Decimals]	4 bytes	A small number with a floating decimal point
DOUBLE[Length, Decimals]	8 bytes	A large number with a floating decimal point
DECIMAL[Length, Decimals]	Length + 1 or 2 bytes	A **DOUBLE** stored as a string, allowing for a fixed decimal point
DATE	3 bytes	In the format of YYYY-MM-DD
DATETIME	8 bytes	In the format of YYYY-MM-DD HH:MM:SS
TIMESTAMP	4 bytes	In the format of YYYYMMDDHHMMSS; acceptable range starts in 1970 and ends in the year 2038
TIME	3 bytes	In the format of HH:MM:SS
ENUM	1 or 2 bytes	Short for enumeration, which means that each column can have one of several possible values
SET	1, 2, 3, 4, or 8 bytes	Like **ENUM** except that each column can have more than one of several possible values

To select the column types:

1. Identify whether a column should be a text, number, or date/time type (Table 4.3).

   This is normally an easy and obvious step, but you want to be as specific as possible. For example, the date *2006-08-02* (MySQL format) could be stored as a string—*August 2, 2006*. But if you use the proper date format, you'll have a more useful database (and, as you'll see, there are functions that can turn *2006-08-02* into *August 2, 2006*).

2. Choose the most appropriate subtype for each column (Table 4.4).

   For this example, the *user_id* is set as a **MEDIUMINT**, allowing for up to nearly 17 million values (as an *unsigned*, or non-negative, number). The *registration_date* will be a **DATETIME**. It can store both the date and the specific time a user registered. When deciding among the date types, consider whether or not you'll want to access just the date, the time, or possibly both. *If unsure, err on the side of storing too much information*.

   The other fields will be mostly **VARCHAR**, since their lengths will differ from record to record. The only exception is the password column, which will be a fixed-length **CHAR** (you'll see why when inserting records in the next chapter). See the sidebar "**CHAR** vs. **VARCHAR**" for more information on these two types.

TABLE 4.3 users Table

Column Name	Type
user_id	number
first_name	text
last_name	text
email	text
pass	text
registration_date	date/time

TABLE 4.4 users Table

Column Name	Type
user_id	MEDIUMINT
first_name	VARCHAR
last_name	VARCHAR
email	VARCHAR
pass	CHAR
registration_date	DATETIME

TABLE 4.5 users Table

Column Name	Type
user_id	MEDIUMINT
first_name	VARCHAR(20)
last_name	VARCHAR(40)
email	VARCHAR(60)
pass	CHAR(40)
registration_date	DATETIME

CHAR vs. VARCHAR

Both of these types store strings and can be set with a maximum length. The primary difference between the two is that anything stored as a **CHAR** will always be stored as a string the length of the column (using spaces to pad it; these spaces will be removed when you retrieve the stored value from the database). Conversely, strings stored in a **VARCHAR** column will require only as much space as the string itself. So the word *cat* in a **VARCHAR(10)** column requires 4 bytes of space (the length of the string plus 1), but in a **CHAR(10)** column, that same word requires 10 bytes of space. Hence, generally speaking, **VARCHAR** columns tend to require less disk space than **CHAR** columns.

However, databases are normally faster when working with fixed-size columns, which is an argument in favor of **CHAR**. And that same three-letter word—*cat*—in a **CHAR(3)** only uses 3 bytes but in a **VARCHAR(10)** requires 4. So how do you decide which to use?

If a string field will *always* be of a set length (e.g., a state abbreviation), use **CHAR**; otherwise, use **VARCHAR**. You may notice, though, that in some cases MySQL defines a column as the one type (like **CHAR**) even though you created it as the other (**VARCHAR**). This is perfectly normal and is MySQL's way of improving performance.

3. Set the maximum length for text columns (**Table 4.5**).

The size of any field should be restricted to the smallest possible value, based upon the largest possible input. For example, if a column stores a state abbreviation, it would be defined as a **CHAR(2)**. Other times you might have to guess somewhat: I can't think of any first names longer than about 10 characters, but just to be safe I'll allow for up to 20.

TIP The length attribute for numeric types does not affect the range of values that can be stored in the column. Columns defined as TINYINT(1) or TINYINT(20) can store the exact same values. Instead, for integers, the length dictates the display width; for decimals, the length is the total number of digits that can be stored.

TIP If you need absolute precision when using non-integers, DECIMAL is preferred over FLOAT or DOUBLE.

TIP MySQL has a BOOLEAN type, which is just a TINYINT(1), with 0 meaning FALSE and 1 meaning TRUE.

TIP Many of the data types have synonymous names: INT and INTEGER, DEC and DECIMAL, etc.

TIP Depending upon the version of MySQL in use, the TIMESTAMP field type is automatically set as the current date and time when an INSERT or UPDATE occurs, even if no value is specified for that particular field. If a table has multiple TIMESTAMP columns, only the first one will be updated when an INSERT or UPDATE is performed.

TIP MySQL also has several variants on the text types that allow for storing binary data. These types are BINARY, VARBINARY, TINYBLOB, MEDIUMBLOB, and LONGBLOB. Such types can be used for storing files or encrypted data.

Choosing Other Column Properties

Besides deciding what data types and sizes you should use for your columns, you should consider a handful of other properties.

First, every column, regardless of type, can be defined as **NOT NULL**. The **NULL** value, in databases and programming, is equivalent to saying that the field has no known value. Ideally, in a properly designed database, every column of every row in every table should have a value, but that isn't always the case. To force a field to have a value, add the **NOT NULL** description to its column type. For example, a required dollar amount can be described as

```
cost DECIMAL(5,2) NOT NULL
```

Indexes, Keys, and AUTO_INCREMENT

Two concepts closely related to database design are indexes and keys. An *index* in a database is a way of requesting that the database keep an eye on the values of a specific column or combination of columns (loosely stated). The end result of this is improved performance when retrieving records but marginally hindered performance when inserting records or updating them.

A *key* in a database table is integral to the "normalization" process used for designing more complicated databases (see Chapter 6). There are two types of keys: *primary* and *foreign*. Each table should have exactly one primary key, and the primary key in one table is often linked as a foreign key in another.

A table's primary key is an artificial way to refer to a record and has to abide by three rules:

1. It must always have a value.
2. That value must never change.
3. That value must be unique for each record in the table.

In the *users* table, the *user_id* will be designated as a **PRIMARY KEY**, which is both a description of the column and a directive to MySQL to index it. Since the *user_id* is a number (which primary keys almost always will be), the **AUTO_INCREMENT** description is also added to the column, which tells MySQL to use the next-highest number as the *user_id* value for each added record. You'll see what this means in practice when you begin inserting records.

When creating a table, you can also specify a default value for any column, regardless of type. In cases where a majority of the records will have the same value for a column, presetting a default will save you from having to specify a value when inserting new rows (unless that row's value for that column is different from the norm).

```
gender ENUM('M', 'F') default 'F'
```

With the *gender* column, if no value is specified when adding a record, the default will be used.

If a column does not have a default value and one is not specified for a new record, that field will be given a default value based upon its type. For numeric types, the default value is 0. For most date and time types, the type's version of "zero" will be the default (e.g., *0000-00-00*). The first **TIMESTAMP** column in a table will have a default value of the current date and time. String types use an empty string ('') as the default value, except for **ENUM**, whose default value (again, if not otherwise specified) is the first possible enumerated value (*M* in the above example).

The number types can be marked as **UNSIGNED,** which limits the stored data to positive numbers and zero. This also effectively doubles the range of positive numbers that can be stored (because no negative numbers will be kept, see Table 4.2). You can also flag the number types as **ZEROFILL**, which means that any extra room will be padded with zeros (**ZEROFILL**s are also automatically **UNSIGNED**).

Finally, when designing a database, you'll need to consider creating indexes, adding keys, and using the **AUTO_INCREMENT** property. Chapter 6 discusses these concepts in greater detail, but in the meantime, check out the sidebar "Indexes, Keys, and **AUTO_INCREMENT**" to learn how they affect the *users* table.

To finish defining your columns:

1. Identify your primary key.

   The primary key is quixotically both arbitrary and critically important. Almost always a number value, the primary key is a unique way to refer to a particular record. For example, your phone number has no inherent value but is unique to you (your home or mobile phone).

   In the *users* table, the *user_id* will be the primary key: an arbitrary number used to refer to a row of data. Again, Chapter 6 will go into the concept of primary keys in more detail.

2. Identify which columns cannot have a **NULL** value.

   In this example, every field is required (cannot be **NULL**). As an example of a column that could have **NULL** values, if you stored peoples' addresses, you might have *address_line1* and *address_line2*, with the latter one being optional. In general, tables that have a lot of **NULL** values suggest a poor design (more on this in...you guessed it...Chapter 6).

continues on next page

3. Make any numeric type **UNSIGNED** if it won't ever store negative numbers.

The *user_id*, which will be a number, should be **UNSIGNED** so that it's always positive (primary keys should be unsigned). Other examples of **UNSIGNED** numbers would be the price of items in an e-commerce example, a telephone extension for a business, or a zip code.

4. Establish the default value for any column.

None of the columns here logically implies a default value.

5. Confirm the final column definitions **(Table 4.6)**.

Before creating the tables, you should revisit the type and range of data you'll store to make sure that your database effectively accounts for everything.

TIP Text columns can also have defined *character sets* and *collations*. This will mean more...in Chapter 6.

TIP Default values must always be a static value, not the result of executing a function, with one exception: the default value for a TIMESTAMP column can be assigned as CURRENT_TIMESTAMP.

TIP TEXT columns cannot be assigned default values.

TABLE 4.6 users Table

Column Name	Type
user_id	MEDIUMINT UNSIGNED NOT NULL
first_name	VARCHAR(20) NOT NULL
last_name	VARCHAR(40) NOT NULL
email	VARCHAR(60) NOT NULL
pass	CHAR(40) NOT NULL
registration_date	DATETIME NOT NULL

Accessing MySQL

In order to create tables, add records, and request information from a database, some sort of *client* is necessary to communicate with the MySQL server. Later in the book, PHP scripts will act in this role, but being able to use another interface is necessary. Although there are oodles of client applications available, I'll focus on two: the *mysql client* and the Web-based phpMyAdmin. A third option, the MySQL Query Browser, is not discussed in this book but can be found at the MySQL Web site (**www.mysql.com**), should you not be satisfied with these two choices.

The rest of this chapter assumes you have access to a running MySQL server. If you are working on your own computer, see Appendix A, "Installation," for instructions on installing MySQL, starting MySQL, and creating MySQL users (all of which must already be done in order to finish this chapter). If you are using a hosted server, your Web host should provide you with the database access. Depending upon the hosting, you may be provided with phpMyAdmin, but not be able to use the command-line mysql client.

Using the mysql Client

The mysql client is normally installed with the rest of the MySQL software. Although the mysql client does not have a pretty graphical interface, it's a reliable, standard tool that's easy to use and behaves consistently on many different operating systems.

The mysql client is accessed from a command-line interface, be it the Terminal application in Linux or Mac OS X **Ⓐ**, or a DOS prompt in Windows **Ⓑ**. If you're not comfortable with command-line interactions, you might find this interface to be challenging, but it becomes easy to use in no time.

To start the application from the command line, type its name and press Return or Enter:

```
mysql
```

Depending upon the server (or your computer), you may need to enter the full path in order to start the application. For example:

/Applications/MAMP/Library/bin/mysql (Mac OS X, using MAMP)

C:\xampp\mysql\bin\mysql (Windows, using XAMPP)

When invoking this application, you can add arguments to affect how it runs. The most common arguments are the username,

continues on next page

Ⓐ A Terminal window in Mac OS X.

Ⓑ A Windows DOS prompt or console (although the default is for white text on a black background).

password, and hostname (computer name, URL, or IP address) you want to connect using. You establish these arguments like so:

```
mysql -u username -h hostname -p
```

The **-p** option will cause the client to prompt you for the password. You can also specify the password on this line if you prefer— by typing it directly after the **-p** prompt— but it will be visible, which is insecure. The **-h hostname** argument is optional, and you can leave it off unless you cannot connect to the MySQL server without it.

Within the mysql client, every statement (SQL command) needs to be terminated by a semicolon. These semicolons are an indication to the client that the query is complete and should be run. The semicolons are not part of the SQL itself (this is a common point of confusion). What this also means is that you can continue the same SQL statement over several lines within the mysql client, which makes it easier to read and to edit, should that be necessary.

As a quick demonstration of accessing and using the mysql client, these next steps will show you how to start the mysql client, select a database to use, and quit the client. Before following these steps,

- The MySQL server must be running.
- You must have a username and password with proper access.

Both of these ideas are explained in Appendix A.

As a side note, in the following steps and throughout the rest of the book, I will continue to provide images using the mysql client on both Windows and Mac OS X. While the appearance differs, the steps and results will be identical. So in short, don't be concerned about why one image shows the DOS prompt and the next a Terminal.

To use the mysql client:

1. Access your system from a command-line interface.

   On Unix systems and Mac OS X, this is just a matter of bringing up the Terminal or a similar application.

   If you are using Windows and installed MySQL on your computer, choose Run from the Start menu (or press Windows Key+R), type **cmd** in the window **C**, and press Enter (or click OK) to bring up a DOS prompt.

2. Invoke the mysql client, using the appropriate command **D**.

   ```
   /path/to/mysql/bin/mysql -u
   → username -p
   ```

   The **/path/to/mysql** part of this step will be largely dictated by the operating system you are running and where MySQL was installed. I've already

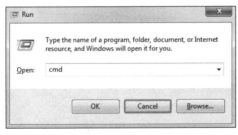

C Executing **cmd** within the Run prompt in Windows is one way to access a DOS prompt interface.

D Access the mysql client by entering the full path to the utility, along with the proper arguments.

provided two options, based upon installations of MAMP on Mac OS X or XAMPP on Windows (both are installed in Appendix A).

The basic premise is that you are running the mysql client, connecting as *username*, and requesting to be prompted for the password. Not to overstate the point, but the username and password values that you use must already be established in MySQL as a valid user (see Appendix A).

3. Enter the password at the prompt and press Return/Enter.

The password you use here should be for the user you specified in the preceding step. If you used the proper username/password combination (i.e., someone with valid access), you should be greeted as shown in . If access is denied, you're probably not using the correct values (see Appendix A for instructions on creating users).

4. Select the database you want to use .

USE test;

The **USE** command selects the database to be used for every subsequent command. The *test* database is one that MySQL installs by default. Assuming it exists on your server, all users should be able to access it.

continues on next page

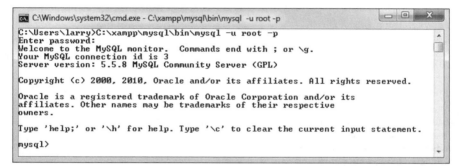

```
C:\Windows\system32\cmd.exe - C:\xampp\mysql\bin\mysql  -u root -p

C:\Users\larry>C:\xampp\mysql\bin\mysql -u root -p
Enter password:
Welcome to the MySQL monitor.  Commands end with ; or \g.
Your MySQL connection id is 3
Server version: 5.5.8 MySQL Community Server (GPL)

Copyright (c) 2000, 2010, Oracle and/or its affiliates. All rights reserved.

Oracle is a registered trademark of Oracle Corporation and/or its
affiliates. Other names may be trademarks of their respective
owners.

Type 'help;' or '\h' for help. Type '\c' to clear the current input statement.

mysql>
```

E If you are successfully able to log in, you'll see a welcome message like this.

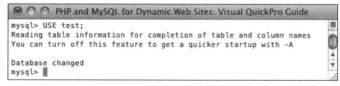

```
          PHP and MySQL for Dynamic Web Sites: Visual QuickPro Guide
mysql> USE test;
Reading table information for completion of table and column names
You can turn off this feature to get a quicker startup with -A

Database changed
mysql>
```

F After getting into the mysql client, run a **USE** command to choose the database with which you want to work.

5. Quit out of mysql .

   `exit`

   You can also use the command **quit** to leave the client. This step—unlike most other commands you enter in the mysql client—does not require a semicolon at the end.

6. Quit the Terminal or DOS console session.

   `exit`

   The command **exit** will terminate the current session. On Windows, it will also close the DOS prompt window.

TIP If you know in advance which database you will want to use, you can simplify matters by starting mysql with

/path/to/mysql/bin/mysql -u *username* -p *databasename*

TIP To see what else you can do with the mysql client, type

/path/to/mysql/bin/mysql --help

TIP The mysql client on most systems allows you to use the up and down arrows to scroll through previously entered commands. If you make a mistake in typing a query, you can scroll up to find it, and then correct the error.

TIP In the mysql client, you can also terminate SQL commands using \G instead of the semicolon. For queries that return results, using \G displays those results as a vertical list, as opposed to a horizontal table, which is sometimes easier to peruse.

TIP If you are in a long statement and make a mistake, cancel the current operation by typing c and pressing Return or Enter. If mysql thinks a closing single or double quotation mark is missing (as indicated by the '> and "> prompts), you'll need to enter the appropriate quotation mark first.

Using phpMyAdmin

phpMyAdmin (**www.phpmyadmin.net**) is one of the best and most popular applications written in PHP. Its sole purpose is to provide an interface to a MySQL server. It's somewhat easier and more natural to use than the mysql client but requires a PHP installation and must be accessed through a Web browser. If you're running MySQL on your own computer, you might find that using the mysql client makes more sense, as installing and configuring phpMyAdmin constitutes unnecessary extra work (although all-in-one PHP and MySQL installers may do this for you). If using a hosted server, your Web host is virtually guaranteed to provide phpMyAdmin as the primary way to work with MySQL and the mysql client may not be an option.

Using phpMyAdmin isn't hard, but the next steps run through the basics so that you'll know what to do in the following chapters.

G Type either **exit** or **quit** to terminate your MySQL session and leave the mysql client.

To use phpMyAdmin:

1. Access phpMyAdmin through your Web browser **H**.

   The URL you use will depend upon your situation. If running on your own computer, this might be **http://localhost/phpMyAdmin/**. If running on a hosted site, your Web host will provide you with the proper URL. In all likelihood, phpMyAdmin would be available through the site's control panel (should one exist).

   Note that phpMyAdmin will only work if it's been properly configured to connect to MySQL with a valid username/password/hostname combination. If you see a message like the one in **I**, you're probably not using the correct values (see Appendix A for instructions on creating users).

continues on next page

H The first phpMyAdmin page (when connected as a MySQL user that can access multiple databases).

I Every client application requires a proper username/password/hostname combination in order to interact with the MySQL server.

2. If possible and necessary, use the list on the left to select a database to use .

What options you have here will vary depending upon what MySQL user phpMyAdmin is connecting as. That user might have access to one database, several databases, or every database. On a hosted site where you have just one database, that database will probably already be selected for you. On your own computer, with phpMyAdmin connecting as the MySQL root user, you would see a pull-down menu or a simple list of available databases **J**.

3. Click on a table name in the left column to select that table **K**.

You don't always have to select a table—in fact you never will if you just use the SQL commands in this book, but doing so can often simplify some tasks.

4. Use the tabs and links (on the right side of the page) to perform common tasks.

For the most part, the tabs and links are shortcuts to common SQL commands. For example, the Browse tab performs a **SELECT** query and the Insert tab creates a form for adding new records.

J Use the list of databases on the left side of the window to choose with which database you want to work. This is the equivalent of running a **USE** *databasename* query within the mysql client.

K Selecting a table from the left column changes the options on the right side of the page.

5. Use the SQL tab or the SQL query window **M** to enter SQL commands.

The next three chapters, and a couple more later in the book, will provide SQL commands that must be run to create, populate, and manipulate tables. These might look like

```
INSERT INTO tablename (col1, col2)
→ VALUES (x, y)
```

These commands can be run using the mysql client, phpMyAdmin, or any other interface. To run them within phpMyAdmin, just enter them into one of the SQL prompts and click *Go*.

TIP There's a lot more that can be done with phpMyAdmin, but full coverage would require a chapter in its own right (and a long chapter at that). The information presented here will be enough for you to follow any of the examples in the book, should you not want to use the mysql client.

TIP phpMyAdmin can be configured to use a special database that will record your query history, allow you to bookmark queries, and more. See the phpMyAdmin documentation for details.

TIP One of the best reasons to use phpMyAdmin is to transfer a database from one computer to another. Use the Export tab in phpMyAdmin connected to the source computer to create a file of data. Then, on the destination computer, use the Import tab in phpMyAdmin (connected to that MySQL server) to complete the transfer.

L The SQL tab, in the main part of the window, can be used to run any SQL command.

M The SQL window can also be used to run commands. It pops up after clicking the SQL icon at the top of the left side of the browser (see the second icon from the left in **K**).

Review and Pursue

If you have any problems with the review questions or the pursue prompts, turn to the book's supporting forum (**www.LarryUllman.com/forums/**).

Review

- What version of MySQL are you using? If you don't know, find out now!

- What characters can be used in database, table, and column names?

- Should you treat database, table, and column names as case-sensitive or case-insensitive?

- What are the three general column types?

- What are the differences between **CHAR** and **VARCHAR**?

- How do you determine what size (in terms of subtype or length) a column should be?

- What are some of the other properties that can be assigned to columns?

- What is a primary key?

- If you're using the command-line mysql client to connect to MySQL, what username and password combination is required?

Pursue

- Find the online MySQL manual for your version of MySQL. Bookmark it!

- Start thinking about what databases you may need for your projects.

- If you haven't yet changed the MySQL root user password (assuming you've installed MySQL on your own computer), use the instructions in Appendix A to do so now.

Introduction
to SQL

The preceding chapter provides a quick introduction to MySQL. The focus there is on two topics: using MySQL's rules and data types to define a database, and how to interact with the MySQL server. This chapter moves on to the *lingua franca* of databases: SQL.

SQL, short for Structured Query Language, is a group of special words used exclusively for interacting with databases. SQL is surprisingly easy to learn and use, and yet, amazingly powerful. In fact, the hardest thing to do in SQL is use it to its full potential!

In this chapter you'll learn all the SQL you need to know to create tables, populate them, and run other basic queries. The examples will all use the *users* table discussed in the preceding chapter. Also, as with that other chapter, this chapter assumes you have access to a running MySQL server and know how to use a client application to interact with it.

In This Chapter

Creating Databases and Tables

The first logical use of SQL will be to create a database. The syntax for creating a new database is simply

`CREATE DATABASE databasename`

That's all there is to it (as I said, SQL is easy to learn)!

The **CREATE** term is also used for making tables:

```
CREATE TABLE tablename (
column1name description,
column2name description
...)
```

As you can see from this syntax, after naming the table, you define each column within parentheses. Each column-description pair should be separated from the next by a comma. Should you choose to create indexes at this time, you can add those at the end of the creation statement, but you can add indexes at a later time as well. (Indexes are more formally discussed in Chapter 6, "Database Design," but Chapter 4, "Introduction to MySQL," introduced the topic.)

In case you were wondering, SQL is *case-insensitive*. However, I make it a habit to capitalize the SQL keywords as in the preceding example syntax and the following steps. Doing so helps to contrast the SQL terms from the database, table, and column names.

To create databases and tables:

1. Access MySQL using whichever client you prefer.

   Chapter 4 shows how to use two of the most common interfaces—the *mysql* command-line client and *phpMyAdmin*—to communicate with a MySQL server. Using the steps in the last chapter, you should now connect to MySQL.

   Throughout the rest of this chapter, most of the SQL examples will be entered using the mysql client, but they will work just the same in phpMyAdmin or most other client tools.

2. Create and select the new database 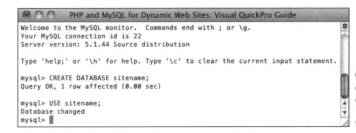:

   ```
   CREATE DATABASE sitename;
   USE sitename;
   ```

   This first line creates the database (assuming that you are connected to MySQL as a user with permission to create new databases). The second line tells MySQL that you want to work within this database from here on out. Remember that within the mysql client, you must terminate every SQL command with a semicolon, although these semicolons aren't technically part of SQL itself. If executing multiple queries at once within phpMyAdmin, they should also be separated by semicolons **B**. If running only a single query within phpMyAdmin, no semicolons are necessary.

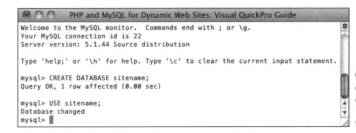

A A new database, called *sitename*, is created in MySQL. It is then selected for future queries.

If you are using a hosting company's MySQL, they will probably create the database for you. In that case, just connect to MySQL and select the database.

3. Create the *users* table :

```
CREATE TABLE users (
user_id MEDIUMINT UNSIGNED NOT NULL
AUTO_INCREMENT,
first_name VARCHAR(20) NOT NULL,
last_name VARCHAR(40) NOT NULL,
email VARCHAR(60) NOT NULL,
pass CHAR(40) NOT NULL,
registration_date DATETIME NOT NULL,
PRIMARY KEY (user_id)
);
```

The design for the *users* table was developed in Chapter 4. There, the names, types, and attributes of each column in the table are determined based upon a number of criteria (see that chapter for more information). Here, that information is placed within the **CREATE** table syntax to actually make the table in the database.

Because the mysql client will not run a query until it encounters a semicolon (or **\G** or **\g**), you can enter statements over multiple lines as in (by pressing Return or Enter at the end of each line). This often makes a query easier to read and debug. In phpMyAdmin, you can also run queries over multiple lines, although they will not be executed until you click Go.

continues on next page

B The same commands for creating and selecting a database can be run within phpMyAdmin's SQL window.

C This **CREATE** SQL command will make the *users* table.

4. Confirm the existence of the table **D**:

```
SHOW TABLES;
SHOW COLUMNS FROM users;
```

The **SHOW** command reveals the tables in a database or the column names and types in a table.

Also, you might notice in **D** that the default value for *user_id* is **NULL**, even though this column was defined as **NOT NULL**. This is actually correct and has to do with *user_id* being an automatically incremented primary key. MySQL will often make minor changes to a column's definition for better performance or other reasons.

In phpMyAdmin, a database's tables are listed on the left side of the browser window, under the database's name **E**. Click a table's name to view its columns **F**.

> **TIP** The rest of this chapter assumes that you are using the mysql client or comparable tool and have already selected the *sitename* database with USE.

> **TIP** The order you list the columns when creating a table has no functional impact, but there are stylistic suggestions for how to order them. I normally list the primary-key column first, followed by any foreign-key columns (more on this subject in the next chapter), followed by the rest of the columns, concluding with any date columns.

> **TIP** When creating a table, you have the option of specifying its *type*. MySQL supports many table types, each with its own strengths and weaknesses. If you do not specify a table type, MySQL will automatically create the table using the default type for that MySQL installation. Chapter 6 discusses this in more detail.

> **TIP** When creating tables and text columns, you have the option to specify its *collation* and *character set*. Both come into play when using multiple languages or languages other than the default for the MySQL server. Chapter 6 also covers these subjects.

> **TIP** DESCRIBE *tablename* is the same statement as SHOW COLUMNS FROM *tablename*.

D Confirm the existence of, and columns in, a table using the **SHOW** command.

E phpMyAdmin shows that the *sitename* database contains one table, named *users*.

Field	Type	Collation	Attributes	Null	Default	Extra
user_id	mediumint(8)		UNSIGNED	No	*None*	auto_increment
first_name	varchar(20)	latin1_swedish_ci		No	*None*	
last_name	varchar(40)	latin1_swedish_ci		No	*None*	
email	varchar(60)	latin1_swedish_ci		No	*None*	
pass	char(40)	latin1_swedish_ci		No	*None*	
registration_date	datetime			No	*None*	

F phpMyAdmin shows a table's definition on this screen (accessed by clicking the table's name in the left-hand column).

Inserting Records

After a database and its table(s) have been created, you can start populating them using the **INSERT** command. There are two ways that an **INSERT** query can be written. With the first method, you name the columns to be populated:

```
INSERT INTO tablename (column1,
→ column2…) VALUES (value1, value2 …)
INSERT INTO tablename (column4,
→ column8) VALUES (valueX, valueY)
```

Using this structure, you can add rows of records, populating only the columns that matter. The result will be that any columns not given a value will be treated as **NULL** (or given a default value, if one was defined). Note that if a column cannot have a **NULL** value (it was defined as **NOT NULL**) and does not have a default value, not specifying a value will cause an error or warning **A**.

The second format for inserting records is not to specify any columns at all but to include values for every one:

```
INSERT INTO tablename VALUES (value1,
→ NULL, value2, value3, …)
```

If you use this second method, you must specify a value, even if it's **NULL**, for every column. If there are six columns in the table, you must list six values. Failure to match the number of values to the number of columns will cause an error **B**. For this and other reasons, the first format of inserting records is generally preferable.

MySQL also allows you to insert multiple rows at one time, separating each record by a comma.

```
INSERT INTO tablename (column1,
→ column4) VALUES (valueA, valueB),
(valueC, valueD),
(valueE, valueF)
```

continues on next page

```
● ○ ○    PHP and MySQL for Dynamic Web Sites: Visual QuickPro Guide
mysql> INSERT INTO users
    -> (first_name, email)
    -> VALUES ('Larry', 'Larry@LarryUllman.com');
Query OK, 1 row affected, 3 warnings (0.00 sec)

mysql> SHOW WARNINGS;
+---------+------+-------------------------------------------------------+
| Level   | Code | Message                                               |
+---------+------+-------------------------------------------------------+
| Warning | 1364 | Field 'last_name' doesn't have a default value        |
| Warning | 1364 | Field 'pass' doesn't have a default value             |
| Warning | 1364 | Field 'registration_date' doesn't have a default value |
+---------+------+-------------------------------------------------------+
3 rows in set (0.00 sec)

mysql> █
```

A Failure to provide, or predefine, a value for a **NOT NULL** column results in errors or warnings.

```
● ○ ○    PHP and MySQL for Dynamic Web Sites: Visual QuickPro Guide
mysql> INSERT INTO users VALUES
    -> ('Larry', 'Ullman', 'Larry@LarryUllman.com');
ERROR 1136 (21S01): Column count doesn't match value count at row 1
mysql> █
```

B Not providing a value for every column in a table, or named in an **INSERT** query, also causes an error.

While you can do this with MySQL, it is not acceptable within the SQL standard and is therefore not supported by all database applications. In MySQL, however, this syntax is faster than using individual **INSERT** queries.

Note that in all of these examples, placeholders are used for the actual table names, column names, and values. Furthermore, the examples forgo quotation marks. In real queries, you must abide by certain rules to avoid errors (see the "Quotes in Queries" sidebar).

To insert data into a table:

1. Insert one row of data into the *users* table, naming the columns to be populated :

```
INSERT INTO users
(first_name, last_name, email,
→ pass, registration_date)
VALUES ('Larry', 'Ullman', 'email@
→ example.com', SHA1('mypass'),
→ NOW( ));
```

Again, this syntax (where the specific columns are named) is more foolproof but not always the most convenient. For the first name, last name, and email columns, simple strings are used for the values (and strings must always be quoted).

Quotes in Queries

In every SQL command:

- Numeric values shouldn't be quoted.
- String values (for **CHAR**, **VARCHAR**, and **TEXT** column types) must always be quoted.
- Date and time values must always be quoted.
- Functions cannot be quoted.
- The word **NULL** must not be quoted.

Unnecessarily quoting a numeric value normally won't cause problems (although you still shouldn't do it), but misusing quotation marks in the other situations will almost always mess things up. Also, it does not matter if you use single or double quotation marks, so long as you consistently pair them (an opening mark with a matching closing one).

And, as with PHP, if you need to use a quotation mark in a value, either use the other quotation mark type to encapsulate it or escape the mark by preceding it with a backslash:

```
INSERT INTO tablename (last_name)
→ VALUES ('O\'Toole')
```

C This query inserts a single record into the *users* table. The *1 row affected* message indicates the success of the insertion.

For the password and registration date columns, two functions are being used to generate the values (see the sidebar "Two MySQL Functions"). The **SHA1( )** function will encrypt the password (*mypass* in this example). The **NOW( )** function will set the *registration_date* as this moment.

When using any function in an SQL statement, do not place it within quotation marks. You also must not have any spaces between the function's name and the following parenthesis (so **NOW( )** not **NOW ( )**).

2. Insert one row of data into the *users* table, without naming the columns **D**:

```
INSERT INTO users VALUES
(NULL, 'Zoe', 'Isabella',
 'email2@example.com',
 SHA1('mojito'), NOW());
```

In this second syntactical example, every column must be provided with a value. The *user_id* column is given a **NULL** value, which will cause MySQL to use the next logical number, per its **AUTO_INCREMENT** description. In other words, the first record will be assigned a *user_id* of 1, the second, 2, and so on.

continues on next page

D Another record is inserted into the table, this time by providing a value for every column in the table.

3. Insert several values into the *users* table **Ⓔ**:

```
INSERT INTO users (first_name,
→last_name, email, pass,
→registration_date) VALUES
('John', 'Lennon', 'john@beatles.com',
→SHA1('Happin3ss'), NOW( )),
('Paul', 'McCartney',
→'paul@beatles.com',
→SHA1('letITbe'), NOW( )),
('George', 'Harrison',
→'george@beatles.com ',
→SHA1('something'), NOW( )),
('Ringo', 'Starr', 'ringo@beatles.com',
→SHA1('thisboy'), NOW( ));
```

Since MySQL allows you to insert multiple values at once, you can take advantage of this and fill up the table with records.

4. Continue Steps 1 and 2 until you've thoroughly populated the *users* table.

Throughout the rest of this chapter I will be performing queries based upon the records I entered into my database. Should your database not have the same specific records as mine, change the particulars accordingly. The fundamental thinking behind the following queries should still apply regardless of the data, since the *sitename* database has a set column and table structure.

Ⓔ This one query—which MySQL allows but other database applications will not—inserts several records into the table at once.

TIP On the downloads page of the book's supporting Web site (www.LarryUllman.com), you can download all of the **SQL commands** for the book. Using some of those commands, you can populate your *users* table exactly as I have.

TIP The term INTO in INSERT statements is optional in MySQL.

TIP phpMyAdmin's INSERT tab allows you to insert records using an HTML form **F**.

TIP Depending upon the version of MySQL in use, failure to provide a value for a column that cannot be NULL may issue warnings with the INSERT still working **A**, or issue errors, with the INSERT failing.

TIP You'll occasionally see uses of the backtick (`) in **SQL commands**. This character, found on the same key as the tilde (~), is different than a single quotation mark. The backtick is used to safely reference a table or column name that might be the same as an existing keyword.

TIP If MySQL warns you about the previous query, the SHOW WARNINGS command will display the problem **A**.

TIP An interesting variation on INSERT is REPLACE. If the value used for the table's primary key, or a UNIQUE index, already exists, then REPLACE updates that row. If not, REPLACE inserts a new row.

Field	Type	Function	Null	Value
user_id	mediumint(8) unsigned	▾		
first_name	varchar(20)	▾		Larry
last_name	varchar(40)	▾		Ullman
email	varchar(60)	▾		email@example.com
pass	char(40)	SHA1 ▾		mypass
registration_date	datetime	NOW ▾		▦

Go

F phpMyAdmin's **INSERT** form shows a table's columns and provides text boxes for entering values. The pull-down menu lists functions that can be used, like **SHA1( )** for the password or **NOW( )** for the registration date.

Selecting Data

Now that the database has some records in it, you can retrieve the stored information with the most used of all SQL terms, **SELECT**. A **SELECT** query returns rows of records using the syntax

SELECT *which_columns* **FROM** *which_table*

The simplest **SELECT** query is

SELECT * **FROM** *tablename*

The asterisk means that you want to retrieve every column. The alternative would be to specify the columns to be returned, with each separated from the next by a comma:

SELECT *column1, column3* **FROM** *tablename*

There are a few benefits to being explicit about which columns are selected. The first is performance: There's no reason to fetch columns you will not be using. The second is order: You can return columns in an order other than their layout in the table. Third—and you'll see this later in the chapter—naming the columns allows you to manipulate the values in those columns using functions.

```
mysql> SELECT * FROM users;
+---------+------------+-----------+----------------------+----------------------------------+---------------------+
| user_id | first_name | last_name | email                | pass                             | registration_date   |
+---------+------------+-----------+----------------------+----------------------------------+---------------------+
|       1 | Larry      | Ullman    | email@example.com    | e727d1464ae12436e899a726da5b2f11d8381b26 | 2011-03-31 21:12:52 |
|       2 | Zoe        | Isabella  | email2@example.com   | 6b793ca1c216835ba85c1fbd1399ce729e34b4e5 | 2011-03-31 21:14:23 |
|       3 | John       | Lennon    | john@beatles.com     | 2a50435b0f512f60988db719106a258fb7e338ff | 2011-03-31 21:15:07 |
|       4 | Paul       | McCartney | paul@beatles.com     | 6ae16792c502a5b47da180ce8456e5ae7d65e262 | 2011-03-31 21:15:07 |
|       5 | George     | Harrison  | george@beatles.com   | 1af17e73721dbe0c40011b82ed4bb1a7dbe3ce29 | 2011-03-31 21:15:07 |
|       6 | Ringo      | Starr     | ringo@beatles.com    | 520f73691bcf89d508d923a2dbc8e6fa58efb522 | 2011-03-31 21:15:07 |
|       7 | David      | Jones     | davey@monkees.com    | ec23244e40137ef72763267f17ed6c7ebb2b019f | 2011-03-31 21:16:47 |
|       8 | Peter      | Tork      | peter@monkees.com    | b8f6bc0c646f68ec6f27653f8473ae4ae81fd302 | 2011-03-31 21:16:47 |
|       9 | Micky      | Dolenz    | micky@monkees.com    | 0599b6e3c9206ef135c83a921294ba6417dbc673 | 2011-03-31 21:16:47 |
|      10 | Mike       | Nesmith   | mike@monkees.com     | 804a1773e9985abeb1f2605e0cc22211cc58cb1b | 2011-03-31 21:16:47 |
|      11 | David      | Sedaris   | david@authors.com    | f54e748ae9624210402eeb2c15a9f506a110ef72 | 2011-03-31 21:16:47 |
|      12 | Nick       | Hornby    | nick@authors.com     | 815f12d7b9d7cd690d4781015c2a0a5b3ae207c0 | 2011-03-31 21:16:47 |
|      13 | Melissa    | Bank      | melissa@authors.com  | 15ac6793642add347cbf24b8884b97947f637091 | 2011-03-31 21:16:47 |
|      14 | Toni       | Morrison  | toni@authors.com     | ce3a79105879624f762c01ecb8abee7b31e67df5 | 2011-03-31 21:16:47 |
|      15 | Jonathan   | Franzen   | jonathan@authors.com | c969581a0a7d6f790f4b520225f34fd90a09c86f | 2011-03-31 21:16:47 |
|      16 | Don        | DeLillo   | don@authors.com      | 01a3ff9a11b328afd3e5affcba4cc9e539c4c455 | 2011-03-31 21:16:47 |
|      17 | Graham     | Greene    | graham@authors.com   | 7c16ec1fcbc8c3ec99790f25c310ef63febb1bb3 | 2011-03-31 21:16:47 |
|      18 | Michael    | Chabon    | michael@authors.com  | bd58cc413f97c33930778416a6dbd2d67720dc41 | 2011-03-31 21:16:47 |
|      19 | Richard    | Brautigan | richard@authors.com  | b1f8414005c218fb53b661f17b4f671bccecea3d | 2011-03-31 21:16:47 |
|      20 | Russell    | Banks     | russell@authors.com  | 6bc4056557e33f1e209870ab578ed362f8b3c1b8 | 2011-03-31 21:16:47 |
|      21 | Homer      | Simpson   | homer@simpson.com    | 54a0b2dcbc5a944907d29304405f0552344b3847 | 2011-03-31 21:16:47 |
|      22 | Marge      | Simpson   | marge@simpson.com    | cea9be7b57e183dea0e4cf000489fe073908c0ca | 2011-03-31 21:16:47 |
|      23 | Bart       | Simpson   | bart@simpson.com     | 73265774abd1028ed8ef06afc5fa0f9a7ccbb6aa | 2011-03-31 21:16:47 |
|      24 | Lisa       | Simpson   | lisa@simpson.com     | a09bb16971ec0759dfff75c088f004e205c9e27b | 2011-03-31 21:16:47 |
|      25 | Maggie     | Simpson   | maggie@simpson.com   | 0e87350b393ceced1d4751b828d18102be123edb | 2011-03-31 21:16:47 |
|      26 | Abe        | Simpson   | abe@simpson.com      | 6591827c8e3d4624e8fc1ee324f31fa389fdafb4 | 2011-03-31 21:16:47 |
+---------+------------+-----------+----------------------+----------------------------------+---------------------+
26 rows in set (0.00 sec)

mysql>
```

A The **SELECT * FROM** *tablename* query returns every column for every record stored in the table.

```
mysql> SELECT first_name, last_name
    -> FROM users;
+------------+------------+
| first_name | last_name  |
+------------+------------+
| Larry      | Ullman     |
| Zoe        | Isabella   |
| John       | Lennon     |
| Paul       | McCartney  |
| George     | Harrison   |
| Ringo      | Starr      |
| David      | Jones      |
| Peter      | Tork       |
| Micky      | Dolenz     |
| Mike       | Nesmith    |
| David      | Sedaris    |
| Nick       | Hornby     |
| Melissa    | Bank       |
| Toni       | Morrison   |
| Jonathan   | Franzen    |
| Don        | DeLillo    |
| Graham     | Greene     |
| Michael    | Chabon     |
| Richard    | Brautigan  |
| Russell    | Banks      |
| Homer      | Simpson    |
| Marge      | Simpson    |
| Bart       | Simpson    |
| Lisa       | Simpson    |
| Maggie     | Simpson    |
| Abe        | Simpson    |
+------------+------------+
26 rows in set (0.00 sec)

mysql>
```

B Only two of the columns for every record in the table are returned by this query.

```
mysql> SELECT NOW();
+---------------------+
| NOW()               |
+---------------------+
| 2011-03-31 21:38:41 |
+---------------------+
1 row in set (0.00 sec)

mysql>
```

C Many queries can be run without specifying a database or table. This query selects the result of calling the NOW( ) function, which returns the current date and time (according to MySQL).

```
mysql> SELECT last_name, first_name
    -> FROM users;
+------------+------------+
| last_name  | first_name |
+------------+------------+
| Ullman     | Larry      |
| Isabella   | Zoe        |
| Lennon     | John       |
| McCartney  | Paul       |
| Harrison   | George     |
| Starr      | Ringo      |
| Jones      | David      |
| Tork       | Peter      |
| Dolenz     | Micky      |
| Nesmith    | Mike       |
| Sedaris    | David      |
| Hornby     | Nick       |
| Bank       | Melissa    |
| Morrison   | Toni       |
| Franzen    | Jonathan   |
| DeLillo    | Don        |
| Greene     | Graham     |
| Chabon     | Michael    |
| Brautigan  | Richard    |
| Banks      | Russell    |
| Simpson    | Homer      |
| Simpson    | Marge      |
| Simpson    | Bart       |
| Simpson    | Lisa       |
| Simpson    | Maggie     |
| Simpson    | Abe        |
+------------+------------+
26 rows in set (0.00 sec)

mysql>
```

D If a SELECT query specifies the columns to be returned, they'll be returned in that order.

To select data from a table:

1. Retrieve all the data from the *users* table **A**:

   `SELECT * FROM users;`

   This very basic SQL command will retrieve every column of every row stored within that table.

2. Retrieve just the first and last names from *users* **B**:

   `SELECT first_name, last_name FROM users;`

   Instead of showing the data from every column in the *users* table, you can use the **SELECT** statement to limit the results to only the fields you need.

TIP In phpMyAdmin, the Browse tab runs a simple SELECT query.

TIP You can actually use SELECT without naming tables or columns. For example, SELECT NOW( ) **C**.

TIP The order in which you list columns in your SELECT statement dictates the order in which the values are presented (compare **B** with **D**).

TIP With SELECT queries, you can even retrieve the same column multiple times, a feature that enables you to manipulate the column's data in many different ways.

Using Conditionals

The **SELECT** query as used thus far will always retrieve every record from a table. But often you'll want to limit what rows are returned, based upon certain criteria. This can be accomplished by adding conditionals to **SELECT** queries. Conditionals use the SQL term **WHERE** and are written much as you'd write a conditional in PHP:

```
SELECT which_columns FROM which_table
→ WHERE condition(s)
```

Table 5.1 lists the most common operators you would use within a conditional. For example, a simple equality check:

```
SELECT name FROM people
WHERE birth_date = '2011-01-26'
```

The operators can be used together, along with parentheses, to create more complex expressions:

```
SELECT * FROM items WHERE
(price BETWEEN 10.00 AND 20.00) AND
(quantity > 0)
SELECT * FROM cities WHERE
(zip_code = 90210) OR (zip_code =
→ 90211)
```

This last example could also be written as:

```
SELECT * FROM cities WHERE
zip_code IN (90210, 90211)
```

To demonstrate using conditionals, let's run some more **SELECT** queries on the *sitename* database. The examples that follow will be just a few of the nearly limitless possibilities. Over the course of this chapter and the entire book you will see how conditionals are used in all types of queries.

TABLE 5.1 MySQL Operators

Operator	Meaning
=	Equals
<	Less than
>	Greater than
<=	Less than or equal to
>=	Greater than or equal to
!= (also < >)	Not equal to
IS NOT NULL	Has a value
IS NULL	Does not have a value
IS TRUE	Has a true value
IS FALSE	Has a false value
BETWEEN	Within a range
NOT BETWEEN	Outside of a range
IN	Found within a list of values
NOT IN	Not found within a list of values
OR (also ||)	Where at least one of two conditionals is true
AND (also &&)	Where both conditionals are true
NOT (also !)	Where the condition is not true
XOR	Where *only one* of two conditionals is true

To use conditionals:

1. Select all of the users whose last name is *Simpson* Ⓐ:

   ```
   SELECT * FROM users
   WHERE last_name = 'Simpson';
   ```

   This simple query returns every column of every row whose *last_name* value is *Simpson*. (Again, if the data in your table differs, you can change any of these queries accordingly.)

2. Select just the first names of users whose last name is *Simpson* Ⓑ:

   ```
   SELECT first_name FROM users
   WHERE last_name = 'Simpson';
   ```

   Here only one column (*first_name*) is being returned for each row. Although it may seem strange, you do not have

to select a column on which you are performing a **WHERE**. The reason for this is that the columns listed after **SELECT** dictate only what *columns* to return and the columns listed in a **WHERE** dictate which *rows* to return.

3. Select every column from every record in the *users* table that does not have an email address Ⓒ:

   ```
   SELECT * FROM users
   WHERE email IS NULL;
   ```

   The **IS NULL** conditional is the same as saying *does not have a value*. Keep in mind that an empty string is different than **NULL** and therefore would not match this condition. An empty string would, however, match

   ```
   SELECT * FROM users WHERE email='';
   ```

continues on next page

```
PHP and MySQL for Dynamic Web Sites: Visual QuickPro Guide
mysql> SELECT * FROM users
    -> WHERE last_name = 'Simpson';
+---------+------------+-----------+-------------------+----------------------------------+---------------------+
| user_id | first_name | last_name | email             | pass                             | registration_date   |
+---------+------------+-----------+-------------------+----------------------------------+---------------------+
|      21 | Homer      | Simpson   | homer@simpson.com | 54a0b2dcbc5a944907d29304405f0552344b3847 | 2011-03-31 21:16:47 |
|      22 | Marge      | Simpson   | marge@simpson.com | cea9be7b57e183dea0e4cf000489fe073908c0ca | 2011-03-31 21:16:47 |
|      23 | Bart       | Simpson   | bart@simpson.com  | 73265774abd1028ed8ef06afc5fa0f9a7ccbb6aa | 2011-03-31 21:16:47 |
|      24 | Lisa       | Simpson   | lisa@simpson.com  | a09bb16971ec0759dfff75c088f004e205c9e27b | 2011-03-31 21:16:47 |
|      25 | Maggie     | Simpson   | maggie@simpson.com| 0e87350b393ceced1d4751b828d18102be123edb | 2011-03-31 21:16:47 |
|      26 | Abe        | Simpson   | abe@simpson.com   | 6591827c8e3d4624e8fc1ee324f31fa389fdafb4 | 2011-03-31 21:16:47 |
+---------+------------+-----------+-------------------+----------------------------------+---------------------+
6 rows in set (0.01 sec)

mysql>
```

Ⓐ All of the Simpsons who have registered.

```
C:\Windows\system32\cmd.exe ...
mysql> SELECT first_name FROM users
    -> WHERE last_name = 'Simpson';
+------------+
| first_name |
+------------+
| Homer      |
| Marge      |
| Bart       |
| Lisa       |
| Maggie     |
| Abe        |
+------------+
6 rows in set (0.00 sec)

mysql> _
```

Ⓑ Just the first names of all of the Simpsons who have registered.

```
C:\Windows\system32\...
mysql> SELECT * FROM users
    -> WHERE email IS NULL;
Empty set (0.00 sec)

mysql>
```

Ⓒ No records are returned by this query because the email column cannot have a **NULL** value. So this query *did* work; it just had no matching records.

---

4. Select the user ID, first name, and last name of all records in which the password is *mypass* :

```
SELECT user_id, first_name,
→ last_name
FROM users
WHERE pass = SHA1('mypass');
```

Since the stored passwords were encrypted with the **SHA1( )** function, you can match a password by using that same encryption function in a conditional. **SHA1( )** is case-sensitive, so this query will work only if the passwords (stored vs. queried) match exactly.

5. Select the user names whose user ID is less than 10 or greater than 20 **E**:

```
SELECT first_name, last_name
FROM users WHERE
(user_id < 10) OR (user_id > 20);
```

This same query could also be written as

```
SELECT first_name, last_name FROM
users WHERE user_id
NOT BETWEEN 10 and 20;
```

or even

```
SELECT first_name, last_name FROM
users WHERE user_id NOT IN
(10, 11, 12, 13, 14, 15, 16, 17, 18,
→ 19, 20);
```

TIP You can perform mathematical calculations within your queries using the mathematic addition (+), subtraction (-), multiplication (*), and division (/) characters.

TIP MySQL supports the keywords TRUE and FALSE, *case-insensitive*. Internally, TRUE evaluates to 1 and FALSE evaluates to 0. So, in MySQL, TRUE + TRUE equals 2.

D Conditionals can make use of functions, like **SHA1( )** here.

E This query uses two conditions and the **OR** operator.

Using LIKE and NOT LIKE

Using numbers, dates, and **NULL**s in conditionals is a straightforward process, but strings can be trickier. You can check for string equality with a query such as

```
SELECT * FROM users
WHERE last_name = 'Simpson'
```

However, comparing strings in a more liberal manner requires extra operators and characters. If, for example, you wanted to match a person's last name that could be *Smith* or *Smiths* or *Smithson*, you would need a more flexible conditional. This is where the **LIKE** and **NOT LIKE** terms come in. These are used—primarily with strings—in conjunction with two

wildcard characters: the underscore (_), which matches a single character, and the percentage sign (**%**), which matches zero or more characters. In the last-name example, the query would be

```
SELECT * FROM users
WHERE last_name LIKE 'Smith%'
```

This query will return all rows whose *last_name* value begins with *Smith*. Because it's a case-insensitive search by default, it would also apply to names that begin with *smith*.

To use LIKE:

1. Select all of the records in which the last name starts with *Bank* **Ⓐ**:

   ```
   SELECT * FROM users
   WHERE last_name LIKE 'Bank%';
   ```

   continues on next page

```
mysql> SELECT * FROM users
    -> WHERE last_name LIKE 'Bank%';
+---------+------------+-----------+---------------------+----------------------------------+---------------------+
| user_id | first_name | last_name | email               | pass                             | registration_date   |
+---------+------------+-----------+---------------------+----------------------------------+---------------------+
|      13 | Melissa    | Bank      | melissa@authors.com | 15ac6793642add347cbf24b8884b97947f637091 | 2011-03-31 21:16:47 |
|      20 | Russell    | Banks     | russell@authors.com | 6bc4056557e33f1e209870ab578ed362f8b3c1b8 | 2011-03-31 21:16:47 |
+---------+------------+-----------+---------------------+----------------------------------+---------------------+
2 rows in set (0.00 sec)

mysql>
```

Ⓐ The **LIKE** SQL term adds flexibility to your conditionals. This query matches any record where the last name value begins with *Bank*.

2. Select the name for every record whose email address is not of the form *something@authors.com* **B**:

```
SELECT first_name, last_name
FROM users WHERE
email NOT LIKE '%@authors.com';
```

To rule out the presence of values in a string, use **NOT LIKE** with the wildcard.

TIP Queries with a LIKE conditional are generally slower because they can't take advantage of indexes. Use LIKE and NOT LIKE only if you absolutely have to.

TIP The wildcard characters can be used at the front and/or back of a string in your queries.

```
SELECT * FROM users
WHERE last_name LIKE '_smith%'
```

TIP Although LIKE and NOT LIKE are normally used with strings, they can also be applied to numeric columns.

TIP To use either the literal underscore or the percentage sign in a LIKE or NOT LIKE query, you will need to escape it (by preceding the character with a backslash) so that it is not confused with a wildcard.

TIP The underscore can be used in combination with itself; as an example, LIKE '__' would find any two-letter combination.

TIP In Chapter 7, "Advanced SQL and MySQL," you'll learn about FULLTEXT searches, which can be more useful than LIKE searches.

```
C:\Windows\system32\cmd.exe - c:\xa...

mysql> SELECT first_name, last_name
    -> FROM users WHERE
    -> email NOT LIKE '%@authors.com';
+------------+------------+
| first_name | last_name  |
+------------+------------+
| Larry      | Ullman     |
| Zoe        | Isabella   |
| John       | Lennon     |
| Paul       | McCartney  |
| George     | Harrison   |
| Ringo      | Starr      |
| David      | Jones      |
| Peter      | Tork       |
| Micky      | Dolenz     |
| Mike       | Nesmith    |
| Homer      | Simpson    |
| Marge      | Simpson    |
| Bart       | Simpson    |
| Lisa       | Simpson    |
| Maggie     | Simpson    |
| Abe        | Simpson    |
+------------+------------+
16 rows in set (0.00 sec)

mysql>
```

B A **NOT LIKE** conditional returns records based upon what a value does not contain.

Sorting Query Results

By default, a **SELECT** query's results will be returned in a meaningless order (for many new to databases, this is an odd concept). To give a meaningful order to a query's results, use an **ORDER BY** clause:

```
SELECT * FROM tablename ORDER BY column
SELECT * FROM orders ORDER BY total
```

The default order when using **ORDER BY** is ascending (abbreviated **ASC**), meaning that numbers increase from small to large, dates go from oldest to most recent, and text is sorted alphabetically. You can reverse this by specifying a descending order (abbreviated **DESC**):

```
SELECT * FROM tablename
ORDER BY column DESC
```

You can even order the returned values by multiple columns:

```
SELECT * FROM tablename
ORDER BY column1, column2
```

You can, and frequently will, use **ORDER BY** with **WHERE** or other clauses. When doing so, place the **ORDER BY** after the conditions:

```
SELECT * FROM tablename WHERE conditions
ORDER BY column
```

To sort data:

1. Select all of the users in alphabetical order by last name **A**:

   ```
   SELECT first_name, last_name FROM
   users ORDER BY last_name;
   ```

   If you compare these results with those in **B** in the "Selecting Data" section, you'll see the benefits of using **ORDER BY**.

2. Display all of the users in alphabetical order by last name and then first name **B**:

   ```
   SELECT first_name, last_name FROM
   users ORDER BY last_name ASC,
   first_name ASC;
   ```

   continues on next page

```
mysql> SELECT first_name, last_name FROM
    -> users ORDER BY last_name;
+------------+-----------+
| first_name | last_name |
+------------+-----------+
| Melissa    | Bank      |
| Russell    | Banks     |
| Richard    | Brautigan |
| Michael    | Chabon    |
| Don        | DeLillo   |
| Micky      | Dolenz    |
| Jonathan   | Franzen   |
| Graham     | Greene    |
| George     | Harrison  |
| Nick       | Hornby    |
| Zoe        | Isabella  |
| David      | Jones     |
| John       | Lennon    |
| Paul       | McCartney |
| Toni       | Morrison  |
| Mike       | Nesmith   |
| David      | Sedaris   |
| Bart       | Simpson   |
| Lisa       | Simpson   |
| Maggie     | Simpson   |
| Marge      | Simpson   |
| Homer      | Simpson   |
| Abe        | Simpson   |
| Ringo      | Starr     |
| Peter      | Tork      |
| Larry      | Ullman    |
+------------+-----------+
26 rows in set (0.00 sec)

mysql>
```

A The records in alphabetical order by last name.

```
mysql> SELECT first_name, last_name FROM
    -> users ORDER BY last_name ASC,
    -> first_name ASC;
+------------+-----------+
| first_name | last_name |
+------------+-----------+
| Melissa    | Bank      |
| Russell    | Banks     |
| Richard    | Brautigan |
| Michael    | Chabon    |
| Don        | DeLillo   |
| Micky      | Dolenz    |
| Jonathan   | Franzen   |
| Graham     | Greene    |
| George     | Harrison  |
| Nick       | Hornby    |
| Zoe        | Isabella  |
| David      | Jones     |
| John       | Lennon    |
| Paul       | McCartney |
| Toni       | Morrison  |
| Mike       | Nesmith   |
| David      | Sedaris   |
| Abe        | Simpson   |
| Bart       | Simpson   |
| Homer      | Simpson   |
| Lisa       | Simpson   |
| Maggie     | Simpson   |
| Marge      | Simpson   |
| Ringo      | Starr     |
| Peter      | Tork      |
| Larry      | Ullman    |
+------------+-----------+
26 rows in set (0.00 sec)

mysql>
```

B The records in alphabetical order, first by last name, and then by first name within that.

In this query, the effect would be that every row is returned, first ordered by the *last_name*, and then by *first_name* within the *last_name*s. The effect is most evident among the Simpsons.

3. Show all of the non-Simpson users by date registered **C**:

```
SELECT * FROM users
WHERE last_name != 'Simpson'
ORDER BY registration_date DESC;
```

You can use an **ORDER BY** on any column type, including numbers and dates. The clause can also be used in a query with a conditional, placing the **ORDER BY** after the **WHERE**.

TIP Because MySQL works naturally with any number of languages, the ORDER BY will be based upon the *collation* being used (see Chapter 6).

TIP If the column that you choose to sort on is an ENUM type, the sort will be based upon the order of the possible ENUM values when the column was created. For example, if you have the column *gender*, defined as ENUM('M', 'F'), the clause ORDER BY gender returns the results with the *M* records first.

```
mysql> SELECT * FROM users
    -> WHERE last_name != 'Simpson'
    -> ORDER BY registration_date DESC;
+---------+------------+-----------+----------------------+----------------------------------+---------------------+
| user_id | first_name | last_name | email                | pass                             | registration_date   |
+---------+------------+-----------+----------------------+----------------------------------+---------------------+
|      20 | Russell    | Banks     | russell@authors.com  | 6bc4056557e33f1e209870ab578ed362f8b3c1b8 | 2011-03-31 21:16:47 |
|      12 | Nick       | Hornby    | nick@authors.com     | 815f12d7b9d7cd690d4781015c2a0a5b3ae207c0 | 2011-03-31 21:16:47 |
|      13 | Melissa    | Bank      | melissa@authors.com  | 15ac6793642add347cbf24b8884b97947f637091 | 2011-03-31 21:16:47 |
|      14 | Toni       | Morrison  | toni@authors.com     | ce3a79105879624f762c01ecb8abee7b31e67df5 | 2011-03-31 21:16:47 |
|      15 | Jonathan   | Franzen   | jonathan@authors.com | c969581a0a7d6f790f4b520225f34fd90a09c86f | 2011-03-31 21:16:47 |
|      16 | Don        | DeLillo   | don@authors.com      | 01a3ff9a11b328afd3e5affcba4cc9e539c4c455 | 2011-03-31 21:16:47 |
|      17 | Graham     | Greene    | graham@authors.com   | 7c16ec1fcbc8c3ec99790f25c310ef63febb1bb3 | 2011-03-31 21:16:47 |
|      18 | Michael    | Chabon    | michael@authors.com  | bd58cc413f97c33930778416a6dbd2d67720dc41 | 2011-03-31 21:16:47 |
|      19 | Richard    | Brautigan | richard@authors.com  | b1f8414005c218fb53b661f17b4f671bccecea3d | 2011-03-31 21:16:47 |
|      11 | David      | Sedaris   | david@authors.com    | f54e748ae9624210402eeb2c15a9f506a110ef72 | 2011-03-31 21:16:47 |
|      10 | Mike       | Nesmith   | mike@monkees.com     | 804a1773e9985abeb1f2605e0cc22211cc58cb1b | 2011-03-31 21:16:47 |
|       9 | Micky      | Dolenz    | micky@monkees.com    | 0599b6e3c9206ef135c83a921294ba6417dbc673 | 2011-03-31 21:16:47 |
|       8 | Peter      | Tork      | peter@monkees.com    | b8f6bc0c646f68ec6f27653f8473ae4ae81fd302 | 2011-03-31 21:16:47 |
|       7 | David      | Jones     | davey@monkees.com    | ec23244e40137ef72763267f17ed6c7ebb2b019f | 2011-03-31 21:16:47 |
|       3 | John       | Lennon    | john@beatles.com     | 2a50435b0f512f60988db719106a258fb7e338ff | 2011-03-31 21:15:07 |
|       4 | Paul       | McCartney | paul@beatles.com     | 6ae16792c502a5b47da180ce8456e5ae7d65e262 | 2011-03-31 21:15:07 |
|       5 | George     | Harrison  | george@beatles.com   | 1af17e73721dbe0c40011b82ed4bb1a7dbe3ce29 | 2011-03-31 21:15:07 |
|       6 | Ringo      | Starr     | ringo@beatles.com    | 520f73691bcf89d508d923a2dbc8e6fa58efb522 | 2011-03-31 21:15:07 |
|       2 | Zoe        | Isabella  | email2@example.com   | 6b793ca1c216835ba85c1fbd1399ce729e34b4e5 | 2011-03-31 21:14:23 |
|       1 | Larry      | Ullman    | email@example.com    | e727d1464ae12436e899a726da5b2f11d8381b26 | 2011-03-31 21:12:52 |
+---------+------------+-----------+----------------------+----------------------------------+---------------------+
20 rows in set (0.00 sec)

mysql>
```

C All of the users not named *Simpson*, displayed by date registered, with the most recent listed first.

A Using the **LIMIT** clause, a query can return a specific number of records.

Limiting Query Results

Another SQL clause that can be added to most queries is **LIMIT**. In a **SELECT** query, **WHERE** dictates which records to return, and **ORDER BY** decides how those records are sorted, but **LIMIT** states how many records to return. It is used like so:

SELECT * FROM *tablename* **LIMIT** *x*

In such queries, only the initial *x* records from the query result will be returned. To return only three matching records, use:

SELECT * FROM *tablename* **LIMIT 3**

Using this format

SELECT * FROM *tablename* **LIMIT** *x, y*

you can have *y* records returned, starting at *x*. To have records 11 through 20 returned, you would write

SELECT * FROM *tablename* **LIMIT 10, 10**

Like arrays in PHP, result sets begin at 0 when it comes to **LIMIT**s, so 10 is the 11th record.

Because **SELECT** does not return results in any meaningful order, you almost always want to apply an **ORDER BY** clause when using **LIMIT**. You can use **LIMIT** with **WHERE** and/or **ORDER BY** clauses, always placing **LIMIT** last:

SELECT *which_columns* **FROM** *tablename*
→ **WHERE**
conditions **ORDER BY** *column* **LIMIT** *x*

To limit the amount of data returned:

1. Select the last five registered users **A**:

   ```
   SELECT first_name, last_name
   FROM users ORDER BY
   registration_date DESC LIMIT 5;
   ```

   To return the latest of anything, sort the data by date, in descending order. Then, to see just the most recent five, add **LIMIT 5** to the query.

   continues on next page

2. Select the second person to register **B**:

```
SELECT first_name, last_name
FROM users ORDER BY
registration_date ASC LIMIT 1, 1;
```

This may look strange, but it's just a good application of the information learned so far. First, order all of the records by *registration_date* ascending, so the first people to register would be returned first. Then, limit the returned results to start at 1 (which is the second row) and to return just one record.

B Thanks to the `LIMIT` clause, a query can even return records from the middle of a group, using the `LIMIT` *x, y* format.

TIP The LIMIT *x, y* clause is most frequently used when paginating query results (showing them in blocks over multiple pages). You'll see this in Chapter 10, "Common Programming Techniques."

TIP A LIMIT clause does not improve the execution speed of a query, since MySQL still has to assemble the entire result and then truncate the list. But a LIMIT clause will minimize the amount of data to handle when it comes to the mysql client or your PHP scripts.

TIP The LIMIT term is not part of the SQL standard and is therefore (sadly) not available on all databases.

TIP The LIMIT clause can be used with most types of queries, not just SELECTs.

Updating Data

Once tables contain some data, you have the potential need to edit those existing records. This might be necessary if information was entered incorrectly or if the data changes (such as a last name or email address). The syntax for updating records is:

UPDATE *tablename* **SET** *column=value*

You can alter multiple columns at a single time, separating each from the next by a comma.

UPDATE *tablename* **SET** *column1=valueA, column5=valueB...*

You will almost always want to use a **WHERE** clause to specify what rows should be updated:

UPDATE *tablename* **SET** *column2=value* **WHERE** *column5=value*

If you don't use a **WHERE** clause, the changes would be applied to every record.

Updates, along with deletions, are one of the most important reasons to use a primary key. This value—which should never change—can be a reference point in **WHERE** clauses, even if every other field needs to be altered.

To update a record:

1. Find the primary key for the record to be updated **A**:

   SELECT user_id **FROM** users
   WHERE first_name = 'Michael'
   AND last_name='Chabon';

   In this example, I'll change the email for this author's record. To do so, I must first find that record's primary key, which this query accomplishes.

2. Update the record **B**:

   UPDATE users
   SET email='mike@authors.com'
   WHERE user_id = 18;

   To change the email address, use an **UPDATE** query, using the primary key (*user_id*) to specify to which record the update should apply. MySQL will report upon the success of the query and how many rows were affected.

   continues on next page

```
mysql> SELECT user_id FROM users
    -> WHERE first_name = 'Michael'
    -> AND last_name='Chabon';
+---------+
| user_id |
+---------+
|      18 |
+---------+
1 row in set (0.00 sec)

mysql>
```

A Before updating a record, determine which primary key to use in the **UPDATE**'s **WHERE** clause.

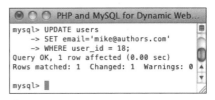

```
mysql> UPDATE users
    -> SET email='mike@authors.com'
    -> WHERE user_id = 18;
Query OK, 1 row affected (0.00 sec)
Rows matched: 1  Changed: 1  Warnings: 0

mysql>
```

B This query altered the value of one column in just one row.

3. Confirm that the change was made **C**:

```
SELECT * FROM users
WHERE user_id=18;
```

Although MySQL already indicated the update was successful **B**, it can't hurt to select the record again to confirm that the proper changes occurred.

TIP Be extra certain to use a WHERE conditional whenever you use UPDATE unless you want the changes to affect every row.

TIP If you run an update query that doesn't actually change any values (like UPDATE users SET first_name='mike' WHERE first_name='mike'), you won't see any errors but no rows will be affected. More recent versions of MySQL would show that *X* rows matched the query but that 0 rows were changed **D**.

TIP To protect yourself against accidentally updating too many rows, apply a LIMIT clause to your UPDATEs:

```
UPDATE users SET email='mike@authors.
com' WHERE user_id = 18 LIMIT 1
```

TIP You should never perform an UPDATE on a primary-key column, because the primary key value should never change. Altering the value of a primary key could have serious repercussions.

TIP To update a record in phpMyAdmin, you can run an UPDATE query using the SQL window or tab. Alternatively, run a SELECT query to find the record you want to update, and then click the pencil next to the record. This will bring up a form similar to the insert form, where you can edit the record's current values.

```
PHP and MySQL for Dynamic Web Sites: Visual QuickPro Guide
mysql> SELECT * FROM users
    -> WHERE user_id=18;
+---------+------------+-----------+------------------+------------------------------------------+---------------------+
| user_id | first_name | last_name | email            | pass                                     | registration_date   |
+---------+------------+-----------+------------------+------------------------------------------+---------------------+
|      18 | Michael    | Chabon    | mike@authors.com | bd58cc413f97c33930778416a6dbd2d67720dc41 | 2011-03-31 21:16:47 |
+---------+------------+-----------+------------------+------------------------------------------+---------------------+
1 row in set (0.00 sec)

mysql>
```

C As a final step, you can confirm the update by selecting the record again.

```
PHP and MySQL for Dynamic Web Sites: Visual QuickPro Guide
mysql> UPDATE users SET first_name='mike' WHERE first_name='mike';
Query OK, 0 rows affected (0.00 sec)
Rows matched: 1  Changed: 0  Warnings: 0

mysql>
```

D Recent versions of MySQL will report upon both matching and changed records for **UPDATE** queries.

Deleting Data

Along with updating existing records, another step you might need to take is to entirely remove a record from the database. To do this, you use the **DELETE** command:

```
DELETE FROM tablename
```

That command as written will delete every record in a table, making it empty again. Once you have deleted a record, there is no way of retrieving it.

In most cases you'll want to delete individual rows, not all of them. To do so, apply a **WHERE** clause:

```
DELETE FROM tablename WHERE condition
```

To delete a record:

1. Find the primary key for the record to be deleted **A**:

   ```
   SELECT user_id FROM users
   WHERE first_name='Peter'
   AND last_name='Tork';
   ```

   Just as in the **UPDATE** example, I first need to determine which primary key to use for the delete.

2. Preview what will happen when the delete is made **B**:

   ```
   SELECT * FROM users
   WHERE user_id = 8;
   ```

   A really good trick for safeguarding against errant deletions is to first run the query using **SELECT** * instead of **DELETE**. The results of this query will represent which row(s) will be affected by the deletion.

   continues on next page

```
mysql> SELECT user_id FROM users
    -> WHERE first_name='Peter'
    -> AND last_name='Tork';
+---------+
| user_id |
+---------+
|       8 |
+---------+
1 row in set (0.00 sec)

mysql>
```

A The *user_id* value will be used to refer to this record in a **DELETE** query.

```
mysql> SELECT * FROM users
    -> WHERE user_id = 8;
+---------+------------+-----------+------------------+----------------------------------+---------------------+
| user_id | first_name | last_name | email            | pass                             | registration_date   |
+---------+------------+-----------+------------------+----------------------------------+---------------------+
|       8 | Peter      | Tork      | peter@monkees.com | b8f6bc0c646f68ec6f27653f8473ae4ae81fd302 | 2011-03-31 21:16:47 |
+---------+------------+-----------+------------------+----------------------------------+---------------------+
1 row in set (0.00 sec)

mysql>
```

B To preview the effect of a **DELETE** query, first run a syntactically similar **SELECT** query.

3. Delete the record 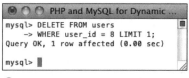:

```
DELETE FROM users
WHERE user_id = 8 LIMIT 1;
```

As with the update, MySQL will report on the successful execution of the query and how many rows were affected. At this point, there is no way of reinstating the deleted records unless you backed up the database beforehand.

Even though the **SELECT** query (Step 2 and **B**) only returned the one row, just to be extra careful, a **LIMIT 1** clause is added to the **DELETE** query.

4. Confirm that the change was made **D**:

```
SELECT user_id FROM users
WHERE first_name='Peter'
AND last_name='Tork';
```

TIP The preferred way to empty a table is to use TRUNCATE:

TRUNCATE TABLE *tablename*

TIP To delete all of the data in a table, as well as the table itself, use DROP TABLE:

DROP TABLE *tablename*

TIP To delete an entire database, including every table therein and all of its data, use

DROP DATABASE *databasename*

```
● ○ ○   PHP and MySQL for Dynamic ...
mysql> DELETE FROM users
    -> WHERE user_id = 8 LIMIT 1;
Query OK, 1 row affected (0.00 sec)

mysql>
```

C Deleting one record from the table.

```
● ○ ○   PHP and MySQL for Dynami...
mysql> SELECT user_id FROM users
    -> WHERE first_name='Peter'
    -> AND last_name='Tork';
Empty set (0.00 sec)

mysql>
```

D The record is no longer part of this table.

Aliases

An *alias* is merely a symbolic renaming of an item used in a query, normally applied to tables, columns, or function calls. Aliases are created using the term **AS**:

```
SELECT registration_date AS reg
FROM users
```

Aliases are case-sensitive strings composed of numbers, letters, and the underscore but are normally kept to a very short length. As you'll see in the following examples, aliases are also reflected in the captions for the returned results. For the preceding example, the query results returned will contain one column of data, named *reg* (not *registration_date*).

In MySQL, if you've defined an alias for a table or a column used in a query, the entire query should consistently use that same alias rather than the original name. For example,

```
SELECT first_name AS name FROM
users WHERE name='Sam'
```

This differs from standard SQL, which doesn't support the use of aliases in **WHERE** conditionals.

Using Functions

To wrap up this chapter, you'll learn about a number of functions that you can use in your MySQL queries. You have already seen two—**NOW( )** and **SHA1( )**—but those are just the tip of the iceberg. Most of the functions you'll see here are used with **SELECT** queries to format and alter the returned data, but you may use MySQL functions in other types of queries as well.

To apply a function to a column's values, the query would look like:

```
SELECT FUNCTION(column) FROM tablename
```

To apply a function to one column's values while also selecting some other columns, you can write a query like either of these:

- ```
  SELECT *, FUNCTION(column) FROM
  tablename
  ```

- ```
  SELECT column1, FUNCTION(column2),
  column3 FROM tablename
  ```

Generally speaking, the latter syntax is preferred, as it only returns the columns you need (as opposed to all of them).

Before getting to the actual functions, make note of a couple more things. First, functions are often applied to stored data (i.e., columns) but can also be applied to literal values. Either of these applications of the **UPPER( )** function (which capitalizes a string) is valid:

```
SELECT UPPER(first_name) FROM users
SELECT UPPER('this string')
```

continues on next page

Second, while the function names themselves are case-insensitive, I will continue to write them in an all-capitalized format, to help distinguish them from table and column names (as I also capitalize SQL terms). Third, an important rule with functions is that *you cannot have spaces between the function name and the opening parenthesis in MySQL*, although spaces within the parentheses are acceptable. And finally, when using functions to format returned data, you'll often want to make uses of *aliases*, a concept discussed in the sidebar.

TIP Just as there are different standards of SQL and different database applications have their own slight variations on the language, some functions are common to all database applications and others are particular to MySQL. This chapter, and book, only concerns itself with the MySQL functions.

TIP Chapter 7 discusses two more categories of MySQL functions: grouping and encryption.

Text functions

The first group of functions to demonstrate are those meant for manipulating text. The most common of the functions in this category are listed in **Table 5.2**. As with most functions, these can be applied to either columns or literal values (both represented by *t*, *t1*, *t2*, etc).

CONCAT( ), perhaps the most useful of the text functions, deserves special attention. The **CONCAT( )** function accomplishes concatenation, for which PHP uses the period (see Chapter 1, "Introduction to PHP"). The syntax for concatenation requires you to place, within parentheses, the various values you want assembled, in order and separated by commas:

```
SELECT CONCAT(t1, t2) FROM tablename
```

While you can—and normally will—apply **CONCAT( )** to columns, you can also incorporate strings, entered within quotation marks. For example, to format

TABLE 5.2 Text Functions

Function	Usage	Returns
CONCAT( )	CONCAT(t1, t2, ...)	A new string of the form *t1t2*.
CONCAT_WS( )	CONCAT_WS(S, t1, t2, ...)	A new string of the form *t1St2S...*
LENGTH( )	LENGTH(t)	The number of characters in *t*.
LEFT( )	LEFT(t, y)	The leftmost y characters from *t*.
RIGHT( )	RIGHT(t, x)	The rightmost x characters from *t*.
TRIM( )	TRIM(t)	*t* with excess spaces from the beginning and end removed.
UPPER( )	UPPER(t)	*t* capitalized.
LOWER( )	LOWER(t)	*t* in all-lowercase format.
REPLACE( )	REPLACE(t1, t2, t3)	The string *t1* with instances of *t2* replaced with *t3*.
SUBSTRING( )	SUBSTRING(t, x, y)	y characters from *t* beginning with x (indexed from 1).

a person's name as *First<SPACE>Last*, you would use

```
SELECT CONCAT(first_name, ' ',
→ last_name)
FROM users
```

Because concatenation normally returns values in a new format, it's an excellent time to use an alias (see the sidebar):

```
SELECT CONCAT(first_name, ' ',
→ last_name)
AS Name FROM users
```

To format text:

1. Concatenate the names *without* using an alias **A**:

   ```
   SELECT CONCAT(last_name, ', ',
   → first_name)
   FROM users;
   ```

   This query will demonstrate two things. First, the users' last names, a comma

and a space, plus their first names are concatenated together to make one string (in the format of *Last, First*). Second, as the figure shows, if you don't use an alias, the returned data's column heading will be the function call. In the mysql client or phpMyAdmin, this is just unsightly; when using PHP to connect to MySQL, this will likely be a problem.

2. Concatenate the names while using an alias **B**:

   ```
   SELECT CONCAT(last_name, ', ',
   → first_name)
   AS Name FROM users ORDER BY Name;
   ```

   To use an alias, just add **AS *aliasname*** after the item to be renamed. The alias will be the new title for the returned data. To make the query a little more interesting, the same alias is also used in the **ORDER BY** clause.

   continues on next page

A This simple concatenation returns every registered user's full name. Notice how the column heading is the use of the **CONCAT( )** function.

B By using an alias, the returned data is under the column heading of *Name* (compare with **A**).

3. Find the longest last name :

```
SELECT LENGTH(last_name) AS L,
last_name FROM users
ORDER BY L DESC LIMIT 1;
```

To determine which registered user's last name is the longest (has the most characters in it), use the **LENGTH( )** function. To find the name, select both the last name value and the calculated length, which is given an alias of *L*. To then find the longest name, order all of the results by *L*, in descending order, but only return the first record.

C By using the **LENGTH( )** function, an alias, an **ORDER BY** clause, and a **LIMIT** clause, this query returns the length and value of the longest stored name.

TIP A query like that in Step 3 (also **C**) may be useful for helping to fine-tune your column lengths once your database has some records in it.

TIP MySQL has two functions for performing regular expression searches on text: REGEXP( ) and NOT REGEXP( ). Chapter 14, "Perl-Compatible Regular Expressions," introduces regular expressions using PHP.

TIP CONCAT( ) has a corollary function called CONCAT_WS( ), which stands for *with separator*. The syntax is CONCAT_WS(*separator*, *t1*, *t2*, ...). The separator will be inserted between each of the listed columns or values. For example, to format a person's full name as *First<SPACE>_Middle<SPACE>_Last*, you would write

```
SELECT CONCAT_WS(' ', first, middle,
last) AS Name FROM tablename
```

CONCAT_WS( ) has an added advantage over CONCAT( ) in that it will ignore columns with NULL values. So that query might return *Joe Banks* from one record but *Jane Sojourner Adams* from another.

TABLE 5.3 Numeric Functions

Function	Usage	Returns
ABS( )	ABS(n)	The absolute value of *n*.
CEILING( )	CEILING(n)	The next-highest integer based upon the value of *n*.
FLOOR( )	FLOOR(n)	The integer value of *n*.
FORMAT( )	FORMAT(n1, n2)	*n1* formatted as a number with *n2* decimal places and commas inserted every three spaces.
MOD( )	MOD(n1, n2)	The remainder of dividing *n1* by *n2*.
POW( )	POW(n1, n2)	*n1* to the *n2* power.
RAND( )	RAND( )	A random number between 0 and 1.0.
ROUND( )	ROUND(n1, n2)	*n1* rounded to *n2* decimal places.
SQRT( )	SQRT(n)	The square root of *n*.

D The RAND( ) function returns a random number between 0 and 1.0.

Numeric functions

Besides the standard math operators that MySQL uses (for addition, subtraction, multiplication, and division), there are a couple dozen functions for formatting and performing calculations on numeric values. **Table 5.3** lists the most common of these, some of which will be demonstrated shortly. As with most functions, these can be applied to either columns or literal values (both represented by *n*, *n1*, *n2*, etc.).

I want to specifically highlight three of these functions: **FORMAT( )**, **ROUND( )**, and **RAND( )**. The first—which is not technically number-specific—turns any number into a more conventionally formatted layout. For example, if you stored the cost of a car as 20198.20, **FORMAT(car_cost, 2)** would turn that number into the more common 20,198.20.

ROUND( ) will take one value, presumably from a column, and round that to a specified number of decimal places. If no decimal places are indicated, it will round the number to the nearest integer. If more decimal places are indicated than exist in the original number, the remaining spaces are padded with zeros (to the right of the decimal point).

The **RAND( )** function, as you might infer, is used for returning random numbers **D**:

SELECT RAND( )

A further benefit to the **RAND( )** function is that it can be used with your queries to return the results in a random order:

SELECT * FROM *tablename* ORDER BY → RAND( )

To use numeric functions:

1. Display a number, formatting the amount as dollars **E**:

```
SELECT CONCAT('$', FORMAT(5639.6, 2))
AS cost;
```

Using the **FORMAT( )** function, as just described, with **CONCAT( )**, you can turn any number into a currency format as you might display it in a Web page.

2. Retrieve a random email address from the table **F**:

```
SELECT email FROM users
ORDER BY RAND( ) LIMIT 1;
```

What happens with this query is: All of the email addresses are selected; the order they are in is shuffled (**ORDER BY RAND( )**); and then the first one is returned. Running this same query multiple times will produce different random results. Notice that you do not specify a column to which **RAND( )** is applied.

TIP Along with the mathematical functions listed here, there are several trigonometric, exponential, and other types of numeric functions available.

TIP The MOD( ) function is the same as using the percent sign:

```
SELECT MOD(9,2)
SELECT 9%2
```

It returns the remainder of a division (1 in these examples).

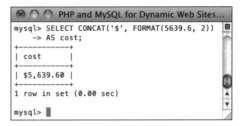

```
mysql> SELECT CONCAT('$', FORMAT(5639.6, 2))
    -> AS cost;
+-----------+
| cost      |
+-----------+
| $5,639.60 |
+-----------+
1 row in set (0.00 sec)

mysql>
```

E Using an arbitrary example, this query shows how the **FORMAT( )** function works.

```
mysql> SELECT email FROM users
    -> ORDER BY RAND() LIMIT 1;
+--------------------+
| email              |
+--------------------+
| graham@authors.com |
+--------------------+
1 row in set (0.00 sec)

mysql>
```

F This query uses the **RAND( )** function to select a random record. Subsequent executions of the same query would return different random results.

Date and time functions

The date and time column types in MySQL are particularly flexible and useful. But because many database users are not familiar with all of the available date and time functions, these options are frequently underused. Whether you want to make calculations based upon a date or return only the month name from a value, MySQL has a function for that purpose. **Table 5.4** lists most of these; see the MySQL manual for a complete list. As with most functions, these can be applied to either columns or literal values (both represented by *dt*, short for *datetime*).

MySQL supports two data types that store both a date and a time (**DATETIME** and

TIMESTAMP), one type that stores just the date (**DATE**), one that stores just the time (**TIME**), and one that stores just a year (**YEAR**). Besides allowing for different types of values, each data type also has its own unique behaviors (again, I'd recommend reading the MySQL manual's pages on this for all of the details). But MySQL is very flexible as to which functions you can use with which type. You can apply a date function to any value that contains a date (i.e., **DATETIME**, **TIMESTAMP**, and **DATE**), or you can apply an hour function to any value that contains the time (i.e., **DATETIME**, **TIMESTAMP**, and **TIME**). MySQL will use the part of the value that it needs and ignore the rest. What you cannot do, however, is apply a date function to a **TIME** value or a time function to a **DATE** or **YEAR** value.

TABLE 5.4 Date and Time Functions

Function	Usage	Returns
DATE( )	DATE(dt)	The date value of *dt*.
HOUR( )	HOUR(dt)	The hour value of *dt*.
MINUTE( )	MINUTE(dt)	The minute value of *dt*.
SECOND( )	SECOND(dt)	The second value of *dt*.
DAYNAME( )	DAYNAME(dt)	The name of the day for *dt*.
DAYOFMONTH( )	DAYOFMONTH(dt)	The numerical day value of dt.
MONTHNAME( )	MONTHNAME(dt)	The name of the month of *dt*.
MONTH( )	MONTH(dt)	The numerical month value of *dt*.
YEAR( )	YEAR(column)	The year value of *dt*.
CURDATE( )	CURDATE( )	The current date.
CURTIME( )	CURTIME( )	The current time.
NOW( )	NOW( )	The current date and time.
UNIX_TIMESTAMP( )	UNIX_TIMESTAMP(dt)	The number of seconds since the epoch until the current moment or until the date specified.
UTC_TIMESTAMP( )	UTC_TIMESTAMP(dt)	The number of seconds since the epoch until the current moment or until the date specified, in Coordinated Universal Time (UTC).

To use date and time functions:

1. Display the date that the last user registered **G**:

   ```
   SELECT DATE(registration_date) AS
   Date FROM users ORDER BY
   registration_date DESC LIMIT 1;
   ```

   The **DATE( )** function returns the date part of a value. To see the date that the last person registered, an **ORDER BY** clause lists the users starting with the most recently registered and this result is limited to just one record.

2. Display the day of the week that the first user registered **H**:

   ```
   SELECT DAYNAME(registration_date) AS
   Weekday FROM users ORDER BY
   registration_date ASC LIMIT 1;
   ```

   This is similar to the query in Step 1, but the results are returned in ascending order and the **DAYNAME( )** function is applied to the *registration_date* column. This function returns *Sunday*, *Monday*, *Tuesday*, etc., for a given date.

3. Show the current date and time, according to MySQL **I**:

   ```
   SELECT CURDATE( ), CURTIME( );
   ```

   To show what date and time MySQL currently thinks it is, you can select the **CURDATE( )** and **CURTIME( )** functions, which return these values. This is another example of a query that can be run without referring to a particular table.

```
mysql> SELECT DATE(registration_date) AS
    -> Date FROM users ORDER BY
    -> registration_date DESC LIMIT 1;
+------------+
| Date       |
+------------+
| 2011-03-31 |
+------------+
1 row in set (0.00 sec)

mysql>
```

G The date functions can be used to extract information from stored values.

```
mysql> SELECT DAYNAME(registration_date) AS
    -> Weekday FROM users ORDER BY
    -> registration_date ASC LIMIT 1;
+----------+
| Weekday  |
+----------+
| Thursday |
+----------+
1 row in set (0.00 sec)

mysql>
```

H This query returns the name of the day that a given date represents.

I This query, not run on any particular table, returns the current date and time on the MySQL server.

J Among the many things MySQL can do with date and time types is determine the last date in a month or the name value of a given date.

4. Show the last day of the current month **J**:

```
SELECT LAST_DAY(CURDATE( )),
MONTHNAME(CURDATE( ));
```

As the last query showed, **CURDATE( )** returns the current date on the server. This value can be used as an argument to the **LAST_DAY( )** function, which returns the last date in the month for a given date. The **MONTHNAME( )** function returns the name of the current month.

TIP The date and time returned by MySQL's date and time functions correspond to those on the server, not on the client accessing the database.

TIP Not mentioned in this section or in Table 5.4 are ADDDATE( ), SUBDATE( ), ADDTIME( ), SUBTIME( ), and DATEDIFF( ). Each can be used to perform arithmetic on date and time values. These can be very useful (for example, to find everyone registered within the past week), but their syntax is cumbersome. As always, see the MySQL manual for more information.

TIP Chapter 6 discusses the concept of time zones in MySQL.

TIP As of MySQL 5.0.2, the server will also prevent invalid dates (e.g., February 31, 2011) from being inserted into a date or date/time column.

Formatting the date and time

There are two additional date and time functions that you might find yourself using more than all of the others combined: **DATE_FORMAT( )** and **TIME_FORMAT( )**. There is some overlap between the two and when you would use one or the other.

DATE_FORMAT( ) can be used to format both the date and time if a value contains both (e.g., *YYYY-MM-DD HH:MM:SS*). Comparatively, **TIME_FORMAT( )** can format only the time value and must be used if only the time value is being stored (e.g., *HH:MM:SS*). The syntax is

SELECT DATE_FORMAT(*datetime*, *formatting*)

The *formatting* relies upon combinations of key codes and the percent sign to indicate what values you want returned. **Table 5.5** lists the available date- and time-formatting parameters. You can use these in any combination, along with literal characters, such as punctuation, to return a date and time in a more presentable form.

Assuming that a column called *the_date* has the date and time of *1996-04-20 11:07:45* stored in it, common formatting tasks and results would be

- Time (11:07:45 AM)

  TIME_FORMAT(the_date, '%r')

- Time without seconds (11:07 AM)

  TIME_FORMAT(the_date, '%l:%i %p')

- Date (April 20th, 1996)

  DATE_FORMAT(the_date, '%M %D, %Y')

TABLE 5.5 *_FORMAT( ) Parameters

Term	Usage	Example
%e	Day of the month	1-31
%d	Day of the month, two digit	01-31
%D	Day with suffix	1st-31st
%W	Weekday name	Sunday-Saturday
%a	Abbreviated weekday name	Sun-Sat
%c	Month number	1-12
%m	Month number, two digit	01-12
%M	Month name	January-December
%b	Month name, abbreviated	Jan-Dec
%Y	Year	2002
%y	Year	02
%l (lowercase L)	Hour	1-12
%h	Hour, two digit	01-12
%k	Hour, 24-hour clock	0-23
%H	Hour, 24-hour clock, two digit	00-23
%i	Minutes	00-59
%S	Seconds	00-59
%r	Time	8:17:02 PM
%T	Time, 24-hour clock	20:17:02
%p	AM or PM	AM or PM

K The current date and time, formatted.

L The current time, in a 24-hour format.

M The `DATE_FORMAT( )` function is used to pre-format the registration date when selecting records from the *users* table.

To format the date and time:

1. Return the current date and time as *Month DD, YYYY - HH:MM* **K**:

   `SELECT DATE_FORMAT(NOW( ),'%M %e, %Y`
   `→%l:%i');`

   Using the **NOW( )** function, which returns the current date and time, you can practice formatting to see what results are returned.

2. Display the current time, using 24-hour notation **L**:

   `SELECT TIME_FORMAT(CURTIME( ),'%T');`

3. Select the email address and date registered, ordered by date registered, formatting the date as *Weekday (abbreviated) Month (abbreviated) Day Year*, for the last five registered users **M**:

   `SELECT email, DATE_FORMAT`
   `→(registration_date, '%a %b %e %Y')`
   `AS Date FROM users`
   `ORDER BY registration_date DESC`
   `LIMIT 5;`

   This is just one more example of how you can use these formatting functions to alter the output of an SQL query.

> **TIP** In your Web applications, you should almost always use MySQL functions to format any dates coming from the database (as opposed to formatting the dates within PHP after retrieving them from the database).

> **TIP** The only way to access the date or time on the client (the user's machine) is to use JavaScript. It cannot be done with PHP or MySQL.

Review and Pursue

If you have any problems with the review questions or the pursue prompts, turn to the book's supporting forum (**www.LarryUllman.com/forums/**).

Review

- What version of MySQL are you using? If you don't know, find out now!

- What SQL command is used to make a new database? What command is used to make a new table in a database?

- What SQL command is used to select the database with which you want to work?

- What SQL commands are used for adding records to a table? Hint: There are multiple options.

- What types of values must be quoted in queries? What types of values shouldn't be quoted?

- What does the asterisk in **SELECT * FROM** *tablename* mean? How do you restrict which columns are returned by a query?

- What does the **NOW( )** function do?

- How do you restrict which *rows* are returned by a query?

- How do **LIKE** and **NOT LIKE** differ from simple equality comparisons? Which type of comparison will be faster? What are the two **LIKE** and **NOT LIKE** wildcard characters?

- How do you affect the sorting of the returned records? What is the default sorting method? How do you inverse the sort? What is the syntax for sorting by multiple columns?

- What does the **LIMIT** clause do? How does **LIMIT** *x* differ from **LIMIT** *x, y*?

- What SQL command is used to change the values already stored in a table? How do you change multiple columns at once? How do you restrict to which rows the changes are applied?

- What SQL command is used to delete rows stored in a table? How do you restrict to which rows the deletions are applied?

- What is an SQL alias? How do you create one? Why is an alias useful?

Pursue

- If you haven't done so already, bookmark the version of the MySQL manual that matches the version of MySQL you are running.

- Go through each of the step sequences in this chapter again, coming up with your own queries to execute (that demonstrate similar concepts as those in the steps).

- Check out the MySQL manual pages for operators used in conditionals.

- Check out the MySQL manual pages for some of MySQL's functions.

- Create, populate, and manipulate your own table of data.

- Do some more practice using functions and aliases.

- Check out the MySQL manual pages for the various date and time types. Also check out **ADDDATE( )** and other date-related functions.

Database
Design

Now that you have a basic understanding of databases, SQL, and MySQL, this chapter begins the process of taking that knowledge deeper. The focus on this chapter, as the title states, is real-world database design. Like the work done in Chapter 4, "Introduction to MySQL," much of the effort herein requires paper and pen, and serious thinking about what your applications will need to do.

The chapter begins with thorough coverage of database *normalization*: a vital approach to the design process. After that, the chapter turns to design-related concepts specific to MySQL: indexes, table types, language support, working with times, and foreign key constraints.

By the end of this chapter, you'll know the steps involved in proper database design, understand how to make the most of MySQL, and plan a couple of multi-table databases. In the next chapter, you'll learn more advanced SQL and MySQL, using these new databases as examples.

In This Chapter

Normalization

Whenever you are working with a relational database management system such as MySQL, the first step in creating and using a database is to establish the database's structure (also called the database *schema*). Database design, aka *data modeling*, is crucial for successful long-term management of information. Using a process called *normalization*, you carefully eliminate redundancies and other problems that would undermine the integrity of your database.

The techniques you will learn over the next few pages will help to ensure the viability, usefulness, and reliability of your databases. The primary example to be discussed—a forum where users can post messages—will be more explicitly used in Chapter 17, "Example—Message Board," but the principles of normalization apply to any database you might create. (The *sitename* example as created and used in the past two chapters *was* properly normalized, even though normalization was never discussed.)

Normalization was developed by an IBM researcher named E.F. Codd in the early 1970s (he also invented the relational database). A relational database is merely a collection of data, organized in a particular manner, and Dr. Codd created a series of rules called *normal forms* that help define that organization. This chapter discusses the first three of the normal forms, which are sufficient for most database designs.

Before you begin normalizing your database, you must define the role of the application being developed. Whether it means that you thoroughly discuss the subject with a client or figure it out for yourself, understanding how the information will be accessed dictates the modeling. Thus, this process will require paper and

pen rather than the MySQL software itself (although database design is applicable to any relational database, not just MySQL).

In this example, I want to create a message board where users can post messages and other users can reply. I imagine that users will need to register, then log in with an email address/password combination, in order to post messages. I also expect that there could be multiple forums for different subjects. I have listed a sample row of data in **Table 6.1**. The database itself will be called *forum*.

TIP One of the best ways to determine what information should be stored in a database is to think about what questions will be asked of the database and what data would be included in the answers.

TIP Always err on the side of storing *more* information than you might need. It's easy to ignore unnecessary data but impossible to later manufacture data that was never stored in the first place.

TIP Normalization can be hard to learn if you fixate on the little things. Each of the normal forms is defined in a very cryptic way; even when put into layman's terms, they can still be confounding. My best advice is to focus on the big picture as you follow along. Once you've gone through normalization and seen the end result, the overall process should be clear enough.

TABLE 6.1 Sample Forum Data

Item	Example
username	troutster
password	mypass
actual name	Larry Ullman
user email	email@example.com
forum	MySQL
message subject	Question about normalization.
message body	I have a question about...
message date	November 2, 2011 12:20 AM

Keys

As briefly mentioned in Chapter 4, *keys* are integral to normalized databases. There are two types of keys: *primary* and *foreign*. A primary key is a unique identifier that has to abide by certain rules. They must

- Always have a value (they cannot be **NULL**)
- Have a value that remains the same (never changes)
- Have a unique value for each record in a table

A good real-world example of a primary key is the U.S. Social Security number: each individual has a unique Social Security number, and that number never changes. Just as the Social Security number is an artificial construct used to identify people, you'll frequently find creating an arbitrary primary key for each table to be the best design practice.

The second type of key is a foreign key. Foreign keys are the representation in Table B of the primary key from Table A. If you have a *cinema* database with a *movies* table and a *directors* table, the primary key from *directors* would be linked as a foreign key in *movies*. You'll see better how this works as the normalization process continues.

TABLE 6.2 Sample Forum Data

Item	Example
message ID	325
username	troutster
password	mypass
actual name	Larry Ullman
user email	email@example.com
forum	MySQL
message subject	Question about normalization.
message body	I have a question about...
message date	November 2, 2011 12:20 AM

The *forum* database is just a simple table as it stands (Table 6.1), but before beginning the normalization process, identify at least one primary key (the foreign keys will come in later steps).

To assign a primary key:

1. Look for any fields that meet the three tests for a primary key.

   In this example (Table 6.1), no column really fits all of the criteria for a primary key. The username and email address will be unique for each forum user but will not be unique for each record in the database (because the same user could post multiple messages). The same subject could be used multiple times as well. The message body will likely be unique for each message but could change (if edited), violating one of the rules of primary keys.

2. If no logical primary key exists, invent one (**Table 6.2**).

   Frequently, you will need to create a primary key because no good solution presents itself. In this example, a *message ID* is manufactured. When you create a primary key that has no other meaning or purpose, it's called a *surrogate* primary key.

TIP As a rule of thumb, I name my primary keys using at least part of the table's name (e.g., *message*) and the word *id*. Some database developers like to add the abbreviation *pk* to the name as well. Some developers just use *id*.

TIP MySQL allows for only one primary key per table, although you can base a primary key on multiple columns (this means the combination of those columns must be unique and never change).

TIP Ideally, your primary key should always be an integer, which results in better MySQL performance.

Relationships

Database relationships refer to how the data in one table relates to the data in another. There are three types of relationships between any two tables: *one-to-one*, *one-to-many*, or *many-to-many*. (Two tables in a database may also be unrelated.)

A relationship is one-to-one if one and only one item in Table A applies to one and only one item in Table B. For example, each U.S. citizen has only one Social Security number, and each Social Security number applies to only one U.S. citizen; no citizen can have two Social Security numbers, and no Social Security number can refer to two citizens.

A relationship is one-to-many if one item in Table A can apply to multiple items in Table B. The terms *female* and *male* will apply to many people, but each person can be only one or the other (in theory). A one-to-many relationship is the most common one between tables in normalized databases.

Finally, a relationship is many-to-many if multiple items in Table A can apply to multiple items in Table B. A book can be written by multiple authors, and authors can write multiple books. Although many-to-many relationships are common in the real word, *you should avoid many-to-many relationships in your design* because they lead to data redundancy and integrity problems. Instead of having many-to-many relationships, properly designed databases use *intermediary tables* that break down one many-to-many relationship into two one-to-many relationships 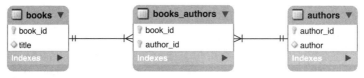.

Relationships and keys work together in that a key in one table will normally relate to a key in another, as mentioned earlier.

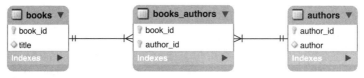

Ⓐ A many-to-many relationship between two tables will be better represented as two one-to-many relationships those tables have with an intermediary table.

TIP Database modeling uses certain conventions to represent the structure of the database, which I'll follow through a series of images in this chapter. The symbols for the three types of relationships are shown in **B**.

TIP The process of database design results in an *ERD* (entity-relationship diagram) or *ERM* (entity-relationship model). This graphical representation of a database uses shapes for tables and columns and the symbols from **B** to represent the relationships.

TIP There are many programs available to help create a database schema, including MySQL Workbench (http://wb.mysql.com). Many of the images in this chapter will come from MySQL Workbench.

TIP The term "relational" in RDBMS actually stems from the tables, which are technically called *relations*.

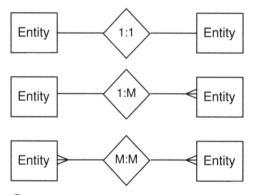

B These symbols, or variations on them, are commonly used to represent relationships in database modeling schemes.

First Normal Form

As already stated, normalizing a database is the process of changing the database's structure according to several rules, called *forms*. Your database should adhere to each rule exactly, and the forms must be followed in order.

Every table in a database must have the following two qualities in order to be in First Normal Form (1NF):

- Each column must contain only one value (this is sometimes described as being *atomic* or *indivisible*).

- No table can have repeating groups of related data.

A table containing one field for a person's entire address (street, city, state, zip code, country) would *not* be 1NF compliant, because it has multiple values in one column, violating the first property above. As for the second, a *movies* table that had columns such as *actor1*, *actor2*, *actor3*, and so on would fail to be 1NF compliant because of the repeating columns all listing the exact same kind of information.

To begin the normalization process, check the existing structure (Table 6.2) for 1NF compliance. Any columns that are not atomic should be broken into multiple columns. If a table has repeating similar columns, then those should be turned into their own, separate table.

To make a database 1NF compliant:

1. Identify any field that contains multiple pieces of information.

   Looking at Table 6.2, one field is not 1NF compliant: *actual name*. The example record contained both the first name and the last name in this one column.

   The *message date* field contains a day, a month, and a year, plus a time, but subdividing past that level of specificity is really not warranted. And, as the end of the last chapter shows, MySQL can handle dates and times quite nicely using the `DATETIME` type.

   Other examples of problems would be if a table used just one column for multiple phone numbers (mobile, home, work), or stored a person's multiple interests (cooking, dancing, skiing, etc.) in a single column.

2. Break up any fields found in Step 1 into distinct fields (**Table 6.3**).

   To fix this problem for the current example, create separate *first name* and *last name* fields, each of which contains only one value.

3. Turn any repeating column groups into their own table.

   The *forum* database doesn't have this problem currently, so to demonstrate what would be a violation, consider **Table 6.4**. The repeating columns (the multiple actor fields) introduce two problems. First of all, there's no getting around the fact that each movie will be limited to a certain number of actors when stored this way. Even if you add columns *actor 1* through *actor 100*, there will still be that limit (of a hundred).

TABLE 6.3 Forum Database, Atomic

Item	Example
message ID	325
username	troutster
password	mypass
first name	Larry
last name	Ullman
user email	email@example.com
forum	MySQL
message subject	Question about normalization.
message body	I have a question about...
message date	November 2, 2011 12:20 AM

TABLE 6.4 Movies Table

Column	Value
movie ID	976
movie title	Casablanca
year released	1943
director	Michael Curtiz
actor 1	Humphrey Bogart
actor 2	Ingrid Bergman
actor 3	Peter Lorre

TABLE 6.5 Movies-Actors Table

ID	Movie	Actor First Name	Actor Last Name
1	Casablanca	Humphrey	Bogart
2	Casablanca	Ingrid	Bergman
3	Casablanca	Peter	Lorre
4	The Maltese Falcon	Humphrey	Bogart
5	The Maltese Falcon	Peter	Lorre

Second, any record that doesn't have the maximum number of actors will have **NULL** values in those extra columns. You should generally avoid columns with **NULL** values in your database schema. As another concern, the actor and director columns are not atomic.

To fix the problems in the *movies* table, a second table would be created (**Table 6.5**). This table uses one row for each actor in a movie, which solves the problems mentioned in the last paragraph. The actor names are also broken up to be atomic. Notice as well that a primary-key column should be added to the new table. The notion that each table has a primary key is implicit in the First Normal Form.

4. Double-check that all new columns and tables created in Steps 2 and 3 pass the 1NF test.

TIP The simplest way to think about 1NF is that this rule analyzes a table *horizontally*: inspect all of the columns within a single row to guarantee specificity and avoid repetition of similar data.

TIP Various resources will describe the normal forms in somewhat different ways, likely with much more technical jargon. What is most important is the spirit—and end result—of the normalization process, not the technical wording of the rules.

Second Normal Form

For a database to be in Second Normal Form (2NF), the database must first already be in 1NF (you must normalize in order). Then, every column in the table that is not a key (i.e., a foreign key) must be dependent upon the primary key. You can normally identify a column that violates this rule when it has non-key values that are the same in multiple rows. Such values should be stored in their own table and related back to the original table through a key.

Going back to the *cinema* example, a *movies* table (Table 6.4) would have the director Martin Scorsese listed 20+ times. This violates the 2NF rule as the column(s) that store the directors' names would not be keys and would not be dependent upon the primary key (the movie ID). The

fix is to create a separate *directors* table that stores the directors' information and assigns each director a primary key. To tie the director back to the movies, the director's primary key would also be a foreign key in the *movies* table.

Looking at Table 6.5 (for actors in movies), both the movie name and the actor names are also in violation of the 2NF rule (they aren't keys and they aren't dependent on the table's primary key). In the end, the *cinema* database in this minimal form requires four tables ●. Each director's name, movie name, and actor's name will be stored only once, and any non-key column in a table is dependent upon that table's primary key. In fact, normalization could be summarized as the process of creating more and more tables until potential redundancies have been eliminated.

● To make the *cinema* database 2NF compliant (given the information being represented), four tables are necessary. The directors are represented in the *movies* table through the *director ID* key; the movies are represented in the *movies-actors* table through the *movie ID* key; and the actors are represented in the *movies-actors* table through the *actor ID* key.

To make a database 2NF compliant:

1. Identify any non-key columns that aren't dependent upon the table's primary key.

   Looking at Table 6.3, the username, first name, last name, email, and forum values are all non-keys (message ID is the only key column currently), and none are dependent upon the message ID. Conversely, the message subject, body, and date are also non-keys, but these do depend upon the message ID.

2. Create new tables accordingly **D**.

   The most logical modification for the forum database is to make three tables: *users*, *forums*, and *messages*.

   In a visual representation of the database, create a box for each table, with the table name as a header and all of its columns (also called its *attributes*) underneath.

3. Assign or create new primary keys **E**.

   Using the techniques described earlier in the chapter, ensure that each new table has a primary key. Here I've added a *user ID* field to the *users* table and a *forum ID* field to *forums*. These are both surrogate primary keys. Because the *username* field in the *users* table and the *name* field in the *forums* table must be unique for each record and must always have a value, you could have them act as the primary keys for their tables. However, this would mean that these values could never change (per the rules of primary keys) and the database will be a little slower, using text-based keys instead of numeric ones.

   continues on next page

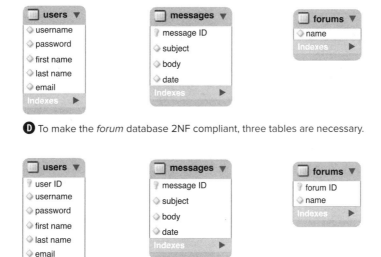

D To make the *forum* database 2NF compliant, three tables are necessary.

E Each table needs its own primary key.

4. Create the requisite foreign keys and indicate the relationships **F**.

The final step in achieving 2NF compliance is to incorporate foreign keys to link associated tables. Remember that a primary key in one table will often be a foreign key in another.

With this example, the *user ID* from the *users* table links to the *user ID* column in the *messages* table. Therefore, *users* has a one-to-many relationship with *messages* (because each user can post multiple messages, but each message can only be posted by one user).

Also, the two *forum ID* columns are linked, creating a one-to-many relationship between *messages* and *forums* (each message can only be in one forum, but each forum can have multiple messages).

There is no direct relationship between the *users* and *forums* tables.

TIP Another way to test for 2NF is to look at the relationships between tables. The ideal is to create one-to-one or one-to-many situations. Tables that have a many-to-many relationship may need to be restructured.

TIP Looking back at **C**, the *movies-actors* table is an *intermediary table*, which turns the many-to-many relationship between movies and actors into two one-to-many relationships. You can often tell a table is acting as an intermediary when all of its columns are keys. In fact, in that table, the primary key could be the combination of the *movie ID* and the *actor ID*.

TIP A properly normalized database should never have duplicate rows in the same table (two or more rows in which the values in every non–primary key column match).

TIP To simplify how you conceive of the normalization process, remember that 1NF is a matter of inspecting a table *horizontally*, and 2NF is a *vertical* analysis (hunting for repeating values over multiple rows).

F To relate the three tables, two foreign keys are added to the *messages* table, each key representing one of the other two tables.

Third Normal Form

A database is in Third Normal Form (3NF) if it is in 2NF and every non-key column is mutually independent. If you followed the normalization process properly to this point, you may not have 3NF issues. You would know that you have a 3NF violation if changing the value in one column would require changing the value in another. In the *forum* example thus far, there aren't any 3NF problems, but I'll explain a hypothetical situation where this rule would come into play.

Take, as an example, a database about books. After applying the first two normal forms, you might end up with one table listing the books, another listing the authors, and a third acting as an intermediary table between books and authors, as there's a many-to-many relationship there. If the *books* table listed the publisher's name and address, that table would be in violation of 3NF **G**. The publisher's address isn't related to the book, but rather to the publisher itself. In other words, that version of the *books* table has a column that's dependent upon a non-key column (the publisher's name).

As I said, the *forum* example is fine as is, but I'll outline the 3NF steps just the same, showing how to fix the books example just mentioned.

To make a database 3NF compliant:

1. Identify any fields in any tables that are interdependent.

    As just stated, what to look for are columns that depend more upon each other than they do on the record as a whole. In the *forum* database, this isn't an issue. Just looking at the *messages* table, each *subject* will be specific to a *message ID*, each *body* will be specific to that *message ID*, and so forth.

    With a books example, the problematic fields are those in the *books* table that pertain to the publisher.

2. Create new tables accordingly.

    If you found any problematic columns in Step 1, like *address1*, *address2*, *city*, *state*, and *zip* in a books example, you would create a separate *publishers* table. (Addresses would be more complex once you factor international publishers in.)

continues on next page

G This database as currently designed fails the 3NF test.

3. Assign or create new primary keys.

Every table must have a primary key, so add *publisher ID* to the new tables.

4. Create the requisite foreign keys that link any of the relationships 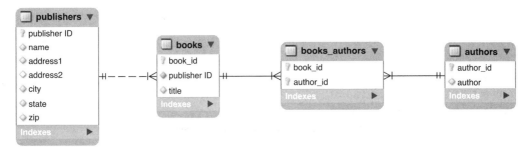.

Finally, add a *publisher ID* to the *books* table. This effectively links each book to its publisher.

TIP Despite there being set rules for how to normalize a database, two different people could normalize the same example in slightly different ways. Database design does allow for personal preference and interpretations. The important thing is that a database has no clear and obvious NF violations. Any NF violation will likely lead to problems down the road.

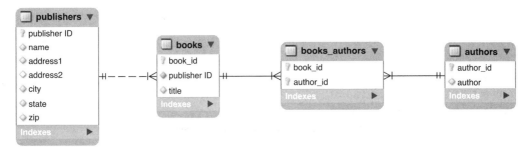

H Going with a minimal version of a hypothetical *books* database, one new table is created for storing the publisher's information.

Overruling Normalization

As much as ensuring that a database is in 3NF will help guarantee reliability and viability, you won't fully normalize every database with which you work. Before undermining the proper methods, though, understand that doing so may have devastating long-term consequences.

The two primary reasons to overrule normalization are convenience and performance. Fewer tables are easier to manipulate and comprehend than more. Further, because of their more intricate nature, normalized databases will most likely be slower for updating, retrieving data from, and modifying. Normalization, in short, is a trade-off between data integrity/scalability and simplicity/speed. On the other hand, there are ways to improve your database's performance but few to remedy corrupted data that can result from poor design.

This chapter includes an example where normalization is ignored: a message's post date and time is stored in one field. As mentioned, because MySQL is so good with dates, there are no dangers to this approach. Another situation where you would overrule normalization is a table that stored a person's gender, among other information. If stored as just M/F or Male/Female (instead of linking to a *genders* table), there would be many repeating values. But that is fine in this case, as those labels are stable values, not likely to change over time (i.e., it's unlikely that a third option will be invented, or that "Female" will be renamed, forcing a mass update of half the records in the table).

Practice and experience will teach you how best to model your database, but do try to err on the side of abiding by the normal forms, particularly as you are still mastering the concept.

Reviewing the Design

After walking through the normalization process, it's best to review the design one more time. You want to make sure that the database stores all of the data you may ever need. Often the creation of new tables, thanks to normalization, implies additional information to record. For example, although the original focus of the *cinema* database was on the movies, now that there are separate *actors* and *directors* tables, additional facts about those people could be reflected in those tables.

With that in mind, although there are a number of additional columns that could be added to the *forum* database, particularly regarding the user, one more field should be added to the *messages* table. Because one message might be a reply to another, some method of indicating that relationship is required. One solution is to add a *parent_id* column to *messages* . If a message is a reply, its *parent_id* value will be the *message_id* of the original message (so *message_id* is acting as a foreign key to this same table). If a message has a *parent_id* of 0, then it's a new thread, not a reply .

continues on next page

I To reflect a message hierarchy, the *parent_id* column is added to *messages*.

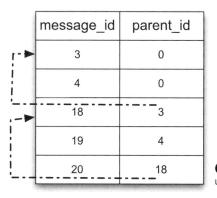

message_id	parent_id
3	0
4	0
18	3
19	4
20	18

J How the *parent_id* field is used to track message threads.

After making any changes to the tables, you must run through the normal forms one more time to ensure that the database is still normalized. Finally, choose the column types and names, per the steps in Chapter 4 . Note that every integer column is **UNSIGNED**, the three primary key columns are also designated as **AUTO_INCREMENT**, and every column is set as **NOT NULL**.

Once the schema is fully developed, it can be created in MySQL, using the commands shown in Chapter 5, "Introduction to SQL." You'll do that later in the chapter, after learning a few more things.

TIP When you have a primary key–foreign key link (like *forum_id* in *forums* to *forum_id* in *messages*), both columns should be of the same type (in this case, TINYINT UNSIGNED NOT NULL).

K The final ERD for the *forums* database.

Creating Indexes

Indexes are a special system that databases use to improve the performance of **SELECT** queries. Indexes can be placed on one or more columns, of any data type, effectively telling MySQL to pay particular attention to those values.

While the maximum number of indexes that a table can have varies, MySQL always guarantees that you can create at least 16 indexes for each table, and each index can incorporate up to 15 columns. While the need for a multicolumn index may not seem obvious, it will come in handy for searches frequently performed on the same combinations of columns (e.g., first and last name, city and state, etc.).

Although indexes are an integral part of any table, not everything needs to be indexed. While an index does improve the speed of reading from databases, it slows down queries that alter data in a database (because the changes need to be recorded in the index).

Indexes are best used on columns

- That are frequently used in the **WHERE** part of a query
- That are frequently used in an **ORDER BY** part of a query
- That are frequently used as the focal point of a **JOIN** (joins are discussed in the next chapter)

Generally speaking, you should *not* index columns that:

- Allow for **NULL** values
- Have a very limited range of values (such as just Y/N or 1/0)

MySQL has four types of indexes: **INDEX** (the standard), **UNIQUE** (which requires each row to have a unique value for that column), **FULLTEXT** (for performing **FULLTEXT** searches, also discussed in Chapter 7, "Advanced SQL and MySQL"), and **PRIMARY KEY** (which is just a particular **UNIQUE** index and one you've already been using). Note that a column should only ever have a single index on it, so choose the index type that's most appropriate.

With this in mind, let's continue designing the *forum* database by identifying appropriate indexes. Later in this chapter, the indexes will be defined when the tables are created in the database. To establish an index when creating a table, this clause is added to the **CREATE TABLE** command:

INDEX_TYPE index_name (columns)

The index name is optional. If no name is provided, the index will take the name of the column, or columns, to which it is applied. When indexing multiple columns, separate them by commas, and put them in the order from most to least important:

```
INDEX full_name (last_name,
→ first_name)
```

You've already seen the syntax for creating indexes in Chapter 5. This command creates a table with a **PRIMARY KEY** index on the **user_id** field:

```
CREATE TABLE users (
user_id MEDIUMINT UNSIGNED NOT NULL
→ AUTO_INCREMENT,
first_name VARCHAR(20) NOT NULL,
last_name VARCHAR(40) NOT NULL,
email VARCHAR(40) NOT NULL,
pass CHAR(40) NOT NULL,
registration_date DATETIME NOT NULL,
PRIMARY KEY (user_id)
);
```

continues on next page

The last thing you should know about indexes are the implications of indexing multiple columns. If you add an index on *col1*, *col2*, and *col3* (in that order), this effectively creates an index for uses of *col1*, *col1* and *col2* together, or on all three columns together. It does not provide an index for referencing just *col2* or *col3* or those two together.

To create indexes:

1. Add a **PRIMARY KEY** index on all primary keys.

   Each table should always have a primary key and therefore a **PRIMARY KEY** index. With the *forums* database, the specific columns to be indexed as primary keys are: *forums.forum_id*, *messages.message_id*, and *users.user_id*. (The syntax *table_name.column_name* is a way to refer to a specific column within a specific table.)

2. Add **UNIQUE** indexes to any columns whose values cannot be duplicated within the table.

   The *forums* database has three columns that should always be unique or else there will be problems: *forums.name*, *users.username*, and *users.email*.

3. Add **FULLTEXT** indexes, if appropriate.

   FULLTEXT indexes and **FULLTEXT** searching are discussed in the next chapter, so I won't discuss this topic any more here, but as you'll discover, there is one **FULLTEXT** index to be used in this database.

4. Add standard indexes to columns frequently used in a **WHERE** clause.

   It requires some experience to know in advance which columns will often be used in **WHERE** clauses (and therefore ought to be indexed). With the *forums* database, one common **WHERE** stands out: when a user logs in, they'll provide their email address and password to log in. The query to confirm the user has provided the correct information will be something like:

   ```
   SELECT * FROM users WHERE pass=
   → SHA1('provided_password') AND
   → email='provided_email_address'
   ```

   From this query, one can deduce that indexing the combination of the email address and password would be beneficial.

5. Add standard indexes to columns frequently used in **ORDER BY** clauses.

   Again, in time such columns will stand out while designing the database. In the *forums* example, there's one column left that would be used in **ORDER BY** clauses that isn't already indexed: *messages.date_entered*. This column will frequently be used in **ORDER BY** clauses as the site will, by default, show all messages in the order they were entered.

TABLE 6.6 The forum Database Indexes

Column Name	Table	Index Type
forum_id	forums	PRIMARY
name	forums	UNIQUE
message_id	messages	PRIMARY
forum_id	messages	INDEX
parent_id	messages	INDEX
user_id	messages	INDEX
date_entered	messages	INDEX
user_id	users	PRIMARY
username	users	UNIQUE
pass/email	users	INDEX
email	users	UNIQUE

6. Add standard indexes to columns frequently used in **JOIN**s.

You may not know what a **JOIN** is now, and the topic is thoroughly covered in Chapter 7, but the most obvious candidates are the foreign key columns. Remember that a foreign key in Table B relates to the primary key in Table A. When selecting data from the database, a **JOIN** will be written based upon this relationship. For that **JOIN** to be efficient, the foreign key must be indexed (the primary key will already have been indexed). In the *forums* example, three foreign key fields in the *messages* table ought to be indexed: *forum_id*, *parent_id*, and *user_id*.

Table 6.6 lists all the indexes identified through these steps.

TIP Indexes can be created after you already have a populated table. However, you'll get an error and the index will not be created if you attempt to add a UNIQUE index to a column that has duplicate values.

TIP MySQL uses the term KEY as synonymous for INDEX:

KEY full_name (last_name, first_name)

TIP You can limit the length of an index to a certain number of characters, such as the first 10:

INDEX *index_name* (*column_name*(10))

You might do so in situations where the first X characters will be sufficiently useful in an ORDER BY clause.

Using Different Table Types

A MySQL feature uncommon in other database applications is the ability to use different types of tables (a table's type is also called its *storage engine*). Each table type supports different features, has its own limits (in terms of how much data it can store), and even performs better or worse under certain situations. Still, how you interact with any table type—in terms of running queries—is consistent across them all.

Historically, the most important table type was *MyISAM*. Until version 5.5.5 of MySQL, MyISAM was the default table type on all operating systems (on Windows, the switch to a different default was made in an earlier version of MySQL). MyISAM tables are great for most applications, handling **SELECT**s and **INSERT**s very quickly. The MyISAM storage engine cannot handle *transactions*, though, which is its main drawback (transactions are covered in the next chapter). Between that feature and its lack of row-level *locking* (the entire table must be locked instead), MyISAM tables are more vulnerable to corruption and data loss should a crash occur.

As of MySQL version 5.5.5, MySQL's new default storage engine, on all operating systems, is *InnoDB*. InnoDB tables can be used for transactions and they perform **UPDATE**s nicely. InnoDB tables also support *foreign key constraints* (discussed at the end of the chapter) and row-level locking. But the InnoDB storage engine is generally slower than MyISAM and requires more disk space on the server. Also, an InnoDB table does not support **FULLTEXT** indexes (covered in Chapter 7).

To specify the storage engine when you define a table, add a clause to the end of the creation statement:

```
CREATE TABLE tablename (
column1name COLUMNTYPE,
column2name COLUMNTYPE…
) ENGINE = type
```

If you don't specify a storage engine when creating tables, MySQL will use the default type for that MySQL server.

This feature of MySQL is even more significant because you can mix the table types within the same database. This way you can best customize each table for optimum features and performance. To continue designing the *forums* database, the next step is to identify the storage engine to be used by each table.

To establish a table's type:

1. Find your MySQL server's available table types :

   `SHOW ENGINES;`

   The **SHOW ENGINES** command, when executed on the MySQL server, will reveal not only the available storage engines but also the default storage engine. It will help to know this information when it's time to choose a table type for your database.

2. If any of your tables requires a **FULLTEXT** index, make it a MyISAM table.

   Again, **FULLTEXT** indexes and searches are discussed in the next chapter, but I'll say now that the *messages* table in the *forums* example will require a **FULLTEXT** index. Therefore, this table must be MyISAM.

3. If any of your tables requires support for transactions, make it an InnoDB table.

   Yes, again, transactions are discussed in the next chapter, but the storage engines ought to be determined now. Neither the *forums* nor *users* tables in the *forums* database will require transactions.

4. If neither of the above applies to a table, use the default storage engine.

   Table 6.7 identifies the storage engines to be used by the tables in the *forums* database.

TIP MySQL has several other table types, but MyISAM and InnoDB are the two most important, by far. The MEMORY type creates the table in memory, making it an extremely fast table but with absolutely no permanence.

TIP At the time of this writing, the MySQL documentation claims that the InnoDB table type is overall faster than MyISAM. There are some politics involved with the table types, so I take this claim with a grain of salt.

TABLE 6.7 The forum Database Table Types

Table	Table Type
forums	InnoDB
messages	MyISAM
users	InnoDB

To confirm what table types your MySQL installation supports, run this command (in the mysql client, here, or phpMyAdmin).

Languages and MySQL

Chapter 1, "Introduction to PHP," quickly introduced the concept of *encodings*. An HTML page or PHP script can specify its encoding, which dictates what characters, and therefore languages, are supported. The same is true for a MySQL database: by setting your database's encoding, you can impact what characters can be stored in it. To see a list of encodings supported by your version of MySQL, run a **SHOW CHARACTER SET** command **Ⓐ**. Note that the phrase *character set* is being used in MySQL to mean *encoding* (which I'll generally follow in this section to be consistent with MySQL).

Each character set in MySQL has one or more *collations*. Collation refers to the rules used for comparing characters in a set. It's like alphabetization, but takes into account numbers, spaces, and other characters as well. Collation is tied to the character set being used, reflecting both the kinds of characters present in that language and the cultural habits of people who generally use the language. For example, how text is sorted in English is not the same as it is in Traditional Spanish or in Arabic. Other considerations include: Are upper- and lowercase versions of a character considered to be the same or different (i.e., is it a case-sensitive comparison)? Or, how do accented characters get sorted? Is a space counted or ignored?

```
C:\Windows\system32\cmd.exe - C:\xampp\mysql\bin\mysql  -u root -p sitename

mysql> SHOW CHARACTER SET;
+----------+-----------------------------+--------------------+--------+
| Charset  | Description                 | Default collation  | Maxlen |
+----------+-----------------------------+--------------------+--------+
| big5     | Big5 Traditional Chinese    | big5_chinese_ci    |      2 |
| dec8     | DEC West European           | dec8_swedish_ci    |      1 |
| cp850    | DOS West European           | cp850_general_ci   |      1 |
| hp8      | HP West European            | hp8_english_ci     |      1 |
| koi8r    | KOI8-R Relcom Russian        | koi8r_general_ci   |      1 |
| latin1   | cp1252 West European        | latin1_swedish_ci  |      1 |
| latin2   | ISO 8859-2 Central European | latin2_general_ci  |      1 |
| swe7     | 7bit Swedish                | swe7_swedish_ci    |      1 |
| ascii    | US ASCII                    | ascii_general_ci   |      1 |
| ujis     | EUC-JP Japanese             | ujis_japanese_ci   |      3 |
| sjis     | Shift-JIS Japanese          | sjis_japanese_ci   |      2 |
| hebrew   | ISO 8859-8 Hebrew           | hebrew_general_ci  |      1 |
| tis620   | TIS620 Thai                 | tis620_thai_ci     |      1 |
| euckr    | EUC-KR Korean               | euckr_korean_ci    |      2 |
| koi8u    | KOI8-U Ukrainian            | koi8u_general_ci   |      1 |
| gb2312   | GB2312 Simplified Chinese   | gb2312_chinese_ci  |      2 |
| greek    | ISO 8859-7 Greek            | greek_general_ci   |      1 |
| cp1250   | Windows Central European    | cp1250_general_ci  |      1 |
| gbk      | GBK Simplified Chinese      | gbk_chinese_ci     |      2 |
| latin5   | ISO 8859-9 Turkish          | latin5_turkish_ci  |      1 |
| armscii8 | ARMSCII-8 Armenian          | armscii8_general_ci|      1 |
| utf8     | UTF-8 Unicode               | utf8_general_ci    |      3 |
| ucs2     | UCS-2 Unicode               | ucs2_general_ci    |      2 |
| cp866    | DOS Russian                 | cp866_general_ci   |      1 |
| keybcs2  | DOS Kamenicky Czech-Slovak  | keybcs2_general_ci |      1 |
| macce    | Mac Central European        | macce_general_ci   |      1 |
| macroman | Mac West European           | macroman_general_ci|      1 |
| cp852    | DOS Central European        | cp852_general_ci   |      1 |
| latin7   | ISO 8859-13 Baltic          | latin7_general_ci  |      1 |
| utf8mb4  | UTF-8 Unicode               | utf8mb4_general_ci |      4 |
| cp1251   | Windows Cyrillic            | cp1251_general_ci  |      1 |
| utf16    | UTF-16 Unicode              | utf16_general_ci   |      4 |
| cp1256   | Windows Arabic              | cp1256_general_ci  |      1 |
| cp1257   | Windows Baltic              | cp1257_general_ci  |      1 |
| utf32    | UTF-32 Unicode              | utf32_general_ci   |      4 |
| binary   | Binary pseudo charset       | binary             |      1 |
| geostd8  | GEOSTD8 Georgian            | geostd8_general_ci |      1 |
| cp932    | SJIS for Windows Japanese   | cp932_japanese_ci  |      2 |
| eucjpms  | UJIS for Windows Japanese   | eucjpms_japanese_ci|      3 |
+----------+-----------------------------+--------------------+--------+
39 rows in set (0.00 sec)
```

Ⓐ The list of character sets supported by this MySQL installation.

To view MySQL's available collations, run this query **B**, replacing *charset* with the proper value from the result in the last query **A**:

SHOW COLLATION LIKE 'charset%'

The results of this query will also indicate the default collation for that character set. The names of collations use a concluding *ci* to indicate case-insensitivity, *cs* for case-sensitivity, and *bin* for binary.

Generally speaking, I recommend using the UTF-8 character set, with its default collation. More importantly, *the character set in use by the database should match that of your PHP scripts*. If you're not using UTF-8 in your PHP scripts, use the matching encoding in the database. If the default collation doesn't adhere to the

conventions of the language primarily in use, then adjust the collation accordingly.

In MySQL, the server as a whole, each database, each table, and even every string column can have a defined character set and collation. To set these values when you create a database, use

CREATE DATABASE *name* **CHARACTER SET**
→ *charset* **COLLATE** *collation*

To set these values when you create a table, use

CREATE TABLE *name* **(**
column definitions
) CHARACTER SET *charset* **COLLATE**
→ *collation*

continues on next page

B The list of collations available in the UTF-8 character set. The first one, *utf_general_ci*, is the default.

To establish the character set and collation for a column, add the right clause to the column's definition (you'd only use this for text types):

```
CREATE TABLE name (
something TEXT CHARACTER SET charset
→ COLLATE collation
…)
```

In each of these cases, both clauses are optional. If omitted, a default character set or collation will be used.

Establishing the character set and collation when you define a database affects what data can be stored (e.g., you can't store a character in a column if its encoding doesn't support that character). A second issue is the encoding used to communicate with MySQL. If you want to store Chinese characters in a table with a Chinese encoding, those characters will need to be transferred using the same encoding. To do so within the mysql client, set the encoding using just

```
CHARSET charset
```

With phpMyAdmin, the encoding to be used is established in the application itself (i.e., written in the configuration file).

At this point in time, every aspect of the database design for the *forums* example has been covered, so let's create that database in MySQL, including its indexes, storage engines, character sets, and collations.

To assign character sets and collations:

1. Access MySQL using whatever client you prefer.

   Like the preceding chapter, this one will also use the mysql client for all of its examples. You are welcome to use phpMyAdmin or other tools as the interface to MySQL.

2. Create the *forum* database **C**:

   ```
   CREATE DATABASE forum
   CHARACTER SET utf8
   COLLATE utf8_general_ci;
   USE forum;
   ```

   Depending upon your setup, you may not be allowed to create your own databases. If not, just use the database provided to you and add the following tables to it. Note that in the **CREATE DATABASE** command, the character set and collation are also defined. By doing so at this point, every table will use those settings.

3. Create the *forums* table **D**:

   ```
   CREATE TABLE forums (
   forum_id TINYINT UNSIGNED NOT
   → NULL AUTO_INCREMENT,
   name VARCHAR(60) NOT NULL,
   PRIMARY KEY (forum_id),
   UNIQUE (name)
   ) ENGINE = INNODB;
   ```

```
mysql> CREATE DATABASE forum
    -> CHARACTER SET utf8
    -> COLLATE utf8_general_ci;
Query OK, 1 row affected (0.00 sec)

mysql> USE forum;
Database changed
mysql>
```

C The first steps are to create and select the database.

```
mysql> CREATE TABLE forums (
    -> forum_id TINYINT UNSIGNED NOT NULL AUTO_INCREMENT,
    -> name VARCHAR(60) NOT NULL,
    -> PRIMARY KEY (forum_id),
    -> UNIQUE (name)
    -> ) ENGINE = INNODB;
Query OK, 0 rows affected (0.04 sec)

mysql>
```

D Creating the first table.

It does not matter in what order you create your tables, but I'll make the *forums* table first. Remember that you can enter your SQL queries over multiple lines for convenience.

This table only contains two columns (which will happen frequently in a normalized database). Because I don't expect there to be many forums, the primary key is a really small type (**TINYINT**). If you wanted to add descriptions of each forum, a **VARCHAR(255)** or **TINYTEXT** column could be added to this table. This table uses the InnoDB storage engine.

4. Create the *messages* table 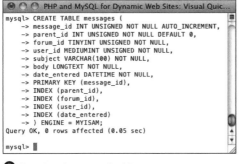:

```
CREATE TABLE messages (
message_id INT UNSIGNED NOT NULL
⇥ AUTO_INCREMENT,
parent_id INT UNSIGNED NOT NULL
⇥ DEFAULT 0,
forum_id TINYINT UNSIGNED NOT NULL,
user_id MEDIUMINT UNSIGNED NOT
⇥ NULL,
subject VARCHAR(100) NOT NULL,
body LONGTEXT NOT NULL,
date_entered DATETIME NOT NULL,
PRIMARY KEY (message_id),
INDEX (parent_id),
INDEX (forum_id),
```

```
INDEX (user_id),
INDEX (date_entered)
) ENGINE = MYISAM;
```

The primary key for this table has to be big, as it could have lots and lots of records. The three foreign key columns—*forum_id*, *parent_id*, and *user_id*—will all be the same size and type as their primary key counterparts. The subject is limited to 100 characters and the body of each message can be a lot of text. The *date_entered* field is a **DATETIME** type.

Unlike the other two tables, this one is of the MyISAM type.

5. Create the *users* table 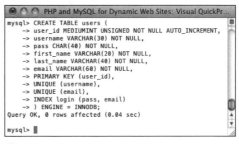:

```
CREATE TABLE users (
user_id MEDIUMINT UNSIGNED NOT
NULL AUTO_INCREMENT,
username VARCHAR(30) NOT NULL,
pass CHAR(40) NOT NULL,
first_name VARCHAR(20) NOT NULL,
last_name VARCHAR(40) NOT NULL,
email VARCHAR(60) NOT NULL,
PRIMARY KEY (user_id),
UNIQUE (username),
UNIQUE (email),
INDEX login (pass, email)
) ENGINE = INNODB;
```

continues on next page

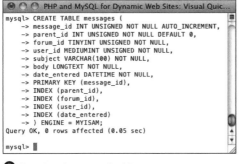

```
PHP and MySQL for Dynamic Web Sites: Visual Quic...
mysql> CREATE TABLE messages (
    -> message_id INT UNSIGNED NOT NULL AUTO_INCREMENT,
    -> parent_id INT UNSIGNED NOT NULL DEFAULT 0,
    -> forum_id TINYINT UNSIGNED NOT NULL,
    -> user_id MEDIUMINT UNSIGNED NOT NULL,
    -> subject VARCHAR(100) NOT NULL,
    -> body LONGTEXT NOT NULL,
    -> date_entered DATETIME NOT NULL,
    -> PRIMARY KEY (message_id),
    -> INDEX (parent_id),
    -> INDEX (forum_id),
    -> INDEX (user_id),
    -> INDEX (date_entered)
    -> ) ENGINE = MYISAM;
Query OK, 0 rows affected (0.05 sec)

mysql>
```

E Creating the second table.

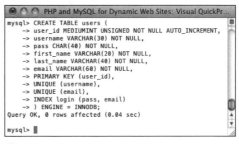

```
PHP and MySQL for Dynamic Web Sites: Visual QuickPr...
mysql> CREATE TABLE users (
    -> user_id MEDIUMINT UNSIGNED NOT NULL AUTO_INCREMENT,
    -> username VARCHAR(30) NOT NULL,
    -> pass CHAR(40) NOT NULL,
    -> first_name VARCHAR(20) NOT NULL,
    -> last_name VARCHAR(40) NOT NULL,
    -> email VARCHAR(60) NOT NULL,
    -> PRIMARY KEY (user_id),
    -> UNIQUE (username),
    -> UNIQUE (email),
    -> INDEX login (pass, email)
    -> ) ENGINE = INNODB;
Query OK, 0 rows affected (0.04 sec)

mysql>
```

F The database's third and final table.

Most of the columns here mimic those in the *sitename* database's *users* table, created in the preceding two chapters. The *pass* column is defined as **CHAR(40)**, because the **SHA1( )** function will be used and it always returns a string 40 characters long (see Chapter 5).

This table uses the InnoDB engine.

6. If desired, confirm the database's structure **G**:

```
SHOW TABLES;
SHOW COLUMNS FROM forums;
SHOW COLUMNS FROM messages;
SHOW COLUMNS FROM users;
```

The **SHOW** command reveals information about a database or a table. This step is optional because MySQL reports on the success of each query as it is entered. Still, it's always nice to remind yourself of a database's structure.

TIP Collations in MySQL can also be specified within a query, to affect the results:

```
SELECT … ORDER BY column COLLATE
→ collation
SELECT … WHERE column LIKE 'value'
→ COLLATE collation
```

TIP The CONVERT( ) function can convert text from one character set to another.

TIP You can change the default character set or collation for a database or table using an ALTER command, discussed in Chapter 7.

TIP Because different character sets require more space to represent a string, you will likely need to increase the size of a column for UTF-8 characters. Do this before changing a column's encoding so that no data is lost.

G Check the structure of any database or table using **SHOW**.

TABLE 6.8 UTC Offsets

City	Time
New York City, U.S.	UTC–4
Cape Town, South Africa	UTC+2
Mumbai, India	UTC+5:30
Auckland, New Zealand	UTC+13
Kathmandu, Nepal	UTC+5:45
Santiago, Chile	UTC–3
Dublin, Ireland	UTC+1

Time Zones and MySQL

Chapter 5 discussed how to use **NOW( )** and other date- and time-related functions. That chapter explained that these functions reflect the time on the server. Therefore, values stored in a database using these functions are also storing the server's time. That may not sound like a problem, but say you move your site from one server to another: you export all the data, import it into the other, and everything's fine… unless the two servers are in different time zones, in which case all of the dates are now technically off. For some sites, such an alteration wouldn't be a big deal, but what if your site features paid memberships? That means some people's membership might expire several hours early and for others, several hours late! At the end of the day, the goal of a database is to reliably store information.

The solution to this particular problem is to store dates and times in a time zone–neutral way. Doing so requires something called UTC (*Coordinated Universal Time*, and, yes, the abbreviation doesn't exactly match the term). UTC, like Greenwich Mean Time (GMT), provides a common point of origin, from which all times in the world can be expressed as UTC plus or minus some hours and minutes (**Table 6.8**).

Fortunately, you don't have to know these values or perform any calculations in order to determine UTC for your server. Instead, the **UTC_DATE( )** function returns the UTC date; **UTC_TIME( )** returns the current UTC time; and **UTC_TIMESTAMP( )** returns the current date and time.

continues on next page

Once you have stored a UTC time, you can retrieve the time adjusted to reflect the server's or the user's location. To change a date and time from any one time zone to another, use CONVERT_TZ( ) **A**:

CONVERT_TZ(*dt, from, to*)

The first argument is a date and time value, like the result of a function or what's stored in a column. The second and third arguments are named time zones. In order to use this function, the list of time zones must already be stored in MySQL, which may or may not be the case for your installation (see the sidebar). If you see **NULL** results **B**, check out the MySQL manual for how to install the time zones on your server.

To use this information, let's start populating the *forums* database, recording the message posted date and time using UTC.

```
C:\Windows\system32\cmd.exe - C:\xampp\mysql\bin\mysql  -u root -p sitename

mysql> SELECT CONVERT_TZ(UTC_TIMESTAMP(), 'UTC', 'America/New_York')
+---------------------------------------------------------------+
| CONVERT_TZ(UTC_TIMESTAMP(), 'UTC', 'America/New_York') |
+---------------------------------------------------------------+
| 2011-04-03 21:18:27                                           |
+---------------------------------------------------------------+
1 row in set (0.02 sec)

mysql>
```

A A conversion of the current UTC date and time to the American Eastern Daylight Time (EDT).

```
PHP and MySQL for Dynamic Web Sites: Visual QuickPro Guide
mysql> SELECT CONVERT_TZ(UTC_TIMESTAMP(), 'UTC', 'America/New_York');
+-------------------------------------------------------+
| CONVERT_TZ(UTC_TIMESTAMP(), 'UTC', 'America/New_York') |
+-------------------------------------------------------+
| NULL                                                  |
+-------------------------------------------------------+
1 row in set (0.00 sec)

mysql>
```

B The CONVERT_TZ( ) function will return NULL if it references an invalid time zone or if the time zones haven't been installed in MySQL (which is the case here).

To work with UTC:

1. Access the *forums* database using whatever client you prefer.

Like the preceding chapter, this one will also use the mysql client for all of its examples. You are welcome to use phpMyAdmin or other tools as the interface to MySQL.

2. If necessary, change the encoding to UTF-8 **C**:

CHARSET utf8;

Because the database uses UTF-8 as its character set, the communication with the database should use the same. This line, explained in the previous section of the chapter, does exactly that. Note that you only need to do this when using the mysql client. Also, if you're not using UTF-8, change the command accordingly.

3. Add some new records to the *forums* table **D**:

INSERT INTO forums (name) VALUES ('MySQL'), ('PHP'), ('Sports'), ('HTML'), ('CSS'), ('Kindling');

Since the *messages* table relies on values retrieved from both the *forums* and *users* tables, those two tables need to be populated first. With this **INSERT** command, only the *name* column must be provided a value (the table's *forum_id* column will be given an automatically incremented integer by MySQL).

4. Add some records to the *users* table **E**:

INSERT INTO users (username, pass, first_name, last_name, email) VALUES ('troutster', SHA1('mypass'), 'Larry', 'Ullman', 'lu@example.com'), ('funny man', SHA1('monkey'), 'David', 'Brent', 'db@example.com'), ('Gareth', SHA1('asstmgr'), 'Gareth', 'Keenan', 'gk@example.com');

If you have any questions on the **INSERT** syntax or use of the **SHA1( )** function here, see Chapter 5.

continues on next page

C The character set used to communicate with MySQL should match that used in the database.

D Adding records to the *forums* table.

E Adding records to the *users* table.

5. Add new records to the *messages* table **F**:

```
SELECT * FROM forums;
SELECT user_id, username FROM
→ users;
INSERT INTO messages (parent_id,
→ forum_id, user_id, subject,
→ body, date_entered) VALUES
(0, 1, 1, 'Question about
→ normalization.', 'I''m confused
→ about normalization. For the
→ second normal form (2NF), I
→ read...', UTC_TIMESTAMP( )),
(0, 1, 2, 'Database Design', 'I''m
→ creating a new database and am
→ having problems with the
→ structure. How many
→ tables should I have?...',
→ UTC_TIMESTAMP( )),
(2, 1, 2, 'Database Design', 'The
→ number of tables your database
→ includes...', UTC_TIMESTAMP( )),
(0, 1, 3, 'Database Design', 'Okay,
→ thanks!', UTC_TIMESTAMP( )),
(0, 2, 3, 'PHP Errors', 'I''m using
→ the scripts from Chapter 3 and
→ I can''t get the first calculator
→ example to work. When I submit
→ the form...', UTC_TIMESTAMP( ));
```

Because two of the fields in the *messages* table (*forum_id* and *user_id*) relate to values in other tables, you need to know those values before inserting new records into this table. For example, when the *troutster* user creates a new message in the *MySQL* forum, the **INSERT** will have a *forum_id* of 1 and a *user_id* of 1.

This is further complicated by the *parent_id* column, which should store the *message_id* to which the new message is a reply. The second message added to the database will have a *message_id* of 2, so replies to that message need a *parent_id* of 2.

F Populating the *messages* table requires knowing foreign key values from *users* and *forums*.

With your PHP scripts—once you've created an interface for this database, this process will be much easier, but it's important to comprehend the theory in SQL terms first.

For the *date_entered* field, the value returned by the **UTC_TIMESTAMP( )** function will be used. Using the **UTC_TIMESTAMP( )** function, the record will store the UTC date and time, not the date and time on the server.

6. Repeat Steps 1 through 3 to populate the database.

The rest of the examples in this chapter and the next will use the populated database. You'll probably want to download the SQL commands from the book's corresponding Web site,

although you can populate the tables with your own examples and then just change the queries in the rest of the chapter accordingly.

7. View the most recent record in the messages table, using the stored date and time **G**:

```
SELECT message_id, subject,
→ date_entered FROM messages
ORDER BY date_entered DESC LIMIT 1;
```

As you can see in the figure and the table definition, UTC times are stored just the same as non-UTC times. What's not obvious in the figure is that the record just inserted reflects a time four hours ahead of the server (because my particular server is in a time zone four hours behind UTC).

continues on next page

G The record that was just inserted, which reflects a time four hours ahead (the server is UTC-4).

8. Retrieve the same record converting the *date_entered* to your time zone **H**:

```
SELECT message_id, subject,
CONVERT_TZ(date_entered, 'UTC',
→ 'America/New_York') AS local
FROM messages ORDER BY
→ date_entered DESC LIMIT 1;
```

Using the **CONVERT_TZ( )** function, you can convert any date and time to a different time zone. For the *from* time zone, use *UTC*. For the *to* time zone, use yours.

If you get a **NULL** result **B**, either the name of one of your time zones is wrong or MySQL hasn't had its time zones loaded yet (see the sidebar).

TIP However you decide to handle dates, the key is to be consistent. If you decide to use UTC, then *always* use UTC.

TIP UTC is also known as Zulu time, represented by the letter *Z*.

TIP Besides being time zone and daylight saving time agnostic, UTC is also more accurate. It factors in irregular leap seconds that compensate for the inexact movement of the planet.

```
C:\Windows\system32\cmd.exe - C:\xampp\mysql\bin\mysql -u root -p sitena...

mysql> SELECT message_id, subject,
    -> CONVERT_TZ(date_entered, 'UTC', 'America/New_York') AS local
    -> FROM messages ORDER BY date_entered DESC LIMIT 1;
+------------+---------+---------------------+
| message_id | subject | local               |
+------------+---------+---------------------+
|         21 | Because | 2011-04-03 21:37:27 |
+------------+---------+---------------------+
1 row in set (0.00 sec)

mysql> _
```

H The UTC-stored date and time converted to my local time.

Foreign Key Constraints

A feature of the InnoDB table type, not supported in other storage engines, is the ability to apply *foreign key constraints*. When you have related tables, the foreign key in Table B relates to the primary key in Table A (for ease of understanding, it may help to think of Table B as the child to Table A's parent). For example, in the *forums* database, the *messages.user_id* is tied to *users.user_id*. If the administrator were to delete a user account, the relationship between those tables would be broken (because the *messages* table would have records with a *user_id* value that doesn't exist in *users*). Foreign key constraints set rules as to what should happen when a break would occur, including preventing that break.

The syntax for creating a foreign key constraint is:

FOREIGN KEY (*item_name*) REFERENCES
→ *table* (*column*)

(This goes within a **CREATE TABLE** or **ALTER TABLE** statement.)

The item name is the foreign key column in the current table. The *table(column)* clause is a reference to the parent table column to which this foreign key should be constrained. If you just use the above, thereby only identifying the relationship, without stating what should happen when the constraint would be broken, MySQL will throw an error if you attempt to delete the parent record while child records exist . MySQL will also throw an error if you attempt to create a child record using a parent ID that doesn't exist **B**.

You can dictate what alternative actions should occur by following the above syntax with one or both of these:

ON DELETE *action*
ON UPDATE *action*

There are five action options, but two—**RESTRICT** and **NO ACTION**—are synonymous and also the default (i.e., the same as if you don't specify the action at all). A third action option—**SET DEFAULT**—doesn't work (don't ask me, ask the MySQL manual!). That leaves **CASCADE** and **SET NULL**. If the action set is **SET NULL**, the removal of a parent record will result in setting the corresponding foreign keys in the child table to **NULL**. If that table defines that column as **NOT NULL** (which it almost always should), deletion of the parent record will trigger an error.

continues on next page

```
● ○ ○    PHP and MySQL for Dynamic Web Sites: Visual QuickPr...
mysql> DELETE FROM parent WHERE parent_id=1;
ERROR 1451 (23000): Cannot delete or update a parent row: a
 foreign key constraint fails (`test`.`child`, CONSTRAINT `
child_ibfk_1` FOREIGN KEY (`parent_id`) REFERENCES `parent`
 (`parent_id`))
mysql>
```

A This error indicates that MySQL is preventing a query from deleting a parent record because the record is constrained to one or more existing children records.

```
● ○ ○    PHP and MySQL for Dynamic Web Sites: Visual QuickPro Guide
mysql> INSERT INTO child
    -> (child_id, parent_id)
    -> VALUES (NULL, 20934);
ERROR 1452 (23000): Cannot add or update a child row: a foreign
key constraint fails (`test`.`child`, CONSTRAINT `child_ibfk_1`
FOREIGN KEY (`parent_id`) REFERENCES `parent` (`parent_id`))
mysql>
```

B Foreign key constraints also affect **INSERT** queries.

The **CASCADE** action is the most useful option. It tells the database to apply the same changes to the related table. With this instruction, if you delete the parent record, MySQL will also delete the child records with that parent ID as its foreign key.

As only the InnoDB table type supports foreign key constraints, both tables in the relationship must be of the InnoDB type. Also, in order for MySQL to be able to compare the foreign key-primary key values, the related columns must be of equitable types. This means that numeric columns must be the same type and size; text columns must use the same character set and collation.

With the *forums* example, it's not possible to use foreign key constraints as the sole table related to another—*messages* relates to both *forums* and *users*—must use the MyISAM table type (to support **FULLTEXT** searches). Instead, let's take a look at a new hypothetical example for banking .

The *customers* table stores all of the information particular to a customer. It would logically also store contact information and so forth. The *accounts* table stores the accounts for each customer, including the type (Checking or Savings) and balance. Each customer may have more than one account, but each account is associated with only one customer (for a bit of simplicity). In the real world, the table might also store the date the account was opened and use a **BIGINT** as the balance (thereby representing all transactions in cents instead of dollars with decimals). Finally, the *transactions* table stores every movement of money from one account to another. Again, to make the example a bit easier to follow, the example assumes that only accounts within this same system will interact. Note that the *transactions* table has two one-to-many relationships with *accounts* (not one many-to-many). Each transaction's *to_account_id* value will be associated with a single account, but each account could be the "to" account multiple times. The same applies to the "from" account. Finally, foreign key constraints are applied to preserve the integrity of the data.

In this next series of steps, you'll create and populate this database, paying attention to the constraints. In the next chapter, this same database will be used to demonstrate transactions and encryption.

C The *banking* database could be used for virtual banking.

To create foreign key constraints:

1. Access MySQL using whatever client you prefer.

   Like the preceding chapter, this one will also use the mysql client for all of its examples. You are welcome to use phpMyAdmin or other tools as the interface to MySQL.

2. Create the *banking* database **D**:

   ```
   CREATE DATABASE banking
   CHARACTER SET utf8
   COLLATE utf8_general_ci;
   USE banking;
   ```

   As always, depending upon your setup, you may not be allowed to create your own databases. If not, just use the database provided to you and add the following tables to it.

3. If necessary, change the communication encoding to UTF-8:

   ```
   CHARSET utf8;
   ```

4. Create the *customers* table **E**:

   ```
   CREATE TABLE customers (
   customer_id INT UNSIGNED NOT NULL
   → AUTO_INCREMENT,
   first_name VARCHAR(20) NOT NULL,
   last_name VARCHAR(40) NOT NULL,
   PRIMARY KEY (customer_id),
   INDEX full_name (last_name,
   → first_name)
   ) ENGINE = INNODB;
   ```

   The *customers* table just stores the customer's ID—the primary key—and name (in two columns). An index is also placed on the full name, in case that might be used in **ORDER BY** and other query clauses. So that the database can use foreign key constraints, every table will use the InnoDB storage engine.

   continues on next page

D A new database is being created for this example.

E Creating the *customers* table.

5. Create the *accounts* table **F**:

```
CREATE TABLE accounts (
account_id INT UNSIGNED NOT NULL
→ AUTO_INCREMENT,
customer_id INT UNSIGNED NOT NULL,
type ENUM('Checking', 'Savings')
→ NOT NULL,
balance DECIMAL(10,2) UNSIGNED NOT
→ NULL DEFAULT 0.0,
PRIMARY KEY (account_id),
INDEX (customer_id),
FOREIGN KEY (customer_id) REFERENCES
→ customers (customer_id)
ON DELETE NO ACTION ON UPDATE NO
→ ACTION
) ENGINE = INNODB;
```

The *accounts* table stores the account ID, customer ID, account type, and balance. The *customer_id* column has an index on it, as it will be used in **JOIN**s (in Chapter 7). More importantly, the column is constrained to *customers. customer_id*, thereby protecting both tables. Even though **NO ACTION** is the default constraint, I've included it in the definition for added clarity.

F Creating the *accounts* table.

6. Create the *transactions* table **G**:

```
CREATE TABLE transactions (
transaction_id INT UNSIGNED NOT
→ NULL AUTO_INCREMENT,
to_account_id INT UNSIGNED NOT
→ NULL,
from_account_id INT UNSIGNED NOT
→ NULL,
amount DECIMAL(5,2) UNSIGNED NOT
→ NULL,
date_entered TIMESTAMP NOT NULL,
PRIMARY KEY (transaction_id),
INDEX (to_account_id),
INDEX (from_account_id),
INDEX (date_entered),
```

```
FOREIGN KEY (to_account_id)
→ REFERENCES accounts (account_id)
ON DELETE NO ACTION ON UPDATE NO
→ ACTION,
FOREIGN KEY (from_account_id)
→ REFERENCES accounts (account_id)
ON DELETE NO ACTION ON UPDATE NO
→ ACTION
) ENGINE = INNODB;
```

The final table will be used to record all movements of monies among the accounts. To do so, it stores both account IDs—the "to" and "from," the amount, and the date/time. Indexes are added accordingly, and both account IDs are constrained to the *accounts* table.

continues on next page

G Creating the third, and final, table: *transactions*.

7. Populate the customers and accounts tables :

```
INSERT INTO customers (first_name,
→ last_name)
VALUES ('Sarah', 'Vowell'),
→ ('David', 'Sedaris'), ('Kojo',
→ 'Nnamdi');
INSERT INTO accounts (customer_id,
→ balance)
VALUES (1, 5460.23), (2, 909325.24),
→ (3, 892.00);
```

First, sample data is entered into the first two tables (the third will be used in the next chapter). Note that because the *accounts.type* column is defined as an **ENUM NOT NULL**, if no value is provided for that column, the first item in the **ENUM** definition—*Checking*—will be used.

8. Attempt to put data into the *accounts* table for which there is no customer :

```
INSERT INTO accounts (customer_id,
→ type, balance)
VALUES (10, 'Savings', 200.00);
```

The foreign key constraint present in the *accounts* table will prevent an account being created without a valid customer ID (a pretty useful check in the real world).

C:\Windows\system32\cmd.exe - C:\xampp\mysql\bin\mysql -u root -p sitename

```
mysql> INSERT INTO customers (first_name, last_name)
    -> VALUES ('Sarah', 'Vowell'), ('David', 'Sedaris'), ('Kojo', 'Nnamdi');
Query OK, 3 rows affected (0.08 sec)
Records: 3  Duplicates: 0  Warnings: 0

mysql> INSERT INTO accounts (customer_id, balance)
    -> VALUES (1, 5460.23), (2, 909325.24), (3, 892.00);
Query OK, 3 rows affected (0.00 sec)
Records: 3  Duplicates: 0  Warnings: 0

mysql> _
```

H Three records are added to both the *customers* and *accounts* tables.

PHP and MySQL for Dynamic Web Sites: Visual QuickPro Guide

```
mysql> INSERT INTO accounts (customer_id, type, balance)
    -> VALUES (10, 'Savings', 200.00);
ERROR 1452 (23000): Cannot add or update a child row: a foreign key
constraint fails (`banking`.`accounts`, CONSTRAINT `accounts_ibfk_1`
 FOREIGN KEY (`customer_id`) REFERENCES `customers` (`customer_id`)
ON DELETE NO ACTION ON UPDATE NO ACTION)
mysql>
```

I Again, as in **B**, the constraint denies the **INSERT** query due to an invalid value from the parent table.

9. Attempt to delete a record from the *customers* table for which there is an *accounts* record :

```
DELETE FROM customers
WHERE customer_id=2;
```

The constraint will also prevent the deletion of customer records when that customer still has an account.

Despite the constraint, you could still delete a customer record if the customer does not have any records in the *accounts* table.

TIP To actually delete constrained records, you must first delete all the children records, and then the parent record.

TIP Foreign key constraints require that all columns in the constraint be indexed. Normal database design would suggest this is the case, but if the correct indexes do not exist, MySQL will create them when the constraint is defined.

TIP Similar to constraints are *triggers*. Simply put, a trigger is a way of telling the database "when X happens to this table, do Y." For example, when inserting a record in Table A, another record might be created or updated in Table B. See the MySQL manual for more on triggers.

```
● ○ ○          PHP and MySQL for Dynamic Web Sites: Visual QuickPro Guide
mysql> DELETE FROM customers
    -> WHERE customer_id=2;
ERROR 1451 (23000): Cannot delete or update a parent row: a foreign key constraint fails (
`banking`.`accounts`, CONSTRAINT `accounts_ibfk_1` FOREIGN KEY (`customer_id`) REFERENCES
`customers` (`customer_id`) ON DELETE NO ACTION ON UPDATE NO ACTION)
mysql>
```

J Because the customer with an ID of 2 has one or more records in the *accounts* table, the *customers* record cannot be deleted.

Review and Pursue

If you have any problems with the review questions or the pursue prompts, turn to the book's supporting forum (www.LarryUllman.com/forums/).

Review

- Why is normalization important?

- What are the two types of keys?

- What are the three types of table relationships?

- How do you fix the problem of a many-to-many relationship between two tables?

- What are the four types of indexes? What general types of columns *should* be indexed? What general types of columns *should not* be indexed?

- What are the two most common MySQL table types? What is the default table type for your MySQL installation?

- What is a *character set*? What is a *collation*? What impact does the character set have on the database? What impact does the collation have? What character set and collation are you using?

- What is *UTC*? How do you find the UTC time in MySQL? How do you convert from UTC to another time zone's time?

- What are *foreign key constraints*? What table type supports foreign key constraints?

Pursue

- You may want to consider downloading, installing, and learning to use the MySQL Workbench application. It can be quite useful.

- If you don't fully grasp the process of normalization—and that's perfectly understandable—search for additional tutorials online or ask a question in my support forums.

- Design your own database using the information presented here.

Advanced SQL and MySQL

This, the last chapter dedicated to SQL and MySQL (although most of the rest of the book will use these technologies in some form or another), discusses the higher-end concepts often needed to work with more complicated databases, like those created in the previous chapter. The first such topic is the **JOIN**, a critical SQL term for querying normalized databases with multiple tables. From there, the chapter introduces a category of functions that are specifically used when grouping query results, followed by more complex ways to select values from a table.

In the middle of the chapter, you'll learn how to perform **FULLTEXT** searches, which can add search engine-like functionality to any site. Next up is the **EXPLAIN** command: it provides a way to test the efficiency of your database schema and your queries. The chapter concludes with coverage of transactions and database encryption.

In This Chapter

Performing Joins

Because relational databases are more complexly structured, they sometimes require special query statements to retrieve the information you need most. For example, if you wanted to know what messages are in the *MySQL* forum (using the *forum* database created in the previous chapter), you would need to first find the *forum_id* for *MySQL*:

```
SELECT forum_id FROM forums WHERE
→ name='MySQL'
```

Then you would use that number to retrieve all the records from the *messages* table that have that *forum_id*:

```
SELECT * FROM messages WHERE
→ forum_id=1
```

This one simple (and, in a forum, often necessary) task would require two separate queries. By using a *join,* you can accomplish all of that in one fell swoop.

A join is an SQL query that uses two or more tables, and produces a virtual table of results. Any time you need to simultaneously retrieve information from more than one table, a join is what you'll probably use.

Joins can be written in many different ways, but the basic syntax is:

```
SELECT what_columns FROM tableA
→ JOIN_TYPE tableB JOIN_CLAUSE
```

Because joins involve multiple tables, the *what_columns* can include columns in any named table. And as joins often return so much information, it's normally best to specify exactly what columns you want returned, instead of selecting them all.

When selecting from multiple tables, you must use the dot syntax (*table.column*) if the tables named in the query have columns with the same name. This is often the case when dealing with relational databases because a primary key from one table may have the same name as a foreign key in another. If you are not explicit when referencing your columns, you'll get an error **Ⓐ**:

```
SELECT forum_id FROM messages INNER
→ JOIN
forums ON messages.forum_id=forums.
→ forum_id
```

The two main types of joins are *inner* and *outer* (there are subtypes within both). As you'll see with outer joins, the order in which you reference the tables does matter.

The join clause is where you indicate the relationship between the joined tables. For example, *forums.forum_id* should equal *messages.forum_id* (as in the above).

You can also use **WHERE** and **ORDER BY** clauses with a join, as you would with any **SELECT** query.

As a last note, before getting into joins more specifically, the SQL concept of an *alias*—introduced in Chapter 5, "Introduction to SQL"—will come in handy when writing joins. Often an alias will just be used as a shorthand way of referencing the same table multiple times within the same query. If you don't recall the syntax for creating aliases, or how they're used, revisit that part of Chapter 5.

```
⬤ ⬤ ◯   PHP and MySQL for Dynamic Web Sites: Visual QuickPro Guide
mysql>
mysql> SELECT forum_id FROM messages INNER JOIN
    -> forums ON messages.forum_id=forums.forum_id;
ERROR 1052 (23000): Column 'forum_id' in field list is ambiguous
mysql> ▮
```

Ⓐ Generically referring to a column name present in multiple tables will cause an ambiguity error.

```
mysql> SELECT m.message_id, m.subject, f.name
    -> FROM messages AS m INNER JOIN forums AS f
    -> ON m.forum_id = f.forum_id
    -> WHERE f.name = 'MySQL';
+------------+-------------------------------+--------+
| message_id | subject                       | name   |
+------------+-------------------------------+--------+
|          1 | Question about normalization. | MySQL  |
|          2 | Database Design               | MySQL  |
|          3 | Database Design               | MySQL  |
|          4 | Database Design               | MySQL  |
+------------+-------------------------------+--------+
4 rows in set (0.00 sec)

mysql>
```

B This join returns three columns from two tables where the *forum_id* value—1—represents the *MySQL* forum.

(As in the previous two chapters, this chapter will use the command-line mysql client to execute queries, but you can also use phpMyAdmin or another tool. The chapter assumes you know how to connect to the MySQL server and declare the character set to use, if necessary.)

Inner Joins

An inner join returns all of the records from the named tables wherever a match is made. For example, to find every message posted in the *MySQL* forum, the inner join would be written as **B**

```
SELECT m.message_id, m.subject, f.name
FROM messages AS m INNER JOIN forums
→ AS f
ON m.forum_id = f.forum_id
WHERE f.name = 'MySQL'
```

This join is selecting three columns from the *messages* table (aliased as *m*) and one column from the *forums* table (aliased as *f*) under two conditions. First, the *f.name* column must have a value of *MySQL* (this will return the *forum_id* of 1). Second, the *forum_id* value in the *forums* table must match the *forum_id* value in the *messages* table. Because of the equality comparison being made across both tables (**m.forum_id = f.forum_id**), this is known as an *equijoin*.

As an alternative syntax, if the column in both tables being used in the equality comparison has the same name, you can simplify your query with **USING**:

```
SELECT m.message_id, m.subject, f.name
FROM messages AS m INNER JOIN forums
→ AS f
USING (forum_id)
WHERE f.name = 'MySQL'
```

To use inner joins:

1. Connect to MySQL and select the *forum* database.

2. Retrieve the forum name and message subject for every record in the *messages* table **ⓒ**:

   ```
   SELECT f.name, m.subject FROM forums
   AS f INNER JOIN messages AS m
   USING (forum_id) ORDER BY f.name;
   ```

   This query will effectively replace the *forum_id* value in the *messages* table with the corresponding *name* value from the *forums* table for each of the records in the *messages* table. The end result is that it displays the textual version of the forum name for each message subject.

   Notice that you can still use **ORDER BY** clauses in joins.

3. Retrieve the subject and date entered for every message posted by the user *funny man* **ⓓ**:

   ```
   SELECT m.subject,
   DATE_FORMAT(m.date_entered,
   → '%M %D, %Y') AS Date
   FROM users AS u
   INNER JOIN messages AS m
   USING (user_id)
   WHERE u.username = 'funny man';
   ```

   This join also uses two tables: *users* and *messages*. The linking column for the two tables is *user_id*, so that's placed in the **USING** clause. The **WHERE** conditional identifies the user being targeted, and the **DATE_FORMAT( )** function will help format the *date_entered* value.

ⓒ A basic inner join that returns only two columns of values.

ⓓ A slightly more complicated version of an inner join, based upon the *users* and *messages* tables.

E An **ORDER BY** clause and a **LIMIT** clause are applied to this join, which returns the forums with the five most recent messages.

4. Find the forums that have had the five most recent postings **E**:

```
SELECT f.name FROM forums AS f
INNER JOIN messages AS m
USING (forum_id)
ORDER BY m.date_entered DESC
→ LIMIT 5;
```

Since the only information that needs to be returned is the forum name, that's the sole column selected by this query. The join is then across the *forums* and *messages* table, linked via the *forum_id*. The query to that point would return every message matched with the forum it's in. That result is then ordered by the *date_entered* column, in descending order, and restricted to just the first five records.

TIP Inner joins can also be written without formally using the phrase INNER JOIN. To do so, place a comma between the table names and turn the ON, or USING, clause into another WHERE condition:

```
SELECT m.message_id, m.subject,
→ f.name FROM messages AS m, forums
→ AS f WHERE m.forum_id = f.forum_id
AND f.name = 'MySQL'
```

TIP Joins that do not include a join clause (ON or USING) or a WHERE clause (e.g., SELECT * FROM urls INNER JOIN url_associations) are called *full* joins and will return every record from both tables. This construct can have unwieldy results with larger tables.

TIP A NULL value in a column referenced in an inner join will never be returned, because NULL matches no other value, including NULL.

TIP MySQL's supported join types differ slightly from the SQL standard. For example, SQL supports a CROSS JOIN and an INNER JOIN as two separate things, but in MySQL they are syntactically the same.

Outer Joins

Whereas an inner join returns records based upon making matches between two tables, an *outer* join will return records that are matched by both tables, *and will return records that don't match*. In other words, an inner join is exclusive but an outer join is inclusive. There are three outer join subtypes: *left*, *right*, and *full*, with left being the most important by far. An example of a left join is:

```
SELECT f.*, m.subject FROM forums AS f
LEFT JOIN messages AS m
ON f.forum_id = m.forum_id
```

The most important consideration with left joins is which table gets named first. In this example, all of the *forums* records will be returned along with all of the *messages* information, if a match is made. If no *messages* records match a *forums* row, then **NULL** values will be returned for the selected *messages* columns instead **F**.

As with an inner join, if the column in both tables being used in the equality comparison has the same name, you can simplify your query with **USING**:

```
SELECT f.*, m.subject FROM forums AS f
LEFT JOIN messages AS m
USING (forum_id)
```

A right outer join does the opposite of a left outer join: it returns all of the applicable records from the right-hand table, along with matches from the left-hand table. This query is equivalent to the above:

```
SELECT f.*, m.subject FROM messages
→ AS m
RIGHT JOIN forums AS f
USING (forum_id)
```

Generally speaking, the left join is preferred over the right (and, arguably, there's no need to have both).

A full outer join is like a combination of a left outer join and a right outer join. In other words, all of the matching records from

```
C:\Windows\system32\cmd.exe - C:\xampp\mysql\bin\mysql  -u root -p

mysql> SELECT f.*, m.subject FROM forums AS f
    -> LEFT JOIN messages AS m
    -> ON f.forum_id = m.forum_id;
+----------+--------------+-----------------------------------+
| forum_id | name         | subject                           |
+----------+--------------+-----------------------------------+
|        5 | CSS          | CSS Resources                     |
|        5 | CSS          | CSS Resources                     |
|        4 | HTML         | HTML vs. XHTML                    |
|        4 | HTML         | HTML vs. XHTML                    |
|        6 | Kindling     | Why?                              |
|        6 | Kindling     | Why? Why? Why?                    |
|        6 | Kindling     | Because                           |
|        7 | Modern Dance | NULL                              |
|        1 | MySQL        | Question about normalization.     |
|        1 | MySQL        | Database Design                   |
|        1 | MySQL        | Database Design                   |
|        1 | MySQL        | Database Design                   |
|        2 | PHP          | PHP Errors                        |
|        2 | PHP          | PHP Errors                        |
|        2 | PHP          | PHP Errors                        |
|        2 | PHP          | PHP Errors                        |
|        2 | PHP          | Dynamic HTML using PHP            |
|        2 | PHP          | Dynamic HTML using PHP            |
|        2 | PHP          | Dynamic HTML using PHP, still not clear |
|        2 | PHP          | Dynamic HTML using PHP, clearer? |
|        3 | Sports       | Chicago Bulls                     |
|        3 | Sports       | Chicago Bulls                     |
+----------+--------------+-----------------------------------+
22 rows in set (0.00 sec)

mysql>
```

F An outer join returns all the records from the first table listed, with non-matching records from the second table replaced with **NULL** values.

G This left join returns for every user, every posted message ID. If a user hasn't posted a message (like *finchy* at the top), the message ID value will be **NULL**.

H This inner join will not return any users who haven't yet posted messages (see *finchy* at the top of **G**).

both tables will be returned, along with all of the records from the left-hand table that do not have matches in the right-hand table, along with all of the records from the right-hand table that do not have matches in the left-hand table. MySQL does not directly support the full outer join, but you can replicate that functionality using a left join, a right join, and a **UNION** statement. A full outer join is not often needed, but see the MySQL manual if you're curious about it or *unions*.

To use outer joins:

1. Connect to MySQL and select the *forum* database, if you have not already.

2. Retrieve every username and every message ID posted by that user **G**:

```
SELECT u.username, m.message_id
FROM users AS u
LEFT JOIN messages AS m
USING (user_id);
```

If you were to run an inner join similar to this, a user who had not yet posted a message would not be listed **H**. Hence, an outer join is required to be inclusive of all users. Note that the fully included table (here, *users*), must be the first table listed in a left join.

continues on next page

3. Retrieve every forum name and every message submission date in that forum in order of submission date 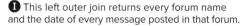:

```
SELECT f.name,
DATE_FORMAT(m.date_entered,
→'%M %D, Y') AS Date
FROM forums AS f
LEFT JOIN messages AS m
USING (forum_id)
ORDER BY date_entered DESC;
```

This is really just a variation on the join in Step 2, this time swapping the *forums* table for the *users* table.

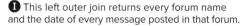

I This left outer join returns every forum name and the date of every message posted in that forum.

Performing Self-Joins

It's possible with SQL to perform a *self-join*: join a table with itself. For example, with the *messages* table, the *parent_id* column is a way of indicating which postings are replies to other postings. To retrieve a single hierarchy of postings, a **SELECT** query must join the *messages* table with itself, equating *parent_id* with *message_id* in the process.

This may sound confusing or impossible, but it's really not. The trick with self-joins is to treat the two references to the same table as if they were single references to two different tables. To pull that off, assign a different alias to each table reference. The already described example would be written like so:

```
SELECT m1.subject, m2.subject AS Reply FROM messages AS m1 LEFT JOIN
→messages AS m2 ON m1.message_id=m2.parent_id WHERE m1.parent_id=0
```

That query first selects every root-level message—those with a 0 *parent_id* value—in the first *messages* table instance, *m1*. Those records are then outer joined with the second *messages* table instance, *m2*. If you run this query yourself, you'll see that the root message's subject is selected, along with the subject of that message's reply, if applicable.

Self-joins aren't the most popular join type, but can sometimes solve a problem better than most other solutions.

TIP Joins can be created using conditionals involving any columns, not just the primary and foreign keys, although that's the most common basis for comparison.

TIP You can perform joins across multiple databases using the *database.table.column* syntax, as long as every database is on the same server (you cannot do this across a network) and you're connected as a user with permission to access every database involved.

TIP The word *OUTER* in a left outer join is optional and often omitted. To be formal, you could write:

```
SELECT f.name, DATE_FORMAT
→ (m.date_entered, '%M %D, Y') AS
→ Date FROM forums AS f LEFT OUTER
→ JOIN messages AS m USING (forum_id)
→ ORDER BY date_entered DESC;
```

Joining Three or More Tables

Joins are a somewhat complicated but important concept, so hopefully you're following along well enough thus far. There are two more ways joins can be used with which you ought to be familiar: *self-joins*, discussed in the sidebar, and joins on three or more tables.

When joining three or more tables, it helps to remember that a join between two tables creates a virtual table of results. When you add a third table, the join is between this initial virtual table and the third referenced table **J**. The syntax for a three-table join is of the format

```
SELECT what_columns FROM tableA
→ JOIN_TYPE tableB JOIN_CLAUSE
→ JOIN_TYPE tableC JOIN_CLAUSE
```

continues on next page

users

user_id	username
1	troutster
2	funny man
3	Gareth
4	tim
5	finchy

messages

message_id	forum_id	user_id	subject
1	1	1	faa
2	1	2	fee
3	1	2	fii
4	1	3	foo
5	2	3	fuu

JOIN virtual table

username	forum_id	subject
troutster	1	faa
funny man	1	fee
Gareth	1	fii
tim	1	foo
finchy	2	fuu

forums

forum_id	name
1	MySQL
2	PHP
3	Sports
4	HTML
5	CSS

JOIN virtual table

username	name	subject
troutster	MySQL	faa
funny man	MySQL	fee
Gareth	MySQL	fii
tim	MySQL	foo
finchy	PHP	fuu

J How a join across three tables works: by first creating a virtual table of results, and then by joining the third table to that.

The join types do not have to be the same in both cases—one could be an inner and the other an outer—and the join clauses are almost certain to be different. You can even add **WHERE**, **ORDER BY**, and **LIMIT** clauses to the end of this. Simply put, to perform a join on more than two tables, just continue to add *JOIN_TYPE tableX JOIN_CLAUSE* sections as needed.

There are three likely problems you'll have with joins that span three or more tables. The first is a simple syntax error, especially when you use parentheses to separate out the clauses. The second is an ambiguous column error, which is common enough among any join type. The third likely problem will be a lack of results returned. Should that happen to you, simplify the join down to just two tables to confirm the result, and then try to reapply the additional join clauses to find where the problem is.

To use joins on three tables or more:

1. Connect to MySQL and select the *forum* database, if you have not already.

2. Retrieve the message ID, subject, and forum name for every message posted by the user *troutster* **K**:

```
SELECT m.message_id, m.subject,
→ f.name
FROM users AS u
INNER JOIN messages AS m
USING (user_id)
INNER JOIN forums AS f
USING (forum_id)
WHERE u.username = 'troutster';
```

This join is similar to one earlier in the chapter, but takes things a step further by incorporating a third table.

K An inner join across all three tables.

3. Retrieve the username, message subject, and forum name for every user **L**:

```
SELECT u.username, m.subject, f.name
FROM users AS u
LEFT JOIN messages AS m
USING (user_id)
LEFT JOIN forums AS f
USING (forum_id);
```

Whereas the query in Step 2 performs two inner joins, this one performs two outer joins. The process behind this query is visually represented by the diagram in **J**.

4. Find the users that have had the five most recent postings, while also selecting the message subject, and the forum name **M**:

```
SELECT u.username, m.subject, f.name
FROM users AS u
INNER JOIN messages AS m
USING (user_id)
INNER JOIN forums AS f
USING (forum_id)
ORDER BY m.date_entered DESC
LIMIT 5;
```

In order to retrieve the username, the message subject, and the forum name, a join across all three tables is required. As the query is only looking for users that have posted, an inner join is appropriate. The result of the two joins will be every username, with every message they posted, in every forum. That result is then ordered by the message's *date_entered* column, and limited to just the first five records.

L This left join returns for every user, every posted message subject, and every forum name. If a user hasn't posted a message (like *finchy* at the top), his or her subject and forum name values will be **NULL**.

M This inner join returns values from all three tables, with applied **ORDER BY** and **LIMIT** clauses.

Grouping Selected Results

Chapter 5 discussed and demonstrated several different categories of functions one can use in MySQL. Another category, used for more complex queries, are the *grouping* or *aggregate* functions (**Table 7.1**).

Whereas most of the functions covered in Chapter 5 manipulate a single value in a single row at a time (e.g., formatting the value in a date column), what the grouping functions return is based upon a value present in a single column over a set of rows. For example, to find the average account balance in the *banking* database, you would run this query **A**:

```
SELECT AVG(balance) FROM accounts
```

To find the smallest and largest account balances, use **B**:

```
SELECT MAX(balance), MIN(balance)
→ FROM accounts
```

To simply count the number of records in a table (or result set), apply **COUNT( )** to either every column or every column that's guaranteed to have a value:

```
SELECT COUNT(*) FROM accounts
```

TABLE 7.1 Grouping Functions

Function	Returns
AVG( )	The average of the values in a column.
COUNT( )	The number of values in a column.
GROUP_CONCAT( )	The concatenation of a column's values.
MAX( )	The largest value in a column.
MIN( )	The smallest value in a column.
SUM( )	The sum of all the values in a column.

A The **AVG( )** function is used to find the average of all the account balances.

B The **MAX( )** and **MIN( )** functions return the largest and smallest account values found in the table.

C The **COUNT( )** function, with or without the **DISTINCT** keyword, simply counts the number of records in a record set.

D Use the **GROUP BY** clause with an aggregating function to group the aggregate results.

The **AVG( )**, **COUNT( )**, and **SUM( )** functions can also use the **DISTINCT** keyword so that the aggregation only applies to distinct values. For example, **SELECT COUNT(customer_id) FROM accounts** will return the number of accounts, but **SELECT COUNT(DISTINCT customer_ID) FROM accounts** will return the number of customers that have accounts **C**.

The aggregate functions as used on their own return individual values (as in **A**, **B**, and **C**). When the aggregate functions are used with a **GROUP BY** clause, a single aggregate value will be returned for each row in the result set **D**:

SELECT AVG(balance), customer_id FROM
→ accounts GROUP BY customer_id

You can apply combinations of **WHERE**, **ORDER BY**, and **LIMIT** conditions to a **GROUP BY**, structuring your query like this:

SELECT *what_columns* **FROM** *table*
WHERE *condition* **GROUP BY** *column*
ORDER BY *column* **LIMIT** *x, y*

A **GROUP BY** clause can also be used in a join. Remember that a join returns a new, virtual table of data, so any grouping would then apply to that virtual table.

To group data:

1. Connect to MySQL and select the *banking* database.

2. Count the number of registered customers ⓔ:

   ```
   SELECT COUNT(*) FROM customers;
   ```

   COUNT( ) is perhaps the most popular grouping function. With it, you can quickly count records, like the number of records in the *customers* table here. The **COUNT( )** function can be applied to any column that's certain to have a value, such as * (i.e., every column) or *customer_id*, the primary key.

   Notice that not all queries using the aggregate functions necessarily have **GROUP BY** clauses.

3. Find the total balance of all accounts by customer, counting the number of accounts in the process ⓕ:

   ```
   SELECT SUM(balance) AS Total,
   COUNT(account_id) AS Number,
   → customer_id
   FROM accounts
   GROUP BY (customer_id);
   ```

   This query is an extension of that in Step 2, but instead of counting just the customers, it counts the number of

accounts associated with each customer and totals the account balances, too.

4. Repeat the query from Step 3, selecting the customer's name instead of their ID ⓖ:

   ```
   SELECT SUM(balance) AS Total,
   COUNT(account_id) AS Number,
   CONCAT(c.last_name, ', ',
   → c.first_name) AS Name
   FROM accounts AS a
   INNER JOIN customers AS c
   USING (customer_id)
   GROUP BY (a.customer_id)
   ORDER BY Name;
   ```

   To retrieve the customer's name, instead of his or her ID, a join is required: **INNER JOIN customers USING (customer_id)**. Next, aliases are added for easier references, and the **GROUP BY** clause is modified to specify to which *customer_id* field the grouping should be applied. Thanks to the join, the customer's name can be selected as the concatenation of the customer's first and last names, a comma, and a space. And finally, the results can be sorted by the customer's name (note that another reference to the alias is used in the **ORDER BY** clause).

```
C:\Windows\system32\cmd.exe - C:\...

mysql> SELECT COUNT(*) FROM customers;
+----------+
| COUNT(*) |
+----------+
|        3 |
+----------+
1 row in set (0.03 sec)

mysql>
```

ⓔ This aggregating query counts the number of records in the *customers* table.

```
C:\Windows\system32\cmd.exe - C:\xampp\mysql...

mysql> SELECT SUM(balance) AS Total,
    -> COUNT(account_id) AS Number, customer_id
    -> FROM accounts
    -> GROUP BY (customer_id);
+-----------+--------+-------------+
| Total     | Number | customer_id |
+-----------+--------+-------------+
|   5460.23 |      1 |           1 |
| 922782.21 |      2 |           2 |
|    892.00 |      1 |           3 |
+-----------+--------+-------------+
3 rows in set (0.00 sec)

mysql>
```

ⓕ This **GROUP BY** query aggregates all of the accounts by *customer_id*, returning the sum of each customer's accounts and the total number of accounts the customer has, in the process.

Remember that if you used an outer join instead of an inner join, you could then retrieve customers who did not have account balances.

5. Concatenate each customer's balance into a single string :

```
SELECT GROUP_CONCAT(balance),
CONCAT(c.last_name, ', ',
→ c.first_name) AS Name
FROM accounts AS a
INNER JOIN customers AS c
USING (customer_id)
GROUP BY (a.customer_id)
ORDER BY Name;
```

The **GROUP_CONCAT( )** function is a useful and often overlooked aggregating tool. As you can see in the figure, by default this function concatenates values, separating each with a comma.

TIP NULL is a peculiar value, and it's interesting to know that GROUP BY will group NULL values together, since they have the same nonvalue.

TIP You have to be careful how you apply the COUNT( ) function, as it only counts non-NULL values. Be certain to use it on either every column (*) or on columns that will never contain NULL values (like the primary key).

TIP The GROUP BY clause, and the functions listed here, take some time to figure out, and MySQL will report an error whenever your syntax is inapplicable. Experiment within the mysql client or phpMyAdmin to determine the exact wording of any query you might want to run from a PHP script.

TIP A related clause is HAVING, which is like a WHERE condition applied to a group.

TIP You cannot apply SUM( ) and AVG( ) to date or time values. Instead, you'll need to convert date and time values to seconds, perform the SUM( ) or AVG( ), and then convert that value back to a date and time.

G This GROUP BY query is like that in **F**, but also returns the customer's name, and sorts the results by name (which requires a join).

H A variation on the query in **G**, this query retrieves the concatenation of all account balances for each customer.

Advanced Selections

The previous two sections of the chapter present more advanced ways to select data from complex structures. But even with the use of the aggregate functions, the data being selected is comparatively straightforward. Sometimes, though, you'll need to select data conditionally, as if you were using an `if-else` clause within the query itself. This is possible in SQL thanks to the *control flow* and *advanced comparison* functions.

To start, **GREATEST( )** returns the largest value in a list **A**:

```
SELECT GREATEST(col1, col2) FROM table
SELECT GREATEST(235, 1209, 59)
```

LEAST( ) returns the smallest value in a list:

```
SELECT LEAST(col1, col2) FROM table
SELECT LEAST(235, 1209, 59)
```

Note that unlike the aggregate functions, which apply to a list of values found in the same column over multiple rows, the comparison and control flow functions apply to multiple columns within the same row (or list of values).

Another useful comparison function is **COALESCE( )**. It returns the first non-**NULL** value in a list:

```
SELECT COALESCE(col1, col2) FROM table
```

If none of the listed items has a value, the function returns **NULL** (you'll see an example in the step sequence to follow).

Whereas **COALESCE( )** simply returns the first non-**NULL** value, you can use **IF( )** to return any value, based upon a condition:

```
SELECT IF (condition, return_if_true,
→ return_if_false)
```

If the condition is true, the second argument to the function is returned, otherwise the third argument is returned. As an example, assuming a table stored the values *M* or *F* in a *gender* column, a query could select *Male* or *Female* instead **B**:

```
SELECT IF(gender='M', 'Male', 'Female')
→ FROM people;
```

As these functions return values, they could even be used in other query types:

```
INSERT INTO people (gender) VALUES
→ (IF(something='Male', 'M', 'F'))
```

```
mysql> SELECT GREATEST(235, 1209, 59);
+-------------------------+
| GREATEST(235, 1209, 59) |
+-------------------------+
|                    1209 |
+-------------------------+
1 row in set (0.00 sec)

mysql>
```

A The **GREATEST( )** function returns the biggest value in a given list.

```
mysql> SELECT gender FROM people;
+--------+
| gender |
+--------+
| M      |
| F      |
+--------+
2 rows in set (0.00 sec)

mysql> SELECT IF(gender='M', 'Male', 'Female')
FROM people;
+---------------------------------+
| IF(gender='M', 'Male', 'Female') |
+---------------------------------+
| Male                            |
| Female                          |
+---------------------------------+
2 rows in set (0.00 sec)

mysql>
```

B The **IF( )** function can dictate the returned value based upon a conditional.

```
mysql> SELECT message_id,
    -> CASE WHEN date_entered > NOW()
    -> THEN 'Future'
    -> ELSE 'PAST'
    -> END AS Posted FROM
    -> messages;
+------------+--------+
| message_id | Posted |
+------------+--------+
|          1 | PAST   |
|          2 | PAST   |
|          3 | PAST   |
|          4 | PAST   |
|          5 | PAST   |
|          6 | PAST   |
|          7 | PAST   |
|          8 | PAST   |
|          9 | PAST   |
|         10 | PAST   |
|         11 | PAST   |
```

C CASE( ) can be used like IF( ) to customize the returned value.

The **CASE( )** function is a more complicated tool that can be used in different ways. The first approach is to treat **CASE( )** like PHP's **switch** conditional:

SELECT CASE *col1* **WHEN** *value1* **THEN** →*return_this* **ELSE** *return_that* **END** → **FROM table**

The gender example could be rewritten as:

SELECT CASE gender WHEN 'M' THEN →**'Male' ELSE 'Female' END FROM people**

The **CASE( )** function can have additional **WHEN** clauses. The **ELSE** is also always optional:

SELECT CASE gender WHEN 'M' THEN →**'Male' WHEN 'F' THEN 'FEMALE' END** → **FROM people**

If you're not looking to perform a simple equality test, you can write conditions into a **CASE( )** **C**:

SELECT message_id, CASE WHEN → **date_entered > NOW( ) THEN 'Future'** → **ELSE 'PAST' END AS Posted FROM** → **messages**

Again, you can add multiple **WHEN...THEN** clauses as needed, and omit the **ELSE**, if that's not necessary.

To practice using these functions, let's run a few more queries on the *forum* database (as a heads up, they're going to get a little complicated).

To perform advanced selections:

1. Connect to MySQL and select the *forum* database.

2. For each forum, find the date and time of the most recent post, or return *N/A* if the forum has no posts :

```
SELECT f.name,
COALESCE(MAX(m.date_entered),
→ 'N/A') AS last_post
FROM forums AS f
LEFT JOIN messages AS m
USING (forum_id)
GROUP BY (m.forum_id)
ORDER BY m.date_entered DESC;
```

To start, in order to find both the forum name and the date of the latest posting in that forum, a join is necessary. Specifically, an outer join, as there may be forums without postings. To find the most recent posting in each forum, the aggregating **MAX( )** function is applied to the *date_entered* column, and the results have to be grouped by the *forum_id* (so that **MAX( )** is applied to each subset of postings within each forum).

The results at that point, without the **COALESCE( )** function call, would return **NULL** for any forum without any messages in it. The final step is to apply **COALESCE( )** so that the string *N/A* is returned should **MAX(m.date_entered)** have a **NULL** value.

3. For each message, append the string *(REPLY)* to the subject if the message is a reply to another message :

```
SELECT message_id,
CASE parent_id WHEN 0 THEN subject
ELSE CONCAT(subject, ' (Reply)')
→ END AS subject
FROM messages;
```

D The **COALESCE( )** function is used to turn NULL values into the string *N/A* (see the last record).

E Here, the string *(Reply)* is appended to the subject of any message that is a reply to another message.

The records in the *messages* tables that have a *parent_id* other than 0 are replies to existing messages. For these messages, let's append *(REPLY)* to the subject value to indicate such. To accomplish that, a **CASE** statement returns just the subject, unadulterated, if the *parent_id* value equals 0. If the *parent_id* value does not equal 0, the string *(REPLY)* is concatenated to the subject, again thanks to **CASE**. This whole construct is assigned the alias of *subject*, so it's still returned under the original "subject" heading.

4. For each user, find the number of messages they've posted, converting zeros to the string *None* **F**:

```
SELECT u.username,
IF(COUNT(message_id) > 0,
→ COUNT(message_id), 'None') AS
→ Posts
FROM users AS u
LEFT JOIN messages AS m
USING (user_id)
GROUP BY (u.user_id);
```

This is somewhat of a variation on the query in Step 2. A left join bridges *users* and *messages*, in order to grab both the username and the count of messages posted. To perform the count, the results are grouped by *users.user_id*. The query to this point would return 0 for every user that has not yet posted **G**. To convert those zeros to the string *None*, while maintaining the non-zero counts, the **IF( )** function is applied. That function's first argument establishes the condition: if the count is greater than zero. The second argument says that the count should be returned when that condition is true. The third argument says that the string *None* should be returned when that condition is false.

TIP The **IFNULL( )** function can sometimes be used instead of **COALESCE( )**. Its syntax is:

```
IFNULL(value, return_if_null)
```

If the first argument, such as a named column, has a NULL value, then the second argument is returned. If argument does not have a NULL value, the value of that argument is returned.

F Thanks to an **IF( )** call, the count of posted messages is displayed as *None* for any user that has not yet posted a message.

G What the query results would look like (compare with **F**) without using **IF( )**.

Performing FULLTEXT Searches

In Chapter 5, the **LIKE** keyword was introduced as a way to perform somewhat simple string matches like

```
SELECT * FROM users
WHERE last_name LIKE 'Smith%'
```

This type of conditional is effective enough but is still very limiting. For example, it would not allow you to do Google-like searches using multiple words. For those kinds of situations, you need **FULLTEXT** searches. Over the next several pages,

Altering Tables

The **ALTER** SQL term is primarily used to modify the structure of an existing table. Commonly this means adding, deleting, or changing the columns therein, but it also includes the addition of indexes. An **ALTER** statement can even be used for renaming the table as a whole. The basic syntax of **ALTER** is

ALTER TABLE *tablename CLAUSE*

There are many possible clauses; **Table 7.2** lists the most common ones, where *t* represents the table's name, *c* a column's name, and *i* an index's name. As always, the MySQL manual covers the topic in exhaustive detail.

TABLE 7.2 ALTER TABLE Clauses

Clause	Usage	Meaning
ADD COLUMN	ALTER TABLE *t* ADD COLUMN *c* TYPE	Adds a new column to the table.
CHANGE COLUMN	ALTER TABLE *t* CHANGE COLUMN *c* *c* TYPE	Changes the data type and properties of a column.
DROP COLUMN	ALTER TABLE *t* DROP COLUMN *c*	Removes a column from a table, including all of its data.
ADD INDEX	ALTER TABLE *t* ADD INDEX *i* (*c*)	Adds a new index on *C*.
DROP INDEX	ALTER TABLE *t* DROP INDEX *i*	Removes an existing index.
RENAME TO	ALTER TABLE *t* RENAME TO *new_t*	Changes the name of a table.

You can also change a table's character set and collation using **ALTER *t* CONVERT TO CHARACTER SET *x* COLLATE *y*.**

```
mysql> SHOW TABLE STATUS\G
*********************** 1. row ***********************
           Name: forums
         Engine: InnoDB
        Version: 10
     Row_format: Compact
           Rows: 7
 Avg_row_length: 2340
    Data_length: 16384
Max_data_length: 0
   Index_length: 16384
      Data_free: 9437184
 Auto_increment: 8
    Create_time: 2011-04-03 21:06:05
    Update_time: NULL
     Check_time: NULL
      Collation: utf8_general_ci
       Checksum: NULL
 Create_options:
        Comment:
*********************** 2. row ***********************
           Name: messages
         Engine: MyISAM
        Version: 10
     Row_format: Dynamic
           Rows: 21
 Avg_row_length: 93
    Data_length: 1956
Max_data_length: 281474976710655
   Index_length: 6144
      Data_free: 0
 Auto_increment: 22
    Create_time: 2011-04-03 21:06:05
    Update_time: 2011-04-03 21:37:28
     Check_time: NULL
      Collation: utf8_general_ci
       Checksum: NULL
 Create_options:
        Comment:
*********************** 3. row ***********************
           Name: users
         Engine: InnoDB
        Version: 10
     Row_format: Compact
           Rows: 5
 Avg_row_length: 3276
    Data_length: 16384
Max_data_length: 0
   Index_length: 49152
      Data_free: 9437184
```

Ⓐ To confirm a table's type, use the **SHOW TABLE STATUS** command.

you'll learn everything you need to know about **FULLTEXT** searches (and you'll learn some more SQL tricks in the process).

Creating a FULLTEXT Index

To start, **FULLTEXT** searches require a **FULLTEXT** index. This index type, as previewed in Chapter 6, "Database Design," can only be created on a MyISAM table. These next examples will use the *messages* table in the *forum* database. The first step, then, is to add a **FULLTEXT** index on the *body* and *subject* columns. Adding indexes to existing tables requires use of the **ALTER** command, as described in the sidebar.

To add a FULLTEXT index:

1. Connect to MySQL and select the *forum* database, if you have not already.

2. Confirm the *messages* table's type Ⓐ:

   SHOW TABLE STATUS\G

   The **SHOW TABLE STATUS** query returns a fair amount of information about each table in the database, including the table's storage engine. Because so much information is returned by the query, the command concludes with **\G** instead of a semicolon. This tells the mysql client to return the results as a vertical list instead of a table (which is sometimes easier to read). If you're using phpMyAdmin or another interface, you can omit the **\G** (just as you can omit concluding semicolons).

   To just find the information for the *messages* table, you can use the query **SHOW TABLE STATUS LIKE 'messages'**.

   continues on next page

3. If the *messages* table is not of the MyISAM type, change the storage engine:

```
ALTER TABLE messages ENGINE =
→ MyISAM;
```

Again, this is only necessary if the table isn't currently of the correct type.

4. Add the **FULLTEXT** index to the *messages* table **B**:

```
ALTER TABLE messages ADD FULLTEXT
→ (body, subject);
```

The syntax for adding any index, regardless of type, is **ALTER TABLE** *tablename* **ADD** *INDEX_TYPE* *index_name* (*columns*). The index name is optional.

Here, the *body* and *subject* columns get a **FULLTEXT** index, to be used in **FULLTEXT** searches later in this chapter.

TIP Inserting records into tables with FULLTEXT indexes can be much slower because of the complex index that's required.

TIP FULLTEXT searches can successfully be used in a simple search engine. But a FULLTEXT index can only be applied to a single table at a time, so more elaborate Web sites, with content stored in multiple tables, would benefit from using a more formal search engine.

Performing Basic FULLTEXT Searches

Once you've established a **FULLTEXT** index on a column or columns, you can start querying against it, using **MATCH...AGAINST** in a **WHERE** conditional:

```
SELECT * FROM tablename WHERE MATCH
(columns) AGAINST (terms)
```

MySQL will return matching rows in order of a mathematically calculated relevance, just like a search engine. When doing so, certain rules apply:

- Strings are broken down into their individual keywords.

- Keywords less than four characters long are ignored.

- Very popular words, called *stopwords*, are ignored.

- If more than 50 percent of the records match the keywords, no records are returned.

This last fact is problematic to many users as they begin with **FULLTEXT** searches and wonder why no results are returned. When you have a sparsely populated table, there just won't be sufficient records for MySQL to return *relevant* results.

B The **FULLTEXT** index is added to the *messages* table.

To perform FULLTEXT searches:

1. Connect to MySQL and select the *forum* database, if you have not already.

2. Thoroughly populate the *messages* table, focusing on adding lengthy bodies.

   Once again, SQL **INSERT** commands can be downloaded from this book's corresponding Web site.

3. Run a simple **FULLTEXT** search on the word *database* **C**:

```
SELECT subject, body FROM messages
WHERE MATCH (body, subject)
AGAINST('database');
```

This is a very simple example that will return some results as long as at least one and less than 50 percent of the records in the *messages* table have the word "database" in their body or subject. Note that the columns referenced in **MATCH** must be the same as those on which the **FULLTEXT** index was made. In this case, you could use either **body, subject** or **subject, body**, but you could not use just **body** or just **subject** **D**.

continues on next page

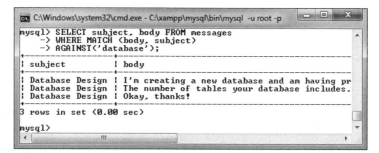

C A basic **FULLTEXT** search.

D A **FULLTEXT** query can only be run on the same column or combination of columns that the **FULLTEXT** index was created on. With this query, even though the combination of *body* and *subject* has a **FULLTEXT** index, attempting to run the match on just *subject* will fail.

4. Run the same **FULLTEXT** search while also showing the relevance **E**:

```
SELECT subject, body, MATCH (body,
subject) AGAINST('database') AS R
FROM messages WHERE MATCH (body,
→ subject) AGAINST('database')\G
```

If you use the same **MATCH…AGAINST** expression as a selected value, the actual relevance will be returned. As in the previous section of the chapter, to make the results easier to view in the mysql client, the query is terminated using **\G**, thereby returning the results as a vertical list.

5. Run a **FULLTEXT** search using multiple keywords **F**:

```
SELECT subject, body FROM messages
WHERE MATCH (body, subject)
AGAINST('html xhtml');
```

With this query, a match will be made if the subject or body contains either word. Any record that contains both words will be ranked higher.

TIP Remember that if a FULLTEXT search returns no records, this means that either no matches were made or that over half of the records match.

TIP For sake of simplicity, all of the queries in this section are simple SELECT statements. You can certainly use FULLTEXT searches within joins or more complex queries.

TIP MySQL comes with several hundred stopwords already defined. These are part of the application's source code.

TIP The minimum keyword length—four characters by default—is a configuration setting you can change in MySQL.

TIP FULLTEXT searches are case-insensitive by default.

```
C:\Windows\system32\cmd.exe - C:\xampp\mysql\bin\mysql -u root -p

mysql> SELECT subject, body, MATCH (body,
    -> subject) AGAINST('database') AS R
    -> FROM messages WHERE MATCH (body, subject) AGAINST('database')\G
*************************** 1. row ***************************
subject: Database Design
   body: I'm creating a new database and am having problems with the str
      R: 2.544002771377565
*************************** 2. row ***************************
subject: Database Design
   body: The number of tables your database includes...
      R: 2.519484281539917
*************************** 3. row ***************************
subject: Database Design
   body: Okay, thanks!
      R: 1.751475572586059
3 rows in set (0.00 sec)

mysql>
```

E The relevance of a **FULLTEXT** search can be selected, too. In this case, you'll see that the two records with the word "database" in both the subject and body have higher relevance than the record that contains the word in just the subject.

```
PHP and MySQL for Dynamic Web Sites: Visual QuickPro Guide

mysql> SELECT subject, body FROM messages
    -> WHERE MATCH (body, subject)
    -> AGAINST('html xhtml');
+-------------------------------------+----------------------------------------------------------------------------------+
| subject                             | body                                                                             |
+-------------------------------------+----------------------------------------------------------------------------------+
| HTML vs. XHTML                      | XHTML is a cross between HTML and XML. The differences are largely syntactic. Blah, blah, blah... |
| HTML vs. XHTML                      | What are the differences between HTML and XHTML?                                  |
| Dynamic HTML using PHP              | Can I use PHP to dynamically generate HTML on the fly? Thanks...                  |
| Dynamic HTML using PHP              | You most certainly can.                                                          |
| Dynamic HTML using PHP, still not clear | Um, how?                                                                      |
| Dynamic HTML using PHP, clearer?    | I think what Larry is trying to say is that you should buy and read his book.     |
| CSS Resources                       | Read Elizabeth Castro's excellent book on (X)HTML and CSS. Or search Google on "CSS". |
+-------------------------------------+----------------------------------------------------------------------------------+
7 rows in set (0.00 sec)

mysql>
```

F Using the **FULLTEXT** search, you can easily find messages that contain multiple keywords.

Performing Boolean FULLTEXT Searches

The basic **FULLTEXT** search is nice, but a more sophisticated **FULLTEXT** search can be accomplished using its Boolean mode. To do so, add the phrase **IN BOOLEAN MODE** to the **AGAINST** clause:

```
SELECT * FROM tablename WHERE
MATCH(columns) AGAINST('terms' IN
→ BOOLEAN
MODE)
```

Boolean mode has a number of operators (**Table 7.3**) to tweak how each keyword is treated:

```
SELECT * FROM tablename WHERE
MATCH(columns) AGAINST('+database
-mysql' IN BOOLEAN MODE)
```

In that example, a match will be made if the word *database* is found and *mysql* is not present. Alternatively, the tilde (~) is used as a milder form of the minus sign, meaning that the keyword can be present in a match, but such matches should be considered less relevant.

TABLE 7.3 Boolean Mode Operators

Operator	Meaning
+	Must be present in every match
-	Must not be present in any match
~	Lowers a ranking if present
*	Wildcard
<	Decrease a word's importance
>	Increase a word's importance
" "	Must match the exact phrase
( )	Create subexpressions

The wildcard character (*) matches variations on a word, so **cata*** matches *catalog*, *catalina*, and so on. Two operators explicitly state what keywords are more (**>**) or less (**<**) important. Finally, you can use double quotation marks to hunt for exact phrases and parentheses to make subexpressions (just be certain to use single quotation marks to wrap the keywords, then).

The following query would look for records with the phrase *Web develop* with the word *html* being required and the word *JavaScript* detracting from a match's relevance:

```
SELECT * FROM tablename WHERE
MATCH(columns) AGAINST('>"Web develop"
+html ~JavaScript' IN BOOLEAN MODE)
```

When using Boolean mode, there are several differences as to how **FULLTEXT** searches work:

- If a keyword is not preceded by an operator, the word is optional but a match will be ranked higher if it is present.

- Results will be returned even if more than 50 percent of the records match the search.

- The results are *not* automatically sorted by relevance.

Because of this last fact, you'll also want to sort the returned records by their relevance, as demonstrated in the next sequence of steps. One important rule that's the same with Boolean searches is that the minimum word length (four characters by default) still applies. So trying to require a shorter word using a plus sign (**+php**) still won't work.

To perform FULLTEXT Boolean searches:

1. Connect to MySQL and select the *forum* database, if you have not already.

2. Run a simple **FULLTEXT** search that finds *HTML*, *XHTML*, or *(X)HTML* **G**:

   ```
   SELECT subject, body FROM
   messages WHERE MATCH(body, subject)
   AGAINST('*HTML' IN BOOLEAN MODE)\G
   ```

   The term HTML may appear in messages in many formats, including *HTML*, *XHTML*, or *(X)HTML*. This Boolean mode query will find all of those, thanks to the wildcard character (*).

   To make the results easier to view, I'm using the **\G** trick mentioned earlier in the chapter, which tells the mysql client to return the results vertically, not horizontally.

3. Find matches involving databases, with an emphasis on normal forms **H**:

   ```
   SELECT subject, body FROM messages
   WHERE MATCH (body, subject)
   AGAINST('>"normal form"* +database*'
   IN BOOLEAN MODE)\G
   ```

G A simple Boolean-mode **FULLTEXT** search.

H This search looks for variations on two different keywords, ranking the one higher than the other.

This query first finds all records that have *database*, *databases*, etc. and *normal form*, *normal forms*, etc. in them. The **database*** term is required (as indicated by the plus sign), but emphasis is given to the normal form clause (which is preceded by the greater-than sign).

4. Repeat the query from Step 2, with a greater importance on XHTML, returning the results in order of relevance ❶:

```
SELECT subject, body, MATCH(body,
→ subject)
AGAINST('*HTML >XHTML' IN BOOLEAN
→ MODE) AS R FROM
messages WHERE MATCH(body, subject)
AGAINST('*HTML >XHTML' IN BOOLEAN
→ MODE) ORDER BY R DESC\G
```

This is similar to the earlier query, but now *XHTML* is specifically given extra weight. This query additionally selects the calculated relevance, and the results are returned in that order.

TIP MySQL 5.1.7 added another FULLTEXT search mode: *natural language*. This is the default mode, if no other mode (like Boolean) is specified.

TIP The WITH QUERY EXPANSION modifier can increase the number of returned results. Such queries perform two searches and return one result set. It bases a second search on terms found in the most relevant results of the initial search. While a WITH QUERY EXPANSION search can find results that would not otherwise have been returned, it can also return results that aren't at all relevant to the original search terms.

```
mysql> SELECT subject, body, MATCH(body, subject)
    -> AGAINST('*HTML >XHTML' IN BOOLEAN MODE) AS R FROM
    -> messages WHERE MATCH(body, subject)
    -> AGAINST('*HTML >XHTML' IN BOOLEAN MODE) ORDER BY R DESC\G
*************************** 1. row ***************************
subject: HTML vs. XHTML
   body: What are the differences between HTML and XHTML?
      R: 2.5
*************************** 2. row ***************************
subject: HTML vs. XHTML
   body: XHTML is a cross between HTML and XML. The differences are largely syntac
      R: 2.5
*************************** 3. row ***************************
subject: CSS Resources
   body: Read Elizabeth Castro's excellent book on (X)HTML and CSS. Or search Goog
      R: 1
*************************** 4. row ***************************
subject: Dynamic HTML using PHP
   body: Can I use PHP to dynamically generate HTML on the fly? Thanks...
      R: 1
*************************** 5. row ***************************
subject: Dynamic HTML using PHP
   body: You most certainly can.
      R: 1
*************************** 6. row ***************************
subject: Dynamic HTML using PHP, still not clear
   body: Um, how?
      R: 1
*************************** 7. row ***************************
subject: Dynamic HTML using PHP, clearer?
   body: I think what Larry is trying to say is that you should buy and read his b
      R: 1
7 rows in set (0.00 sec)

mysql>
```

❶ This modified version of an earlier query selects, and then sorts the results by, the relevance.

Optimizing Queries

Once you have a complete and populated database, and have a sense as to what queries will commonly be run on it, it's a good idea to take some steps to optimize your queries and your database as a whole. Doing so will ensure you're getting the best possible performance out of MySQL (and therefore, your Web site)

To start, the sidebar reemphasizes key design ideas that have already been suggested in this book. Along with these tips, there are two simple techniques for optimizing existing tables. One way to improve MySQL's performance is to run an **OPTIMIZE** command on occasion. This query will rid a table of any unnecessary overhead, thereby improving the speed of any interactions with it:

```
OPTIMIZE TABLE tablename
```

Running this command is particularly beneficial after changing a table via an **ALTER** command, or after a table has had lots of **DELETE** queries run on it, leaving virtual gaps among the records.

Second, you can occasionally use the **ANALYZE** command:

```
ANALYZE TABLE tablename
```

Executing this command updates the indexes on the table, thereby improving their usage in queries. You could execute it whenever massive amounts of data stored in the table changes (e.g., via **UPDATE** or **INSERT** commands).

Speaking of queries, as you're probably realizing by now, there are often many different ways of accomplishing the same goal. To find out the most efficient approach, it helps to understand how exactly MySQL will run that query. This can be accomplished using the **EXPLAIN** SQL keyword. Explaining queries is a very advanced topic, but I'll introduce the fundamentals here, and you can always see the MySQL manual or search the Web for more information.

Database Optimization

The performance of your database is primarily dependent upon its structure and indexes. When creating databases, try to

- Choose the best storage engine
- Use the smallest data type possible for each column
- Define columns as **NOT NULL** whenever possible
- Use integers as primary keys
- Judiciously define indexes, selecting the correct type and applying them to the right column or columns
- Limit indexes to a certain number of characters, if possible
- Avoid creating too many indexes
- Make sure that columns to be used as the basis of joins are of the same type and, in the case of strings, use the same character set and collation

To explain a query:

1. Find a query that may be resource-intensive.

   Good candidates are queries that do any of the following:

   ▸ Join two or more tables

   ▸ Use groupings and aggregate functions

   ▸ Have **WHERE** clauses.

   For example, this query from earlier in the chapter meets two of these criteria:

   ```
   SELECT SUM(balance) AS Total,
   COUNT(account_id) AS Number,
   → CONCAT(c.last_name, ', ',
   → c.first_name) AS Name
   FROM accounts AS a INNER
   → JOIN customers AS c USING
   → (customer_id)
   GROUP BY (a.customer_id) ORDER BY
   → Name;
   ```

2. Connect to MySQL and select the applicable database, if you have not already.

3. Execute the query on the database, prefacing it with **EXPLAIN** Ⓐ:

   ```
   EXPLAIN SELECT SUM(balance) AS
   → Total,
   COUNT(account_id) AS Number,
   → CONCAT(c.last_name, ', ',
   → c.first_name) AS Name
   FROM accounts AS a INNER JOIN
   → customers AS c USING (customer_id)
   GROUP BY (a.customer_id) ORDER BY
   → Name\G
   ```

   If you're using the mysql client, you'll find it also helps to use the concluding **\G** trick (instead of the semicolon), to make the output more legible. The output itself will be one row of information for every table used in the query. The tables are listed in the same order that MySQL must access them to execute the query.

   I'll walk through the key parts of the output, but to begin, the *select_type* value should be *SIMPLE* for most **SELECT** queries, and would be different if the query involves a **UNION** or sub-query (see the MySQL manual for more on either **UNION**s or subqueries).

   continues on next page

```
PHP and MySQL for Dynamic Web Sites: Visual QuickPro Guide
mysql> EXPLAIN SELECT SUM(balance) AS Total,
    -> COUNT(account_id) AS Number, CONCAT(c.last_name, ', ', c.first_name) AS Name
    -> FROM accounts AS a INNER JOIN customers AS c USING (customer_id)
    -> GROUP BY (a.customer_id) ORDER BY Name\G
*************************** 1. row ***************************
           id: 1
  select_type: SIMPLE
        table: c
         type: index
possible_keys: PRIMARY
          key: full_name
      key_len: 184
          ref: NULL
         rows: 3
        Extra: Using index; Using temporary; Using filesort
*************************** 2. row ***************************
           id: 1
  select_type: SIMPLE
        table: a
         type: ALL
possible_keys: customer_id
          key: NULL
      key_len: NULL
          ref: NULL
         rows: 4
        Extra: Using where; Using join buffer
2 rows in set (0.00 sec)

mysql> 
```

Ⓐ This **EXPLAIN** output reveals how MySQL will go about processing the query.

4. Check out the *type* value.

Table 7.4 lists the different type values, from best to worst. The MySQL manual discusses what each means in detail but understand first that *eq_ref* is the best you'll commonly see and *ALL* is the worst. A type of *eq_ref* means that an index is being properly used and an equality comparison is being made.

Note that you'll sometimes see *ALL* because the table has very few records in it, in which case it's more efficient for MySQL to scan the table rather than use an index. This is presumably the case with Ⓐ, as the *accounts* table only has four records.

5. Check out the *possible_keys* value.

The *possible_keys* value indicates which indexes exist that MySQL might be able to use to find the corresponding rows in this table. If you have a **NULL** value here, there are no indexes that MySQL thinks would be useful. Therefore, you might benefit from creating an index on that table's applicable columns.

6. Check out the *key*, *key_len*, and *ref* values.

Whereas *possible_keys* indicates what indexes might be usable, *key* says what index MySQL *will actually use* for that query. Occasionally, you'll find a value here that's not listed in *possible_keys*, which is okay. If no key is being used, that almost always indicates a problem that can be remedied by adding an index or modifying the query.

The *key_len* value indicates the length (i.e., the size) of the key that MySQL used. Generally, shorter is better here, but don't worry about it too much.

The *ref* column indicates which columns MySQL compared to the index named in the key column.

7. Check out the *rows* value.

This column provides an estimate of how many rows in the table MySQL thinks it will need to examine. Once again, lower is better. In fact, on a join, a rough estimate of the efficiency can be determined by multiplying all the rows values together.

Often in a join, the number of rows to be examined should go from more to less, as in Ⓑ.

8. Check out the *Extra* value.

Finally, this column reports any additional information about how MySQL will execute the query that may be useful. Two phrases you don't want to find here are: *Using filesort* and *Using temporary*. Both mean that extra steps are required to complete the query (e.g., a **GROUP BY** clause often requires MySQL creates a temporary table).

TABLE 7.4 Join Types

Type
system
const
eq_ref
ref
fulltext
ref_or_null
index_merge
unique_subquery
index_subquery
range
index
ALL

```
PHP and MySQL for Dynamic Web Sites: Visual QuickPro Guide
mysql> EXPLAIN SELECT u.username, m.subject, f.name
    -> FROM users AS u
    -> LEFT JOIN messages AS m
    -> USING (user_id)
    -> LEFT JOIN forums AS f
    -> USING (forum_id)\G
*************************** 1. row ***************************
         id: 1
select_type: SIMPLE
      table: u
       type: index
possible_keys: NULL
        key: username
    key_len: 92
        ref: NULL
       rows: 5
      Extra: Using index
*************************** 2. row ***************************
         id: 1
select_type: SIMPLE
      table: m
       type: ref
possible_keys: user_id
        key: user_id
    key_len: 3
        ref: forum.u.user_id
       rows: 4
      Extra:
*************************** 3. row ***************************
         id: 1
select_type: SIMPLE
      table: f
       type: eq_ref
possible_keys: PRIMARY
        key: PRIMARY
    key_len: 1
        ref: forum.m.forum_id
       rows: 1
      Extra:
3 rows in set (0.00 sec)

mysql>
```

B Another explanation of a query, this one a join across three tables.

If *Extra* says anything along the lines of *Impossible X* or *No matching Y*, that means your query has clauses that are always false and can be removed.

9. Modify your table or queries and repeat!

If the output suggests problems with how the query is being executed, you can consider doing any of the following:

▸ Changing the particulars of the query

▸ Changing the properties of a table's columns

▸ Adding or modifying a table's indexes

Remember that the validity of the explanation will depend, in part, on how many rows are in the involved tables (as explained in Step 4, MySQL may skip indexes for small tables). Also understand that not all queries are fixable. Simple **SELECT** queries and even joins can sometimes be improved, but there's little one can do to improve the efficiency of a **GROUP BY** query, considering everything MySQL must do to aggregate data.

TIP The **EXPLAIN EXTENDED** command provides a few more details about a query:

`EXPLAIN EXTENDED SELECT…`

TIP Problematic queries can also be found by enabling certain MySQL logging features, but that requires administrative control over the MySQL server.

TIP In terms of performance, MySQL deals with more, smaller tables better than it does fewer, larger tables. That being said, a normalized database structure should always be the primary goal.

TIP In MySQL terms, a "big" database has thousands of tables and millions of rows.

Performing Transactions

A *database transaction* is a sequence of queries run during a single session. For example, you might insert a record into one table, insert another record into another table, and maybe run an update. Without using transactions, each individual query takes effect immediately and cannot be undone (the queries, by default, are automatically committed). With transactions, you can set start and stop points and then enact or retract all of the queries between those points as needed (for example, if one query failed, all of the queries can be undone).

Commercial interactions commonly require transactions, even something as basic as transferring $100 from my bank account to yours. What seems like a simple process is actually several steps:

- Confirm that I have $100 in my account.
- Decrease my account by $100.
- Verify the decrease.
- Increase the amount of money in your account by $100.
- Verify that the increase worked.

If any of the steps failed, all of them should be undone. For example, if the money couldn't be deposited in your account, it should be returned to mine until the entire transaction can go through.

The ability to execute transactions depends upon the features of the storage engine in use. To perform transactions with MySQL, you must use the InnoDB table type (or storage engine).

To begin a new transaction in the mysql client, type

START TRANSACTION;

Once your transaction has begun, you can now run your queries. Once you have finished, you can either enter **COMMIT** to enact all of the queries or **ROLLBACK** to undo the effect of all of the queries.

After you have either committed or rolled back the queries, the transaction is considered complete, and MySQL returns to an *autocommit* mode. This means that any queries you execute take immediate effect. To start another transaction, just type **START TRANSACTION**.

It is important to know that certain types of queries cannot be rolled back. Specifically, those that create, alter, truncate (empty), or delete tables or that create or delete databases cannot be undone. Furthermore, using such a query has the effect of committing and ending the current transaction.

Second, you should understand that transactions are particular to each connection. So one user connected through the mysql client has a different transaction than another mysql client user, both of which are different than a connected PHP script.

Finally, *you cannot perform transactions using phpMyAdmin*. Each submission of a query through phpMyAdmin's SQL window or tab is an individual and complete transaction, which cannot be undone with subsequent submissions.

With this in mind, let's use transactions with the banking database to perform the already mentioned task. In Chapter 19, "Example— E-Commerce," transactions will be run through a PHP script.

To perform transactions:

1. Connect to MySQL and select the *banking* database.

2. Begin a transaction and show the table's current values :

   ```
   START TRANSACTION;
   SELECT * FROM accounts;
   ```

3. Subtract $100 from David Sedaris' (or any user's) checking account.

   ```
   UPDATE accounts
   SET balance = (balance-100)
   WHERE account_id=2;
   ```

   Using an **UPDATE** query, a little math, and a **WHERE** conditional, you can subtract 100 from a balance. Although MySQL will indicate that one row was affected, the effect is not permanent until the transaction is committed.

4. Add $100 to Sarah Vowell's checking account:

   ```
   UPDATE accounts
   SET balance = (balance+100)
   WHERE account_id=1;
   ```

   This is the opposite of Step 3, as if $100 were being transferred from the one person to the other.

5. Confirm the results **B**:

   ```
   SELECT * FROM accounts;
   ```

   As you can see in the figure, the one balance is 100 more and the other is 100 less than they originally were **A**.

6. Roll back the transaction:

   ```
   ROLLBACK;
   ```

   To demonstrate how transactions can be undone, let's undo the effects of these queries. The **ROLLBACK** command returns the database to how it was prior to starting the transaction. The command also terminates the transaction, returning MySQL to its autocommit mode.

   continues on next page

A A transaction is begun and the existing table records are shown.

B Two **UPDATE** queries are executed and the results are viewed.

7. Confirm the results **C**:

```
SELECT * FROM accounts;
```

The query should reveal the contents of the table as they originally were.

8. Repeat Steps 2 through 4.

To see what happens when the transaction is committed, the two **UPDATE** queries will be run again. Be certain to start the transaction first, though, or the queries will automatically take effect!

9. Commit the transaction and confirm the results:

```
COMMIT;
SELECT * FROM accounts;
```

Once you enter **COMMIT**, the entire transaction is permanent, meaning that any changes are now in place. **COMMIT** also ends the transaction, returning MySQL to autocommit mode.

TIP One of the great features of transactions is that they offer protection should a random event occur, such as a server crash. Either a transaction is executed in its entirety or all of the changes are ignored.

TIP To alter MySQL's autocommit nature, type

```
SET AUTOCOMMIT=0;
```

Then you do not need to type START TRANSACTION and no queries will be permanent until you type COMMIT (or use an ALTER, CREATE, etc., query).

TIP You can create *savepoints* in transactions:

```
SAVEPOINT savepoint_name;
```

Then you can roll back to that point:

```
ROLLBACK TO SAVEPOINT savepoint_name;
```

C Because the **ROLLBACK** command was used, the potential effects of the **UPDATE** queries were ignored.

D Invoking the **COMMIT** command makes the transaction's effects permanent.

Database Encryption

Up to this point, pseudo-encryption has been accomplished in the database using the **SHA1( )** function. In the *sitename* and *forum* databases, the user's password has been stored after running it through **SHA1( )**. Although using this function in this way is perfectly fine (and quite common), the function doesn't provide *real* encryption: the **SHA1( )** function returns a *representation* of a value (called a *hash*), not an encrypted version of the value. By storing the hashed version of some data, comparisons can still be made later (such as upon login), but the original data cannot be retrieved from the database. If you need to store data in a protected way while still being able to view the data in its original form at some later point, other MySQL functions are necessary.

MySQL has several encryption and decryption functions built into the software. If you require data to be stored in an encrypted form that can be decrypted, you'll want to use **AES_ENCRYPT( )** and **AES_ DECRYPT( )**. The **AES_ENCRYPT( )** function is considered to be the most secure encryption option.

These functions take two arguments: the data being encrypted or decrypted and a *salt* argument. The salt argument is a string that helps to randomize the encryption. Let's look at the encryption and decryption functions first, and then I'll return to the salt.

To add a record to a table while encrypting the data, the query might look like

```
INSERT INTO users (username, pass)
VALUES ('troutster', AES_ENCRYPT
→('mypass', 'nacl19874salt!'))
```

The encrypted data returned by the **AES_ENCRYPT( )** function will be in binary format. To store that data in a table, the column must be defined as one of the binary types (e.g., **VARBINARY** or **BLOB**).

To run a login query for the record just inserted (matching a submitted username and password against those in the database), you would write

```
SELECT * FROM users WHERE
username='troutster' AND
AES_DECRYPT(pass, 'nacl19874salt!') =
→'mypass'
```

This is equivalent to:

```
SELECT * FROM users WHERE
username = 'troutster' AND
AES_ENCRYPT('mypass', 'nacl19874salt!')
→= pass
```

Returning to the issue of the *salt*, the exact same salt must be used for both encryption and decryption, which means that the salt must be stored somewhere as well. Contrary to what you might think, it's actually safe to store the salt in the database, even in the same row as the salted data. This is because the purpose of the salt is to make the encryption process harder to crack (specifically, by a "rainbow" attack). Such attacks are done remotely, using brute force. Conversely, if someone can see everything stored in your database, you have bigger problems to worry about (i.e., all of your data has been breached).

Finally, to get the maximum benefit from "salting" the stored data, each piece of stored data should use a unique salt, and the longer the salt the better.

To put all this together, let's add PIN and salt columns to the *banking.customers* table, and then store an encrypted version of each customer's PIN.

To encrypt and decrypt data:

1. Access MySQL and select the *banking* database:

2. Add the two new columns to the *customers* table **A**:

```
ALTER TABLE customers ADD COLUMN
→ pin VARBINARY(16) NOT NULL;
ALTER TABLE customers ADD COLUMN
→ nacl CHAR(20) NOT NULL;
```

The first column, *pin*, will store an encrypted version of the user's PIN. As **AES_ENCRYPT( )** returns a binary value 16 characters long, the *pin* column is defined as **VARBINARY(16)**. The second column stores the salt, which will be a string 20 characters long.

3. Update the first customer's PIN **B**:

```
UPDATE customers
SET nacl = SUBSTRING(MD5(RAND( )),
→ -20)
WHERE customer_id=1;
UPDATE customers
SET pin=AES_ENCRYPT(1234, nacl)
WHERE customer_id=1;
```

The first query updates the customer's record, adding a salt value to the *nacl* column. That random value is obtained by applying the **MD5( )** function to the output from the **RAND( )** function. This will create a string 32 characters long, such as *4b8bb06aea7f3d162ad5b4d83687e3ac*. Then the last 20 characters are taken from this string, using **SUBSTRING( )**.

The second query stores the customer's PIN—1234, using the already-stored *nacl* value as the salt.

A Two columns are added to the *customers* table.

```
mysql> UPDATE customers
    -> SET nacl = SUBSTRING(MD5(RAND()), -20)
    -> WHERE customer_id=1;
Query OK, 1 row affected (0.08 sec)
Rows matched: 1  Changed: 1  Warnings: 0

mysql> UPDATE customers
    -> SET pin=AES_ENCRYPT(1234, nacl)
    -> WHERE customer_id=1;
Query OK, 1 row affected (0.00 sec)
Rows matched: 1  Changed: 1  Warnings: 0

mysql>
```

B A record is updated, using an encryption function to protect the PIN.

4. Retrieve the PIN in an unencrypted form **C**:

```
SELECT customer_id, AES_DECRYPT(pin,
nacl) AS pin FROM customers
WHERE customer_id=1;
```

This query returns the decrypted PIN for the customer with a *customer_id* of 1. Any value stored using **AES_ENCRYPT( )** can be retrieved (and matched) using **AES_DECRYPT( )**, as long as the same salt is used.

5. Check out the customer's record without using decryption **D**:

```
SELECT * FROM customers
WHERE customer_id=1;
```

As you can see in the figure, the encrypted version of the PIN is unreadable.

TIP As a rule of thumb, use SHA1( ) for information that will never need to be viewable, such as passwords and perhaps usernames. Use AES_ENCRYPT( ) for information that needs to be protected but may need to be viewable at a later date, such as credit card information, Social Security numbers, addresses (perhaps), and so forth.

TIP As a reminder, never storing credit card numbers and other high-risk data is always the safest option.

TIP The SHA2( ) function is an improvement over SHA1( ) and should be preferred for hashing data. I only chose not to use it in this book because SHA2( ) requires MySQL 5.5.5 or later.

TIP The same salting technique can be applied to SHA1( ), SHA2( ), and other functions.

TIP Be aware that data sent to the MySQL server, or received from it, could be intercepted and viewed. Better security can be had by using an **SSL** connection to the MySQL database.

C The record has been retrieved, decrypting the PIN in the process.

D Encrypted data is stored in an unreadable format (here, as a binary string of data).

Review and Pursue

If you have any problems with the review questions or the pursue prompts, turn to the book's supporting forum (`www.LarryUllman.com/forums/`).

Review

- What are the two primary types of joins?

- Why are aliases often used with joins?

- Why is it considered often necessary and at least a best practice to use the *table.column* syntax in joins?

- What impact does the order of tables used have on an outer join?

- How do you create a self-join?

- What are the aggregate functions?

- What impact does the **DISTINCT** keyword have on an aggregate function? What impact does **GROUP BY** have on an aggregate function?

- What kind of index is required in order to perform **FULLTEXT** searches? What type of storage engine?

- What impact does it have when you conclude a **SELECT** query with **\G** instead of a semicolon in the mysql client?

- How do **IN BOOLEAN MODE FULLTEXT** searches differ from standard **FULLTEXT** searches?

- What commands can you use to improve a table's performance?

- How do you examine the efficiency of a query?

- Why doesn't the *forum* database support transactions?

- How do you begin a transaction? How do you undo the effects of a transaction in progress? How do you make the effects of the current transaction permanent?

- What kind of column type is required to store the output from the **AES_ ENCRYPT( )** function?

- What are the important criteria for the salt used in the encryption process?

Pursue

- Come up with more join examples for the *forum* and *banking* databases. Perform inner joins, outer joins, and joins across all three tables.

- Check out the MySQL manual pages if you're curious about the **UNION** SQL command or about subqueries.

- Perform some more grouping exercises on the *banking* or *forum* databases.

- Practice running **FULLTEXT** searches on the *forum* database.

- Examine other queries to see the results.

- Read the MySQL manual pages, and other online tutorials, on explaining queries and optimizing tables.

- Play with transactions some more.

- Research the subjects of salting passwords and rainbow attacks to learn more.

Error Handling and Debugging

If you're working through this book sequentially (which would be for the best), the next subject to learn is how to use PHP and MySQL together. However, that process will undoubtedly generate errors, errors that can be tricky to debug. So before moving on to new concepts, these next few pages address the bane of the programmer: *errors*. As you gain experience, you'll make fewer errors and learn your own debugging methods, but there are plenty of tools and techniques the beginner can use to help ease the learning process.

This chapter has three main threads. One focus is on learning about the various kinds of errors that can occur when developing dynamic Web sites and what their likely causes are. Second, a multitude of debugging techniques are taught, in a step-by-step format. Finally, you'll see different techniques for handling the errors that do occur in the most graceful manner possible.

Error Types and Basic Debugging

When developing Web applications with PHP and MySQL, you end up with potential bugs in one of four or more technologies. You could have HTML issues, PHP problems, SQL errors, or MySQL mistakes. The first step in fixing any bug is finding its source.

HTML problems are often the least disruptive and the easiest to catch. You normally know there's a problem when your layout is all messed up. Some steps for catching and fixing these, as well as general debugging hints, are discussed in the next section.

PHP errors are the ones you'll see most often, as this language will be at the heart of your applications. PHP errors fall into three general areas:

- Syntactical
- Run-time
- Logical

Syntactical errors are the most common and the easiest to fix. You'll see them if you merely omit a semicolon. Such errors stop the script from executing, and if *display_errors* is on in your PHP configuration, PHP will show an error, including the line PHP thinks it's on Ⓐ. If *display_errors* is off, you'll see a blank page. (You'll learn more about *display_errors* later in this chapter.)

Run-time errors include those things that don't stop a PHP script from executing (like parse errors do) but do stop the script from doing everything it was supposed to do. Examples include calling a function using the wrong number or types of parameters. With these errors, PHP will normally display a message indicating the exact problem Ⓑ (again, assuming that *display_errors* is on).

Parse error: syntax error, unexpected $end in /Users/larryullman/Sites/phpmysql4/display_errors.php on line **21**

Ⓐ Parse errors—which you've probably seen many times over by now—are the most common sort of PHP error, particularly for beginning programmers.

Warning: round() expects at least 1 parameter, 0 given in /Users/larryullman/Sites/phpmysql4/display_errors.php on line **13**

Ⓑ Misusing a function (calling it with improper parameters) will create errors during the execution of the script.

The Right Mentality

Before getting much further, a word regarding errors: they happen to the best of us. Even the author of this here book sees more than enough errors in his Web development duties (but rest assured that the code in this book should be bug-free). Thinking that you'll get to a skill level where errors never occur is a fool's dream, but there are techniques for minimizing errors, and knowing how to quickly catch, handle, and fix errors is a major skill in its own right. So try not to become frustrated as you make errors; instead, bask in the knowledge that you're becoming a better debugger!

The final category of error—logical—is actually the worst, because PHP won't necessarily report it to you. These are out-and-out bugs: problems that aren't obvious and don't stop the execution of a script. Tricks for solving all of these PHP errors will be demonstrated in just a few pages.

SQL errors are normally a matter of syntax, and they'll be reported when you try to run the query in MySQL. For example, I've done this too many times :

`DELETE * FROM tablename`

The syntax is just wrong, a confusion with the **SELECT** syntax (**SELECT * FROM** *tablename*). The correct syntax is

`DELETE FROM tablename`

Again, MySQL will raise a red flag when you have SQL errors, so these aren't that difficult to find and fix. With modern Web sites, the catch is that you don't always have static queries, but often ones dynamically generated by PHP. In such cases, if there's an SQL syntax problem, the issue is probably in your PHP code.

Besides reporting on SQL errors, MySQL has its own errors to consider. An inability

to access the database is a common one and a showstopper at that . You'll also see errors when you misuse a MySQL function or ambiguously refer to a column in a join. Again, MySQL will report any such error in specific detail. Keep in mind that when a query doesn't return the records or otherwise have the result you expect, that's not a MySQL or SQL error, but rather a logical one. Toward the end of this chapter you'll see how to solve SQL and MySQL problems.

But as you have to walk before you can run, the next section covers the fundamentals of debugging dynamic Web sites, starting with the basic checks you should make and how to fix HTML problems.

Basic debugging steps

This first sequence of steps may seem obvious, but when it comes to debugging, missing one of these steps leads to an unproductive and extremely frustrating debugging experience. And while I'm at it, I should mention that the best piece of general debugging advice is this:

When you get frustrated, step away from the computer!

continues on next page

C MySQL will report any errors found in the syntax of an SQL command.

D An inability to connect to a MySQL server or a specific database is a common MySQL error.

I have solved almost all of the most perplexing issues I've come across by taking a break, clearing my head, and coming back to the code with fresh eyes. Readers in the book's supporting forum (**www.LarryUllman.com/forums/**) have frequently found this to be true as well. Trying to forge ahead when you're frustrated tends to make things worse. Much worse.

To begin debugging any problem:

- Make sure that you are running the right page.

    It's altogether too common that you try to fix a problem and no matter what you do, it never goes away. The reason: you've actually been editing a different page than you thought. So verify that the name and location of the file being executed matches that of the file you're editing. In this regard, using an all-in-one IDE, such as Adobe Dreamweaver (**www.adobe.com/go/dreamweaver**), is an advantage.

- Make sure that you have saved your latest changes.

An unsaved document will continue to have the same problems it had before you edited it (because the edits haven't been enacted). One of the many reasons I like the TextMate (**www.macromates.com**) text editor is that it automatically saves every document when the application loses focus.

- Make sure that you run all PHP pages through the URL.

    Because PHP works through a Web server (Apache, IIS, etc.), running any PHP code requires that you access the page through a URL (**http://www.example.com/page.php** or **http://localhost/page.php**). If you double-click a PHP page to open it in a browser (or use the browser's File > Open option), you'll see the PHP code, not the executed result. This also occurs if you load an HTML page without going through a URL (which will work on its own) but then submit the form to a PHP page **Ⓔ**.

Ⓔ PHP code will only be executed if run through a URL. This means that forms that submit to a PHP page must also be loaded through **http://**.

- Know what versions of PHP and MySQL you are running.

  Some problems are specific to a certain version of PHP or MySQL. For example, some functions are added in later versions of PHP, and MySQL added significant new features in versions 4, 4.1, and 5. Run a **phpinfo( )** script 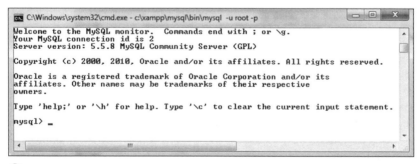(see Appendix A, "Installation," for a script example) and open a mysql client session to determine this information. phpMyAdmin will often report on the versions involved as well (but don't confuse the version of phpMyAdmin, which will likely be 3.*something,* with the versions of PHP or MySQL).

I consider the versions being used to be such an important, fundamental piece of information that I won't normally assist people looking for help until they provide this information!

- Know what Web server you are running.

  Similarly, some problems and features are unique to your Web serving application—Apache, IIS, or Abyss. You should know which one you are using, and which version, from when you installed the application. If you're using a Web host, the hosting company can provide you with this information.

- Try executing pages in a different Web browser.

  Every Web developer should have and use at least two Web browsers. If you test your pages in different ones, you'll be able to see if the problem has to do with your script or a particular browser. Normally, only HTML and CSS problems can arise (or disappear) when you switch browsers; rarely will PHP, let alone MySQL or SQL, errors be browser specific.

  continues on next page

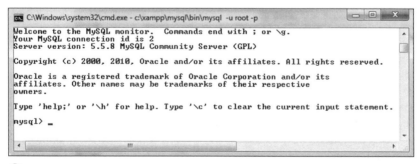

F A **phpinfo( )** script is one of your best tools for debugging, informing you of the PHP version and how it's configured.

G When you connect to a MySQL server, it will let you know the version number in use.

- If possible, try executing the page using a different Web server, version of PHP, and/or version of MySQL.

  PHP and MySQL errors sometimes stem from particular configurations and versions on one server. If something works on one server but not another, then you'll know that the script isn't inherently at fault. From there it's a matter of using `phpinfo( )` scripts to see what server settings may be different.

TIP If taking a break is one thing you should do when you become frustrated, here's what you *shouldn't* do: send off one or multiple panicky and persnickety emails to a writer, to a newsgroup or mailing list, or to anyone else. When it comes to asking for free help from strangers, patience and pleasantries garner much better and faster results.

TIP For that matter, I would strongly advise *against* randomly guessing at solutions. I've seen far too many people only complicate matters further by taking stabs at solutions, without a full understanding of what the attempted changes should or should not do.

TIP There's another different realm of errors that you could classify as *usage* errors: what goes wrong when the site's user doesn't do what you thought they would. As a golden rule, write your code so that it doesn't break even if the user doesn't do anything right or does everything wrong! In other words, make no assumptions. There's a quote from Doug Linder that applies here: "A good programmer is someone who looks both ways before crossing a one-way street."

Debugging HTML

Debugging HTML is relatively easy. The source code is very accessible, most problems are overt, and attempts at fixing the HTML don't normally make things worse (as can happen with PHP). Still, there are some basic steps you should follow to find and fix an HTML problem.

To debug an HTML error:

- Check the source code.

  If you have an HTML problem, you'll almost always need to check the source code of the page to find it. How you view the source code depends upon the browser being used, but normally it's a matter of using something like View > Page Source or View > Source.

- Use a validation tool **H**.

  Validation tools, like the one at **http:// validator.w3.org**, are great for finding mismatched tags, broken tables, and other problems.

- Use Firefox.

  I'm not trying to start a discussion on which is the best Web browser, and as Internet Explorer is (still!) the most used one, you'll need to eventually test using it, but I personally find that Firefox (available for free from **www.mozilla. com**) is the best Web browser for Web developers. Firefox offers reliability and debugging features not available in other browsers. If you want to stick with IE or Safari for your day-to-day browsing, that's up to you, but when doing Web development, turn to Firefox.

- Use Firefox's add-on widgets **I**.

  Besides being just a great Web browser, the very popular Firefox browser has a ton of features that the Web developer will appreciate. Furthermore, you can expand Firefox's functionality by installing any of the free widgets that are available. The Web Developer widget in particular provides quick access to great tools, such as showing a table's borders, revealing the CSS, validating a page, and more. I also frequently use these add-ons: Firebug, DOM Inspector, and HTML Validator, among others.

H Validation tools like the one provided by the W3C (World Wide Web Consortium) are good for finding problems and making sure your HTML conforms to standards.

I Firefox's Web Developer widget provides quick access to lots of useful tools.

- Test the page in another browser.

  PHP code is generally browser-independent, meaning you'll get consistent results regardless of the client. Not so with HTML. Sometimes a particular browser has a quirk that affects the rendered page. Running the same page in another browser is the easiest way to know if it's an HTML problem or a browser quirk.

TIP The first step toward fixing any kind of problem is understanding what's causing it. Remember the role each technology—HTML, PHP, SQL, and MySQL—plays as you debug. If your page doesn't look right, that's an HTML problem. If your HTML is dynamically generated by PHP, it's still an HTML problem, but you'll need to work with the PHP code to make it right.

Book Errors

If you've followed an example in this book and something's not working right, what should you do?

1. Double-check your code or steps against those in the book.

2. Use the index at the back of the book to see if I reference a script or function in an earlier page (you may have missed an important usage rule or tip).

3. View the PHP manual for a specific function to see if it's available in your version of PHP and to verify how the function is used.

4. Check out the book's errata page (through the supporting Web site, **www.LarryUllman.com**) to see if an error in the code does exist and has been reported. Don't post your particular problem there yet, though!

5. Triple-check your code and use all the debugging techniques outlined in this chapter.

6. Search the book's supporting forum to see if others have had this problem and if a solution has already been determined.

7. If all else fails, use the book's supporting forum to ask for assistance. When you do, make sure you include all the pertinent information (version of PHP, version of MySQL, the debugging steps you took and what the results were, etc.).

Displaying PHP Errors

PHP provides remarkably useful and descriptive error messages when things go awry. Unfortunately, PHP doesn't show these errors when running using its default configuration. This policy makes sense for live servers, where you don't want the end users seeing PHP-specific error messages, but it also makes everything that much more confusing for the beginning PHP developer. To be able to see PHP's errors, you must turn on the *display_ errors* directive, either in an individual script or for the PHP configuration as a whole.

To turn on *display_errors* in a script, use the **ini_set( )** function. As its arguments, this function takes a directive name and what setting that directive should have:

```
ini_set('display_errors', 1);
```

Including this line in a script will turn on *display_errors* for that script. The only downside is that if your script has a syntax error that prevents it from running at all, then you'll still see a blank page. To have PHP display errors for the entire server, you'll need to edit its configuration, as is discussed in the "Configuring PHP" section of Appendix A.

To turn on display_errors:

1. Create a new PHP document in your text editor or IDE, to be named **display_errors.php** (Script 8.1):

```
<!DOCTYPE html PUBLIC "-//W3C//DTD
→ XHTML 1.0 Transitional//EN"
"http://www.w3.org/TR/xhtml1/DTD/
→ xhtml1-transitional.dtd">
<html xmlns="http://www.w3.org/
→ 1999/xhtml" xml:lang="en"
→ lang="en">
```

Script 8.1 The **ini_set( )** function can be used to tell a PHP script to reveal any errors that might occur.

```
1    <!DOCTYPE html PUBLIC "-//W3C//DTD XHTML
     1.0 Transitional//EN"
2        "http://www.w3.org/TR/xhtml1/DTD/
         xhtml1-transitional.dtd">
3    <html xmlns="http://www.w3.org/1999/
     xhtml" xml:lang="en" lang="en">
4    <head>
5       <meta http-equiv="Content-Type"
        content="text/html; charset=utf-8" />
6       <title>Displaying Errors</title>
7    </head>
8    <body>
9    <h2>Testing Display Errors</h2>
10   <?php # Script 8.1 - display_errors.php
11
12   // Show errors:
13   ini_set('display_errors', 1);
14
15   // Create errors:
16   foreach ($var as $v) {}
17   $result = 1/0;
18
19   ?>
20   </body>
21   </html>
```

```
<head>
  <meta http-equiv="Content-type"
  → content="text/html;
  → charset=iso-8859-1" />
  <title>Displaying Errors</title>
</head>
<body>
<h2>Testing Display Errors</h2>
<?php # Script 8.1 -
→ display_errors.php
```

2. After the initial PHP tags, add:

```
ini_set('display_errors', 1);
```

From this point in this script forward, any errors that occur will be displayed.

3. Create some errors:

```
foreach ($var as $v) {}
$result = 1/0;
```

To test the *display_errors* setting, the script needs to have at least one error. This first line doesn't even try to do anything, but it's guaranteed to cause an error. There are actually two issues here: first, there's a reference to a variable (**$var**) that doesn't exist; second, a non-array (**$var**) is being used in the **foreach** loop as if it were an array.

The second line is a classic division by zero, which is not allowed in programming languages or in math.

4. Complete the page:

```
?>
</body>
</html>
```

5. Save the file as **display_errors.php**, place it in your Web directory, and test it in your Web browser **A**.

6. If you want, change the first line of PHP code to read:

```
ini_set('display_errors', 0);
```

Then save and retest the script **B**.

TIP There are limits as to what PHP settings the `ini_set( )` function can be used to adjust. See the PHP manual for specifics as to what can and cannot be changed using it.

TIP As a reminder, changing the *display_errors* setting in a script only works so long as that script runs (i.e., it cannot have any parse errors). To be able to *always* see any errors that occur, you'll need to enable *display_errors* in PHP's configuration file (again, see the appendix).

A With *display_errors* turned on (for this script), the page reports the errors when they occur.

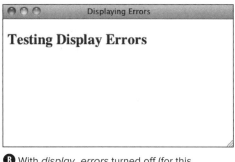

B With *display_errors* turned off (for this page), the same errors are no longer reported. Unfortunately, they still exist.

Adjusting Error Reporting in PHP

Once you have PHP set to display the errors that occur, you might want to adjust the level of error reporting. Your PHP installation as a whole, or individual scripts, can be set to report or ignore different types of errors. **Table 8.1** lists most of the levels, but they can generally be one of these three kinds:

- *Notices*, which do not stop the execution of a script and may not necessarily be a problem.

- *Warnings*, which indicate a problem but don't stop a script's execution.

- *Errors*, which stop a script from continuing (including the ever-common parse error, which prevents scripts from running at all).

As a rule of thumb, you'll want PHP to report on any kind of error while you're developing a site but report no specific errors once the site goes live. For security and aesthetic purposes, it's generally unwise for a public user to see PHP's detailed error messages.

Suppressing Errors with @

Individual errors can be suppressed in PHP using the error suppression operator, **@**. For example, if you don't want PHP to report if it couldn't include a file, you would code

```
@include ('config.inc.php');
```

Or if you don't want to see a "division by zero" error:

```
$x = 8;
$y = 0;
$num = @($x/$y);
```

The **@** symbol will work only on expressions, like function calls or mathematical operations. You cannot use **@** before conditionals, loops, function definitions, and so forth.

As a rule of thumb, I recommend that **@** be used on functions whose execution, should they fail, will not affect the functionality of the script as a whole. Or you can choose not to display PHP's errors by handling them more gracefully yourself (a topic discussed later in this chapter).

TABLE 8.1 Error-Reporting Levels

Number	Constant	Report On
1	E_ERROR	Fatal run-time errors (that stop execution of the script)
2	E_WARNING	Run-time warnings (non-fatal errors)
4	E_PARSE	Parse errors
8	E_NOTICE	Notices (things that could or could not be a problem)
256	E_USER_ERROR	User-generated error messages, generated by the **trigger_error( )** function
512	E_USER_WARNING	User-generated warnings, generated by the **trigger_error( )** function
1024	E_USER_NOTICE	User-generated notices, generated by the **trigger_error( )** function
2048	E_STRICT	Recommendations for compatibility and interoperability
8192	E_DEPRECATED	Warnings about code that won't work in future versions of PHP
30719	E_ALL	All errors, warnings, and recommendations

Script 8.2 This script will demonstrate how error reporting can be manipulated in PHP.

```
1   <!DOCTYPE html PUBLIC "-//W3C//DTD XHTML
    1.0 Transitional//EN"
2        "http://www.w3.org/TR/xhtml1/DTD/
         xhtml1-transitional.dtd">
3   <html xmlns="http://www.w3.org/1999/
    xhtml" xml:lang="en" lang="en">
4   <head>
5      <meta http-equiv="Content-Type"
       content="text/html; charset=utf-8" />
6      <title>Reporting Errors</title>
7   </head>
8   <body>
9   <h2>Testing Error Reporting</h2>
10  <?php # Script 8.2 - report_errors.php
11
12  // Show errors:
13  ini_set('display_errors', 1);
14
15  // Adjust error reporting:
16  error_reporting(E_ALL | E_STRICT);
17
18  // Create errors:
19  foreach ($var as $v) {}
20  $result = 1/0;
21
22  ?>
23  </body>
24  </html>
```

Frequently, error messages—particularly those dealing with the database—will reveal certain behind-the-scenes aspects of your Web application that are best not shown. While you hope all of these will be worked out during the development stage, that may not be the case.

You can universally adjust the level of error reporting following the instructions in Appendix A. Or you can adjust this behavior on a script-by-script basis using the **error_reporting( )** function. This function is used to establish what type of errors PHP should report on within a specific page. The function takes either a number or a constant, using the values in Table 8.1 (the PHP manual lists a few others, related to the core of PHP itself).

error_reporting(0); // Show no errors.

A setting of 0 turns error reporting off entirely (errors will still occur; you just won't see them anymore). Conversely, **error_reporting (E_ALL)** will tell PHP to report on every error that occurs. The numbers can be added up to customize the level of error reporting, or you could use the bitwise operators—**|** (or), **~** (not), **&** (and)—with the constants. With this following setting, any non-notice error will be shown:

error_reporting (E_ALL & ~E_NOTICE);

To adjust error reporting:

1. Open **display_errors.php** (Script 8.1) in your text editor or IDE, if it is not already.

   To play around with error reporting levels, use **display_errors.php** as an example.

2. After adjusting the *display_errors* setting, add (**Script 8.2**):

   error_reporting(E_ALL | E_STRICT);

   continues on next page

For development purposes, have PHP notify you of all errors, notices, warnings, and recommendations. Setting the level of error reporting to **E_ALL** will accomplish that. But **E_ALL** does not include **E_STRICT**, so another clause— | (or) **E_STRICT**—is added.

In short, now PHP will let you know about anything that is, or just may be, a problem.

Because **E_ALL** and **E_STRICT** are constants, they are not enclosed in quotation marks.

3. Save the file as **report_errors.php**, place it in your Web directory, and run it in your Web browser **A**.

I also altered the page's title and the heading, but both are immaterial to the point of this exercise.

4. Change the level of error reporting to something different and retest **B** and **C**.

TIP The numeric value of E_ALL in Table 8.1 can differ from one version of PHP to the next.

TIP Because you'll often want to adjust the *display_errors* and *error_reporting* for every page in a Web site, you might want to place those lines of code in a separate PHP file that can then be included by other PHP scripts.

TIP The scripts in this book were all written with PHP's error reporting on the highest level (with the intention of catching every possible problem).

TIP The trigger_error( ) function is a way to programmatically generate an error in a PHP script. Its first argument is an error message; its second, optional, argument is a numeric error type, corresponding to the values in Table 8.1. By default the type will be E_USER.

```
if (/* some condition */) {
    trigger_error('Something Bad
    ➝ Happened!');
}
```

A On the highest level of error reporting, PHP has two warnings and one notice for this page (Script 8.2).

Reporting Errors

Testing Error Reporting

Warning: Invalid argument supplied for foreach() in /Users/larryullman/Sites/phpmysql4/report_errors.php on line **19**

Warning: Division by zero in /Users/larryullman/Sites/phpmysql4/report_errors.php on line **20**

B The same page (Script 8.2) after disabling the reporting of notices.

Reporting Errors

Testing Error Reporting

C The same page again (Script 8.2) with error reporting turned off (set to 0). The result is the same as if *display_errors* was disabled. Of course, the errors still occur; they're just not being reported.

Creating Custom Error Handlers

Another option for error management with your sites is to alter how PHP handles errors. By default, if *display_errors* is enabled and an error is caught (that falls under the level of error reporting), PHP will print the error, in a somewhat simplistic form, within some minimal HTML tags 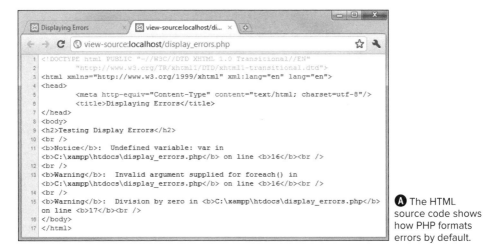.

You can override how errors are handled by creating your own function that will be called when errors occur. For example,

```
function report_errors (arguments) {
    // Do whatever here.
}
set_error_handler ('report_errors');
```

The PHP **set_error_handler( )** function is used to name the user-defined function to be called when an error occurs. The handling function (*report_errors*, in this case) will, at that time, receive several values that can be used in any possible manner.

This function can be written to take up to five arguments. In order, these arguments are: an error number (corresponding to

Table 8.1), a textual error message, the name of the file where the error was found, the specific line number on which it occurred, and the variables that existed at the time of the error. Defining a function that accepts all these arguments might look like

```
function report_errors ($num, $msg,
→ $file, $line, $vars) {...
```

To make use of this concept, the **report_errors.php** file (Script 8.2) will be rewritten one last time.

To create your own error handler:

1. Open **report_errors.php** (Script 8.2) in your text editor or IDE, if it is not already.

2. Remove the **ini_set( )** and **error_reporting( )** lines (**Script 8.3**).

   When you establish your own error-handling function, the error reporting levels no longer have any meaning, so the line that adjusts them can be removed. Adjusting the *display_errors* setting is also meaningless, as the error-handling function will control whether errors are displayed or not.

continues on page 255

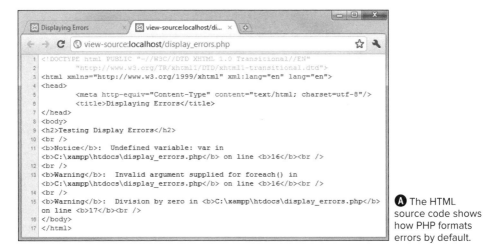

A The HTML source code shows how PHP formats errors by default.

Script 8.3 By defining your own error-handling function, you can customize how errors are treated in your PHP scripts.

```
1    <!DOCTYPE html PUBLIC "-//W3C//DTD XHTML 1.0 Transitional//EN"
2         "http://www.w3.org/TR/xhtml1/DTD/xhtml1-transitional.dtd">
3    <html xmlns="http://www.w3.org/1999/xhtml" xml:lang="en" lang="en">
4    <head>
5       <meta http-equiv="Content-Type" content="text/html; charset=utf-8" />
6       <title>Handling Errors</title>
7    </head>
8    <body>
9
10   <h2>Testing Error Handling</h2>
11   <?php # Script 8.3 - handle_errors.php
12
13   // Flag variable for site status:
14   define('LIVE', FALSE);
15
16   // Create the error handler:
17   function my_error_handler ($e_number, $e_message, $e_file, $e_line, $e_vars) {
18
19      // Build the error message:
20      $message = "An error occurred in script '$e_file' on line $e_line: $e_message\n";
21
22      // Append $e_vars to  $message:
23      $message .= print_r ($e_vars, 1);
24
25      if (!LIVE) { // Development (print the error).
26         echo '<pre>' . $message . "\n";
27         debug_print_backtrace();
28         echo '</pre><br />';
29      } else { // Don't show the error.
30         echo '<div class="error">A system error occurred. We apologize for the
            inconvenience.</div><br />';
31      }
32
33   } // End of my_error_handler() definition.
34
35   // Use my error handler:
36   set_error_handler ('my_error_handler');
37
38   // Create errors:
39   foreach ($var as $v) {}
40   $result = 1/0;
41
42   ?>
43   </body>
44   </html>
```

3. Before the script creates the errors, add:

```
define ('LIVE', FALSE);
```

This constant will be a flag used to indicate whether or not the site is currently live. It's an important distinction, as how you handle errors and what you reveal in the browser should differ greatly when you're developing a site and when a site is live.

This constant is being set outside of the function for two reasons. First, I want to treat the function as a black box that does what I need it to do without having to go in and tinker with it. Second, in many sites, there might be other settings (like the database connectivity information) that are also live versus development-specific. Conditionals could, therefore, also refer to this constant to adjust those settings.

4. Begin defining the error-handling function:

```
function my_error_handler
→ ($e_number, $e_message, $e_file,
→ $e_line, $e_vars) {
```

The `my_error_handler()` function is set to receive the full five arguments that a custom error handler can.

5. Create the error message using the received values.

```
$message = "An error occurred
→ in script '$e_file' on line
→ $e_line: $e_message\n";
```

The error message will begin by referencing the filename and line number where the error occurred. Added to this is the actual error message. All of these values are passed to the function when it is called (when an error occurs).

6. Add any existing variables to the error message:

```
$message .= print_r ($e_vars, 1);
```

The `$e_vars` variable will receive all of the variables that exist, and their values, when the error happens. Because this might contain useful debugging information, it's added to the message.

The `print_r()` function is normally used to print out a variable's structure and value; it is particularly useful with arrays. If you call the function with a second argument (1 or TRUE), the result is returned instead of printed. So this line adds all of the variable information to `$message`.

7. Print a message that will vary, depending upon whether or not the site is live:

```
if (!LIVE) {
    echo '<pre>' . $message . "\n";
    debug_print_backtrace();
    echo '</pre><br />';
} else {
    echo '<div class="error">
    → A system error occurred.
    → We apologize for the
    → inconvenience.</div><br />';
}
```

continues on next page

If the site is not live (if **LIVE** is FALSE), which would be the case while the site is being developed, a detailed error message should be printed **B**. For ease of viewing, the error message is printed within HTML **PRE** tags. Furthermore, a useful debugging function, **debug_print_backtrace( )**, is also called. This function returns a slew of information about what functions have been called, what files have been included, and so forth.

If the site is live, a simple mea culpa will be printed, letting the user know that an error occurred but not what the specific problem is **C**. Under this situation, you could also use the **error_log( )** function (see the sidebar) to have the detailed error message emailed or written to a log.

```
● ○ ○                          Handling Errors

Testing Error Handling

An error occurred in script '/Users/larryullman/Sites/phpmysql4/handle_errors.php' on line 39: Undefined variable: var
Array
(
    [GLOBALS] => Array
 *RECURSION*
    [_ENV] => Array
        (
            [SHELL] => /bin/bash
            [TMPDIR] => /var/folders/P3/P3RIUu4AEC035t0ffrBGXU+++TI/-Tmp-/
            [Apple_PubSub_Socket_Render] => /tmp/launch-zrfx4g/Render
            [USER] => larryullman
            [COMMAND_MODE] => legacy
            [SSH_AUTH_SOCK] => /tmp/launch-wjP9AP/Listeners
            [__CF_USER_TEXT_ENCODING] => 0x1F5:0:0
            [PATH] => /usr/bin:/bin:/usr/sbin:/sbin
            [PWD] => /
            [SHLVL] => 1
            [HOME] => /Users/larryullman
            [DYLD_LIBRARY_PATH] => /Applications/MAMP/Library/lib:
            [LOGNAME] => larryullman
            [DISPLAY] => /tmp/launch-b2WLIf/org.x:0
            [_] => /Applications/MAMP/Library/bin/httpd
        )

    [HTTP_ENV_VARS] => Array
        (
            [SHELL] => /bin/bash
            [TMPDIR] => /var/folders/P3/P3RIUu4AEC035t0ffrBGXU+++TI/-Tmp-/
            [Apple_PubSub_Socket_Render] => /tmp/launch-zrfx4g/Render
            [USER] => larryullman
            [COMMAND_MODE] => legacy
            [SSH_AUTH_SOCK] => /tmp/launch-wjP9AP/Listeners
            [__CF_USER_TEXT_ENCODING] => 0x1F5:0:0
            [PATH] => /usr/bin:/bin:/usr/sbin:/sbin
```

B During the development phase, detailed error messages are printed in the Web browser. (In a more real-world script, with more code, the messages would be more useful.)

```
● ○ ○                     Handling Errors

Testing Error Handling

A system error occurred. We apologize for the inconvenience.

A system error occurred. We apologize for the inconvenience.

A system error occurred. We apologize for the inconvenience.
```

C Once a site has gone live, more user-friendly (and less revealing) errors are printed. Here, one message is printed for each of the three errors in the script.

Logging PHP Errors

In Script 8.3, errors are handled by simply printing them out in detail or not. Another option is to *log* the errors: make a permanent note of them somehow. For this purpose, the **error_log( )** function instructs PHP how to file an error. Its syntax is

```
error_log (message, type,
→ destination, extra headers);
```

The *message* value should be the text of the logged error (i.e., **$message** in Script 8.3). The *type* dictates how the error is logged. The options are the numbers 0, 1, 3, and 4: use the computer's default logging method (0), send it in an email (1), write it to a text file (3), or send it to the Web server's logging handler (4).

The *destination* parameter can be either the name of a file (for log type 3) or an email address (for log type 1). The *extra headers* argument is used only when sending emails (log type 1). Both the destination and extra headers are optional.

8. Complete the function and tell PHP to use it:

```
}
set_error_handler('my_error_
→ handler');
```

This second line is the important one, telling PHP to use the custom error handler instead of PHP's default handler.

9. Save the file as **handle_errors.php**, place it in your Web directory, and test it in your Web browser **B**.

10. Change the value of **LIVE** to TRUE, save, and retest the script **C**.

To see how the error handler behaves with a live site, just change this one value.

TIP If your PHP page uses special HTML formatting—like CSS tags to affect the layout and font treatment—add this information to your error reporting function.

TIP Obviously in a live site you'll probably need to do more than apologize for the inconvenience (particularly if the error significantly affects the page's functionality). Still, this example demonstrates how you can easily adjust error handling to suit the situation.

TIP If you don't want the error-handling function to report on every notice, error, or warning, you could check the error number value (the first argument sent to the function). For example, to ignore notices when the site is live, you would change the main conditional to

```
if (!LIVE) {
    echo '<pre>' . $message . "\n";
    debug_print_backtrace( );
    echo '</pre><br />';
} elseif ($e_number != E_NOTICE) {
    echo '<div class="error">A system
    → error occurred. We apologize
    → for the inconvenience.</div>
    → <br />';
}
```

PHP Debugging Techniques

When it comes to debugging, what you'll best learn from experience are the causes of certain types of errors. Understanding the common causes will shorten the time it takes to fix errors. To expedite the learning process, **Table 8.2** lists the likely reasons for the most common PHP errors.

The first, and most common, type of error that you'll run across is syntactical and will prevent your scripts from executing. An error like this will result in messages like the one in Ⓐ, which every PHP developer has seen too many times. To avoid making this sort of mistake when you program, be sure to:

- End every statement (but not language constructs like loops and conditionals) with a semicolon.

- Balance all quotation marks, parentheses, curly braces, and square brackets (each opening character must be closed).

Parse error: syntax error, unexpected T_ENCAPSED_AND_WHITESPACE, expecting T_STRING or T_VARIABLE or T_NUM_STRING in **/Users/larryullman/Sites/phpmysql4/errors.php** on line **10**

Ⓐ The parse error prevents a script from running because of invalid PHP syntax. This one was caused by failing to enclose `$array['key']` within curly braces when printing its value.

TABLE 8.2 Common PHP Errors

Error	Likely Cause
Blank Page	HTML problem, or PHP error and *display_errors* or *error_reporting* is off.
Parse error	Missing semicolon; unbalanced curly braces, parentheses, or quotation marks; or use of an unescaped quotation mark in a string.
Empty variable value	Forgot the initial $, misspelled or miscapitalized the variable name, or inappropriate variable scope (with functions).
Undefined variable	Reference made to a variable before it is given a value or an empty variable value (see those potential causes).
Call to undefined function	Misspelled function name, PHP is not configured to use that function (like a MySQL function), or document that contains the function definition was not included.
Cannot redeclare function	Two definitions of your own function exist; check within included files.
Headers already sent	White space exists in the script before the PHP tags, data has already been printed, or a file has been included.

- Be consistent with your quotation marks (single quotes can be closed only with single quotes and double quotes with double quotes).

- Escape, using the backslash, all single- and double-quotation marks within strings, as appropriate.

One thing you should also understand about syntactical errors is that just because the PHP error message says the error is occurring on line 12, that doesn't mean that the mistake is actually on that line. At the very least, it is not uncommon for there to be a difference between what PHP thinks is line 12 and what your text editor indicates is line 12. So while PHP's direction is useful in tracking down a problem, treat the line number referenced as more of a starting point than an absolute.

If PHP reports an error on the last line of your document, this is almost always because a mismatched parenthesis, curly brace, or quotation mark was not caught until that moment.

The second type of error you'll encounter results from misusing a function. This error occurs, for example, when a function is called without the proper arguments. This error is discovered by PHP when attempting to execute the code. In later chapters you'll probably see such errors when using the **header( )** function, cookies, or sessions.

To fix errors, you'll need to do a little detective work to see what mistakes were made and where. For starters, though, always thoroughly read and trust the error message PHP offers. Although the referenced line number may not always be correct, a PHP error is very descriptive, normally helpful, and almost always 100 percent correct.

To debug your scripts:

- Turn on *display_errors*.

  Use the earlier steps to enable *display_errors* for a script, or, if possible, the entire server, as you develop your applications.

- Use comments.

  Just as you can use comments to document your scripts, you can also use them to rule out problematic lines. If PHP is giving you an error on line 12, then commenting out that line should get rid of the error. If not, then you know the error is elsewhere. Just be careful that you don't introduce more errors by improperly commenting out only a portion of a code block: the syntax of your scripts must be maintained.

continues on next page

- Use the **print** and **echo** functions.

  In more complicated scripts, I frequently use **echo** statements to leave me notes as to what is happening as the script is executed **B**. When a script has several steps, it may not be easy to know if the problem is occurring in step 2 or step 5. By using an **echo** statement, you can narrow the problem down to the specific juncture.

- Check what quotation marks are being used for printing variables.

  It's not uncommon for programmers to mistakenly use single quotation marks and then wonder why their variables are not printed properly. Remember that single quotation marks treat text literally and that you must use double quotation marks to print out the values of variables.

- Track variables **C**.

  It is pretty easy for a script not to work because you referred to the wrong variable or the right variable by the wrong name or because the variable does not have the value you would expect. To check for these possibilities, use the **print** or **echo** statements to print out the values of variables at important points in your scripts. This is simply a matter of

  ```
  echo "<p>\$var = $var</p>\n";
  ```

  or

  ```
  echo "<p>\$var is $var</p>\n";
  ```

  The first dollar sign is escaped so that the variable's name is printed. The second reference of the variable will print its value.

The form has been submitted.

The data has been validated.

In the calculate_trip_cost() function.

Total Estimated Cost

The total cost of driving 235 miles, averaging 30 mile you drive at an average of 65 miles per hour, the trip

B More complex debugging can be accomplished by leaving yourself notes as to what the script is doing.

The form has been submitted.

The data has been validated.

$_POST['distance'] is 235.

$_POST['gallon_price'] is 3.50.

$_POST['efficiency'] is 30.

In the calculate_trip_cost() function.

$miles is 235.

$mpg is 30.

$ppg is 3.50.

Total Estimated Cost

The total cost of driving 235 miles, averaging 30 mile you drive at an average of 65 miles per hour, the trip

C Printing the names and values of variables is the easiest way to track them over the course of a script.

Using die() and exit()

Two functions that are often used with error management are **die( )** and **exit( )**, (they're technically language constructs, not functions, but who cares?). When a **die( )** or **exit( )** is called in your script, the entire script is terminated. Both are useful for stopping a script from continuing should something important—like establishing a database connection— fail to happen. You can also pass to **die( )** and **exit( )** a string that will be printed out in the browser.

You'll commonly see **die( )** or **exit( )** used in an **OR** conditional. For example:

```
include('config.inc.php') OR die
 →('Could not open the file. ');
```

With a line like that, if PHP could not include the configuration file, the **die( )** statement will be executed and the "Could not open the file." message will be printed. You'll see variations on this throughout this book and in the PHP manual, as it's a quick, but potentially excessive, way to handle errors without using a custom error handler.

■ Print array values.

For more complicated variable types (arrays and objects), the **print_r( )** and **var_dump( )** functions will print out their values without the need for loops. Both functions accomplish the same task, although **var_dump( )** is more detailed in its reporting than **print_r( )**.

TIP Many text editors include utilities to check for balanced parentheses, brackets, and quotation marks.

TIP If you cannot find the parse error in a complex script, begin by using the /* */ comments to render the entire PHP code inert. Then continue to uncomment sections at a time (by moving the opening or closing comment characters) and rerun the script until you deduce what lines are causing the error. Watch how you comment out control structures, though, as the curly braces must continue to be matched in order to avoid parse errors. For example:

```
if (condition) {
        /* Start comment.
        Inert code.
        End comment. */
}
```

TIP To make the results of print_r( ) more readable in the Web browser, wrap it within HTML <pre> (preformatted) tags. This one line is one of my favorite debugging tools:

```
echo '<pre>' . print_r ($var, 1) .
 →'</pre>';
```

SQL and MySQL Debugging Techniques

The most common SQL errors are caused by the following issues:

- Unbalanced use of quotation marks or parentheses
- Unescaped apostrophes in column values
- Misspelling a column name, table name, or function
- Ambiguously referring to a column in a join
- Placing a query's clauses (**WHERE**, **GROUP BY**, **ORDER BY**, **LIMIT**) in the wrong order

Furthermore, when using MySQL you can also run across the following:

- Unpredictable or inappropriate query results
- Inability to access the database

Since you'll be running the queries for your dynamic Web sites from PHP, you need a methodology for debugging SQL and MySQL errors within that context (PHP will not report a problem with your SQL).

Debugging SQL problems

To decide if you are experiencing a MySQL (or SQL) problem rather than a PHP one, you need a system for finding and fixing the issue. Fortunately, the steps you should take to debug MySQL and SQL problems are easy to define and should be followed without thinking. If you ever have any MySQL or SQL errors to debug, just abide by this sequence of steps.

To hammer the point home, this next sequence of steps is probably the most useful debugging technique in this chapter and the entire book. You'll likely need to follow these steps in any PHP-MySQL Web application when you're not getting the results you expected.

To debug your SQL queries:

1. Print out any applicable queries in your PHP script **A**.

   As you'll see in the next chapter, SQL queries will often be assigned to a variable, particularly when you use PHP to dynamically create them. Using the code **echo $query** (or whatever the query variable is called) in your PHP scripts, you can send to the browser the exact query being run. Sometimes this step alone will help you see what the real problem is.

2. Run the query in the mysql client or other tool **B**.

   The most foolproof method of debugging an SQL or MySQL problem is to run the query used in your PHP scripts through an independent application: the mysql client, phpMyAdmin, or the like. Doing so will give you the same result as the original PHP script receives but without the overhead, hassle, or mystery.

Home Page	Register	View Users	Change Password	link five
INSERT INTO users (first_name, last_name, email, password, registration_date) VALUES ('Larry', 'Ullman', 'Larry@example.com', SHA1('pass42'), NOW())				

A Knowing exactly what query a PHP script is attempting to execute is the most useful first step for solving SQL and MySQL problems.

If the independent application returns the expected result but you are still not getting the proper behavior in your PHP script, then you will know that the problem lies within the script itself, not your SQL command or the MySQL database.

3. If the problem still isn't evident, rewrite the query in its most basic form, and then keep adding dimensions back in until you discover which clause is causing the problem. Continue to use a third-party interface to MySQL to do this (i.e., put away the PHP script until you've got the SQL query working properly).

Sometimes it's difficult to debug a query because there's too much going on. Like commenting out most of a PHP script, taking a query down to its bare minimum structure and slowly building it back up can be the easiest way to debug complex SQL commands.

Debugging access problems

Access-denied error messages are the most common problem beginning developers encounter when using PHP to interact with MySQL. These are among the common solutions:

- Reload MySQL after altering the privileges so that the changes take effect. Either use the mysqladmin tool or run **FLUSH PRIVILEGES** in the mysql client. You must be logged in as a user with the appropriate permissions to do this (see Appendix A for more).

- Double-check the password used. The error message *Access denied for user: 'user@localhost' (Using password: YES)* frequently indicates that the password is wrong or mistyped. (This is not always the cause but is the first thing to check.)

- The error message *Can't connect to...* (error number 2002) indicates that MySQL either is not running or is not running on the socket or TCP/IP port tried by the client.

TIP MySQL keeps its own error logs, which are very useful in solving MySQL problems (like why MySQL won't even start). MySQL's error log will be located in the MySQL data directory and titled `hostname.err`.

TIP The MySQL manual is very detailed, containing SQL examples, function references, and the meanings of error codes. Make the manual your friend and turn to it when confusing errors pop up.

B To understand what result a PHP script is receiving, run the same query through a separate interface. In this case the problem is the reference to the *password* column, when the table's column is actually called just *pass*.

Review and Pursue

If you have any problems with the review questions or the pursue prompts, turn to the book's supporting forum (**www.LarryUllman.com/forums/**).

Review

- Why must PHP scripts be run through a URL?

- What version of PHP are you using? What version of MySQL? What version of what Web server application are you using? On what operating system?

- What debugging steps should you take if the rendered Web page doesn't look right in your Web browser?

- Do you have *display_errors* enabled on your server? Why is enabling *display_errors* useful on development servers? Why is revealing errors a bad thing on production servers?

- How does the level of *error_reporting* affect PHP scripts? To what level of *error_reporting* is your PHP server set?

- What does the @ operator do?

- What are the benefits of using your own error-handling function? What impact does the error reporting level have when using your own error-handling function?

- How can **print** or **echo** be used as debugging tools? Hint: There are many correct answers.

- What is the method for fixing PHP-SQL-MySQL bugs?

Pursue

- Install the Firebug and Web Developer extensions for Firefox, if you have not already. Install Firefox if you haven't already installed it!

- Enable *display_errors* on your development server, if you can.

- If you can, set PHP's level of error reporting to **E_ALL | E_STRICT** on your development server.

- Check out the PHP manual's page for the **debug_print_backtrace( )** function to learn more about it.

- Consider using a professional-grade IDE that provides built-in debugging tools.

Using PHP with MySQL

Now that you have a sufficient amount of PHP, SQL, and MySQL experience under your belt, it's time to put all of the technologies together. PHP's strong integration with MySQL is just one reason so many programmers have embraced it; it's impressive how easily you can use the two together.

This chapter will use the existing *sitename* database—created in Chapter 5, "Introduction to SQL"—to build a PHP interface for interacting with the *users* table. The knowledge taught and the examples used here will be the basis for all of your PHP-MySQL Web applications, as the principles involved are the same for any PHP-MySQL interaction.

Before heading into this chapter, you should be comfortable with everything covered in the first eight chapters, including the error debugging and handling techniques just taught in the previous chapter. Finally, remember that you need a PHP-enabled Web server and access to a running MySQL server in order to execute the following examples.

In This Chapter

Modifying the Template

Since all of the pages in this chapter and the next will be part of the same Web application, it'll be worthwhile to use a common template system. Instead of creating a new template from scratch, the layout from Chapter 3, "Creating Dynamic Web Sites," will be used again, with only a minor modification to the header file's navigation links.

To make the header file:

1. Open **header.html** (Script 3.2) in your text editor or IDE.

2. Change the list of links to read (**Script 9.1**):

   ```
   <li><a href="index.php">Home
   → Page</a></li>
   <li><a href="register.php">
   → Register</a></li>
   ```

   ```
   <li><a href="view_users.php">View
   → Users</a></li>
   <li><a href="password.php">Change
   → Password</a></li>
   <li><a href="#">link five</a></li>
   ```

   All of the examples in this chapter will involve the registration, view users, and change password pages. The date form and calculator links from Chapter 3 can be deleted.

3. Save the file as **header.html**.

4. Place the new header file in your Web directory, within the **includes** folder along with **footer.html** (Script 3.3) and **style.css** (available for download from the book's supporting Web site, **www.LarryUllman.com**).

Script 9.1 The site's header file, used for the pages' template, modified with new navigation links.

```
1    <!DOCTYPE html PUBLIC "-//W3C//DTD XHTML 1.0 Strict//EN" "http://www.w3.org/TR/xhtml1/DTD/
     xhtml1-strict.dtd">
2    <html xmlns="http://www.w3.org/1999/xhtml">
3    <head>
4        <title><?php echo $page_title; ?></title>
5        <link rel="stylesheet" href="includes/style.css" type="text/css" media="screen" />
6        <meta http-equiv="content-type" content="text/html; charset=utf-8" />
7    </head>
8    <body>
9        <div id="header">
10           <h1>Your Website</h1>
11           <h2>catchy slogan...</h2>
12       </div>
13       <div id="navigation">
14           <ul>
15               <li><a href="index.php">Home Page</a></li>
16               <li><a href="register.php">Register</a></li>
17               <li><a href="view_users.php">View Users</a></li>
18               <li><a href="password.php">Change Password</a></li>
19               <li><a href="#">link five</a></li>
20           </ul>
21       </div>
22       <div id="content"><!-- Start of the page-specific content. -->
23   <!-- Script 9.1 - header.html -->
```

5. Test the new header file by running `index.php` in your Web browser **A**.

> **TIP** For a preview of this site's structure, see the sidebar "Organizing Your Documents" in the next section.

> **TIP** Remember that you can use any file extension for your template files, including `.inc` or `.php`.

A The dynamically generated home page with new navigation links.

WARNING: READ THIS!

PHP and MySQL have gone through many changes over the past decade. Of these, the most important for this chapter, and one of the most important for the rest of the book, involves what PHP functions you use to communicate with MySQL. For years, PHP developers used the standard MySQL functions (called the *mysql* extension). As of PHP 5 and MySQL 4.1, you can use the newer Improved MySQL functions (called the *mysqli* extension). These functions provide improved performance and take advantage of added features (among other benefits).

As this book assumes you're using at least PHP 5 and MySQL 5, all of the examples will only use the Improved MySQL functions. *If your server does not support this extension, you will not be able to run these examples as they are written!* Most of the examples in the rest of the book will also not work for you.

If the server or home computer you're using does not support the Improved MySQL functions, you have three options: upgrade PHP and MySQL, read the second edition of this book (which teaches and primarily uses the older functions), or learn how to use the older functions and modify all the examples accordingly. For questions or problems, see the book's corresponding forum (**www.LarryUllman.com/forums/**).

Connecting to MySQL

The first step for interacting with MySQL—connecting to the server—requires the appropriately named **mysqli_connect( )** function:

$dbc = mysqli_connect (*hostname,*
→ ***username, password, db_name*);**

The first three arguments sent to the function (hostname, username, and password) are based upon the users and privileges established within MySQL (see Appendix A, "Installation," for more information). Commonly (but not always), the host value will be *localhost*.

The fourth argument is the name of the database to use. This is the equivalent of saying **USE databasename** within the mysql client.

If the connection was made, the **$dbc** variable, short for *database connection* (but you can use any name you want, of course), will become a reference point for all of your subsequent database interactions. Most of the PHP functions for working with MySQL will take this variable as its first argument.

If a connection problem occurred, you can call **mysqli_connect_error( )**, which returns the connection error message. It takes no arguments, so would be called using just

mysqli_connect_error( );

Once you've connected to the database, you should set the encoding for the interaction. You can do so (as of PHP 5.0.5) with the **mysqli_set_charset( )** function:

mysqli_set_charset($dbc, 'utf8');

The value used as the encoding—the second argument—should match that of your PHP scripts and the collation of your database (see Chapter 6, "Database Design," for more on MySQL collations). If you fail to do this, all data will be transferred using the default character set, which could cause problems.

To start using PHP with MySQL, let's create a special script that makes the connection. Other PHP scripts that require a MySQL connection can then include this file.

To connect to and select a database:

1. Create a new PHP document in your text editor or IDE, to be named **mysqli_connect.php** (Script 9.2):

   <?php # Script 9.2 -
   → mysqli_connect.php

   This file will be included by other PHP scripts, so it doesn't need to contain any HTML.

2. Set the MySQL host, username, password, and database name as constants:

   DEFINE ('DB_USER', 'username');
   DEFINE ('DB_PASSWORD', 'password');
   DEFINE ('DB_HOST', 'localhost');
   DEFINE ('DB_NAME', 'sitename');

   I prefer to establish these values as constants for security reasons (they cannot be changed this way), but that isn't required. In general, setting these values as some sort of variable or constant makes sense so that you can separate the configuration parameters from the functions that use them, but again, this is not obligatory.

When writing your script, change these values to ones that will work on your setup. If you have been provided with a MySQL username/password combination and a database (like for a hosted site), use that information here. Or, if possible, follow the steps in Appendix A to create a user that has access to the *sitename* database, and insert those values here. Whatever you do, don't just use the values written in this book's code unless you know for certain they will work on your server.

3. Connect to MySQL:

   $dbc = @mysqli_connect (DB_HOST,
   → DB_USER, DB_PASSWORD, DB_NAME)
   → OR die ('Could not connect to
   → MySQL: ' . mysqli_connect_
   → error( ));

   The **mysqli_connect( )** function, if it successfully connects to MySQL, will return a resource link that corresponds to the open connection. This link will be assigned to the **$dbc** variable, so that other functions can make use of this connection.

   The function call is preceded by the error suppression operator (**@**). This prevents the PHP error from being displayed in the Web browser. This is preferable, as the error will be handled by the **OR die( )** clause.

continues on next page

Script 9.2 The `mysqli_connect.php` script will be used by every other script in this chapter. It establishes a connection to MySQL, selects the database, and sets the encoding.

```
1    <?php # Script 9.2 - mysqli_connect.php
2
3    // This file contains the database access information.
4    // This file also establishes a connection to MySQL,
5    // selects the database, and sets the encoding.
6
7    // Set the database access information as constants:
8    DEFINE ('DB_USER', 'username');
9    DEFINE ('DB_PASSWORD', 'password');
10   DEFINE ('DB_HOST', 'localhost');
11   DEFINE ('DB_NAME', 'sitename');
12
13   // Make the connection:
14   $dbc = @mysqli_connect (DB_HOST, DB_USER, DB_PASSWORD, DB_NAME) OR die ('Could not connect to
     MySQL: ' . mysqli_connect_error( ) );
15
16   // Set the encoding...
17   mysqli_set_charset($dbc, 'utf8');
```

If the **mysqli_connect( )** function cannot return a valid resource link, then the **OR die( )** part of the statement is executed (because the first part of the **OR** will be false, so the second part must be true). As discussed in the preceding chapter, the **die( )** function terminates the execution of the script. The function can also take as an argument a string that will be printed to the Web browser. In this case, the string is a combination of *Could not connect to MySQL:* and the specific MySQL error . Using this blunt error management system makes debugging much easier as you develop your sites.

4. Save the file as **mysqli_connect.php**.

   Since this file contains information—the database access data—that must be kept private, it will use a **.php** extension. With a **.php** extension, even if malicious users ran this script in their Web browser, they would not see the page's actual content.

   You may also note that I did not include a terminating PHP tag: **?>**. This is allowed in PHP (when the script ends with PHP code), and has a benefit to be explained in subsequent chapters.

5. Ideally, place the file outside of the Web document directory 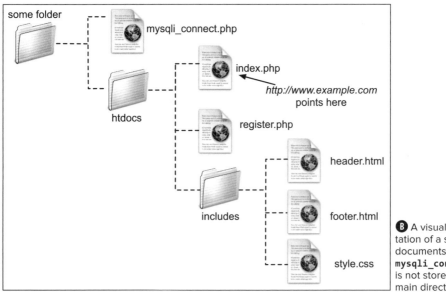.

Ⓐ If there were problems connecting to MySQL, an informative message is displayed and the script is halted.

Ⓑ A visual representation of a server's Web documents, where **mysqli_connect.php** is not stored within the main directory (*htdocs*).

C If the MySQL connection script works properly, the end result will be a blank page (no HTML is generated by the script).

Because the file contains sensitive MySQL access information, it ought to be stored securely. If you can, place it in the directory immediately above or otherwise outside of the Web directory. This way the file will not be accessible from a Web browser. See the "Organizing Your Documents" sidebar for more.

6. Temporarily place a copy of the script within the Web directory and run it in your Web browser **C**.

   In order to test the script, you'll want to place a copy on the server so that it's accessible from the Web browser (which means it must be in the Web directory). If the script works properly, the result should be a blank page **C**. If you see an *Access denied...* or similar message **A**, it means that the combination of username, password, and host does not have permission to access the particular database.

continues on next page

Organizing Your Documents

Chapter 3 introduced the concept of *site structure* while developing the first Web application. Now that pages will begin using a database connection script, the topic is more important.

Should the database connectivity information (username, password, host, and database) fall into malicious hands, it could be used to steal your information or wreak havoc upon the database as a whole. Therefore, you cannot keep a script like `mysqli_connect.php` too secure.

The best recommendation for securing such a file is to store it outside of the Web documents directory. If, for example, the *htdocs* folder in **B** is the root of the Web directory (in other words, the URL **www.example.com** leads there), then not storing `mysqli_connect.php` anywhere within the *htdocs* directory means it will never be accessible via the Web browser. Granted, the source code of PHP scripts is not viewable from the Web browser (only the data sent to the browser by the script is), but you can never be too careful. If you aren't allowed to place documents outside of the Web directory, placing `mysqli_connect.php` in the Web directory is less secure, but not the end of the world.

Secondarily, I recommend using a `.php` extension for your connection scripts. A properly configured and working server will execute rather than display code in such a file. Conversely, if you use just `.inc` as your extension, that page's contents would be displayed in the Web browser if accessed directly.

7. Remove the temporary copy from the Web directory.

TIP If you're using a version of PHP that does not support the `mysqli_set_charset()` function, you'll need to execute a SET NAMES *encoding* query instead:

`mysqli_query($dbc, 'SET NAMES utf8');`

TIP The same values used in Chapter 5 to log in to the mysql client should work from your PHP scripts.

TIP If you receive an error that claims `mysqli_connect()` is an "undefined function", it means that PHP has not been compiled with support for the Improved MySQL Extension. See the appendix for installation information.

TIP If you see a *Could not connect...* error message when running the script **D**, it likely means that MySQL isn't running.

TIP In case you are curious, **E** shows what would happen if you didn't use @ before `mysqli_connect()` and an error occurred.

TIP If you don't need to select the database when establishing a connection to MySQL, omit that argument from the `mysqli_connect()` function:

`$dbc = mysqli_connect (hostname,`
`→ username, password);`

Then, when appropriate, you can select the database using:

`mysqli_select_db($dbc, db_name);`

Could not connect to MySQL: No connection could be made because the target machine actively refused it.

D Another reason why PHP might not be able to connect to MySQL (besides using invalid username/password/hostname/database information) is if MySQL isn't currently running.

Warning: mysqli_connect() [function.mysqli-connect]: (28000/1045): Access denied for user 'username'@'localhost' (using password: YES) in **C:\xampp\htdocs\mysqli_connect.php on line 14** Could not connect to MySQL: Access denied for user 'username'@'localhost' (using password: YES)

E If you don't use the error suppression operator (@), you'll see both the PHP error and the custom OR die() error.

Executing Simple Queries

Once you have successfully connected to and selected a database, you can start executing queries. The queries can be as basic as inserts, updates, and deletions or as involved as complex joins returning numerous rows. Regardless of the SQL command type, the PHP function for executing a query is **mysqli_query( )**:

result = mysqli_query(*dbc*, *query*);

The function takes the database connection as its first argument and the query itself as the second. Within the context of a complete PHP script, I normally assign the query to another variable, called **$query** or just **$q**, so running a query might look like

$r = mysqli_query($dbc, $q);

For simple queries like **INSERT**, **UPDATE**, **DELETE**, etc. (which do not return records), the **$r** variable—short for *result*—will be either TRUE or FALSE, depending upon whether the query executed successfully.

Register

First Name:	Jane
Last Name:	Doe
Email Address:	jd@example.com
Password:	••••••••
Confirm Password:	••••••••

Register

A The registration form.

Keep in mind that "executed successfully" means that it ran without error; it doesn't mean that the query's execution necessarily had the desired result; you'll need to test for that.

For complex queries that return records (**SELECT** being the most important of these), **$r** will be a resource link to the results of the query if it worked or be FALSE if it did not. Thus, you can use this line of code in a conditional to test if the query successfully ran:

$r = mysqli_query ($dbc, $q);
if ($r) { // Worked!

If the query did not successfully run, some sort of MySQL error must have occurred. To find out what that error was, call the **mysqli_error( )** function:

echo mysqli_error($dbc);

The function's lone argument is the database connection.

One final, albeit optional, step in your script would be to close the existing MySQL connection once you're finished with it:

mysqli_close($dbc);

This function call is not required, because PHP will automatically close the connection at the end of a script, but it does make for good programming form to incorporate it.

To demonstrate this process, let's create a registration script. It will show the form when first accessed **A**, handle the form submission, and, after validating all the data, insert the registration information into the *users* table of the *sitename* database.

As a forewarning, this script knowingly has a security hole in it (depending upon the version of PHP in use, and its settings), to be remedied later in the chapter.

To execute simple queries:

1. Begin a new PHP script in your text editor or IDE, to be named **register.php** (Script 9.3):

```php
<?php # Script 9.3 - register.php
$page_title = 'Register';
include ('includes/header.html');
```

The fundamentals of this script—using included files, having the same page both display and handle a form, and creating a sticky form—come from Chapter 3. See that chapter if you're confused about any of these concepts.

2. Create the submission conditional and initialize the **$errors** array:

```php
if ($_SERVER['REQUEST_METHOD'] ==
→'POST') {
  $errors = array();
```

This script will both display and handle the HTML form. This first conditional will check for how the script is being requested, in order to know when to process the form (again, this comes from Chapter 3). The **$errors** variable will be used to store every error message (one for each form input not properly filled out).

3. Validate the first name:

```php
if (empty($_POST['first_name'])) {
  $errors[] = 'You forgot to
  → enter your first name.';
} else {
  $fn = trim($_POST['first_name']);
}
```

As discussed in Chapter 3, the **empty()** function provides a minimal way of ensuring that a text field was filled out. If the first name field was not filled out, an error message is added to the

$errors array. Otherwise, **$fn** is set to the submitted value, after trimming off any extraneous spaces. By using this new variable—which is obviously short for *first_name*—it will be syntactically easier to write the query later.

4. Validate the last name and email address:

```php
if (empty($_POST['last_name'])) {
  $errors[] = 'You forgot to
  → enter your last name.';
} else {
  $ln = trim($_POST['last_name']);
}
if (empty($_POST['email'])) {
  $errors[] = 'You forgot to
  → enter your email address.';
} else {
  $e = trim($_POST['email']);
}
```

These lines are essentially the same as those validating the first name field. In both cases a new variable will be created, assuming that the minimal validation was passed.

5. Validate the passwords:

```php
if (!empty($_POST['pass1'])) {
  if ($_POST['pass1'] != $_POST
  →['pass2']) {
    $errors[] = 'Your password
    → did not match the con-
firmed
    → password.';
  } else {
    $p = trim($_POST['pass1']);
  }
} else {
  $errors[] = 'You forgot to
  → enter your password.';
}
```

continues on page 277

Script 9.3 The registration script adds a record to the database by running an **INSERT** query.

```php
1    <?php # Script 9.3 - register.php
2    // This script performs an INSERT query to add a record to the users table.
3
4    $page_title = 'Register';
5    include ('includes/header.html');
6
7    // Check for form submission:
8    if ($_SERVER['REQUEST_METHOD'] == 'POST') {
9
10       $errors = array(); // Initialize an error array.
11
12       // Check for a first name:
13       if (empty($_POST['first_name'])) {
14          $errors[] = 'You forgot to enter your first name.';
15       } else {
16          $fn = trim($_POST['first_name']);
17       }
18
19       // Check for a last name:
20       if (empty($_POST['last_name'])) {
21          $errors[] = 'You forgot to enter your last name.';
22       } else {
23          $ln = trim($_POST['last_name']);
24       }
25
26       // Check for an email address:
27       if (empty($_POST['email'])) {
28          $errors[] = 'You forgot to enter your email address.';
29       } else {
30          $e = trim($_POST['email']);
31       }
32
33       // Check for a password and match against the confirmed password:
34       if (!empty($_POST['pass1'])) {
35          if ($_POST['pass1'] != $_POST['pass2']) {
36             $errors[] = 'Your password did not match the confirmed password.';
37          } else {
38             $p = trim($_POST['pass1']);
39          }
40       } else {
41          $errors[] = 'You forgot to enter your password.';
42       }
43
44       if (empty($errors)) { // If everything's OK.
45
46          // Register the user in the database...
47
48          require ('../mysqli_connect.php'); // Connect to the db.
49
50          // Make the query:
51          $q = "INSERT INTO users (first_name, last_name, email, pass, registration_date) VALUES
             ('$fn', '$ln', '$e', SHA1('$p'), NOW() )";
```

code continues on next page

```
52        $r = @mysqli_query ($dbc, $q); // Run the query.
53        if ($r) { // If it ran OK.
54
55            // Print a message:
56            echo '<h1>Thank you!</h1>
57        <p>You are now registered. In Chapter 12 you will actually be able to log in!</p><p>
          <br /></p>';
58
59        } else { // If it did not run OK.
60
61            // Public message:
62            echo '<h1>System Error</h1>
63            <p class="error">You could not be registered due to a system error. We apologize for
              any inconvenience.</p>';
64
65            // Debugging message:
66            echo '<p>' . mysqli_error($dbc) . '<br /><br />Query: ' . $q . '</p>';
67
68        } // End of if ($r) IF.
69
70        mysqli_close($dbc); // Close the database connection.
71
72        // Include the footer and quit the script:
73        include ('includes/footer.html');
74        exit();
75
76    } else { // Report the errors.
77
78        echo '<h1>Error!</h1>
79        <p class="error">The following error(s) occurred:<br />';
80        foreach ($errors as $msg) { // Print each error.
81            echo " - $msg<br />\n";
82        }
83        echo '</p><p>Please try again.</p><p><br /></p>';
84
85    } // End of if (empty($errors)) IF.
86
87 } // End of the main Submit conditional.
88 ?>
89 <h1>Register</h1>
90 <form action="register.php" method="post">
91    <p>First Name: <input type="text" name="first_name" size="15" maxlength="20" value="<?php if
       (isset($_POST['first_name'])) echo $_POST['first_name']; ?>" /></p>
92    <p>Last Name: <input type="text" name="last_name" size="15" maxlength="40" value="<?php if
       (isset($_POST['last_name'])) echo $_POST['last_name']; ?>" /></p>
93    <p>Email Address: <input type="text" name="email" size="20" maxlength="60" value="<?php if
       (isset($_POST['email'])) echo $_POST['email']; ?>" /> </p>
94    <p>Password: <input type="password" name="pass1" size="10" maxlength="20" value="<?php if
       (isset($_POST['pass1'])) echo $_POST['pass1']; ?>" /></p>
95    <p>Confirm Password: <input type="password" name="pass2" size="10" maxlength="20"
       value="<?php if (isset($_POST['pass2'])) echo $_POST['pass2']; ?>" /></p>
96    <p><input type="submit" name="submit" value="Register" /></p>
97 </form>
98 <?php include ('includes/footer.html'); ?>
```

To validate the password, the script needs to check the *pass1* input for a value and then confirm that the *pass1* value matches the *pass2* value (meaning the password and confirmed password are the same).

6. Check if it's OK to register the user:

```
if (empty($errors)) {
```

If the submitted data passed all of the conditions, the **$errors** array will have no values in it (it will be empty), so this condition will be true and it's safe to add the record to the database. If the **$errors** array is not empty, then the appropriate error messages should be printed (see Step 11) and the user given another opportunity to register.

7. Include the database connection:

```
require ('../mysqli_connect.php');
```

This line of code will insert the contents of the **mysqli_connect.php** file into this script, thereby creating a connection to MySQL and selecting the database. You may need to change the reference to the location of the file as it is on your server (as written, this line assumes that **mysqli_connect.php** is in the parent folder of the current folder).

8. Add the user to the database:

```
$q = "INSERT INTO users (first_
→ name, last_name, email, pass,
→ registration_date) VALUES ('$fn',
→ '$ln', '$e', SHA1('$p'), NOW() );
$r = @mysqli_query ($dbc, $q);
```

The query itself is similar to those demonstrated in Chapter 5. The **SHA1( )** function is used to encrypt the password, and **NOW( )** is used to set the registration date as this moment.

After assigning the query to a variable, it is run through the **mysqli_query( )** function, which sends the SQL command to the MySQL database. As in the **mysqli_connect.php** script, the **mysqli_query( )** call is preceded by @ in order to suppress any ugly errors. If a problem occurs, the error will be handled more directly in the next step.

9. Report on the success of the registration:

```
if ($r) {
    echo '<h1>Thank you!</h1>
<p>You are now registered. In
→ Chapter 12 you will actually be
→ able to log in!</p><p><br /></p>';
} else {
    echo '<h1>System Error</h1>
    <p class="error">You could
    → not be registered due to a
    → system error. We apologize
    → for any inconvenience.</p>';
    echo '<p>' . mysqli_error($dbc)
    → . '<br /><br />Query: ' . $q .
    → '</p>';
} // End of if ($r) IF.
```

The **$r** variable, which is assigned the value returned by **mysqli_query( )**, can be used in a conditional to test for the successful operation of the query.

continues on next page

If **$r** has a TRUE value, then a *Thank you!* message is displayed **B**. If **$r** has a FALSE value, error messages are printed. For debugging purposes, the error messages will include both the error spit out by MySQL (thanks to the **mysqli_error( )** function) and the query that was run **C**. This information is critical to debugging the problem. You would not want to display this kind of information on a live site, however.

10. Close the database connection and complete the HTML template:

```
mysqli_close($dbc);
include ('includes/footer.html');
exit( );
```

Closing the connection isn't required but is a good policy. Then the footer is included and the script terminated (thanks to the **exit( )** function). If those two lines weren't here, the registration form would be displayed again (which isn't necessary after a successful registration).

11. Print out any error messages and close the submit conditional:

```
} else { // Report the errors.
  echo '<h1>Error!</h1>
  <p class="error">The following
→ error(s) occurred:<br />';
  foreach ($errors as $msg) {
→ // Print each error.
    echo " - $msg<br />\n";
  }
  echo '</p><p>Please try
→ again.</p><p><br /></p>';
} // End of if (empty($errors))
→ IF.
} // End of the main Submit
→ conditional.
```

The **else** clause is invoked if there were any errors. In that case, all of the errors are displayed using a **foreach** loop **D**.

The final closing curly brace closes the main submit conditional. The main conditional is a simple **if**, not an **if-else**, so that the form can be made sticky (again, see Chapter 3).

Thank you!

....

You are now registered. In Chapter 12 you will actually be able to log in!

B If the user could be registered in the database, this message is displayed.

System Error

....

You could not be registered due to a system error. We apologize for any inconvenience.

Unknown column 'password' in 'field list'

Query: INSERT INTO users (first_name, last_name, email, password, registration_date) VALUES ('John', 'Doe', 'jd@example.net', SHA1('pass'), NOW())

C Any MySQL errors caused by the query will be printed, as will the query that was being run.

12. Close the PHP section and begin the HTML form:

```
?>
<h1>Register</h1>
<form action="register.php"
 ↬ method="post">
  <p>First Name: <input type=
    ↬ "text" name="first_name"
    ↬ size="15" maxlength="20"
    ↬ value="<?php if (isset($_POST
    ↬ ['first_name'])) echo $_POST
    ↬ ['first_name']; ?>" /></p>
  <p>Last Name: <input type="text"
    ↬ name="last_name" size="15"
    ↬ maxlength="40" value="<?php if
    ↬ (isset($_POST['last_name']))
    ↬ echo $_POST['last_name'];
    ↬ ?>" /></p>
```

Error!

The following error(s) occurred:
- You forgot to enter your last name.
- Your password did not match the confirmed password.

Please try again.

Register

First Name: | Little |

Last Name: | |

Email Address: | ld@example.edu |

Password: | •••••••• |

Confirm Password: | |

| Register |

D Each form validation error is reported to the user so that they may try registering again.

The form is really simple, with one text input for each field in the *users* table (except for the *user_id* and *registration_date* columns, which will automatically be populated). Each input is made sticky, using code like

```
value="<?php if (isset($_POST
 ↬ ['var'])) echo $_POST['var']; ?>"
```

Also, I would strongly recommend that you use the same name for your form inputs as the corresponding column in the database where that value will be stored. Further, you should set the maximum input length in the form equal to the maximum column length in the database. Both of these habits help to minimize errors.

13. Complete the HTML form:

```
  <p>Email Address: <input
    ↬ type="text" name="email"
    ↬ size="20" maxlength="60"
    ↬ value="<?php if (isset($_POST
    ↬ ['email'])) echo $_POST
    ↬ ['email']; ?>"  /> </p>
  <p>Password: <input type=
    ↬ "password" name="pass1"
    ↬ size="10" maxlength="20"
    ↬ value="<?php if (isset($_POST
    ↬ ['pass1'])) echo $_POST
    ↬ ['pass1']; ?>" /></p>
  <p>Confirm Password: <input
    ↬ type="password" name="pass2"
    ↬ size="10" maxlength="20"
    ↬ value="<?php if (isset($_POST
    ↬ ['pass2'])) echo $_POST
    ↬ ['pass2']; ?>"  /></p>
  <p><input type="submit"
    ↬ name="submit" value=
    ↬ "Register" /></p>
</form>
```

continues on next page

This is all much like that in Step 12, with the addition of a submit button.

As a side note, I don't need to follow my **maxlength** recommendation (from Step 12) with the password inputs, because they will be encrypted with **SHA1( )**, which always creates a string 40 characters long. And since there are two of them, they can't both use the same name as the column in the database.

14. Complete the template:

```php
<?php include ('includes/
   footer.html'); ?>
```

15. Save the file as **register.php**, place it in your Web directory, and test it in your Web browser.

Note that if you use an apostrophe in one of the form values, it will likely break the query ❶. The section "Ensuring Secure SQL" later in this chapter will show how to protect against this.

TIP After running the script, you can always ensure that it worked by using the mysql client or phpMyAdmin to view the records in the *users* table.

TIP You should not end your queries with a semicolon in PHP, as you do when using the mysql client. When working with MySQL, this is a common, albeit harmless, mistake to make. When working with other database applications (Oracle, for one), doing so will make your queries unusable.

TIP As a reminder, the mysqli_query( ) function returns a TRUE value if the query could be executed on the database without error. This does not necessarily mean that the result of the query is what you were expecting. Later scripts will demonstrate how to more accurately gauge the success of a query.

TIP You are not obligated to create a $q variable as I tend to do (you could directly insert your query text into mysqli_query( )). However, as the construction of your queries becomes more complex, using a variable will be the only option.

TIP Practically any query you would run in the mysql client can also be executed using mysqli_query( ).

TIP Another benefit of the Improved MySQL Extension over the standard extension is that the mysqli_multi_query( ) function lets you execute multiple queries at one time. The syntax for doing so, particularly if the queries return results, is a bit more complicated, so see the PHP manual if you have this need.

System Error

You could not be registered due to a system error. We apologize for any inconvenience.

You have an error in your SQL syntax; check the manual that corresponds to your MySQL server version for the right syntax to use near 'Toole', 'pete@example.net', SHA1('pass'), NOW())' at line 1

Query: INSERT INTO users (first_name, last_name, email, pass, registration_date) VALUES ('Peter', 'O'Toole', 'pete@example.net', SHA1('pass'), NOW())

---

❶ Apostrophes in form values (like the last name here) will conflict with the apostrophes used to delineate values in the query.

Retrieving Query Results

The preceding section of this chapter demonstrates how to execute simple queries on a MySQL database. A *simple query*, as I'm calling it, could be defined as one that begins with **INSERT**, **UPDATE**, **DELETE**, or **ALTER**. What all four of these have in common is that they return no data, just an indication of their success. Conversely, a **SELECT** query generates information (i.e., it will return rows of records) that has to be handled by other PHP functions.

The primary tool for handling **SELECT** query results is `mysqli_fetch_array()`, which uses the query result variable (that I've been calling `$r`) and returns one row of data at a time, in an array format. You'll want to use this function within a loop that will continue to access every returned row as long as there are more to be read. The basic construction for reading every record from a query is

```
while ($row = mysqli_fetch_array($r))
{
        // Do something with $row.
}
```

You will almost always want to use a **while** *loop to fetch the results from a* **SELECT** *query.*

The `mysqli_fetch_array()` function takes an optional second parameter specifying what type of array is returned: associative, indexed, or both. An associative array allows you to refer to column values by name, whereas an indexed array requires you to use only numbers (starting at 0 for the first column returned). Each parameter is defined by a constant listed in **Table 9.1**, with **MYSQLI_BOTH** being the default. The **MYSQLI_NUM** setting is marginally faster (and uses less memory) than the other options. Conversely, **MYSQLI_ASSOC** is more overt (`$row['column']` rather than `$row[3]`) and may continue to work even if the query changes.

An optional step you can take when using `mysqli_fetch_array()` would be to free up the query result resources once you are done using them:

```
mysqli_free_result ($r);
```

This line removes the overhead (memory) taken by `$r`. It's an optional step, since PHP will automatically free up the resources at the end of a script, but—like using `mysqli_close()`—it does make for good programming form.

To demonstrate how to handle results returned by a query, let's create a script for viewing all of the currently registered users.

TABLE 9.1 mysqli_fetch_array() Constants

Constant	Example
MYSQLI_ASSOC	`$row['column']`
MYSQLI_NUM	`$row[0]`
MYSQLI_BOTH	`$row[0]` or `$row['column']`

To retrieve query results:

1. Begin a new PHP document in your text editor or IDE, to be named **view_users.php** (Script 9.4):

```
<?php # Script 9.4 -
→ view_users.php
$page_title = 'View the Current
→ Users';
include ('includes/header.html');
echo '<h1>Registered Users</h1>';
```

2. Connect to and query the database:

```
require ('../mysqli_connect.php');
$q = "SELECT CONCAT(last_name,
→', ', first_name) AS name,
→ DATE_FORMAT(registration_date,
→'%M %d, %Y') AS dr FROM users
→ ORDER BY registration_date ASC";
$r = @mysqli_query ($dbc, $q);
```

The query here will return two columns **A**: the users' names (formatted as *Last Name, First Name*) and the date they registered (formatted as *Month DD, YYYY*). Because both columns are formatted using MySQL functions, aliases are given to the returned results (*name* and *dr*, accordingly). See Chapter 5 if you are confused by any of this syntax.

3. Create an HTML table for displaying the query results:

```
if ($r) {
   echo '<table align="center"
→ cellspacing="3" cellpadding="3"
   width="75%">
   <tr><td align="left"><b>Name
→ </b></td><td align="left">
→ <b>Date Registered</b></td></tr>
';
```

If the **$r** variable has a TRUE value, then the query ran without error and the results can be displayed. To do that, start by making a table and a header row in HTML.

4. Fetch and print each returned record:

```
while ($row = mysqli_fetch_array
→ ($r, MYSQLI_ASSOC)) {
   echo '<tr><td align="left">' .
→ $row['name'] . '</td><td align=
→ "left">' . $row['dr'] . '</td>
→ </tr>
';
}
```

Next, loop through the results using **mysqli_fetch_array()** and print each fetched row. Notice that within the **while** loop, the code refers to each returned value using the proper alias: **$row['name']** and **$row['dr']**. The script could not refer to **$row['first_name']** or **$row['date_registered']** because no such field name was returned **A**.

continues on page 284

A The query results as run within the mysql client.

Script 9.4 The `view_users.php` script runs a static query on the database and prints all of the returned rows.

```php
1    <?php # Script 9.4 - view_users.php
2    // This script retrieves all the records from the users table.
3
4    $page_title = 'View the Current Users';
5    include ('includes/header.html');
6
7    // Page header:
8    echo '<h1>Registered Users</h1>';
9
10   require ('../mysqli_connect.php'); // Connect to the db.
11
12   // Make the query:
13   $q = "SELECT CONCAT(last_name, ', ', first_name) AS name, DATE_FORMAT(registration_date, '%M %d, %Y') AS dr FROM users ORDER BY registration_date ASC";
14   $r = @mysqli_query ($dbc, $q); // Run the query.
15
16   if ($r) { // If it ran OK, display the records.
17
18       // Table header.
19       echo '<table align="center" cellspacing="3" cellpadding="3" width="75%">
20       <tr><td align="left"><b>Name</b></td><td align="left"><b>Date Registered</b></td></tr>
21   ';
22
23       // Fetch and print all the records:
24       while ($row = mysqli_fetch_array($r, MYSQLI_ASSOC)) {
25           echo '<tr><td align="left">' . $row['name'] . '</td><td align="left">' . $row['dr'] .
             '</td></tr>
26           ';
27       }
28
29       echo '</table>'; // Close the table.
30
31       mysqli_free_result ($r); // Free up the resources.
32
33   } else { // If it did not run OK.
34
35       // Public message:
36       echo '<p class="error">The current users could not be retrieved. We apologize for any
         inconvenience.</p>';
37
38       // Debugging message:
39       echo '<p>' . mysqli_error($dbc) . '<br /><br />Query: ' . $q . '</p>';
40
41   } // End of if ($r) IF.
42
43   mysqli_close($dbc); // Close the database connection.
44
45   include ('includes/footer.html');
46   ?>
```

5. Close the HTML table and free up the query resources:

```
echo '</table>';
mysqli_free_result ($r);
```

Again, this is an optional step but a good one to take.

6. Complete the main conditional:

```
} else {
    echo '<p class="error">The
    → current users could not be
    → retrieved. We apologize for
    → any inconvenience.</p>';
    echo '<p>' . mysqli_error($dbc)
    → . '<br /><br />Query: ' . $q .
    → '</p>';
} // End of if ($r) IF.
```

As in the **register.php** example, there are two kinds of error messages here. The first is a generic message, the type you'd show in a live site. The second is much more detailed, printing both the MySQL error and the query, both being critical for debugging purposes.

7. Close the database connection and finish the page:

```
mysqli_close($dbc);
include ('includes/footer.html');
?>
```

8. Save the file as **view_users.php**, place it in your Web directory, and test it in your browser **B**.

TIP The function mysqli_fetch_row( ) is the equivalent of mysqli_fetch_array ($r, MYSQLI_NUM);

TIP The function mysqli_fetch_assoc( ) is the equivalent of mysqli_fetch_array ($r, MYSQLI_ASSOC);

TIP As with any associative array, when you retrieve records from the database, you must refer to the selected columns or aliases exactly as they are in the database or query. This is to say that the keys are case-sensitive.

TIP If you are in a situation where you need to run a second query inside of your while loop, be certain to use different variable names for that query. For example, the inner query would use $r2 and $row2 instead of $r and $row. If you don't do this, you'll encounter logical errors.

TIP I sometimes see beginning PHP developers muddle the process of fetching query results. Remember that you must execute the query using mysqli_query( ), and then use mysqli_fetch_array( ) to retrieve a single row of information. If you have multiple rows to retrieve, use a while loop.

Registered Users

Name	Date Registered
Ullman, Larry	March 31, 2011
Isabella, Zoe	March 31, 2011
Starr, Ringo	March 31, 2011
Harrison, George	March 31, 2011
McCartney, Paul	March 31, 2011
Lennon, John	March 31, 2011
Brautigan, Richard	March 31, 2011
Banks, Russell	March 31, 2011
Simpson, Homer	March 31, 2011
Simpson, Marge	March 31, 2011
Simpson, Bart	March 31, 2011
Simpson, Lisa	March 31, 2011
Simpson, Maggie	March 31, 2011
Simpson, Abe	March 31, 2011
Chabon, Michael	March 31, 2011
Greene, Graham	March 31, 2011
DeLillo, Don	March 31, 2011
Jones, David	March 31, 2011
Dolenz, Micky	March 31, 2011
Nesmith, mike	March 31, 2011
Sedaris, David	March 31, 2011
Hornby, Nick	March 31, 2011
Bank, Melissa	March 31, 2011
Morrison, Toni	March 31, 2011
Franzen, Jonathan	March 31, 2011
Doe, Jane	April 15, 2011

B All of the user records are retrieved from the database and displayed in the Web browser.

Ensuring Secure SQL

Database security with respect to PHP comes down to three broad issues:

1. Protecting the MySQL access information
2. Not revealing too much about the database
3. Being cautious when running queries, particularly those involving user-submitted data

You can accomplish the first objective by securing the MySQL connection script outside of the Web directory so that it is never viewable through a Web browser (see ⓒ in "Connecting to MySQL"). I discuss this in some detail earlier in the chapter. The second objective is attained by not letting the user see PHP's error messages or your queries (in these scripts, that information is printed out for your debugging purposes; you'd never want to do that on a live site).

For the third objective, there are numerous steps you can and should take, all based upon the premise of never trusting user-supplied data. First, validate that some value has been submitted, or that it is of the proper type (number, string, etc.). Second, use regular expressions to make sure that submitted data matches what you would expect it to be (this topic is covered in Chapter 14, "Perl-Compatible Regular Expressions"). Third, you can typecast some values to guarantee that they're numbers (discussed in Chapter 13, "Security Methods"). A fourth recommendation is to run user-submitted data through the `mysqli_real_escape_string()` function. This function makes data safe to use in a query by escaping what could be problematic characters. It's used like so:

```
$safe = mysqli_real_escape_string
→($dbc, data);
```

To understand why this is necessary, see ⒠ in "Executing Simple Queries." The use of the apostrophe in the user's last name made the query syntactically invalid:

```
INSERT INTO users (first_name,
→last_name, email, pass,
→registration_date) VALUES ('Peter',
→'O'Toole', 'pete@example.net',
→SHA1('aPass8'), NOW() )
```

In that particular example, valid user data broke the query, which is not good. But if your PHP script allows for this possibility, a malicious user can purposefully submit problematic characters (the apostrophe being one example) in order to hack into, or damage, your database. For security purposes, `mysqli_real_escape_string()` should be used on every text input in a form. To demonstrate this, let's revamp **register.php** (Script 9.3).

To use mysqli_real_escape_string():

1. Open **register.php** (Script 9.3) in your text editor or IDE, if it is not already.

2. Move the inclusion of the **mysqli_connect.php** file (line 48 in Script 9.3) to just after the main conditional (**Script 9.5**).

   Because the **mysqli_real_escape_string( )** function requires a database connection, the **mysqli_connect.php** script must be required earlier in the script.

continues on page 288

Script 9.5 The **register.php** script now uses the **mysqli_real_escape_string( )** function to make submitted data safe to use in a query.

```
1   <?php # Script 9.5 - register.php #2
2   // This script performs an INSERT query to add a record to the users table.
3
4   $page_title = 'Register';
5   include ('includes/header.html');
6
7   // Check for form submission:
8   if ($_SERVER['REQUEST_METHOD'] == 'POST') {
9
10      require ('../mysqli_connect.php'); // Connect to the db.
11
12      $errors = array(); // Initialize an error array.
13
14      // Check for a first name:
15      if (empty($_POST['first_name'])) {
16          $errors[] = 'You forgot to enter your first name.';
17      } else {
18          $fn = mysqli_real_escape_string($dbc, trim($_POST['first_name']));
19      }
20
21      // Check for a last name:
22      if (empty($_POST['last_name'])) {
23          $errors[] = 'You forgot to enter your last name.';
24      } else {
25          $ln = mysqli_real_escape_string($dbc, trim($_POST['last_name']));
26      }
27
28      // Check for an email address:
29      if (empty($_POST['email'])) {
```

code continues on next page

```
30          $errors[] = 'You forgot to enter your email address.';
31      } else {
32          $e = mysqli_real_escape_string($dbc, trim($_POST['email']));
33      }
34
35      // Check for a password and match against the confirmed password:
36      if (!empty($_POST['pass1'])) {
37          if ($_POST['pass1'] != $_POST['pass2']) {
38              $errors[] = 'Your password did not match the confirmed password.';
39          } else {
40              $p = mysqli_real_escape_string($dbc, trim($_POST['pass1']));
41          }
42      } else {
43          $errors[] = 'You forgot to enter your password.';
44      }
45
46      if (empty($errors)) { // If everything's OK.
47
48          // Register the user in the database...
49
50          // Make the query:
51          $q = "INSERT INTO users (first_name, last_name, email, pass, registration_date) VALUES
              ('$fn', '$ln', '$e', SHA1('$p'), NOW() )";
52          $r = @mysqli_query ($dbc, $q); // Run the query.
53          if ($r) { // If it ran OK.
54
55              // Print a message:
56              echo '<h1>Thank you!</h1>
57          <p>You are now registered. In Chapter 12 you will actually be able to log in!</p><p>
              <br /></p>';
58
59          } else { // If it did not run OK.
60
61              // Public message:
62              echo '<h1>System Error</h1>
63          <p class="error">You could not be registered due to a system error. We apologize for
              any inconvenience.</p>';
64
65              // Debugging message:
66              echo '<p>' . mysqli_error($dbc) . '<br /><br />Query: ' . $q . '</p>';
67
68          } // End of if ($r) IF.
69
70          mysqli_close($dbc); // Close the database connection.
71
72          // Include the footer and quit the script:
73          include ('includes/footer.html');
74          exit();
75
76      } else { // Report the errors.
```

code continues on next page

3. Change the validation routines to use the `mysqli_real_escape_string( )` function, replacing each occurrence of `$var = trim($_POST['var'])` with `$var = mysqli_real_escape_string($dbc, trim($_POST['var']))`:

```
$fn = mysqli_real_escape_string
→ ($dbc, trim($_POST['first_name']));
$ln = mysqli_real_escape_string
→ ($dbc, trim($_POST['last_name']));
$e = mysqli_real_escape_string
→ ($dbc, trim($_POST['email']));
$p = mysqli_real_escape_string
→ ($dbc, trim($_POST['pass1']));
```

Instead of just assigning the submitted value to each variable (**$fn, $ln**, etc.), the values will be run through the `mysqli_real_escape_string( )` function first. The `trim( )` function is still used to get rid of any unnecessary spaces.

4. Add a second call to `mysqli_close( )` before the end of the main conditional:

```
mysqli_close($dbc);
```

To be consistent, since the database connection is opened as the first step of the main conditional, it should be closed as the last step of this same conditional. It still needs to be closed before including the footer and terminating the script (lines 73 and 74), though.

Script 9.5 *continued*

```
77
78           echo '<h1>Error!</h1>';
79           <p class="error">The following error(s) occurred:<br />';
80           foreach ($errors as $msg) { // Print each error.
81               echo " - $msg<br />\n";
82           }
83           echo '</p><p>Please try again.</p><p><br /></p>';
84
85       } // End of if (empty($errors)) IF.
86
87       mysqli_close($dbc); // Close the database connection.
88
89   } // End of the main Submit conditional.
90   ?>
91   <h1>Register</h1>
92   <form action="register.php" method="post">
93       <p>First Name: <input type="text" name="first_name" size="15" maxlength="20" value="<?php if
         (isset($_POST['first_name'])) echo $_POST['first_name']; ?>" /></p>
94       <p>Last Name: <input type="text" name="last_name" size="15" maxlength="40" value="<?php if
         (isset($_POST['last_name'])) echo $_POST['last_name']; ?>" /></p>
95       <p>Email Address: <input type="text" name="email" size="20" maxlength="60" value="<?php if
         (isset($_POST['email'])) echo $_POST['email']; ?>" /> </p>
96       <p>Password: <input type="password" name="pass1" size="10" maxlength="20" value="<?php if
         (isset($_POST['pass1'])) echo $_POST['pass1']; ?>" /></p>
97       <p>Confirm Password: <input type="password" name="pass2" size="10" maxlength="20"
         value="<?php if (isset($_POST['pass2'])) echo $_POST['pass2']; ?>" /></p>
98       <p><input type="submit" name="submit" value="Register" /></p>
99   </form>
100  <?php include ('includes/footer.html'); ?>
```

Register

First Name: Peter

Last Name: O'Toole

Email Address: pete@example.net

Password: ••••••••

Confirm Password: ••••••••

Register

A Values with apostrophes in them, like a person's last name, will no longer break the **INSERT** query, thanks to the `mysqli_real_ escape_string( )` function.

5. Save the file as **register.php**, place it in your Web directory, and test it in your Web browser **A** and **B**.

TIP The `mysqli_real_escape_string( )` function escapes a string in accordance with the language being used (i.e., the collation), which is an advantage using this function has over alternative solutions.

TIP If you see results like those in **C**, it means that the `mysqli_real_escape_string( )` function cannot access the database (because it has no connection, like `$dbc`).

TIP If Magic Quotes is enabled on your server, you'll need to remove any slashes added by Magic Quotes, prior to using the `mysqli_real_escape_string( )` function. The code (cumbersome as it is) would look like:

```
$fn = mysqli_real_escape_string
→ ($dbc, trim(stripslashes($_POST
→ ['first_name'])));
```

If you don't use `stripslashes( )` and Magic Quotes is enabled, the form values will be doubly escaped.

TIP If you look at the values stored in the database (using the mysql client, phpMyAdmin, or the like), you will not see the apostrophes and other problematic characters stored with preceding backslashes. This is correct. The backslashes keep the problematic characters from breaking the query but the backslashes are not themselves stored.

Thank you!

You are now registered. In Chapter 12 you will actually be able to log in!

B Now the registration process will handle problematic characters and be more secure.

Notice: Undefined variable: dbc in **C:\xampp\htdocs\register.php** on line 18

Warning: mysqli_real_escape_string() expects parameter 1 to be mysqli, null given in **C:\xampp\htdocs\register.php** on line 18

C Since the `mysqli_real_escape_string( )` requires a database connection, using it without that connection (e.g., before including the connection script) can lead to other errors.

Counting Returned Records

The next logical function to discuss is **mysqli_num_rows( )**. This function returns the number of rows retrieved by a **SELECT** query. It takes one argument, the query result variable:

$num = mysqli_num_rows($r);

Although simple in purpose, this function is very useful. It's necessary if you want to paginate your query results (an example of this can be found in the next chapter). It's also a good idea to use this function before you attempt to fetch any results using a **while** loop (because there's no need to fetch the results if there aren't any, and attempting to do so may cause errors). In this next sequence of steps, let's modify **view_users.php** to list the total number of registered users.

To modify view_users.php:

1. Open **view_users.php** (refer to Script 9.4) in your text editor or IDE, if it is not already.

2. Before the **if ($r)** conditional, add this line (**Script 9.6**):

   $num = mysqli_num_rows ($r);

   This line will assign the number of rows returned by the query to the **$num** variable.

3. Change the original **$r** conditional to:

   if ($num > 0) {

   The conditional as it was written before was based upon whether the query did or did not successfully run, not whether or not any records were returned. Now it will be more accurate.

Script 9.6 Now the **view_users.php** script will display the total number of registered users, thanks to the **mysqli_num_rows( )** function.

```
1   <?php # Script 9.6 - view_users.php #2
2   // This script retrieves all the records
    from the users table.
3
4   $page_title = 'View the Current Users';
5   include ('includes/header.html');
6
7   // Page header:
8   echo '<h1>Registered Users</h1>';
9
10  require ('../mysqli_connect.php');
    // Connect to the db.
11
12  // Make the query:
13  $q = "SELECT CONCAT(last_name, ', ',
    first_name) AS name, DATE_FORMAT
    (registration_date, '%M %d, %Y') AS dr
    FROM users ORDER BY registration_date ASC";
14  $r = @mysqli_query ($dbc, $q); // Run
    the query.
15
16  // Count the number of returned rows:
17  $num = mysqli_num_rows($r);
18
19  if ($num > 0) { // If it ran OK,
    display the records.
20
21      // Print how many users there are:
22      echo "<p>There are currently $num
        registered users.</p>\n";
23
24      // Table header.
25      echo '<table align="center"
        cellspacing="3" cellpadding="3"
        width="75%">
26      <tr><td align="left"><b>Name</
        b></td><td align="left"><b>Date
        Registered</b></td></tr>
27      ';
28
29      // Fetch and print all the records:
30      while ($row = mysqli_fetch_array($r,
        MYSQLI_ASSOC)) {
31          echo '<tr><td align="left">' .
            $row['name'] . '</td><td align=
            "left">' . $row['dr'] . '</td></tr>
32          ';
33      }
```

code continues on next page

Script 9.6 *continued*

```
34
35      echo '</table>'; // Close the table.
36
37      mysqli_free_result ($r); // Free up
        the resources.
38
39  } else { // If no records were returned.
40
41      echo '<p class="error">There are
        currently no registered users.</p>';
42
43  }
44
45  mysqli_close($dbc); // Close the database
    connection.
46
47  include ('includes/footer.html');
48  ?>
```

Registered Users

There are currently 26 registered users.

Name	Date Registered
Ullman, Larry	March 31, 2011
Isabella, Zoe	March 31, 2011
Starr, Ringo	March 31, 2011
Harrison, George	March 31, 2011

Ⓐ The number of registered users is now displayed at the top of the page.

4. Before creating the HTML table, print the number of registered users:

   ```
   echo "<p>There are currently $num
   → registered users.</p>\n";
   ```

5. Change the **else** part of the main conditional to read:

   ```
   echo '<p class="error">There are
   → currently no registered users.</p>';
   ```

   The original conditional was based upon whether or not the query worked. Hopefully, you've successfully debugged the query so that it is working and the original error messages are no longer needed. Now the error message just indicates if no records were returned.

6. Save the file as **view_users.php**, place it in your Web directory, and test it in your Web browser Ⓐ.

Modifying register.php

The **mysqli_num_rows( )** function could be applied to **register.php** to prevent someone from registering with the same email address multiple times. Although the **UNIQUE** index on that column in the database will prevent that from happening, such attempts will create a MySQL error. To prevent this using PHP, run a **SELECT** query to confirm that the email address isn't currently registered. That query would be simply

```
SELECT user_id FROM users WHERE → email='$e'
```

You would run this query (using the **mysqli_query( )** function) and then call **mysqli_num_rows( )**. If **mysqli_num_rows( )** returns 0, you know that the email address hasn't already been registered and it's safe to run the **INSERT**.

Updating Records with PHP

The last technique in this chapter shows how to update database records through a PHP script. Doing so requires an **UPDATE** query, and its successful execution can be verified with PHP's `mysqli_affected_rows()` function.

While the `mysqli_num_rows()` function will return the number of rows generated by a **SELECT** query, `mysqli_affected_rows()` returns the number of rows affected by an **INSERT**, **UPDATE**, or **DELETE** query. It's used like so:

`$num = mysqli_affected_rows($dbc);`

Unlike `mysqli_num_rows()`, the one argument the function takes is the database connection (**$dbc**), not the results of the previous query (**$r**).

The following example will be a script that allows registered users to change their password. It demonstrates two important ideas:

- Checking a submitted username and password against registered values (the key to a login system as well)
- Updating database records using the primary key as a reference

As with the registration example, this one PHP script will both display the form and handle it.

To update records with PHP:

1. Begin a new PHP script in your text editor or IDE, to be named **password.php** (Script 9.7):

   ```php
   <?php # Script 9.7 - password.php
   $page_title = 'Change Your Password';
   include ('includes/header.html');
   ```

   continues on page 294

A The form for changing a user's password.

Script 9.7 The **password.php** script runs an **UPDATE** query on the database and uses the `mysqli_affected_rows()` function to confirm the change.

```
1    <?php # Script 9.7 - password.php
2    // This page lets a user change their
     password.
3
4    $page_title = 'Change Your Password';
5    include ('includes/header.html');
6
7    // Check for form submission:
8    if ($_SERVER['REQUEST_METHOD'] == 'POST') {
9
10       require ('../mysqli_connect.php');
         // Connect to the db.
11
12       $errors = array(); // Initialize an
         error array.
13
14       // Check for an email address:
15       if (empty($_POST['email'])) {
16           $errors[] = 'You forgot to enter
             your email address.';
17       } else {
18           $e = mysqli_real_escape_string
             ($dbc, trim($_POST['email']));
19       }
20
21       // Check for the current password:
22       if (empty($_POST['pass'])) {
23           $errors[] = 'You forgot to enter
             your current password.';
24       } else {
25           $p = mysqli_real_escape_string
             ($dbc, trim($_POST['pass']));
26       }
27
28       // Check for a new password and match
29       // against the confirmed password:
```

code continues on next page

```
30      if (!empty($_POST['pass1'])) {
31          if ($_POST['pass1'] != $_POST['pass2']) {
32              $errors[] = 'Your new password did not match the confirmed password.';
33          } else {
34              $np = mysqli_real_escape_string($dbc, trim($_POST['pass1']));
35          }
36      } else {
37          $errors[] = 'You forgot to enter your new password.';
38      }
39
40      if (empty($errors)) { // If everything's OK.
41
42          // Check that they've entered the right email address/password combination:
43          $q = "SELECT user_id FROM users WHERE (email='$e' AND pass=SHA1('$p') )";
44          $r = @mysqli_query($dbc, $q);
45          $num = @mysqli_num_rows($r);
46          if ($num == 1) { // Match was made.
47
48              // Get the user_id:
49              $row = mysqli_fetch_array($r, MYSQLI_NUM);
50
51              // Make the UPDATE query:
52              $q = "UPDATE users SET pass=SHA1('$np') WHERE user_id=$row[0]";
53              $r = @mysqli_query($dbc, $q);
54
55              if (mysqli_affected_rows($dbc) == 1) { // If it ran OK.
56
57                  // Print a message.
58                  echo '<h1>Thank you!</h1>
59                  <p>Your password has been updated. In Chapter 12 you will actually be able to log
                    in!</p><p><br /></p>';
60
61              } else { // If it did not run OK.
62
63                  // Public message:
64                  echo '<h1>System Error</h1>
65                  <p class="error">Your password could not be changed due to a system error. We
                    apologize for any inconvenience.</p>';
66
67                  // Debugging message:
68                  echo '<p>' . mysqli_error($dbc) . '<br /><br />Query: ' . $q . '</p>';
69
70              }
71
72              mysqli_close($dbc); // Close the database connection.
73
74              // Include the footer and quit the script (to not show the form).
75              include ('includes/footer.html');
76              exit();
77
78          } else { // Invalid email address/password combination.
79              echo '<h1>Error!</h1>
```

code continues on next page

2. Start the main conditional:

```
if ($_SERVER['REQUEST_METHOD'] ==
→ 'POST') {
```

Since this page both displays and handles the form, it'll use the standard conditional to check for the form's submission.

3. Include the database connection and create an array for storing errors:

```
require ('../mysqli_connect.php');
$errors = array();
```

The initial part of this script mimics the registration form.

4. Validate the email address and current password fields:

```
if (empty($_POST['email'])) {
  $errors[] = 'You forgot to
  → enter your email address.';
} else {
  $e = mysqli_real_escape_string
  → ($dbc, trim($_POST['email']));
}
if (empty($_POST['pass'])) {
  $errors[] = 'You forgot to
  → enter your current password.';
} else {
  $p = mysqli_real_escape_string
  → ($dbc, trim($_POST['pass']));
}
```

The form Ⓐ has four inputs: the email address, the current password, and two for the new password. The process for validating each of these is the same as it is in **register.php**. Any data that passes the validation test will be trimmed and run through the **mysqli_real_escape_string( )** function, so that it is safe to use in a query.

Script 9.7 *continued*

```
80            <p class="error">The email
              address and password do not
              match those on file.</p>';
81        }
82
83    } else { // Report the errors.
84
85        echo '<h1>Error!</h1>
86        <p class="error">The following
          error(s) occurred:<br />';
87        foreach ($errors as $msg) { //
          Print each error.
88            echo " - $msg<br />\n";
89        }
90        echo '</p><p>Please try again.</
          p><p><br /></p>';
91
92    } // End of if (empty($errors)) IF.
93
94    mysqli_close($dbc); // Close the
      database connection.
95
96 } // End of the main Submit conditional.
97 ?>
98 <h1>Change Your Password</h1>
99 <form action="password.php"
   method="post">
100    <p>Email Address: <input type="text"
       name="email" size="20" maxlength="60"
       value="<?php if (isset($_POST['email']))
       echo $_POST['email']; ?>"  /> </p>
101    <p>Current Password: <input
       type="password" name="pass" size="10"
       maxlength="20" value="<?php if
       (isset($_POST['pass'])) echo $_
       POST['pass']; ?>"  /></p>
102    <p>New Password: <input
       type="password" name="pass1"
       size="10" maxlength="20" value="<?php
       if (isset($_POST['pass1'])) echo $_
       POST['pass1']; ?>"  /></p>
103    <p>Confirm New Password: <input
       type="password" name="pass2"
       size="10" maxlength="20" value="<?php
       if (isset($_POST['pass2'])) echo $_
       POST['pass2']; ?>"  /></p>
104    <p><input type="submit" name="submit"
       value="Change Password" /></p>
105 </form>
106 <?php include ('includes/footer.html');
    ?>
```

5. Validate the new password:

```php
if (!empty($_POST['pass1'])) {
  if ($_POST['pass1'] != $_POST
  → ['pass2']) {
    $errors[] = 'Your new
    → password did not match the
    → confirmed password.';
  } else {
    $np = mysqli_real_escape_
    → string($dbc, trim
    → ($_POST['pass1']));
  }
} else {
  $errors[] = 'You forgot to
  → enter your new password.';
}
```

This code is also exactly like that in the registration script, except that a valid new password is assigned to a variable called **$np** (because **$p** represents the current password).

6. If all the tests are passed, retrieve the user's ID:

```php
if (empty($errors)) {
  $q = "SELECT user_id FROM
  → users WHERE (email='$e' AND
  → pass=SHA1('$p') )";
  $r = @mysqli_query($dbc, $q);
  $num = @mysqli_num_rows($r);
  if ($num == 1) {
  $row = mysqli_fetch_array($r,
  → MYSQLI_NUM);
```

This first query will return just the *user_id* field for the record that matches the submitted email address and password **B**. To compare the submitted password against the stored one, encrypt it again with the **SHA1( )** function. If the user is registered and has correctly entered both the email address and password, exactly one column from one row will be selected (since the email value must be unique across all rows). Finally, this one record is assigned as an array (of one element) to the **$row** variable.

If this part of the script doesn't work for you, apply the standard debugging methods: remove the error suppression operators (@) so that you can see what errors, if any, occur; use the **mysqli_ error( )** function to report any MySQL errors; and print, then run the query using another interface **B**.

7. Update the database for the new password:

```php
$q = "UPDATE users SET pass=
→ SHA1('$np') WHERE user_id=$row[0]";
$r = @mysqli_query($dbc, $q);
```

This query will change the password—using the new submitted value—where the *user_id* column is equal to the number retrieved from the previous query.

continues on next page

```
● ○ ○   PHP and MySQL for Dynamic Web...
mysql> SELECT user_id FROM users
    -> WHERE (email='email@example.com'
    -> AND pass=SHA1('mypass') );
+---------+
| user_id |
+---------+
|       1 |
+---------+
1 row in set (0.00 sec)

mysql>
```

B The result when running the **SELECT** query from the script (the first of two queries it has) within the mysql client.

8. Check the results of the query:

```
if (mysqli_affected_rows($dbc)
→ == 1) {
  echo '<h1>Thank you!</h1>
  <p>Your password has been
  → updated. In Chapter 12 you
  → will actually be able to log
  → in!</p><p><br /></p>';
} else {
  echo '<h1>System Error</h1>
  <p class="error">Your password
  → could not be changed due to
  → a system error. We apologize
for any inconvenience.</p>';
  echo '<p>' . mysqli_error($dbc) .
  → '<br /><br />Query: ' . $q .
  → '</p>';
}
```

This part of the script again works similar to **register.php**. In this case, if **mysqli_affected_rows( )** returns the number 1, the record has been updated, and a success message will be printed. If not, both a public, generic message and a more useful debugging message will be printed.

9. Close the database connection, include the footer, and terminate the script:

```
mysqli_close($dbc);
include ('includes/footer.html');
exit( );
```

At this point in the script, the **UPDATE** query has been run. It either worked or it did not (because of a system error). In both cases, there's no need to show the form again, so the footer is included (to complete the page) and the script is terminated, using the **exit( )** function. Prior to that, just to be thorough, the database connection is closed.

10. Complete the **if ($num == 1)** conditional:

```
} else {
  echo '<h1>Error!</h1>
  <p class="error">The email
  → address and password do not
  → match those on file.</p>';
}
```

If **mysqli_num_rows( )** does not return a value of 1, then the submitted email address and password do not match those in the database and this error is printed. In this case, the form will be displayed again so that the user can enter the correct information.

11. Print any validation error messages:

```
} else {
  echo '<h1>Error!</h1>
  <p class="error">The following
  → error(s) occurred:<br />';
  foreach ($errors as $msg) {
  → // Print each error.
    echo " - $msg<br />\n";
  }
  echo '</p><p>Please try again.
  → </p><p><br /></p>';
}
```

This **else** clause applies if the **$errors** array is not empty (which means that the form data did not pass all the validation tests). As in the registration page, the errors will be printed.

12. Close the database connection and complete the PHP code:

```
  mysqli_close($dbc);
}
?>
```

13. Display the form:

```
<h1>Change Your Password</h1>
<form action="password.php"
→ method="post">
```

```
<p>Email Address: <input type=
→"text" name="email" size="20"
→maxlength="60" value="<?php
→if (isset($_POST['email'])) echo
→$_POST['email']; ?>"  /> </p>
<p>Current Password: <input
→type="password" name="pass"
→size="10" maxlength="20"
→value="<?php if (isset($_POST
→['pass'])) echo $_POST['pass'];
→?>"  /></p>
<p>New Password: <input type=
→"password" name="pass1" size=
→"10" maxlength="20" value=
→"<?php if (isset($_POST
→['pass1'])) echo $_POST['pass1'];
→?>"  /></p>
<p>Confirm New Password:
→<input type="password"
→name="pass2" size="10"
→maxlength="20" value="<?php
→if (isset($_POST['pass2'])) echo
→$_POST['pass2']; ?>"  /></p>
<p><input type="submit"
→name="submit" value="Change
→Password" /></p>
</form>
```

The form takes three different inputs of type password—the current password, the new one, and a confirmation of the new password—and one text input for the email address. Every input is sticky, too.

14. Include the footer file:

```
<?php include ('includes/footer.
→html'); ?>
```

15. Save the file as **password.php**, place it in your Web directory, and test it in your Web browser **C** and **D**.

TIP If you delete every record from a table using the command TRUNCATE *tablename*, mysqli_affected_rows( ) will return 0, even if the query was successful and every row was removed. This is just a quirk.

TIP If an UPDATE query runs but does not actually change the value of any column (for example, a password is replaced with the same password), mysqli_affected_rows( ) will return 0.

TIP The mysqli_affected_rows( ) conditional used here could (and maybe should) also be applied to the register.php script to confirm that one record was added. That would be a more exacting condition to check than if ($r).

Thank you!

Your password has been updated. In Chapter 12 you will actually be able to log in!

C The password was changed in the database.

Error!

The email address and password do not match those on file.

Change Your Password

Email Address: email@example.com

Current Password: •••••

New Password: ••••••••

Confirm New Password: ••••••••

Change Password

D If the entered email address and password don't match those on file, the password will not be updated.

Review and Pursue

If you have any problems with the review questions or the pursue prompts, turn to the book's supporting forum (**www.LarryUllman.com/forums/**).

Review

- What version of PHP are you using? What version of MySQL? Does your PHP-MySQL combination support the MySQL Improved extension?

- What is the most important sequence of steps for debugging PHP-MySQL problems (explicitly covered at the end of Chapter 8, "Error Handling and Debugging"?

- What hostname, username, and password combination do you, specifically, use to connect to MySQL?

- What PHP code is used to connect to a MySQL server, select the database, and establish the encoding?

- What encoding are you using? Why is it necessary for the PHP scripts to use the same encoding that is used to interact with MySQL that is used for storing the text in the database?

- Why is it preferable to store the **mysqli_connect.php** script outside of the Web root directory? And what is the Web root directory?

- Why shouldn't live sites show MySQL errors and the queries being run?

- What syntax will you almost always use to handle the results of a **SELECT** query? What syntax could you use if the **SELECT** query returns only a single row?

- Why is it important to use the **mysqli_real_escape_string()** function?

- After what kind of queries would you use the **mysqli_num_rows()** function?

- After what types of queries would you use the **mysqli_affected_rows()** function?

Pursue

- If you don't remember how the template system works, or how to use the **include()** function, revisit Chapter 3.

- Use the information covered in Chapter 8 to apply your own custom error handler to this site's examples.

- Change the use of **mysqli_num_rows()** in **view_users.php** so that it's only called if the query had a TRUE result.

- Apply the **mysqli_num_rows()** function to **register.php**, as suggested in an earlier sidebar.

- Apply the **mysqli_affected_rows()** function to **register.php** to confirm that the **INSERT** worked.

- If you want, create scripts that interact with the *banking* database. Easy projects to begin with include: viewing all customers, viewing all accounts (do a **JOIN** to also show the customer's name), and adding to or subtracting from an account's balance.

Common Programming Techniques

Now that you have a little PHP and MySQL interaction under your belt, it's time to take things up a notch. This chapter is similar to Chapter 3, "Creating Dynamic Web Sites," in that it covers myriad independent topics. But what all of these have in common is that they demonstrate common PHP-MySQL programming techniques. You won't learn any new functions here; instead, you'll see how to use the knowledge you already possess to create standard Web functionality.

The examples themselves will broaden the Web application started in the preceding chapter by adding new, popular features. You'll see several tricks for managing database information, in particular editing and deleting records using PHP. At the same time, a couple of new ways of passing data to your PHP pages will be introduced. The final sections of the chapter add features to the **view_users.php** page.

Sending Values to a Script

In the examples so far, all of the data received in the PHP script came from what the user entered in a form. There are, however, two different ways you can pass variables and values to a PHP script, both worth knowing.

The first method is to make use of HTML's **hidden** input type:

```
<input type="hidden" name="do"
→ value="this" />
```

As long as this code is anywhere between the **form** tags, the variable **$_POST['do']** will have a value of *this* in the handling PHP script, assuming that the form uses the POST method. If the form uses the GET method, then **$_GET['do']** would have that value. With that in mind, you can actually skip the creation of the form, and just directly append a *name=value* pair to the URL:

www.example.com/page.php?do=this

Again, with this specific example, **page.php** receives a variable called **$_GET['do']** with a value of *this*.

To demonstrate this GET method trick, a new version of the **view_users.php** script, first created in the last chapter, will be written. This one will provide links to pages that will allow you to edit or delete an existing user's record. The links will pass the user's ID to the handling pages, both of which will also be written in this chapter.

To manually send values to a PHP script:

1. Open **view_users.php** (Script 9.6) in your text editor or IDE.

2. Change the SQL query to read (**Script 10.1**):

   ```
   $q = "SELECT last_name,
   → first_name, DATE_FORMAT
   → (registration_date, '%M %d, %Y')
   → AS dr, user_id FROM users ORDER
   → BY registration_date ASC";
   ```

Script 10.1 The **view_users.php** script, started in Chapter 9, "Using PHP with MySQL," now modified so that it presents Edit and Delete links, passing the user's ID number along in each URL.

```
1    <?php # Script 10.1 - view_users.php #3
2    // This script retrieves all the records from the users table.
3    // This new version links to edit and delete pages.
4
5    $page_title = 'View the Current Users';
6    include ('includes/header.html');
7    echo '<h1>Registered Users</h1>';
8
9    require_once ('../mysqli_connect.php');
10
11   // Define the query:
12   $q = "SELECT last_name, first_name, DATE_FORMAT(registration_date, '%M %d, %Y') AS dr,
      user_id FROM users ORDER BY registration_date ASC";
13   $r = @mysqli_query ($dbc, $q);
14
15   // Count the number of returned rows:
16   $num = mysqli_num_rows($r);
17
18   if ($num > 0) { // If it ran OK, display the records.
```

code continues on next page

The query has been changed in a couple of ways. First, the first and last names are selected separately, not concatenated together. Second, the *user_id* is also now being selected, as that value will be necessary in creating the links.

3. Add three more columns to the main table:

```
echo '<table align="center"
→ cellspacing="3" cellpadding="3"
→ width="75%">
```

```
<tr>
   <td align="left"><b>Edit</b></td>
   <td align="left"><b>Delete</b>
   → </td>
   <td align="left"><b>Last Name
   → </b></td>
   <td align="left"><b>First Name
   → </b></td>
   <td align="left"><b>Date
   → Registered</b></td>
</tr>
';
```

continues on next page

Script 1.10 *continued*

```
19
20      // Print how many users there are:
21      echo "<p>There are currently $num registered users.</p>\n";
22
23      // Table header:
24      echo '<table align="center" cellspacing="3" cellpadding="3" width="75%">
25      <tr>
26          <td align="left"><b>Edit</b></td>
27          <td align="left"><b>Delete</b></td>
28          <td align="left"><b>Last Name</b></td>
29          <td align="left"><b>First Name</b></td>
30          <td align="left"><b>Date Registered</b></td>
31      </tr>
32      ';
33
34      // Fetch and print all the records:
35      while ($row = mysqli_fetch_array($r, MYSQLI_ASSOC)) {
36          echo '<tr>
37              <td align="left"><a href="edit_user.php?id=' . $row['user_id'] . '">Edit</a></td>
38              <td align="left"><a href="delete_user.php?id=' . $row['user_id'] . '">Delete</a></td>
39              <td align="left">' . $row['last_name'] . '</td>
40              <td align="left">' . $row['first_name'] . '</td>
41              <td align="left">' . $row['dr'] . '</td>
42          </tr>
43          ';
44      }
45
46      echo '</table>';
47      mysqli_free_result ($r);
48
49  } else { // If no records were returned.
50      echo '<p class="error">There are currently no registered users.</p>';
51  }
52
53  mysqli_close($dbc);
54
55  include ('includes/footer.html');
56  ?>
```

In the previous version of the script, there were only two columns: one for the name and another for the date the user registered. The name column has been separated into its two parts and two new columns added: one for the *Edit* link and another for the *Delete* link.

4. Change the `echo` statement within the `while` loop to match the table's new structure:

```
echo '<tr>
    <td align="left"><a href=
    "edit_user.php?id=' . $row
    ['user_id'] . '">Edit</a></td>
    <td align="left"><a href=
    "delete_user.php?id=' . $row
    ['user_id'] . '">Delete</a></td>
    <td align="left">' .
    $row['last_name'] . '</td>
    <td align="left">' .
    $row['first_name'] . '</td>
    <td align="left">' . $row['dr'] .
    '</td>
</tr>
';
```

For each record returned from the database, this line will print out a row with five columns. The last three columns are obvious and easy to create: just refer to the returned column name.

For the first two columns, which provide links to edit or delete the user, the syntax is slightly more complicated. The desired end result is HTML code like `<a href="edit_user.php?id=X">Edit </a>`, where *X* is the user's ID. Knowing this, all the PHP code has to do is print `$row['user_id']` for *X*, being mindful of the quotation marks to avoid parse errors.

Because the HTML attributes use a lot of double quotation marks and this `echo` statement requires a lot of variables to be printed, I find it easiest to use single quotes for the HTML and then to concatenate the variables to the printed text.

5. Save the file as `view_users.php`, place it in your Web directory, and run it in your Web browser **A**.

There's no point in clicking the new links, though, as those scripts have not yet been created.

Registered Users

There are currently 26 registered users.

Edit	Delete	Last Name	First Name	Date Registered
Edit	Delete	Ullman	Larry	March 31, 2011
Edit	Delete	Isabella	Zoe	March 31, 2011
Edit	Delete	Starr	Ringo	March 31, 2011
Edit	Delete	Harrison	George	March 31, 2011
Edit	Delete	McCartney	Paul	March 31, 2011
Edit	Delete	Lennon	John	March 31, 2011
Edit	Delete	Brautigan	Richard	March 31, 2011
Edit	Delete	Banks	Russell	March 31, 2011

A The revised version of the `view_users.php` page, with new columns and links.

6. If you want, view the HTML source of the page to see each dynamically generated link **B**.

TIP To append multiple variables to a URL, use this syntax: `page.php?name1=value1&name2=value2&name3=value3`. It's simply a matter of using the ampersand, plus another *name=value* pair.

TIP One trick to adding variables to URLs is that strings should be encoded to ensure that the value is handled properly. For example, the space in the string *Elliott Smith* would be problematic. The solution then is to use the `urlencode()` function:

```
$url = 'page.php?name=' . urlencode
→('Elliott Smith');
```

You only need to do this when programmatically adding values to a URL. When a form uses the GET method, it automatically encodes the data.

```
<tr>
        <td align="left"><a href="edit_user.php?id=2">Edit</a></td>
        <td align="left"><a href="delete_user.php?id=2">Delete</a></td>
        <td align="left">Isabella</td>
        <td align="left">Zoe</td>
        <td align="left">March 31, 2011</td>
</tr>
<tr>
        <td align="left"><a href="edit_user.php?id=6">Edit</a></td>
        <td align="left"><a href="delete_user.php?id=6">Delete</a></td>
        <td align="left">Starr</td>
        <td align="left">Ringo</td>
        <td align="left">March 31, 2011</td>
</tr>
<tr>
        <td align="left"><a href="edit_user.php?id=5">Edit</a></td>
        <td align="left"><a href="delete_user.php?id=5">Delete</a></td>
        <td align="left">Harrison</td>
        <td align="left">George</td>
        <td align="left">March 31, 2011</td>
</tr>
```

B Part of the HTML source of the page (see **A**) shows how the user's ID is added to each link's URL.

Using Hidden Form Inputs

In the preceding example, a new version of the **view_users.php** script was written. This one now includes links to the **edit_user.php** and **delete_user.php** pages, passing each a user's ID through the URL. This next example, **delete_user.php**, will take the passed user ID and allow the administrator to delete that user. Although you could have this page simply execute a **DELETE** query as soon as the page is accessed, for security purposes (and to prevent an inadvertent deletion), there should be multiple steps **ⓐ**:

1. The page must check that it received a numeric user ID.

2. A message will confirm that this user should be deleted.

3. The user ID will be stored in a hidden form input.

4. Upon submission of this form, the user will actually be deleted.

To use hidden form inputs:

1. Begin a new PHP document in your text editor or IDE, to be named **delete_user.php** (Script 10.2):

   ```
   <?php # Script 10.2 -
   → delete_user.php
   ```

2. Include the page header:

   ```
   $page_title = 'Delete a User';
   include ('includes/header.html');
   echo '<h1>Delete a User</h1>';
   ```

   This document will use the same template system as the other pages in the application. See Chapters 9 and 3 for clarification, if needed.

3. Check for a valid user ID value:

   ```
   if ( (isset($_GET['id'])) &&
   → (is_numeric($_GET['id'])) ) {
      $id = $_GET['id'];
   } elseif ( (isset($_POST['id'])) &&
   → (is_numeric($_POST['id'])) ) {
      $id = $_POST['id'];
   } else {
      echo '<p class="error">This page
   → has been accessed in error.</p>';
      include ('includes/footer.html');
      exit( );
   }
   ```

continues on page 306

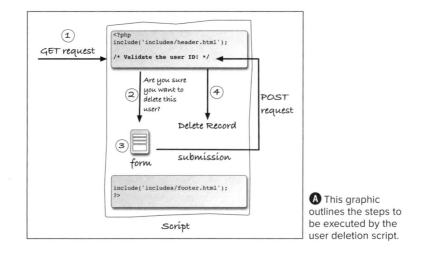

ⓐ This graphic outlines the steps to be executed by the user deletion script.

Script 10.2 This script expects a user ID to be passed to it through the URL. It then presents a confirmation form and deletes the user upon submission.

```
1   <?php # Script 10.2 - delete_user.php
2   // This page is for deleting a user record.
3   // This page is accessed through view_
    users.php
4
5   $page_title = 'Delete a User';
6   include ('includes/header.html');
7   echo '<h1>Delete a User</h1>';
8
9   // Check for a valid user ID, through
    GET or POST:
10  if ( (isset($_GET['id'])) && (is_numeric
    ($_GET['id'])) ) { // From view_users.php
11      $id = $_GET['id'];
12  } elseif ( (isset($_POST['id'])) &&
    (is_numeric($_POST['id'])) ) { // Form
    submission.
13      $id = $_POST['id'];
14  } else { // No valid ID, kill the script.
15      echo '<p class="error">This page has
        been accessed in error.</p>';
16      include ('includes/footer.html');
17      exit();
18  }
19
20  require_once ('../mysqli_connect.php');
21
22  // Check if the form has been submitted:
23  if ($_SERVER['REQUEST_METHOD'] == 'POST') {
24
25      if ($_POST['sure'] == 'Yes') {
        // Delete the record.
26
27          // Make the query:
28          $q = "DELETE FROM users WHERE
            user_id=$id LIMIT 1";
29          $r = @mysqli_query ($dbc, $q);
30          if (mysqli_affected_rows($dbc) ==
            1) { // If it ran OK.
31
32              // Print a message:
33              echo '<p>The user has been
                deleted.</p>';
34
35          } else { // If the query did not
            run OK.
36              echo '<p class="error">The user
                could not be deleted due to a
                system error.</p>'; // Public
                message.
```

Script 10.2 *continued*

```
37              echo '<p>' . mysqli_error($dbc)
                . '<br />Query: ' . $q . '</p>';
                // Debugging message.
38          }
39
40      } else { // No confirmation of deletion.
41          echo '<p>The user has NOT been
            deleted.</p>';
42      }
43
44  } else { // Show the form.
45
46      // Retrieve the user's information:
47      $q = "SELECT CONCAT(last_name, ',
        ', first_name) FROM users WHERE
        user_id=$id";
48      $r = @mysqli_query ($dbc, $q);
49
50      if (mysqli_num_rows($r) == 1) {
        // Valid user ID, show the form.
51
52          // Get the user's information:
53          $row = mysqli_fetch_array ($r,
            MYSQLI_NUM);
54
55          // Display the record being deleted:
56          echo "<h3>Name: $row[0]</h3>
57          Are you sure you want to delete
            this user?";
58
59          // Create the form:
60          echo '<form action="delete_user.
            php" method="post">
61  <input type="radio" name="sure"
    value="Yes" /> Yes
62  <input type="radio" name="sure"
    value="No" checked="checked" /> No
63  <input type="submit" name="submit"
    value="Submit" />
64  <input type="hidden" name="id"
    value="' . $id . '" />
65  </form>';
66
67      } else { // Not a valid user ID.
68          echo '<p class="error">This page
            has been accessed in error.</p>';
69      }
70
71  } // End of the main submission conditional.
72
73  mysqli_close($dbc);
74
75  include ('includes/footer.html');
76  ?>
```

This script relies upon having a valid user ID, to be used in a **DELETE** query's **WHERE** clause. The first time this page is accessed, the user ID should be passed in the URL (the page's URL will end with **delete_user.php?id=X**), after clicking the *Delete* link in the **view_users.php** page. The first **if** condition checks for such a value and that the value is numeric.

As you will see, the script will then store the user ID value in a hidden form input. When the form is submitted (back to this same page), the script will receive the ID through **$_POST**. The second condition checks this and, again, that the ID value is numeric.

If neither of these conditions is TRUE, then the page cannot proceed, so an error message is displayed and the script's execution is terminated **B**.

4. Include the MySQL connection script:

```
require_once ('../mysqli_
→ connect.php');
```

Both of this script's processes—showing the form and handling the form—require a database connection, so this line is outside of the main submit conditional (Step 5).

5. Begin the main submit conditional:

```
if ($_SERVER['REQUEST_METHOD'] ==
→ 'POST') {
```

To test for a form submission, the script uses the same conditional first explained in Chapter 3, and also used in Chapter 9.

6. Delete the user, if appropriate:

```
if ($_POST['sure'] == 'Yes') {
  $q = "DELETE FROM users WHERE
  → user_id=$id LIMIT 1";
  $r = @mysqli_query ($dbc, $q);
```

The form **C** will force the user to click a radio button to confirm the deletion. This little requirement prevents any accidents. Thus, the handling process first checks that the correct radio button was selected. If so, a basic **DELETE** query is defined, using the user's ID in the **WHERE** clause. A **LIMIT** clause is added to the query as an extra precaution.

7. Check if the deletion worked and respond accordingly:

```
if (mysqli_affected_rows($dbc)
→ == 1) {
  echo '<p>The user has been
  → deleted.</p>';
```

Delete a User

Name: Dolenz, Micky
Are you sure you want to delete this user?
○ Yes ● No Submit

C The page confirms the user deletion using this simple form.

Delete a User

The user has been deleted.

D If you select *Yes* in the form (see **C**) and click Submit, this should be the result.

---

http://localhost/delete_user.php?id=cat

| Home Page | Register |

Delete a User

This page has been accessed in error.

Copyright © Plain and Simple 2007 | Desig

B If the page does not receive a number ID value, this error is shown.

```
} else {
  echo '<p class="error">The user
  → could not be deleted due to a
  → system error.</p>';
  echo '<p>' . mysqli_error($dbc) .
  → '<br />Query: ' . $q . '</p>';
}
```

The `mysqli_affected_rows()` function checks that exactly one row was affected by the **DELETE** query. If so, a happy message is displayed . If not, an error message is sent out.

Keep in mind that it's possible that no rows were affected without a MySQL error occurring. For example, if the query tries to delete the record where the user ID is equal to 42000 (and if that doesn't exist), no rows will be deleted but no MySQL error will occur. Still, because of the checks made when the form is first loaded, it would take a fair amount of hacking by the user to get to that point.

8. Complete the `$_POST['sure']` conditional:

```
} else {
  echo '<p>The user has NOT been
  → deleted.</p>';
}
```

If the user did not explicitly check the *Yes* button, the user will *not* be deleted and this message is displayed .

9. Begin the **else** clause of the main submit conditional:

```
} else {
```

The page will either handle the form or display it. Most of the code prior to this takes effect if the form has been submitted (if **$_SERVER['REQUEST_METHOD']** equals *POST*). The code from here on takes effect if the form has not yet been submitted, in which case the form should be displayed.

10. Retrieve the information for the user being deleted:

```
$q = "SELECT CONCAT(last_name, ',
→ ', first_name) FROM users WHERE
→ user_id=$id";
$r = @mysqli_query ($dbc, $q);
if (mysqli_num_rows($r) == 1) {
  $row = mysqli_fetch_array ($r,
  → MYSQLI_NUM);
```

To confirm that the script received a valid user ID and to state exactly who is being deleted (refer back to), the to-be-deleted user's name is retrieved from the database .

The conditional—checking that a single row was returned—ensures that a valid user ID was provided to the script. If so, that one record is fetched into the `$row` variable.

11. Display the record being deleted:

```
echo "<h3>Name: $row[0]</h3>
Are you sure you want to delete
→ this user?";
```

continues on next page

Delete a User

The user has NOT been deleted.

Ⓔ If you do not select *Yes* in the form, no database changes are made.

```
⬤ ⬤ ⬤  PHP and MySQL for Dynamic Web Sites: Visu...
mysql> SELECT CONCAT(last_name, ', ', first_name)
FROM users WHERE user_id=12;
+-------------------------------------+
| CONCAT(last_name, ', ', first_name) |
+-------------------------------------+
| Hornby, Nick                        |
+-------------------------------------+
1 row in set (0.00 sec)

mysql> ▌
```

Ⓕ Running the same **SELECT** query in the mysql client.

To help prevent accidental deletions of the wrong record, the name of the user to be deleted is first displayed. That value is available in **$row[0]**, because the **mysqli_fetch_array( )** function (in Step 10), uses the **MYSQLI_NUM** constant, thereby assigning the returned record to **$row** as an indexed array. The user's name is the first, and only, column in the returned record, so it's indexed at 0 (as arrays normally begin indexing at 0).

12. Create the form:

```
echo '<form action="delete_user.php"
→ method="post">
<input type="radio" name="sure"
→ value="Yes" /> Yes
<input type="radio" name="sure"
→ value="No" checked="checked" /> No
<input type="submit" name="submit"
→ value="Submit" />
<input type="hidden" name="id"
→ value="' . $id . '" />
</form>';
```

The form posts back to this same page. It contains two radio buttons, with the same name but different values, a submit button, and a hidden input. The most important step here is that the user ID (**$id**) is stored as a hidden form input so that the handling process can also access this value **G**.

13. Complete the **mysqli_num_rows( )** conditional:

```
} else {
   echo '<p class="error">This page
   → has been accessed in error.</p>';
}
```

If no record was returned by the **SELECT** query (because an invalid user ID was submitted), this message is displayed.

If you see this message when you test this script but don't understand why, apply the standard debugging steps outlined at the end of Chapter 8, "Error Handling and Debugging."

14. Complete the PHP page:

```
}
mysqli_close($dbc);
include ('includes/footer.html');
?>
```

The closing brace finishes the main submission conditional. Then the MySQL connection is closed and the footer is included.

15. Save the file as **delete_user.php** and place it in your Web directory (it should be in the same directory as **view_users.php**).

16. Run the page by first clicking a *Delete* link in the **view_users.php** page.

TIP Hidden form elements don't display in the Web browser but are still present in the HTML source code **G**. For this reason, never store anything there that must be kept truly secure.

TIP Using hidden form inputs and appending values to a URL are just two ways to make data available to other PHP pages. Two more methods—cookies and sessions—are thoroughly covered in Chapter 12, "Cookies and Sessions."

```
ript 9.1 - header.html --><h1>Delete a User</h1><h3>Name: Nesmith, mike</h3>
        Are you sure you want to delete this user?<form action="delete_user.php" method="post">
<input type="radio" name="sure" value="Yes" /> Yes
<input type="radio" name="sure" value="No" checked="checked" /> No
<input type="submit" name="submit" value="Submit" />
<input type="hidden" name="id" value="10" />
</form><!-- Script 3.3 - footer.html -->
```

G The user ID is stored as a hidden input so that it's available when the form is submitted.

Edit a User

First Name: **Richard**

Last Name: **Brautigan**

Email Address: **richard@authors.com**

Submit

A The form for editing a user's record.

Script 10.3 The **edit_user.php** page first displays the user's current information in a form. Upon submission of the form, the record will be updated in the database.

```
1    <?php # Script 10.3 - edit_user.php
2    // This page is for editing a user
     record.
3    // This page is accessed through view_
     users.php.
4
5    $page_title = 'Edit a User';
6    include ('includes/header.html');
7    echo '<h1>Edit a User</h1>';
8
9    // Check for a valid user ID, through
     GET or POST:
10   if ( (isset($_GET['id'])) && (is_numeric($_
     GET['id'])) ) { // From view_users.php
11       $id = $_GET['id'];
12   } elseif ( (isset($_POST['id'])) &&
     (is_numeric($_POST['id'])) ) { // Form
     submission.
13       $id = $_POST['id'];
14   } else { // No valid ID, kill the script.
15       echo '<p class="error">This page has
         been accessed in error.</p>';
16       include ('includes/footer.html');
17       exit();
18   }
19
20   require_once ('../mysqli_connect.php');
21
22   // Check if the form has been submitted:
23   if ($_SERVER['REQUEST_METHOD'] == 'POST') {
24
25       $errors = array();
```

code continues on next page

Editing Existing Records

A common practice with database-driven Web sites is having a system in place so that you can easily edit existing records. This concept seems daunting to many beginning programmers, but the process is surprisingly straightforward. For the following example—editing registered user records—the process combines skills the book has already taught:

- Making sticky forms
- Using hidden inputs
- Validating registration data
- Executing simple queries

This next example is generally very similar to **delete_user.php** and will also be linked from the **view_users.php** script (when a person clicks *Edit*). A form will be displayed with the user's current information, allowing for those values to be changed **A**. Upon submitting the form, if the data passes all of the validation routines, an **UPDATE** query will be run to update the database.

To edit an existing database record:

1. Begin a new PHP document in your text editor or IDE, to be named **edit_user.php** (Script 10.3):

   ```
   <?php # Script 10.3 - edit_user.php
   $page_title = 'Edit a User';
   include ('includes/header.html');
   echo '<h1>Edit a User</h1>';
   ```

   continues on page 311

```
26
27      // Check for a first name:
28      if (empty($_POST['first_name'])) {
29          $errors[] = 'You forgot to enter
            your first name.';
30      } else {
31          $fn = mysqli_real_escape_string($dbc,
            trim($_POST['first_name']));
32      }
33
34      // Check for a last name:
35      if (empty($_POST['last_name'])) {
36          $errors[] = 'You forgot to enter
            your last name.';
37      } else {
38          $ln = mysqli_real_escape_string($dbc,
            trim($_POST['last_name']));
39      }
40
41      // Check for an email address:
42      if (empty($_POST['email'])) {
43          $errors[] = 'You forgot to enter
            your email address.';
44      } else {
45          $e = mysqli_real_escape_string
            ($dbc, trim($_POST['email']));
46      }
47
48      if (empty($errors)) { // If
        everything's OK.
49
50          //  Test for unique email address:
51          $q = "SELECT user_id FROM users
            WHERE email='$e' AND user_id != $id";
52          $r = @mysqli_query($dbc, $q);
53          if (mysqli_num_rows($r) == 0) {
54
55              // Make the query:
56              $q = "UPDATE users SET first_
                name='$fn', last_name='$ln',
                email='$e' WHERE user_id=$id
                LIMIT 1";
57              $r = @mysqli_query ($dbc, $q);
58              if (mysqli_affected_rows($dbc)
                == 1) { // If it ran OK.
59
60                  // Print a message:
61                  echo '<p>The user has been
                    edited.</p>';
62
```

```
63              } else { // If it did not run OK.
64                  echo '<p class="error">The user
                    could not be edited due to a
                    system error. We apologize for
                    any inconvenience.</p>';
                    // Public message.
65                  echo '<p>' . mysqli_error($dbc)
                    . '<br />Query: ' . $q . '</
                    p>'; // Debugging message.
66              }
67
68          } else { // Already registered.
69              echo '<p class="error">The
                email address has already been
                registered.</p>';
70          }
71
72      } else { // Report the errors.
73
74          echo '<p class="error">The
            following error(s) occurred:<br />';
75          foreach ($errors as $msg) {
            // Print each error.
76              echo " - $msg<br />\n";
77          }
78          echo '</p><p>Please try again.</p>';
79
80      } // End of if (empty($errors)) IF.
81
82  } // End of submit conditional.
83
84  // Always show the form...
85
86  // Retrieve the user's information:
87  $q = "SELECT first_name, last_name,
    email FROM users WHERE user_id=$id";
88  $r = @mysqli_query ($dbc, $q);
89
90  if (mysqli_num_rows($r) == 1) { // Valid
    user ID, show the form.
91
92      // Get the user's information:
93      $row = mysqli_fetch_array ($r,
        MYSQLI_NUM);
94
95      // Create the form:
96      echo '<form action="edit_user.php"
        method="post">
97  <p>First Name: <input type="text"
    name="first_name" size="15" maxlength="15"
    value="' . $row[0] . '" /></p>
```

code continues on next page

Script 10.3 *continued*

```
98    <p>Last Name: <input type="text"
      name="last_name" size="15" maxlength="30"
      value="' . $row[1] . '" /></p>
99    <p>Email Address: <input type="text"
      name="email" size="20" maxlength="60"
      value="' . $row[2] . '"  /> </p>
100   <p><input type="submit" name="submit"
      value="Submit" /></p>
101   <input type="hidden" name="id" value="' .
      $id . '" />
102   </form>';
103
104   } else { // Not a valid user ID.
105       echo '<p class="error">This page has
          been accessed in error.</p>';
106   }
107
108   mysqli_close($dbc);
109
110   include ('includes/footer.html');
111   ?>
```

2. Check for a valid user ID value:

```
if ( (isset($_GET['id'])) &&
→ (is_numeric($_GET['id'])) ) {
  $id = $_GET['id'];
} elseif ( (isset($_POST['id'])) &&
→ (is_numeric($_POST['id'])) ) {
  $id = $_POST['id'];
} else {
  echo '<p class="error">This page
  → has been accessed in error.</p>';
  include ('includes/footer.html');
  exit( );
}
```

This validation routine is exactly the same as that in **delete_user.php**, confirming that a numeric user ID has been received, whether the page has first been accessed from **view_users.php** (the first condition) or upon submission of the form (the second condition).

3. Include the MySQL connection script and begin the main submit conditional:

```
require_once ('../mysqli_connect.
→ php');
if ($_SERVER['REQUEST_METHOD'] ==
→ 'POST') {
  $errors = array( );
```

Like the registration examples you have already done, this script makes use of an array to track errors.

continues on next page

4. Validate the first name:

```
if (empty($_POST['first_name'])) {
  $errors[] = 'You forgot to
  ⇥ enter your first name.';
} else {
  $fn = mysqli_real_escape_string
  ⇥ ($dbc, trim($_POST
  ⇥ ['first_name']));
}
```

The form Ⓐ is like a registration page but without the password fields (see the second tip). The form data can therefore be validated by applying the same techniques used in a registration script. As with a registration example, the validated data is trimmed and then run through **mysqli_real_escape_string( )** for security.

5. Validate the last name and email address:

```
if (empty($_POST['last_name'])) {
  $errors[] = 'You forgot to
  ⇥ enter your last name.';
} else {
  $ln = mysqli_real_escape_string
  ⇥ ($dbc, trim($_POST
  ⇥ ['last_name']));
}
if (empty($_POST['email'])) {
  $errors[] = 'You forgot to
  ⇥ enter your email address.';
} else {
  $e = mysqli_real_escape_string
  ⇥ ($dbc, trim($_POST['email']));
}
```

6. If there were no errors, check that the submitted email address is not already in use:

```
if (empty($errors)) {
$q = "SELECT user_id FROM users
⇥ WHERE email='$e' AND user_id
⇥ != $id";
$r = @mysqli_query($dbc, $q);
if (mysqli_num_rows($r) == 0) {
```

The integrity of the database and of the application as a whole partially depends upon having unique email address values in the *users* table. That requirement guarantees that the login system, which uses a combination of the email address and password (to be developed in Chapter 12), works. Because the form allows for altering the user's email address (see Ⓐ), special steps have to be taken to ensure uniqueness of that value across every database record. To understand this query, consider two possibilities....

In the first, the user's email address is being changed. In this case you just need to run a query making sure that that particular email address isn't already registered: **SELECT user_id FROM users WHERE email='$e'**.

In the second possibility, the user's email address will remain the same. In this case, it's okay if the email address is already in use, because it's already in use *for this user*.

To write one query that will work for both possibilities, don't check to see if the email address is being used, but rather see if it's being used by *anyone else*, hence:

```
SELECT user_id FROM users WHERE email='$e' AND user_id != $id
```

If this query returns no records, it's safe to run the **UPDATE** query.

7. Update the database:

```
$q = "UPDATE users SET
→ first_name='$fn', last_name=
→ '$ln', email='$e' WHERE user_id=
→ $id LIMIT 1";
$r = @mysqli_query ($dbc, $q);
```

The **UPDATE** query is similar to examples you could have seen in Chapter 5, "Introduction to SQL." The query updates three fields—first name, last name, and email address—using the values submitted by the form. This system works because the form is preset with the existing values. So, if you edit the first name in the form but nothing else, the first name value in the database is updated using this new value, but the last name and email address values are "updated" using their current values. This system is much easier than trying to determine which form values have changed and updating just those in the database.

8. Report on the results of the update:

```
if (mysqli_affected_rows($dbc) ==
→ 1) {
  echo '<p>The user has been
  → edited.</p>';
} else {
  echo '<p class="error">The user
  → could not be edited due to a
  → system error. We apologize
  → for any inconvenience.</p>';
  echo '<p>' . mysqli_error($dbc) .
  → '<br />Query: ' . $q . '</p>';
}
```

The **mysqli_affected_rows( )** function will return the number of rows in the database affected by the most recent query. If any of the three form values was altered, then this function will return the value 1. This conditional tests for that and prints a message indicating success or failure.

Keep in mind that the **mysqli_ affected_rows( )** function will return a value of 0 if an **UPDATE** command successfully ran but didn't actually affect any records. Therefore, if you submit this form without changing any of the form values, a system error is displayed, which may not technically be correct. Once you have this script effectively working, you could change the error message to indicate that no alterations were made if **mysqli_ affected_rows( )** returns 0.

continues on next page

9. Complete the email conditional:

```
} else {
  echo '<p class="error">The
    → email address has already
    → been registered.</p>';
}
```

This **else** completes the conditional that checked if an email address was already being used by another user. If so, that message is printed.

10. Complete the **$errors** conditional:

```
} else {
echo '<p class="error">The following
  → error(s) occurred:<br />';
  foreach ($errors as $msg) {
    echo " - $msg<br />\n";
  }
  echo '</p><p>Please try again.</p>';
}
```

The **else** is used to report any errors in the form (namely, a lack of a first name, last name, or email address), just like in the registration script.

11. Complete the submission conditional:

```
} // End of submit conditional.
```

The final closing brace completes the main submit conditional. In this example, the form will be displayed whenever the page is accessed. After submitting the form, the database will be updated, and the form will be shown again, now displaying the latest information.

12. Retrieve the information for the user being edited:

```
$q = "SELECT first_name,
  → last_name, email FROM users
  → WHERE user_id=$id";
$r = @mysqli_query ($dbc, $q);
if (mysqli_num_rows($r) == 1) {
  $row = mysqli_fetch_array ($r,
    → MYSQL_NUM);
```

In order to populate the form elements, the current information for the user must be retrieved from the database. This query is similar to the one in **delete_user.php**. The conditional—checking that a single row was returned—ensures that a valid user ID was provided.

13. Display the form:

```
echo '<form action="edit_user.php"
  → method="post">
<p>First Name: <input type="text"
  → name="first_name" size="15"
  → maxlength="15" value="' .
  → $row[0] . '" /></p>
<p>Last Name: <input type="text"
  → name="last_name" size="15"
  → maxlength="30" value="' .
  → $row[1] . '" /></p>
<p>Email Address: <input type=
  → "text" name="email" size="20"
  → maxlength="60" value="' .
  → $row[2] . '" /> </p>
<p><input type="submit" name=
  → "submit" value="Submit" /></p>
<input type="hidden" name="id"
  → value="' . $id . '" />
</form>';
```

The form has but three text inputs, each of which is made sticky using the data retrieved from the database. Again, the user ID (**$id**) is stored as a hidden form input so that the handling process can also access this value.

14. Complete the **mysqli_num_rows( )** conditional:

```
} else {
  echo '<p class="error">This page
    → has been accessed in error.</p>';
}
```

If no record was returned from the database, because an invalid user ID was submitted, this message is displayed.

Edit a User

The user has been edited.

First Name: Richard

Last Name: Brautigan

Email Address: rich@authors.com

Submit

Ⓑ The new values are displayed in the form after successfully updating the database (compare with the form values in Ⓐ).

Edit a User

The email address has already been registered.

First Name: Richard

Last Name: Brautigan

Email Address: richard@authors.com

Submit

Ⓒ If you try to change a record to an existing email address or if you omit an input, errors are reported.

15. Complete the PHP page:

```
mysqli_close($dbc);
include ('includes/footer.html');
?>
```

16. Save the file as **edit_user.php** and place it in your Web directory (in the same folder as **view_users.php**).

17. Run the page by first clicking an *Edit* link in the **view_users.php** page Ⓑ and Ⓒ.

TIP As written, the sticky form always shows the values retrieved from the database. This means that if an error occurs, the database values will be used, not the ones the user just entered (if those are different). To change this behavior, the sticky form would have to check for the presence of $_POST variables, using those if they exist, or the database values if not.

TIP This edit page does not include the functionality to change the password. That concept was already demonstrated in password.php (Script 9.7). If you would like to incorporate that functionality here, keep in mind that you cannot display the current password, as it is stored in a hashed format (i.e., it's not decryptable). Instead, just present two boxes for changing the password (the new password input and a confirmation). If these values are submitted, update the password in the database as well. If these inputs are left blank, do not update the password in the database.

Paginating Query Results

Pagination is a concept you're familiar with even if you don't know the term. When you use a search engine like Google, it displays the results as a series of pages and not as one long list. The `view_users.php` script could benefit from this feature.

Paginating query results makes extensive use of the **LIMIT** SQL clause introduced in Chapter 5. **LIMIT** restricts which subset of the matched records is actually returned. To paginate the returned results of a query, each iteration of the page will run the same query using different **LIMIT** parameters. The first page viewing will request the first *X* records; the second page viewing, the second group of *X* records; and so forth. To make this work, two values must be passed from page to page in the URL, like the user IDs passed from the `view_users.php` page. The first value is the total number of pages to be displayed. The second value is an indicator of which records the page should display with this iteration (i.e., where to begin fetching records).

Another, more cosmetic technique will be demonstrated here: displaying each row of the table—each returned record—using an alternating background color **A**. This effect will be achieved with ease, using the ternary operator (see the sidebar "The Ternary Operator").

There's a lot of good, new information to be covered here, so to make it easier to follow along, let's write this version from scratch instead of trying to modify Script 10.1.

To paginate view_users.php:

1. Begin a new PHP document in your text editor or IDE, to be named `view_users.php` (Script 10.4):

   ```
   <?php # Script 10.4 -
   → view_users.php #4
   $page_title = 'View the Current
   → Users';
   include ('includes/header.html');
   echo '<h1>Registered Users</h1>';
   require_once ('../mysqli_connect.
   → php');
   ```

2. Set the number of records to display per page:

   ```
   $display = 10;
   ```

   By establishing this value as a variable here, you'll make it easy to change the number of records displayed on each page at a later date. Also, this value will be used multiple times in this script, so it's best represented as a single variable (you could also represent this value as a constant, if you'd rather).

3. Check if the number of required pages has been already determined:

   ```
   if (isset($_GET['p']) && is_numeric
   → ($_GET['p'])) {
     $pages = $_GET['p'];
   } else {
   ```

A Alternating the table row colors makes this list of users more legible (every other row has a light gray background).

Script 10.4 This new version of `view_users.php` incorporates *pagination* so that the users are listed over multiple Web browser pages.

```
1    <?php # Script 10.4 - view_users.php #4
2    // This script retrieves all the records
     from the users table.
3    // This new version paginates the query
     results.
4
5    $page_title = 'View the Current Users';
6    include ('includes/header.html');
7    echo '<h1>Registered Users</h1>';
8
9    require_once ('../mysqli_connect.php');
10
11   // Number of records to show per page:
12   $display = 10;
13
14   // Determine how many pages there are...
15   if (isset($_GET['p']) && is_numeric
     ($_GET['p'])) { // Already been
     determined.
16
17       $pages = $_GET['p'];
18
19   } else { // Need to determine.
20
```

code continues on next page

For this script to display the users over several page viewings, it will need to determine how many total pages of results will be required. The first time the script is run, this number has to be calculated. For every subsequent call to this page, the total number of pages will be passed to the script in the URL, making it available in **$_GET['p']**. If this variable is set and is numeric, its value will be assigned to the **$pages** variable. If not, then the number of pages will need to be calculated.

4. Count the number of records in the database:

```
$q = "SELECT COUNT(user_id) FROM
→ users";
$r = @mysqli_query ($dbc, $q);
$row = @mysqli_fetch_array ($r,
→ MYSQLI_NUM);
$records = $row[0];
```

continues on page 319

The Ternary Operator

This example uses an operator not introduced before, called the *ternary* operator. Its structure is

(condition) ? valueT : valueF

The condition in parentheses will be evaluated; if it is TRUE, the first value will be returned (*valueT*). If the condition is FALSE, the second value (*valueF*) will be returned.

Because the ternary operator returns a value, the entire structure is often used to assign a value to a variable or used as an argument for a function. For example, the line

```
echo (isset($var)) ? 'SET' : 'NOT SET';
```

will print out *SET* or *NOT SET*, depending upon the status of the variable **$var**.

In this version of the **view_users.php** script, the ternary operator is used to toggle the value of a variable between two options. The variable itself will then be used to dictate the background color of each record in the table. There are certainly other ways to set this value, but the ternary operator is the most concise.

```
21     // Count the number of records:
22     $q = "SELECT COUNT(user_id) FROM
       users";
23     $r = @mysqli_query ($dbc, $q);
24     $row = @mysqli_fetch_array ($r,
       MYSQL_NUM);
25     $records = $row[0];
26
27     // Calculate the number of pages...
28     if ($records > $display) { // More
       than 1 page.
29         $pages = ceil ($records/$display);
30     } else {
31         $pages = 1;
32     }
33
34     } // End of p IF.
35
36     // Determine where in the database to
       start returning results...
37     if (isset($_GET['s']) && is_numeric
       ($_GET['s'])) {
38         $start = $_GET['s'];
39     } else {
40         $start = 0;
41     }
42
43     // Define the query:
44     $q = "SELECT last_name, first_name,
       DATE_FORMAT(registration_date, '%M
       %d, %Y') AS dr, user_id FROM users
       ORDER BY registration_date ASC LIMIT
       $start, $display";
45     $r = @mysqli_query ($dbc, $q);
46
47     // Table header:
48     echo '<table align="center" cellspacing="0"
       cellpadding="5" width="75%">
49     <tr>
50         <td align="left"><b>Edit</b></td>
51         <td align="left"><b>Delete</b></td>
52         <td align="left"><b>Last Name</b></td>
53         <td align="left"><b>First Name</b></
td>
54         <td align="left"><b>Date Registered
       </b></td>
55     </tr>
56     ';
57
58     // Fetch and print all the records....
59
```

```
60     $bg = '#eeeeee'; // Set the initial
       background color.
61
62     while ($row = mysqli_fetch_array($r,
       MYSQL_ASSOC)) {
63
64         $bg = ($bg=='#eeeeee' ? '#ffffff' :
           '#eeeeee'); // Switch the
           background color.
65
66         echo '<tr bgcolor="' . $bg . '">
67             <td align="left"><a href="edit_
           user.php?id=' . $row['user_id'] .
           '">Edit</a></td>
68             <td align="left"><a href="delete_
           user.php?id=' . $row['user_id'] .
           '">Delete</a></td>
69             <td align="left">' . $row['last_
           name'] . '</td>
70             <td align="left">' . $row['first_
           name'] . '</td>
71             <td align="left">' . $row['dr'] .
           '</td>
72         </tr>
73         ';
74
75     } // End of WHILE loop.
76
77     echo '</table>';
78     mysqli_free_result ($r);
79     mysqli_close($dbc);
80
81     // Make the links to other pages, if
       necessary.
82     if ($pages > 1) {
83
84         // Add some spacing and start a
           paragraph:
85         echo '<br /><p>';
86
87         // Determine what page the script is
on:
88         $current_page = ($start/$display)
           + 1;
89
90         // If it's not the first page, make a
           Previous link:
91         if ($current_page != 1) {
92             echo '<a href="view_users.
               php?s=' . ($start - $display) .
               '&p=' . $pages . '">Previous</a> ';
93         }
```

code continues on next page

```
94
95      // Make all the numbered pages:
96      for ($i = 1; $i <= $pages; $i++) {
97          if ($i != $current_page) {
98              echo '<a href="view_users.
                php?s=' . (($display *
                ($i - 1))) . '&p=' . $pages .
                '">' . $i . '</a> ';
99          } else {
100             echo $i . ' ';
101         }
102     } // End of FOR loop.
103
104     // If it's not the last page, make a
        Next button:
105     if ($current_page != $pages) {
106         echo '<a href="view_users.
            php?s=' . ($start + $display) .
            '&p=' . $pages . '">Next</a>';
107     }
108
109     echo '</p>'; // Close the paragraph.
110
111 } // End of links section.
112
113 include ('includes/footer.html');
114 ?>
```

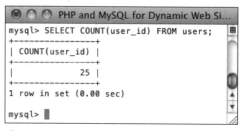

```
  ●●●    PHP and MySQL for Dynamic Web Si...
mysql> SELECT COUNT(user_id) FROM users;
+----------------+
| COUNT(user_id) |
+----------------+
|             25 |
+----------------+
1 row in set (0.00 sec)

mysql>
```

B The result of running the counting query in the mysql client.

Using the **COUNT( )** function, introduced in Chapter 8, "Advanced SQL and MySQL," you can easily find the number of records in the *users* table (i.e., the number of records to be paginated). This query will return a single row with a single column: the number of records **B**.

5. Mathematically calculate how many pages are required:

```
if ($records > $display) {
    $pages = ceil ($records/$display);
} else {
    $pages = 1;
}
```

The number of pages required to display all of the records is based upon the total number of records to be shown and the number to display per page (as assigned to the **$display** variable). If there are more records in the result set than there are records to be displayed per page, multiple pages will be required. To calculate exactly how many pages, take the next highest integer from the division of the two (the **ceil( )** function returns the next highest integer). For example, if there are 25 records returned and 10 are being displayed per page, then 3 pages are required (the first page will display 10, the second page 10, and the third page 5). If **$records** is not greater than **$display**, only one page is necessary.

6. Complete the number of pages **if-else**:

```
} // End of p IF.
```

7. Determine the starting point in the database:

```
if (isset($_GET['s']) && is_numeric
→ ($_GET['s'])) {
    $start = $_GET['s'];
} else {
    $start = 0;
}
```

continues on next page

The second parameter the script will receive—on subsequent viewings of the page—will be the starting record. This corresponds to the first number in a **LIMIT** *x, y* clause. Upon initially calling the script, the first ten records—0 through 10—should be retrieved (because **$display** has a value of 10). The second page would show records 10 through 19; the third, 20 through 29; and so forth.

The first time this page is accessed, the **$_GET['s']** variable will not be set, and so **$start** should be 0 (the first record in a **LIMIT** clause is indexed at 0). Subsequent pages will receive the **$_GET['s']** variable from the URL, and it will be assigned to **$start**.

8. Write the **SELECT** query with a **LIMIT** clause:

```
$q = "SELECT last_name,
→ first_name, DATE_FORMAT
→ (registration_date, '%M %d, %Y')
→ AS dr, user_id FROM users ORDER
→ BY registration_date ASC LIMIT
→ $start, $display";
$r = @mysqli_query ($dbc, $q);
```

The **LIMIT** clause dictates with which record to begin retrieving (**$start**) and how many to return (**$display**) from that point. The first time the page is run, the query will be **SELECT last_name, first_name … LIMIT 0, 10**. Clicking to the next page will result in **SELECT last_name, first_name … LIMIT 10, 10**.

9. Create the HTML table header:

```
echo '<table align="center"
→ cellspacing="0" cellpadding="5"
→ width="75%">
<tr>
  <td align="left"><b>Edit</b></td>
  <td align="left"><b>Delete</b>
  → </td>
  <td align="left"><b>Last Name
  → </b></td>
```

```
  <td align="left"><b>First Name
  → </b></td>
  <td align="left"><b>Date
  → Registered</b></td>
</tr>
';
```

In order to simplify this script a little bit, I'm assuming that there are records to be displayed. To be more formal, this script, prior to creating the table, would invoke the **mysqli_num_rows()** function and have a conditional that confirms that some records were returned.

10. Initialize the background color variable:

```
$bg = '#eeeeee';
```

To make each row have its own background color, a variable will be used to store that color. To start, the **$bg** variable is assigned a value of *#eeeeee*, a light gray. This color will alternate with white (*#ffffff*).

11. Begin the **while** loop that retrieves every record, and then swap the background color:

```
while ($row = mysqli_fetch_array
→ ($r, MYSQLI_ASSOC)) {
  $bg = ($bg=='#eeeeee' ?
  → '#ffffff' : '#eeeeee');
```

The background color used by each row in the table is assigned to the **$bg** variable. Because the background color should alternate, this one line of code will, upon each iteration of the loop, assign the opposite color to **$bg**. If **$bg** is equal to *#eeeeee*, then it will be assigned the value of *#ffffff* and vice versa (again, see the sidebar for the syntax and explanation of the ternary operator). For the first row fetched, **$bg** is initially equal to *#eeeeee* (see Step 10) and will therefore be assigned *#ffffff*, making a white background.

For the second row, **$bg** is not equal to *#eeeeee*, so it will be assigned that value, making a gray background.

12. Print the records in a table row:

```
echo '<tr bgcolor="' . $bg . '">
  <td align="left"><a href=
  →"edit_user.php?id=' . $row
  →['user_id'] . '">Edit</a></td>
  <td align="left"><a href=
  "delete_user.php?id=' . $row
  →['user_id'] . '">Delete</a></td>
  <td align="left">' . $row['last_
  →name'] . '</td>
  <td align="left">' . $row
  →['first_name'] . '</td>
  <td align="left">' . $row['dr'] .
  →'</td>
</tr>
';
```

This code only differs in one way from that in the previous version of this script: the initial **TR** tag now includes the **bgcolor** attribute, whose value will be the **$bg** variable (so *#eeeeee* and *#ffffff*, alternating).

13. Complete the **while** loop and the table, free up the query result resources, and close the database connection:

```
} // End of WHILE loop.
echo '</table>';
mysqli_free_result ($r);
mysqli_close($dbc);
```

14. Begin a section for displaying links to other pages, if necessary:

```
if ($pages > 1) {
  echo '<br /><p>';
```

If the script requires multiple pages to display all of the records, it needs the appropriate links at the bottom of the page 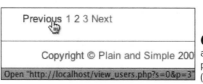.

15. Determine the current page being viewed:

```
$current_page = ($start/$display)
→ + 1;
```

To make the links, the script must first determine the current page. This can be calculated as the starting number divided by the display number, plus 1. For example, on the second viewing of this page, **$start** will be 10 (because on the first instance, **$start** is 0), making the **$current_page** value 2: $(10/10) + 1 = 2$.

16. Create a link to the previous page, if necessary:

```
if ($current_page != 1) {
  echo '<a href="view_users.
  →php?s=' . ($start - $display) .
  →'&p=' . $pages . '">Previous
  →</a> ';
}
```

If the current page is not the first page, it should also have a *Previous* link to the earlier result set **C**. This isn't strictly necessary, but is nice.

Each link will be made up of the script name, plus the starting point and the number of pages. The starting point for the previous page will be the current starting point minus the number being displayed. These values must be passed in every link, or else the pagination will fail.

continues on next page

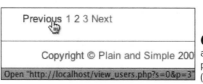

C The *Previous* link will appear only if the current page is not the first one (compare with **A**).

17. Make the numeric links:

```
for ($i = 1; $i <= $pages; $i++) {
  if ($i != $current_page) {
    echo '<a href="view_users.
    ↪php?s=' . (($display *
    ↪($i - 1))) . '&p=' . $pages
    ↪. '">' . $i . '</a> ';
  } else {
    echo $i . ' ';
  }
}
```

The bulk of the links will be created by looping from 1 to the total number of pages. Each page will be linked except for the current one. For each link, the starting point value, s, will be calculated by multiplying the number of records to display per page times one less than $i. For example, on page 3, $i - 1 is 2, meaning s will be 20.

18. Create a *Next* link:

```
if ($current_page != $pages) {
  echo '<a href="view_users.
  ↪php?s=' . ($start + $display) .
  ↪'&p=' . $pages . '">Next</a>';
}
```

Finally, a *Next* page link will be displayed, assuming that this is not the final page **D**.

19. Complete the page:

```
  echo '</p>';
} // End of links section.
include ('includes/footer.html');
?>
```

20. Save the file as **view_users.php**, place it in your Web directory, and test it in your Web browser.

TIP This example paginates a simple query, but if you want to paginate a more complex query, like the results of a search, it's not that much more complicated. The main difference is that whatever terms are used in the query must be passed from page to page in the links. If the main query is not *exactly the same* from one viewing of the page to the next, the pagination will fail.

TIP If you run this example and the pagination doesn't match the number of results that should be returned (for example, the counting query indicates there are 150 records but the pagination only creates 3 pages, with 10 records on each), it's most likely because the main query and the COUNT( ) query are too different. These two queries will never be the same, but they must perform the same join (if applicable) and have the same WHERE and/or GROUP BY clauses to be accurate.

TIP No error handling has been included in this script, as I know the queries function as written. If you have problems, remember your MySQL/SQL debugging steps: print the query, run it using the mysql client or phpMyAdmin to confirm the results, and invoke the mysqli_ error( ) function as needed.

Registered Users

Edit	Delete	Last Name	First Name
Edit	Delete	Bank	Melissa
Edit	Delete	Morrison	Toni
Edit	Delete	Franzen	Jonathan
Edit	Delete	DeLillo	Don
Edit	Delete	Doe	Jane

Previous 1 2 3

D The final results page will not display a *Next* link (compare with **A** and **C**).

```
1    <?php # Script 10.5 - view_users.php #5
2    // This script retrieves all the records
     from the users table.
3    // This new version allows the results
     to be sorted in different ways.
4
5    $page_title = 'View the Current Users';
6    include ('includes/header.html');
7    echo '<h1>Registered Users</h1>';
8
9    require_once ('../mysqli_connect.php');
10
11   // Number of records to show per page:
12   $display = 10;
13
14   // Determine how many pages there are...
15   if (isset($_GET['p']) && is_numeric($_GET
     ['p'])) { // Already been determined.
16       $pages = $_GET['p'];
17   } else { // Need to determine.
18       // Count the number of records:
19       $q = "SELECT COUNT(user_id) FROM users";
20       $r = @mysqli_query ($dbc, $q);
21       $row = @mysqli_fetch_array ($r,
         MYSQLI_NUM);
22       $records = $row[0];
23       // Calculate the number of pages...
24       if ($records > $display) { // More
         than 1 page.
25           $pages = ceil ($records/$display);
26       } else {
27           $pages = 1;
28       }
29   } // End of p IF.
30
31   // Determine where in the database to
     start returning results...
32   if (isset($_GET['s']) && is_numeric($_GET
     ['s'])) {
33       $start = $_GET['s'];
34   } else {
35       $start = 0;
36   }
37
```

code continues on next page

Making Sortable Displays

To wrap up this chapter, there's one final feature that could be added to `view_users.php`. In its current state, the list of users is displayed in order by the date they registered. It would be nice to be able to view them by name as well.

From a MySQL perspective, accomplishing this task is easy: just change the **ORDER BY** clause of the **SELECT** query. Therefore, to add a sorting feature to the script merely requires additional PHP code that will change the **ORDER BY** clause. A logical way to do this is to link the column headings so that clicking them changes the display order. As you hopefully can guess, this involves using the GET method to pass a parameter back to this page indicating the preferred sort order.

To make sortable links:

1. Open **view_users.php** (Script 10.4) in your text editor or IDE, if it is not already.

2. After determining the starting point (**$s**), define a **$sort** variable (**Script 10.5**):

   $sort = (isset($_GET['sort'])) ?
   → **$_GET['sort'] : 'rd';**

   The **$sort** variable will be used to determine how the query results are to be ordered. This line uses the ternary operator (see the sidebar in the previous section of the chapter) to assign a value to **$sort**. If **$_GET['sort']** is set, which will be the case after the user clicks any link, then **$sort** should be assigned that value. If **$_GET['sort']** is not set, then **$sort** is assigned a default value of *rd* (short for *registration date*).

continues on page 325

```
38    // Determine the sort...
39    // Default is by registration date.
40    $sort = (isset($_GET['sort'])) ?
      $_GET['sort'] : 'rd';
41
42    // Determine the sorting order:
43    switch ($sort) {
44       case 'ln':
45          $order_by = 'last_name ASC';
46          break;
47       case 'fn':
48          $order_by = 'first_name ASC';
49          break;
50       case 'rd':
51          $order_by = 'registration_date
             ASC';
52          break;
53       default:
54          $order_by = 'registration_date
             ASC';
55          $sort = 'rd';
56          break;
57    }
58
59    // Define the query:
60    $q = "SELECT last_name, first_name,
      DATE_FORMAT(registration_date, '%M %d,
      %Y') AS dr, user_id FROM users ORDER
      BY $order_by LIMIT $start, $display";
61    $r = @mysqli_query ($dbc, $q); // Run the
      query.
62
63    // Table header:
64    echo '<table align="center" cellspacing="0"
      cellpadding="5" width="75%">
65    <tr>
66       <td align="left"><b>Edit</b></td>
67       <td align="left"><b>Delete</b></td>
68       <td align="left"><b><a href="view_users.
          php?sort=ln">Last Name</a></b></td>
69       <td align="left"><b><a href="view_users.
          php?sort=fn">First Name</a></b></td>
70       <td align="left"><b><a href="view_users.
          php?sort=rd">Date Registered</a></b></td>
71    </tr>
72    ';
73
```

```
74    // Fetch and print all the records....
75    $bg = '#eeeeee';
76    while ($row = mysqli_fetch_array($r,
      MYSQLI_ASSOC)) {
77       $bg = ($bg=='#eeeeee' ? '#ffffff' :
          '#eeeeee');
78       echo '<tr bgcolor="' . $bg . '">
79          <td align="left"><a href="edit_
             user.php?id=' . $row['user_id'] .
             '">Edit</a></td>
80          <td align="left"><a href="delete_
             user.php?id=' . $row['user_id'] .
             '">Delete</a></td>
81          <td align="left">' . $row['last_
             name'] . '</td>
82          <td align="left">' . $row['first_
             name'] . '</td>
83          <td align="left">' . $row['dr'] .
             '</td>
84       </tr>
85       ';
86    } // End of WHILE loop.
87
88    echo '</table>';
89    mysqli_free_result ($r);
90    mysqli_close($dbc);
91
92    // Make the links to other pages, if
      necessary.
93    if ($pages > 1) {
94
95       echo '<br /><p>';
96       $current_page = ($start/$display) +
          1;
97
98       // If it's not the first page, make a
          Previous button:
99       if ($current_page != 1) {
100         echo '<a href="view_users.
             php?s=' . ($start - $display) .
             '&p=' . $pages . '&sort=' .
             $sort . '">Previous</a> ';
101      }
102
103      // Make all the numbered pages:
104      for ($i = 1; $i <= $pages; $i++) {
105         if ($i != $current_page) {
```

code continues on next page

```
106          echo '<a href="view_users.
             php?s=' . (($display * ($i -
             1))) . '&p=' . $pages .
             '&sort=' . $sort . '">' .
             $i . '</a> ';
107      } else {
108          echo $i . ' ';
109      }
110  } // End of FOR loop.
111
112  // If it's not the last page, make a
     Next button:
113  if ($current_page != $pages) {
114      echo '<a href="view_users.
             php?s=' . ($start + $display) .
             '&p=' . $pages . '&sort=' .
             $sort . '">Next</a>';
115  }
116
117  echo '</p>'; // Close the paragraph.
118
119  } // End of links section.
120
121  include ('includes/footer.html');
122  ?>
```

3. Determine how the results should be ordered:

```
switch ($sort) {
    case 'ln':
        $order_by = 'last_name ASC';
        break;
    case 'fn':
        $order_by = 'first_name ASC';
        break;
    case 'rd':
        $order_by = 'registration_
        → date ASC';
        break;
    default:
        $order_by = 'registration_
        → date ASC';
        $sort = 'rd';
        break;
}
```

The **switch** checks **$sort** against several expected values. If, for example, it is equal to *ln*, then the results should be ordered by the last name in ascending order. The assigned **$order_by** variable will be used in the SQL query.

If **$sort** has a value of *fn*, then the results should be in ascending order by first name. If the value is *rd*, then the results will be in ascending order of registration date. This is also the default case. Having this default case here protects against a malicious user changing the value of **$_GET['sort']** to something that could break the query.

continues on next page

4. Modify the query to use the new **$order_by** variable:

```
$q = "SELECT last_name, first_
→ name, DATE_FORMAT(registration_
→ date, '%M %d, %Y') AS dr, user_
→ id FROM users ORDER BY $order_by
→ LIMIT $start, $display";
```

By this point, the **$order_by** variable has a value indicating how the returned results should be ordered (for example, *registration_date ASC)*, so it can be easily added to the query. Remember that the **ORDER BY** clause comes before the **LIMIT** clause. If the resulting query doesn't run properly for you, print it out and inspect its syntax.

5. Modify the table header **echo** statement to create links out of the column headings:

```
echo '<table align="center"
→ cellspacing="0" cellpadding="5"
→ width="75%">
<tr>
  <td align="left"><b>Edit</b></td>
  <td align="left"><b>Delete</b></td>
  <td align="left"><b><a href=
  → "view_users.php?sort=ln">Last
  → Name</a></b></td>
  <td align="left"><b><a href=
  → "view_users.php?sort=fn">First
  → Name</a></b></td>
  <td align="left"><b><a href=
  → "view_users.php?sort=rd">Date
  → Registered</a></b></td>
</tr>
';
```

To turn the column headings into clickable links, just surround them with the **A** tag. The value of the **href** attribute for each link corresponds to the acceptable values for **$_GET['sort']** (see the **switch** in Step 3).

6. Modify the **echo** statement that creates the *Previous* link so that the sort value is also passed:

```
echo '<a href="view_users.php?s=' .
→ ($start - $display) . '&p=' .
→ $pages . '&sort=' . $sort . '">
→ Previous</a> ';
```

Add another *name=value* pair to the *Previous* link so that the sort order is also sent to each page of results. If you don't, then the pagination will fail, as the **ORDER BY** clause will differ from one page to the next.

7. Repeat Step 6 for the numbered pages and the *Next* link:

```
echo '<a href="view_users.php?s=' .
→ (($display * ($i - 1))) . '&p=' .
→ $pages . '&sort=' . $sort . '">' .
→ $i . '</a> ';
echo '<a href="view_users.php?s=' .
→ ($start + $display) . '&p=' .
→ $pages . '&sort=' . $sort . '">
→ Next</a>';
```

8. Save the file as **view_users.php**, place it in your Web directory, and run it in your Web browser **Ⓐ** and **Ⓑ**.

TIP A very important security concept was also demonstrated in this example. Instead of using the value of $_GET['sort'] directly in the query, it's checked against assumed values in a switch. If, for some reason, $_GET['sort'] has a value other than would be expected, the query uses a default sorting order. The point is this: don't make assumptions about received data, and don't use unvalidated data in an SQL query.

Ⓐ After clicking the first name column, the results are shown in ascending order by first name.

Ⓑ After clicking the *Last Name* column, and then clicking to the second paginated display, the page shows the second group of results in ascending order by last name.

Review and Pursue

If you have any problems with the review questions or the pursue prompts, turn to the book's supporting forum (**www.LarryUllman.com/forums/**).

Review

- What is the standard sequence of steps for debugging PHP-MySQL problems (explicitly conveyed at the end of Chapter 8)?

- What are the two ways of passing values to a PHP script (aside from user input)?

- What security measures do the **delete_user.php** and **edit_user.php** scripts take to prevent malicious or accidental deletions?

- Why is it safe to use the **$id** value in queries without running it through **mysqli_real_escape_string( )** first?

- In what situation will the **mysqli_affected_rows( )** function return a false negative (i.e., report that no records were affected despite the fact that the query ran without error)?

- What is the ternary operator? How is it used?

- What two values are required to properly paginate query results?

- How do you alter a query so that its results are paginated?

- If a paginated query is based upon additional criteria (beyond those used in a **LIMIT** clause), what would happen if those criteria are not also passed along in every pagination link?

- Why is it important not to directly use the value of **$_GET['sort']** in a query?

- Why is it important to pass the sorting value along in each pagination link?

Pursue

- Change the **delete_user.php** and **edit_user.php** pages so that they both display the user being affected in the browser window's title bar.

- Modify **edit_user.php** so that you can also change a user's password.

- If you're up for a challenge, modify **edit_user.php** so that the form elements' values come from **$_POST**, if set, and the database if not.

- Change the value of the **$display** variable in **view_users.php** to alter the pagination.

- Paginate another query result, such as a list of accounts or customers found in the *banking* database.

- Create delete and edit scripts for the *banking* database. You'll have to factor in the foreign key constraints in place, which limit, for example, the deletion of customers that still have accounts.

Web Application Development

The preceding two chapters focus on using PHP and MySQL together (which is, after all, the primary point of this book). But there's still a lot of PHP-centric material to be covered. Taking a quick break from using PHP with MySQL, this chapter covers a handful of techniques that are often used in more complex Web applications.

The first topic covered in this chapter is sending email using PHP. It's a very common thing to do and is surprisingly simple (assuming that the server is properly set up). After that, the chapter has uses-related examples to cover three new ideas: handling file uploads through an HTML form, using PHP and JavaScript together, and how to use the **header( )** function to manipulate the Web browser. The chapter concludes by touching upon some of the date and time functions present in PHP.

In This Chapter

Sending Email

One of my absolute favorite things about PHP is how easy it is to send an email. On a properly configured server, the process is as simple as using the `mail()` function:

```
mail (to, subject, body, [headers]);
```

The *to* value should be an email address or a series of addresses, separated by commas. Any of these are allowed:

- email@example.com

- email1@example.com, email2@example.com

- Actual Name <email@example.com>

- Actual Name <email@example.com>, This Name <email2@example.com>

The *subject* value will create the email's subject line, and *body* is where you put the contents of the email. To make things more legible, variables are often assigned values and then used in the `mail()` function call:

```
$to = 'email@example.com';
$subject = 'This is the subject';
$body = 'This is the body.
It goes over multiple lines.';
mail ($to, $subject, $body);
```

As you can see in the assignment to the **$body** variable, you can create an email message that goes over multiple lines by having the text do exactly that within the quotation marks. You can also use the newline character (**\n**) within double quotation marks to accomplish this:

```
$body = "This is the body.\nIt goes
→ over multiple lines.";
```

This is all very straightforward, and there are only a couple of caveats. First, the subject line cannot contain the newline character (**\n**). Second, each line of the

PHP mail() Dependencies

PHP's `mail()` function doesn't actually send the email itself. Instead, it tells the mail server running on the computer to do so. What this means is that the computer on which PHP is running must have a working mail server in order for this function to work.

If you have a computer running a Unix variant or if you are running your Web site through a professional host, this should not be a problem. But if you are running PHP on your own desktop or laptop computer, you'll probably need to make adjustments.

If you are running Windows and have an Internet service provider (ISP) that provides you with an SMTP server (like *smtp.comcast.net*), this information can be set in the **php.ini** file (download Appendix A, "Installation," from peachpit.com to see how to edit this file). Unfortunately, this will only work if your ISP does not require authentication—a username and password combination—to use the SMTP server. Otherwise, you'll need to install an SMTP server on your computer. There are plenty available: just search the Internet for *free windows smtp server* and you'll see some options. The XAMPP application, which Appendix A recommends you use, includes the Mercury mail server.

If you are running Mac OS X, you'll need to enable the built-in SMTP server (either sendmail or postfix, depending upon the specific version of Mac OS X you are running). You can find instructions online for doing so (search with *enable sendmail "Mac OS X"*). If you're using MAMP, per the recommendation in Appendix A, search online for sending email with MAMP.

body should be no longer than 70 characters in length (this is more of a recommendation than a requirement). You can accomplish this using the **wordwrap( )** function. It will insert a newline into a string every *X* number of characters. To wrap text to 70 characters, use

```
$body = wordwrap($body, 70);
```

The **mail( )** function takes a fourth, optional parameter for additional headers. This is where you could set the From, Reply-To, Cc, Bcc, and similar settings. For example,

```
mail ($to, $subject, $body, 'From:
→ reader@example.com');
```

To use multiple headers of different types in your email, separate each with **\r\n**:

```
$headers = "From: John@example.com\
→ r\n";
$headers .= "Cc: Jane@example.com,
→ Joe@example.com\r\n";
mail ($to, $subject, $body, $headers);
```

Although this fourth argument is optional, it is advised that you always include a From value (although that can also be established in PHP's configuration file).

To use the **mail( )** function, let's create a page that shows a contact form Ⓐ and then handles the form submission, validating the data and sending it along in an email. This example will also provide a nice tip you'll sometimes use on pages with sticky forms.

Note two things before running this script: First, for this example to work, the computer on which PHP is running must have a working mail server. If you're using a hosted site, this shouldn't be an issue; on your own computer, you'll likely need to take preparatory steps (see the sidebar). I will say in advance that these steps can be daunting for the beginner; it will likely be easiest and most gratifying to use a hosted site for this particular script.

Second, this example, while functional, could be manipulated by bad people, allowing them to send spam through your contact form (not just to you but to anyone). The steps for preventing such attacks are provided in Chapter 13, "Security Methods." Following along and testing this example is just fine; relying upon it as your long-term contact form solution is a bad idea.

Ⓐ A standard contact form.

To send email:

1. Begin a new PHP script in your text editor or IDE, to be named **email.php** (Script 11.1):

```
<!DOCTYPE html PUBLIC "-//W3C//
→ DTD XHTML 1.0 Transitional//EN"
→ "http://www.w3.org/TR/xhtml1/DTD/
→ xhtml1-transitional.dtd">
<html xmlns="http://www.w3.org/
→ 1999/xhtml" xml:lang="en"
→ lang="en">
<head>
   <meta http-equiv="Content-Type"
   → content="text/html;
   → charset=utf-8" />
   <title>Contact Me</title>
</head>
<body>
<h1>Contact Me</h1>
<?php # Script 11.1 - email.php
```

None of the examples in this chapter will use a template, like those in the past two chapters, so it starts with the standard HTML.

2. Create the conditional for checking if the form has been submitted and validate the form data:

```
if ($_SERVER['REQUEST_METHOD'] ==
→ 'POST') {
   if (!empty($_POST['name'])
   → && !empty($_POST['email']) &&
   → !empty($_POST['comments']) ) {
```

The form contains three text inputs (technically, one is a textarea). The **empty( )** function will confirm that something was entered into each. In Chapter 13, you'll learn how to use the **Filter** extension to confirm that the supplied email address has a valid format.

Script 11.1 This page displays a contact form that, upon submission, will send an email with the form data to an email address.

```
1   <!DOCTYPE html PUBLIC "-//W3C//DTD XHTML
    1.0 Transitional//EN" "http://www.w3.org/
    TR/xhtml1/DTD/xhtml1-transitional.dtd">
2   <html xmlns="http://www.w3.org/1999/
    xhtml" xml:lang="en" lang="en">
3   <head>
4       <meta http-equiv="Content-Type"
        content="text/html; charset=utf-8" />
5       <title>Contact Me</title>
6   </head>
7   <body>
8   <h1>Contact Me</h1>
9   <?php # Script 11.1 - email.php
10
11  // Check for form submission:
12  if ($_SERVER['REQUEST_METHOD'] == 'POST') {
13
14      // Minimal form validation:
15      if (!empty($_POST['name']) && !empty
        ($_POST['email']) && !empty($_POST
        ['comments']) ) {
16
17          // Create the body:
18          $body = "Name: {$_POST['name']}\n
            \nComments: {$_POST['comments']}";
19
20          // Make it no longer than 70
            characters long:
21          $body = wordwrap($body, 70);
22
23          // Send the email:
24          mail('your_email@example.com',
            'Contact Form Submission',
            $body, "From: {$_POST['email']}");
25
26          // Print a message:
27          echo '<p><em>Thank you for
            contacting me. I will reply some
            day.</em></p>';
28
29          // Clear $_POST (so that the form's
            not sticky):
30          $_POST = array();
31
32      } else {
33          echo '<p style="font-weight: bold;
            color: #C00">Please fill out the
            form completely.</p>';
34      }
```

code continues on next page

Script 11.1 *continued*

```
35
36    } // End of main isset() IF.
37
38    // Create the HTML form:
39    ?>
40    <p>Please fill out this form to contact
      me.</p>
41    <form action="email.php" method="post">
42        <p>Name: <input type="text"
          name="name" size="30" maxlength="60"
          value="<?php if (isset($_POST['name']))
          echo $_POST['name']; ?>" /></p>
43        <p>Email Address: <input type="text"
          name="email" size="30" maxlength="80"
          value="<?php if (isset($_POST['email']))
          echo $_POST['email']; ?>" /></p>
44        <p>Comments: <textarea name="comments"
          rows="5" cols="30"><?php if (isset
          ($_POST['comments'])) echo $_POST
          ['comments']; ?></textarea></p>
45        <p><input type="submit" name="submit"
          value="Send!" /></p>
46    </form>
47    </body>
48    </html>
```

Contact Me

Please fill out the form completely.

Please fill out this form to contact me.

Name: Not Larry Ullman

Email Address:

Comments: Your book isn't just the
greatest computer book ever
written, it's the greatest
book ever written, period! It
totally blows "One Hundred

[Send!]

B The contact form will remember the user-supplied values in case it is not completely filled out.

3. Create the body of the email:

```
$body = "Name: {$_POST['name']}\n\
 nComments: {$_POST['comments']}";
$body = wordwrap($body, 70);
```

The email's body will start with the prompt *Name:*, followed by the name entered into the form. Then the same treatment is given to the comments. The **wordwrap( )** function then formats the whole body so that each line is only 70 characters long.

4. Send the email and print a message in the Web browser:

```
mail('your_email@example.com',
 'Contact Form Submission',
 $body, "From: {$_POST['email']}");
echo '<p><em>Thank you for
 contacting me. I will reply
 some day.</em></p>';
```

Assuming the server is properly configured, this one line will send the email. You will need to change the *to* value to your actual email address. The *From* value will be the email address from the form. The subject will be a literal string.

There's no easy way of confirming that the email was successfully sent, let alone received, but a generic message is printed.

5. Clear the **$_POST** array;

```
$_POST = array( );
```

In this example, the form will always be shown, even upon successful submission. The form will be sticky in case the user omitted something **B**. However, if the mail was sent, there's no need to show the values in the form again. To avoid that, the **$_POST** array can be cleared of its values using the **array( )** function.

continues on next page

6. Complete the conditionals:

```
    } else {
        echo '<p style="font-weight:
        → bold; color: #C00">Please
        → fill out the form
        → completely.</p>';
    }
} // End of main isset() IF.
```

The error message contains some inline CSS, so that it's in red and made bold.

7. Begin the form:

```
<p>Please fill out this form to
→ contact me.</p>
<form action="email.php"
→ method="post">
    <p>Name: <input type="text"
    → name="name" size="30"
    → maxlength="60" value="<?php
    → if (isset($_POST['name'])) echo
    → $_POST['name']; ?>" /></p>
    <p>Email Address: <input
    → type="text" name="email"
    → size="30" maxlength="80"
    → value="<?php if (isset($_POST
    → ['email'])) echo $_POST
    → ['email']; ?>" /></p>
```

The form will submit back to this same page using the POST method. The first two inputs are of type text; both are made sticky by checking if the corresponding **$_POST** variable has a value. If so, that value is printed as the current value for that input. Because the **$_POST** array is cleared out in Step 5, **$_POST['name']** and the like will not be set when this form is viewed again, after its previous successful completion and submission.

8. Complete the form:

```
    <p>Comments: <textarea name=
    → "comments" rows="5" cols="30">
    → <?php if (isset($_POST
    → ['comments'])) echo $_POST
    → ['comments']; ?></textarea></p>
    <p><input type="submit" name=
    → "submit" value="Send!" /></p>
</form>
```

The comments input is a textarea, which does not use a **value** attribute. Instead, to be made sticky, the value is printed between the opening and closing **textarea** tags.

9. Complete the HTML page:

```
</body>
</html>
```

Contact Me

Thank you for contacting me. I will reply some day.

Please fill out this form to contact me.

Name: [   ]

Email Address: [   ]

Comments: [   ]

[Send!]

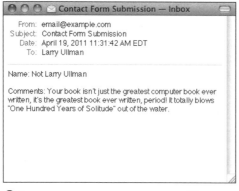 Successful completion and submission of the form.

● ● ● ☐ Contact Form Submission — Inbox

From: email@example.com
Subject: Contact Form Submission
Date: April 19, 2011 11:31:42 AM EDT
To: Larry Ullman

Name: Not Larry Ullman

Comments: Your book isn't just the greatest computer book ever written, it's the greatest book ever written, period! It totally blows "One Hundred Years of Solitude" out of the water.

D The resulting email (from the data in **A**).

10. Save the file as **email.php**, place it in your Web directory, and test it in your Web browser **C**.

11. Check your email to confirm that you received the message **D**.

If you don't actually get the email, you'll need to do some debugging work. With this example, you should confirm with your host (if using a hosted site) or yourself (if running PHP on your server), that there's a working mail server installed. You should also test this using different email addresses (for both the *to* and *from* values). Also, watch that your spam filter isn't eating up the message.

TIP The mail( ) function takes an optional fifth argument, for additional parameters to be sent to the mail-sending application.

TIP The mail( ) function returns a 1 or a 0 indicating the success of the function call. This is not the same thing as the email successfully being sent or received. Again, you cannot easily test for either using PHP.

TIP While it's easy to send a simple message with the mail( ) function, sending HTML emails or emails with attachments involves more work. I discuss how you can do both in my book *PHP 5 Advanced: Visual QuickPro Guide* (Peachpit Press, 2007).

TIP Using a contact form that has PHP send an email is a great way to minimize the spam you receive. With this system, your actual email address is not visible in the Web browser, meaning it can't be harvested by spambots.

Handling File Uploads

Chapters 2, "Programming with PHP," and 3, "Creating Dynamic Web Sites," go over the basics of handling HTML forms with PHP. For the most part, every type of form element can be handled the same in PHP, with one exception: file uploads. The process of uploading a file has two dimensions. First the HTML form must be displayed, with the proper code to allow for file uploads. Upon submission of the form, the server will first store the uploaded file in a temporary directory, so the next step is for the PHP script to copy the uploaded file to its final destination.

For this process to work, several things must be in place:

- PHP must run with the correct settings.
- A temporary storage directory must exist with the correct permissions.
- The final storage directory must exist with the correct permissions.

With this in mind, this next section will cover the server setup to allow for file uploads; then a PHP script will be created that actually does the uploading.

Allowing for file uploads

As I said, certain settings must be established in order for PHP to be able to handle file uploads. I'll first discuss why or when you'd need to make these adjustments before walking you through the steps.

The first issue is PHP itself. There are several settings in PHP's configuration file (**php.ini**) that dictate how PHP handles uploads, specifically stating how large of a file can be uploaded and where the upload should temporarily be stored (**Table 11.1**). Generally speaking, you'll need to edit this file if any of these conditions apply:

- *file_uploads* is disabled.
- PHP has no temporary directory to use.
- You will be uploading very large files (larger than 2MB).

If you don't have access to your **php.ini** file—like if you're using a hosted site—presumably the host has already configured PHP to allow for file uploads.

The second issue is the location of, and permissions on, the temporary directory. This is where PHP will store the uploaded file until your PHP script moves it to its final

TABLE 11.1 File Upload Configurations

Setting	Value Type	Importance
file_uploads	Boolean	Enables PHP support for file uploads
max_input_time	integer	Indicates how long, in seconds, a PHP script is allowed to run
post_max_size	integer	Size, in bytes, of the total allowed **POST** data
upload_max_filesize	integer	Size, in bytes, of the largest possible file upload allowed
upload_tmp_dir	string	Indicates where uploaded files should be temporarily stored

destination. If you installed PHP on your own Windows computer, you might need to take steps here. Mac OS X and Unix users need not worry about this, as a temporary directory already exists for such purposes (namely, a special directory called **/tmp**).

Finally, the destination folder must be created and have the proper permissions established on it. This is a step that *everyone* must take for *every* application that handles file uploads. Because there are important security issues involved in this step, please also make sure that you read and understand the sidebar, "Secure Folder Permissions."

With all of this in mind, let's go through the steps.

Secure Folder Permissions

There's normally a trade-off between security and convenience. With this example, it'd be more convenient to place the *uploads* folder within the Web document directory (the convenience arises with respect to how easily the uploaded images can be viewed in the Web browser), but doing that is less secure.

For PHP to be able to place files in the *uploads* folder, it needs to have write permissions on that directory. On most servers, PHP is running as the same user as the Web server itself. On a hosted server, this means that all *X* number of sites being hosted are running as the same user. Creating a folder that PHP can write to means creating a folder that *everyone* can write to. Literally anyone with a site hosted on the server can now move, copy, or write files to your *uploads* folder (assuming that they know it exists). This even means that a malicious user could copy a troublesome PHP script to your *uploads* directory. However, since the *uploads* directory in this example is not within the Web directory, such a PHP script cannot be run in a Web browser. It's less convenient to do things this way, but more secure.

If you must keep the *uploads* folder publicly accessible, and if you're using the Apache Web server, you could limit access to the *uploads* folder using an **.htaccess** file. Basically, you would state that only image files in the folder be publicly viewable, meaning that even if a PHP script were to be placed there, it could not be executed. Or, because you'll learn how to use *proxy scripts* later in this chapter, you could deny all external access to that folder. Information on how to use **.htaccess** files can be found in Appendix A, a free download from peachpit.com.

Sometimes even the most conservative programmer will make security concessions. The important point is that you're aware of the potential concerns and that you do the most you can to minimize the danger.

To prepare the server:

1. Run the `phpinfo()` function to confirm your server settings (A).

   The `phpinfo()` function prints out a slew of information about your PHP setup. It's one of the most important functions in PHP, if not the most (in my opinion). Search for the settings listed in Table 11.1 and confirm their values. Make sure that *file_uploads* has a value of *On* and that the limit for *upload_max_filesize* (2MB, by default) and *post_max_size* (8MB) won't be a restriction for you. If running PHP on Windows, see if *upload_tmp_dir* has a value. If it doesn't, that might be a problem (you'll know for certain after running the PHP script that handles the file upload). For non-Windows users, if this value says *no value*, that's perfectly fine.

   By the way, another advantage of using an all-in-one installer, such as XAMPP for Windows or MAMP for Mac OS X, is that the installer should properly configure these settings, too.

2. If necessary, open `php.ini` in your text editor.

   If there's anything you saw in Step 1 that needs to be changed, or if something happens when you actually go to handle a file upload using PHP, you'll need to edit the `php.ini` file. To find this file, see the *Configuration File (php.ini) path* value in the `phpinfo()` output. This indicates exactly where this file is on your computer (also download Appendix A for more).

   If you are not allowed to edit your `php.ini` file (if, for instance, you're using a hosted server), then presumably any necessary edits would have already been made to allow for file uploads. If not, you'll need to request these changes from your hosting company (which may or may not agree to make them).

PHP Version 5.3.5	*php*
System	Windows NT LARRY-PC 6.1 build 7601 (Unknow Windows version Home Premium Edition Service Pack 1) i586
Build Date	Jan 6 2011 17:50:45
Compiler	MSVC6 (Visual C++ 6.0)
Architecture	x86
Configure Command	cscript /nologo configure.js "--enable-snapshot-build" "--disable-isapi" "--enable-debug-pack" "--disable-isapi" "--without-mssql" "--without-pdo-mssql" "--without-pi3web" "--with-pdo-oci=D:\php-sdk\oracle\instantclient10\sdk,shared" "--with-oci8=D:\php-sdk\oracle\instantclient10\sdk,shared" "--with-oci8-11g=D:\php-sdk\oracle\instantclient11\sdk,shared" "--enable-object-out-dir=../obj/" "--enable-com-dotnet" "--with-mcrypt=static"
Server API	Apache 2.0 Handler
Virtual Directory Support	enabled

(A) A `phpinfo()` script returns all the information regarding your PHP setup, including all the file-upload handling stuff.

3. Search the **php.ini** file for the configuration to be changed and make any edits **B**.

For example, in the File Uploads section, you'll see these three lines:

```
file_uploads = On
;upload_tmp_dir =
upload_max_filesize = 2M
```

The first line dictates whether or not uploads are allowed. The second states where the uploaded files should be temporarily stored. On most operating systems, including Mac OS X and Unix, this setting can be left commented out (preceded by a semicolon) without any problem.

If you are running Windows and need to create a temporary directory, set this value to **C:\tmp**, making sure that the line is *not* preceded by a semicolon.

Again, using XAMPP on Windows 7, I did not need to create a temporary directory, so you may be able to get away without one too.

Finally, a maximum upload file size is set (the *M* is shorthand for megabytes in configuration settings).

4. Save the **php.ini** file and restart your Web server.

How you restart your Web server depends upon the operating system and Web-serving application being used. See Appendix A for instructions.

5. Confirm the changes by rerunning the **phpinfo( )** script.

Before going any further, confirm that the necessary changes have been enacted by repeating Step 1.

continues on next page

```
864   ;;;;;;;;;;;;;;;;
865   ; File Uploads ;
866   ;;;;;;;;;;;;;;;;
867   |
868   ; Whether to allow HTTP file uploads.
869   ; http://php.net/file-uploads
870   file_uploads = On
871
872   ; Temporary directory for HTTP uploaded files (will use system default if not
873   ; specified).
874   ; http://php.net/upload-tmp-dir
875   ;upload_tmp_dir =
876
877   ; Maximum allowed size for uploaded files.
878   ; http://php.net/upload-max-filesize
879   upload_max_filesize = 2M
880
881   ; Maximum number of files that can be uploaded via a single request
882   max_file_uploads = 20
```

B The File Uploads subsection of the **php.ini** file.

6. If you are running Windows and need to create a temporary directory, add a **tmp** folder within **C:** and make sure that everyone can write to that directory .

PHP, through your Web server, will temporarily store the uploaded file in the *upload_tmp_dir*. For this to work, the Web user (if your Web server runs as a particular user) must have permission to write to the folder.

In all likelihood, you may not actually have to change the permissions, but to do so, depending upon what version of Windows you are running, you can normally adjust the permissions by right-clicking the folder and selecting Properties. With the Properties window, there should be a Security tab where permissions are set. It may also be under Sharing. Windows uses a more lax permissions system, so you probably won't have to change anything unless the folder is deliberately restricted.

Mac OS X and Unix users can skip this step as the temporary directory—**/tmp**—has open permissions already.

C Windows users need to make sure that the **C:\tmp** (or whatever directory is used) is writable by PHP.

D Assuming that *htdocs* is the Web root directory (**http://www.example.com** or **http://localhost** points there), then the *uploads* directory needs to be placed outside of it.

7. Create a new directory, called *uploads*, in a directory outside of the Web root directory.

All of the uploaded files will be permanently stored in the *uploads* directory. If you'll be placing your PHP script in the **C:\xampp\htdocs\ch11** directory, then create a **C:\xampp\uploads** directory. Or if the files are going in **/Users/~<username>/Sites/ch11**, make a **/Users/~<username>/uploads** folder. Figure **D** shows the structure you should establish, and the sidebar discusses why this step is necessary.

8. Set the permissions on the *uploads* directory so that the Web server can write to it.

E Adjusting the properties on the *uploads* folder in Mac OS X.

Again, Windows users can use the Properties window to make these changes, although it may not be necessary. Mac OS X users can...

A. Select the folder in the Finder.

B. Press Command+I.

C. Allow everyone to Read & Write, under the Ownership & Permissions panel **E**.

If you're using a hosted site, the host likely provides a control panel through which you can tweak a folder's settings or you might be able to do this within your FTP application.

Depending upon your operating system, you may be able to upload files without first taking this step. You can try the following script before altering the permissions, just to see. If you see messages like those in **F**, then you will need to make some adjustments.

TIP Unix users can use the chmod command to adjust a folder's permissions. The proper permissions in Unix terms can be either 755 or 777.

TIP Because of the time it can take to upload a large file, you may also need to change the *max_input_time* value in the php.ini file or temporarily bypass it using the set_time_limit( ) function in your script.

TIP File and directory permissions can be complicated stuff, particularly if you've never dealt with them before. If you have problems with these steps or the next script, search the Web or turn to the book's corresponding forum (www.LarryUllman.com/forums/).

Warning: move_uploaded_file(../uploads/trout.jpg) [function.move-uploaded-file]: failed to open stream: Permission denied in **/Users/larryullman/Sites/phpmysql4/upload_image.php** on line **27**

Warning: move_uploaded_file() [function.move-uploaded-file]: Unable to move '/Applications/MAMP/tmp/php/php0EKXMX' to '../uploads/trout.jpg' in **/Users/larryullman/Sites/phpmysql4/upload_image.php** on line **27**

F If PHP could not move the uploaded image over to the *uploads* folder because of a permissions issue, you'll see an error message like this one. Fix the permissions on *uploads* to correct this.

Uploading files with PHP

Now that the server has (hopefully) been set up to properly allow for file uploads, you can create the PHP script that does the actual file handling. There are two parts to such a script: the HTML form and the PHP code.

The required syntax for a form to handle a file upload has three parts:

```
<form enctype="multipart/form-data"
→ action="script.php" method="post">
<input type="hidden" name="MAX_FILE_
→ SIZE" value="30000" />
File <input type="file" name=
→ "upload" />
```

The **enctype** part of the initial **form** tag indicates that the form should be able to handle multiple types of data, including files. If you want to accept file uploads, you must include this **enctype**! Also note that the form *must use* the POST method. The **MAX_FILE_SIZE** hidden input is a form restriction on how large the chosen file can be, in bytes, and must come before the file input. While it's easy for a user to circumvent this restriction, it should still be used. Finally, the file input type will create the proper button in the form (**G** and **H**).

Upon form submission, the uploaded file can be accessed using the **$_FILES** superglobal. The variable will be an array of values, listed in **Table 11.2**.

Once the file has been received by the PHP script, the **move_uploaded_file()** function can transfer it from the temporary directory to its permanent location.

```
move_uploaded_file
→ (temporary_filename,
/path/to/destination/filename);
```

G The file input as it appears in IE 9 on Windows.

Choose File No file chosen

H The file input as it appears in Google Chrome on Mac OS X.

TABLE 11.2 The $_FILES Array

Index	Meaning
name	The original name of the file (as it was on the user's computer).
type	The MIME type of the file, as provided by the browser.
size	The size of the uploaded file in bytes.
tmp_name	The temporary filename of the uploaded file as it was stored on the server.
error	The error code associated with any problem.

```
1    <!DOCTYPE html PUBLIC "-//W3C//DTD XHTML
     1.0 Transitional//EN" "http://www.w3.org/
     TR/xhtml1/DTD/xhtml1-transitional.dtd">
2    <html xmlns="http://www.w3.org/1999/
     xhtml" xml:lang="en" lang="en">
3    <head>
4        <meta http-equiv="Content-Type"
         content="text/html; charset=utf-8" />
5        <title>Upload an Image</title>
6        <style type="text/css" title="text/css"
         media="all">
7        .error {
8            font-weight: bold;
9            color: #C00;
10       }
11       </style>
12   </head>
13   <body>
14   <?php # Script 11.2 - upload_image.php
15
16   // Check if the form has been submitted:
17   if ($_SERVER['REQUEST_METHOD'] == 'POST') {
18
19       // Check for an uploaded file:
20       if (isset($_FILES['upload'])) {
21
22           // Validate the type. Should be
             JPEG or PNG.
23           $allowed = array ('image/pjpeg',
             'image/jpeg', 'image/JPG', 'image/
             X-PNG', 'image/PNG', 'image/png',
             'image/x-png');
24           if (in_array($_FILES['upload']
             ['type'], $allowed)) {
25
26               // Move the file over.
27               if (move_uploaded_file
                 ($_FILES['upload']['tmp_name'],
                 "../uploads/{$_FILES['upload']
                 ['name']}")) {
28                   echo '<p><em>The file has
                     been uploaded!</em></p>';
29               } // End of move... IF.
30
31           } else { // Invalid type.
32               echo '<p class="error">Please
                 upload a JPEG or PNG image.</p>';
33           }
34
35       } // End of isset($_FILES['upload']) IF.
```

code continues on next page

This next script will let the user select a file on their computer and will then store it in the *uploads* directory. The script will check that the file is of an image type, specifically a JPEG or PNG. In the next section of this chapter, another script will list, and create links to, the uploaded images.

To handle file uploads in PHP:

1. Create a new PHP document in your text editor or IDE, to be named **upload_image.php** (Script 11.2):

```
<!DOCTYPE html PUBLIC "-//W3C//
→ DTD XHTML 1.0 Transitional//EN"
→ "http://www.w3.org/TR/xhtml1/DTD/
→ xhtml1-transitional.dtd">
<html xmlns="http://www.w3.org/
→ 1999/xhtml" xml:lang="en"
→ lang="en">
<head>
    <meta http-equiv="Content-Type"
    → content="text/html;
    → charset=utf-8" />
    <title>Upload an Image</title>
    <style type="text/css" title=
    → "text/css" media="all">
    .error {
        font-weight: bold;
        color: #C00;
    }
    </style>
</head>
<body>
<?php # Script 11.2 -
→ upload_image.php
```

This script will make use of one CSS class to format any errors.

continues on next page

2. Check if the form has been submitted and that a file was selected:

```
if ($_SERVER['REQUEST_METHOD'] ==
→'POST') {
    if (isset($_FILES['upload'])) {
```

Since this form will have no other fields to be validated , this is the only conditional required. You could also validate the size of the uploaded file to determine if it fits within the acceptable range (refer to the **$_FILES['upload'] ['size']** value).

3. Check that the uploaded file is of the proper type:

```
$allowed = array ('image/pjpeg',
→'image/jpeg', 'image/JPG',
→'image/X-PNG', 'image/PNG',
→'image/png', 'image/x-png');
if (in_array($_FILES['upload']
→['type'], $allowed)) {
```

The file's type is its *MIME* type, indicating what kind of file it is. The browser can determine and may provide this information, depending upon the properties of the selected file.

To validate the file's type, first create an array of allowed options. The list of allowed types is based upon accepting JPEGs and PNGs. Some browsers have variations on the MIME types, so those are included here as well. If the uploaded file's type is in this array, the file is valid and should be handled.

Script 11.2 *continued*

```
36
37      // Check for an error:
38      if ($_FILES['upload']['error'] > 0) {
39          echo '<p class="error">The file could
            not be uploaded because: <strong>';
40
41          // Print a message based upon the
            error.
42          switch ($_FILES['upload']['error']) {
43              case 1:
44                  print 'The file exceeds the
                    upload_max_filesize setting
                    in php.ini.';
45                  break;
46              case 2:
47                  print 'The file exceeds the
                    MAX_FILE_SIZE setting in the
                    HTML form.';
48                  break;
49              case 3:
50                  print 'The file was only
                    partially uploaded.';
51                  break;
52              case 4:
53                  print 'No file was uploaded.';
54                  break;
55              case 6:
56                  print 'No temporary folder
                    was available.';
57                  break;
58              case 7:
59                  print 'Unable to write to
                    the disk.';
60                  break;
61              case 8:
62                  print 'File upload stopped.';
63                  break;
```

code continues on next page

❶ This very basic HTML form only takes one input: a file.

Script 11.2 *continued*

```
64          default:
65              print 'A system error
                occurred.';
66              break;
67          } // End of switch.
68
69          print '</strong></p>';
70
71      } // End of error IF.
72
73      // Delete the file if it still exists:
74      if (file_exists ($_FILES['upload']
        ['tmp_name']) && is_file($_FILES
        ['upload']['tmp_name']) ) {
75          unlink ($_FILES['upload']
            ['tmp_name']);
76      }
77
78  } // End of the submitted conditional.
79  ?>
80
81  <form enctype="multipart/form-data"
    action="upload_image.php" method="post">
82
83      <input type="hidden" name="MAX_FILE_
        SIZE" value="524288" />
84
85      <fieldset><legend>Select a JPEG or
        PNG image of 512KB or smaller to be
        uploaded:</legend>
86
87      <p><b>File:</b> <input type="file"
        name="upload" /></p>
88
89      </fieldset>
90      <div align="center"><input type="submit"
        name="submit" value="Submit" /></div>
91
92  </form>
93  </body>
94  </html>
```

Please upload a JPEG or PNG image.

┌─ Select a JPEG or PNG image of 512KB or sma

 File: (Choose File) No file chosen

J If the user uploads a file that's not a JPEG or PNG, this is the result.

---

4. Copy the file to its new location on the server:

```
if (move_uploaded_file ($_FILES
→['upload']['tmp_name'],
→"../uploads/{$_FILES['upload']
→['name']}")) {
  echo '<p><em>The file has been
  → uploaded!</em></p>';
} // End of move... IF.
```

The `move_uploaded_file()` function will move the file from its temporary to its permanent location (in the *uploads* folder). The file will retain its original name. In Chapter 18, "Example—E-Commerce," you'll see how to give the file a new name, which is generally a good idea.

As a rule, you should always use a conditional to confirm that a file was successfully moved, instead of just assuming that the move worked.

5. Complete the image type and `isset ($_FILES['upload'])` conditionals:

```
    } else { // Invalid type.
      echo '<p class="error">Please
      → upload a JPEG or PNG
      → image.</p>';
    }
} // End of isset($_FILES
→['upload']) IF.
```

The first `else` clause completes the `if` begun in Step 3. It applies if a file was uploaded but it wasn't of the right MIME type **J**.

6. Check for, and report on, any errors:

```
if ($_FILES['upload']['error'] > 0) {
  echo '<p class="error">The file
  → could not be uploaded
  → because: <strong>';
```

If an error occurred, then `$_FILES ['upload']['error']` will have a value greater than 0. In such cases, this script will report what the error was.

continues on next page

7. Begin a **switch** that prints a more detailed error:

```
switch ($_FILES['upload']['error']) {
  case 1:
    print 'The file exceeds the
    → upload_max_filesize setting
    → in php.ini.';
    break;
  case 2:
    print 'The file exceeds the
    → MAX_FILE_SIZE setting in
    → the HTML form.';
    break;
  case 3:
    print 'The file was only
    → partially uploaded.';
    break;
  case 4:
    print 'No file was uploaded.';
    break;
```

There are several possible reasons a file could not be uploaded and moved. The first and most obvious one is if the permissions are not set properly on the destination directory. In such a case, you'll see an appropriate error message (see **ⓕ** in the previous section of the chapter). PHP will often also store an error number in the **$_FILES['upload']['error']** variable. The numbers correspond to specific problems, from 0 to 4, plus 6 through 8 (oddly enough, there is no 5). The **switch** conditional here prints out the problem according to the error number. The **default** case is added for future support (if different numbers are added in later versions of PHP).

For the most part, these errors are useful to you, the developer, and not things you'd indicate to the average user.

8. Complete the **switch**:

```
  case 6:
    print 'No temporary folder
    → was available.';
    break;
  case 7:
    print 'Unable to write to the
    → disk.';
    break;
  case 8:
    print 'File upload stopped.';
    break;
  default:
    print 'A system error
    → occurred.';
    break;
} // End of switch.
```

9. Complete the error **if** conditional:

```
    print '</strong></p>';
} // End of error IF.
```

10. Delete the temporary file if it still exists:

```
if (file_exists ($_FILES['upload']
→ ['tmp_name']) && is_file($_FILES
→ ['upload']['tmp_name']) ) {
  unlink ($_FILES['upload']
  → ['tmp_name']);
}
```

If the file was uploaded but it could not be moved to its final destination or some other error occurred, then that file is still sitting on the server in its temporary location. To remove it, apply the **unlink( )** function. Just to be safe, prior to applying **unlink( )**, a conditional checks that the file exists and that it is a file (because the **file_exists( )** function will return TRUE if the named item is a directory).

11. Complete the PHP section:

```
} // End of the submitted
→ conditional.
?>
```

12. Create the HTML form:

```
<form enctype="multipart/form-data"
→ action="upload_image.php"
→ method="post">
<input type="hidden" name=
→ "MAX_FILE_SIZE" value="524288" />
  <fieldset><legend>Select a JPEG
  → or PNG image of 512KB or
  → smaller to be uploaded:
  → </legend>
  <p><b>File:</b> <input type=
  → "file" name="upload" /></p>
  </fieldset>
  <div align="center"><input
  → type="submit" name="submit"
  → value="Submit" /></div>
</form>
```

This form is very simple ⦿, but it contains the three necessary parts for file uploads: the form's **enctype** attribute, the **MAX_FILE_SIZE** hidden input, and the file input.

13. Complete the HTML page:

```
</body>
</html>
```

14. Save the file as **upload_image.php**, place it in your Web directory, and test it in your Web browser (⦿ and ⦿).

If you want, you can confirm that the script works by checking the contents of the *uploads* directory.

TIP Omitting the **enctype** form attribute is a common reason for file uploads to mysteriously fail.

TIP The existence of an uploaded file can also be validated with the **is_uploaded_file( )** function.

TIP Windows users must use either forward slashes or double backslashes to refer to directories (so C:\\ or C:/ but not C:\). This is because the backslash is the escape character in PHP.

TIP The **move_uploaded_file( )** function will overwrite an existing file without warning if the new and existing files both have the same name.

TIP The **MAX_FILE_SIZE** is a restriction in the browser as to how large a file can be, although not all browsers abide by this restriction. The PHP configuration file has its own restrictions. You can also validate the uploaded file size within the receiving PHP script.

TIP In Chapter 13, you'll learn a method for improving the security of this script by validating the uploaded file's type more reliably.

The file has been uploaded!

┌ Select a JPEG or PNG image of 512KB or sma

File: (Choose File) No file chosen

⦿ The result upon successfully uploading and moving a file.

Please upload a JPEG or PNG image.

The file could not be uploaded because: The file exceeds the MAX_FILE_SIZE setting in the HTML form.

┌ Select a JPEG or PNG image of 512KB or smaller to be uploaded:

File: (Choose File) No file chosen

(Submit)

⦿ The result upon attempting to upload a file that is too large.

PHP and JavaScript

Although PHP and JavaScript are fundamentally different technologies, they can be used together to make better Web sites. The most significant difference between the two languages is that JavaScript is primarily client-side (meaning it runs in the Web browser) and PHP is always server-side. Therefore, JavaScript can do such things as detect the size of the browser window, create pop-up windows, make image mouseovers, whereas PHP can do nothing like these things. Conversely, PHP can interact with MySQL on the server, but JavaScript cannot.

Although PHP cannot do certain things that JavaScript can, PHP can be used to create JavaScript, just as PHP can create HTML. To be clear, in a Web browser, JavaScript is incorporated by, and interacts with HTML, but PHP can dynamically generate JavaScript code, just as you've been using PHP to dynamically generate HTML.

To demonstrate this, one PHP script will be created that lists all the images uploaded by the **upload_image.php** script **A**. The PHP script will also create each image name as a clickable link. The links themselves will call a JavaScript function **B** that creates a pop-up window. The pop-up window will actually show the clicked image. This example will in no way be a thorough discussion of JavaScript, but it does adequately demonstrate how the various technologies—PHP, HTML, and JavaScript—can be used together. In Chapter 15, "Introducing jQuery," you'll learn how to use the jQuery JavaScript framework to add all sorts of functionality to PHP-based scripts.

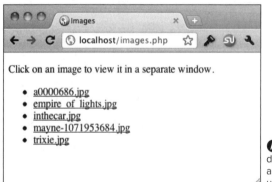

A This PHP page dynamically creates a list of all the uploaded images.

```
<li><a href="javascript:create_window('a0000686.jpg',481,390)">a0000686.jpg</a></li>
<li><a href="javascript:create_window('empire_of_lights.jpg',575,897)">empire_of_lights.jpg</a></li>
<li><a href="javascript:create_window('inthecar.jpg',1009,841)">inthecar.jpg</a></li>
<li><a href="javascript:create_window('mayne-1071953684.jpg',1280,1024)">mayne-
1071953684.jpg</a></li>
<li><a href="javascript:create_window('trixie.jpg',1280,1024)">trixie.jpg</a></li>
```

B Each image's name is linked as a call to a JavaScript function. The function call's parameters are created by PHP.

Creating the JavaScript File

Even though JavaScript and PHP are two different languages, they are similar enough that it's possible to dabble with JavaScript without any formal training. Before creating the JavaScript code for this example, I'll explain a few of the fundamentals.

First, JavaScript code can be added to an HTML page in one of two ways: inline or through an external file. To add inline JavaScript, place the JavaScript code between HTML **script** tags:

```
<script type="text/javascript">
// Actual JavaScript code.
</script>
```

To use an external JavaScript file, add a **src** attribute to the **script** tag:

```
<script type="text/javascript"
→ src="somefile.js"></script>
```

Your HTML pages can have multiple uses of the **script** tag, but each can only include an external file or have some JavaScript code, but not both.

As you can see in the above, JavaScript files use a **.js** extension. The file should use the same encoding (as set in your text editor or IDE) as the HTML script that will include the file. You can indicate the file's encoding in the **script** tag:

```
<script type="text/javascript"
→ charset="utf-8" src="somefile.js">
→ </script>
```

Whether you place your JavaScript code within **script** tags or in an external file, there are no opening and closing JavaScript tags, like the opening and closing PHP tags.

Next, know that variables in JavaScript are case-sensitive, just like PHP, but variables in JavaScript do not begin with dollar signs.

Finally, one of the main differences between JavaScript and PHP is that JavaScript is an Object-Oriented Programming (OOP) language. Whereas PHP can be used in both a procedural approach, as most of this book demonstrates, and an object-oriented approach (introduced in Chapter 16, "An OOP Primer"), JavaScript is only ever an object-oriented language. This means you'll see the "dot" syntax like *something.something( )* or *something.something.something*.

That's enough of the basics; in the following script I'll explain the particulars of each bit of code in sufficient detail. In this next sequence of steps, you'll create a separate JavaScript file that will define one JavaScript function. The function itself will take three arguments—an image's name, width, and height. The function will use these values to create a pop-up window specifically for that image.

To create JavaScript with PHP:

1. Begin a new JavaScript document in your text editor or IDE, to be named **function.js** (Script 11.3):

```
// Script 11.3 - function.js
```

Again, there are no opening JavaScript tags here, you can just start writing JavaScript code. Comments in JavaScript can use either the single line (**//**) or multiline (**/* */**) syntax.

2. Begin the JavaScript function:

```
function create_window (image,
→ width, height) {
```

The JavaScript **create_window( )** function will accept three parameters: the image's name, its width, and its height. Each of these will be passed to this function when the user clicks a link. The exact values of the image name, width, and height will be determined by PHP.

The syntax for creating a function in JavaScript is very similar to a user-defined function in PHP, except that the variables do not have initial dollar signs.

3. Add ten pixels to the received **width** and **height** values:

```
width = width + 10;
height = height + 10;
```

Some pixels will be added to the width and height values to create a window slightly larger than the image itself. Math in JavaScript uses the same operators as in pretty much every language.

4. Resize the pop-up window if it is already open:

```
if (window.popup && !window.popup.
→ closed) {
  window.popup.resizeTo(width,
    → height);
}
```

Later in the function, a window will be created, associated with the **popup**

Script 11.3 The **function.js** script defines a JavaScript function for creating the pop-up window that will show an individual image.

```
1    // Script 11.3 - function.js
2
3    // Make a pop-up window function:
4    function create_window (image, width,
     height) {
5
6       // Add some pixels to the width and
        height:
7       width = width + 10;
8       height = height + 10;
9
10      // If the window is already open,
11      // resize it to the new dimensions:
12      if (window.popup && !window.popup.
        closed) {
13         window.popup.resizeTo(width, height);
14      }
15
16      // Set the window properties:
17      var specs = "location=no,
        scrollbars=no, menubars=no,
        toolbars=no, resizable=yes,
        left=0, top=0, width=" + width + ",
        height=" + height;
18
19      // Set the URL:
20      var url = "show_image.php?image=" +
        image;
21
22      // Create the pop-up window:
23      popup = window.open(url, "ImageWindow",
        specs);
24      popup.focus( );
25
26   } // End of function.
```

variable. If the user clicks one image name, creating the pop-up window, and then clicks another image's name without having closed the first pop-up window, the new image will be displayed in a mis-sized window. To prevent that, a bit of code here first checks if the pop-up window exists and if it is not closed. If both conditions are TRUE (which is to say that the window is already open), the window will be resized according to the new image dimensions. This is accomplished by calling the **resizeTo( )** method of the **popup** object (a *method* is the OOP term for a function).

5. Determine the properties of the pop-up window:

```
var specs = "location=no,
→ scrollbars=no, menubars=no,
→ toolbars=no, resizable=yes,
→ left=0, top=0, width=" +
→ width + ", height=" + height;
```

This line creates a new JavaScript variable with a name of **specs**. The **var** keyword before the variable name is the preferred way to create variables within a function (specifically, it creates a variable *local* to the function). Note that the **image**, **width**, and **height** variables didn't use this keyword, as they were created as the arguments to a function.

This variable will be used to establish the properties of the pop-up window. The window will have no location bar, scroll bars, menus, or toolbars; it should be resizable; it will be located in the upper-left corner of the screen; and it will have a width of **width** and a height of **height** .

With strings in JavaScript, the plus sign is used to perform concatenation (whereas PHP uses the period).

6. Define the URL:

```
var url = "show_image.php?image="
→ + image;
```

This code sets the URL of the pop-up window, which is to say what page the window should load. That page is **show_image.php**, to be created later in this chapter. The **show_image.php** script expects to receive an image's name in the URL, so the value of the **url** variable is *show_image. php?image=* plus the name of the image concatenated to the end 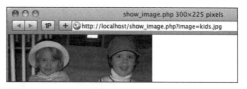.

7. Create the pop-up window:

```
popup = window.open(url,
→ "ImageWindow", specs);
popup.focus( );
```

Finally, the pop-up window is created using the **open( )** method of the **window** object. The **window** object is a global JavaScript object created by the browser to refer to the open windows. The **open( )** method's first argument is the page to load, the second is the title to be given to the window, and the

continues on next page

C The pop-up window, created by JavaScript.

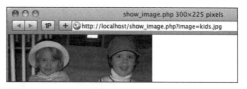

D The address of the pop-up window shows how the image value is passed in the URL.

third is a list of properties. Note that the creation of this window is assigned to the **popup** variable. Because this variable's creation does not begin with the keyword **var**, **popup** will be a global variable. This is necessary in order for multiple calls of this function to reference that same variable.

Finally, focus is given to the new window, meaning it should appear above the current window.

8. Save the script as **function.js**.

9. Place the script, or a copy, in the **js** folder of your Web directory.

JavaScript, like CSS, ought to be separated out when organizing your Web directory. Normally, external JavaScript files are placed in a folder named *js*, *javascript*, or *scripts*.

Creating the PHP Script

Now that the JavaScript code required by the page has been created, it's time to create the PHP script itself (which will output the HTML that calls the JavaScript function). The purpose of this script is to list all of the images already uploaded by **upload_image.php**. To do this, PHP needs to dynamically retrieve the contents of the **uploads** directory. That can be done via the **scandir( )** function. It returns an array listing the files in a given directory (it was added in PHP 5).

The PHP script must link each displayed image name as a call to the just-defined JavaScript function. That function expects to receive three arguments: the image's name, its width, and its height. For PHP to find these last two values, the script will use the **getimagesize( )** function. It returns an array of information for a given image (**Table 11.3**).

To create JavaScript with PHP:

1. Begin a new PHP document in your text editor or IDE, to be named **images.php** (**Script 11.4**):

```
<!DOCTYPE html PUBLIC "-//W3C//
→ DTD XHTML 1.0 Transitional//EN"
→ "http://www.w3.org/TR/xhtml1/DTD/
→ xhtml1-transitional.dtd">
<html xmlns="http://www.w3.org/
→ 1999/xhtml" xml:lang="en"
→ lang="en">
<head>
  <meta http-equiv="Content-Type"
  → content="text/html;
  → charset=utf-8" />
  <title>Images</title>
```

2. Include the JavaScript file:

```
<script type="text/javascript"
→ charset="utf-8" src="js/
→ function.js"></script>
```

You can use the **script** tags anywhere in an HTML page, but inclusions of external files are commonly performed

TABLE 11.3 The getimagesize( ) Array

Element	Value	Example
0	image's width in pixels	423
1	image's height in pixels	368
2	image's type	2 (representing JPG)
3	appropriate HTML **img** tag data	height="368" width="423"
mime	image's MIME type	image/png

Script 11.4 The `images.php` script uses JavaScript and PHP to create links to images stored on the server. The images will be viewable through `show_image.php` (Script 11.5).

```
1   <!DOCTYPE html PUBLIC "-//W3C//DTD XHTML
    1.0 Transitional//EN" "http://www.w3.org/
    TR/xhtml1/DTD/xhtml1-transitional.dtd">
2   <html xmlns="http://www.w3.org/1999/
    xhtml" xml:lang="en" lang="en">
3   <head>
4       <meta http-equiv="Content-Type"
        content="text/html; charset=utf-8" />
5       <title>Images</title>
6       <script type="text/javascript" charset=
        "utf-8" src="js/function.js"></script>
7   </head>
8   <body>
9   <p>Click on an image to view it in a
    separate window.</p>
10  <ul>
11  <?php # Script 11.4 - images.php
12  // This script lists the images in the
    uploads directory.
13
14  $dir = '../uploads'; // Define the
    directory to view.
15
16  $files = scandir($dir); // Read all the
    images into an array.
17
18  // Display each image caption as a link
    to the JavaScript function:
19  foreach ($files as $image) {
20
21      if (substr($image, 0, 1) != '.') { //
        Ignore anything starting with a period.
22
23          // Get the image's size in pixels:
24          $image_size = getimagesize
            ("$dir/$image");
25
26          // Make the image's name URL-safe:
27          $image_name = urlencode($image);
28
29          // Print the information:
30          echo "<li><a href=\"javascript:
            create_window('$image_name',
            $image_size[0],$image_size[1])\">
            $image</a></li>\n";
31
32      } // End of the IF.
33
34  } // End of the foreach loop.
35  ?>
36  </ul>
37  </body>
38  </html>
```

in the document's head. The reference to **function.js** assumes that the file will be found in the **js** directory, with the **js** directory being in the same directory as this current script (see ⓓ under "Handling File Uploads").

3. Complete the HTML head and begin the body:

```
</head>
<body>
<p>Click on an image to view it
→ in a separate window.</p>
```

4. Begin an HTML unordered list:

```
<ul>
```

To make things simple, this script displays each image as an item in an unordered list.

5. Start the PHP code and create an array of images by referring to the *uploads* directory:

```
<?php # Script 11.4 - images.php
$dir = '../uploads';
$files = scandir($dir);
```

This script will automatically list and link all of the images stored in the *uploads* folder (presumably put there by **upload_image.php**, Script 11.3). The code begins by defining the directory as a variable, so that it's easier to refer to. Then the **scandir( )** function, which returns an array of files and directories found within a folder, assigns that information to an array called **$files**.

6. Begin looping through the **$files** array:

```
foreach ($files as $image) {
    if (substr($image, 0, 1) != '.') {
```

This loop will go through every image in the array and create a list item for it. Within the loop, there is one conditional that checks if the first character in the

continues on next page

file's name is a period. On non-Windows systems, hidden files start with a period, the current directory is referred to using just a single period, and two periods refers to the parent directory. Since all of these might be included in **$files**, they need to be weeded out.

7. Get the image information and encode its name:

```
$image_size = getimagesize
→ ("$dir/$image");
$image_name = urlencode($image);
```

The **getimagesize( )** function returns an array of information about an image (Table 11.3). The values returned by this function will be used to set the width and height sent to the **create_window( )** JavaScript function.

Next, the **urlencode( )** function makes a string safe to pass in a URL. Because the image name may contain characters not allowed in a URL (and it will be passed in the URL when invoking **show_image. php**), the name should be encoded.

8. Print the list item:

```
echo "<li><a href=\"javascript:
→ create_window('$image_name',
→ $image_size[0],$image_size[1])\">
→ $image</a>\n";
```

Finally, the loop creates the HTML list item, consisting of the linked image name. The link itself is a call to the JavaScript **create_window( )** function. In order to execute the JavaScript function from within HTML, preface it with **javascript:**. (There's much more to calling JavaScript from within HTML, but just use this syntax for now.)

The function's three arguments are: the image's name, the image's width, and the image's height. Because the image's name will be a string, it must be wrapped in quotation marks.

9. Complete the **if** conditional, the **foreach** loop, and the PHP section:

```
} // End of the IF.
} // End of the foreach loop.
?>
```

10. Complete the unordered list and the HTML page:

```
</ul>
</body>
</html>
```

11. Save the file as **images.php**, place it in your Web directory (in the same directory as **upload_image.php**), and test it in your Web browser Ⓐ.

Note that clicking the links will not work yet, as **show_image.php**—the page the pop-up window attempts to load—hasn't been created.

12. View the source code to see the dynamically generated links Ⓑ.

Notice how the parameters to each function call are appropriate to the specific image.

TIP Different browsers will handle the sizing of the window differently. In my tests, for example, Google Chrome always required that the window be at least a certain width and Internet Explorer 9 would pad the displayed image on all four sides.

TIP Some versions of Windows create a **Thumbs.db** file in a folder of images. You might want to check for this value in the conditional in Step 6 that weeds out some returned items. That code would be

```
if ( (substr($image, 0, 1) != '.') &&
→ ($image != 'Thumbs.db') ) {
```

TIP Not to belabor the point, but most everything Web developers do with JavaScript (for example, resize or move the browser window) cannot be done using the server-side PHP.

TIP There is *a little* overlap between the PHP and JavaScript. Both can set and read cookies, create HTML, and do some browser detection.

Understanding HTTP Headers

The **images.php** script, just created, displays a list of image names, each of which is linked to a JavaScript function call. That JavaScript function creates a pop-up window which loads a PHP script that will actually reveal the image. This may sound like a lot of work for little effort, but there's a method to my madness. A trivial reason for this approach is that JavaScript is required in order to create a window sized to fit the image (as opposed to creating a pop-up window of any size, with the image in it). More importantly, because the images are being stored in the **uploads** directory, ideally stored outside of the Web root directory, the images cannot be viewed directly in the Web browser using either of the following:

```
http://www.example.com/uploads/
→ image.png
```

or

```
<img src="image.png" />
```

The reason why neither of the above will work is that files and folders located outside of the Web root directory are, by definition, unavailable via a Web browser. This is actually a good thing, because it allows you to safeguard content, providing it only when appropriate. To make that content available through a Web browser, you need to create a *proxy script* in PHP. A proxy script just fulfills a role, such as providing a file (displaying an image is actually the same thing as providing a file to the browser). Thus, given the proxy script **proxy.php**, the above examples could be made to work using either 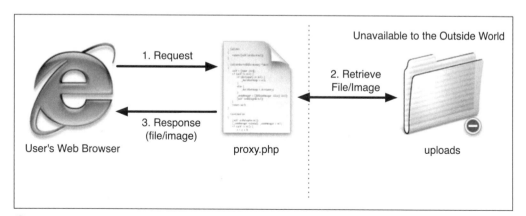:

```
http://www.example.com/proxy.php?
→ image=image.png
```

or

```
<img src="proxy.php?image=image.png" />
```

This, of course, is exactly what's being done with **show_image.php**, linked in the **create_window( )** JavaScript function. But how does **proxy.php**, or **show_image.php**, work? The answer lies in an understanding of *HTTP headers*.

continues on next page

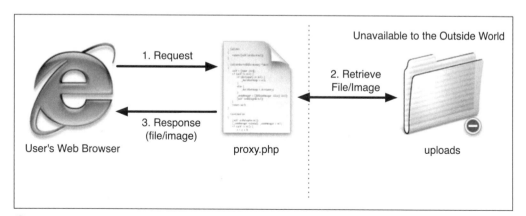

1. Request

2. Retrieve File/Image

Unavailable to the Outside World

3. Response (file/image)

User's Web Browser

proxy.php

uploads

A A proxy script is able to provide access to content on the server that would otherwise be unavailable.

HTTP (Hypertext Transfer Protocol) is the technology at the heart of the World Wide Web and defines the way clients and servers communicate (in layman's terms). When a browser requests a Web page, it receives a series of HTTP headers in return. This happens behind the scenes; most users aren't aware of this at all.

PHP's built-in **header( )** function can be used to take advantage of this protocol. The most common example of this will be demonstrated in the next chapter, when the **header( )** function will be used to redirect the Web browser from the current page to another. Here, you'll use it to send files to the Web browser.

In theory, the **header( )** function is easy to use. Its syntax is

header(*header string*);

The list of possible header strings is quite long, as headers are used for everything from redirecting the Web browser, to sending files, to creating cookies, to controlling page caching, and much, much more. Starting with something simple, to

use **header( )** to redirect the Web browser, type

**header ('Location: http://www.
→ example.com/page.php');**

That line will send the Web browser from the page it's on over to that other URL. You'll see examples of this in the next chapter.

In this next example, which will send an image file to the Web browser, three header calls are used. The first is *Content-Type*. This is an indication to the Web browser of what kind of data is about to follow. The *Content-Type* value matches the data's MIME type. This line lets the browser know it's about to receive a PDF file:

**header("Content-Type:application/
→ pdf\n");**

Next, you can use *Content-Disposition*, which tells the browser how to treat the data:

**header ("Content-Disposition:
→ attachment; filename=\
→ "somefile.pdf\"\n");**

The *attachment* value will prompt the browser to download the file **B**. An

B Firefox prompts the user to download the file because of the *attachment Content-Disposition* value.

alternative is to use *inline*, which tells the browser to display the data, assuming that the browser can. The `filename` attribute is just that: it tells the browser the name associated with the data. Some browsers abide by this instruction, others do not.

A third header to use for downloading files is *Content-Length*. This is a value, in bytes, corresponding to the amount of data to be sent.

```
header ("Content-Length: 4096\n");
```

That's the basics with respect to using the `header( )` function. Before getting to the example, note that if a script uses multiple `header( )` calls, each should be terminated by a newline (`\n`) as in the preceding code snippets. More importantly, the absolutely critical thing to remember about the `header( )` function is that it must be called before *anything* is sent to the Web browser. This includes HTML or even blank spaces. If your code has any `echo` or `print` statements, has blank lines outside of PHP tags, or includes files that do any of these things before calling `header( )`, you'll see an error message like that in **C**.

Warning: Cannot modify header information - headers already sent by (output started at /Users/larryullman/Sites/phpmysql4/proxy.php:2) in **/Users/larryullman/Sites/phpmysql4/proxy.php** on line **3**

Warning: Cannot modify header information - headers already sent by (output started at /Users/larryullman/Sites/phpmysql4/proxy.php:2) in **/Users/larryullman/Sites/phpmysql4/proxy.php** on line **4**

C The *headers already sent* error means that the Web browser was sent something—HTML, plain text, even a space—prior to using the `header( )` function.

To use the header() function:

1. Begin a new PHP document in your text editor or IDE, to be named **show_image.php** (Script 11.5):

   ```php
   <?php # Script 11.5 -
   → show_image.php
   $name = FALSE;
   ```

   Because this script will use the **header()** function, nothing—absolutely nothing—can be sent to the Web browser. No HTML, not even a blank line, tab, or space before the opening PHP tag.

   The **$name** variable will be used as a flag, indicating if all of the validation routines have been passed.

2. Check for an image name:

   ```php
   if (isset($_GET['image'])) {
   ```

   The script needs to receive a valid image name in the URL. This should be appended to the URL in the JavaScript function that calls this page (see **function.js**, Script 11.3).

3. Validate the image's extension:

   ```php
   $ext = strtolower ( substr
   → ($_GET['image'], -4));
     if (($ext == '.jpg') OR ($ext ==
   → 'jpeg') OR ($ext == '.png')) {
   ```

   The next check is that the file to be sent to the Web browser has a **.jpeg**, **.jpg**, or **.png** extension. This way the script won't try to send something bad to the user. For example, if a malicious user changed the address in the pop-up window from **http://www.example.com/show_image.php?image=image.png** to **http://www.example.com/show_image.php?image=../../../path/to/something/important**, this conditional would catch, and prevent, that hack.

   To validate the extension, the **substr()** function returns the last four characters from the image's name (the **-4**

Script 11.5 This script retrieves an image from the server and sends it to the browser, using HTTP headers.

```php
1    <?php # Script 11.5 - show_image.php
2    // This page displays an image.
3
4    $name = FALSE; // Flag variable:
5
6    // Check for an image name in the URL:
7    if (isset($_GET['image'])) {
8
9        // Make sure it has an image's
         extension:
10       $ext = strtolower ( substr ($_GET
         ['image'], -4));
11
12       if (($ext == '.jpg') OR ($ext ==
         'jpeg') OR ($ext == '.png')) {
13
14           // Full image path:
15           $image = "../uploads/{$_GET['image']}";
16
17           // Check that the image exists and
             is a file:
18           if (file_exists ($image) &&
             (is_file($image))) {
19
20               // Set the name as this image:
21               $name = $_GET['image'];
22
23           } // End of file_exists() IF.
24
25       } // End of $ext IF.
26
27   } // End of isset($_GET['image']) IF.
28
29   // If there was a problem, use the
     default image:
30   if (!$name) {
31       $image = 'images/unavailable.png';
32       $name = 'unavailable.png';
33   }
34
35   // Get the image information:
36   $info = getimagesize($image);
37   $fs = filesize($image);
38
39   // Send the content information:
40   header ("Content-Type: {$info['mime']}\n");
41   header ("Content-Disposition: inline;
     filename=\"$name\"\n");
42   header ("Content-Length: $fs\n");
43
44   // Send the file:
45   readfile ($image);
```

accomplishes this). The extension is also run through the **strtolower( )** function so that **.PNG** and **.png** are treated the same. Then a conditional checks to see if **$ext** is equal to any of the three allowed values.

4. Check that the image is a file on the server:

```
$image = "../uploads/
→ {$_GET['image']}";
if (file_exists ($image) &&
→ (is_file($image))) {
```

Before attempting to send the image to the Web browser, make sure that it exists and that it is a file (as opposed to a directory). As a security measure, the image's full path is defined as a combination of *../uploads* and the received image name.

5. Set the value of the flag variable to the image's name:

```
$name = $_GET['image'];
```

Once the image has passed all of these tests, the **$name** variable is assigned the value of the image.

6. Complete the conditionals begun in Steps 2, 3, and 4:

```
      } // End of file_exists() IF.
   } // End of $ext IF.
} // End of isset($_GET['image']) IF.
```

There are no **else** clauses for any of these three conditions. If all three conditions aren't TRUE, then the flag variable **$name** will still have a FALSE value.

7. If no valid image was received by this page, use a default image:

```
if (!$name) {
   $image = 'images/unavailable.png';
   $name = 'unavailable.png';
}
```

If the image doesn't exist, if it isn't a file, or if it doesn't have the proper extension, then the **$name** variable will still have a value of FALSE. In such cases, a default image will be used instead . The image itself can be downloaded from the book's corresponding Web site (**www.LarryUllman.com**, found with all the downloadable code) and should be placed in an **images** folder. The **images** folder should be in the same directory as this script, not in the same directory as the **uploads** folder.

8. Retrieve the image's information:

```
$info = getimagesize($image);
$fs = filesize($image);
```

continues on next page

D This image will be shown any time there's a problem with showing the requested image.

To send a file to the Web browser, the script needs to know the file's MIME type and size. An image file's type can be found using **getimagesize( )**. The file's size, in bytes, is found using **filesize( )**. Because the **$image** variable represents either **../uploads/{$_GET['image']}** or **images/unavailable.png**, these lines will work on both the correct and the unavailable image.

9. Send the file:

```
header ("Content-Type:
→ {$info['mime']}\n");
header ("Content-Disposition:
→ inline; filename=\"$name\"\n");
header ("Content-Length: $fs\n");
```

These **header( )** calls will send the file data to the Web browser. The first line uses the image's MIME type for the value of the *Content-Type* header. The second line tells the browser the name of the file and that it should be displayed in the browser (*inline*). The last **header( )** function indicates how much data is to be expected.

The file data itself is sent using the **readfile( )** function, which reads in a file and immediately sends the content to the Web browser.

10. Save the file as **show_image.php**, place it in your Web directory, in the same folder as **images.php**, and test it in your Web browser by clicking a link in **images.php** .

Notice that this page contains no HTML. It only sends an image file to the Web browser. Also note that I omitted the terminating PHP tag. This is acceptable, and in certain situations like this, preferred. If you included the closing PHP tag, and you inadvertently had an extra space or blank line after that tag, the browser could have problems displaying the image (because the browser will have received the image data of *X* length, matching the *Content-Length* header, plus a bit of extra data).

E This image is displayed by having PHP send the file to the Web browser.

TIP I cannot stress strongly enough that *nothing* can be sent to the Web browser before using the `header()` function. Even an included file that has a blank line after the closing **PHP** tag will make the `header()` function unusable.

TIP To avoid problems when using `header()`, you can call the `headers_sent()` function first. It returns a Boolean value indicating if something has already been sent to the Web browser:

```
if (!headers_sent()) {
        // Use the header() function.
} else {
        // Do something else.
}
```

Output buffering, demonstrated in Chapter 17, "Example—User Registration," can also prevent problems when using `header()`.

TIP Debugging scripts like this, where PHP sends data, not text, to the Web browser, can be challenging. For help, use one of the many developer plug-ins for the Firefox browser **F**.

TIP You can also indicate to the Web browser the page's encoding using PHP and the `header()` function:

```
<?php header ('Content-Type: text/
html; charset=UTF-8'); ?>
```

This can be more effective than using a META tag, but it does require the page to be a PHP script. If using this, it must be the first line in the page, before any HTML.

TIP A proxy script can only ever send to the browser a single file (or image) at a time.

⚙ **Response Headers - http://localhost/show_image.php?image=kids.jpg**

```
Date: Wed, 20 Apr 2011 03:20:52 GMT
Server: Apache
X-Powered-By: PHP/5.3.2
Content-Disposition: inline; filename="kids.jpg"
Content-Length: 106403
Keep-Alive: timeout=15, max=99
Connection: Keep-Alive
Content-Type: image/jpeg

200 OK
```

F The Web Developer Toolbar extension for Firefox includes the ability to see what headers were sent by a page and/or server. This can be useful debugging information.

Date and Time Functions

Chapter 5, "Introduction to SQL," demonstrates a handful of great date and time functions that MySQL supports. Naturally, PHP has its own date and time functions. To start, there's **date_default_timezone_set( )**. This function is used to establish the default time zone (which can also be set in PHP's configuration file).

```
date_default_timezone_set(tz);
```

The *tz* value is a string like *America/New_York* or *Pacific/Auckland*. There are too many to list here (Africa alone has over 50), but see the PHP manual for them all. Note that as of PHP 5.1, the default time zone must be set, either in a script or in PHP's configuration file, prior to calling any of the date and time functions, or else you'll see an error.

Next up, the **checkdate( )** function takes a month, a day, and a year and returns a Boolean value indicating whether that date actually exists (or existed). It even takes into account leap years. This function can be used to ensure that a user supplied a valid date (birth date or other):

```
if (checkdate(month, day, year)) { // OK!
```

Perhaps the most frequently used function is the aptly named **date( )**. It returns the date and/or time as a formatted string. It takes two arguments:

```
date (format, [timestamp]);
```

The timestamp is an optional argument representing the number of seconds since the Unix Epoch (midnight on January 1, 1970) for the date in question. It allows you to get information, like the day of the week, for a particular date. If a timestamp is not specified, PHP will just use the current time on the server.

TABLE 11.4 Date( ) Function Formatting

Character	Meaning	Example
Y	Year as 4 digits	2011
y	Year as 2 digits	11
L	Is it a leap year?	1 (for yes)
n	Month as 1 or 2 digits	2
m	Month as 2 digits	02
F	Month	February
M	Month as 3 letters	Feb
j	Day of the month as 1 or 2 digits	8
d	Day of the month as 2 digits	08
l (lower-case L)	Day of the week	Monday
D	Day of the week as 3 letters	Mon
w	Day of the week as a single digit	0 (Sunday)
z	Day of the year: 0 to 365	189
t	Number of days in the month	31
S	English ordinal suffix for a day, as 2 characters	rd
g	Hour; 12-hour format as 1 or 2 digits	6
G	Hour; 24-hour format as 1 or 2 digits	18
h	Hour; 12-hour format as 2 digits	06
H	Hour; 24-hour format as 2 digits	18
i	Minutes	45
s	Seconds	18
u	Microseconds	1234
a	am or pm	am
A	AM or PM	PM
U	Seconds since the epoch	1048623008
e	Timezone	UTC
I (capital i)	Is it daylight savings?	1 (for yes)
O	Difference from GMT	+0600

TABLE 11.5 The getdate() Array

Key	Value	Example
year	year	2011
mon	month	11
month	month name	November
mday	day of the month	24
weekday	day of the week	Thursday
hours	hours	11
minutes	minutes	56
seconds	seconds	47

There are myriad formatting parameters available (**Table 11.4**), and these can be used in conjunction with literal text. For example,

```
echo date('F j, Y'); // January 26, 2011
echo date('H:i'); // 23:14
echo date('D'); // Sat
```

You can find the timestamp for a particular date using the **mktime( )** function:

```
$stamp = mktime (hour, minute,
→ second, month, day, year);
```

If called with no arguments, **mktime( )** returns the current timestamp, which is the same as calling the **time( )** function.

Finally, the **getdate( )** function can be used to return an array of values (**Table 11.5**) for a date and time. For example,

```
$today = getdate( );
echo $today['month']; // October
```

This function also takes an optional timestamp argument. If that argument is not used, **getdate( )** returns information for the current date and time.

These are just a handful of the many date and time functions PHP has. For more, see the PHP manual. To practice working with these functions, let's modify **images.php** (Script 11.4) in a couple of ways. First, the script will show each image's uploaded date and time. Second, while a change is being made to the layout, the script will show each image's file size, too **A**.

Click on an image to view it in a separate window.

- a0000686.jpg 57kb (April 19, 2011 13:40:55)
- empire_of_lights.jpg 41kb (April 19, 2011 13:40:33)
- fountain.jpg 99kb (April 19, 2011 23:25:54)
- inthecar.jpg 220kb (April 19, 2011 13:40:48)
- kids.jpg 104kb (April 19, 2011 22:08:40)
- mayne-1071953684.jpg 433kb (April 19, 2011 13:41:34)
- trixie.jpg 412kb (April 19, 2011 13:41:15)

A The revised **images.php** shows two more pieces of information about each image.

To use the date and time functions:

1. Open **images.php** (Script 11.4) in your text editor or IDE, if it is not already.

2. As the first line of code after the opening PHP tag, establish the time zone (**Script 11.6**):

   ```
   date_default_timezone_set
   → ('America/New_York');
   ```

   Before calling any of the date and time functions, the time zone has to be established. To find your time zone, see **www.php.net/timezones**.

3. Within the **foreach** loop, after getting the image's dimensions, calculate its file size:

   ```
   $file_size = round ( (filesize
   → ("$dir/$image")) / 1024) . "kb";
   ```

   The **filesize( )** function was first used in the **show_image.php** script. It returns the size of a file in bytes. To calculate the kilobytes of a file, divide this number by 1,024 (there are that many bytes in a kilobyte) and round it off.

4. On the next line, determine the image's modification date and time:

   ```
   $image_date = date("F d, Y H:i:s",
   → filemtime("$dir/$image"));
   ```

   To find a file's modification date and time, call the **filemtime( )** function, providing the function with the file, or directory, to be examined. This function returns a timestamp, which can then be used as the second argument to the **date( )**, which will format the timestamp accordingly.

If you're perplexed by what's happening here, you can break the code into two steps:

```
$filemtime = filemtime
→ ("$dir/$image");
$image_date = date("F d, Y H:i:s ",
→ $filemtime);
```

5. Change the echo statement so that it also prints the file size and modification date:

   ```
   echo "<li><a href=\"javascript:
   → create_window('$image_name',
   → $image_size[0],$image_size[1])\">
   → $image</a> $file_size
   → ($image_date)</li>\n";
   ```

   Both are printed outside of the **A** tag, so they aren't part of the links.

6. Save the file as **images.php**, place it in your Web directory, and test it in your Web browser.

TIP The **date( )** function has some parameters that are used for informative purposes, not formatting. For example, **date('L')** returns 1 or 0 indicating if it's a leap year; **date('t')** returns the number of days in the current month; and **date('I')** returns a 1 if it's currently daylight saving time.

TIP PHP's date functions reflect the time on the server (because PHP runs on the server); you'll need to use JavaScript if you want to determine the date and time on the user's computer.

TIP In Chapter 16, you'll learn how to use the new **DateTime** class to work with dates and times in PHP.

Script 11.6 This modified version of `images.php` (Script 11.4) uses PHP's date and time functions in order to report some information to the user.

```
1    <!DOCTYPE html PUBLIC "-//W3C//DTD XHTML 1.0 Transitional//EN" "http://www.w3.org/TR/xhtml1/DTD/
     xhtml1-transitional.dtd">
2    <html xmlns="http://www.w3.org/1999/xhtml" xml:lang="en" lang="en">
3    <head>
4       <meta http-equiv="Content-Type" content="text/html; charset=utf-8" />
5       <title>Images</title>
6       <script type="text/javascript" charset="utf-8" src="js/function.js"></script>
7    </head>
8    <body>
9    <p>Click on an image to view it in a separate window.</p>
10   <ul>
11   <?php # Script 11.6 - images.php
12   // This script lists the images in the uploads directory.
13   // This version now shows each image's file size and uploaded date and time.
14
15   // Set the default timezone:
16   date_default_timezone_set ('America/New_York');
17
18   $dir = '../uploads'; // Define the directory to view.
19
20   $files = scandir($dir); // Read all the images into an array.
21
22   // Display each image caption as a link to the JavaScript function:
23   foreach ($files as $image) {
24
25       if (substr($image, 0, 1) != '.') { // Ignore anything starting with a period.
26
27           // Get the image's size in pixels:
28           $image_size = getimagesize ("$dir/$image");
29
30           // Calculate the image's size in kilobytes:
31           $file_size = round ( (filesize ("$dir/$image")) / 1024) . "kb";
32
33           // Determine the image's upload date and time:
34           $image_date = date("F d, Y H:i:s", filemtime("$dir/$image"));
35
36           // Make the image's name URL-safe:
37           $image_name = urlencode($image);
38
39           // Print the information:
40           echo "<li><a href=\"javascript:create_window('$image_name',$image_size[0],
                 $image_size[1])\">$image</a> $file_size ($image_date)</li>\n";
41
42       } // End of the IF.
43
44   } // End of the foreach loop.
45
46   ?>
47   </ul>
48   </body>
49   </html>
```

Review and Pursue

If you have any problems with the review questions or the pursue prompts, turn to the book's supporting forum (**www.LarryUllman.com/forums/**).

Review

- What function is used to send email? What are the function's arguments? What does the server need in order to send email?

- Does it make a difference whether **\n** is used within single or double quotation marks?

- Can you easily know for certain if, or when, a recipient received an email sent by PHP?

- What debugging steps can you take if you aren't receiving any email that should be sent from a PHP script?

- How do folder permissions come into play for handling uploaded files?

- What two directories are used in handling file uploads?

- What additional attribute must be made to the opening **form** tag in order to handle a file upload?

- What is a MIME type?

- In what ways are PHP and JavaScript alike? How are they different?

- What tag is used to add JavaScript to an HTML page?

- What does the **var** keyword mean in JavaScript?

- What is the concatenation operator in JavaScript?

- What does the PHP **header()** function do?

- What do *headers already sent* error messages mean?

- What is a *proxy script*? When might a proxy script be necessary?

- What does the **readfile()** function do?

Pursue

- Create a more custom contact form. Have the PHP script also send a more custom email, including any other data requested by the form.

- Search online using the keywords *php email spam filters* to learn techniques for improving the successful delivery of PHP-sent email (i.e., to minimize the chances of spam filters eating legitimate emails).

- Make a variation on **upload_image.php** that supports the uploading of different file types. Create a corresponding version of **show_image.php**. Note: You'll need to do some research on MIME types to complete these challenges.

- Check out the PHP manual page for the **glob()** function.

- A lot of information and new functions were introduced in this chapter. Check out the PHP manual for some of them to learn more.

Cookies and Sessions

The Hypertext Transfer Protocol (HTTP) is a *stateless* technology, meaning that each individual HTML page is an unrelated entity. HTTP has no method for tracking users or retaining variables as a person traverses a site. Without the server being able to track a user, there can be no shopping carts or custom Web-site personalization. Using a server-side technology like PHP, you can overcome the statelessness of the Web. The two best PHP tools for this purpose are *cookies* and *sessions*.

The key difference between cookies and sessions is that cookies store data in the user's Web browser and sessions store data on the server itself. Sessions are generally more secure than cookies and can store much more information. As both technologies are easy to use with PHP and are worth knowing, this chapter covers both cookies and sessions. The examples for demonstrating this information will be a login system, based upon the existing *sitename* database.

Making a Login Page

A login process involves just a few components **Ⓐ**:

- A form for submitting the login information

- A validation routine that confirms the necessary information was submitted

- A database query that compares the submitted information against the stored information

- Cookies or sessions to store data that reflects a successful login

Subsequent pages can then have checks to confirm that the user is logged in (to limit access to that page or add features). There is also, of course, a logging-out process, which involves clearing out the cookies or session data that represent a logged-in status.

To start all this, let's take some of these common elements and place them into separate files. Then, the pages that require this functionality can include the necessary files. Breaking up the logic this way will make some of the following scripts easier to read and write, plus cut down on their redundancies. You'll define two includable files. This first script will contain the bulk of a login page, including the header, the error reporting, the form, and the footer **Ⓑ**.

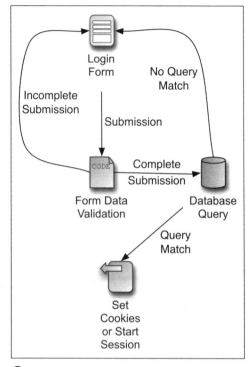

Ⓐ The login process.

Ⓑ The login form and page.

Script 12.1 The `login_page.inc.php` script creates the complete login page, including the form, and reports any errors. It will be included by other pages that need to show the login page.

```php
1   <?php # Script 12.1 - login_page.inc.php
2   // This page prints any errors
    associated with logging in
3   // and it creates the entire login page,
    including the form.
4
5   // Include the header:
6   $page_title = 'Login';
7   include ('includes/header.html');
8
9   // Print any error messages, if they exist:
10  if (isset($errors) && !empty($errors)) {
11      echo '<h1>Error!</h1>
12      <p class="error">The following
        error(s) occurred:<br />';
13      foreach ($errors as $msg) {
14          echo " - $msg<br />\n";
15      }
16      echo '</p><p>Please try again.</p>';
17  }
18
19  // Display the form:
20  ?><h1>Login</h1>
21  <form action="login.php" method="post">
22      <p>Email Address: <input type="text"
        name="email" size="20" maxlength="60" />
        </p>
23      <p>Password: <input type="password"
        name="pass" size="20" maxlength="20" />
        </p>
24      <p><input type="submit" name="submit"
        value="Login" /></p>
25  </form>
26
27  <?php include ('includes/footer.html');
    ?>
```

To make a login page:

1. Begin a new PHP page in your text editor or IDE, to be named `login_page.inc.php` (Script 12.1):

   ```php
   <?php # Script 12.1 -
   → login_page.inc.php
   ```

2. Include the header:

   ```php
   $page_title = 'Login';
   include ('includes/header.html');
   ```

   This chapter will make use of the same template system first created in Chapter 3, "Creating Dynamic Web Sites," then modified in Chapter 9, "Using PHP with MySQL."

3. Print any error messages, if they exist:

   ```php
   if (isset($errors) &&
   → !empty($errors)) {
       echo '<h1>Error!</h1>
       <p class="error">The following
       → error(s) occurred:<br />';
       foreach ($errors as $msg) {
         echo " - $msg<br />\n";
       }
       echo '</p><p>Please try
       → again.</p>';
   }
   ```

continues on next page

This code was also developed back in Chapter 9, although an additional **isset( )** clause has been added as an extra precaution. If any errors exist (in the **$errors** array variable), they'll be printed as an unordered list **C**.

4. Display the form:

```
?><h1>Login</h1>
<form action="login.php"
→ method="post">
  <p>Email Address: <input type=
  → "text" name="email" size="20"
  → maxlength="60" /> </p>
  <p>Password: <input type=
  → "password" name="pass" size=
  → "20" maxlength="20" /></p>
  <p><input type="submit" name=
  → "submit" value="Login" /></p>
</form>
```

The HTML form only needs two text inputs: one for an email address and a second for the password. The names of the inputs match those in the *users* table of the *sitename* database (which this login system is based upon).

To make it easier to create the HTML form, the PHP section is closed first. The form is not sticky, but you could easily add code to accomplish that.

5. Complete the page:

```
<?php include ('includes/
→ footer.html'); ?>
```

6. Save the file as **login_page.inc.php** and place it in your Web directory (in the **includes** folder, along with the files from Chapter 3 and Chapter 9: **header. html**, **footer.html**, and **style.css**).

The page will use a **.inc.php** extension to indicate both that it's an includable file and that it contains PHP code.

TIP It may seem illogical that this script includes the header and footer file from within the **includes** directory when this script will also be within that same directory. This code works because this script will be included by pages within the main directory; thus the include references are with respect to the parent file, not this one.

Error!

The following error(s) occurred:
- You forgot to enter your email address.
- You forgot to enter your password.

Please try again.

Login

Email Address:

C As with other scripts in this book, form errors are displayed above the form itself.

Making the Login Functions

Along with the login page that was stored in `login_page.inc.php`, there's a little bit of functionality that will be common to several scripts in this chapter. In this next script, also to be included by other pages in the login/logout system, two functions will be defined.

First, many pages will end up redirecting the user from one page to another. For example, upon successfully logging in, the user will be taken to `loggedin.php`. If a user accesses `loggedin.php` and they aren't logged in, they should be taken to `index.php`. Redirection uses the `header( )` function, introduced in Chapter 11, "Web Application Development." The syntax for redirection is

```
header ('Location: http://www.
→ example.com/page.php');
```

Because this function will send the browser to `page.php`, the current script should be terminated using `exit( )` immediately after this:

```
header ('Location: http://www.
→ example.com/page.php');
exit( );
```

If you don't call `exit( )`, the current script will continue to run (just not in the Web browser).

The location value in the `header( )` call should be an absolute URL (`www.example.com/page.php` instead of just `page.php`). You can hard-code this value into every `header( )` call or, better yet, have PHP dynamically determine it. The first function in this next script will do just that, and then redirect the user to that absolute URL.

The other bit of code that will be used by multiple scripts in this chapter validates the login form. This is a three-step process:

1. Confirm that an email address was provided.

2. Confirm that a password was provided.

3. Confirm that the provided email address and password match those stored in the database (during the registration process).

This next script will define two different functions. The details of how each function works will be explained in the steps that follow.

To create the login functions:

1. Begin a new PHP document in your text editor or IDE, to be named **login_functions.inc.php** (Script 12.2):

   ```
   <?php # Script 12.2 -
   → login_functions.inc.php
   ```

   As this file will be included by other files, it does not need to contain any HTML.

2. Begin defining a new function:

   ```
   function redirect_user ($page =
   → 'index.php') {
   ```

   The **redirect_user( )** function will create an absolute URL that's correct for the site running these scripts, and then redirect the user to that page. The benefit of doing this dynamically (as opposed to just hard-coding **http://www.example.com/page.php**) is that you can develop your code on one server (like your own computer) and then move it to another server without ever needing to change this code.

   The function takes one optional argument: the final destination page name. The default value is *index.php*.

3. Start defining the URL:

   ```
   $url = 'http://' . $_SERVER
   → ['HTTP_HOST'] . dirname($_SERVER
   → ['PHP_SELF']);
   ```

   To start, **$url** is assigned the value of *http://* plus the host name (which could be either *localhost* or *www.example.com*). To this is added the name of the current directory using the **dirname( )** function, in case the redirection is taking place within a subfolder. **$_SERVER['PHP_SELF']** refers to the current script (which will be the one calling this function), including the

Script 12.2 The **login_functions.inc.php** script defines two functions that will be used by different scripts in the login/logout process.

```
1    <?php # Script 12.2 - login_functions.
     inc.php
2    // This page defines two functions used
     by the login/logout process.
3
4    /* This function determines an absolute
     URL and redirects the user there.
5     * The function takes one argument: the
     page to be redirected to.
6     * The argument defaults to index.php.
7     */
8    function redirect_user ($page = 'index.
     php') {
9
10       // Start defining the URL...
11       // URL is http:// plus the host name
         plus the current directory:
12       $url = 'http://' . $_SERVER['HTTP_
         HOST'] . dirname($_SERVER['PHP_SELF']);
13
14       // Remove any trailing slashes:
15       $url = rtrim($url, '/\\');
16
17       // Add the page:
18       $url .= '/' . $page;
19
20       // Redirect the user:
21       header("Location: $url");
22       exit(); // Quit the script.
23
24   } // End of redirect_user() function.
25
26
27   /* This function validates the form data
     (the email address and password).
28    * If both are present, the database is
     queried.
29    * The function requires a database
     connection.
30    * The function returns an array of
     information, including:
31    * - a TRUE/FALSE variable indicating
     success
32    * - an array of either errors or the
     database result
33    */
34   function check_login($dbc, $email = '',
     $pass = '') {
35
36       $errors = array(); // Initialize
         error array.
```

code continues on next page

```
37
38        // Validate the email address:
39        if (empty($email)) {
40            $errors[] = 'You forgot to enter
          your email address.';
41        } else {
42            $e = mysqli_real_escape_
          string($dbc, trim($email));
43        }
44
45        // Validate the password:
46        if (empty($pass)) {
47            $errors[] = 'You forgot to enter
          your password.';
48        } else {
49            $p = mysqli_real_escape_
          string($dbc, trim($pass));
50        }
51
52        if (empty($errors)) { // If
          everything's OK.
53
54            // Retrieve the user_id and
          first_name for that email/password
          combination:
55            $q = "SELECT user_id, first_name
          FROM users WHERE email='$e' AND
          pass=SHA1('$p')";
56            $r = @mysqli_query ($dbc, $q);
          // Run the query.
57
58            // Check the result:
59            if (mysqli_num_rows($r) == 1) {
60
61                // Fetch the record:
62                $row = mysqli_fetch_array ($r,
              MYSQLI_ASSOC);
63
64                // Return true and the record:
65                return array(true, $row);
66
67            } else { // Not a match!
68                $errors[] = 'The email address
              and password entered do not
              match those on file.';
69            }
70
71        } // End of empty($errors) IF.
72
73        // Return false and the errors:
74        return array(false, $errors);
75
76    } // End of check_login() function.
```

directory name. That whole value might be */somedir/page.php*. The **dirname( )** function will return just the directory part from that value (i.e., */somedir/*).

4. Remove any ending slashes from the URL:

$url = rtrim($url, '/\\');

Because the existence of a subfolder might add an extra slash (**/**) or backslash (****, for Windows), the function needs to remove that. To do so, apply the **rtrim( )** function. By default, this function removes spaces from the right side of a string. If provided with a list of characters to remove as the second argument, it'll chop those off instead. The characters to be removed are **/** and ****. But since the backslash is the escape character in PHP, you need to use **** to refer to a single backslash. With this one line of code, if **$url** concludes with either of these characters, the **rtrim( )** function will remove them.

5. Append the specific page to the URL:

$url .= '/' . $page;

Next, the specific page name is concatenated to the **$url**. It's preceded by a slash because any trailing slashes were removed in Step 4 and you can't have **www.example.compage.php** as the URL.

This may all seem to be quite complicated, but it's a very effective way to ensure that the redirection works no matter on what server, or from what directory, the script is being run (as long as the redirection is taking place within that directory).

continues on next page

6. Redirect the user and complete the function:

```
header("Location: $url");
exit( ); // Quit the script.
} // End of redirect_user( )
→ function.
```

The final steps are to send a *Location* header and terminate the execution of the script.

7. Begin a new function:

```
function check_login($dbc,
→ $email = '', $pass = '') {
```

This function will validate the login information. It takes three arguments: the database connection, which is required; the email address, which is optional; and the password, which is also optional.

Although this function could access **$_POST['email']** and **$_POST['pass']** directly, it's better if the function is passed these values, making the function more independent.

8. Validate the email address and password:

```
$errors = array( );
if (empty($email)) {
  $errors[] = 'You forgot to
  → enter your email address.';
} else {
  $e = mysqli_real_escape_string
  → ($dbc, trim($email));
}
if (empty($pass)) {
  $errors[] = 'You forgot to
  → enter your password.';
} else {
  $p = mysqli_real_escape_string
  → ($dbc, trim($pass));
}
```

This validation routine is similar to that used in the registration page. If any problems occur, they'll be added to the **$errors** array, which will eventually be used on the login page (see Ⓒ under "Making a Login Page"). Note that this **$errors** array is *local* to the function. Even though it has the same name, this is not the same **$errors** variable that is used in the login page. Code later in the function will return this **$errors** variable's value, and code in the scripts that call this function will then assign this returned value to the proper, global **$errors** array, usable on the login page.

9. If no errors occurred, run the database query:

```
if (empty($errors)) {
  $q = "SELECT user_id, first_name
  → FROM users WHERE email='$e'
  → AND pass=SHA1('$p')";
  $r = @mysqli_query ($dbc, $q);
```

The query selects the *user_id* and *first_name* values from the database where the submitted email address (from the form) matches the stored email address and the **SHA1( )** version of the submitted password matches the stored password Ⓐ.

Ⓐ The results of the login query, shown in the mysql client, if the user submitted the proper email address/password combination.

10. Check the results of the query:

```
if (mysqli_num_rows($r) == 1) {
  $row = mysqli_fetch_array ($r,
  → MYSQLI_ASSOC);
  return array(true, $row);
```

If the query returned one row, then the login information was correct. The results are then fetched into **$row**. The final step in a successful login is to return two pieces of information back to the requesting script: the Boolean *true*, indicating that the login was a success; and the data fetched from MySQL. Using the **array( )** function, both the Boolean value and the **$row** array can be returned by this function.

11. If no record was selected by the query, create an error:

```
} else { // Not a match!
  $errors[] = 'The email address
  → and password entered do not
  → match those on file.';
}
```

If the query did not return one row, then an error message is added to the array. It will end up being displayed on the login page **B**.

Error!

The following error(s) occurred:
- The email address and password entered do not match those on file.

Please try again.

Login

Email Address:

B If the user entered an email address and password, but they don't match the values stored in the database, this is the result in the Web browser.

12. Complete the conditional begun in Step 9 and complete the function:

```
  } // End of empty($errors) IF.
  return array(false, $errors);
} // End of check_login() function.
```

The final step is for the function to return a value of *false*, indicating that login failed, and to return the **$errors** array, which stores the reason(s) for failure. This **return** statement can be placed here—at the end of the function instead of within a conditional—because the function will only get to this point if the login failed. If the login succeeded, the **return** line in Step 10 will stop the function from continuing (a function stops as soon as it executes a **return**).

13. Save the file as **login_functions. inc.php** and place it in your Web directory (in the **includes** folder, along with **header.html**, **footer.html**, and **style.css**).

This page will also use a **.inc.php** extension to indicate both that it's an includable file and that it contains PHP code.

As with some other includable files created in this book (although not **login_page.inc.php**), the closing PHP tag—**?>**—is omitted. Doing so prevents potential complications that can arise should an includable file have an errant blank space or line after the closing tag.

TIP The scripts in this chapter include no debugging code (like the MySQL error or query). If you have problems with these scripts, apply the debugging techniques outlined in Chapter 8, "Error Handling and Debugging."

TIP You can add *name=value* pairs to the URL in a header( ) call to pass values to the target page:

```
$url .= '?name=' . urlencode(value);
```

Using Cookies

Cookies are a way for a server to store information on the user's machine. This is one way that a site can remember or track a user over the course of a visit. Think of a cookie as being like a name tag: you tell the server your name and it gives you a sticker to wear. Then it can know who you are by referring back to that name tag 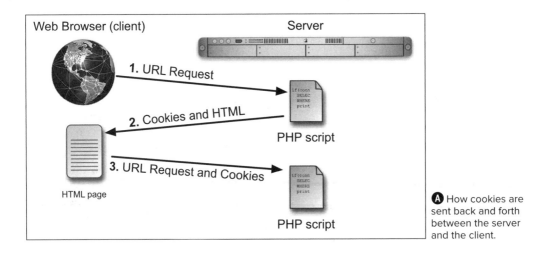.

In this section, you will learn how to set a cookie, retrieve information from a stored cookie, alter a cookie's settings, and then delete a cookie.

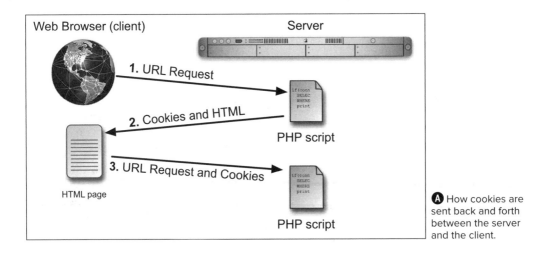

Web Browser (client)   Server

1. URL Request

2. Cookies and HTML

PHP script

3. URL Request and Cookies

HTML page

PHP script

A How cookies are sent back and forth between the server and the client.

Testing for Cookies

To effectively program using cookies, you need to be able to accurately test for their presence. The best way to do so is to have your Web browser ask what to do when receiving a cookie. In such a case, the browser will prompt you with the cookie information each time PHP attempts to send a cookie.

Different versions of different browsers on different platforms all define their cookie-handling policies in different places. I'll quickly run through a couple of options for popular Web browsers.

To set this up using Internet Explorer on Windows, choose Tools > Internet Options. Then click the Privacy tab, followed by the Advanced button under Settings. Click "Override automatic cookie handling" and then choose "Prompt" for First-party Cookies.

Using Firefox, you'll want to select "ask me every time" in the "Keep until" drop-down menu. To get to that point on Windows, choose Tools > Options > Privacy. If you are using Firefox on Mac OS X, start by choosing Firefox > Preferences. Then, on the Privacy tab, select "Use custom settings for history" and you'll see the "Keep until" selector.

Unfortunately, Safari and Google Chrome do not have options to prompt you when cookies are sent (not so far as I can see, that is, without installing extensions or plug-ins). Both do allow you to view existing cookies, which is still a useful debugging tool.

Setting cookies

The most important thing to understand about cookies is that they must be sent from the server to the client prior to *any other information*. Should the server attempt to send a cookie after the Web browser has already received HTML—even an extraneous white space—an error message will result and the cookie will not be sent **B**. This is by far the most common cookie-related error but is easily fixed. If you see such a message:

1. Note the script and line number following *output started at*.

2. Open that script and head to that line number.

3. Remove the blank space, line, text, HTML, or whatever that is outputted by that line.

Cookies are sent via the `setcookie()` function:

```
setcookie (name, value);
setcookie ('name', 'Nicole');
```

The second line of code will send a cookie to the browser with a name of *name* and a value of *Nicole* **C**.

You can continue to send more cookies to the browser with subsequent uses of the `setcookie()` function:

```
setcookie ('ID', 263);
setcookie ('email', 'email@example.com');
```

As for the cookies name, it's best not to use white spaces or punctuation, and pay attention to the exact case used.

Warning: Cannot modify header information - headers already sent by (output started at /Users/larryullman/Sites/phpmysql4/includes/login_functions.inc.php:80) in **/Users/larryullman/Sites/phpmysql4/login.php** on line **22**

B The *headers already sent...* error message is all too common when creating cookies. Pay attention to what the error message says in order to find and fix the problem.

The site localhost wants to set a cookie.

☐ Use my choice for all cookies from this site

(Hide Details)　(Allow for Session)　(Deny)　(**Allow**)

Name: name
Content: Nicole
Host: localhost
Path: /
Send For: Any type of connection
Expires: At end of session

C If the browser is set to ask for permission when receiving cookies, you'll see a message like this when a site attempts to send one (this is Firefox's version of the prompt).

To send a cookie:

1. Begin a new PHP document in your text editor or IDE, to be named **login.php** (Script 12.3):

   ```
   <?php # Script 12.3 - login.php
   ```

   For this example, let's make a **login. php** script that works in conjunction with the scripts from Chapter 9. This script will also require the two files created at the beginning of the chapter.

2. If the form has been submitted, include the two helper files:

   ```
   if ($_SERVER['REQUEST_METHOD'] ==
   → 'POST') {
     require ('includes/
     → login_functions.inc.php');
     require ('../mysqli_connect.php');
   ```

   This script will do two things: handle the form submission and display the form. This conditional checks for the submission.

   Within the conditional, the script must include both **login_functions.inc. php** and **mysqli_connect.php** (which was created in Chapter 9 and should still be in the same location relative to this script; change your code here if your **mysqli_connect.php** is not in the parent directory of the current directory).

   I've chosen to use **require( )** in both cases, instead of **include( )**, because a failure to include either of these scripts makes the login process impossible.

Script 12.3 Upon a successful login, the **login.php** script creates two cookies and redirects the user.

```
1   <?php # Script 12.3 - login.php
2   // This page processes the login form
    submission.
3   // Upon successful login, the user is
    redirected.
4   // Two included files are necessary.
5   // Send NOTHING to the Web browser prior
    to the setcookie() lines!
6
7   // Check if the form has been submitted:
8   if ($_SERVER['REQUEST_METHOD'] == 'POST') {
9
10      // For processing the login:
11      require ('includes/login_functions.
        inc.php');
12
13      // Need the database connection:
14      require ('../mysqli_connect.php');
15
16      // Check the login:
17      list ($check, $data) = check_login($dbc,
        $_POST['email'], $_POST['pass']);
18
19      if ($check) { // OK!
20
21          // Set the cookies:
22          setcookie ('user_id',
            $data['user_id']);
23          setcookie ('first_name',
            $data['first_name']);
24
25          // Redirect:
26          redirect_user('loggedin.php');
27
28      } else { // Unsuccessful!
29
30          // Assign $data to $errors for
            error reporting
31          // in the login_page.inc.php file.
32          $errors = $data;
33
34      }
35
36      mysqli_close($dbc); // Close the
        database connection.
37
38  } // End of the main submit conditional.
39
40  // Create the page:
41  include ('includes/login_page.inc.php');
42  ?>
```

3. Validate the form data:

```
list ($check, $data) = check_login
→ ($dbc, $_POST['email'],
→ $_POST['pass']);
```

After including both files, the **check_login( )** function can be called. It's passed the database connection (which comes from **mysqli_connect.php**), along with the email address and the password (both of which come from the form). As an added precaution, the script could confirm that both variables are set and not empty prior to invoking the function.

This function returns an array of two elements: a Boolean value and an array (of user data or errors). To assign those returned values to variables, apply the **list( )** function. The first value returned by the function (the Boolean) will be assigned to **$check**. The second value returned (either the **$row** or **$errors** array) will be assigned to **$data**.

4. If the user entered the correct information, log them in:

```
if ($check) { // OK!
  setcookie ('user_id',
  → $data['user_id']);
  setcookie ('first_name',
  → $data['first_name']);
```

The **$check** variable indicates the success of the login attempt. If it has a TRUE value, then **$data** contains the user's ID and first name. These two values can be used in cookies.

Generally speaking, you should never store a database table's primary key value, such as **$data['user_id']**, in a cookie, because cookies can be manipulated easily. In this situation, it's

not going to be a problem as the *user_id* value isn't actually used anywhere in the site (it's being stored in the cookie for demonstration purposes).

5. Redirect the user to another page:

```
redirect_user('loggedin.php');
```

Using the function defined earlier in the chapter, the user will be redirected to another script upon a successful login. The specific page to be redirected to is **loggedin.php**.

6. Complete the **$check** conditional (started in Step 4) and then close the database connection:

```
} else {
  $errors = $data;
}
mysqli_close($dbc);
```

If **$check** has a FALSE value, then the **$data** variable is storing the errors generated within the **check_login( )** function. If so, the errors should be assigned to the **$errors** variable, because that's what the code in the script that displays the login page—**login_page.inc.php**—is expecting.

7. Complete the main submit conditional and include the login page:

```
}
include ('includes/
→ login_page.inc.php');
?>
```

This **login.php** script itself primarily performs validation, by calling the **check_login( )** function, and handles the cookies and redirection. The **login_page.inc.php** file contains the login page itself, so it just needs to be included.

continues on next page

8. Save the file as **login.php**, place it in your Web directory (in the same folder as the files from Chapter 9), and load this page in your Web browser (see **B** under "Making a Login Page").

If you want, you can submit the form erroneously, but you cannot correctly log in yet, as the final destination—**loggedin.php**—hasn't been written.

TIP Cookies are limited to about 4 KB of total data, and each Web browser can remember a limited number of cookies from any one site. This limit is 50 cookies for most of the current Web browsers (but if you're sending out 50 different cookies, you may want to rethink how you do things).

TIP The setcookie( ) function is one of the few functions in PHP that could have different results in different browsers, since each browser treats cookies in its own way. Be sure to test your Web sites in multiple browsers on different platforms to ensure consistency.

TIP If the first two included files send anything to the Web browser or even have blank lines or spaces after the closing PHP tag, you'll see a *headers already sent* error. This is why neither includes the terminating PHP tag.

Accessing cookies

To retrieve a value from a cookie, you only need to refer to the **$_COOKIE** superglobal, using the appropriate cookie name as the key (as you would with any array). For example, to retrieve the value of the cookie established with the line

```
setcookie ('username', 'Trout');
```

you would refer to **$_COOKIE['username']**.

In the following example, the cookies set by the **login.php** script will be accessed in two ways. First, a check will be made that the user is logged in (otherwise, they shouldn't be accessing this page). Second, the user will be greeted by their first name, which was stored in a cookie.

To access a cookie:

1. Begin a new PHP document in your text editor or IDE, to be named **loggedin.php** (Script 12.4):

```
<?php # Script 12.4 - loggedin.php
```

The user will be redirected to this page after successfully logging in. The script will greet the user by first name, using the cookie.

2. Check for the presence of a cookie.

```
if (!isset($_COOKIE['user_id'])) {
```

Since a user shouldn't be able to access this page unless they are logged in, check for a cookie that should have been set (in **login.php**).

3. Redirect the user if they are not logged in:

```
require ('includes/
→ login_functions.inc.php');
redirect_user( );
}
```

If the user is not logged in, they will be automatically redirected to the main page. This is a simple way to limit access to content.

4. Include the page header:

```
$page_title = 'Logged In!';
include ('includes/header.html');
```

Script 12.4 The `loggedin.php` script prints a greeting to a user thanks to a stored cookie.

```php
1   <?php # Script 12.4 - loggedin.php
2   // The user is redirected here from
    login.php.
3
4   // If no cookie is present, redirect the
    user:
5   if (!isset($_COOKIE['user_id'])) {
6
7       // Need the functions:
8       require ('includes/login_functions.
        inc.php');
9       redirect_user();
10
11  }
12
13  // Set the page title and include the
    HTML header:
14  $page_title = 'Logged In!';
15  include ('includes/header.html');
16
17  // Print a customized message:
18  echo "<h1>Logged In!</h1>
19  <p>You are now logged in, {$_COOKIE
    ['first_name']}!</p>
20  <p><a href=\"logout.php\">Logout</a></p>";
21
22  include ('includes/footer.html');
23  ?>
```

5. Welcome the user, referencing the cookie:

```php
echo "<h1>Logged In!</h1>
<p>You are now logged in,
 {$_COOKIE['first_name']}!</p>
<p><a href=\"logout.php\">Logout
 </a></p>";
```

To greet the user by name, refer to the `$_COOKIE['first_name']` variable (enclosed within curly braces to avoid parse errors). A link to the logout page (to be written later in the chapter) is also printed.

6. Complete the HTML page:

```php
include ('includes/footer.html');
?>
```

7. Save the file as **loggedin.php**, place it in your Web directory (in the same folder as **login.php**), and test it in your Web browser by logging in through **login.php** **D**.

Since these examples use the same database as those in Chapter 9, you should be able to log in using the registered username and password submitted at that time.

continues on next page

D If you used the correct email address and password, you'll see this page after logging in.

8. To see the cookies being set **E** and **F**, change the cookie settings for your browser and test again.

> **TIP** Some browsers (e.g., Internet Explorer) will not adhere to your cookie-prompting preferences for cookies sent over localhost.

> **TIP** A cookie is not accessible until the setting page (e.g., `login.php`) has been reloaded or another page has been accessed (in other words, you cannot set and access a cookie in the same page).

> **TIP** If users decline a cookie or have their Web browser set not to accept them, they will automatically be redirected to the home page in this example, even if they successfully logged in. For this reason, you may want to let the user know that cookies are required.

Setting cookie parameters

Although passing just the name and value arguments to the `setcookie()` function will suffice, you ought to be aware of the other arguments available. The function can take up to five more parameters, each of which will alter the definition of the cookie.

```
setcookie (name, value, expiration,
  path, host, secure, httponly);
```

The expiration argument is used to set a definitive length of time for a cookie to exist, specified in seconds since the *epoch* (the epoch is midnight on January 1, 1970). If it is not set or if it's set to a value of 0, the cookie will continue to be functional until the user closes their browser. These cookies are said to last for the browser session (also indicated in **E** and **F**).

To set a specific expiration time, add a number of minutes or hours to the current moment, retrieved using the `time()` function. The following line will set the expiration time of the cookie to be 30 minutes (60 seconds times 30 minutes) from the current moment:

```
setcookie (name, value, time()+1800);
```

The path and host arguments are used to limit a cookie to a specific folder within a Web site (the path) or to a specific host (**www.example.com** or *192.168.0.1*). For example, you could restrict a cookie to exist only while a user is within the *admin* folder of a domain (and the *admin* folder's subfolders):

```
setcookie (name, value, expire,
  '/admin/');
```

Setting the path to **/** will make the cookie visible within an entire domain (Web site). Setting the domain to **.example.com** will make the cookie visible within an entire domain and every subdomain (**www.example.com**, **admin.example.com**, **pages.example.com**, etc.).

E The `user_id` cookie with a value of 1.

F The `first_name` cookie with a value of *Larry* (yours will probably be different).

Script 12.5 The `login.php` script now uses every argument the `setcookie()` function can take.

```php
1    <?php # Script 12.5 - login.php #2
2    // This page processes the login form
     submission.
3    // The script now adds extra parameters
     to the setcookie() lines.
4
5    // Check if the form has been submitted:
6    if ($_SERVER['REQUEST_METHOD'] == 'POST') {
7
8        // Need two helper files:
9        require ('includes/login_functions.
         inc.php');
10       require ('../mysqli_connect.php');
11
12       // Check the login:
13       list ($check, $data) = check_login
         ($dbc, $_POST['email'], $_POST['pass']);
14
15       if ($check) { // OK!
16
17           // Set the cookies:
18           setcookie ('user_id', $data
             ['user_id'], time()+3600,
             '/', '', 0, 0);
19           setcookie ('first_name', $data
             ['first_name'], time()+3600,
             '/', '', 0, 0);
20
21           // Redirect:
22           redirect_user('loggedin.php');
23
24       } else { // Unsuccessful!
25
26           // Assign $data to $errors for
             login_page.inc.php:
27           $errors = $data;
28
29       }
30
31       mysqli_close($dbc); // Close the
         database connection.
32
33   } // End of the main submit conditional.
34
35   // Create the page:
36   include ('includes/login_page.inc.php');
37   ?>
```

The secure value dictates that a cookie should only be sent over a secure HTTPS connection. A 1 indicates that a secure connection must be used, and a 0 says that a standard connection is fine.

```
setcookie (name, value, expire,
→path, host, 1);
```

If your site is using a secure connection, you ought to restrict any cookies to HTTPS as well.

Finally, added in PHP 5.2 is the *httponly* argument. A Boolean value is used to make the cookie only accessible through HTTP (and HTTPS). Enforcing this restriction will make the cookie more secure (preventing some hack attempts) but is not supported by all browsers at the time of this writing.

```
setcookie (name, value, expire,
→path, host, secure, TRUE);
```

As with all functions that take arguments, you must pass the **setcookie()** values in order. To skip any parameter, use **NULL**, 0, or an empty string (don't use **FALSE**). The expiration and secure values are both integers and are therefore not quoted.

To demonstrate this information, let's add an expiration setting to the login cookies so that they last for only one hour.

To set a cookie's parameters:

1. Open **login.php** in your text editor (refer to Script 12.3), if it is not already.

2. Change the two **setcookie()** lines to include an expiration date that's 60 minutes away (**Script 12.5**):

```
setcookie ('user_id', $data['user_
→id'], time()+3600, '/', '', 0, 0);
setcookie ('first_name',
→$data['first_name'],
→time()+3600, '/', '', 0, 0);
```

continues on next page

With the expiration date set to `time()` `+ 3600` (60 minutes times 60 seconds), the cookie will continue to exist for an hour after it is set. While making this change, every other parameter is explicitly addressed.

For the final parameter, which accepts a Boolean value, you can also use 0 to represent FALSE (PHP will handle the conversion for you). Doing so is a good idea, as using *false* in any of the cookie arguments can cause problems.

3. Save the script, place it in your Web directory, and test it in your Web browser by logging in **G**.

TIP Some browsers have difficulties with cookies that do not list every argument. Explicitly stating every parameter—even as an empty string—will achieve more reliable results across all browsers.

TIP Here are some general guidelines for cookie expirations: If the cookie should last as long as the user's session, do not set an expiration time; if the cookie should continue to exist after the user has closed and reopened his or her browser, set an expiration time weeks or months ahead; and if the cookie can constitute a security risk, set an expiration time of an hour or fraction thereof so that the cookie does not continue to exist too long after a user has left his or her browser.

TIP For security purposes, you could set a 5- or 10-minute expiration time on a cookie and have the cookie resent with every new page the user visits (assuming that the cookie exists). This way, the cookie will continue to persist as long as the user is active but will automatically die 5 or 10 minutes after the user's last action.

TIP E-commerce and other privacy-related Web applications should use an SSL (Secure Sockets Layer) connection for all transactions, including the cookie.

TIP Be careful with cookies created by scripts within a directory. If the path isn't specified, then that cookie will only be available to other scripts within that same directory.

Deleting cookies

The final thing to understand about using cookies is how to delete one. While a cookie will automatically expire when the user's browser is closed or when the expiration date/time is met, often you'll want to manually delete the cookie instead. For example, in Web sites that have login capabilities, you will want to delete any cookies when the user logs out.

Although the **setcookie()** function can take up to seven arguments, only one is actually required—the cookie name. If you send a cookie that consists of a name without a value, it will have the same effect as deleting the existing cookie of the same name. For example, to create the cookie *first_name*, you use this line:

```
setcookie('first_name', 'Tyler');
```

To delete the *first_name* cookie, you would code:

```
setcookie('first_name');
```

As an added precaution, you can also set an expiration date that's in the past:

```
setcookie('first_name', '',
→ time()-3600);
```

To demonstrate all of this, let's add a logout capability to the site. The link to the logout page appears on **loggedin.php**.

G Changes to the **setcookie()** parameters, like an expiration date and time, will be reflected in the cookie sent to the Web browser (compare with **F**).

As an added feature, the header file will be altered so that a *Logout* link appears when the user is logged in and a *Login* link appears when the user is logged out.

To delete a cookie:

1. Begin a new PHP document in your text editor or IDE, to be named **logout.php** (Script 12.6):

   ```
   <?php # Script 12.6 - logout.php
   ```

2. Check for the existence of a *user_id* cookie; if it is not present, redirect the user:

   ```
   if (!isset($_COOKIE['user_id'])) {
       require ('includes/
       →login_functions.inc.php');
       redirect_user( );
   ```

Script 12.6 The **logout.php** script deletes the previously established cookies.

```
1    <?php # Script 12.6 - logout.php
2    // This page lets the user logout.
3
4    // If no cookie is present, redirect the
     user:
5    if (!isset($_COOKIE['user_id'])) {
6
7        // Need the function:
8        require ('includes/login_functions.
         inc.php');
9        redirect_user( );
10
11   } else { // Delete the cookies:
12       setcookie ('user_id', '', time( )-3600,
         '/', '', 0, 0);
13       setcookie ('first_name', '',
         time( )-3600, '/', '', 0, 0);
14   }
15
16   // Set the page title and include the
     HTML header:
17   $page_title = 'Logged Out!';
18   include ('includes/header.html');
19
20   // Print a customized message:
21   echo "<h1>Logged Out!</h1>
22   <p>You are now logged out, {$_COOKIE
     ['first_name']}!</p>";
23
24   include ('includes/footer.html');
25   ?>
```

As with **loggedin.php**, if the user is not already logged in, this page should redirect the user to the home page. There's no point in trying to log out a user who isn't logged in!

3. Delete the cookies, if they exist:

   ```
   } else {
       setcookie ('user_id', '',
       →time( )-3600, '/', '', 0, 0);
       setcookie ('first_name', '',
       →time( )-3600, '/', '', 0, 0);
   }
   ```

   If the user is logged in, these two cookies will effectively delete the existing ones. Except for the value and the expiration, the other arguments should have the same values as they do when the cookies were created.

4. Make the remainder of the PHP page:

   ```
   $page_title = 'Logged Out!';
   include ('includes/header.html');
   echo "<h1>Logged Out!</h1>
   <p>You are now logged out,
   →{$_COOKIE['first_name']}!</p>";
   include ('includes/footer.html');
   ?>
   ```

   The page itself is also much like the **loggedin.php** page. Although it may seem odd that you can still refer to the *first_name* cookie (that was just deleted in this script), it makes perfect sense considering the process:

   A. This page is requested by the client.

   B. The server reads the available cookies from the client's browser.

   C. The page is run and does its thing (including sending new cookies that delete the existing ones).

   continues on next page

Thus, in short, the original *first_name* cookie data is available to this script when it first runs. The set of cookies sent by this page (the delete cookies) aren't available to this page, so the original values are still usable.

5. Save the file as **logout.php** and place it in your Web directory (in the same folder as **login.php**).

To create the logout link:

1. Open **header.html** (refer to Script 9.1) in your text editor or IDE.

2. Change the fifth and final link to (**Script 12.7**):

```
<li><?php
if ( (isset($_COOKIE['user_id']))
→ && (basename($_SERVER['PHP_SELF'])
→ != 'logout.php') ) {
  echo '<a href="logout.php">
  → Logout</a>';
} else {
  echo '<a href="login.php">
  → Login</a>';
}
?></li>
```

Instead of having a permanent login link in the navigation area, it should display a *Login* link if the user is not logged in ❽ or a *Logout* link if the user is ❶. The preceding conditional will accomplish just that, depending upon the presence of a cookie.

For that condition, if the cookie is set, the user is logged in and can be shown the logout link. If the cookie is not set, the user should be shown the login link. There is one catch, however: Because the **logout.php** script would ordinarily display a logout link (because the cookie exists when the page is first being viewed), the conditional has to also check that the current page is not the **logout.php** script. An easy way to dynamically determine the

Script 12.7 The **header.html** file now displays either a *Login* or a *Logout* link, depending upon the user's current status.

```
1   <!DOCTYPE html PUBLIC "-//W3C//DTD XHTML
    1.0 Strict//EN" "http://www.w3.org/TR/
    xhtml1/DTD/xhtml1-strict.dtd">
2   <html xmlns="http://www.w3.org/1999/
    xhtml">
3   <head>
4     <title><?php echo $page_title; ?>
      </title>
5     <link rel="stylesheet" href="includes/
      style.css" type="text/css"
      media="screen" />
6     <meta http-equiv="content-type"
      content="text/html; charset=utf-8" />
7   </head>
8   <body>
9     <div id="header">
10      <h1>Your Website</h1>
11      <h2>catchy slogan...</h2>
12    </div>
13    <div id="navigation">
14      <ul>
15        <li><a href="index.php">Home
          Page</a></li>
16        <li><a href="register.
          php">Register</a></li>
17        <li><a href="view_users.
          php">View Users</a></li>
18        <li><a href="password.
          php">Change Password</a></li>
19        <li><?php // Create a login/
          logout link:
20   if ( (isset($_COOKIE['user_id']))
     && (basename($_SERVER['PHP_SELF'])
     != 'logout.php') ) {
21       echo '<a href="logout.php">Logout
         </a>';
22   } else {
23       echo '<a href="login.php">Login</a>';
24   }
25   ?></li>
26      </ul>
27    </div>
28    <div id="content"><!-- Start of the
      page-specific content. -->
29   <!-- Script 12.7 - header.html -->
```

current page is to apply the `basename()` function to `$_SERVER['PHP_SELF']`.

3. Save the file, place it in your Web directory (within the `includes` folder), and test the login/logout process in your Web browser **J**.

TIP To see the result of the `setcookie()` calls in the `logout.php` script, turn on cookie prompting in your browser **K**.

TIP Due to a bug in how Internet Explorer on Windows handles cookies, you may need to set the *host* parameter to `false` (without quotes) in order to get the logout process to work when developing on your own computer (i.e., through *localhost*).

TIP When deleting a cookie, you should always use the same parameters that set the cookie (aside from the value and expiration, naturally). If you set the host and path in the creation cookie, use them again in the deletion cookie.

TIP To hammer the point home, remember that the deletion of a cookie does not take effect until the page has been reloaded or another page has been accessed. In other words, the cookie will still be available to a page after that page has deleted it.

H The home page with a *Login* link.

I After the user logs in, the page now has a *Logout* link.

J The result after logging out.

K This is how the deletion cookie appears in a Firefox prompt (compare with **G**).

Using Sessions

Another method of making data available to multiple pages of a Web site is to use *sessions*. The premise of a session is that data is stored on the server, not in the Web browser, and a session identifier is used to locate a particular user's record (the session data). This session identifier is normally stored in the user's Web browser via a cookie, but the sensitive data itself—like the user's ID, name, and so on—always remains on the server.

The question may arise: why use sessions at all when cookies work just fine? First of all, sessions are likely more secure in that all of the recorded information is stored on the server and not continually sent back and forth between the server and the client. Second, you can store more data in a session. Third, some users reject cookies or turn them off completely. Sessions, while designed to work with a cookie, can function without them, too.

To demonstrate sessions—and to compare them with cookies—let's rewrite the previous set of scripts.

Setting session variables

The most important rule with respect to sessions is that each page that will use them must begin by calling the **session_start( )** function. This function tells PHP to either begin a new session or access an existing one. This function must be called before anything is sent to the Web browser!

The first time this function is used, **session_start( )** will attempt to send a cookie with a name of *PHPSESSID* (the default session name) and a value of something like *a61f8670baa8e90a30c878df89a2074b* (32 hexadecimal letters, the session ID). Because of this attempt to send a cookie, **session_start( )** must be called before any data is sent to the Web browser, as is the case when using the **setcookie( )** and **header( )** functions.

Sessions vs. Cookies

This chapter has examples accomplishing the same tasks—logging in and logging out—using both cookies and sessions. Obviously, both are easy to use in PHP, but the true question is when to use one or the other.

Sessions have the following advantages over cookies:

- They are generally more secure (because the data is being retained on the server).
- They allow for more data to be stored.
- They can be used without cookies.

Whereas cookies have the following advantages over sessions:

- They are easier to program.
- They require less of the server.
- They can be made to last far longer.

In general, to store and retrieve just a couple of small pieces of information, or to store information for a longer duration, use cookies. For most of your Web applications, though, you'll use sessions.

Script 12.8 This version of the **login.php** script uses sessions instead of cookies.

```
1    <?php # Script 12.8 - login.php #3
2    // This page processes the login form
     submission.
3    // The script now uses sessions.
4
5    // Check if the form has been submitted:
6    if ($_SERVER['REQUEST_METHOD'] == 'POST') {
7
8        // Need two helper files:
9        require ('includes/login_functions.
         inc.php');
10       require ('../mysqli_connect.php');
11
12       // Check the login:
13       list ($check, $data) = check_login($dbc,
         $_POST['email'], $_POST['pass']);
14
15       if ($check) { // OK!
16
17           // Set the session data:
18           session_start();
19           $_SESSION['user_id'] =
             $data'user_id'];
20           $_SESSION['first_name'] =
             $data['first_name'];
21
22           // Redirect:
23           redirect_user('loggedin.php');
24
25       } else { // Unsuccessful!
26
27           // Assign $data to $errors for
             login_page.inc.php:
28           $errors = $data;
29
30       }
31
32       mysqli_close($dbc); // Close the
         database connection.
33
34   } // End of the main submit conditional.
35
36   // Create the page:
37   include ('includes/login_page.inc.php');
38   ?>
```

Once the session has been started, values can be registered to the session using the normal array syntax, using the **$_SESSION** superglobal:

```
$_SESSION['key'] = value;
$_SESSION['name'] = 'Roxanne';
$_SESSION['id'] = 48;
```

Let's update the **login.php** script with this in mind.

To begin a session:

1. Open **login.php** (refer to Script 12.5) in your text editor or IDE.

2. Replace the **setcookie()** lines (18–19) with these lines (**Script 12.8**):

   ```
   session_start();
   $_SESSION['user_id'] =
   $data['user_id'];
   $_SESSION['first_name'] =
   $data['first_name'];
   ```

   The first step is to begin the session. Since there are no **echo** statements, inclusions of HTML files, or even blank spaces prior to this point in the script, it will be safe to use **session_start()** at this point in the script (although the function call could be placed at the top of the script as well). Then, two *key-value* pairs are added to the **$_SESSION** superglobal array to register the user's first name and user ID to the session.

   continues on next page

3. Save the page as `login.php`, place it in your Web directory, and test it in your Web browser .

Although `loggedin.php` and the header and script will need to be rewritten, you can still test the login script and see the resulting cookie 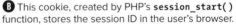. The `loggedin.php` page should redirect you back to the home page, though, as it's still checking for the presence of a `$_COOKIE` variable.

TIP Because sessions will normally send and read cookies, you should always try to begin them as early in the script as possible. Doing so will help you avoid the problem of attempting to send a cookie after the headers (HTML or white space) have already been sent.

TIP If you want, you can set *session.auto_start* in the `php.ini` file to 1, making it unnecessary to use `session_start( )` on each page. This does put a greater toll on the server and, for that reason, shouldn't be used without some consideration of the circumstances.

TIP You can store arrays in sessions (making `$_SESSION` a multidimensional array), just as you can store strings or numbers.

Accessing session variables

Once a session has been started and variables have been registered to it, you can create other scripts that will access those variables. To do so, each script must first enable sessions, again using `session_start( )`.

This function will give the current script access to the previously started session (if it can read the *PHPSESSID* value stored in the cookie) or create a new session if it cannot. Understand that if the current session ID cannot be found and a new session ID is generated, none of the data stored under the old session ID will be available. I mention this here and now because if you're having problems with sessions, checking the session ID value to see if it changes from one page to the next is the first debugging step.

Assuming that there was no problem accessing the current session, to then refer to a session variable, use `$_SESSION['var']`, as you would refer to any other array.

A The login form remains unchanged to the end user, but the underlying functionality now uses sessions.

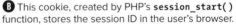

B This cookie, created by PHP's `session_start( )` function, stores the session ID in the user's browser.

Script 12.9 The `loggedin.php` script is updated so that it refers to **$_SESSION** and not **$_COOKIE** (changes are required on two lines).

```
1    <?php # Script 12.9 - loggedin.php #2
2    // The user is redirected here from
     login.php.
3
4    session_start( ); // Start the session.
5
6    // If no session value is present,
     redirect the user:
7    if (!isset($_SESSION['user_id'])) {
8
9        // Need the functions:
10       require ('includes/login_functions.
         inc.php');
11       redirect_user( );
12
13   }
14
15   // Set the page title and include the
     HTML header:
16   $page_title = 'Logged In!';
17   include ('includes/header.html');
18
19   // Print a customized message:
20   echo "<h1>Logged In!</h1>
21   <p>You are now logged in, {$_SESSION
     ['first_name']}!</p>
22   <p><a href=\"logout.php\">Logout</a></p>";
23
24   include ('includes/footer.html');
25   ?>
```

To access session variables:

1. Open **loggedin.php** (refer to Script 12.4) in your text editor or IDE.

2. Add a call to the **session_start( )** function (**Script 12.9**):

    session_start( );

    Every PHP script that either sets or accesses session variables must use the **session_start( )** function. This line must be called before the **header.html** file is included and before anything is sent to the Web browser.

3. Replace the references to **$_COOKIE** with **$_SESSION** (lines 5 and 19 of the original file):

    if (!isset($_SESSION['user_id'])) {

    and

    echo "<h1>Logged In!</h1>
    <p>You are now logged in,
    → {$_SESSION['first_name']}!</p>
    <p><a href=\"logout.php\">Logout
    → </a></p>";

    Switching a script from cookies to sessions requires only that you change uses of **$_COOKIE** to **$_SESSION** (assuming that the same names were used).

4. Save the file as **loggedin.php**, place it in your Web directory, and test it in your browser **C**.

continues on next page

Home Page	Register	View Users	Change Password	Login

Logged In!

You are now logged in, Larry!

Logout

C After logging in, the user is redirected to **loggedin.php**, which will welcome the user by name using the stored session value.

5. Replace the reference to **$_COOKIE** with **$_SESSION** in **header.html** (from Script 12.7 to **Script 12.10**):

```
if (isset($_SESSION['user_id'])) {
```

For the *Login/Logout* links to function properly (notice the incorrect link in **C**), the reference to the cookie variable within the header file must be switched over to sessions. The header file does not need to call the **session_start( )** function, as it'll be included by pages that do.

Note that this conditional does not need to check if the current page is the logout page, as session data behaves differently than cookie data (I'll explain this further in the next section of the chapter).

6. Save the header file, place it in your Web directory (in the **includes** folder), and test it in your browser **D**.

TIP For the *Login/Logout* links to work on the other pages (**register.php**, **index.php**, etc.), you'll need to add the **session_start( )** command to each of those.

TIP As a reminder of what I already said, if you have an application where the session data does not seem to be accessible from one page to the next, it could be because a new session is being created on each page. To check for this, compare the session ID (the last few characters of the value will suffice) to see if it is the same. You can see the session's ID by viewing the session cookie as it is sent or by invoking the **session_id( )** function:

```
echo session_id( );
```

TIP Session variables are available as soon as you've established them. So, unlike when using cookies, you can assign a value to **$_SESSION['*var*']** and then refer to **$_SESSION['*var*']** later in that same script.

Script 12.10 The **header.html** file now also references **$_SESSION** instead of **$_COOKIE**.

```
1   <!DOCTYPE html PUBLIC "-//W3C//DTD XHTML
     1.0 Strict//EN" "http://www.w3.org/TR/
     xhtml1/DTD/xhtml1-strict.dtd">
2   <html xmlns="http://www.w3.org/1999/xhtml">
3   <head">
4       <title><?php echo $page_title; ?>
        </title>
5       <link rel="stylesheet" href="includes/
        style.css" type="text/css"
        media="screen" />
6       <meta http-equiv="content-type"
        content="text/html; charset=utf-8" />
7   </head>
8   <body>
9       <div id="header">
10          <h1>Your Website</h1>
11          <h2>catchy slogan...</h2>
12      </div>
13      <div id="navigation">
14          <ul>
15              <li><a href="index.php">Home
                Page</a></li>
16              <li><a href="register.php">
                Register</a></li>
17              <li><a href="view_users.php">
                View Users</a></li>
18              <li><a href="password.php">
                Change Password</a></li>
19              <li><?php // Create a login/
                logout link:
20  if (isset($_SESSION['user_id'])) {
21      echo '<a href="logout.php">Logout</a>';
22  } else {
23      echo '<a href="login.php">Login</a>';
24  }
25  ?></li>
26          </ul>
27      </div>
28      <div id="content"><!-- Start of the
        page-specific content. -->
29  <!-- Script 12.10 - header.html -->
```

Home Page	Register	View Users	Change Password		Logout

Logged In!

You are now logged in, Larry!

Logout

D With the header file altered for sessions, the proper *Login/Logout* links will be displayed (compare with **C**).

Script 12.11 Destroying a session, as you would in a logout page, requires special syntax to delete the session cookie and the session data on the server, as well as to clear out the **$_SESSION** array.

```php
1    <?php # Script 12.11 - logout.php #2
2    // This page lets the user logout.
3    // This version uses sessions.
4
5    session_start(); // Access the
     existing session.
6
7    // If no session variable exists,
     redirect the user:
8    if (!isset($_SESSION['user_id'])) {
9
10       // Need the functions:
11       require ('includes/login_functions.
         inc.php');
12       redirect_user();
13
14   } else { // Cancel the session:
15
16       $_SESSION = array(); // Clear the
         variables.
17       session_destroy(); // Destroy the
         session itself.
18       setcookie ('PHPSESSID', '', time()-3600,
         '/', '', 0, 0); // Destroy the cookie.
19
20   }
21
22   // Set the page title and include the
     HTML header:
23   $page_title = 'Logged Out!';
24   include ('includes/header.html');
25
26   // Print a customized message:
27   echo "<h1>Logged Out!</h1>
28   <p>You are now logged out!</p>";
29
30   include ('includes/footer.html');
31   ?>
```

Deleting session variables

When using sessions, you ought to create a method of deleting the session data. In the current example, this would be necessary when the user logs out.

Whereas a cookie system only requires that another cookie be sent to destroy the existing cookie, sessions are slightly more demanding, since there are both the cookie on the client and the data on the server to consider.

To delete an individual session variable, you can use the **unset( )** function (which works with any variable in PHP):

unset($_SESSION['*var*']);

But to delete every session variable, you shouldn't use **unset( )**, instead, reset the **$_SESSION** array:

$_SESSION = array( );

Finally, to remove all of the session data from the server, call **session_destroy( )**:

session_destroy( );

Note that prior to using any of these methods, the page must begin with **session_start( )** so that the existing session is accessed. Let's update the **logout.php** script to clean out the session data.

To delete a session:

1. Open **logout.php** (Script 12.6) in your text editor or IDE.

2. Immediately after the opening PHP line, start the session (**Script 12.11**):

   session_start( );

   Anytime you are using sessions, you must call the **session_start( )** function, preferably at the very beginning of a page. This is true even if you are deleting a session.

continues on next page

3. Change the conditional so that it checks for the presence of a session variable:

```
if (!isset($_SESSION['user_id'])) {
```

As with the **logout.php** script in the cookie examples, if the user is not currently logged in, they will be redirected.

4. Replace the **setcookie( )** lines (that delete the cookies) with:

```
$_SESSION = array( );
session_destroy( );
setcookie ('PHPSESSID', '',
→ time( )-3600, '/', '', 0, 0);
```

The first line here will reset the entire **$_SESSION** variable as a new array, erasing its existing values. The second line removes the data from the server, and the third sends a cookie to delete the existing session cookie in the browser.

Garbage Collection

Garbage collection with respect to sessions is the process of the server automatically deleting the session files (where the actual data is stored). Creating a logout system that destroys a session is ideal, but there's no guarantee all users will formally log out as they should. For this reason, PHP includes a cleanup process.

Whenever the **session_start( )** function is called, PHP's garbage collection kicks in, checking the last modification date of each session (a session is modified whenever variables are set or retrieved). Two settings dictate garbage collection: *session.gc_maxlifetime* and *session.gc_probability*. The first states after how many seconds of inactivity a session is considered idle and will therefore be deleted. The second setting determines the probability that garbage collection is performed, on a scale of 1 to 100. With the default settings, each call to **session_start( )** has a 1 percent chance of invoking garbage collection. If PHP does start the cleanup, any sessions that have not been used in more than 1,440 seconds will be deleted.

You can change these settings using the **ini_set( )** function, although be careful in doing so. Too frequent or too probable garbage collection can bog down the server and inadvertently end the sessions of slower users.

5. Remove the reference to **$_COOKIE** in the message:

```
echo "<h1>Logged Out!</h1>
<p>You are now logged out!</p>";
```

Unlike when using the cookie version of the **logout.php** script, you cannot refer to the user by their first name anymore, as all of that data has been deleted.

6. Save the file as **logout.php**, place it in your Web directory, and test it in your browser **E**.

TIP The **header.html** file only needs to check if **$_SESSION['user_id']** is set, and not if the page is the logout page, because by the time the header file is included by **logout. php**, all of the session data will have already been destroyed. The destruction of session data applies immediately, unlike with cookies.

TIP Never set **$_SESSION** equal to NULL and never use **unset($_SESSION)**. Either could cause problems on some servers.

TIP In case it's not absolutely clear what's going on, there exists three kinds of information with a session: the session identifier (which is stored in a cookie by default), the session data (which is stored in a text file on the server), and the **$_SESSION** array (which is how a script accesses the session data in the text file). Just deleting the cookie doesn't remove the data file and vice versa. Clearing out the **$_SESSION** array would erase the data from the text file, but the file itself would still exist, as would the cookie. The three steps outlined in this logout script effectively remove all traces of the session.

Home Page	Register	View Users	Change Password	Login

Logged Out!

You are now logged out!

E The logout page (now featuring sessions).

Improving Session Security

Because important information is normally stored in a session (you should never store sensitive data in a cookie), security becomes more of an issue. With sessions there are two things to pay attention to: the session ID, which is a reference point to the session data, and the session data itself, stored on the server. A malicious person is far more likely to hack into a session through the session ID than the data on the server, so I'll focus on that side of things here (in the tips at the end of this section I mention two ways to protect the session data itself).

The session ID is the key to the session data. By default, PHP will store this in a cookie, which is preferable from a security standpoint. It is possible in PHP to use sessions without cookies, but that leaves

Changing the Session Behavior

As part of PHP's support for sessions, there are over 20 different configuration options you can set for how PHP handles sessions. For the full list, see the PHP manual, but I'll highlight a few of the most important ones here. Note two rules about changing the session settings:

1. All changes must be made before calling **session_start( )**.

2. The same changes must be made on every page that uses sessions.

Most of the settings can be set within a PHP script using the **ini_set( )** function (discussed in Chapter 8):

```
ini_set (parameter, new_setting);
```

For example, to require the use of a session cookie (as mentioned, sessions can work without cookies but it's less secure), use

```
ini_set ('session.use_only_cookies', 1);
```

Another change you can make is to the name of the session (perhaps to use a more user-friendly one). To do so, call the **session_name( )** function:

```
session_name('YourSession');
```

The benefits of creating your own session name are twofold: it's marginally more secure and it may be better received by the end user (since the session name is the cookie name the end user will see). The **session_name( )** function can also be used when deleting the session cookie:

```
setcookie (session_name(), '', time()-3600);
```

If not provided with an argument, this function instead returns the current session name.

Finally, there's also the **session_set_cookie_params( )** function. It's used to tweak the settings of the session cookie:

```
session_set_cookie_params(expire, path, host, secure, httponly);
```

Note that the expiration time of the cookie refers only to the longevity of the cookie in the Web browser, not to how long the session data will be stored on the server.

Script 12.12 This final version of the `login.php` script also stores an encrypted form of the user's *HTTP_USER_AGENT* (the browser and operating system of the client) in a session.

```php
1   <?php # Script 12.12 - login.php #4
2   // This page processes the login form
    submission.
3   // The script now stores the HTTP_USER_
    AGENT value for added security.
4
5   // Check if the form has been submitted:
6   if ($_SERVER['REQUEST_METHOD'] == 'POST')
    {
7
8       // Need two helper files:
9       require ('includes/login_functions.
        inc.php');
10      require ('../mysqli_connect.php');
11
12      // Check the login:
13      list ($check, $data) = check_login($dbc,
        $_POST['email'], $_POST['pass']);
14
15      if ($check) { // OK!
16
17          // Set the session data:
18          session_start();
19          $_SESSION['user_id'] =
            $data['user_id'];
20          $_SESSION['first_name'] =
            $data['first_name'];
21
22          // Store the HTTP_USER_AGENT:
23          $_SESSION['agent'] = md5($_SERVER
            ['HTTP_USER_AGENT']);
24
25          // Redirect:
26          redirect_user('loggedin.php');
27
28      } else { // Unsuccessful!
29
30          // Assign $data to $errors for
            login_page.inc.php:
31          $errors = $data;
32
33      }
34
35      mysqli_close($dbc); // Close the
        database connection.
36
37  } // End of the main submit conditional.
38
39  // Create the page:
40  include ('includes/login_page.inc.php');
41  ?>
```

the application vulnerable to *session hijacking*: If malicious user Alice can learn user Bob's session ID, Alice can easily trick a server into thinking that Bob's session ID is also *Alice's* session ID. At that point, Alice would be riding coattails on Bob's session and would have access to Bob's data. Storing the session ID in a cookie makes it somewhat harder to steal.

One method of preventing hijacking is to store some sort of user identifier in the session, and then to repeatedly double-check this value. The *HTTP_USER_AGENT*—a combination of the browser and operating system being used—is a likely candidate for this purpose. This adds a layer of security in that one person could only hijack another user's session if they are both running the exact same browser and operating system. As a demonstration of this, let's modify the examples one last time.

To use sessions more securely:

1. Open `login.php` (refer to Script 12.8) in your text editor or IDE.

2. After assigning the other session variables, also store the *HTTP_USER_AGENT* value (**Script 12.12**):

   ```
   $_SESSION['agent'] =
   → md5($_SERVER['HTTP_USER_AGENT']);
   ```

   The *HTTP_USER_AGENT* is part of the **$_SERVER** array (you may recall using it way back in Chapter 1, "Introduction to PHP"). It will have a value like *Mozilla/4.0 (compatible; MSIE 8.0; Windows NT 6.1...).*

   continues on next page

Instead of storing this value in the session as is, it'll be run through the md5( ) function for added security. That function returns a 32-character hexadecimal string (called a *hash*) based upon a value. In theory, no two strings will have the same md5( ) result.

3. Save the file and place it in your Web directory.

4. Open **loggedin.php** (Script 12.9) in your text editor or IDE.

5. Change the !isset($_SESSION['user_id']) conditional to (**Script 12.13**):

   ```
   if (!isset($_SESSION['agent']) OR
   → ($_SESSION['agent'] != md5($_SERVER
   → ['HTTP_USER_AGENT']) )) {
   ```

   This conditional checks two things. First, it sees if the **$_SESSION['agent']** variable is not set (this part is just as it was before, although *agent* is being used instead of *user_id*). The second part of the conditional checks if the md5( ) version of **$_SERVER['HTTP_USER_AGENT']** does not equal the value stored in **$_SESSION['agent']**. If either of these conditions is true, the user will be redirected.

6. Save this file, place in your Web directory, and test in your Web browser by logging in.

Script 12.13 This `loggedin.php` script now confirms that the user accessing this page has the same *HTTP_USER_AGENT* as they did when they logged in.

```
1    <?php # Script 12.13 - loggedin.php #3
2    // The user is redirected here from
     login.php.
3
4    session_start( ); // Start the session.
5
6    // If no session value is present,
     redirect the user:
7    // Also validate the HTTP_USER_AGENT!
8    if (!isset($_SESSION['agent']) OR
     ($_SESSION['agent'] != md5($_SERVER
     ['HTTP_USER_AGENT']) )) {
9
10       // Need the functions:
11       require ('includes/login_functions.
         inc.php');
12       redirect_user( );
13
14   }
15
16   // Set the page title and include the
     HTML header:
17   $page_title = 'Logged In!';
18   include ('includes/header.html');
19
20   // Print a customized message:
21   echo "<h1>Logged In!</h1>
22   <p>You are now logged in, {$_SESSION
     ['first_name']}!</p>
23   <p><a href=\"logout.php\">Logout</a></p>";
24
25   include ('includes/footer.html');
26   ?>
```

Preventing Session Fixation

Another specific kind of session attack is known as *session fixation*. This approach is the opposite of *session hijacking*. Instead of malicious user Alice finding and using Bob's session ID, she instead creates her own session ID (perhaps by logging in legitimately), and then gets Bob to access the site using that session. The hope is that Bob would then do something that would unknowingly benefit Alice.

You can help protect against these types of attacks by changing the session ID after a user logs in. The `session_ regenerate_id( )` does just that, providing a new session ID to refer to the current session data. You can use this function on sites for which security is paramount (like e-commerce or online banking) or in situations when it'd be particularly bad if certain users (i.e., administrators) had their sessions manipulated.

TIP For critical uses of sessions, require the use of cookies and transmit them over a secure connection, if at all possible. You can even set PHP to only use cookies by setting *session.use_only_cookies* to 1.

TIP By default, a server stores every session file for every site within the same temporary directory, meaning any site could theoretically read any other site's session data. If you are using a server shared with other domains, changing the *session.save_path* from its default setting will be more secure. For example, it'd be better if you stored your site's session data in a dedicated directory particular to your site.

TIP The session data itself can also be stored in a database rather than a text file. This is a more secure, but more programming-intensive, option. I teach how to do this in my book *PHP 5 Advanced: Visual QuickPro Guide*.

TIP The user's IP address (the network address from which the user is connecting) is *not* a good unique identifier, for two reasons. First, a user's IP address can, and normally does, change frequently (ISPs dynamically assign them for short periods of time). Second, many users accessing a site from the same network (like a home network or an office) could all have the same IP address.

Review and Pursue

If you have any problems with the review questions or the pursue prompts, turn to the book's supporting forum (**www.LarryUllman.com/forums/**).

Review

- What code is used to redirect the user's browser from one page to the next?

- What does the *headers already sent* error message mean?

- What value does **$_SERVER['HTTP_HOST']** store? What value does **$_SERVER['PHP_SELF']** store?

- What does the **dirname( )** function do?

- What does the **rtrim( )** function do? What arguments can it take?

- How do you write a function that returns multiple values? How do you call such a function?

- What arguments can the **setcookie( )** function take?

- How do you reference values previously stored in a cookie?

- How do you delete an existing cookie?

- Are cookies available immediately after being sent (on the same page)? Why can you still refer to a cookie (on the same page) after it is deleted?

- What debugging steps can you take when you have problems with cookies?

- What does the **basename( )** function do?

- How do you begin a session?

- How do you reference values previously stored in a session?

- Is session data available immediately after being assigned (on the same page)?

- How do you terminate a session?

- What debugging steps can you take when you have problems with sessions?

Pursue

- If you have not already done so, learn how to view cookie data in your Web browser. When developing sites that use cookies, enable the option so that the browser prompts you when cookies are received.

- Make the login form sticky.

- Add code to the handling of the **$errors** variable on the login page that uses a **foreach** loop if **$errors** is an array, or just prints the value of **$errors** otherwise.

- Modify the **redirect_user( )** function so that it can be used to redirect the user to a page within another directory.

- Implement another cookie example, such as storing a user's preference in the cookie, then base a look or feature of a page upon the stored value (when present).

- Change the code in **logout.php** (Script 12.11) so that it uses the **session_name( )** function to dynamically set the name value of the session cookie being deleted.

- Implement another session example, if you'd like more practice with sessions (you'll get more practice later in the book, too).

- Check out the PHP manual pages for any new function introduced in this chapter with which you're not comfortable.

- Check out the PHP manual pages on cookies and sessions (two separate sections) to learn more. Also read some of the user-submitted comments for additional tips.

Security Methods

The security of your Web applications is such an important topic that it really cannot be overstressed. Although security-related issues have been mentioned throughout this book, this chapter will help to fill in certain gaps, finalize other points, and teach several new things.

The topics discussed here include: preventing spam; typecasting variables; preventing cross-site scripting (XSS) and SQL injection attacks; the new Filter extension; and validating uploaded files by type. This chapter will use five discrete examples to best demonstrate these concepts. Some other common security issues and best practices will be mentioned in sidebars as well.

Preventing Spam

Spam is nothing short of a plague, cluttering up the Internet and email inboxes. There are steps you can take to avoid receiving spam at your email accounts, but in this book the focus is on preventing spam being sent through your PHP scripts.

Chapter 11, "Web Application Development," shows how easy it is to send email using PHP's **mail( )** function. The example there, a contact form, took some information from the user 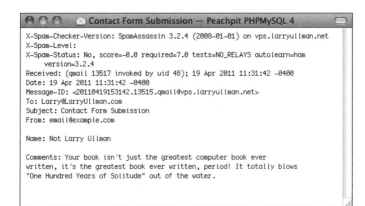 and sent it to an email address. Although it may seem like there's no harm in this system, there's actually a big security hole. But first, some background on what an email actually is.

Regardless of how an email is sent, how it's formatted, and what it looks like when it's received, an email contains two parts: a header and a body. The header includes such information as the *to* and *from* addresses, the subject, the date, and more **B**. Each item in the header is on its own line, in the format *Name*: *value*. The body of the email is exactly what you think it is: the body of the email.

Contact Me

Please fill out this form to contact me.

Name: Not Larry Ullman

Email Address: email@example.com

Comments: Your book isn't just the greatest computer book ever written, it's the greatest book ever written, period! It totally blows "One Hundred

Send!

A A simple, standard HTML contact form.

```
Contact Form Submission — Peachpit PHPMySQL 4
X-Spam-Checker-Version: SpamAssassin 3.2.4 (2008-01-01) on vps.larryullman.net
X-Spam-Level:
X-Spam-Status: No, score=-0.0 required=7.0 tests=NO_RELAYS autolearn=ham
     version=3.2.4
Received: (qmail 13517 invoked by uid 48); 19 Apr 2011 11:31:42 -0400
Date: 19 Apr 2011 11:31:42 -0400
Message-ID: <20110419153142.13515.qmail@vps.larryullman.net>
To: Larry@LarryUllman.com
Subject: Contact Form Submission
From: email@example.com

Name: Not Larry Ullman

Comments: Your book isn't just the greatest computer book ever
written, it's the greatest book ever written, period! It totally blows
"One Hundred Years of Solitude" out of the water.
```

B The raw source version of the email sent by the contact form **A**.

In looking at PHP's **mail( )** function—

mail (*to, subject, body* [,*headers*]);

—you can see that one of the arguments goes straight to the email's body and the rest appear in its header. To send spam to *your address* (as in Chapter 11's example), all a person would have to do is enter the spam message into the comments section of the form **A**. That's bad enough, but to send spam to *anyone else* at the same time, all the user would have to do is add *Bcc: poorsap@example.org*, followed by some sort of line terminator (like a newline or carriage return), to the email's header. With the example as is, this just means entering this into the *from* value of the contact form: *me@example.com\ nBcc:poorsap@example.org*.

You might think that safeguarding everything that goes into an email's header would be sufficiently safe, but as an email is just one document, bad input in a body can impact the header, too.

There are a couple of preventive techniques that can be applied to this contact form. First, validate any email addresses using regular expressions, covered in Chapter 13, "Perl-Compatible Regular Expressions," or the Filter extension, discussed in just a few pages. Second, now that you know what an evildoer must enter to send spam (**Table 13.1**), watch for those characters and strings in form values. If a value contains anything from that list, don't use that value in a sent email. (The last four values in Table 13.1 are all different ways of creating newlines.)

In this next example, a modification of the email script from Chapter 11, I'll define a function that scrubs all potentially dangerous characters from provided data. Two new PHP functions will be used as well: **str_replace( )** and **array_map( )**. Both will be explained in detail in the steps that follow.

TABLE 13.1 Spam Tip-offs

Strings
content-type:
mime-version:
multipart-mixed:
content-transfer-encoding:
bcc:
cc:
to:
\r
\n
%0a
%0d

A Security Approach

The most important concept to understand about security is that it's not a binary state: don't think of a Web site or script as being either *secure* or *not secure*. Security isn't a switch that you turn on and off; it's a scale that you can move up and down. When you program, think about what you can do to make your site *more secure* and what you've done that makes it *less secure*. Also, keep in mind that improved security normally comes at a cost of convenience (both to you, the programmer, and to the end user) and performance. Increased security normally means more code, more checks, and more required of the server. When developing Web applications, the goal is to achieve a level of security that's appropriate for the particular situation. And then err on the side of being a tad too secure, just to be prudent.

To prevent spam:

1. Open **email.php** (Script 11.1) in your text editor or IDE.

   To complete this spam-purification, the email script needs to be modified.

2. After checking for the form submission, begin defining a function (**Script 13.1**):

   ```php
   function spam_scrubber($value) {
   ```

   This function will take one argument: a string. Normally, I would define functions at the top of the script, or in a separate file, but to make things simpler, it'll be defined within the submission-handling block of code.

3. Create a list of really bad things that wouldn't be in a legitimate contact form submission:

   ```php
   $very_bad = array('to:', 'cc:',
   → 'bcc:', 'content-type:',
   → 'mime-version:',
   → 'multipart-mixed:',
   → 'content-transfer-encoding:');
   ```

   Any of these strings should not be present in an honest contact form submission (it's possible someone might legitimately use *to:* in their comments, but unlikely). If any of these strings are present, then this is a spam attempt. To make it easier to test for all these, they're placed in an array, which will be looped through (Step 4). The comparison in Step 4 will be case-insensitive, so each of the dangerous strings is written in all lowercase letters.

4. Loop through the array. If a very bad thing is found, return an empty string instead:

   ```php
   foreach ($very_bad as $v) {
     if (stripos($value, $v) !==
   → false) return '';
   }
   ```

Script 13.1 This version of the script can now safely send emails without concern for spam. Any problematic characters will be caught by the **spam_scrubber( )** function.

```php
1    <!DOCTYPE html PUBLIC "-//W3C//DTD XHTML
     1.0 Transitional//EN" "http://www.w3.org/
     TR/xhtml1/DTD/xhtml1-transitional.dtd">
2    <html xmlns="http://www.w3.org/1999/
     xhtml" xml:lang="en" lang="en">
3    <head>
4        <meta http-equiv="Content-Type"
         content="text/html; charset=utf-8" />
5        <title>Contact Me</title>
6    </head>
7    <body>
8    <h1>Contact Me</h1>
9    <?php # Script 13.1 - email.php #2
10   // This version now scrubs dangerous
     strings from the submitted input.
11
12   // Check for form submission:
13   if ($_SERVER['REQUEST_METHOD'] == 'POST') {
14
15       /* The function takes one argument: a
         string.
16       * The function returns a clean
         version of the string.
17       * The clean version may be either an
         empty string or
18       * just the removal of all newline
         characters.
19       */
20       function spam_scrubber($value) {
21
22           // List of very bad values:
23           $very_bad = array('to:',
             'cc:', 'bcc:', 'content-type:',
             'mime-version:', 'multipart-mixed:',
             'content-transfer-encoding:');
24
25           // If any of the very bad strings
             are in
26           // the submitted value, return an
             empty string:
27           foreach ($very_bad as $v) {
28               if (stripos($value, $v) !==
                 false) return '';
29           }
30
```

code continues on next page

```
31        // Replace any newline characters
          with spaces:
32        $value = str_replace(array( "\r",
          "\n", "%0a", "%0d"), ' ', $value);
33
34        // Return the value:
35        return trim($value);
36
37        } // End of spam_scrubber()
          function.
38
39    // Clean the form data:
40    $scrubbed = array_map
          ('spam_scrubber', $_POST);
41
42    // Minimal form validation:
43    if (!empty($scrubbed['name']) &&
          !empty($scrubbed['email']) &&
          !empty($scrubbed['comments']) ) {
44
45        // Create the body:
46        $body = "Name: {$scrubbed
          ['name']}\n\nComments:
          {$scrubbed['comments']}";
47
48        // Make it no longer than 70
          characters long:
49        $body = wordwrap($body, 70);
50
51        // Send the email:
52        mail('your_email@example.com',
          'Contact Form Submission', $body,
          "From: {$scrubbed['email']}");
53
54        // Print a message:
55        echo '<p><em>Thank you for
          contacting me. I will reply some
          day.</em></p>';
56
57        // Clear $_POST (so that the form's
          not sticky):
58        $_POST = array();
59
60    } else {
61        echo '<p style="font-weight: bold;
          color: #C00">Please fill out the
          form completely.</p>';
62    }
63
64    } // End of main isset() IF.
```

code continues on next page

The **foreach** loop will access each item in the **$very_bad** array one at a time, assigning each item to **$v**. Within the loop, the **stripos( )** function will check if the item is in the string provided to this function as **$value**. The **stripos( )** function performs a case-insensitive search (so it would match *bcc:*, *Bcc:*, *bCC:*, etc.). The function returns a Boolean TRUE if the needle is found in the haystack (e.g., looking for occurrences of **$v** in **$value**). The conditional therefore says that if that function's results do not equal FALSE (i.e., **$v** was not found in **$value**), return an empty string.

Therefore, for each of the dangerous character strings, the first time that any of them is found in the submitted value, the function will return an empty string and terminate (functions automatically stop executing once they hit a **return**).

5. Replace any newline characters with spaces:

   $value = str_replace(array("\r",
   →"\n", "%0a", "%0d"), ' ', $value);

   Newline characters, which are represented by **\r**, **\n** , **%0a**, and **%0d**, may or may not be problematic. A newline character is required to send spam (or else you can't create the proper header) but will also appear if a user just hits Enter or Return while typing in a textarea box. For this reason, any found newlines will just be replaced by a space. This means that the submitted value could lose some of its formatting, but that's a reasonable price to pay to stop spam.

   continues on next page

The **str_replace( )** function looks through the value in the third argument and replaces any occurrences of the characters in the first argument with the character or characters in the second. Or as the PHP manual puts it:

```
mixed str_replace (mixed $search,
→ mixed $replace, mixed $subject)
```

This function is very flexible in that it can take strings or arrays for its three arguments (the *mixed* means it accepts a mix of argument types). Hence, this line of code in the script assigns to the **$value** variable its original value, with any newline characters replaced by a single space.

There is a case-insensitive version of this function, but it's not necessary here, as, for example, **\r** is a carriage return but **\R** is not.

6. Return the value and complete the function:

```
    return trim($value);
} // End of spam_scrubber( )
→ function.
```

Finally, this function returns the value, trimmed of any leading and ending spaces. Keep in mind that the function will only get to this point if none of the very bad things was found.

7. After the function definition, invoke the **spam_scrubber( )** function:

```
$scrubbed = array_map
→ ('spam_scrubber', $_POST);
```

This approach is beautiful in its simplicity! The **array_map( )** function has two required arguments. The first is the name of the function to call. In this case, that's *spam_scrubber* (without the parentheses, because you're providing the function's *name*, not calling the function). The second argument is an array.

What **array_map( )** does is apply the named function once for each array element, sending each array element's value to that function call. In this script, **$_POST** has four elements—*name*, *email*, *comments*, and *submit*, meaning that the **spam_scrubber( )** function will be called four times, thanks to **array_map( )**. After this line of code, the **$scrubbed** array will end up with four elements: **$scrubbed['name']** will

Script 13.1 *continued*

```
65
66    // Create the HTML form:
67    ?>
68    <p>Please fill out this form to contact me.</p>
69    <form action="email.php" method="post">
70        <p>Name: <input type="text" name="name" size="30" maxlength="60" value="<?php if
          (isset($scrubbed['name'])) echo $scrubbed['name']; ?>" /></p>
71        <p>Email Address: <input type="text" name="email" size="30" maxlength="80"
          value="<?php if (isset($scrubbed['email'])) echo $scrubbed['email']; ?>" /></p>
72        <p>Comments: <textarea name="comments" rows="5" cols="30"><?php if
          (isset($scrubbed['comments'])) echo $scrubbed['comments']; ?></textarea></p>
73        <p><input type="submit" name="submit" value="Send!" /></p>
74    </form>
75    </body>
76    </html>
```

Contact Me

Please fill out this form to contact me.

Name: `Not Larry Ullman`

Email Address: `Larry@LarryUllman.com\r\ncc:l`

Comments:
```
This is spam!!!
```

[Send!]

C The presence of *CC:* in the email address field will prevent this submission from being sent in an email **D**.

Contact Me

Please fill out the form completely.

Please fill out this form to contact me.

Name: `Not Larry Ullman`

Email Address: [   ]

Comments:
```
This is spam!!!
```

[Send!]

D The email was not sent because of the very bad characters used in the email address, which gets turned into an empty string by the spam prevention function.

have the value of **$_POST['name']** after running it through **spam_scrubber( )**; **$scrubbed['email']** will have the same value as **$_POST['email']** after running it through **spam_scrubber( )**; and so forth.

This one line of code then takes an entire array of potentially tainted data (**$_POST**), cleans it using **spam_scrubber( )**, and assigns the result to a new variable. Here's the most important thing about this technique: from here on out, the script must use the **$scrubbed** array, which is clean, not **$_POST**, which is still potentially dirty.

8. Change the form validation to use this new array:

```
if (!empty($scrubbed['name']) &&
→ !empty($scrubbed['email']) &&
→ !empty($scrubbed['comments']) ) {
```

Each of these elements could have an empty value for two reasons. First, if the user left them empty. Second, if the user entered one of the bad strings in the field **C**, which would be turned into an empty string by the **spam_scrubber( )** function **D**.

9. Change the creation of the **$body** variable so that it uses the clean values:

```
$body = "Name: {$scrubbed
→ ['name']}\n\nComments:
→ {$scrubbed['comments']}";
```

10. Change the invocation of the **mail( )** function to use the clean email address:

```
mail('your_email@example.com',
→ 'Contact Form Submission', $body,
→ "From: {$scrubbed['email']}");
```

Remember to use your own email address in the **mail( )** call, or you'll never get the message!

continues on next page

11. Change the form so that it uses the **$scrubbed** version of the values:

```
<p>Name: <input type="text"
→ name="name" size="30"
→ maxlength="60" value="<?php if
→ (isset($scrubbed['name'])) echo
→ $scrubbed['name']; ?>" /></p>
<p>Email Address: <input
→ type="text" name="email"
→ size="30" maxlength="80"
→ value="<?php if (isset
→ ($scrubbed['email'])) echo
→ $scrubbed['email']; ?>" /></p>
<p>Comments: <textarea
→ name="comments" rows="5"
→ cols="30"><?php if (isset
→ ($scrubbed['comments'])) echo
→ $scrubbed['comments']; ?>
→ </textarea></p>
```

12. Save the script as **email.php**, place it in your Web directory, and test it in your Web browser **E** and **F**.

TIP Using the `array_map()` function as I have in this example is convenient but not without its downsides. First, it blindly applies the `spam_scrubber()` function to the entire `$_POST` array, even to the submit button. This isn't harmful but is unnecessary. Second, any multidimensional arrays within `$_POST` will be lost. In this specific example, that's not a problem, but it is something to be aware of.

TIP To prevent automated submissions to any form, you could use a CAPTCHA test. These are prompts that can only be understood by humans (in theory). While this is commonly accomplished using an image of random characters, the same thing can be achieved using a question like *What is two plus two?* or *On what continent is China?*. Checking for the correct answer to this question would then be part of the validation routine.

E Although the comments field contains newline characters (created by pressing Enter or Return), the email will still be sent **F**.

F The received email, with the newlines in the comments **E** turned into spaces.

TABLE 13.2 Type Validation Functions

Function	Checks For
`is_array()`	Arrays
`is_bool()`	Booleans (`TRUE`, `FALSE`)
`is_float()`	Floating-point numbers
`is_int()`	Integers
`is_null()`	`NULL`s
`is_numeric()`	Numeric values, even as a string (e.g., `'20'`)
`is_resource()`	Resources, like a database connection
`is_scalar()`	Scalar (single-valued) variables
`is_string()`	Strings

Validating Data by Type

For the most part, the form validation used in this book thus far has been rather minimal, often just checking if a variable has any value at all. In many situations, this really is the best you can do. For example, there's no perfect test for what a valid street address is or what a user might enter into a comments field. Still, much of the data you'll work with can be validated in stricter ways. In the next chapter, the sophisticated concept of regular expressions will demonstrate just that. But here I'll cover the more approachable ways you can validate some data by type.

PHP supports many types of data: strings, numbers (integers and floats), arrays, and so on. For each of these, there's a specific function that checks if a variable is of that type (**Table 13.2**). You've already seen the `is_numeric()` function in action in earlier chapters, and `is_array()` is great for

continues on next page

Two Validation Approaches

A large part of security is based upon validation: if data comes from outside of the server—from HTML forms, the URL, cookies, it can't be trusted. (A higher level of security also validates any data coming from outside of the *script*, including sessions and databases.) There are two types of validation: *whitelist* and *blacklist*. In the calculator example, we know that all values must be positive, that they must all be numbers, and that the quantity must be an integer (the other two numbers could be integers or floats, it makes no difference). Typecasting forces the inputs to be numbers, and a check confirms that they are positive. At this point, the assumption is that the input is valid. This is a whitelist approach: these values are good; anything else is bad.

The preventing spam example uses a blacklist approach. That script knows exactly which characters are bad and invalidates input that contains them. All other input is considered to be good.

Many security experts prefer the whitelist approach, but it can't always be used. Each example will dictate which approach will work best, but it's important to use one or the other. Don't just assume that data is safe without some sort of validation.

confirming a variable is acceptable to use in a **foreach** loop. Each function returns TRUE if the submitted variable is of a certain type and FALSE otherwise.

In PHP, you can even change a variable's type, after it's been assigned a value. Doing so is called *typecasting* and is accomplished by preceding a variable's name by the destination type in parentheses:

```
$var = 20.2;
echo (int) $var; // 20
```

Depending upon the original and destination types, PHP will convert the variable's value accordingly:

```
$var = 20;
echo (float) $var; // 20.0
```

With numeric values, the conversion is straightforward, but with other variable types, more complex rules apply:

```
$var = 'trout';
echo (int) $var; // 0
```

In most circumstances you don't need to cast a variable from one type to another, as PHP will often automatically do so as needed. But forcibly casting a variable's type can be a good security measure in your Web applications. To show how you might use this notion, let's create a calculator script for determining the total purchase price of an item **A**.

To use typecasting:

1. Begin a new PHP document in your text editor or IDE, to be named **calculator.php** (Script 13.2):

```
<!DOCTYPE html PUBLIC "-//W3C//
→ DTD XHTML 1.0 Transitional//EN"
→ "http://www.w3.org/TR/xhtml1/DTD/
→ xhtml1-transitional.dtd">
<html xmlns="http://www.w3.org/
→ 1999/xhtml" xml:lang="en"
→ lang="en">
```

A The HTML form takes three inputs: a quantity, a price, and a tax rate.

Script 13.2 By *typecasting* variables, this script more definitively validates that data is of the correct format.

```
1    <!DOCTYPE html PUBLIC "-//W3C//DTD XHTML
     1.0 Transitional//EN" "http://www.w3.org/
     TR/xhtml1/DTD/xhtml1-transitional.dtd">
2    <html xmlns="http://www.w3.org/1999/
     xhtml" xml:lang="en" lang="en">
3    <head>
4        <meta http-equiv="Content-Type"
         content="text/html; charset=utf-8" />
5        <title>Widget Cost Calculator</title>
6    </head>
7    <body>
8    <?php # Script 13.2 - calculator.php
9    // This script calculates an order total
     based upon three form values.
10
11   // Check if the form has been submitted:
12   if ($_SERVER['REQUEST_METHOD'] == 'POST') {
13
14       // Cast all the variables to a
         specific type:
15       $quantity = (int) $_POST['quantity'];
16       $price = (float) $_POST['price'];
17       $tax = (float) $_POST['tax'];
18
19       // All variables should be positive!
20       if ( ($quantity > 0) && ($price >
         0) && ($tax > 0) ) {
```

code continues on next page

```
21
22            // Calculate the total:
23            $total = $quantity * $price;
24            $total += $total * ($tax/100);
25
26            // Print the result:
27            echo '<p>The total cost of purchasing
              ' . $quantity . ' widget(s) at $' .
              number_format ($price, 2) . ' each,
              plus tax, is $' . number_format
              ($total, 2) . '.</p>';
28
29        } else { // Invalid submitted values.
30            echo '<p style="font-weight: bold;
              color: #C00">Please enter a valid
              quantity, price, and tax rate.</p>';
31        }
32
33    } // End of main isset() IF.
34
35    // Leave the PHP section and create the
      HTML form.
36    ?>
37    <h2>Widget Cost Calculator</h2>
38    <form action="calculator.php"
      method="post">
39        <p>Quantity: <input type="text"
          name="quantity" size="5" maxlength="10"
          value="<?php if (isset($quantity)) echo
          $quantity; ?>" /></p>
40        <p>Price: <input type="text"
          name="price" size="5" maxlength="10"
          value="<?php if (isset($price)) echo
          $price; ?>" /></p>
41        <p>Tax (%): <input type="text"
          name="tax" size="5" maxlength="10"
          value="<?php if (isset($tax)) echo
          $tax; ?>" /></p>
42        <p><input type="submit" name="submit"
          value="Calculate!" /></p>
43    </form>
44    </body>
45    </html>
```

```
<head>
    <meta http-equiv="Content-Type"
    → content="text/html;
    → charset=utf-8" />
    <title>Widget Cost Calculator
    → </title>
</head>
<body>
<?php # Script 13.2 -
→ calculator.php
```

2. **Check if the form has been submitted:**

```
if ($_SERVER['REQUEST_METHOD'] ==
→ 'POST') {
```

Like many previous examples, this one script will both display the HTML form and handle its submission.

3. **Cast all the variables to a specific type:**

```
$quantity = (int) $_POST['quantity'];
$price = (float) $_POST['price'];
$tax = (float) $_POST['tax'];
```

The form itself has three text boxes Ⓐ, into which practically anything could be typed (there's no number type of input for forms in HTML 4 or XHTML 1.1). But the quantity must be an integer, and both price and tax are acceptable as floats (i.e., could contain decimal points). To force these constraints, cast each one to a specific type.

4. **Check if the variables have proper values:**

```
if ( ($quantity > 0) &&
→ ($price > 0) && ($tax > 0) ) {
```

For this calculator to work, the three variables must be specific types (see Step 3). More importantly, they must all be positive numbers. This conditional checks for that prior to performing the calculations. Note that, per the rules of typecasting, if the posted values are not numbers, they will be cast to 0 and therefore not pass this conditional.

continues on next page

5. Calculate and print the results:

```php
$total = $quantity * $price;
$total += $total * ($tax/100);
echo '<p>The total cost of
→ purchasing ' . $quantity . '
→ widget(s) at $' . number_format
→ ($price, 2) . ' each, plus tax,
→ is $' . number_format
→ ($total, 2) . '.</p>';
```

To calculate the total, first the quantity is multiplied by the price. To apply the tax to the total, the value of the total times the tax divided by 100 (e.g., 6.5% becomes .065) is then added, using the addition assignment shortcut operator. The **number_format( )** function is used to print both the price and total values in the proper format **B**.

6. Complete the conditionals:

```php
    } else {
        echo '<p style="font-weight:
→ bold; color: #C00">Please
→ enter a valid quantity,
→ price, and tax rate.</p>';
    }
} // End of main isset( ) IF.
```

A little CSS is used to create a bold, red error message, should there be a problem **C**.

7. Begin the HTML form:

```php
?>
<h2>Widget Cost Calculator</h2>
<form action="calculator.php"
→ method="post">
    <p>Quantity: <input type="text"
→ name="quantity" size="5"
→ maxlength="10" value="<?php
→ if (isset($quantity)) echo
→ $quantity; ?>" /></p>
```

The HTML form is really simple and posts back to this same page. The inputs will have a sticky quality, so the user can see what was previously

B The results of the calculation when the form is properly completed.

C An error message is printed in bold, red text if any of the three fields does not contain a positive number.

entered. By referring to **$quantity** etc. instead of **$_POST['quantity']** etc., the form will reflect the value for each input *as it was typecast*.

8. Complete the HTML form:

```
<p>Price: <input type="text"
→ name="price" size="5"
→ maxlength="10" value="<?php
→ if (isset($price)) echo
→ $price; ?>" /></p>
<p>Tax (%): <input type="text"
→ name="tax" size="5"
→ maxlength="10" value="<?php
→ if (isset($tax)) echo
→ $tax; ?>" /></p>
<p><input type="submit"
→ name="submit" value=
→ "Calculate!" /></p>
</form>
```

9. Complete the HTML page:

```
</body>
</html>
```

10. Save the file as **calculator.php**, place it in your Web directory, and test it in your Web browser ❶ and ❷.

TIP You should definitely use typecasting when working with numbers within SQL queries. Numbers aren't quoted in queries, so if a string is somehow used in a number's place, there will be an SQL syntax error. If you typecast such variables to an integer or float first, the query may not work (in terms of returning a record) but will still be syntactically valid. You'll frequently see this in the book's last three chapters.

TIP As I implied, regular expressions are a more advanced method of data validation and are sometimes your best bet. But using type-based validation, when feasible, will certainly be faster (in terms of processor speed) and less prone to programmer error (did I mention that regular expressions are complex?).

TIP To repeat myself, the rules of how values are converted from one data type to another are somewhat complicated. If you want to get into the details, see the PHP manual.

❶ If invalid values are entered, such as floats for the quantity or strings for the tax...

❷ ...they'll be cast into more appropriate formats. The negative price will also keep this calculation from being made (although the casting won't change that value).

Validating Files by Type

Chapter 11 includes an example of handling file uploads in PHP. As uploading files allows users to place a more potent type of content on your server (compared with just the text sent via a form), one cannot be too mindful of security when it comes to handling them. In that particular example, the uploaded file was validated by checking its MIME type. Specifically, with an uploaded file, `$_FILES['upload']['type']` refers to the MIME type provided by the uploading browser. This is a good start, but it's easy for a malicious user to trick the browser into providing a false MIME type. A more reliable way of confirming a file's type is to use the Fileinfo extension.

Added in PHP 5.3, the Fileinfo extension determines a file's type (and encoding) by hunting for "magic bytes" or "magic numbers" within the file. For example, the data that makes up a GIF image must begin with the ASCII code that represents either *GIF89a* or *GIF87a*; the data that makes up a PDF file starts with *%PDF*.

To use Fileinfo, start by creating a Fileinfo resource:

`$fileinfo = finfo_open(kind);`

The *kind* value will be one of several constants, indicating the type of resource you want to create. To determine a file's type, the constant is `FILEINFO_MIME_TYPE`:

```
$fileinfo = finfo_open
→ (FILEINFO_MIME_TYPE);
```

Next, call the `finfo_file()` function, providing the Fileinfo resource and a reference to the file you want to examine:

`finfo_file($fileinfo, $filename);`

This function returns the file's MIME type (given the already created resource), based upon the file's actual magic bytes.

Finally, once you're done, you should close the Fileinfo resource:

`finfo_close($fileinfo);`

This next script will use this information to confirm that an uploaded file is an RTF (Rich Text Format). Note that you'll only be able to test this example if you are using version 5.3 of PHP or later **A**. If you are using an earlier version, you'll need to install the Fileinfo extension through PECL (PHP Extension Community Library, `http://pecl.php.net`). On Windows, if you are using PHP 5.3 or later, the Fileinfo DLL file should be included with your installation, but you may need to enable it in your `php.ini` configuration file (download Appendix A, "Installation" from peachpit.com).

Fatal error: Call to undefined function finfo_open() in C:\xampp\htdocs\upload_rtf.php on line **18**

A If your PHP installation does not support the Fileinfo extension, you'll see an error message like this one.

Script 13.3 Using the Fileinfo extension, this script does a good job of confirming an uploaded file's type.

```
1    <!DOCTYPE html PUBLIC "-//W3C//DTD XHTML
     1.0 Transitional//EN" "http://www.w3.org/
     TR/xhtml1/DTD/xhtml1-transitional.dtd">
2    <html xmlns="http://www.w3.org/1999/
     xhtml" xml:lang="en" lang="en">
3    <head>
4        <meta http-equiv="Content-Type"
         content="text/html; charset=utf-8" />
5        <title>Upload a RTF Document</title>
6    </head>
7    <body>
8    <?php # Script 13.3 - upload_rtf.php
9
10   // Check if the form has been submitted:
11   if ($_SERVER['REQUEST_METHOD'] == 'POST')
     {
12
13       // Check for an uploaded file:
14       if (isset($_FILES['upload']) && file_
         exists($_FILES['upload']['tmp_name'])) {
15
16           // Validate the type. Should be
     RTF.
17           // Create the resource:
18           $fileinfo = finfo_open
             (FILEINFO_MIME_TYPE);
19
20           // Check the file:
21           if (finfo_file($fileinfo,
             $_FILES['upload']['tmp_name']) ==
             'text/rtf') {
22
23               // Indicate it's okay!
24               echo '<p><em>The file would be
                 acceptable!</em></p>';
25
26               // In theory, move the file over.
                 In reality, delete the file:
27               unlink($_FILES['upload']
                 ['tmp_name']);
28
29           } else { // Invalid type.
30               echo '<p style="font-weight:
                 bold; color: #C00">Please
                 upload an RTF document.</p>';
31           }
32
```

code continues on next page

To validate files by type:

1. Begin a new PHP script in your text editor or IDE, to be named **upload_rtf.php** (Script 13.3):

   ```
   <!DOCTYPE html PUBLIC "-//W3C//
   → DTD XHTML 1.0 Transitional//EN"
   → "http://www.w3.org/TR/xhtml1/DTD/
   → xhtml1-transitional.dtd">
   <html xmlns="http://www.w3.org/
   → 1999/xhtml" xml:lang="en"
   → lang="en">
   <head>
       <meta http-equiv="Content-Type"
       → content="text/html;
       → charset=utf-8" />
       <title>Upload a RTF Document
       → </title>
   </head>
   <body>
   <?php # Script 13.3 -
   → upload_rtf.php
   ```

2. Check if the form has been submitted:

   ```
   if ($_SERVER['REQUEST_METHOD'] ==
   → 'POST') {
   ```

   This same script will both display and handle the form.

3. Check for an uploaded file:

   ```
   if (isset($_FILES['upload']) &&
   → file_exists($_FILES['upload']
   → ['tmp_name'])) {
   ```

   This script first confirms that the **$_FILES['upload']** variable is set, which would be the case after a form submission. The conditional then confirms that the uploaded file exists (by default, in the temporary directory). This clause prevents attempts to validate the file's type should the upload have failed (e.g., because the selected file was too large).

continues on next page

4. Create the Fileinfo resource:

```
$fileinfo = finfo_open
→(FILEINFO_MIME_TYPE);
```

This line, as already explained, creates a Fileinfo resource whose specific purpose is to retrieve a file's MIME type.

5. Check the file's type:

```
if (finfo_file($fileinfo,
→$_FILES['upload']['tmp_name']) ==
→'text/rtf') {
    echo '<p><em>The file would be
    →acceptable!</em></p>';
```

If the **finfo_file( )** function returns a value of *text/rtf* for the uploaded file, then the file has the proper type for the purposes of this script. In that case, a message is printed **B**.

6. Delete the uploaded file:

```
unlink($_FILES['upload']
→['tmp_name']);
```

In a real-world example, the script would now move the file over to its final destination on the server. As this script is simply for the purpose of validating a file's type, the file can be removed instead.

7. Complete the type conditional:

```
} else { // Invalid type.
    echo '<p style="font-weight:
    →bold; color: #C00">Please
    →upload an RTF document.</p>';
}
```

Script 13.3 *continued*

```
33        // Close the resource:
34        finfo_close($fileinfo);
35
36    } // End of isset($_FILES['upload'])
IF.
37
38        // Add file upload error handling, if
          desired.
39
40    } // End of the submitted conditional.
41    ?>
42
43    <form enctype="multipart/form-data"
      action="upload_rtf.php" method="post">
44        <input type="hidden" name="MAX_FILE_
          SIZE" value="524288" />
45        <fieldset><legend>Select an RTF
          document of 512KB or smaller to be
          uploaded:</legend>
46        <p><b>File:</b> <input type="file"
          name="upload" /></p>
47        </fieldset>
48        <div align="center"><input
          type="submit" name="submit"
          value="Submit" /></div>
49    </form>
50    </body>
51    </html>
```

B If the selected and uploaded document has a valid RTF MIME type, the user will see this result.

If the uploaded file's MIME type is not *text/rtf*, the script will print an error message **C**.

8. Close the Fileinfo resource:

```
finfo_close($fileinfo);
```

The final step is to close the open Fileinfo resource, once it's no longer needed.

9. Complete the remaining conditionals:

```
} // End of isset($_FILES
→['upload']) IF.
} // End of the submitted
→conditional.
?>
```

You could also add debugging information, such as the related uploaded error message, if an error occurs.

10. Create the form:

```
<form enctype="multipart/
→form-data" action="upload_rtf.
→php" method="post">
  <input type="hidden" name=
  →"MAX_FILE_SIZE" value="524288" />
```

```
<fieldset><legend>Select an RTF
→document of 512KB or smaller
→to be uploaded:</legend>
<p><b>File:</b> <input type=
→"file" name="upload" /></p>
</fieldset>
<div align="center"><input
→type="submit" name="submit"
→value="Submit" /></div>
</form>
```

The form uses the proper **enctype** attribute, has a **MAX_FILE_SIZE** recommendation in a hidden form input, and uses a file input type: the three requirements for accepting file uploads. That's all there is to this example (as in **B** and **C**).

11. Complete the page:

```
</body>
</html>
```

12. Save the file as **upload_rtf.php**, place it in your Web directory, and test it in your Web browser.

TIP The same Fileinfo resource can be applied to multiple files. Just close the resource after the script is done with the resource.

C Uploaded files without the proper MIME type are rejected.

Preventing XSS Attacks

HTML is simply plain text, like **<b>**, which is given special meaning by Web browsers (as by making text bold). Because of this fact, your Web-site's user could easily put HTML in their form data, like in the comments field in the email example. What's wrong with that, you might ask?

Many dynamically driven Web applications take the information submitted by a user, store it in a database, and then redisplay that information on another page. Think of a forum, as just one example. At the very least, if a user enters HTML code in their data, such code could throw off the layout and aesthetic of your site. Taking this a step further, JavaScript is also just plain text, but text that has special meaning—*executable* meaning—within a Web browser. If malicious code entered into a form were re-displayed in a Web browser **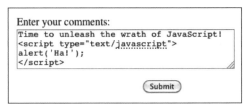**, it could create pop-up windows ****, steal cookies, or redirect the browser to other sites. Such attacks are referred to as *cross-site scripting* (XSS). As in the email example, where you need to look for and nullify bad strings found in data, prevention of XSS attacks is accomplished by addressing any potentially dangerous PHP, HTML, or JavaScript.

PHP includes a handful of functions for handling HTML and other code found within strings. These include:

- **htmlspecialchars( )**, which turns &, ', ", <, and > into an HTML *entity* format (*&*, *"*, etc.)

- **htmlentities( )**, which turns all applicable characters into their HTML entity format

- **strip_tags( )**, which removes all HTML and PHP tags

These three functions are roughly listed in order from least disruptive to most. Which

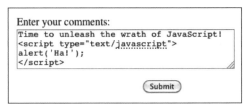

A The malicious and savvy user can enter HTML, CSS, and JavaScript into textual form fields.

B The JavaScript entered into the comments field **A** would create this alert window when the comments were displayed in the Web browser.

C Thanks to the **htmlentities( )** and **strip_tags( )** functions, malicious code entered into a form field **A** can be rendered inert.

Script 13.4 Applying the `htmlentities()` and `strip_tags()` functions to submitted text can prevent XSS attacks.

```
1   <!DOCTYPE html PUBLIC "-//W3C//DTD XHTML
    1.0 Transitional//EN" "http://www.w3.org/
    TR/xhtml1/DTD/xhtml1-transitional.dtd">
2   <html xmlns="http://www.w3.org/1999/
    xhtml" xml:lang="en" lang="en">
3   <head>
4       <meta http-equiv="Content-Type"
        content="text/html; charset=utf-8" />
5       <title>XSS Attacks</title>
6   </head>
7   <body>
8   <?php # Script 13.4 - xss.php
9
10  if ($_SERVER['REQUEST_METHOD'] == 'POST') {
11
12      // Apply the different functions,
        printing the results:
13      echo "<h2>Original</h2><p>{$_POST
        ['data']}</p>";
14      echo '<h2>After htmlentities()
        </h2><p>' . htmlentities($_POST
        ['data']). '</p>';
15      echo '<h2>After strip_tags()
        </h2><p>' . strip_tags($_POST
        ['data']). '</p>';
16
17  }
18  // Display the form:
19  ?>
20  <form action="xss.php" method="post">
21      <p>Do your worst! <textarea name="data"
        rows="3" cols="40"></textarea></p>
22      <div align="center"><input
        type="submit" name="submit"
        value="Submit" /></div>
23  </form>
24  </body>
25  </html>
```

function you'll want to use depends upon the application at hand. To demonstrate how these functions work and differ, let's just create a simple PHP page that takes some text and runs it through these functions, printing the results **C**.

To prevent XSS attacks:

1. Begin a new PHP document in your text editor or IDE, to be named **xss.php** (**Script 13.4**):

   ```
   <!DOCTYPE html PUBLIC "-//W3C//
   → DTD XHTML 1.0 Transitional//EN"
   → "http://www.w3.org/TR/xhtml1/DTD/
   → xhtml1-transitional.dtd">
   <html xmlns="http://www.w3.org/
   → 1999/xhtml" xml:lang="en"
   → lang="en">
   <head>
     <meta http-equiv="Content-Type"
   → content="text/html;
   → charset=utf-8" />
     <title>XSS Attacks</title>
   </head>
   <body>
   <?php # Script 13.4 - xss.php
   ```

2. Check for the form submission and print the received data in its original format:

   ```
   if ($_SERVER['REQUEST_METHOD'] ==
   → 'POST') {
     echo "<h2>Original</h2>
   → <p>{$_POST['data']}</p>";
   ```

   To compare and contrast what was originally received with the result after applying the functions, the original value must first be printed.

3. Apply the **htmlentities()** function, printing the results:

   ```
   echo '<h2>After htmlentities()
   → </h2><p>' . htmlentities($_POST
   → ['data']). '</p>';
   ```

continues on next page

To keep submitted information from messing up a page or hacking the Web browser, it's run through the **htmlentities( )** function. With this function, any HTML entity will be translated; for instance, **<** and **>** will become *<* and *>* respectively.

4. Apply the **strip_tags( )** function, printing the results:

```
echo '<h2>After strip_tags()
→ </h2><p>' . strip_tags($_POST
→ ['data']). '</p>';
```

The **strip_tags( )** function completely takes out any HTML, JavaScript, or PHP tags. It's therefore the most foolproof function to use on submitted data.

5. Complete the PHP section:

```
}
?>
```

6. Display the HTML form:

```
<form action="xss.php" method=
→ "post">
  <p>Do your worst! <textarea
→ name="data" rows="3"
→ cols="40"></textarea></p>
  <div align="center"><input
→ type="submit" name="submit"
→ value="Submit" /></div>
</form>
```

The form **A** has only one field for the user to complete: a textarea.

7. Complete the page:

```
</body>
</html>
```

8. Save the page as **xss.php**, place it in your Web directory, and test it in your Web browser.

9. View the source code of the page to see the full effect of these functions **D**.

TIP Both htmlspecialchars( ) and htmlentities( ) take an optional parameter indicating how quotation marks should be handled. See the PHP manual for specifics.

TIP The strip_tags( ) function takes an optional parameter indicating what tags should *not* be stripped.

```
$var = strip_tags ($var, '<p><br />');
```

TIP The strip_tags( ) function will remove even invalid HTML tags, which may cause problems. For example, strip_tags( ) will yank out all of the code it thinks is an HTML tag, even if it's improperly formed, like *<b I forgot to close the tag*.

TIP Unrelated to security but quite useful is the nl2br( ) function. It turns every return (such as those entered into a text area) into an HTML <br /> tag.

```
<h2>Original</h2><p>Time to unleash the wrath of
  JavaScript! <script type="text/javascript">
alert('Ha!');
</script></p><h2>After htmlentities()</h2><p>Time to
  unleash the wrath of JavaScript! &lt;script
  type=&quot;text/javascript&quot;&gt;
alert('Ha!');
&lt;/script&gt;</p><h2>After strip_tags()</h2><p>Time to
  unleash the wrath of JavaScript!
alert('Ha!');
</p><form action="xss.php" method="post">
```

D This snippet of the page's HTML source **C** shows the original, submitted value, the value after using **html_entities( )**, and the value after using **strip_tags( )**.

Using the Filter Extension

Earlier, this chapter introduced the concept of *typecasting*, which is a good way to force a variable to be of the right type. In the next chapter, you'll learn about *regular expressions*, which can validate both the type of data and its specific contents or format. Introduced in PHP 5.2 is the Filter extension (**www.php.net/filter**), an important tool that bridges the gap between the relatively simple approach of typecasting and the more complex concept of regular expressions.

The Filter extension can be used for one of two purposes: *validating* data or *sanitizing* it. A validation process, as you know well by now, confirms that data matches expectations. Sanitization, by comparison, alters data by removing inappropriate characters in order to make the data meet expectations.

The most important function in the Filter extension is `filter_var( )`:

```
filter_var(variable, filter
→ [,options]);
```

The function's first argument is the variable to be filtered; the second is the filter to apply; and, the optional third argument is for adding additional criteria. **Table 13.3** lists the validation filters, each of which is represented as a constant.

For example, to confirm that a variable has a decimal value, you would use:

```
if (filter_var($var, FILTER_VALIDATE_
→ FLOAT)) {
```

A couple of filters take an optional parameter, the most common being the **FILTER_VALIDATE_INT** filter, which has *min_range* and *max_range* options for controlling the smallest and largest acceptable values. For example, this next bit of code confirms that the **$age** variable is an integer between 1 and 120 (inclusive):

```
if (filter_var($var, FILTER_VALIDATE_
→ INT, array('min_range' => 1,
→ 'max_range' => 120))) {
```

To sanitize data, you'll still use the **filter_var( )** function, but use one of the sanitation filters as listed in **Table 13.4**.

continues on next page

TABLE 13.3 Validation Filters

Constant
FILTER_VALIDATE_BOOLEAN
FILTER_VALIDATE_EMAIL
FILTER_VALIDATE_FLOAT
FILTER_VALIDATE_INT
FILTER_VALIDATE_IP
FILTER_VALIDATE_REGEXP
FILTER_VALIDATE_URL

TABLE 13.4 Sanitization Filters

Constant
FILTER_SANITIZE_EMAIL
FILTER_SANITIZE_ENCODED
FILTER_SANITIZE_MAGIC_QUOTES
FILTER_SANITIZE_NUMBER_FLOAT
FILTER_SANITIZE_NUMBER_INT
FILTER_SANITIZE_SPECIAL_CHARS
FILTER_SANITIZE_STRING
FILTER_SANITIZE_STRIPPED
FILTER_SANITIZE_URL
FILTER_UNSAFE_RAW

Many of the filters duplicate other PHP functions. For example, **FILTER_SANITIZE_MAGIC_QUOTES** is the same as applying **addslashes( )**; **FILTER_SANITIZE_SPECIAL_CHARS** can be used in lieu of **htmlspecialchars( )**, and **FILTER_SANITIZE_STRING( )** can be used as a replacement for **strip_tags( )**. The PHP manual lists several additional flags, as constants, that can be used as the optional third argument to affect how each filter behaves. As an example of applying a sanitizing filter, this code is equivalent to how **strip_tags( )** is used in **xss.php** (Script 13.4):

```
echo '<h2>After strip_tags( )</h2>
→ <p>' . filter_var($_POST['data'],
→ FILTER_SANITIZE_STRING) . '</p>';
```

If you get hooked on using the Filter extension, you may appreciate the consistency of being able to use it for all data sanitization, even when functions such as **strip_tags( )** exist.

To practice this, the next example will update **calculator.php** (Script 13.2) so that it sanitizes all of the incoming data. Remember that you need PHP 5.2 or later to use the Filter extension. If you're using an earlier version of PHP, you can install the Filter extension using PECL.

To use the Filter extension:

1. Open **calculator.php** (Script 13.2) in your text editor or IDE.

2. Change the assignment of the **$quantity** variable to (**Script 13.5**):

```
$quantity = (isset($_POST
→ ['quantity'])) ? filter_var
→ ($_POST['quantity'], FILTER_
→ VALIDATE_INT, array('min_range'
→ => 1)) : NULL;
```

Script 13.5 Using the Filter extension, this script sanitizes incoming data rather than typecasting it, as in the earlier version of the script.

```
1    <!DOCTYPE html PUBLIC "-//W3C//DTD XHTML
     1.0 Transitional//EN" "http://www.w3.org/
     TR/xhtml1/DTD/xhtml1-transitional.dtd">
2    <html xmlns="http://www.w3.org/1999/
     xhtml" xml:lang="en" lang="en">
3    <head>
4        <meta http-equiv="Content-Type"
         content="text/html; charset=utf-8" />
5        <title>Widget Cost Calculator</title>
6    </head>
7    <body>
8    <?php # Script 13.5 - calculator.php #2
9    // This version of the script uses the
         Filter extension instead of typecasting.
10
11   // Check if the form has been submitted:
12   if ($_SERVER['REQUEST_METHOD'] == 'POST') {
13
14       // Sanitize the variables:
15       $quantity = (isset($_POST
         ['quantity'])) ? filter_var($_POST
         ['quantity'], FILTER_VALIDATE_INT,
         array('min_range' => 1)) : NULL;
16       $price = (isset($_POST['price']))
         ? filter_var($_POST['price'],
         FILTER_SANITIZE_NUMBER_FLOAT,
         FILTER_FLAG_ALLOW_FRACTION) : NULL;
17       $tax = (isset($_POST['tax'])) ?
         filter_var($_POST['tax'], FILTER_
         SANITIZE_NUMBER_FLOAT, FILTER_FLAG_
         ALLOW_FRACTION) : NULL;
18
19       // All variables should be positive!
20       if ( ($quantity > 0) && ($price > 0)
         && ($tax > 0) ) {
21
22           // Calculate the total:
23           $total = $quantity * $price;
24           $total += $total * ($tax/100);
25
26           // Print the result:
27           echo '<p>The total cost of
             purchasing ' . $quantity . '
             widget(s) at $' . number_format
             ($price, 2) . ' each, plus tax,
             is $' . number_format ($total, 2) .
             '.</p>';
28
```

code continues on next page

```
29      } else { // Invalid submitted values.
30          echo '<p style="font-weight: bold;
            color: #C00">Please enter a valid
            quantity, price, and tax rate.</p>';
31      }
32
33  } // End of main isset() IF.
34
35  // Leave the PHP section and create the
    HTML form.
36  ?>
37  <h2>Widget Cost Calculator</h2>
38  <form action="calculator.php"
    method="post">
39      <p>Quantity: <input type="text"
        name="quantity" size="5" maxlength="10"
        value="<?php if (isset($quantity)) echo
        $quantity; ?>" /></p>
40      <p>Price: <input type="text"
        name="price" size="5" maxlength="10"
        value="<?php if (isset($price)) echo
        $price; ?>" /></p>
41      <p>Tax (%): <input type="text"
        name="tax" size="5" maxlength="10"
        value="<?php if (isset($tax)) echo
        $tax; ?>" /></p>
42      <p><input type="submit" name="submit"
        value="Calculate!" /></p>
43  </form>
44  </body>
45  </html>
```

This version of the script will improve upon its predecessor in a couple of ways. First, each POST variable is checked for existence using **isset( )**, instead of assuming the variable exists. If the variable is not set, then **$quantity** is assigned **NULL**. If the variable is set, it's run through **filter_var( )**, sanitizing the value as an integer greater than 1. The sanitized value is then assigned to **$quantity**. All of this code is written using the ternary operator, introduced in Chapter 10, "Common Programming Techniques," for brevity's sake. As an **if-else** conditional, the same code would be written as:

```
if (isset($_POST['quantity'])) {
    $quantity = filter_var($_POST
    ['quantity'], FILTER_VALIDATE_
    INT, array('min_range' => 1));
} else {
    $quantity = NULL;
}
```

3. Change the assignment of the **$price** variable to:

```
$price = (isset($_POST['price'])) ?
filter_var($_POST['price'],
FILTER_SANITIZE_NUMBER_FLOAT,
FILTER_FLAG_ALLOW_FRACTION) :
NULL;
```

This code is a repetition of that in Step 2, except that the sanitizing filter insists that the data be a float. The additional argument, **FILTER_FLAG_ALLOW_FRACTION**, says that it's acceptable for the value to use a decimal point.

continues on next page

4. Change the assignment of the **$tax** variable to:

```
$tax = (isset($_POST['tax'])) ?
→ filter_var($_POST['tax'],
→ FILTER_SANITIZE_NUMBER_FLOAT,
→ FILTER_FLAG_ALLOW_FRACTION) :
→ NULL;
```

This is a repetition of the code in Step 3.

5. Save the page, place it in your Web directory, and test it in your Web browser **Ⓐ** and **Ⓑ**.

> **TIP** The `filter_has_var( )` function confirms if a variable with a given name exists.

> **TIP** The `filter_input_array( )` function allows you to apply an array of filters to an array of variables in one step. For details (and perhaps to be blown away), see the PHP manual.

Widget Cost Calculator

Quantity: `1.5`

Price: `-20.9`

Tax (%): `cat`

(Calculate!)

Ⓐ Invalid values in submitted form data...

Please enter a valid quantity, price, and tax rate.

Widget Cost Calculator

Quantity: [   ]

Price: `-20.9`

Tax (%): [   ]

(Calculate!)

Ⓑ ...will be nullified by the Filter extension (as opposed to typecasting, which, for example, converted the string *cat* to the number 0).

Preventing SQL Injection Attacks

Another type of attack that malicious users can attempt is *SQL injection* attacks. As the name implies, these are endeavors to insert bad code into a site's SQL queries. One aim of such attacks is that they would create a syntactically invalid query, thereby revealing something about the script or database in the resulting error message **A**. An even bigger aspiration is that the injection attack could alter, destroy, or expose the stored data.

Fortunately, SQL injection attacks are rather easy to prevent. Start by validating all data to be used in queries (and perform typecasting, or apply the Filter extension, whenever possible). Second, use a function like `mysqli_real_escape_string( )`, which makes data safe to use in queries. This function was introduced in Chapter 9, "Using PHP and MySQL." Third, don't show detailed errors on live sites.

An alternative to using `mysqli_real_escape_string( )` is to use *prepared statements*. Prepared statements were added to MySQL in version 4.1, and PHP

continues on next page

You could not be registered due to a system error. We apologize for any inconvenience.

You have an error in your SQL syntax; check the manual that corresponds to your MySQL server version for the right syntax to use near '";DELETE TABLE user', 'Ullman', 'email3@example.com', SHA1('password'), NOW())' at line 1

Query: INSERT INTO users (first_name, last_name, email, pass, registration_date) VALUES ('";DELETE TABLE user', 'Ullman', 'email3@example.com', SHA1('password'), NOW())

A If a site reveals a detailed error message and doesn't properly handle problematic characters in submitted values, hackers can learn a lot about your server.

Prepared Statement Performance

Prepared statements can be more secure than running queries in the old-fashioned way, but they may also be faster. If a PHP script sends the same query to MySQL multiple times, using different values each time, prepared statements can really speed things up. In such cases, the query itself is only sent to MySQL and parsed once. Then, the values are sent to MySQL separately.

As a trivial example, the following code would run 100 queries in MySQL:

```
$q = 'INSERT INTO counter (num) VALUES (?)';
$stmt = mysqli_prepare($dbc, $q);
mysqli_stmt_bind_param($stmt, 'i', $n);
for ($n = 1; $n <= 100; $n++) {
        mysqli_stmt_execute($stmt);
}
```

Even though the query is being run 100 times, the full text is only being transferred to, and parsed by, MySQL once. MySQL versions 5.1.17 and later include a caching mechanism that may also improve the performance of other uses of prepared statements.

can use them as of version 5 (thanks to the Improved MySQL extension). When not using prepared statements, the entire query, including the SQL syntax and the specific values, is sent to MySQL as one long string. MySQL then parses and executes it. With a prepared query, the SQL syntax is sent to MySQL first, where it is parsed, making sure it's syntactically valid (e.g., confirming that the query does not refer to tables or columns that don't exist). Then the specific values are sent separately; MySQL assembles the query using those values, then executes it. The benefits of prepared statements are important: greater security and potentially better performance. I'll focus on the security aspect here, but see the sidebar for a discussion of performance.

Prepared statements can be created out of any **INSERT**, **UPDATE**, **DELETE**, or **SELECT** query. Begin by defining your query, marking *placeholders* using question marks. As an example, take the **SELECT** query from **edit_user.php** (Script 10.3):

```
$q = "SELECT first_name, last_name,
→ email FROM users WHERE user_id=$id";
```

As a prepared statement, this query becomes

```
$q = "SELECT first_name, last_name,
→ email FROM users WHERE user_id=?";
```

Next, *prepare* the statement in MySQL, assigning the results to a PHP variable:

```
$stmt = mysqli_prepare($dbc, $q);
```

At this point, MySQL will parse the query, but it won't execute it.

Next, you *bind* PHP variables to the query's placeholders. In other words, you state that one variable should be used for the first question mark, another variable for the next question mark, and so on. Continuing with the same example, you would code

```
mysqli_stmt_bind_param($stmt, 'i', $id);
```

The *i* part of the command indicates what kind of value should be expected, using

the characters listed in **Table 13.5**. In this case, the query expects to receive one integer. As another example, here's how the login query from Chapter 12, "Cookies and Sessions," would be handled:

```
$q = "SELECT user_id, first_name
→ FROM users WHERE email=? AND
→ pass=SHA1(?)";
$stmt = mysqli_prepare($dbc, $q);
mysqli_stmt_bind_param($stmt, 'ss',
→ $e, $p);
```

In this example, something interesting is also revealed: even though both the email address and password values are strings, *they are not placed within quotes* in the query. This is another difference between a prepared statement and a standard query.

Once the statement has been bound, you can assign values to the PHP variables (if that hasn't happened already) and then execute the statement. Using the login example, that'd be:

```
$e = 'email@example.com';
$p = 'mypass';
mysqli_stmt_execute($stmt);
```

The values of **$e** and **$p** will be used when the prepared statement is executed.

To see this process in action, let's write a script that adds a post to the *messages* table in the *forum* database (created in Chapter 6, "Database Design"). I'll also use the opportunity to demonstrate a couple of the other prepared statement-related functions.

TABLE 13.5 Bound Value Types

Letter	Represents
d	Decimal
i	Integer
b	Blob (binary data)
s	All other types

Script 13.6 This script, which represents a simplified version of a message posting page, uses prepared statements as a way of preventing SQL injection attacks.

```
1    <!DOCTYPE html PUBLIC "-//W3C//DTD XHTML
     1.0 Transitional//EN" "http://www.w3.org/
     TR/xhtml1/DTD/xhtml1-transitional.dtd">
2    <html xmlns="http://www.w3.org/1999/
     xhtml" xml:lang="en" lang="en">
3    <head>
4        <meta http-equiv="Content-Type"
         content="text/html; charset=utf-8" />
5        <title>Post a Message</title>
6    </head>
7    <body>
8    <?php # Script 13.6 - post_message.php
9
10   if ($_SERVER['REQUEST_METHOD'] == 'POST') {
11
12       // Validate the data (omitted)!
13
14       // Connect to the database:
15       $dbc = mysqli_connect ('localhost',
         'username', 'password', 'forum');
16
17       // Make the query:
18       $q = 'INSERT INTO messages
         (forum_id, parent_id, user_id,
         subject, body, date_entered)
         VALUES (?, ?, ?, ?, ?, NOW( ))';
19
20       // Prepare the statement:
21       $stmt = mysqli_prepare($dbc, $q);
22
23       // Bind the variables:
24       mysqli_stmt_bind_param($stmt,
         'iiiss', $forum_id, $parent_id,
         $user_id, $subject, $body);
25
26       // Assign the values to variables:
27       $forum_id = (int) $_POST['forum_id'];
28       $parent_id = (int) $_POST['parent_id'];
29       $user_id = 3; // The user_id value
         would normally come from the session.
30       $subject = strip_tags($_POST['subject']);
31       $body = strip_tags($_POST['body']);
32
33       // Execute the query:
34       mysqli_stmt_execute($stmt);
35
```

code continues on next page

To use prepared statements:

1. Begin a new PHP script in your text editor or IDE, to be named **post_message.php** (Script 13.6):

```
<!DOCTYPE html PUBLIC "-//W3C//
DTD XHTML 1.0 Transitional//EN"
"http://www.w3.org/TR/xhtml1/DTD/
xhtml1-transitional.dtd">
<html xmlns="http://www.w3.org/
1999/xhtml" xml:lang="en"
lang="en">
<head>
    <meta http-equiv="Content-Type"
    content="text/html;
    charset=utf-8" />
    <title>Post a Message</title>
</head>
<body>
<?php # Script 13.6 -
post_message.php
```

2. Check for form submission and connect to the *forum* database:

```
if ($_SERVER['REQUEST_METHOD'] ==
'POST') {
    $dbc = mysqli_connect
    ('localhost', 'username',
    'password', 'forum');
```

Note that, for brevity's sake, I'm omitting basic data validation and error reporting. Although a real site (a more realized version of this script can be found in Chapter 17, "Example— Message Board"), would check that the message subject and body aren't empty and that the various ID values are positive integers, this script will still be relatively safe, thanks to the security offered by prepared statements.

This example will use the *forum* database, created in Chapter 6.

continues on next page

3. Define and prepare the query:

```
$q = 'INSERT INTO messages
→(forum_id, parent_id, user_id,
→subject, body, date_entered)
→VALUES (?, ?, ?, ?, ?, NOW( ))';
$stmt = mysqli_prepare($dbc, $q);
```

This syntax has already been explained. The query is defined, using placeholders for values to be assigned later. Then the `mysqli_prepare( )` function sends this to MySQL, assigning the result to `$stmt`.

The query itself was first used in Chapter 6. It populates six fields in the *messages* table. The value for the `date_entered` column will be the result of the `NOW( )` function, not a bound value.

4. Bind the appropriate variables and create a list of values to be inserted:

```
mysqli_stmt_bind_param($stmt,
→'iiiss', $forum_id, $parent_id,
→$user_id, $subject, $body);
$forum_id = (int)
→$_POST['forum_id'];
$parent_id = (int)
→$_POST['parent_id'];
$user_id = 3;
$subject = strip_tags($_POST
→['subject']);
$body = strip_tags($_POST['body']);
```

The first line says that three integers and two strings will be used in the prepared statement. The values will be found in the variables to follow.

For those variables, the subject and body values come straight from the form **B**, after running them through `strip_tags( )` to remove any potentially dangerous code. The forum ID and parent ID (which indicates if the message is a reply to an existing message or not) also come from the form. They'll be typecast to integers (for added security, you would confirm that they're positive

Script 13.6 *continued*

```
36      // Print a message based upon the result:
37      if (mysqli_stmt_affected_rows($stmt)
        == 1) {
38          echo '<p>Your message has been
            posted.</p>';
39      } else {
40          echo '<p style="font-weight: bold;
            color: #C00">Your message could
            not be posted.</p>';
41          echo '<p>' . mysqli_stmt_error
            ($stmt) . '</p>';
42      }
43
44      // Close the statement:
45      mysqli_stmt_close($stmt);
46
47      // Close the connection:
48      mysqli_close($dbc);
49
50  } // End of submission IF.
51
52  // Display the form:
53  ?>
54  <form action="post_message.php"
    method="post">
55
56      <fieldset><legend>Post a message:
        </legend>
57
58      <p><b>Subject</b>: <input
        name="subject" type="text" size="30"
        maxlength="100" /></p>
59
60      <p><b>Body</b>: <textarea name="body"
        rows="3" cols="40"></textarea></p>
61
62      </fieldset>
63      <div align="center"><input type="submit"
        name="submit" value="Submit" /></div>
64      <input type="hidden" name="forum_id"
        value="1" />
65      <input type="hidden" name="parent_id"
        value="0" />
66
67  </form>
68  </body>
69  </html>
```

numbers after typecasting them, or you could use the Filter extension).

The user ID value, in a real script, would come from the session, where it would be stored when the user logged in.

5. Execute the query:

```
mysqli_stmt_execute($stmt);
```

Finally, the prepared statement is executed.

6. Print the results of the execution and complete the loop:

```
if (mysqli_stmt_affected_rows
→ ($stmt) == 1) {
  echo '<p>Your message has been
  → posted.</p>';
} else {
  echo '<p style="font-weight:
  → bold; color: #C00">Your message
  → could not be posted.</p>';
  echo '<p>' . mysqli_stmt_error
  → ($stmt) . '</p>';
}
```

The successful insertion of a record can be confirmed using the

mysqli_stmt_affected_rows( ) function, which works as you expect it would (returning the number of affected rows). In that case, a simple message is printed **C**. If a problem occurred, the m**ysqli_stmt_error( )** function returns the specific MySQL error message. This is for your debugging purposes, not to be used in a live site. That being said, often the PHP error message is more useful than that returned by **mysqli_stmt_error( ) D**.

7. Close the statement and the database connection:

```
mysqli_stmt_close($stmt);
mysqli_close($dbc);
```

The first function closes the prepared statement, freeing up the resources. At this point, **$stmt** no longer has a value. The second function closes the database connection.

8. Complete the PHP section:

```
} // End of submission IF.
?>
```

continues on next page

B The simple HTML form.

C If one record in the database was affected by the query, this will be the result.

Warning: mysqli_stmt_bind_param() [function.mysqli-stmt-bind-param]: Number of elements in type definition string doesn't match number of bind variables in **/Users/larryullman/Sites/phpmysql4/post_message.php** on line 24

Your message could not be posted.

No data supplied for parameters in prepared statement

D Error reporting with prepared statements can be confounding sometimes!

9. Begin the form:

```
<form action="post_message.php"
→ method="post">
  <fieldset><legend>Post a
  → message:</legend>
  <p><b>Subject</b>: <input name=
  → "subject" type="text" size="30"
  → maxlength="100" /></p>
```

```
<p><b>Body</b>: <textarea
→ name="body" rows="3"
→ cols="40"></textarea></p>
</fieldset>
```

The form begins with just a subject text input and a textarea for the message's body.

More Security Recommendations

This chapter covers many specific techniques for improving your Web security. Here are a handful of other recommendations:

- Do your best to limit what information is requested from the user, and what the site stores. The less information handled by the site in any way means there's less data to worry about being stolen.

- Make it your job to study, follow, and abide by security recommendations. Don't just rely upon the advice of one chapter, one book, or one author.

- Don't retain user-supplied names for uploaded files. You'll see an alternative solution in Chapter 19, "Example—E-Commerce."

- Watch how database references are used. For example, if a person's user ID is their primary key from the database and this is stored in a cookie (as in Chapter 12), a malicious user just needs to change that cookie value to access another user's account.

- Don't show detailed error messages (this point was repeated in Chapter 8, "Error Handling and Debugging").

- Use cryptography (this is discussed in Chapter 7, "Advanced SQL and MySQL," with respect to the database, and in my book *PHP 5 Advanced: Visual QuickPro Guide* (Peachpit Press, 2007) with respect to the server).

- Don't store credit card numbers, social security numbers, banking information, and the like. The only exception to this would be if you have deep enough pockets to pay for the best security and to cover the lawsuits that arise when this data is stolen from your site (which will inevitably happen).

- Use SSL, when appropriate. A secure connection is one of the best protections a server can offer a user.

- Reliably and consistently protect every page and directory that needs it. Never assume that people won't find sensitive areas just because there's no link to them. If access to a page or directory should be limited, make sure it is.

My final recommendation is to be aware of your own limitations. As the programmer, you probably approach a script thinking how it *should be* used. This is not the same as to how it *will be* used, either accidentally or on purpose. Try to break your site to see what happens. Do bad things, do the wrong thing. Have other people try to break it, too (it's normally easy to find such volunteers). When you code, if you assume that no one will ever use a page properly, it'll be much more secure than if you assume people always will.

10. Complete the form:

```
<div align="center"><input
→ type="submit" name="submit"
→ value="Submit" /></div>
<input type="hidden" name=
→ "forum_id" value="1" />
<input type="hidden" name=
→ "parent_id" value="0" />
</form>
```

The form contains two fields the user would fill out and two hidden inputs that store values the query needs. In a real version of this script, the `forum_id` and `parent_id` values would be determined dynamically.

11. Complete the page:

```
</body>
</html>
```

12. Save the file as **post_message.php**, place it in your Web directory, and test it in your Web browser **E**.

TIP There are two kinds of prepared statements. Here I have demonstrated bound parameters, where PHP variables are bound to a query. The other type is bound results, where the results of a query are bound to PHP variables.

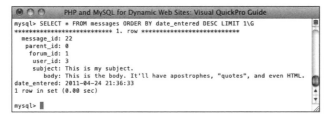

```
PHP and MySQL for Dynamic Web Sites: Visual QuickPro Guide
mysql> SELECT * FROM messages ORDER BY date_entered DESC LIMIT 1\G
*************************** 1. row ***************************
  message_id: 22
   parent_id: 0
    forum_id: 1
     user_id: 3
     subject: This is my subject.
        body: This is the body. It'll have apostrophes, "quotes", and even HTML.
date_entered: 2011-04-24 21:36:33
1 row in set (0.00 sec)

mysql>
```

E Selecting the most recent entry in the *messages* table confirms that the prepared statement (Script 13.6) worked. Notice that the HTML was stripped out of the post but the quotes are still present.

Preventing Brute Force Attacks

A brute force attack is an attempt to log in to a secure system by making lots of attempts in the hopes of eventual success. It's not a sophisticated type of attack, hence the name "brute force." For example, if you have a login process that requires a username and password, there is a limit as to the possible number of username/password combinations. That limit may be in the billions or trillions, but still, it's a finite number. Using algorithms and automated processes, a brute force attack repeatedly tries combinations until they succeed.

The best way to prevent brute force attacks from succeeding is requiring users to register with good, hard-to-guess passwords: containing letters, numbers, and punctuation; both upper and lowercase; words not in the dictionary; at least eight characters long, etc. Also, don't give indications as to why a login failed: saying that a username and password combination isn't correct gives away nothing, but saying that a username isn't right or that the password isn't right for that username says too much.

To stop a brute force attack in its tracks, you could also limit the number of incorrect login attempts by a given IP address. IP addresses do change frequently, but in a brute force attack, the same IP address would be trying to log in multiple times in a matter of minutes. You would have to track incorrect logins by IP address, and then, after *X* number of invalid attempts, block that IP address for 24 hours (or something). Or, if you didn't want to go that far, you could use an "incremental delay" defense: each incorrect login from the same IP address creates an added delay in the response (use PHP's **sleep( )** function to create the delay). Humans might not notice or be bothered by such delays, but automated attacks most certainly would.

Review and Pursue

If you have any problems with the review questions or the pursue prompts, turn to the book's supporting forum (www.LarryUllman.com/forums/).

Review

- What are some of the inappropriate strings and characters that could be indicators of potential spam attempts?

- What does the `stripos()` function do? What is its syntax?

- What does the `str_replace()` function do? What is its syntax?

- What does the `array_map()` function do? What is its syntax?

- What is *typecasting*? How do you typecast a variable in PHP?

- What function is used to move an uploaded file to its final destination on the server?

- What is the Fileinfo extension? How is it used?

- What does the `htmlspecialchars()` function do?

- What does the `htmlentities()` function do?

- What does the `strip_tags()` function do?

- What function converts newline characters into HTML break tags?

- What is the most important function in the Filter extension? How is it used?

- What are prepared statements? What benefits might prepared statements have over the standard method of querying a database?

- What is the syntax for using prepared statements?

Pursue

- If you haven't applied the Filter function, for email validation, and the `spam_scrubber()` function to a contact form used on one of your sites, do so now!

- Change `calculator.php` to allow for no tax rate.

- Update `calculator.php`, from Chapter 3, "Creating Dynamic Web Sites," so that it also uses typecasting or the Filter extension. (As a reminder, that calculator determined the cost of a car trip, based upon the distance, average miles per gallon, and average price paid per gallon.)

- Modify `upload_rtf.php` so that it reports the actual MIME type for the uploaded file, should it not be *text/rtf*.

- Create a PHP script that reports the MIME type of any uploaded file.

- Apply the `strip_tags()` function to a previous script in the book, such as the registration example, to prevent inappropriate code from being stored in the database.

- Apply the Filter function to the login process in Chapter 12 to guarantee that the submitted email address meets the email address format, prior to using it in a query.

- Apply the Filter function, or typecasting, to the `delete_user.php` and `edit_user.php` scripts from Chapter 10.

- Apply the Fileinfo extension to the `show_image.php` script from Chapter 11.

14

Perl-Compatible Regular Expressions

Regular expressions are an amazingly powerful (but tedious) tool available in most of today's programming languages and even in many applications. Think of regular expressions as an elaborate system of matching patterns. You first write the pattern and then use one of PHP's built-in functions to apply the pattern to a value (regular expressions are applied to strings, even if that means a string with a numeric value). Whereas a string function could see if the name *John* is in some text, a regular expression could just as easily find *John*, *Jon*, and *Jonathon*.

Because the regular expression syntax is so complex, while the functions that use them are simple, the focus in this chapter will be on mastering the syntax in little bites. The PHP code will be very simple; later chapters will better incorporate regular expressions into real-world scripts.

Creating a Test Script

As already stated, regular expressions are a matter of applying patterns to values. The application of the pattern to a value is accomplished using one of a handful of functions, the most important being **preg_match( )**. This function returns a 0 or 1, indicating whether or not the pattern matched the string. Its basic syntax is

preg_match(*pattern, subject*);

The **preg_match( )** function will stop once it finds a single match. If you need to find all the matches, use **preg_match_all( )**. That function will be discussed toward the end of the chapter.

When providing the pattern to **preg_ match( )**, it needs to be placed within quotation marks, as it'll be a string. Because many escaped characters within double quotation marks have special meaning (like **\n**), I advocate using single quotation marks to define your patterns.

Secondarily, within the quotation marks, the pattern needs to be encased within *delimiters*. The delimiter can be any character that's not alphanumeric or the backslash, and the same character must be used to mark the beginning and end of the pattern. Commonly, you'll see forward slashes used. To see if the word *cat* contains the letter *a*, you would code (spoiler alert: it does):

if (preg_match('/a/', 'cat')) {

If you need to match a forward slash in the pattern, use a different delimiter, like the pipe (|) or an exclamation mark (!).

The bulk of this chapter covers all the rules for defining patterns. In order to best learn by example, let's start by creating a simple PHP script that takes a pattern and a string **A** and returns the regular expression result **B**.

A The HTML form, which will be used for practicing regular expressions.

B The script will print what values were used in the regular expression and what the result was. The form will also be made sticky to remember previously submitted values.

```
1    <!DOCTYPE html PUBLIC "-//W3C//DTD XHTML
     1.0 Transitional//EN" "http://www.w3.org/
     TR/xhtml1/DTD/xhtml1-transitional.dtd">
2    <html xmlns="http://www.w3.org/1999/
     xhtml" xml:lang="en" lang="en">
3    <head>
4       <meta http-equiv="Content-Type"
        content="text/html; charset=utf-8" />
5       <title>Testing PCRE</title>
6    </head>
7    <body>
8    <?php // Script 14.1 - pcre.php
9    // This script takes a submitted string
     and checks it against a submitted pattern.
10
11   if ($_SERVER['REQUEST_METHOD'] == 'POST') {
12
13      // Trim the strings:
14      $pattern = trim($_POST['pattern']);
15      $subject = trim($_POST['subject']);
16
17      // Print a caption:
18      echo "<p>The result of checking<br />
        <b>$pattern</b><br />against<br />
        $subject<br />is ";
19
20      // Test:
21      if (preg_match ($pattern,
        $subject) ) {
22         echo 'TRUE!</p>';
23      } else {
24         echo 'FALSE!</p>';
25      }
26
27   } // End of submission IF.
28   // Display the HTML form.
29   ?>
30   <form action="pcre.php" method="post">
31      <p>Regular Expression Pattern:
        <input type="text" name="pattern"
        value="<?php if (isset($pattern)) echo
        htmlentities($pattern); ?>" size="40" />
        (include the delimiters)</p>
32      <p>Test Subject: <input type="text"
        name="subject" value="<?php if (isset
        ($subject)) echo htmlentities($subject);
        ?>" size="40" /></p>
33      <input type="submit" name="submit"
        value="Test!" />
34   </form>
35   </body>
36   </html>
```

To match a pattern:

1. Begin a new PHP document in your text editor or IDE, to be named **pcre.php** (Script 14.1).

   ```
   <!DOCTYPE html PUBLIC "-//W3C//
   → DTD XHTML 1.0 Transitional//EN"
   → "http://www.w3.org/TR/xhtml1/DTD/
   → xhtml1-transitional.dtd">
   <html xmlns="http://www.w3.org/
   → 1999/xhtml" xml:lang="en"
   → lang="en">
   <head>
      <meta http-equiv="Content-Type"
      → content="text/html;
      → charset=utf-8" />
      <title>Testing PCRE</title>
   </head>
   <body>
   <?php // Script 14.1 - pcre.php
   ```

2. Check for the form submission:

   ```
   if ($_SERVER['REQUEST_METHOD'] ==
   → 'POST') {
   ```

3. Treat the incoming values:

   ```
   $pattern = trim($_POST['pattern']);
   $subject = trim($_POST['subject']);
   ```

   The form will submit two values to this same script. Both should be trimmed, just to make sure the presence of any extraneous spaces doesn't skew the results. I've omitted a check that each input isn't empty, but you could include that if you wanted.

   continues on next page

Note that if Magic Quotes is enabled on your server, you'll see extra slashes added to the form data **C**. To combat this, you'll need to apply **stripslashes( )** here as well:

```
$pattern = stripslashes(trim
→ ($_POST['pattern']));
$subject = stripslashes(trim
→ ($_POST['subject']));
```

4. Print a caption:

```
echo "<p>The result of checking
→ <br /><b>$pattern</b><br />against
<br />$subject<br />is ";
```

As you can see **B**, the form-handling part of this script will start by printing the values submitted.

5. Run the regular expression:

```
if (preg_match ($pattern,
→ $subject) ) {
  echo 'TRUE!</p>';
} else {
  echo 'FALSE!</p>';
}
```

To test the pattern against the string, feed both to the **preg_match( )** function. If this function returns 1, that means a match was made, this condition will be TRUE, and the word *TRUE* will be printed. If no match was made, the condition will be FALSE and that will be stated **D**.

C With Magic Quotes enabled on your server, the script will add slashes to certain characters, most likely making the regular expressions fail.

D If the pattern does not match the string, this will be the result. This submission and response also conveys that regular expressions are case-sensitive by default.

6. Complete the submission conditional and the PHP block:

```
} // End of submission IF.
?>
```

7. Create the HTML form:

```
<form action="pcre.php" method=
→"post">
  <p>Regular Expression Pattern:
  →<input type="text" name=
  →"pattern" value="<?php if
  →(isset($pattern)) echo
  →htmlentities($pattern);
  →?>" size="40" /> (include
  →the delimiters)</p>
  <p>Test Subject: <input type=
  →"text" name="subject" value=
  →"<?php if (isset($subject))
  →echo htmlentities($subject);
  →?>" size="40" /></p>
  <input type="submit" name=
  →"submit" value="Test!" />
</form>
```

The form contains two text boxes, both of which are sticky (using the trimmed version of the values). Because the two values might include quotation marks and other characters that would conflict with the form's "stickiness," each variable's value is sent through **htmlentities( )**, too.

8. Complete the HTML page:

```
</body>
</html>
```

9. Save the file as **pcre.php**, place it in your Web directory, and test it in your Web browser.

Although you don't know the rules for creating patterns yet, you could use any other literal value. Remember to use delimiters around the pattern or else you'll see an error message **E**.

TIP Some text editors, such as BBEdit and emacs, allow you to use regular expressions to match and replace patterns within and throughout several documents.

TIP The PCRE functions all use the established locale. A *locale* reflects a computer's designated country and language, among other settings.

TIP Previous versions of PHP supported another type of regular expressions, called *POSIX*. These have since been deprecated, meaning they'll be dropped from future versions of the language.

E If you fail to wrap the pattern in matching delimiters, you'll see an error message.

Defining Simple Patterns

Using one of PHP's regular expression functions is really easy, defining patterns to use is hard. There are lots of rules for creating a pattern. You can use these rules separately or in combination, making your pattern either quite simple or very complex. To start, then, you'll see what characters are used to define a simple pattern. As a formatting rule, I'll define patterns in **bold** and will indicate what the pattern matches in *italics*. The patterns in these explanations won't be placed within delimiters or quotes (both being needed when used within **preg_match( )**), just to keep things cleaner.

The first type of character you will use for defining patterns is a *literal*. A literal is a value that is written exactly as it is interpreted. For example, the pattern **a** will match the letter *a*, **ab** will match *ab*, and so forth. Therefore, assuming a case-insensitive search is performed, **rom** will match any of the following strings, since they all contain *rom*:

- CD-ROM
- Rommel crossed the desert.
- I'm writing a roman à clef.

Along with literals, your patterns will use *meta-characters*. These are special symbols that have a meaning beyond their literal value (Table 14.1). While **a** simply means *a*, the period (.) will match any single character except for a newline (. matches *a*, *b*, *c*, the underscore, a space, etc., just not **\n**). To match any meta-character, you will need to escape it, much as you escape a quotation mark to print it. Hence **\.** will match the period itself. So **1.99** matches *1.99* or *1B99* or *1299*

(a 1 followed by any character followed by 99) but **1\.99** only matches *1.99*.

Two meta-characters specify where certain characters must be found. There is the caret (^), which marks the beginning of a pattern. There is also the dollar sign (**$**), which marks the conclusion of a pattern. Accordingly, **^a** will match any string beginning with an *a*, while **a$** will correspond to any string ending with an *a*. Therefore, **^a$** will only match *a* (a string that both begins and ends with *a*).

These two meta-characters—the caret and the dollar sign—are crucial to *validation*, as validation normally requires checking the value of an entire string, not just the presence of one string in another. For example, using an email-matching pattern without those two characters will match any string containing an email address. Using an email-matching pattern that begins with a caret and ends with a dollar sign will match a string that contains *only* a valid email address.

TABLE 14.1 Meta-Characters

Character	Meaning
\	Escape character
^	Indicates the beginning of a string
$	Indicates the end of a string
.	Any single character except newline
|	Alternatives (or)
[	Start of a class
]	End of a class
(	Start of a subpattern
)	End of a subpattern
{	Start of a quantifier
}	End of a quantifier

A Looking for a cat in a string.

B PCRE performs a case-sensitive comparison by default.

Regular expressions also make use of the pipe (|) as the equivalent of *or*: **a|b** will match strings containing either *a* or *b*. (Using the pipe within patterns is called *alternation* or *branching*). So **yes|no** accepts either of those two words in their entirety (the alternation is *not* just between the two letters surrounding it: *s* and *n*).

Once you comprehend the basic symbols, then you can begin to use parentheses to group characters into more involved patterns. Grouping works as you might expect: **(abc)** will match *abc*, **(trout)** will match *trout*. Think of parentheses as being used to establish a new literal of a larger size. Because of precedence rules in PCRE, **yes|no** and **(yes)|(no)** are equivalent. But **(even|heavy) handed** will match either *even handed* or *heavy handed*.

To use simple patterns:

1. Load **pcre.php** in your Web browser, if it is not already.

2. Check if a string contains the letters *cat* **A**.

   To do so, use the literal **cat** as the pattern and any number of strings as the subject. Any of the following would be a match: *catalog*, *catastrophe*, *my cat left*, etc. For the time being, use all lowercase letters, as **cat** will not match *Cat* **B**.

   Remember to use delimiters around the pattern, as well (see the figures).

continues on next page

3. Check if a string starts with *cat* **C**.

   To have a pattern apply to the start of a string, use the caret as the first character (^cat). The sentence *my cat left* will not be a match now.

4. Check if a string contains the word *color* or *colour* **D**.

   The pattern to look for the American or British spelling of this word is **col(o|ou)r**. The first three letters—*col*—must be present. This needs to be followed by either an *o* or *ou*. Finally, an *r* is required.

TIP If you are looking to match an exact string within another string, use the `strstr( )` function, which is faster than regular expressions. In fact, as a rule of thumb, you should use regular expressions only if the task at hand cannot be accomplished using any other function or technique.

TIP You can escape a bunch of characters in a pattern using \Q and \E. Every character within those will be treated literally (so \Q$2.99?\E matches *$2.99?*).

TIP To match a single backslash, you have to use \\\\. The reason is that matching a backslash in a regular expression requires you to escape the backslash, resulting in \\. Then to use a backslash in a PHP string, it also has to be escaped, so escaping both backslashes means a total of four.

C The caret in a pattern means that the match has to be found at the start of the string.

D By using the pipe meta-character, the performed search can be more flexible.

Using Quantifiers

You've just seen and practiced with a couple of the meta-characters, the most important of which are the caret and the dollar sign. Next, there are three meta-characters that allow for multiple occurrences: **a*** will match zero or more *a*'s (no *a*'s, *a*, *aa*, *aaa*, etc.); **a+** matches one or more *a*'s (*a*, *aa*, *aaa*, etc., but there must be at least one); and **a?** will match up to one *a* (*a* or no *a*'s match). These meta-characters all act as quantifiers in your patterns, as do the curly braces. **Table 14.2** lists all of the quantifiers.

To match a certain quantity of a thing, put the quantity between curly braces (**{}**), stating a specific number, just a minimum, or both a minimum and a maximum. Thus, **a{3}** will match *aaa*; **a{3,}** will match *aaa*, *aaaa*, etc. (three or more *a*'s); and **a{3,5}** will match just *aaa*, *aaaa*, and *aaaaa* (between three and five).

Note that quantifiers apply to the thing that came before it, so **a?** matches zero or one *a*'s, **ab?** matches an *a* followed by zero or one *b*'s, but **(ab)?** matches zero or one *ab*'s. Therefore, to match *color* or *colour*, you could also use **colou?r** as the pattern.

TABLE 14.2 Quantifiers

Character	Meaning
?	0 or 1
*	0 or more
+	1 or more
{x}	Exactly x occurrences
{x,y}	Between x and y (inclusive)
{x,}	At least x occurrences

To use quantifiers:

1. Load **pcre.php** in your Web browser, if it is not already.

2. Check if a string contains the letters *c* and *t*, with one or more letters in between .

   To do so, use **c.+t** as the pattern and any number of strings as the subject. Remember that the period matches any character (except for the newline). Each of the following would be a match: *cat*, *count*, *coefficient*, etc. The word *doctor* would not match, as there are no letters between the *c* and the *t* (although *doctor* would match **c.*t**).

3. Check if a string matches either *cat* or *cats* .

continues on next page

continues on next page

A The plus sign, when used as a quantifier, requires that one or more of a thing be present.

B You can check for the plural form of many words by adding *s?* to the pattern.

To start, if you want to make an exact match, use both the caret and the dollar sign. Then you'd have the literal text *cat*, followed by an *s*, followed by a question mark (representing 0 or 1 *s*'s). The final pattern—**^cats?$**—matches *cat* or *cats* but not *my cat left* or *I like cats*.

4. Check if a string ends with *.33*, *.333*, or *.3333* **C**.

To find a period, escape it with a backslash: \.. To find a three, use a literal **3**. To find a range of 3's, use the curly brackets (**{}**). Putting this together, the pattern is **\.3{2,4}**. Because the string should end with this (nothing else can follow), conclude the pattern with a dollar sign: **\.3{2,4}$**.

Admittedly, this is kind of a stupid example (not sure when you'd need to do exactly this), but it does demonstrate several things. This pattern will match lots of things—*12.333*, *varmit.3333*, *.33*, look *.33*—but not *12.3* or *12.334*.

5. Match a five-digit number **D**.

A number can be any one of the numbers 0 through 9, so the heart of the pattern is **(0|1|2|3|4|5|6|7|8|9)**. Plainly said, this means: a number is a 0 or a 1 or a 2 or a 3.... To make it a five-digit number, follow this with a quantifier: **(0|1|2|3|4|5|6|7|8|9){5}**. Finally, to match this exactly (as opposed to matching a five-digit number within a string), use the caret and the dollar sign: **^(0|1|2|3|4|5|6|7|8|9){5}$**.

This, of course, is one way to match a United States zip code, a very useful pattern.

TIP When using curly braces to specify a number of characters, you must always include the minimum number. The maximum is optional: a{3} and a{3,} are acceptable, but a{,3} is not.

TIP Although it demonstrates good dedication to programming to learn how to write and execute your own regular expressions, numerous working examples are available already by searching the Internet.

The result of checking
/\.3{2,4}$/
against
;lksajfls;dajfsad;lsdkjfl;k.333
is TRUE!

Regular Expression Pattern: /\.3{2,4}$/
(include the delimiters)

Test Subject: ;lksajfls;dajfsad;lsdkjfl;k.333

Test!

C The curly braces let you dictate the acceptable range of quantities present.

The result of checking
/^(0|1|2|3|4|5|6|7|8|9){5}$/
against
16803
is TRUE!

Regular Expression Pattern: /^(0|1|2|3|4|5|6|7|8|9){5}$/
(include the delimiters)

Test Subject: 16803

Test!

D The proper test for confirming that a number contains five digits.

Using Character Classes

As the last example demonstrated (**D** in the previous section), relying solely upon literals in a pattern can be tiresome. Having to write out all those digits to match any number is silly. Imagine if you wanted to match any four-letter word: **^(a|b|c|d...){4}$** (and that doesn't even take into account uppercase letters)! To make these common references easier, you can use *character classes*.

Classes are created by placing characters within square brackets (**[]**). For example, you can match any one vowel with **[aeiou]**. This is equivalent to **(a|e|i|o|u)**. Or you can use the hyphen to indicate a range of characters: **[a-z]** is any single lowercase letter and **[A-Z]** is any uppercase, **[A-Za-z]** is any letter in general, and **[0-9]** matches any digit. As an example, **[a-z]{3}** would match *abc*, *def*, *oiw*, etc.

Within classes, most of the meta-characters are treated literally, except for four. The backslash is still the escape, but the caret (**^**) is a negation operator when used as the first character in the class. So **[^aeiou]** will match any non-vowel. The only other meta-character within a class is the dash, which indicates a range. (If the dash is used as the last character in a class, it's a literal dash.) And, of course, the closing bracket (**]**) still has meaning as the terminator of the class.

Naturally, a class can have both ranges and literal characters. A person's first name, which can contain letters, spaces, apostrophes, and periods, could be represented by **[A-z '.]** (again, the period doesn't need to be escaped within the class, as it loses its meta-meaning there).

Along with creating your own classes, there are six already-defined classes that have their own shortcuts (**Table 14.3**). The digit and space classes are easy to understand. The word character class doesn't mean "word" in the language sense but rather as in a string unbroken by spaces or punctuation.

Using this information, the five-digit number (aka, zip code) pattern could more easily be written as **^[0-9]{5}$** or **^\d{5}$**. As another example, **can\s?not** will match both *can not* and *cannot* (the word *can*, followed by zero or one space characters, followed by *not*).

TABLE 14.3 Character Classes

Class	Shortcut	Meaning
[0-9]	\d	Any digit
[\f\r\t\n\v]	\s	Any white space
[A-Za-z0-9_]	\w	Any word character
[^0-9]	\D	Not a digit
[^\f\r\t\n\v]	\S	Not white space
[^A-Za-z0-9_]	\W	Not a word character

To use character classes:

1. Load **pcre.php** in your Web browser, if it is not already.

2. Check if a string is formatted as a valid United States zip code **A**.

   A United States zip code always starts with five digits (^\d{5}). But a valid zip code could also have a dash followed by another four digits (-\d{4}$). To make this last part optional, use the question mark (the 0 or 1 quantifier). This complete pattern is then ^(\d{5}) (-\d{4})?$. To make it all clearer, the first part of the pattern (matching the five digits) is also grouped in parentheses, although this isn't required in this case.

3. Check if a string contains no spaces **B**.

   The **\S** character class shortcut will match non-space characters. To make sure that the entire string contains no spaces, use the caret and the dollar sign: ^\S$. If you don't use those, then all the pattern is confirming is that the subject contains at least one non-space character.

A The pattern to match a United States zip code, in either the five-digit or five plus four format.

B The no-white-space shortcut can be used to ensure that a submitting string is contiguous.

Using Boundaries

Boundaries are shortcuts for helping to find, um, boundaries. In a way, you've already seen this: using the caret and the dollar sign to match the beginning or end of a value. But what if you wanted to match boundaries within a value?

The clearest boundary is between a word and a non-word. A "word" in this case is not *cat, month,* or *zeitgeist*, but in the **\w** shortcut sense: the letters A through Z (both upper- and lowercase), plus the numbers 0 through 9, and the underscore. To use words as boundaries, there's the **\b** shortcut. To use non-word characters as boundaries, there's **\B**. So the pattern **\bfor\b** matches *they've come for you* but doesn't match *force* or *forebode*. Therefore **\bfor\B** would match *force* but not *they've come for you* or *informal*.

4. Validate an email address .

The pattern ^[\w.-]+@[\w.-]+\.[A-Za-z]{2,6}$ provides for reasonably good email validation. It's wrapped in the caret and the dollar sign, so the string must be a valid email address and nothing more. An email address starts with letters, numbers, and the underscore (represented by \w), plus a period (.) and a dash. This first block will match *larryullman*, *larry77*, *larry.ullman*, *larry-ullman*, and so on. Next, all email addresses include one and only one @. After that, there can be any number of letters, numbers, periods, and dashes. This is the domain name: *larryullman*, *smith-jones*, *amazon.co* (as in *amazon.co.uk*), etc. Finally, all email addresses conclude with one period and between two and six letters. This accounts for *.com*, *.edu*, *.info*, *.travel*, etc.

TIP I think that the zip code example is a great demonstration as to how complex and useful regular expressions are. One pattern accurately tests for both formats of the zip code, which is fantastic. But when you put this into your PHP code, with quotes and delimiters, it's not easily understood:

```
if (preg_match ('/^(\d{5})(-\d{4})?$/',
→ $zip)) {
```

That certainly looks like gibberish, right?

TIP This email address validation pattern is pretty good, although not perfect. It will allow some invalid addresses to pass through (like ones starting with a period or containing multiple periods together). However, a 100 percent foolproof validation pattern is ridiculously long, and frequently using regular expressions is really a matter of trying to exclude the bulk of invalid entries without inadvertently excluding any valid ones.

TIP Regular expressions, particularly PCRE ones, can be extremely complex. When starting out, it's just as likely that your use of them will break the validation routines instead of improving them. That's why practicing like this is important.

C A pretty good and reliable validation for email addresses.

Finding All Matches

Going back to the PHP functions used with Perl-Compatible regular expressions, **preg_match( )** has been used just to see if a pattern matches a value or not. But the script hasn't been reporting what, exactly, in the value did match the pattern. You can find out this information by providing a variable as a third argument to the function:

```
preg_match(pattern, subject, $match);
```

The **$match** variable will contain the first match found (because this function only returns the first match in a value). To find every match, use **preg_match_all( )**. Its syntax is the same:

```
preg_match_all(pattern, subject,
→$matches);
```

This function will return the number of matches made, or FALSE if none were found. It will also assign to **$matches** every match made. Let's update the PHP script to print the returned matches, and then run a couple more tests.

To report all matches:

1. Open **pcre.php** (Script 14.1) in your text editor or IDE, if it is not already.

2. Change the invocation of **preg_match( )** to (**Script 14.2**):

```
if (preg_match_all ($pattern,
→$subject, $matches) ) {
```

There are two changes here. First, the actual function being called is different. Second, the third argument is provided a variable name that will be assigned every match.

Script 14.2 To reveal exactly what values in a string match which patterns, this revised version of the script will print out each match. You can retrieve the matches by naming a variable as the third argument in **preg_match( )** or **preg_match_all( )**.

```
1   <!DOCTYPE html PUBLIC "-//W3C//DTD XHTML
    1.0 Transitional//EN" "http://www.w3.org/
    TR/xhtml1/DTD/xhtml1-transitional.dtd">
2   <html xmlns="http://www.w3.org/1999/
    xhtml" xml:lang="en" lang="en">
3   <head>
4       <meta http-equiv="Content-Type"
        content="text/html; charset=utf-8" />
5       <title>Testing PCRE</title>
6   </head>
7   <body>
8   <?php // Script 14.2 - matches.php
9   // This script takes a submitted string
    and checks it against a submitted pattern.
10  // This version prints every match made.
11
12  if ($_SERVER['REQUEST_METHOD'] == 'POST') {
13
14      // Trim the strings:
15      $pattern = trim($_POST['pattern']);
16      $subject = trim($_POST['subject']);
17
18      // Print a caption:
19      echo "<p>The result of checking<br />
        <b>$pattern</b><br />against<br />
        $subject<br />is ";
20
21      // Test:
22      if (preg_match_all ($pattern,
        $subject, $matches) ) {
23          echo 'TRUE!</p>';
24
25          // Print the matches:
26          echo '<pre>' . print_r($matches,
            1) . '</pre>';
27
28      } else {
29          echo 'FALSE!</p>';
30      }
31
32  } // End of submission IF.
```

code continues on next page

```
33   // Display the HTML form.
34   ?>
35   <form action="matches.php"
     method="post">
36       <p>Regular Expression Pattern:
         <input type="text" name="pattern"
         value="<?php if (isset($pattern)) echo
         htmlentities($pattern); ?>" size="40" />
         (include the delimiters)</p>
37       <p>Test Subject: <textarea
         name="subject" rows="5"
         cols="40"><?php if (isset($subject))
         echo htmlentities($subject); ?>
         </textarea></p>
38       <input type="submit" name="submit"
         value="Test!" />
39   </form>
40   </body>
41   </html>
```

3. After printing the value *TRUE*, print the contents of **$matches**:

   echo '<pre>' . print_r($matches,
   → 1) . '</pre>';

   Using **print_r( )** to output the contents of the variable is the easiest way to know what's in **$matches** (you could use a **foreach** loop instead). As you'll see when you run this script, this variable will be an array whose first element is an array of matches made.

4. Change the form's **action** attribute to *matches.php*:

   <form action="matches.php"
   → method="post">

   This script will be renamed, so the **action** attribute must be changed, too.

5. Change the subject input to be a textarea:

   <p>Test Subject: <textarea name=
   → "subject" rows="5" cols="40">
   → <?php if (isset($subject)) echo
   → htmlentities($subject); ?>
   → </textarea></p>

   continues on next page

Being Less Greedy

A key component to Perl-Compatible regular expressions is the concept of *greediness*. By default, PCRE will attempt to match as much as possible. For example, the pattern <.+> matches any HTML tag. When tested on a string like *<a href="page.php">Link</a>*, it will actually match that entire string, from the opening < to the closing one. This string contains three possible matches, though: the entire string, the opening tag (from *<a* to *">*), and the closing tag (*</a>*).

To overrule greediness, make the match *lazy*. A lazy match will contain as little data as possible. Any quantifier can be made lazy by following it with the question mark. For example, the pattern <.+?> would return two matches in the preceding string: the opening tag and the closing tag. It would not return the whole string as a match. (This is one of the confusing aspects of the regular expression syntax: the same character—here, the question mark—can have different meanings depending on its context.)

Another way to make patterns less greedy is to use negative classes. The pattern <[^>]+> matches everything between the opening and closing <> except for a closing >. So using this pattern would have the same result as using <.+?>. This pattern would also match strings that contain newline characters, which the period excludes.

In order to be able to enter in more text for the subject, this element will become a textarea.

6. Save the file as **matches.php**, place it in your Web directory, and test it in your Web browser.

For the first test, use **for** as the pattern and *This is a formulaic test for informal matches.* as the subject **Ⓐ**. It may not be proper English, but it's a good test subject.

For the second test, change the pattern to **for.*** **Ⓑ**. The result may surprise you, the cause of which is discussed in the sidebar, "Being Less Greedy." To make this search less greedy, the pattern could be changed to **for.*?**, whose results would be the same as those in **Ⓐ**.

The result of checking
/for/
against
This is a formulaic test for informal matches.
is TRUE!

```
Array
(
    [0] => Array
        (
            [0] => for
            [1] => for
            [2] => for
        )

)
```

Regular Expression Pattern: `/for/` (include the delimiters)

Test Subject:
```
This is a formulaic test for informal
matches.
```

(Test!)

Ⓐ This first test returns three matches, as the literal text *for* was found three times.

The result of checking
/for.*/
against
This is a formulaic test for informal matches.
is TRUE!

```
Array
(
    [0] => Array
        (
            [0] => formulaic test for informal matches.
        )

)
```

Regular Expression Pattern: `/for.*/` (include the delimiters)

Test Subject:
```
This is a formulaic test for informal
matches.
```

(Test!)

Ⓑ Because regular expressions are "greedy" by default (see the sidebar), this pattern only finds one match in the string. That match happens to start with the first instance of *for* and continues until the end of the string.

The result of checking
/for[\S]*/
against
This is a formulaic test for informal matches.
is TRUE!

```
Array
(
    [0] => Array
        (
            [0] => formulaic
            [1] => for
            [2] => formal
        )

)
```

Regular Expression Pattern: /for[\S]*/
(include the delimiters)

Test Subject: This is a formulaic test for informal matches.

Test!

C This revised pattern matches strings that begin with *for* and end on a word.

The result of checking
/\b[a-z]*for[a-z]*\b/
against
This is a formulaic test for informal matches.
is TRUE!

```
Array
(
    [0] => Array
        (
            [0] => formulaic
            [1] => for
            [2] => informal
        )

)
```

Regular Expression Pattern: /\b[a-z]*for[a-z]*\b/
(include the delimiters)

Test Subject: This is a formulaic test for informal matches.

Test!

D Unlike the pattern in **C**, this one matches entire words that contain *for* (*informal* here, *formal* in **C**).

For the third test, use **for[\S]***, or, more simply **for\S*** **C**. This has the effect of making the match stop as soon as a white space character is found (because the pattern wants to match *for* followed by any number of non–white space characters).

For the final test, use **\b[a-z]*for[a-z]*\b** as the pattern **D**. This pattern makes use of boundaries, discussed in the sidebar "Using Boundaries," earlier in the chapter.

TIP The `preg_split( )` function will take a string and break it into an array using a regular expression pattern.

Using Modifiers

The majority of the special characters you can use in regular expression patterns are introduced in this chapter. One final type of special character is the pattern modifier. **Table 14.4** lists these. Pattern modifiers are different than the other metacharacters in that they are placed after the closing delimiter.

Of these delimiters, the most important is *i*, which enables case-insensitive searches. All of the examples using variations on *for* (in the previous sequence of steps) would not match the word *For*. However, **/for.*/i** would be a match. Note that I am including the delimiters in that pattern, as the modifier goes after the closing one. Similarly, the last step in the previous sequence referenced the sidebar "Being Less Greedy" and stated how **for.*?** would perform a lazy search. So would **/for.*/U**.

The multiline mode is interesting in that you can make the caret and the dollar sign behave differently. By default, each applies to the entire value. In multiline mode, the caret matches the beginning of any line and the dollar sign matches the end of any line.

To use modifiers:

1. Load **matches.php** in your Web browser, if it is not already.

2. Validate a list of email addresses **A**.

   To do so, use **/^[\w.-]+@[\w.-]+\.[A-Za-z]{2,6}\r?$/m** as the pattern. You'll see that I've added an optional carriage return (\r?) before the dollar sign. This is necessary because some of the lines will contain returns and others won't. And in multiline mode, the dollar sign matches the end of a line. (To be more flexible, you could use \s? instead.)

TABLE 14.4 Pattern Modifiers

Character	Result
A	Anchors the pattern to the beginning of the string
i	Enables case-insensitive mode
m	Enables multiline matching
s	Has the period match every character, including newline
x	Ignores most white space
U	Performs a non-greedy match

A A list of email addresses, one per line, can be validated using the multiline mode. Each valid address is stored in **$matches**.

The result of checking
/^\d{5})(-\d{4})?\s?$/m
against
12345 trout 13245-0001 45678-002 89765 b 78944
is TRUE!

```
Array
(
    [0] => Array
        (
            [0] => 12345
            [1] => 13245-0001
            [2] => 78944
        )

    [1] => Array
        (
            [0] => 12345
            [1] => 13245
            [2] => 78944
        )

    [2] => Array
        (
            [0] =>
            [1] => -0001
            [2] =>
        )

)
```

Regular Expression Pattern: /^\d{5})(-\d{4})?\s?$/m
(include the delimiters)

Test Subject:
```
12345
trout
13245-0001
45678-002
89765 b
```

Test!

B Validating a list of zip codes, one per line.

3. Validate a list of United States zip codes **B**.

Very similar to the example in Step 2, the pattern is now /^(\d{5})(-\d{4})?\s?$/m. You'll see that I'm using the more flexible \s? instead of \r?.

You'll also notice when you try this yourself (or in **B**) that the $matches variable contains a lot more information now. This will be explained in the next section of the chapter.

TIP To always match the start or end of a pattern, regardless of the multiline setting, there are shortcuts you can use. Within the pattern, the shortcut \A will match only the very beginning of the value, \z matches the very end, and \Z matches any line end, like $ in single-line mode.

TIP If your version of PHP supports it, it's probably best to use the Filter extension to validate an email address or a URL. But if you have to validate a list of either, the Filter extension won't cut it, and regular expressions will be required.

Matching and Replacing Patterns

The last subject to discuss in this chapter is how to match and replace patterns in a value. While **preg_match( )** and **preg_match_all( )** will find things for you, if you want to do a search and replace, you'll need to use **preg_replace( )**. Its syntax is

```
preg_replace(pattern, replacement,
→ subject);
```

This function takes an optional fourth argument limiting the number of replacements made.

To replace all instances of *cat* with *dog*, you would use

```
$str = preg_replace('/cat/', 'dog',
→ 'I like my cat.');
```

This function returns the altered value (or unaltered value if no matches were made), so you'll likely want to assign it to a variable or use it as an argument to another function (like printing it by calling **echo**). Also, as a reminder, the above is just an example: you'd never want to replace one literal string with another using regular expressions, use **str_replace( )** instead.

There is a related concept to discuss that is involved with this function: *back referencing*. In a zip code matching pattern—^(\d{5})(-\d{4})?$—there are two groups within parentheses: the first five digits and the optional dash plus four-digit extension. Within a regular expression pattern, PHP will automatically number parenthetical groupings beginning at 1. Back referencing allows you to refer to each individual section by using **$** plus the corresponding number. For example, if you match the zip code *94710-0001* with this pattern, referring back to **$2** will give you *-0001*. The code **$0** refers to the whole

initial string. This is why **B** in the previous section shows entire zip code matches in **$matches[0]**, the matching first five digits in **$matches[1]**, and any matching dash plus four digits in **$matches[2]**.

To practice with this, let's modify Script 14.2 to also take a replacement input **A**.

To match and replace patterns:

1. Open **matches.php** (Script 14.2) in your text editor or IDE, if it is not already.

2. Add a reference to a third incoming variable (**Script 14.3**):

   ```
   $replace = trim($_POST['replace']);
   ```

   As you can see in **A**, the third form input (added between the existing two) takes the replacement value. That value is also trimmed to get rid of any extraneous spaces.

   If your server has Magic Quotes enabled, you'll again need to apply **stripslashes( )** here.

continues on page 454

A One use of **preg_replace( )** would be to replace variations on inappropriate words with symbols representing their omission.

Script 14.3 To test the `preg_replace( )` function, which replaces a matched pattern in a string with another value, you can use this third version of the PCRE test script

```
1    <!DOCTYPE html PUBLIC "-//W3C//DTD XHTML 1.0 Transitional//EN" "http://www.w3.org/TR/xhtml1/DTD/
     xhtml1-transitional.dtd">
2    <html xmlns="http://www.w3.org/1999/xhtml" xml:lang="en" lang="en">
3    <head>
4       <meta http-equiv="Content-Type" content="text/html; charset=utf-8" />
5       <title>Testing PCRE Replace</title>
6    </head>
7    <body>
8    <?php // Script 14.3 - replace.php
9    // This script takes a submitted string and checks it against a submitted pattern.
10   // This version replaces one value with another.
11
12   if ($_SERVER['REQUEST_METHOD'] == 'POST') {
13
14      // Trim the strings:
15      $pattern = trim($_POST['pattern']);
16      $subject = trim($_POST['subject']);
17      $replace = trim($_POST['replace']);
18
19      // Print a caption:
20      echo "<p>The result of replacing<br /><b>$pattern</b><br />with<br />$replace
         <br />in<br />$subject<br /><br />";
21
22      // Check for a match:
23      if (preg_match ($pattern, $subject) ) {
24         echo preg_replace($pattern, $replace, $subject) . '</p>';
25      } else {
26         echo 'The pattern was not found!</p>';
27      }
28
29   } // End of submission IF.
30   // Display the HTML form.
31   ?>
32   <form action="replace.php" method="post">
33      <p>Regular Expression Pattern: <input type="text" name="pattern" value="<?php if
         (isset($pattern)) echo htmlentities($pattern); ?>" size="40" /> (include the delimiters)</p>
34      <p>Replacement: <input type="text" name="replace" value="<?php if (isset($replace))
         echo htmlentities($replace); ?>" size="40" /></p>
35      <p>Test Subject: <textarea name="subject" rows="5" cols="40"><?php if (isset($subject)) echo
         htmlentities($subject); ?></textarea></p>
36      <input type="submit" name="submit" value="Test!" />
37   </form>
38   </body>
39   </html>
```

3. Change the caption:

```
echo "<p>The result of replacing
→ <br /><b>$pattern</b><br />
→ with<br />$replace<br />in
→ <br />$subject<br /><br />";
```

The caption will print out all of the incoming values, prior to applying `preg_replace()`.

4. Change the regular expression conditional so that it only calls `preg_replace()` if a match is made:

```
if (preg_match ($pattern,
→ $subject) ) {
    echo preg_replace($pattern,
    → $replace, $subject) . '</p>';
} else {
    echo 'The pattern was not
    → found!</p>';
}
```

You can call `preg_replace()` without running `preg_match()` first. If no match was made, then no replacement will occur. But to make it clear when a match is or is not being made (which is always good to confirm, considering how tricky regular expressions are), the `preg_match()` function will be applied first. If it returns a TRUE value, then `preg_replace()` is called, printing the results **B**. Otherwise, a message is printed indicating that no match was made **C**.

5. Change the form's **action** attribute to *replace.php*:

```
<form action="replace.php"
→ method="post">
```

This file will be renamed, so this value needs to be changed accordingly.

B The resulting text has uses of bleep, bleeps, bleeped, bleeper, and bleeping replaced with *****.

C If the pattern is not found within the subject, the subject will not be changed.

6. Add a text input for the replacement string:

```
<p>Replacement: <input
→ type="text" name="replace"
→ value="<?php if (isset($replace))
→ echo htmlentities($replace); ?>"
→ size="40" /></p>
```

7. Save the file as **replace.php**, place it in your Web directory, and test it in your Web browser **D**.

As a good example, you can turn an email address found within some text into its HTML link equivalent: **<a href="mailto:email@example. com">email@example.com</a>**. The pattern for matching an email address should be familiar by now: ^[\w.-]+@ [\w.-]+\.[A-Za-z]{2,6}$. However, because the email address could be found within some text, the caret and dollar sign need to be replaced by the word boundaries shortcut: **\b**. The final pattern is therefore /**\b[\w.-]+@[\w.-] +\.[A-Za-z]{2,6}\b/**.

To refer to this matched email address, you can refer to **$0** (because **$0** refers to the entire match, whether or not parentheses are used). So the replacement value would be *<a href="mailto:$0"> $0</a>*. Because HTML is involved here, look at the HTML source code of the resulting page for the best idea of what happened.

TIP Back references can even be used within the pattern. For example, if a pattern included a grouping (i.e., a subpattern) that would be repeated.

TIP I've introduced, somewhat quickly, the bulk of the PCRE syntax here, but there's much more to it. Once you've mastered all this, you can consider moving on to *anchors, named subpatterns, comments, lookarounds, possessive quantifiers*, and more.

D Another use of **preg_replace()** is dynamically turning email addresses into clickable links. See the HTML source code for the full effect of the replacement.

Review and Pursue

If you have any problems with the review questions or the pursue prompts, turn to the book's supporting forum (**www.LarryUllman.com/forums/**).

Review

- What function is used to match a regular expression? What function is used to find all matches of a regular expression? What function is used to replace matches of a regular expression?

- What characters can you use and not use to delineate a regular expression?

- How do you match a literal character or string of characters?

- What are meta-characters? How do you escape a meta-character?

- What meta-character do you use to bind a pattern to the beginning of a string? To the end?

- How do you create subpatterns (aka groupings)?

- What are the quantifiers? How do you require 0 or 1 of a character or string? 0 or more? 1 or more? Precisely *X* occurrences? A range of occurrences? A minimum of occurrences?

- What are character classes?

- What meta-characters still have meaning within character classes?

- What shortcut represents the "any digit" character class? The "any white space" class? "Any word"? What shortcuts represent the opposite of these?

- What are boundaries? How do you create boundaries in patterns?

- How do you make matches "lazy"? And what does that mean anyway?

- What are the pattern modifiers?

- What is *back referencing*? How does it work?

Pursue

- Search online for a PCRE "cheat sheet" (PHP or otherwise) that lists all the meaningful characters and classes. Print out the cheat sheet and keep it beside your computer.

- Practice, practice, practice!

Introducing jQuery

New in this edition of the book is this chapter, introducing the jQuery JavaScript framework. As JavaScript has developed into a more valuable language over the past decade, its meaningful usage has become commonplace in today's Web sites. Accordingly, many PHP developers are expected to know a bit of JavaScript as well.

Although this chapter cannot present full coverage of JavaScript or jQuery, you'll learn more than enough to be able to add to your PHP-based projects the features that users have come to expect. In the process, you'll also learn some basics of programming in JavaScript in general, and get a sense of into what areas of jQuery you may want to further delve.

What is jQuery?

In order to grasp jQuery, you must have a solid sense of what JavaScript is. As discussed in Chapter 11, "Web Application Development," JavaScript is a programming language that's primarily used to add dynamic features to Web pages. Unlike PHP, which always runs on the server, JavaScript generally runs on the client (JavaScript is starting to be used as a server-side tool, too, although that's still more on the fringe). PHP, precisely because it is server-side, is browser-agnostic for the most part: very few things you'll do in PHP will have different results from one browser to the next. Conversely, precisely because

it's running in the Web browser, JavaScript code often has to be customized for the variations in browsers. For many years, this was the bane of the Web developer: creating reliable cross-browser code. Overcoming this particular hurdle is one of the many strengths of jQuery (**www.jquery.com** Ⓐ).

jQuery is a JavaScript framework, a framework just being a library of code whose use can expedite and simplify development. The core of the jQuery framework is able to handle all key JavaScript functionality, as you'll see in this chapter. But the framework is extendable via plug-ins to provide other features, such as the ability to create a dynamic, paginated, sortable table of data. In fact, a number of useful user interface

Ⓐ The home page for the jQuery JavaScript framework.

Ⓑ The home page for the jQuery User Interface library (jQuery UI), which works in conjunction with jQuery.

tools have been wrapped inside their own bundle, jQuery UI (**www.jqueryui.com** Ⓑ).

There are many JavaScript frameworks out there, and in no way am I claiming jQuery is the best. I do prefer jQuery, however, and it's quickly earned a place as one of the premier JavaScript frameworks. As you'll soon see, jQuery has a simple, albeit cryptic, syntax, and by using it, you can manipulate the Document Object Model (DOM) with aplomb. This is to say that you can easily reference elements within an HTML page, thereby grabbing the values of form inputs, adding or removing any kind of HTML element, changing element properties, and so forth.

Before getting into the particulars of using jQuery, do understand that jQuery is just a JavaScript framework, meaning that what you'll actually be doing over the next several pages is JavaScript programming. JavaScript as a language, while similar in some

ways to PHP, differs in other ways, such as how variables are created, what character is used to perform concatenation, and so forth. Moreover, JavaScript is an *object-oriented language*, meaning the syntax you'll sometimes see will be that much different than the procedural PHP programming you've done to this point (the next chapter introduces Object-Oriented Programming—OOP—in PHP). Because you'll inevitably have problems—like simply omitting a semicolon, you'll need to know a bit about how to debug JavaScript. For a quick introduction to that subject, see the sidebar.

For examples of server-side JavaScript, check out Node (**www.nodejs.org**) or Jaxer (**www.jaxer.org**).

TIP I've written a several-part series on jQuery, covering many of the same topics as this chapter. You can find the series on my Web site (**www.LarryUllman.com**).

Debugging JavaScript

To this point, you may not have thought it so wonderful that PHP dumped all its errors into your Web browser, shoving your mistakes in your face. Until now. When Web pages have JavaScript errors, you rarely are notified. In order to debug problematic JavaScript code, the first thing you'll need to do is see what actual errors exist.

The first tool you'll need when programming in JavaScript is a good Web browser. Not a good Web browser for *users*, but a good one for *developers*. Firefox (**www.mozilla.com**) is the clear champion in this regard, although Opera (**www.opera.com**) and Google Chrome (**www.google.com/chrome/**) may be close seconds. By opening Firefox's built-in error console (found under the Tools menu), you'll be able to see any JavaScript errors as they occur.

An added advantage that Firefox has over the other browsers is a long history of excellent third-party extensions. In particular, Firebug and Web Developer are fantastic assets for understanding what's happening within the Web page. There are also extensions such as FireQuery, which add jQuery-aware development tools to Firefox.

Before beginning this chapter, I would recommend that you download and install the latest version of Firefox, and the aforementioned extensions (if you have not already). Running your JavaScript-enabled Web pages in Firefox will make it easier for you to see the errors as they happen, thereby making it that much easier to debug.

Incorporating jQuery

JavaScript is built into all graphical Web browsers by default, meaning no special steps must be taken to include JavaScript in a Web page (users have the option of disabling JavaScript, although statistically few do). jQuery is a framework of code, though; in order to use it, a Web page must first incorporate the jQuery library. To include any external JavaScript file in a Web page involves the HTML **script** tag, providing the name of the external file as the value of its **src** attribute:

```
<script src="file.js" type="text/
→ javascript" charset="utf-8"></script>
```

The jQuery framework file will have a name like **jquery-X.Y.Z.min.js**, where *X.Y.Z* is the version number (1.6.1 at the time of this writing). The *min* part of the file's name indicates that the JavaScript file has been *minified*. *Minification* is the removal of spaces, newlines, and comments from code. The result is code that's barely legible Ⓐ, but still completely functional. The benefit of minified code is that it will load in the browser slightly faster because it will be a marginally smaller file size.

Ⓐ What the minified jQuery code looks like.

B The form for downloading the current version of jQuery.

The following set of steps will walk you through installing the jQuery library on your Web server and incorporating it into a Web page; see the sidebar for an alternative approach.

To incorporate jQuery:

1. Load **www.jquery.com** in your Web browser.

2. At the top of the page, select *PRODUCTION* (it's the default option), and click *Download(jQuery);* **B**.

   Because the resulting file is just JavaScript, it will load directly in your Web browser **A**.

3. Save the page on your computer.

   Most browsers offer a Save Page, Save As, or Save Page As option. Save the file as **jquery-*X.Y.Z*.min.js**, where *X.Y.Z* is the actual version number.

   continues on next page

Using Hosted jQuery

This chapter recommends that you download a copy of jQuery and place it in your Web directory. Upon doing so, you just need to update the **script** tag to point to the location of the jQuery file on your Web site. I want to mention an alternative solution, though: using a *hosted* version of jQuery. By this, I mean that instead of using a version of the jQuery library stored on your own Web server, you could use a version stored elsewhere online. For example, Google provides copies of many JavaScript frameworks for public use (**http://code.google.com/apis/libraries/**). To use Google's copy of the jQuery library, the code would be:

```
<script type="text/javascript" src="https://ajax.googleapis.com/ajax/libs/
→ jquery/1.6.1/jquery.min.js" charset="utf-8"></script>
```

By using Google's hosted version of jQuery, your site (i.e., your site's visitors) will likely see a performance boost, due to Google's Content Delivery Network (CDN) and the way browsers cache media. I've only chosen *not* to use the Google-provided version of jQuery in this chapter because not all readers will have constant Internet connections and because knowing how to use local JavaScript files is a critical skill.

4. Move the downloaded file to a **js** folder within your Web server directory.

All of the JavaScript files to be used by this chapter's examples will be placed within a subdirectory named **js**.

5. Begin a new HTML document in your text editor or IDE, to be named **test. html** (Script 15.1):

```
<!DOCTYPE html PUBLIC "-//W3C//
 DTD XHTML 1.0 Transitional//EN"
 "http://www.w3.org/TR/xhtml1/DTD/
 xhtml1-transitional.dtd">
<html xmlns="http://www.w3.org/
 1999/xhtml" xml:lang="en"
 lang="en">
<head>
  <meta http-equiv="Content-Type"
   content="text/html;
   charset=utf-8" />
  <title>Testing jQuery</title>
</head>
<body>
  <!-- Script 15.1 - test.html -->
</body>
</html>
```

This very first example will simply test the incorporation and basic use of the jQuery library.

6. Within the HTML head, include jQuery:

```
<script type="text/javascript"
 src="js/jquery-1.6.1.min.js"
 charset="utf-8"></script>
```

The **script** tag is used to include a JavaScript file. Conventionally, **script** tags are placed within the HTML page's head, although that's not required (or always the case). The value of the **src** attribute needs to match the name and location of your jQuery library. In this case, the assumption is that this HTML page is in the same directory as the **js** folder, created as part of Step 4.

7. Save the file as **test.html**.

Because this script won't be executing any PHP, it uses the **.html** extension.

8. If you want, load the page in your Web browser and check for errors.

As this is just an HTML page, you can load it directly in a Web browser, without going through a URL. You can then use your browser's error console or other development tools (see the "Debugging JavaScript" sidebar) to check that no errors occurred in loading the JavaScript file.

Script 15.1 This blank HTML page shows how the jQuery library can be included.

```
1    <!DOCTYPE html PUBLIC "-//W3C//DTD XHTML 1.0 Transitional//EN" "http://www.w3.org/TR/xhtml1/DTD/
     xhtml1-transitional.dtd">
2    <html xmlns="http://www.w3.org/1999/xhtml" xml:lang="en" lang="en">
3    <head>
4       <meta http-equiv="Content-Type" content="text/html; charset=utf-8" />
5       <title>Testing jQuery</title>
6       <script type="text/javascript" src="js/jquery-1.6.1.min.js" charset="utf-8"></script>
7    </head>
8    <body>
9       <!-- Script 15.1 - test.html -->
10   </body>
11   </html>
```

Using jQuery

Once you successfully have jQuery incorporated into a Web page, you can begin using it. jQuery, or any JavaScript code, can be written between opening and closing **script** tags:

```
<script type="text/javascript">
// JavaScript goes here.
</script>
```

(Note that in JavaScript, the double slashes create comments, just as in PHP.)

Alternatively, you can place jQuery and JavaScript code within a separate file, and then include that file using the **script** tags, just as you included the jQuery library. This is the route to be used in this chapter, in order to further separate the JavaScript from the HTML.

To be clear, a Web page can have multiple uses of the **script** tags, and the same **script** tag cannot both include an external file and contain JavaScript code.

The code placed within a **script** tag will be executed as soon as the browser encounters it. This is often problematic, though, as JavaScript is frequently used to interact with the DOM: if immediately executed JavaScript code references a DOM element, the code will fail, as that DOM element will not have been encountered by the browser at that point **Ⓐ**. The only reliable way to reference DOM elements is after the browser has knowledge of the entire DOM.

In standard JavaScript, you can have code be executed after the page is completely loaded by referencing **window.onLoad**. In jQuery, the preferred method is to confirm that the Web document is *ready*:

```
$(document).ready(some_function);
```

As mentioned already, the jQuery syntax can seem especially strange for the uninitiated, so I'll explain this in detail. First of all, the code **$(*something*)** is how elements and such within the Web browser are selected in jQuery. In this particular case, the item being selected is the entire Web document. To this selection, the **ready()** function is applied. It takes one argument: a function to be called. Note that the argument is a reference to the function: its name, without quotation marks. Separately, **some_function()** would have to be defined, wherein the actual work—that which should be done when the document is loaded—takes place.

continues on next page

HTML Page   Browser Load

```
<html>
<head>
    <script type="text/javascript">
    // Making a reference to #something
    // here won't work!
    </script>
</head>
<body>
    <p id="something">This is something.</p>
</body>
</html>
```

Execute | JavaScript

Encounter | Document
Object | Model

Ⓐ A browser reads a Web page as the HTML is loaded, meaning that JavaScript code cannot reference DOM elements until the browser has seen them all.

An alternative syntax is to use an *anonymous function*, which is a function definition without a name. Anonymous functions are common to JavaScript (anonymous functions are possible in PHP, too, but not common). To create an anonymous function, the function's definition is placed inline, in lieu of the function's name:

```
$(document).ready(function( ) {
    // Function code.
});
```

Because the need to execute code when the browser is ready is so common, this whole construct is often simplified in jQuery to just:

```
$(function( ) {
    // Function code.
});
```

The syntax is unusual, especially the `});` at the end, so be mindful of this as you program. As with any programming language, incorrect JavaScript syntax will make the code inoperable.

To test jQuery, this next sequence of steps will create a JavaScript alert once the document is ready ❸. After you have this simple test working, you can safely begin using jQuery more practically.

To use jQuery:

1. Create a new JavaScript document in your text editor or IDE, to be named **test.js** (Script 15.2):

   // Script 15.2 - test.js

   A JavaScript file has no **script** tags—those are in the HTML document—or other opening tags. You can just begin entering JavaScript code. Again, a double slash creates a comment.

The page at http://localhost says:

⚠ Ready!

OK

❸ This JavaScript alert is created once jQuery recognizes that the Web document is ready in the browser.

Script 15.2 This simple JavaScript file creates an alert to test successful incorporation and use of the jQuery library.

```
1    // Script 15.2 - test.js
2    // This script is included by test.html.
3    // This script just creates an alert to
     test jQuery.
4
5    // Do something when the document is
     ready:
6    $(function( ) {
7
8        // Alert!
9        alert('Ready!');
10
11   });
```

2. Create an alert when the document is ready:

```
$(function() {
  alert('Ready!');
});
```

This is just the syntax already explained, with a call to **alert( )** in place of the *Function code.* comment shown earlier. The **alert( )** function takes a string as its argument, which will be used in the presented alert box **B**.

3. Save the file as **test.js**, in your Web server's **js** directory.

4. Open **test.html** (Script 15.1), in your text editor or IDE.

The next step is to update the HTML page so that it includes the new JavaScript file.

5. After including the jQuery library, include the new JavaScript file (**Script 15.3**):

```
<script type="text/javascript"
➞ src="js/test.js" charset="utf-8">
➞ </script>
```

Assuming that the **test.js** JavaScript file is placed in the same directory as the jQuery library, with the same relative location to **test.html**, this code will successfully incorporate it.

6. Save the HTML page and test it in your Web browser **B**.

If you do not see the alert window, you'll need to debug the JavaScript code.

> **TIP** Technically, in OOP, a *function* is called a *method*. **For the duration of this chapter, I'll continue to use the term "function" as it's likely to be more familiar to you.**

> **TIP** The code **$( )** is shorthand for calling the **jQuery( )** function.

> **TIP** jQuery's "ready" status is slightly different than JavaScript's onLoad: the latter also waits for the loading of images and other media, whereas jQuery's ready status is triggered by the full loading of the DOM.

Script 15.3 The updated test HTML page loads a new JavaScript file.

```
1   <!DOCTYPE html PUBLIC "-//W3C//DTD XHTML 1.0 Transitional//EN" "http://www.w3.org/TR/xhtml1/DTD/
    xhtml1-transitional.dtd">
2   <html xmlns="http://www.w3.org/1999/xhtml" xml:lang="en" lang="en">
3   <head>
4       <meta http-equiv="Content-Type" content="text/html; charset=utf-8" />
5       <title>Testing jQuery</title>
6       <script type="text/javascript" src="js/jquery-1.6.1.min.js" charset="utf-8"></script>
7       <script type="text/javascript" src="js/test.js" charset="utf-8"></script>
8   </head>
9   <body>
10      <!-- Script 15.3 - test.html #2 -->
11  </body>
12  </html>
```

Selecting Page Elements

Once you've got basic jQuery functionality working, the next thing to learn is how to select page elements. Being able to do so will allow you to hide and show images or blocks of text, manipulate forms, and more.

You've already seen how to select the Web document itself: **$(document)**. To select other page elements, use *CSS selectors* in place of **document**:

- **#something** selects the element with an **id** value of *something*

- **.something** selects every element with a **class** value of *something*

- **something** selects every element of *something* type (e.g., **p** selects every paragraph)

Those three rules are more than enough to get you started, but know that unlike **document**, each of these gets placed

within quotation marks. For example, the code **$('a')** selects every link and **$('#caption')** selects the element with an **id** value of *caption*. By definition, no two elements in a single Web page should have the same identifying value, thus to reference individual elements on the page, **#something** is the easiest solution.

These rules can be combined as well:

- **$('img.landscape')** selects every image with a **class** of *landscape*

- **$('#register input')** selects every input element found within an element that has an **id** of *register*

For the next jQuery example, a JavaScript-driven version of the Widget Cost Calculator form, similar to the one developed in Chapter 13, "Security Methods," will be developed. In these next few steps, the HTML page will be created, with the appropriate elements, classes, and unique identifiers to be easily manipulated by jQuery **Ⓐ**.

Ⓐ The Widget Cost Calculator as an HTML form.

To create the HTML form:

1. Open **test.html** (Script 15.3) in your text editor or IDE, if it is not already.

   Since this file is already jQuery-enhanced, it'll be easiest to just update it.

2. Change the page's title (**Script 15.4**):

   ```
   <title>Widget Cost Calculator
   → </title>
   ```

3. After the page title, incorporate a CSS file:

   ```
   <link rel="stylesheet" href="css/
   → style.css" type="text/css"
   → media="screen" />
   ```

   To make the form a bit more attractive, some CSS code will style it. You can find the CSS file in the book's corresponding downloads at **www.LarryUllman.com**.

The CSS file also defines two significant classes—*error* and *errorMessage*, to be manipulated by jQuery later in the chapter. The first turns everything red; the second italicizes text (but the class will be more meaningful as a way of identifying a group of similar items). In time, you'll see how these classes are used.

4. Change the second **script** tag so that it references **calculator.js**, not **test.js**:

   ```
   <script type="text/javascript"
   → src="js/calculator.js"
   → charset="utf-8"></script>
   ```

   The JavaScript for this example will go in **calculator.js**, to be written subsequently. It will be stored in the same **js** folder as the other JavaScript documents.

   continues on next page

Script 15.4 In this HTML page is a form with three textual inputs for performing a calculation.

```
1    <!DOCTYPE html PUBLIC "-//W3C//DTD XHTML 1.0 Transitional//EN" "http://www.w3.org/TR/xhtml1/DTD/
     xhtml1-transitional.dtd">
2    <html xmlns="http://www.w3.org/1999/xhtml" xml:lang="en" lang="en">
3    <head>
4        <meta http-equiv="Content-Type" content="text/html; charset=utf-8" />
5        <title>Widget Cost Calculator</title>
6        <link rel="stylesheet" href="css/style.css" type="text/css" media="screen" />
7        <script type="text/javascript" src="js/jquery-1.6.1.min.js" charset="utf-8"></script>
8        <script type="text/javascript" src="js/calculator.js" charset="utf-8"></script>
9    </head>
10   <body>
11       <!-- Script 15.4 - calculator.html -->
12   <h1>Widget Cost Calculator</h1>
13   <p id="results"></p>
14   <form action="calculator.php" method="post" id="calculator">
15       <p id="quantityP">Quantity: <input type="text" name="quantity" id="quantity" /></p>
16       <p id="priceP">Price: <input type="text" name="price" id="price" /></p>
17       <p id="taxP">Tax (%): <input type="text" name="tax" id="tax" /></p>
18       <p><input type="submit" name="submit" id="submit" value="Calculate!" /></p>
19   </form>
20   </body>
21   </html>
```

5. Within the HTML body, create an empty paragraph and begin a form:

```
<h1>Widget Cost Calculator</h1>
<p id="results"></p>
<form action="calculator.php"
→ method="post" id="calculator">
```

The paragraph with the **id** of *results* but no content will be used later in the chapter to present the results of the calculations. It has a unique **id** value, for easy reference. The form, too, has a unique **id** value. The form, in theory, would be submitted to **calculator.php** (a separate script, not actually written in this chapter), but that submission will be interrupted by JavaScript.

6. Create the first form element:

```
<p id="quantityP">Quantity: <input
→ type="text" name="quantity"
→ id="quantity" /></p>
```

Each form input, as originally written in Chapter 13, involved the textual prompt, the element itself, and a paragraph surrounding both. To the paragraph and form input, unique **id** values are added.

Note that I tend to use "camel-case" style names—*quantityP*—in object-oriented languages such as JavaScript. This approach just better follows OOP conventions (conversely, I would use *quantity_p* in procedural PHP code).

7. Create the remaining two form elements:

```
<p id="priceP">Price: <input
→ type="text" name="price"
→ id="price" /></p>
<p id="taxP">Tax (%): <input
→ type="text" name="tax"
→ id="tax" /></p>
```

8. Complete the form and the HTML page:

```
    <p><input type="submit"
→ name="submit" id="submit"
→ value="Calculate!" /></p>
</form>
</body>
</html>
```

The submit button also has a unique **id**, but that's for the benefit of the CSS; it won't actually be referenced in the JavaScript.

9. Save the page as **calculator.html** and load it in your Web browser **Ⓐ**.

Even though the second JavaScript file, **calculator.js**, has not yet been written, the form is still loadable.

TIP jQuery has its own additional, custom selectors, allowing you to select page elements in more sophisticated ways. For examples, see the jQuery manual.

Event Handling

JavaScript, like PHP, is often used to respond to events. Differently, though, events in JavaScript terms are primarily user actions within the Web browser, such as:

- Moving the cursor over an image or piece of text
- Clicking a link
- Changing the value of a form element
- Submitting a form

To handle events in JavaScript, you apply an *event listener* (also called an *event handler*) to an element, which is to say, you tell JavaScript that when A event happens to B element, the C function should be called. In jQuery, event listeners are assigned using the syntax

selection.*eventType*(*function*);

The *selection* part would be like **$('.something')** or **$('a')**: whatever element or elements to which the event listener should be applied. The *eventType* value will differ based upon the selection. Common values are *change*, *focus*, *mouseover*, *click*, *submit*, and *select*: different events can be triggered by different HTML elements. In jQuery, these are all actually the names of functions being called on the selection. These functions take one argument: a function to be called when the event occurs on that selection. Commonly, the function to be invoked is written inline, anonymously. For example, to handle the event of any image being moused-over, you would code:

```
$('img').mouseover(function( ) {
    // Do this!
});
```

This construct should look familiar, as **test.js** assigns an event handler that listens for the *ready* event occurring on the Web document.

Let's take this new information and apply it to the HTML page already begun. At this point, an event listener can be added to the form so that its submission can be handled. In this particular case, the form's three inputs will be minimally validated, the total calculation will be performed, and the results of the calculation displayed in an alert **A**. In order to do all this, you need to know one more thing: to fetch the values entered into the textual form inputs requires the **val( )** function. It returns the value for the selection, as you'll see in these next steps.

A The calculations are displayed using an alert box (for now).

To handle the form submission:

1. Open **test.js** in your text editor or IDE:

   Since the **test.js** file already has the proper syntax for executing code when the browser is ready, it'll be easiest and most foolproof to start with it.

2. Remove the existing **alert( )** call (**Script 15.5**).

   All of the following code will go in place of the original **alert( )**.

3. In place of the **alert( )** call, add an event handler to the form's submission:

   **$('#calculator').submit(function( ) {
   }); // End of form submission.**

   The selector grabs a reference to the form, which has an **id** value of *calculator*. To this selection the **submit( )** function is applied, so that when the form is submitted, the inline anonymous function will be called. Because the syntax can be so tricky, my recommendation is to add this block of code, and then write the contents of the anonymous function—found in the following steps—secondarily. Note that this and the following code goes within the existing **$(document).ready( ) { }** block.

4. Within the new anonymous function, initialize four variables:

   var quantity, price, tax, total;

   In JavaScript, the **var** keyword is used to declare a variable. It can also declare multiple variables at once, if separated by commas. Note that variables in JavaScript do not have an initial dollar sign, like those in PHP.

Script 15.5 This JavaScript file is included by **calculator.html** (Script 15.4). Upon submission of the form, the form's values are validated and a calculation performed.

```
1   // Script 15.5 - calculator.js
2   // This script is included by
    calculator.html.
3   // This script handles and validates the
    form submission.
4
5   // Do something when the document is
    ready:
6   $(function() {
7
8       // Assign an event handler to the form:
9       $('#calculator').submit(function() {
10
11          // Initialize some variables:
12          var quantity, price, tax, total;
13
14          // Validate the quantity:
15          if ($('#quantity').val() > 0) {
16
17              // Get the quantity:
18              quantity = $('#quantity').val();
19
20          } else { // Invalid quantity!
21
22              // Alert the user:
23              alert('Please enter a valid
                quantity!');
24
25          }
26
27          // Validate the price:
28          if ($('#price').val() > 0) {
29              price = $('#price').val();
30          } else {
31              alert('Please enter a valid
                price!');
32          }
33
34          // Validate the tax:
35          if ($('#tax').val() > 0) {
36              tax = $('#tax').val();
37          } else {
38              alert('Please enter a valid
                tax!');
39          }
40
```

code continues on next page

Script 15.5 *continued*

```
41        // If appropriate, perform the
          calculations:
42        if (quantity && price && tax) {
43
44            total = quantity * price;
45            total += total * (tax/100);
46
47            // Display the results:
48            alert('The total is $' + total);
49
50        }
51
52        // Return false to prevent an
          actual form submission:
53        return false;
54
55    }); // End of form submission.
56
57  }); // End of document ready.
```

The page at http://localhost says:

⚠ Please enter a valid quantity!

[OK]

B If a form element does not have a positive numeric value, an alert box indicates the error.

5. Validate the quantity:

```
if ($('#quantity').val( ) > 0) {
  quantity = $('#quantity').val( );
} else {
  alert('Please enter a valid
   → quantity!');
}
```

For each of the three form inputs, the value needs to be a number greater than zero. The value entered can be found by calling the **val( )** function on the selected element. If the returned value is greater than zero, then the value is assigned to the local variable **quantity**. Otherwise, an alert box indicates the problem to the user **B**. This is admittedly a tedious use of alerts; you'll learn a smoother approach in the next section of the chapter.

6. Repeat the validation for the other two form inputs:

```
if ($('#price').val( ) > 0) {
  price = $('#price').val( );
} else {
  alert('Please enter a valid
   → price!');
}
if ($('#tax').val( ) > 0) {
  tax = $('#tax').val( );
} else {
  alert('Please enter a valid
   → tax!');
}
```

continues on next page

7. If all three variables have valid values, perform the calculations:

```
if (quantity && price && tax) {
    total = quantity * price;
    total += total * (tax/100);
```

This code should be fairly obvious by now: it looks almost exactly as it would in PHP, save for the lack of dollar signs in front of each variable's name.

8. Report the total:

```
alert('The total is $' + total);
```

Again, a crude alert window will be used to display the results of the calculation **Ⓐ**. As you can see in this code, the plus sign performs concatenation in JavaScript.

9. Complete the conditional begun in Step 7 and return the value **false**:

```
}
return false;
```

Having the function return **false** prevents the form from actually being submitted to the script that's identified as the form's **action**.

10. Save the page as **calculator.js** (in the **js** folder) and test the calculator in your Web browser.

Note that if you already had **calculator.html** loaded in your Web browser, you'll need to refresh the browser to load the updated JavaScript.

TIP There are many jQuery plug-ins specifically for validating forms, but I wanted to keep this simple (and explain core JavaScript concepts in the process).

TIP It is possible to format numbers in JavaScript, for example, so they always contain two decimals, but it's not easily done. For this reason, and because I didn't want to detract from the more important information being covered, the results of the calculation may not always look as good as they should.

TIP With jQuery, if the browser supports it, the JavaScript code will perform the calculations. If the user has JavaScript disabled, or if she or he is using a really old browser, the JavaScript will not take effect and the form will be submitted as per usual (here, to the non-existent **calculator.php**).

DOM Manipulation

One of the most critical uses of JavaScript in general, and jQuery in particular, is manipulation of the DOM: changing, in any way, the contents of the Web browser. Normally, DOM manipulation is manifested by altering what the user sees; how easily you can do this in jQuery is one of its strengths.

Once you've selected the element or elements to be manipulated, applying any number of jQuery functions to the selection will change its properties. For starters, the **hide( )** and **show( )** functions ...um...hide and show the selection. Thus, to hide a form (perhaps after the user has successfully completed it), you would use:

$('#actualFormId').hide( );

The **toggle( )** function, when called, will hide a visible element and show a hidden one (i.e., it toggles between those two states). Note that these functions neither create nor destroy the selection (i.e., the selection will remain part of the DOM, whether it's visible or not).

Similar to **show( )** and **hide( )** are **fadeIn( )** and **fadeOut( )**. These functions also reveal or hide the selection, but do so with a bit of effect added in.

Another way to impact the DOM is to change the CSS classes that apply to a selection. The **addClass( )** function applies a CSS class and **removeClass( )** removes one. The following code adds the *emphasis* class to a specific blockquote and removes it from all paragraphs:

$('#blockquoteID').addClass
→ ('emphasis');
$('p').removeClass('emphasis');

The **toggleClass( )** function can be used to toggle the application of a class to a selection.

The already mentioned functions generally change the *properties* of the page's elements, but you can also change the *contents* of those elements. In the previous section, you used the **val( )** function, which returns the value of a form element. But when provided with an argument, **val( )** assigns a new value to that form element:

$('#something').val('cat');

Similarly, the **html( )** function returns the HTML contents of an element and **text( )** returns the textual contents. Both functions can also take arguments used to assign new HTML and text, accordingly.

continues on next page

Let's use all this information to finish off the widget cost calculator. A few key changes will be made:

- Errors will be indicated by applying the *error* class
- Errors will also be indicated by hiding or showing error messages Ⓐ
- The final total will be written to the page Ⓑ
- Alerts will not be used

There are a couple of ways of showing and hiding error messages. The simplest, to be implemented here, is to manually add the messages to the form, and then toggle their visibility using JavaScript. Accordingly, these steps begin by updating the HTML page.

To manipulate the DOM:

1. Open **calculator.html** in your text editor or IDE, if it is not already.

2. Between the quantity form element and its closing paragraph tag, add an error message (**Script 15.6**):

   ```
   <p id="quantityP">Quantity:
   → <input type="text"
   name="quantity" id="quantity" />
   → <span class="errorMessage"
   → id="quantityError">Please enter
   → a valid quantity!</span></p>
   ```

   Now following the input is a textual error, which also has a unique **id**. The span containing the error also uses the *errorMessage* class. This impacts the message's formatting, thanks to the external CSS document, and makes it easier for jQuery to globally hide all error messages upon first loading the page.

Ⓐ Error messages are now displayed next to the problematic form inputs.

Ⓑ The results of the calculations are now displayed above the form.

3. Repeat Step 2 for the other two form inputs:

```
<p id="priceP">Price: <input
→ type="text" name="price"
→ id="price" /><span class=
→ "errorMessage" id="priceError">
→ Please enter a valid price!
→ </span></p>
<p id="taxP">Tax (%): <input
→ type="text" name="tax"
→ id="tax" /><span class=
→ "errorMessage" id="taxError">
→ Please enter a valid tax!
→ </span></p>
```

4. Save the file.

5. Open **calculator.js** in your text editor or IDE, if it is not already.

continues on next page

Script 15.6 The updated HTML page has hardcoded error messages beside the key form inputs.

```
1   <!DOCTYPE html PUBLIC "-//W3C//DTD XHTML 1.0 Transitional//EN" "http://www.w3.org/TR/xhtml1/DTD/
    xhtml1-transitional.dtd">
2   <html xmlns="http://www.w3.org/1999/xhtml" xml:lang="en" lang="en">
3   <head>
4       <meta http-equiv="Content-Type" content="text/html; charset=utf-8" />
5       <title>Widget Cost Calculator</title>
6       <link rel="stylesheet" href="css/style.css" type="text/css" media="screen" />
7       <script type="text/javascript" src="js/jquery-1.6.1.min.js" charset="utf-8"></script>
8       <script type="text/javascript" src="js/calculator.js" charset="utf-8"></script>
9   </head>
10  <body>
11      <!-- Script 15.6 - calculator.html #2 -->
12  <h1>Widget Cost Calculator</h1>
13  <p id="results"></p>
14  <form action="calculator.php" method="post" id="calculator">
15      <p id="quantityP">Quantity: <input type="text" name="quantity" id="quantity" />
    <span class="errorMessage" id="quantityError">Please enter a valid quantity!</span></p>
16      <p id="priceP">Price: <input type="text" name="price" id="price" /><span class=
    "errorMessage" id="priceError">Please enter a valid price!</span></p>
17      <p id="taxP">Tax (%): <input type="text" name="tax" id="tax" /><span class="errorMessage"
    id="taxError">Please enter a valid tax!</span></p>
18      <p><input type="submit" name="submit" id="submit" value="Calculate!" /></p>
19  </form>
20  </body>
21  </html>
```

6. Remove all existing **alert( )** calls (**Script 15.7**).

7. Before the submit event handler, hide every element with the *errorMessage* class:

$('.errorMessage').hide( );

The selector grabs a reference to any element of any type that has a class of *errorMessage*. In the HTML form, this applies only to the three **span** tags.

8. In the **if** clause code after assigning a value to the local **quantity** variable, remove the *error* class and hide the error message:

$('#quantityP').removeClass
→ ('error');
$('#quantityError').hide( );

As you'll see in Step 9, when the user enters an invalid quantity, the quantity paragraph (with an **id** value of *quantityP*) will be assigned the *error* class and the quantity error message (i.e., *#quantityError*) will be shown. If the user entered an invalid quantity, but then entered a valid one, those two effects must be undone, using this code here.

In the case that an invalid quantity was never submitted, the quantity paragraph will not have the *error* class and the quantity error message will still be hidden. In situations where jQuery is asked to do something that's not possible, such as hiding an already hidden element, jQuery just ignores the request.

9. If the quantity is not valid, add the error class and show the error message:

$('#quantityP').addClass('error');
$('#quantityError').show( );

This is the converse of the code in Step 8. Note that it goes within the **else** clause.

Script 15.7 Using jQuery, the JavaScript code now manipulates the DOM instead of using **alert( )** calls.

```
1    // Script 15.7 - calculator.js #2
2    // This script is included by calculator.
     html.
3    // This script handles and validates the
     form submission.
4
5    // Do something when the document is
     ready:
6    $(function() {
7
8        // Hide all error messages:
9        $('.errorMessage').hide( );
10
11       // Assign an event handler to the
         form:
12       $('#calculator').submit(function( ) {
13
14           // Initialize some variables:
15           var quantity, price, tax, total;
16
17           // Validate the quantity:
18           if ($('#quantity').val( ) > 0) {
19
20               // Get the quantity:
21               quantity = $('#quantity').val( );
22
23               // Clear an error, if one
                 existed:
24               $('#quantityP').removeClass
                 ('error');
25
26               // Hide the error message, if
                 it was visible:
27               $('#quantityError').hide( );
28
29           } else { // Invalid quantity!
30
31               // Add an error class:
32               $('#quantityP').addClass
                 ('error');
33
34               // Show the error message:
35               $('#quantityError').show( );
36
37           }
38
```

code continues on next page

```
39          // Validate the price:
40          if ($('#price').val( ) > 0) {
41              price = $('#price').val( );
42              $('#priceP').removeClass
                ('error');
43              $('#priceError').hide( );
44          } else {
45              $('#priceP').addClass
                ('error');
46              $('#priceError').show( );
47          }
48
49          // Validate the tax:
50          if ($('#tax').val( ) > 0) {
51              tax = $('#tax').val( );
52              $('#taxP').removeClass
                ('error');
53              $('#taxError').hide( );
54          } else {
55              $('#taxP').addClass('error');
56              $('#taxError').show( );
57          }
58
59          // If appropriate, perform the
            calculations:
60          if (quantity && price && tax) {
61
62              total = quantity * price;
63              total += total * (tax/100);
64
65              // Display the results:
66              $('#results').html('The total
                is <b>$' + total + '</b>.');
67
68          }
69
70          // Return false to prevent an
            actual form submission:
71          return false;
72
73      }); // End of form submission.
74
75  }); // End of document ready.
```

10. Repeat Steps 8 and 9 for the price, making that **if-else** read:

```
if ($('#price').val( ) > 0) {
    price = $('#price').val( );
    $('#priceP').removeClass
     ('error');
    $('#priceError').hide( );
} else {
    $('#priceP').addClass('error');
    $('#priceError').show( );
}
```

11. Repeat Steps 8 and 9 for the tax, making that **if-else** read:

```
if ($('#tax').val( ) > 0) {
    tax = $('#tax').val( );
    $('#taxP').removeClass('error');
    $('#taxError').hide( );
} else {
    $('#taxP').addClass('error');
    $('#taxError').show( );
}
```

12. After calculating the total, within the same **if** clause, update the *results* paragraph:

```
$('#results').html('The total is
 <b>$' + total + '</b>.');
```

Instead of using an alert box, the total message can just be written to the HTML page dynamically. One way of doing so is by changing the text or HTML of an element on the page. The page already has an empty paragraph for this purpose, with an **id** value of *results*. To change the text found within the paragraph, one would apply the **text( )** function. To change the HTML found within the paragraph, use **html( )** instead.

continues on next page

13. Save the page as **calculator.js** (in the **js** folder) and test the calculator in your Web browser.

Again, remember that you must reload the HTML page (because both the HTML and the JavaScript have been updated).

TIP jQuery will not throw an error if you attempt to select page elements that don't exist. jQuery will also not throw an error if you call a function on non-existent elements.

TIP In JavaScript, as in other OOP languages, you can "chain" function calls together, performing multiple actions at one time. This code reveals a previously hidden paragraph, adds a new class, and changes its textual content, all in one line:

```
$('#pId').show( ).addClass('thisClass').
→ text('Hello, world!');
```

TIP You can change the attributes of a selection using the `attr( )` function. Its first argument is the attribute to be impacted; the second, the new value. For example, the following code will disable a submit button by adding the property `disabled="disabled"`:

```
$('#submitButtonId').attr('disabled',
→ 'disabled');
```

TIP You can add, move, or remove elements using the `prepend( )`, `append( )`, `remove( )`, and other functions. See the jQuery manual for specifics.

Using Ajax

Along with DOM manipulation, another key use of JavaScript and jQuery is *Ajax*. The term Ajax was first coined in 2005, although browser support was mixed for years. Come 2011, Ajax is a standard feature of many dynamic Web sites, and its straightforward use is supported by all the major browsers. But what is Ajax?

Ajax can mean many things, involving several different technologies and approaches, but at the end of the day, Ajax is simply the use of JavaScript to perform a server-side request unbeknownst to the user. In a standard request model, which is to say pretty much every other example in this book, the user may begin on, say, `login.html`. Upon submission of the form, the browser will be taken to perhaps `login.php`, where the actual form validation is done, the registration in the database takes place, and the results are displayed **A**. (Even if the same PHP script both displays and handles a form, the standard request model requires two separate and overt requests of that same page.)

continues on next page

A A standard client-server request model, with the browser constantly reloading entire Web pages.

With the Ajax model, the form submission will be *hijacked* by JavaScript, which will in turn send the form data to a server-side PHP script. That PHP script does whatever validation and other tasks necessary, and then returns only data to the client-side JavaScript, indicating the results of the operation. The client-side JavaScript then uses the returned data to update the Web page 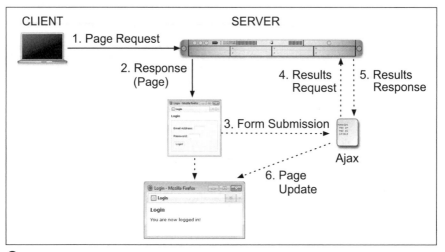. Although there are more steps, the user will be unaware of most of them, and be able to continue interacting with the Web page while this process takes place.

Incorporating Ajax into a Web site results in an improved user experience, more similar to how desktop applications behave. Secondarily, there can be better performance, with less data being transmitted back and forth (e.g., an entire second page of HTML, like `login.php`, does not need to be transmitted).

You already know much of the information required for performing Ajax transactions: form validation with JavaScript, form validation with PHP, and using JavaScript to update the DOM. The last bit of knowledge you need is how to perform the actual Ajax request using jQuery. Over the next several pages, you'll create the HTML form, the server-side PHP script, and the intermediary JavaScript, all for the sake of handling a login form. In order to shorten and simplify the code a bit, I've cut a couple of corners, but I'll indicate exactly when I do so, and every cut will be in an area you could easily flesh out on your own.

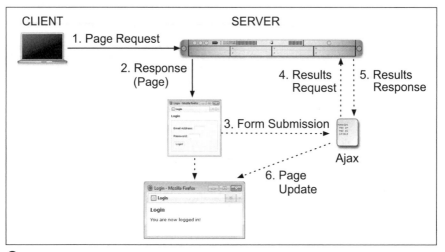

B With Ajax, server requests are made behind the scenes, and the Web browser can be updated without reloading.

Creating the Form

The login form simply needs two inputs: one for an email address and another for a password **C**. The form will use the same techniques for displaying errors and indicating results as `calculator.html` **D**.

To create the form:

1. Begin a new PHP document in your text editor or IDE, to be named `login.php` (Script 15.8):

   <!DOCTYPE html PUBLIC "-//W3C//
   → DTD XHTML 1.0 Transitional//EN"
   → "http://www.w3.org/TR/xhtml1/DTD/
   → xhtml1-transitional.dtd">
   <html xmlns="http://www.w3.org/
   → 1999/xhtml" xml:lang="en"
   → lang="en">
   <head>

continues on next page

C The login form.

D Error messages are revealed beside each form element.

Script 15.8 The login form has one text input for the email address, a password input, and a submit button. Other elements exist to be manipulated by jQuery.

```
1    <!DOCTYPE html PUBLIC "-//W3C//DTD XHTML 1.0 Transitional//EN" "http://www.w3.org/TR/xhtml1/DTD/
     xhtml1-transitional.dtd">
2    <html xmlns="http://www.w3.org/1999/xhtml" xml:lang="en" lang="en">
3    <head>
4        <meta http-equiv="Content-Type" content="text/html; charset=utf-8" />
5        <title>Login</title>
6        <link rel="stylesheet" href="css/style.css" type="text/css" media="screen" />
7        <script type="text/javascript" src="js/jquery-1.6.1.min.js" charset="utf-8"></script>
8        <script type="text/javascript" src="js/login.js" charset="utf-8"></script>
9    </head>
10   <body>
11       <!-- Script 15.8 - login.php -->
12   <h1>Login</h1>
13   <p id="results"></p>
14   <form action="login.php" method="post" id="login">
15       <p id="emailP">Email Address: <input type="text" name="email" id="email" /><span
         class="errorMessage" id="emailError">Please enter your email address!</span></p>
16       <p id="passwordP">Password: <input type="password" name="password" id="password" /><span
         class="errorMessage" id="passwordError">Please enter your password!</span></p>
17       <p><input type="submit" name="submit" id="submit" value="Login!" /></p>
18   </form>
19   </body>
20   </html>
```

```
<meta http-equiv="Content-Type"
→ content="text/html;
→ charset=utf-8" />
<title>Login</title>
<link rel="stylesheet"
→ href="css/style.css"
→ type="text/css" media=
→ "screen" />
```

This will actually be a PHP script, not just an HTML file. The page uses the same external CSS file as `calculator.html`.

2. Incorporate the jQuery library and a second JavaScript file:

```
<script type="text/javascript"
→ src="js/jquery-1.6.1.min.js"
→ charset="utf-8"></script>
<script type="text/javascript"
→ src="js/login.js" charset=
→ "utf-8"></script>
```

The page will use the same jQuery library as `calculator.html`. The page-specific JavaScript will go in `login.js`. Both will be stored in the `js` folder, found in the same directory as this script.

3. Complete the HTML head and begin the body:

```
</head>
<body>
  <!-- Script 15.8 - login.php -->
<h1>Login</h1>
<p id="results"></p>
```

Within the body, before the form, is an empty paragraph with an **id** of *results*, to be dynamically populated with jQuery later **E**.

4. Create the form:

```
<form action="login.php"
→ method="post" id="login">
  <p id="emailP">Email Address:
  → <input type="text" name=
  → "email" id="email" /><span
  → class="errorMessage"
  → id="emailError">Please enter
  → your email address!</span></p>
  <p id="passwordP">Password:
  → <input type="password"
  → name="password" id="password" />
  <span class="errorMessage"
  → id="passwordError">Please
  → enter your password!</span></p>
  <p><input type="submit"
  → name="submit" id="submit"
  → value="Login!" /></p>
</form>
```

This form is quite similar to that in `calculator.html`. Both form elements are wrapped within paragraphs that have unique **id** values, making it easy for jQuery to apply the *error* class when needed. Both elements are followed by the default error message, to be hidden and shown by jQuery as warranted.

5. Complete the HTML page:

```
</body>
</html>
```

6. Save the page as `login.php` and load in your Web browser.

Remember that this is a PHP script, so it must be accessed through a URL (*http://something*).

E Upon successfully logging in, the form will disappear and a message will appear just under the header.

Creating the Server-Side Script

The previous sequence of steps goes through creating the client side of the process: the HTML form. Next, I'm going to skip ahead and look at the server side: the PHP script that handles the form data. This script has to do two things:

1. Validate the submitted data.

2. Return a string indicating the results.

For simplicity's sake, the PHP script will merely compare the submitted values against hardcoded ones, but you could easily modify this code to perform a database query instead.

In terms of the Ajax process, the important thing is that this PHP script only ever returns a single string **F**, without any HTML or other markup **G**. This is mandatory, as the entire output of the PHP script is what the JavaScript performing the Ajax request will receive. And, as you'll see in the JavaScript for this example, the PHP script's output will be the basis for the error reporting and DOM manipulation to be performed.

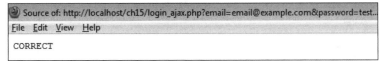

F The results of the server-side PHP script when a proper request is made.

> Source of: http://localhost/ch15/login_ajax.php?email=email@example.com&password=test...
>
> File Edit View Help
>
> CORRECT

G The HTML source of the server-side PHP script shows that the only output is a simple string, without any HTML at all.

To handle the Ajax request:

1. Begin a new PHP document in your text editor or IDE, to be named `login_ajax.php` (Script 15.9):

```
<?php # Script 15.9 -
→ login_ajax.php
```

Again, this script is not meant to be executed directly, so it contains no HTML.

2. Validate that an email address and a password were received in the URL:

```
if (isset($_GET['email'],
→ $_GET['password'])) {
```

A GET request will be made of this script, hence, the first thing the code does is confirm that both an email address and a password were passed to it.

3. Validate that the submitted email address is of the proper syntax:

```
if (filter_var($_GET['email'],
→ FILTER_VALIDATE_EMAIL)) {
```

Using the Filter extension, the provided email address is also checked for basic syntax. If your version of PHP does not support the Filter extension, you can use a regular expression here instead (see Chapter 14, "Perl-Compatible Regular Expressions").

4. If the submitted values are correct, indicate success:

```
if ( ($_GET['email'] ==
→ 'email@example.com') &&
→ ($_GET['password'] ==
→ 'testpass') ) {
  echo 'CORRECT';
```

As already said, this code just compares the submitted values against two static strings. You could easily swap out this code for a database query, like those in Chapter 12, "Cookies and Sessions." At this point you could also set a cookie

Script 15.9 This PHP script will receive the Ajax request from JavaScript. It performs some validation and returns simple strings to indicate the results.

```
1   <?php # Script 15.9 - login_ajax.php
2   // This script is called via Ajax from
    login.php.
3   // The script expects to receive two
    values in the URL: an email address and
    a password.
4   // The script returns a string
    indicating the results.
5
6   // Need two pieces of information:
7   if (isset($_GET['email'], $_GET['password'])) {
8
9       // Need a valid email address:
10      if (filter_var($_GET['email'], FILTER_
        VALIDATE_EMAIL)) {
11
12          // Must match specific values:
13          if ( ($_GET['email'] == 'email@
            example.com') && ($_GET['password']
            == 'testpass') ) {
14
15              // Set a cookie, if you want,
                or start a session.
16
17              // Indicate success:
18              echo 'CORRECT';
19
20          } else { // Mismatch!
21              echo 'INCORRECT';
22          }
23
24      } else { // Invalid email address!
25          echo 'INVALID_EMAIL';
26      }
27
28  } else { // Missing one of the two
    variables!
29      echo 'INCOMPLETE';
30  }
31
32  ?>
```

or begin a session (although see the following tip for the "gotchas" involved with doing so).

Most importantly, the script simply echoes the word *CORRECT*, without any other HTML (Ⓕ and Ⓖ).

5. Complete the three conditionals:

```
   } else {
      echo 'INCORRECT';
   }
} else {
   echo 'INVALID_EMAIL';
}
} else {
   echo 'INCOMPLETE';
}
```

These three **else** clauses complete the conditionals begun in Steps 2, 3, and 4. Each simply prints a string indicating a certain status. The JavaScript associated with the login form, to be written next, will take different actions based upon each of the possible results.

6. Complete the PHP page:

```
?>
```

7. Save the file as **login_ajax.php**, and place it in the same folder of your Web directory as **login.php**.

It's important that the two files are in the same directory in order for the Ajax request to work.

TIP It's perfectly acceptable for the server-side PHP script in an Ajax process to set cookies or begin a session. Keep in mind, however, that the page in the Web browser has already been loaded, meaning that page cannot access cookies or sessions created after the fact. You'll need to use JavaScript to update the page after creating a cookie or starting a session, but subsequent pages loaded in the browser will have full access to cookie or session data.

Creating the JavaScript

The final step is to create the JavaScript that interrupts the form submission, sends the data to the server-side PHP script, reads the PHP script's results, and updates the DOM accordingly. This is the "glue" between the client-side HTML form and the server-side PHP. All of the JavaScript form validation and DOM manipulation will be quite similar to what you've already seen in this chapter. Two new concepts will be introduced, though.

First, you'll need to know how to create a *generic object* in JavaScript. In this particular case, one object will represent the data to be sent to the PHP script and another will represent the options for the Ajax request. Here is how you create a new object in JavaScript:

```
var objectName = new Object();
```

The next chapter gets into OOP in more detail, but understand now that this just creates a new variable of type *Object*. The capital letter "O" **Object** is a blank template in JavaScript (being an object-oriented language, most variables in JavaScript are objects of some type). Once you've created the object, you can add values to it using the syntax:

```
objectName.property = value;
```

If you're new to JavaScript or OOP, it may help to think of the generic object as being like an indexed array, with a name and a corresponding value.

The second new piece of information is the usage of jQuery's **ajax()** function. This function performs an Ajax request. It takes as its lone argument the request's settings. Being part of the jQuery library, it's invoked like so:

```
$.ajax(settings);
```

That's the basic premise; the particulars will be discussed in detail in the following code.

To perform an Ajax request:

1. Begin a new JavaScript file in your text editor or IDE, to be named **login.js** (Script 15.10):

   ```
   // Script 15.10 - login.js
   ```

2. Add the jQuery code for handling the "ready" state of the document:

   ```
   $(function( ) {
   });
   ```

   The JavaScript needs to start with this code, in order to set the table once the Web browser is ready. Because of the complicated syntax, I think it's best to add this entire block of code first and then place all of the subsequent code within the curly braces.

3. Hide every element that has the *errorMessage* class:

   ```
   $('.errorMessage').hide( );
   ```

   The selector grabs a reference to any element of any type that has a **class** of *errorMessage*. In the HTML form, this applies only to the three **span** tags. Those will be hidden by this code as soon as the DOM is loaded.

4. Create an event listener for the form's submission:

   ```
   $('#login').submit(function( ) {
   });
   ```

   This code is virtually the same as that in the calculator form. All of the remaining code will go within these curly brackets.

5. Initialize two variables:

   ```
   var email, password;
   ```

   These two variables will act as local representations of the form data.

Script 15.10 The JavaScript code in this file performs an Ajax request of a server-side script and updates the DOM based upon the returned response.

```
1   // Script 15.10 - login.js
2   // This script is included by login.php.
3   // This script handles and validates the
    form submission.
4   // This script then makes an Ajax
    request of login_ajax.php.
5
6   // Do something when the document is
    ready:
7   $(function( ) {
8
9       // Hide all error messages:
10      $('.errorMessage').hide( );
11
12      // Assign an event handler to the form:
13      $('#login').submit(function( ) {
14
15          // Initialize some variables:
16          var email, password;
17
18          // Validate the email address:
19          if ($('#email').val( ).length >= 6) {
20
21              // Get the email address:
22              email = $('#email').val( );
23
24              // Clear an error, if one existed:
25              $('#emailP').removeClass('error');
26
27              // Hide the error message, if
                it was visible:
28              $('#emailError').hide( );
29
30          } else { // Invalid email address!
31
32              // Add an error class:
33              $('#emailP').addClass('error');
34
35              // Show the error message:
36              $('#emailError').show( );
37
38          }
39
```

code continues on next page

```
40      // Validate the password:
41      if ($('#password').val( ).length > 0) {
42          password = $('#password').val( );
43          $('#passwordP').removeClass
            ('error');
44          $('#passwordError').hide( );
45      } else {
46          $('#passwordP').addClass
            ('error');
47          $('#passwordError').show( );
48      }
49
50      // If appropriate, perform the
        Ajax request:
51      if (email && password) {
52
53          // Create an object for the
            form data:
54          var data = new Object( );
55          data.email = email;
56          data.password = password;
57
58          // Create an object of Ajax
            options:
59          var options = new Object( );
60
61          // Establish each setting:
62          options.data = data;
63          options.dataType = 'text';
64          options.type = 'get';
65          options.success = function
            (response) {
66
67              // Worked:
68              if (response == 'CORRECT') {
69
70                  // Hide the form:
71                  $('#login').hide( );
72
```

code continues on next page

6. Validate the email address:

```
if ($('#email').val( ).length >= 6) {
   email = $('#email').val( );
   $('#emailP').removeClass
 ➝ ('error');
   $('#emailError').hide( );
```

The calculator form validated that all of the numbers were greater than zero, which isn't an appropriate validation for the login form. Instead, the conditional confirms that the string length of the value of the email input is greater than or equal to 6 (six characters being the absolute minimum required for a valid email address, such as *a@b.cc*). You could also use regular expressions in JavaScript to perform more stringent validation, but I'm trying to keep this simple (and the server-side PHP script will validate the email address as well, as you've already seen).

If the email address value passes the minimal validation, it's assigned to the local variable. Next, the *error* class is removed from the paragraph, in case it was added previously, and the email-specific error is hidden, in case it was shown previously.

7. Complete the email address conditional:

```
} else {
   $('#emailP').addClass('error');
   $('#emailError').show( );
}
```

This code completes the conditional begun in Step 6. The code is the same as that used in **calculator.html**, adding the error class to the entire paragraph and showing the error message Ⓓ.

continues on next page

8. Validate the password:

```
if ($('#password').val( ).length >
→ 0) {
  password = $('#password').val( );
  $('#passwordP').removeClass
  → ('error');
  $('#passwordError').hide( );
} else {
  $('#passwordP').addClass
  → ('error');
  $('#passwordError').show( );
}
```

For the password, the minimum length would likely be determined by the registration process. As a placeholder, this code just confirms a positive string length. Otherwise, this code is essentially the same as that in the previous two steps.

9. If both values were received, store them in a new object:

```
if (email && password) {
  var data = new Object( );
  data.email = email;
  data.password = password;
```

Script 15.10 *continued*

```
73               // Show a message:
74               $('#results').removeClass('error');
75               $('#results').text('You are now logged in!');
76
77             } else if (response == 'INCORRECT') {
78               $('#results').text('The submitted credentials do not match those on file!');
79               $('#results').addClass('error');
80             } else if (response == 'INCOMPLETE') {
81               $('#results').text('Please provide an email address and a password!');
82               $('#results').addClass('error');
83             } else if (response == 'INVALID_EMAIL') {
84               $('#results').text('Please provide your email address!');
85               $('#results').addClass('error');
86             }
87
88           }; // End of success.
89           options.url = 'login_ajax.php';
90
91         // Perform the request:
92         $.ajax(options);
93
94       } // End of email && password IF.
95
96       // Return false to prevent an actual form submission:
97       return false;
98
99     }); // End of form submission.
100
101 }); // End of document ready.
```

The premise behind this code was explained before these steps. First a new, generic object is created. Then a property of that object named *email* is created, and assigned the value of the email address. Finally, a property named *password* is created, and assigned the value of the entered password. If it helps to imagine this code in PHP terms, the equivalent would be:

```
$data = array( );
$data['email'] = $email;
$data['password'] = $password;
```

10. Create a new object for the Ajax options, and establish the first three settings:

```
var options = new Object( );
options.data = data;
options.dataType = 'text';
options.type = 'get';
```

Here, another generic object is created. Next, a property named *data* is assigned the value of the **data** object. This property of the **options** object stores the data being passed to the PHP script as part of the Ajax request.

The second setting is the data type expected back from the server-side request. As the PHP script **login_ajax. php** returns (i.e., prints) a simple string, the value here is *text*. The **dataType** setting impacts how the JavaScript will attempt to work with the returned response: it needs to match what the actual server response will be.

The *type* setting is the type of request being made, with *get* and *post* being the two most common. A GET request

is the default, so it does not need to be assigned here, but the code is being explicit anyway.

To be clear, because of the name of the properties in the **data** object—*email* and *password*—and because of the *type* value of *get*, the **login_ajax.php** script will receive **$_GET['email']** and **$_GET['password']**. If you were to change the names of the properties in **data**, or the value of **options.type**, the server-side PHP script would receive the Ajax data in different superglobal variables.

11. Begin defining what should happen upon a successful Ajax request:

```
options.success = function
→(response) {
}; // End of success.
```

The **success** property defines what the JavaScript should do when the Ajax query works. By "work," I mean that the JavaScript is able to perform a request of the server-side page and receive a result. For what should *actually* happen, an anonymous function is assigned to this property. In this step, the anonymous function is defined and the assignment line is completed. The code in subsequent steps will go between these curly brackets.

As you can see, the anonymous function takes one argument: the response from the server-side script, assigned to the **response** variable. As already explained, the response received by the JavaScript will be the entirety of whatever is outputted by the PHP script.

continues on next page

12. Within the anonymous function created in Step 11, if the server response equals *CORRECT*, hide the form and update the page:

```
if (response == 'CORRECT') {
  $('#login').hide( );
  $('#results').removeClass
  → ('error');
  $('#results').text('You are now
  → logged in!');
```

When the user submits the correct credentials—*email@example.com* and *testpass*, `login_ajax.php` will return the string *CORRECT*. In that case, the JavaScript will hide the entire login form and assign a string to the *results* paragraph, indicating such Ⓔ. Because incorrect submissions may have added the *error* class to this paragraph (see Step 13), that class is also removed here.

13. If the server response equals *INCORRECT*, indicate an error:

```
} else if (response ==
→ 'INCORRECT') {
  $('#results').text('The submitted
  → credentials do not match
  → those on file!');
  $('#results').addClass('error');
```

When the user submits a password and a syntactically valid email address, but does not provide the correct specific values, the server-side PHP script will return the string *INCORRECT*. In that case, a different string is assigned to the *results* paragraph and the *error* class is applied to the paragraph as well Ⓗ.

Login

The submitted credentials do not match those on file!

Email Address: test@example.com

Password: ••••••••

Login!

Ⓗ The results upon providing invalid login credentials.

14. Add clauses for the other two possible server responses:

```
} else if (response ==
→'INCOMPLETE') {
  $('#results').text('Please
  →provide an email address and
  →a password!');
  $('#results').addClass('error');
} else if (response ==
→'INVALID_EMAIL') {
  $('#results').text('Please
  →provide your email address!');
  $('#results').addClass('error');
}
```

These are repetitions of the code in Step 13, with different messages. This is the end of the code that goes within the **success** property's anonymous function.

15. Add the **url** property and make the request:

```
options.url = 'login_ajax.php';
$.ajax(options);
```

The **url** property of the Ajax object names the actual server-side script to which the request should be sent. As long as **login.php** and **login_ajax.php** are in the same directory, this reference will work.

Finally, after establishing all of the request options, the request is performed.

16. Complete the conditional begun in Step 9 and return **false**:

```
} // End of email && password IF.
return false;
```

If the **email** and **password** variables do not have TRUE values, no Ajax request is made (i.e., that conditional has no **else** clause). Finally, the value **false** is returned here to prevent the actual submission of the form.

17. Save the page as **login.js** (in the **js** folder) and test the login form in your Web browser.

TIP As a debugging tip, it often helps to run the server-side script directly **F**, to confirm that it works (e.g., that it doesn't contain a parse or other error).

TIP The Firefox Firebug extension can reveal the details about Ajax requests made by a Web page **I**.

TIP The Opera Web browser has a built-in tool named *Dragonfly*, which is also an excellent development resource.

TIP Because JavaScript can be disabled by users, you can never rely strictly upon JavaScript form validation. You must always also use server-side PHP validation in order to protect your Web site.

I Thanks to the Firebug extension, you can see what transpires in a behind-the-scenes Ajax request.

Review and Pursue

If you have any problems with the review questions or the pursue prompts, turn to the book's supporting forum (www.LarryUllman.com/forums/).

Review

- What is JavaScript? How does JavaScript compare to PHP?

- What is jQuery? What is the relationship between jQuery and JavaScript?

- How is an external JavaScript file incorporated into an HTML page? How is JavaScript code placed within the HTML page itself?

- Why is it important to wait until the entire DOM has been loaded in order to execute JavaScript code that references DOM elements?

- Why are unique identifiers in the DOM necessary?

- In jQuery, how do you select elements of a given tag type? How do you select elements that have a certain class? How do you select a specific element?

- In jQuery, how do you add an event listener to a page element (or elements)? What *is* an event listener?

- Why must you reload HTML pages after altering its JavaScript?

- What are some of the jQuery functions one can use to manipulate the DOM?

- What is Ajax? Why is Ajax a "good thing"?

- Why must an HTML page that performs a server-side request be loaded through a URL?

- How do you create a generic object in JavaScript?

- What impact does the Ajax request's **type** property have? What impact do the names of the properties in the **data** object have?

Pursue

- Head to the jQuery Web site and start perusing the jQuery documentation.

- Check out jQuery UI and what it can do for your Web pages.

- Use the jQuery documentation, or simply search online, for some of jQuery's plug-ins. Attempt to use one or more of them in a Web page.

- Once you feel comfortable with the Ajax process, search online for information about performing Ajax requests using *JSON* (JavaScript Object Notation) or *XML* (eXtensible Markup Language) to represent the data transmitted back to the JavaScript.

- See what happens when you reference a DOM element in JavaScript before the entire DOM has been loaded. Witnessing this should help you recognize what's happening when you inevitably and accidentally fail to wait until the browser is ready before referencing the DOM.

- Update **calculator.js** so that the *results* paragraph is initially cleared upon each form submission. By doing so, the results of previous submissions won't be shown upon subsequent invalid submissions.

- Modify **login_ajax.php** so that it uses a database to confirm successful login.

- Modify **login_ajax.php** so that it sends a cookie or begins a session. Create a secondary PHP script that accesses the created cookie or session.

- Modify **login.php** so that it also performs the login validation, should the user have JavaScript disabled. Hint: This is simpler than you might think—just use PHP to handle the form submission (in the same file) as if JavaScript were not present at all.

An OOP Primer

PHP is somewhat unusual as a language in that it can be used both *procedurally*, as most of this book demonstrates, and as an *Object-Oriented Programming* (OOP) language. There are merits to both approaches, and one ought to be familiar with each as well (eventually).

Unfortunately, mastery of OOP requires lots of time and information: my *PHP 5 Advanced: Visual QuickPro Guide* (Peachpit Press) spends 150 pages on the subject! Still, one of the great things about OOP is that you can *use* it without fully *knowing* it. You'll see what this means shortly.

In this chapter, which is new to this edition of the book, is a primer for OOP in PHP. Some of the examples will replicate procedural ones already shown in the book, in order to best compare and contrast the two approaches. Various sidebars and tips will mention other uses of OOP in PHP, many of which will not have procedural equivalents.

Fundamentals and Syntax

If you've never done any Object-Oriented Programming before, both the concept and the syntax can be quite foreign. Simply put, all applications, or scripts, involve *taking actions with information*: validating it, manipulating it, storing it in a database, and so forth. Philosophically, procedural programming is written with a focus on the actions: do this, then this, then this; OOP is data-centric, focusing more on the kinds of information being used.

OOP Fundamentals

OOP begins with the definition of a *class*, which is a template for a particular type of data: an employee, a user, a page of content, and so forth. A class definition contains both variables and functions. Syntactically, a variable in a class definition is called an *attribute* or *property*, and a function in a class definition is called

OOP vs. Procedural

Discussions as to the merits of OOP vs. procedural programming can quickly escalate to verbal wars, with each side fiercely advocating for their approach. PHP is somewhat unique in that you have a choice (by comparison, C is strictly a procedural language and Java object-oriented). In my opinion, each programming style has its strengths and weaknesses, but neither is "better" than the other.

Procedural programming is arguably faster to learn and use, particularly for smaller projects. But procedural code can be harder to maintain and expand, especially in more complicated sites, and has the potential to be buggier.

Code written using OOP, on the other hand, may be easier to maintain, specifically on larger projects, and may be more appropriate in team environments. But OOP is harder to master, and when not done well, is that much more challenging to remedy.

In time, you'll naturally come up with your own opinions and preferences. The real lesson, to me, is to take advantage of the fact that PHP allows for both syntaxes, and not to limit yourself to just one style regardless of the situation.

a *method*. Combined, the attributes and methods are the *members* of the class.

As a theoretical example, you might have a class called *Car*. Note that class names conventionally begin with an uppercase letter. The properties of a **Car** would include **make**, **model**, **year**, **odometer**, and so forth: all information that can be known about a car. A **Car**'s properties can be set, changed, and retrieved, and the values of the properties distinguish *this* **Car** from *that* **Car**. A **Car**'s methods—the things that the car can do—would include: **start( )**, **drive( )**, **park( )**, and **turnOff( )**. These actions are common to all **Car**s.

In the introduction to this chapter, I stated that you can *use* OOP without really *knowing* it. By that I mean that it's very easy, and common enough, to use an existing class definition for your own needs. In fact, the reusability of code—particularly code created by others—is one of the key benefits of OOP. What actually takes a lot of effort, at least to do it right, is to master the design process: understanding what members to define and, more importantly, how to implement sophisticated OOP concepts such as:

- Inheritance
- Access control
- Overriding methods
- Scope resolution
- Abstraction
- And so on

When you're interested in learning how to properly create your own classes, you can look into these subjects in my *PHP 5 Advanced: Visual QuickPro Guide*, among other resources, but in this chapter, let's focus on using existing classes instead of creating your own custom ones.

OOP Syntax in PHP

So let's say someone has gone through the process of designing and defining a **Car** class. Most classes are not used directly; rather, you create an *instance* of that class—a specific variable of the class's type. That instance is called an *object*. In PHP, an instance is created using the **new** keyword:

```
$obj = new ClassName( );
$mine = new Car( );
```

Whereas the code **$name = 'Larry'** creates a variable of type string, the above code creates a variable of type **Car**. Everything that's part of **Car**'s definition—every property (i.e., variable) and method (i.e., function)—is now embedded in **$mine**.

Behind the scenes (i.e., in the class definition), a special method called the *constructor* is automatically invoked when a new object of that type is generated. The constructor normally provides whatever initial setup would be required by the subsequent usage of that object. For example, the **MySQLi** class's constructor establishes a connection to the database and the **DateTime** class's constructor creates a reference to an exact date and time (both the **MySQLi** and **DateTime** classes will be explicitly used in this chapter).

If the constructor takes arguments, like any function can, those may be provided when the object is created:

```
$mine = new Car('Honda', 'Fit', 2008);
```

Once you have an object, you reference its properties (i.e., variables) and call its methods (i.e., functions) using the syntax **$object_name->member_name**:

```
$mine->color = 'Purple';
$mine->start( );
```

continues on next page

The first line (theoretically) assigns the value *Purple* to the object's **color** property. The second line invokes the object's **start( )** method. As with any function call, the parentheses are required. If the method takes arguments, those can be provided, too:

```
$mine->drive('Forward');
```

Sometimes you'll use an object's properties as you would any other variable:

```
$mine->odometer += 20;
echo "My car currently has $mine->
 odometer miles on it.";
```

If an object's method returns a value, the method can be invoked in the same manner as any function that returns a value:

```
// The fill() method takes a number of
// gallons being added and returns
// how full the tank is:
$tank = $mine->fill(8.5);
```

And that's really enough to know about OOP in order to start using it. As you'll see, the examples over the next few pages will replicate functionality explained earlier in the book, so that the contrasting approaches to the same end result should help you better understand what's going on.

TIP In documentation, you'll see the *ClassName*::*method_name*( ) syntax. This is a way of specifying to which class a method belongs.

TIP One of the major changes in PHP 5.3 is support for *namespaces*. Namespaces, in layman's terms, provide a way to group multiple class definitions under a single title. Namespaces are useful for organizing code, as well as preventing conflicts (e.g., differentiating between my Car class and your Car class).

TIP Classes can also have their own constants, just as they have their own variables and functions. Class constants are normally used without an instance of that class, as in:

echo *ClassName*::*CONSTANT_NAME*;

TIP OOP in PHP has changed dramatically from PHP 3 to PHP 4 to PHP 5. The syntax discussed in this chapter will only work with PHP 5 and above.

More OOP Classes

There are more OOP classes defined in PHP than just those illustrated in this chapter, although I think the **MySQLi** and **DateTime** classes are the two most obviously accessible and usable. The largest body of classes can be found in the *Standard PHP Library* (SPL), built into PHP as of version 5.0, and greatly expanded in version 5.3.

The SPL provides high-end classes in several categories: exception handling, *iterators* (loops that can work on any collection of data), custom data types, and more. The SPL is definitely for more advanced PHP programmers and is most beneficial for otherwise strongly or entirely OOP-based code.

There are several good classes defined for internationalization purposes, too (**www.php.net/intl**). These classes define some of the functionality originally intended as part of the now-defunct PHP 6, including the ability to sort words, format numbers, and so forth, in a manner customized to the given *locale* (a locale is a combination of the language, cultural habits, and other unique choices for a region).

Working with MySQL

Just as you can write PHP code in both procedural and object-oriented styles, the MySQL Improved extension can similarly be used either way to interact with a database. Chapter 9, "Using PHP with MySQL," introduced the basics of the procedural approach. As a comparison, this chapter will run through the same functionality using OOP.

There are three defined classes that you will use herein:

- **MySQLi**, the primary class, provides a database connection, a querying method, and more.

- **MySQLi_Result**, is used to handle the results of **SELECT** queries (among others).

- **MySQLi_STMT** is for performing prepared statements (introduced in Chapter 13, "Security Methods").

For each, I'll explain the basic usage and walk you through an example script. For a full listing of all the possibilities—all the properties and methods of each class—see the PHP manual.

Creating a Connection

As with the procedural approach, creating a connection is the first step in interacting with MySQL when using object notation. With the **MySQLi** class, a connection is established when the object is instantiated (i.e., when the object is created), by passing the appropriate connection values to the constructor:

```
$mysqli = new MySQLi(hostname,
  username, password, database);
```

Even though this is OOP, you would use the same MySQL values as you would when programming procedurally, or when connecting to MySQL using the command-line client or other interface.

If a connection could not be made, the **connect_error** property will store the reason why Ⓐ:

```
if ($mysqli->connect_error) {
        echo $mysqli->connect_error;
}
```

Unfortunately, that approach was buggy (or just plain broken) in versions of PHP prior to 5.2.9, so you'll see this *kludge* (an unseemly fix) in the PHP manual instead:

```
if (mysqli_connect_error()) {
        echo mysqli_connect_error();
}
```

continues on next page

Warning: mysqli_mysqli() [mysqli.mysqli]: (28000/1045): Access denied for user 'usernae'@'localhost' (using password: YES) in
C:\xampp\htdocs\mysqli_oop_connect.php on line **14**
Access denied for user 'usernae'@'localhost' (using password: YES)

Ⓐ A MySQL connection error.

If you are not using PHP 5.2.9 or later, you'll have to use this last bit of code in your own scripts.

Next, you should establish the character set:

`$mysqli->set_charset(charset);`
`$mysqli->set_charset('utf8');`

At this point, you're ready to execute your queries, to be covered next.

After executing the queries, call the **close( )** method to close the database connection:

`$mysqli->close( );`

To be extra tidy, you can delete the object, too:

`unset($mysqli);`

To practice this, let's write a PHP script that connects to MySQL. As the subsequent two scripts will be updates of scripts from Chapter 9, and will use the same template as Chapter 9, you'll want to place these next three scripts in the same Web directories you used for Chapter 9.

To make an OOP MySQL connection:

1. Begin a new PHP script in your text editor or IDE, to be named **mysqli_oop_ connect.php** (Script 16.1):

   `<?php # Script 16.1 -`
   `→ mysqli_oop_connect.php`

   This script will largely follow the same approach as **mysqli_connect.php** in Chapter 9. It will contain no HTML.

Script 16.1 This script creates a new **MySQLi** object, through which database interactions will take place.

```
1   <?php # Script 16.1 - mysqli_oop_
        connect.php
2   // This file contains the database
        access information.
3   // This file also establishes a
        connection to MySQL,
4   // selects the database, and sets the
        encoding.
5   // The MySQL interactions use OOP!
6
7   // Set the database access information
        as constants:
8   DEFINE ('DB_USER', 'username');
9   DEFINE ('DB_PASSWORD', 'password');
10  DEFINE ('DB_HOST', 'localhost');
11  DEFINE ('DB_NAME', 'sitename');
12
13  // Make the connection:
14  $mysqli = new MySQLi(DB_HOST,
        DB_USER, DB_PASSWORD, DB_NAME);
15
16  // Verify the connection:
17  if ($mysqli->connect_error) {
18      echo $mysqli->connect_error;
19      unset($mysqli);
20  } else { // Establish the encoding.
21      $mysqli->set_charset('utf8');
22  }
```

2. Set the database connection parameters as constants:

```
DEFINE ('DB_USER', 'username');
DEFINE ('DB_PASSWORD', 'password');
DEFINE ('DB_HOST', 'localhost');
DEFINE ('DB_NAME', 'sitename');
```

As always, you'll need to change the particulars to be correct for your server. As with Chapter 9, this chapter's examples will make use of the *sitename* database.

3. Create a `MySQLi` object:

```
$mysqli = new MySQLi(DB_HOST,
  → DB_USER, DB_PASSWORD, DB_NAME);
```

This is the syntax already explained, using the constants as the values to be passed to the constructor.

4. If an error occurred, show it:

```
if ($mysqli->connect_error) {
  echo $mysqli->connect_error;
  unset($mysqli);
```

If the `MySQLi` object's `connect_error` property has a value, it means that the script could not establish a connection to the database. In that case, the connection error is displayed Ⓐ, and the object variable is unset, since it's useless.

Remember that if you're using a version of PHP prior to 5.2.9 (and you do know what, exact, version you're using, correct?), you'll need to change this code to:

```
if (mysqli_connect_error( )) {
  echo mysqli_connect_error( );
  unset($mysqli);
```

5. If a connection was made, establish the encoding:

```
} else {
  $mysqli->set_charset('utf8');
}
```

Remember that the encoding used to communicate with MySQL needs to match the encoding set by the HTML pages and by the database.

6. Save the script as `mysqli_oop_connect.php`.

As with most files in this book that are meant to be included by other scripts, this one omits the closing PHP tag.

7. Ideally, place the file outside of the Web document directory.

Because the file contains sensitive MySQL access information, it ought to be stored securely. If you can, place it in the directory immediately above or otherwise outside of the Web directory (see Chapter 9 for particulars).

Again, the following two scripts will use the template that Chapter 9 used, so you should store this connection script in the same directory as `mysqli_connect.php` from Chapter 9.

continues on next page

8. Temporarily place a copy of the script within the Web directory and run it in your Web browser.

In order to test the script, you'll want to place a copy on the server so that it's accessible from the Web browser (which means it must be in the Web directory). If the script works properly, the result should be a blank page. If you see an *Access denied...* or similar message **A**, it means that the combination of username, password, and host does not have permission to access the particular database.

9. Remove the temporary copy from the Web directory.

TIP You can use `print_r( )` to learn about, and debug, objects in PHP code **B**:

```
echo '<pre>' . print_r($mysqli, 1) .
→ '</pre>';
```

TIP Since the `$mysqli` object is unset if no connection is made, any script that needs it can be written to test for a successful connection by just using:

```
if (isset($mysqli)) { // Do whatever.
```

For brevity sake, this test is omitted in subsequent scripts, but know it's possible.

TIP The MySQLi constructor takes two more arguments: the port to use and the socket. When running **MAMP** or **XAMPP** (see Appendix A, "Installation" which you can download from peachpit.com), you may need to provide the port.

TIP The `MySQLi::character_set_name( )` method returns the current character set. The `MySQLi::get_charset( )` method returns the character set, collation, and more.

TIP You can change the database used by the current connection via the `select_db( )` method:

```
$mysqli->select_db(dbname);
```

```
mysqli Object
(
    [affected_rows] => 0
    [client_info] => mysqlnd 5.0.7-dev - 091210 - $Revision: 304625 $
    [client_version] => 50007
    [connect_errno] => 0
    [connect_error] =>
    [errno] => 0
    [error] =>
    [field_count] => 0
    [host_info] => localhost via TCP/IP
    [info] =>
    [insert_id] => 0
    [server_info] => 5.5.8
    [server_version] => 50508
    [sqlstate] => 00000
    [protocol_version] => 10
    [thread_id] => 6
    [warning_count] => 0
)
```

B Using `print_r( )` on an object, perhaps wrapped within preformatted tags to make its output easier to read, reveals the object's many property names and values.

Executing Simple Queries

Once you've successfully established a connection to the MySQL server, you can begin using the **MySQLi** object to query the database. For that, call the appropriately named **query( )** method:

```
$mysqli->query(query);
```

Its lone argument is the SQL command to be executed, which I normally assign to a separate variable beforehand:

```
$q = 'SELECT * FROM tablename';
$mysqli->query($q);
```

You can test for the query's error-free execution by using the method call as a condition:

```
if ($mysqli->query($q)) { // Worked!
```

Alternatively, you can check the **error** property **C**:

```
if ($mysqli->error) { // Did not
→ work!
        echo $mysqli->error;
}
```

If the query just executed was an **INSERT**, you can retrieve the automatically generated primary key value via the **insert_id** property:

```
$id = $mysqli->insert_id;
```

If the query just executed was an **UPDATE**, **INSERT**, or **DELETE**, you can retrieve the number of affected rows—how many rows were updated, inserted, or deleted—from the **affected_rows** property:

```
echo "$mysqli->affected_rows rows
→ were affected by the query.";
```

The last thing to know, before executing any queries, is how to *sanctify* data used in the query. To do so, apply the **real_ escape_method( )** to a string variable beforehand:

```
$var = $mysqli->real_escape_
→ string($var);
```

This is equivalent to invoking **mysqli_ real_escape_string( )**, and prevents apostrophes and other problematic characters from breaking the syntax of the SQL command.

Using all this information, the next set of steps will rewrite **register.php** (Script 9.5) from Chapter 9, using OOP.

System Error

You could not be registered due to a system error. We apologize for any inconvenience.

Table 'sitename.user' doesn't exist

Query: INSERT INTO user (first_name, last_name, email, pass, registration_date) VALUES ('this', 'that', 'email@example.com', SHA1('password'), NOW())

C A problem with a query results in a MySQL error.

To execute simple queries:

1. Open **register.php** (Script 9.5) in your text editor or IDE.

2. Change the inclusion of the MySQL connection script to (**Script 16.2**):

   ```
   require ('../mysqli_oop_connect.php');
   ```

   Assuming that **mysqli_oop_connect. php** is in the directory above this one, this code will work. If your directory structure differs, change the reference to the file accordingly.

3. Change each use of **mysqli_ real_escape_string( )** to: **$mysqli->real_escape_string( )**:

   ```
   $fn = $mysqli->real_escape_string
   ➝ (trim($_POST['first_name']));
   $ln = $mysqli->real_escape_string
   ➝ (trim($_POST['last_name']));
   $e = $mysqli->real_escape_string
   ➝ (trim($_POST['email']));
   $p = $mysqli->real_escape_string
   ➝ (trim($_POST['pass1']));
   ```

   Four pieces of data—all strings, naturally—are escaped for added protection in the query. Because the script now uses the MySQL Improved extension using an object-oriented approach, these four lines should be changed.

4. Update how the query is executed (line 52 of the original script):

   ```
   $mysqli->query($q);
   ```

   To execute a query on the database using OOP, call the object's **query( )** method, providing it with the query to be run.

Script 16.2 This updated version of the registration script uses the MySQL Improved extension via OOP.

```
1   <?php # Script 16.2 - register.php
2   // This script performs an INSERT query
    to add a record to the users table.
3   // This is an OOP version of the script
    from Chapter 9.
4
5   $page_title = 'Register';
6   include ('includes/header.html');
7
8   // Check for form submission:
9   if ($_SERVER['REQUEST_METHOD'] == 'POST') {
10
11      require ('../mysqli_oop_connect.php');
        // Connect to the db.
12
13      $errors = array(); // Initialize an
        error array.
14
15      // Check for a first name:
16      if (empty($_POST['first_name'])) {
17          $errors[] = 'You forgot to enter
            your first name.';
18      } else {
19          $fn = $mysqli->real_escape_
            string(trim($_POST['first_name']));
20      }
21
22      // Check for a last name:
23      if (empty($_POST['last_name'])) {
24          $errors[] = 'You forgot to enter
            your last name.';
25      } else {
26          $ln = $mysqli->real_escape_
            string(trim($_POST['last_name']));
27      }
28
29      // Check for an email address:
30      if (empty($_POST['email'])) {
31          $errors[] = 'You forgot to enter
            your email address.';
32      } else {
33          $e = $mysqli->real_escape_
            string(trim($_POST['email']));
34      }
35
36      // Check for a password and match
        against the confirmed password:
37      if (!empty($_POST['pass1'])) {
```

code continues on next page

Script 16.2 *continued*

```
38        if ($_POST['pass1'] != $_POST
          ['pass2']) {
39            $errors[] = 'Your password
              did not match the confirmed
              password.';
40        } else {
41            $p = $mysqli->real_escape_
              string(trim($_POST['pass1']));
42        }
43     } else {
44        $errors[] = 'You forgot to enter
          your password.';
45     }
46
47     if (empty($errors)) { // If
       everything's OK.
48
49        // Register the user in the
          database...
50
51        // Make the query:
52        $q = "INSERT INTO users
          (first_name, last_name, email,
          pass, registration_date) VALUES
          ('$fn', '$ln', '$e', SHA1('$p'),
          NOW( ) )";
53
54        // Execute the query:
55        $mysqli->query($q);
56
57        if ($mysqli->affected_rows ==
          1) { // If it ran OK.
58
59            // Print a message:
60            echo '<h1>Thank you!</h1>
61        <p>You are now registered. In
          Chapter 12 you will actually be
          able to log in!</p><p><br /></p>';
62
63        } else { // If it did not run OK.
64
65            // Public message:
66            echo '<h1>System Error</h1>
67        <p class="error">You could not
          be registered due to a system
          error. We apologize for any
          inconvenience.</p>';
68
69            // Debugging message:
70            echo '<p>' . $mysqli->error .
              '<br /><br />Query: ' . $q .
              '</p>';
```

5. Change the confirmation of the query's execution to read (originally line 53):

```
if ($mysqli->affected_rows == 1) {
```

The previous version of the script used the result variable to confirm that the query worked:

```
if ($r) {
```

Here, the conditional more formally asserts that the number of affected rows equals 1.

continues on next page

Script 16.2 *continued*

```
71
72            } // End of if ($r) IF.
73
74            $mysqli->close( ); // Close the
              database connection.
75            unset($mysqli);
76
77            // Include the footer and quit the
              script:
78            include ('includes/footer.html');
79            exit( );
80
81        } else { // Report the errors.
82
83            echo '<h1>Error!</h1>
84        <p class="error">The following
          error(s) occurred:<br />';
85            foreach ($errors as $msg) {
          // Print each error.
86                echo " - $msg<br />\n";
87            }
88            echo '</p><p>Please try again.
              </p><p><br /></p>';
89
90        } // End of if (empty($errors)) IF.
91
92        $mysqli->close( ); // Close the
          database connection.
93        unset($mysqli);
94
95     } // End of the main Submit conditional.
96     ?>
```

code continues on next page

6. Update the debugging error message to use the object (line 66 of the original script):

```
echo '<p>' . $mysqli->error .
→ '<br /><br />Query: ' . $q .
→ '</p>';
```

Instead of invoking the **mysqli_error( )** function, the **error** property of the object will store the database reported problem **C**.

7. Finally, change both instances where the database connection is closed to:

```
$mysqli->close( );
unset($mysqli);
```

The first line closes the connection. The second line removes the variable from existence. This step frees up the used memory and while not obligatory, is a professional touch.

The original script closed the database connection in two places; make sure you update both.

8. Save the script, place it in your Web directory, and test it in your Web browser **D**.

> **Thank you!**
> ....
> You are now registered. In Chapter 12 you will actually be able to log in!

D If all of the code was updated as appropriate, the registration script should work as it did before.

Script 16.2 *continued*

```
97    <h1>Register</h1>
98    <form action="register.php" method="post">
99        <p>First Name: <input type="text" name="first_name" size="15" maxlength="20" value="<?php if
          (isset($_POST['first_name'])) echo $_POST['first_name']; ?>" /></p>
100       <p>Last Name: <input type="text" name="last_name" size="15" maxlength="40" value="<?php if
          (isset($_POST['last_name'])) echo
          $_POST['last_name']; ?>" /></p>
101       <p>Email Address: <input type="text" name="email" size="20" maxlength="60" value="<?php if
          (isset($_POST['email'])) echo $_POST['email']; ?>" /> </p>
102       <p>Password: <input type="password" name="pass1" size="10" maxlength="20" value="<?php if
          (isset($_POST['pass1'])) echo $_POST['pass1']; ?>" /></p>
103       <p>Confirm Password: <input type="password" name="pass2" size="10" maxlength="20" value="<?php
          if (isset($_POST['pass2'])) echo $_POST['pass2']; ?>" /></p>
104       <p><input type="submit" name="submit" value="Register" /></p>
105   </form>
106   <?php include ('includes/footer.html'); ?>
```

Fetching Results

The previous section demonstrated how to execute "simple" queries, which is how I categorize queries that don't return rows of results. When executing **SELECT** queries, the code is a bit different, as you have to handle the query's results. First, after establishing the **MySQLi** object, you run the query on the database using the **query( )** method. If the query is expected to return a result set, assign the results of the method invocation to another variable:

```
$q = 'SELECT * FROM tablename';
$result = $mysqli->query($q);
```

The **$result** variable will be an object of type **MySQLi_Result**: just as some functions return a string or an integer, **MySQLi::query( )** will return a **MySQLi_Result** object. Its **num_rows** property will reflect the number of records in the query result:

```
if ($result->num_rows > 0) {
→ // Handle the results.
```

If you have only one row returned by the query, you can just call the **fetch_array( )** method to get it:

```
$row = $result->fetch_array( );
```

This method, like the procedural **mysqli_fetch_array( )** counterpart, takes a constant as an optional argument to indicate whether the returned row should be treated as an associative array (**MYSQLI_ASSOC**), an indexed array (**MYSQLI_NUM**), or both (**MYSQLI_BOTH**). **MYSQLI_BOTH** is the default value.

When you have multiple records to fetch, you can do so using a loop:

```
while ($row = $result->fetch_array
→ (MYSQLI_NUM)) {
        // Use $row.
}
```

With that code, **$row** within the loop will be an array, meaning you access individual columns using either **$row[0]** or **$row['column']** (assuming you're using the appropriate constant). If you're really enjoying the OOP syntax, you can use the **fetch_object( )** method instead, thereby creating an object instead of an array:

```
$q = 'SELECT user_id, first_name
→ FROM users';
$result = $mysqli->query($q);
while ($row = $result->fetch_
→ object( )) {
        // Use $row->user_id
// Use $row->first_name
}
```

Once you're done with the results, you should free the resources they required:

```
$result->free( );
```

Let's take this information to update **view_users.php** (Script 9.6).

To retrieve query results:

1. Open **view_users.php** (Script 9.6) in your text editor or IDE.

2. Change the inclusion of the MySQL connection script to (**Script 16.3**):

   require ('../mysqli_oop_connect.php');

   Again, the path needs to be correct for your setup.

3. Change the execution of the query to (originally line 14):

   $r = $mysqli->query($q);

   Regardless of the type of query being executed, the same **MySQLi::query( )** method is called. Here, though, the results of executing the query are assigned to a new variable, which will be an object of type **MySQLi_Result**.

   For brevity, I'm calling this variable just **$r**, but you can use the more formal **$result**, if you'd prefer.

4. Alter how the number of returned rows is determined to (line 17 of the original script):

   $num = $r->num_rows;

   The result object's **num_rows** property reflects the number of records returned by the query. This value is assigned to the variable **$num**, as before.

   Note that this is a *property*, not a *method* (it's **$r->num_rows**, not **$r->num_rows( )**).

5. Change the **while** loop to read:

   while ($row = $r->fetch_object( )) {

   The change here is that the **MySQLi_Result** object's **fetch_object( )** function is called instead of invoking **mysqli_fetch_array( )**.

Script 16.3 The MySQLi and MySQLi_Result classes are used in this script to fetch records from the database.

```
1    <?php # Script 16.3 - view_users.php
2    // This script retrieves all the records
     from the users table.
3    // This is an OOP version of the script
     from Chapter 9.
4
5    $page_title = 'View the Current Users';
6    include ('includes/header.html');
7
8    // Page header:
9    echo '<h1>Registered Users</h1>';
10
11   require ('../mysqli_oop_connect.php');
     // Connect to the db.
12
13   // Make the query:
14   $q = "SELECT CONCAT(last_name, ', ',
     first_name) AS name, DATE_FORMAT
     (registration_date, '%M %d, %Y')
     AS dr FROM users ORDER BY
     registration_date ASC";
15   $r = $mysqli->query($q); // Run the
     query.
16
17   // Count the number of returned rows:
18   $num = $r->num_rows;
19
20   if ($num > 0) { // If it ran OK, display
     the records.
21
22       // Print how many users there are:
23       echo "<p>There are currently $num
         registered users.</p>\n";
24
25       // Table header.
26       echo '<table align="center"
         cellspacing="3" cellpadding="3"
         width="75%">
27       <tr><td align="left"><b>Name</b>
         </td><td align="left"><b>Date
         Registered</b></td></tr>
28       ';
29
30       // Fetch and print all the records:
31       while ($row = $r->fetch_object( )) {
32           echo '<tr><td align="left">' .
             $row->name . '</td><td align=
             "left">' . $row->dr . '</td></tr>
33           ';
34       }
```

code continues on next page

Script 16.3 *continued*

```
35
36      echo '</table>'; // Close the table.
37
38      $r->free(); // Free up the
        resources.
39      unset($r);
40
41    } else { // If no records were returned.
42
43      echo '<p class="error">There are
        currently no registered users.</p>';
44
45    }
46
47    // Close the database connection.
48    $mysqli->close();
49    unset($mysqli);
50
51    include ('includes/footer.html');
52    ?>
```

Registered Users

There are currently 28 registered users.

Name	Date Registered
Ullman, Larry	March 31, 2011
Isabella, Zoe	March 31, 2011
Starr, Ringo	March 31, 2011
Harrison, George	March 31, 2011
McCartney, Paul	March 31, 2011
Lennon, John	March 31, 2011
Chabon, Michael	March 31, 2011
Brautigan, Richard	March 31, 2011
Banks, Russell	March 31, 2011
Simpson, Homer	March 31, 2011

E The object-oriented version of `view_users.php` (Script 16.3) looks the same as the original procedural version.

6. Within the **while** loop, change how each column's value is printed:

```
echo '<tr><td align="left">' .
→ $row->name . '</td><td align=
→ "left">' . $row->dr . '</td></tr>
';
```

Since the **$row** variable is now an object, object notation, instead of array notation, must be used to refer to the columns in each row: **$row->name** and **$row->dr** instead of **$row['name']** and **$row['dr']**.

7. Change how the resources are freed:

```
$r->free();
unset($r);
```

To free the memory taken by the returned results, call the **MySQLi_Result** object's **free()** method. Furthermore, since that object won't be used anymore in the script, it can be unset.

8. Update how the database connection is closed:

```
$mysqli->close();
unset($mysqli);
```

9. Save the script, place it in your Web directory, and test it in your Web browser **E**.

> **TIP** The real benefit of using the **fetch_object()** method is that you can have the results fetched as a *particular type of object*. For example, say you have defined a **Car** class in PHP and a script fetches all of the stored information about cars from the database. In the PHP script, each record can be fetched as an object of **Car** class type. By doing so, you'll have created a PHP **Car** object, whose data is populated from the database record, but can still invoke the methods of the **Car** class.

Prepared Statements

Chapter 13 introduced another way of executing queries: using *prepared statements*. Prepared statements can offer improved security, and possibly even better performance, over the standard approach to running queries. Naturally, you can execute prepared statements using the MySQL Improved extension as objects. The steps are the same: after creating a **MySQLi** object (and therefore a connection to the database), you

- Prepare the query
- Bind the parameters
- Execute the query

In actual code that looks like:

```
$q = 'INSERT INTO tablename (this,
→ that) VALUES (?, ?)';
$stmt = $mysqli->prepare($q);
$stmt->bind_param('si', $this, $that);
$this = 'Larry';
$that = 234;
$stmt->execute( );
```

The **MySQLi::prepare( )** method returns an object of type **MySQLi_STMT**. That object has a few key properties:

- **affected_rows** stores how many rows were affected by the statement, normally applicable to **INSERT**, **UPDATE**, and **DELETE** queries.

- **num_rows** reflects the number of records in the result set for a **SELECT** query.

- **insert_id** stores the automatically generated ID value for the previous **INSERT** query.

- **error** represents any error that might have occurred.

Once you're done executing the prepared statement, you should close the statement:

```
$stmt->close( );
```

Let's apply this information by updating **post_message.php** (Script 13.6). This is a stand-alone script that uses the *forum* database and isn't, in Chapter 13 or this chapter, tied to any other scripts.

To execute prepared statements:

1. Open **post_message.php** (Script 13.6) in your text editor or IDE.

2. Change the creation of the database connection to (**Script 16.4**):

   ```
   $mysqli = new MySQLi('localhost',
   → 'username', 'password', 'forum');
   $mysqli->set_charset('utf8');
   ```

   The previous version of the script did not use a separate connection script, and neither will this one. Make sure your values are correct for connecting to the *forum* database on your server.

3. Alter the preparation of the query to read (line 21 of the original script):

   ```
   $stmt = $mysqli->prepare($q);
   ```

   The **MySQLi::prepare( )** method prepares a statement, taking the query as its lone argument. It returns an object of type **MySQLi_STMT**, assigned to **$stmt** here.

4. Change the binding of parameters to:

   ```
   $stmt->bind_param('iiiss',
   → $forum_id, $parent_id, $user_id,
   → $subject, $body);
   ```

   This code change is simply from **mysqli_stmt_bind_param($stmt...** to **$stmt->bind_param(...** The method's first argument is an indicator of the data types to follow. The subsequent arguments are the PHP variables to which the query's placeholders are bound.

5. Update the execution of the statement to:

   ```
   $stmt->execute( );
   ```

continues on page 510

Script 16.4 In this version of a script from Chapter 13, the `MySQLi_STMT` class is used to execute a prepared statement.

Script 16.4 *continued*

```
1    <!DOCTYPE html PUBLIC "-//W3C//DTD XHTML
     1.0 Transitional//EN" "http://www.w3.org/
     TR/xhtml1/DTD/xhtml1-transitional.dtd">
2    <html xmlns="http://www.w3.org/1999/
     xhtml" xml:lang="en" lang="en">
3    <head>
4        <meta http-equiv="Content-Type"
         content="text/html; charset=utf-8" />
5        <title>Post a Message</title>
6    </head>
7    <body>
8    <?php # Script 16.4 - post_message.php
9    // This is an OOP version of the script
     from Chapter 13.
10
11   if ($_SERVER['REQUEST_METHOD'] == 'POST') {
12
13       // Validate the data (omitted)!
14
15       // Connect to the database:
16       $mysqli = new MySQLi('localhost',
         'username', 'password', 'forum');
17       $mysqli->set_charset('utf8');
18
19       // Make the query:
20       $q = 'INSERT INTO messages (forum_id,
         parent_id, user_id, subject, body,
         date_entered) VALUES (?, ?, ?, ?, ?,
         NOW())';
21
22       // Prepare the statement:
23       $stmt = $mysqli->prepare($q);
24
25       // Bind the variables:
26       $stmt->bind_param('iiiss',
         $forum_id, $parent_id, $user_id,
         $subject, $body);
27
28       // Assign the values to variables:
29       $forum_id = (int) $_POST['forum_id'];
30       $parent_id = (int) $_POST['parent_id'];
31       $user_id = 3; // The user_id value
         would normally come from the session.
32       $subject = strip_tags($_POST
         ['subject']);
33       $body = strip_tags($_POST['body']);
34
35       // Execute the query:
36       $stmt->execute();
```

```
37
38       // Print a message based upon the
         result:
39       if ($stmt->affected_rows == 1) {
40           echo '<p>Your message has been
             posted.</p>';
41       } else {
42           echo '<p style="font-weight: bold;
             color: #C00">Your message could
             not be posted.</p>';
43           echo '<p>' . $stmt->error . '</p>';
44       }
45
46       // Close the statement:
47       $stmt->close();
48       unset($stmt);
49
50       // Close the connection:
51       $mysqli->close();
52       unset($mysqli);
53
54   } // End of submission IF.
55
56   // Display the form:
57   ?>
58   <form action="post_message.php"
     method="post">
59
60       <fieldset><legend>Post a message:
         </legend>
61
62       <p><b>Subject</b>: <input
         name="subject" type="text" size="30"
         maxlength="100" /></p>
63
64       <p><b>Body</b>: <textarea name="body"
         rows="3" cols="40"></textarea></p>
65
66       </fieldset>
67       <div align="center"><input
         type="submit" name="submit"
         value="Submit" /></div>
68       <input type="hidden" name="forum_id"
         value="1" />
69       <input type="hidden" name="parent_id"
         value="0" />
70
71   </form>
72   </body>
73   </html>
```

6. Change the conditional that tests the success to:

```
if ($stmt->affected_rows == 1) {
```

To confirm the success of an **INSERT** query, check the number of affected rows, here referencing the **affected_rows** property of the **MySQLi_STMT** object.

7. Change the error reporting to use:

```
echo '<p>' . $stmt->error . '</p>';
```

At this point in the script, an error would most likely be because of something like using a duplicate value for a column that must be unique. If there was a syntactical error in the query, that would be in **$mysqli->error** after preparing the query.

8. Update how the statement is closed:

```
$stmt->close( );
unset($stmt);
```

9. Alter how the database connection is closed:

```
$mysqli->close( );
unset($mysqli);
```

10. Save the script, place it in your Web directory, and test it in your Web browser **F** and **G**.

F The HTML form for posting a new message.

G The new message has been successfully stored in the database.

Outbound Parameters

As in Chapter 13, the **post_message.php** script is a demonstration of using *inbound* parameters: associating placeholders in a query with PHP variables. You can also use *outbound* parameters: binding the values returned by a query to PHP variables. To start, you prepare the query:

```
$q = 'SELECT this, that FROM
→ tablename';
$stmt = $mysqli->prepare($q);
```

Then you bind the returned rows to variables:

```
$stmt->bind_result($this, $that);
```

Next, you call the **MySQLi_STMT::fetch( )** method, most likely as part of a **while** loop:

```
while ($stmt->fetch( )) {
}
```

Within the **while** loop, **$this** and **$that** will store each record's returned columns.

Outbound parameters don't offer added security, like inbound parameters, or necessarily better performance, but if you have a query that uses prepared statements, it would make sense to use both inbound and outbound parameters. For example, take a login query:

```
SELECT user_id, first_name
→ FROM users WHERE email='?' AND
→ pass=SHA1('?')
```

You would use inbound parameters to represent the submitted email address and password but use outbound parameters for the retrieved user ID and first name from that same query.

The DateTime Class

Added in version 5.2 of the language is the **DateTime** class. An alternative to the date- and time-related functions introduced in Chapter 11, "Web Application Development," the **DateTime** class packages together all the functionality you might need for manipulating dates and times. It's especially useful for converting and comparing dates and times.

To begin, create a new **DateTime** object:

```
$dt = new DateTime( );
```

If created without providing any arguments to the constructor, the generated **DateTime** argument will represent the current date and time. To create a representation of a specific date and time, provide that as the first argument:

```
$dt = new DateTime('2011-04-20');
$dt = new DateTime('2011-04-20 11:15');
```

There are many acceptable formats for specifying the date and time, detailed in the PHP manual. You can also establish the date or time after creating the object using the **setDate( )** and **setTime( )** methods. The **setDate( )** method expects to receive, in order, the desired year, month, and day. The **setTime( )** method takes the hour, minute, and optional seconds, as its arguments:

```
$dt = new DateTime( );
$dt->setDate(2001, 4, 20);
$dt->setTime(11, 15);
```

The **DateTime** object will only allow you to establish valid dates and times, throwing an *exception* for invalid ones **Ⓐ**:

```
$dt = new DateTime('2011-13-42');
```

Exceptions are a topic not previously introduced. Whereas procedural code may generate errors, objects *throw exceptions* (yes, it's said that they're *thrown*). When you get further along with OOP, you'll learn how to use **try...catch** blocks to "catch" and handle thrown exceptions.

The **DateTime** constructor takes an optional second argument, which is the time zone to use. If not provided, the default time zone for that PHP installation applies. You can also change the time zone after the fact, using **setTimezone( )**. Note that both the **setTimezone( )** method, and the constructor, take **DateTimeZone** objects as arguments, not strings:

```
$tz = new DateTimeZone('America/
→ New_York');
$dt->setTimezone($tz);
```

Once you have a **DateTime** object, you can manipulate its value by adding and subtracting time periods. One way to do so is the **modify( )** method:

```
$dt->modify('+1 day');
$dt->modify('-1 month');
$dt->modify('next Thursday');
```

The values you can provide to the method are quite flexible, and correspond to those that are usable in the **strtotime( )** function (which converts a string to a timestamp; see the PHP manual for details).

The **add( )** method is used to add a time period to the represented date and time.

continues on next page

Fatal error: Uncaught exception 'Exception' with message 'DateTime::__construct() [<a href='datetime.--construct'>datetime.--construct</a>]: Failed to parse time string (2011-13-42) at position 6 (3): Unexpected character' in /Users/larryullman/Sites/phpmysql4/ch16/test.php:2 Stack trace: #0 /Users/larryullman/Sites/phpmysql4/ch16/test.php(2): DateTime->__construct('2011-13-42') #1 {main} thrown in **/Users/larryullman/Sites/phpmysql4/ch16/test.php** on line **2**

Ⓐ Attempting to create a **DateTime** object with an invalid date or time results in an exception.

It takes as its lone argument an object of type **DateInterval**:

```
$di = new DateInterval(interval);
$dt->add($di);
```

There's a specific notation used to set the interval, always starting with the letter *P*, for "period." After that, add an integer and a period designator: *Y*, for years; *M*, for months; *D*, for days; *W*, for weeks; *H*, for hours; *M*, for minutes; and *S*, for seconds. You may wonder how the letter *M* can represent both months and minutes: this is possible because hours, minutes, and seconds should also be preceded by a *T*, for time. These characters should be combined in order from largest to smallest (i.e., from years to seconds). Here are some examples:

- *P3W* represents three weeks
- *P2Y3M* represents two years and three months
- *P2M3DT4H18M43S* represents two months, three days, four hours, 18 minutes, and 43 seconds

The **sub( )** method functions just the same as **add( )**, but subtracts the time period from the object:

```
$di = new DateInterval('P2W');
→ // 2 weeks
$dt->sub($di);
```

The **diff( )** method returns a **DateInterval** object that reflects the amount of time between two **DateTime** objects:

```
$diff = $dt->diff($dt2);
```

The **DateInterval** class defines several properties for representing the calculated interval: **y** for years, **m** for months, **d** for days, **h** for hours, **i** for minutes, **s** for seconds, and **days**, which also represents days.

The last **DateTime** class method you should be familiar with is **format( )**, which returns the represented date formatted as you want it:

```
echo $dt->format(format);
```

For the formatting, you can use the same characters as the **date( )** function, covered in Chapter 11.

To demonstrate all of this information, this next script will perform a task needed by many Web sites: allow the user to enter two dates to create a range 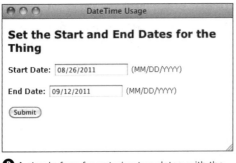. This script will perform top-quality validation of the submitted dates, and calculate the number of days between them **C**. The information presented could easily be applied to, say, a hotel registration system or the like. The script will use much of the information just presented, and even do a straight comparison of two **DateTime** objects, a feature possible since PHP 5.2.2.

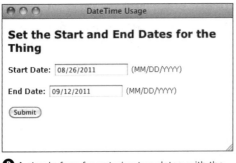

B A simple form for entering two dates, with the format specified.

C If two valid dates are submitted, with the ending date being after the starting date, the dates are displayed again, along with the calculated interval.

Script 16.5 Emulating common date selection functionality, this script accepts and validates two dates.

```
1    <!DOCTYPE html PUBLIC "-//W3C//DTD XHTML
     1.0 Transitional//EN" "http://www.w3.org/
     TR/xhtml1/DTD/xhtml1-transitional.dtd">
2    <html xmlns="http://www.w3.org/1999/
     xhtml" xml:lang="en" lang="en">
3    <head>
4       <meta http-equiv="Content-Type"
        content="text/html; charset=utf-8" />
5       <title>DateTime Usage</title>
6       <style type="text/css" media="screen">
7       body {
8          font-family: Verdana, Arial,
           Helvetica, sans-serif;
9          font-size: 12px;
10         margin: 10px;
11      }
12      label { font-weight: bold; }
13      .error { color: #F00; }
14      </style>
15   </head>
16   <body>
17   <?php # Script 16.5 - datetime.php
18
19   // Set the start and end date as today
     and tomorrow by default:
20   $start = new DateTime( );
21   $end = new DateTime( );
22   $end->modify('+1 day');
23
24   // Default format for displaying dates:
25   $format = 'm/d/Y';
26
27   // This function validates a provided
     date string.
28   // The function returns an array--month,
     day, year--if valid.
29   function validate_date($date) {
30
31      // Break up the string into its parts:
32      $date_array = explode('/', $date);
33
34      // Return FALSE if there aren't 3 items:
35      if (count($date_array) != 3) return
        false;
36
```

code continues on next page

To use the DateTime class:

1. Begin a new PHP script in your text editor or IDE, to be named **datetime.php**, starting with the HTML (**Script 16.5**):

```
<!DOCTYPE html PUBLIC "-//W3C//
→ DTD XHTML 1.0 Transitional//EN"
→ "http://www.w3.org/TR/xhtml1/DTD/
→ xhtml1-transitional.dtd">
<html xmlns="http://www.w3.org/
→ 1999/xhtml" xml:lang="en"
→ lang="en">
<head>
   <meta http-equiv="Content-Type"
   → content="text/html;
   → charset=utf-8" />
   <title>DateTime Usage</title>
```

2. Add a splash of CSS:

```
<style type="text/css"
→ media="screen">
body {
   font-family: Verdana, Arial,
   → Helvetica, sans-serif;
   font-size: 12px;
   margin: 10px;
}
label { font-weight: bold; }
.error { color: #F00; }
</style>
```

Only the *error* class here is significant in terms of the functionality. It will format error messages in red text.

3. Complete the head and begin the body and the PHP section:

```
</head>
<body>
<?php # Script 16.5 - datetime.php
```

continues on page 515

```
37      // Return FALSE if it's not a valid date:
38      if (!checkdate($date_array[0], $date_array[1], $date_array[2])) return false;
39
40      // Return the array:
41      return $date_array;
42
43   } // End of validate_date() function.
44
45   // Check for a form submission:
46   if (isset($_POST['start'], $_POST['end'])) {
47
48      // Call the validation function on both dates:
49      if ( (list($sm, $sd, $sy) = validate_date($_POST['start'])) && (list($em, $ed, $ey) =
         validate_date($_POST['end'])) ) {
50
51         // If it's okay, adjust the DateTime objects:
52         $start->setDate($sy, $sm, $sd);
53         $end->setDate($ey, $em, $ed);
54
55         // The start date must come first:
56         if ($start < $end) {
57
58            // Determine the interval:
59            $interval = $start->diff($end);
60
61            // Print the results:
62            echo "<p>The event has been planned starting on {$start->format($format)} and ending
               on {$end->format($format)}, which is a period of $interval->days day(s).</p>";
63
64         } else { // End date must be later!
65            echo '<p class="error">The starting date must precede the ending date.</p>';
66         }
67
68      } else { // An invalid date!
69         echo '<p class="error">One or both of the submitted dates was invalid.</p>';
70      }
71
72   } // End of form submission.
73
74   // Show the form:
75   ?>
76   <h2>Set the Start and End Dates for the Thing</h2>
77   <form action="datetime.php" method="post">
78
79      <p><label for="start_date">Start Date:</label> <input type="text" name="start_date"
         value="<?php echo $start->format($format); ?>" /> (MM/DD/YYYY)</p>
80      <p><label for="end_date">End Date:</label> <input type="text" name="end_date" value="<?php
         echo $end->format($format); ?>" /> (MM/DD/YYYY)</p>
81
82      <p><input type="submit" value="Submit" /></p>
83   </form>
84   </body>
85   </html>
```

4. Create two **DateTime** objects:

```
$start = new DateTime( );
$end = new DateTime( );
```

Whether the form has been submitted or not, two **DateTime** objects are first created, both of which will be instantiated using the current date and time. Subsequently, one or both objects will be assigned new values.

5. Add one day to the end date:

```
$end->modify('+1 day');
```

By default, when the page is first loaded, the form will be preset with today as the starting date and tomorrow as the ending date. To determine the ending date, simply modify the object's current value, adding one day.

Using the **DateInterval** object and the **DateTime::add( )** method, the same thing can be done like so:

```
$day = new DateInterval('P1D');
$end->add($day);
```

6. Establish the default format for displayed dates:

```
$format = 'm/d/Y';
```

The script will display a formatted version of the date in four places. Assigning the preferred format—*MM/DD/YYYY*—to a variable makes it easier to change later, if desired.

7. Begin defining a function:

```
function validate_date($date) {
  $array = explode('/', $date);
```

Both submitted dates will need to be validated in a couple of ways, and whenever you have repeating code in a script or application, defining a function to execute that code may make sense. This function takes a date string (not a

DateTime object) as its lone argument. The string will be the user-submitted value, something like *08/02/2011*. The first thing the function does is break up the string into its three separate parts—month, day, and year—using the **explode( )** function. The resulting array is assigned to the **$array** variable.

8. If the array does not contain three elements, return **false**:

```
if (count($array) != 3) return
→ false;
```

The first thing the function does is confirm that it has exactly three discrete values to work with, representing a month, day, and year. If the array does not contain three elements, the function returns the value **false** to indicate an invalid date. The **explode( )** line in Step 7 and this line invalidates any submitted value that doesn't fit the pattern *X/Y/Z* (although that could still be *cat/dog/zebra*).

Note that normally I would recommend always using curly brackets in conditionals, but I've made this code as short as possible by omitting them, and keeping the entire construct on a single line. Also remember that as soon as a function executes a **return** statement, the function is exited.

9. If the provided date isn't a valid date, return **false**:

```
if (!checkdate($array[0],
→ $array[1], $array[2])) return
→ false;
```

Similar to Step 8, this code invokes PHP's **checkdate( )** function to confirm that the provided date actually exists. If the date does not exist, such as *13/43/2011*, the function again returns **false**.

continues on next page

10. Return the date array and complete the function:

```
   return $array;
} // End of validate_date()
→ function.
```

If the provided date is of the correct format and corresponds to an existing date, the array of date elements is returned by the function.

11. If the form has been submitted, validate the user-submitted values:

```
if (isset($_POST['start'],
→ $_POST['end'])) {
if ( (list($sm, $sd, $sy) =
→ validate_date($_POST['start']))
→ && (list($em, $ed, $ey) =
→ validate_date($_POST['end'])) ) {
```

If the two variables are set, meaning the form has been submitted, both are run through the **validate_date( )** function. If that function returns **FALSE** for either date, this conditional will be **FALSE**. If the function returns an array for both dates, assigned to corresponding month, day, and year variables, then the results can be determined and displayed.

12. Reset the dates to the user-submitted dates:

```
$start->setDate($sy, $sm, $sd);
$end->setDate($ey, $em, $ed);
```

Because the provided dates are valid at this point, both objects can be updated to represent the user-entered dates. To do so, the **setDate( )** method is invoked, providing it with the individual values.

13. If the end date comes after the start date, calculate the interval between them:

```
if ($start < $end) {
   $interval = $start->diff($end);
```

Just as you can compare two numbers to see if one is greater than or less than the other, you can compare two **DateTime** objects. If the end date does come later, then the difference between the two dates is calculated by invoking the **diff( )** method on one object and providing the other as its argument. The result is assigned to the **$interval** variable, which will be an object of type **DateInterval**.

14. Print the results:

```
echo "<p>The event has been
→ planned starting on {$start->
→ format($format)} and ending on
→ {$end->format($format)}, which
→ is a period of $interval->days
→ day(s).</p>";
```

Finally, the results are displayed Ⓒ. As you can see, it's possible to invoke object methods within quotation marks, thereby printing the output of that function call, but you have to wrap the whole construct in curly brackets. Referencing attributes, such as **$interval->days**, does not require the curly brackets.

15. Complete the conditionals begun in Steps 11 and 13:

```
   } else { // End date must be
   → later!
      echo '<p class="error">The
      → starting date must precede
      → the ending date.</p>';
   }
} else { // An invalid date!
   echo '<p class="error">One or
   → both of the submitted dates
   → was invalid.</p>';
}
```

The first **else** clause applies if both dates are valid, but the end date does not follow the start date **D**. The second **else** clause applies if either of the submitted dates does not pass the **validate_date()** test. In this case, both dates will retain the default settings **E**.

16. Complete the form submission conditional, close the PHP block, and begin the HTML form:

```
} // End of form submission.
?>
<h2>Set the Start and End Dates
→ for the Thing</h2>
<form action="datetime.php"
→ method="post">
```

17. Create the two inputs for the dates:

```
<p><label for="start">Start
→ Date:</label> <input type="text"
→ name="start" value="<?php echo
→ $start->format($format); ?>" />
→ (MM/DD/YYYY)</p>
<p><label for="end">End Date:
→ </label> <input type="text"
→ name="end" value="<?php echo
→ $end->format($format); ?>" />
→ (MM/DD/YYYY)</p>
```

For each input, the value is preset by calling the **format()** method of the associated object. The required format that the date needs to be entered in is also indicated in parentheticals.

18. Complete the form and the HTML page:

```
<p><input type="submit"
value="Submit" /></p>
</form>
</body>
</html>
```

19. Save the script as **datetime.php**, place it in your Web directory, and test it in your Web browser.

If, when you run this script, you see an exception about relying upon the system's time zone setting, invoke **date_default_timezone_set()**, as explained in Chapter 11, prior to creating the **DateTime** objects.

TIP The DateTime::getTimestamp() method returns the Unix timestamp for the represented date and time.

TIP Internally, the DateTime class represents the dates and times as a 64-bit number, meaning it can represent dates from approximately 292 billion years ago to 292 billion years from now.

TIP Several constants in the DateTime class represent common date-time formats, such as DateTime::COOKIE.

TIP The DateTime methods are also represented in procedural versions.

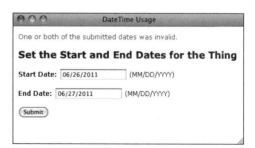

D The result if the provided starting date actually follows the entered ending date.

E The result if either submitted date does not correspond to a valid date.

Review and Pursue

If you have any problems with the review questions or the pursue prompts, turn to the book's supporting forum (**www.LarryUllman.com/forums/**).

Review

- What is a *class*? What is a *method*? What are variables defined within classes called?

- What is an object? How do you create an object in PHP? How do you call an object's methods?

- What is a *constructor*?

- What is the syntax for creating a **MySQLi** object?

- How do you execute any kind of query using **MySQLi**?

- How do you make string data safe to use in a query, when using **MySQLi**? Hint: there are two answers.

- How do you check for, and display, a **MySQLi** error?

- How do you fetch the results of **SELECT** queries using the **MySQLi** (and other) objects? What is the difference between using **MySQLi_Result::fetch_array( )** and **MySQLi_Result::fetch_object( )**?

- How do you execute a prepared statement using the **MySQLi** and **MySQLi_STMT** classes?

- What syntax is used to create a new **DateTime** object? What are the two ways you can set the object's date and/or time?

- What is an *exception*?

Pursue

- When you're interested in learning more about OOP, consider reading a book or tutorial on the generic subject of OOP, without respect to any given programming language.

- Check out the PHP manual's documentation on OOP in PHP (**www.php.net/oop**).

- Revisit Chapter 9 if you're unclear as to the need to apply **real_escape_string( )** to string data used in queries.

- Rewrite some of the other scripts from Chapter 9, "Using PHP with MySQL," and Chapter 10, "Common Programming Techniques," using **MySQLi**.

- Read through the full documentation for the **DateTime** class in the PHP manual (**www.php.net/datetime**).

- Learn about the **strtotime( )** function in the PHP manual (**www.php.net/strtotime**).

- If you want a big challenge, apply the information presented in the previous chapter, along with the jQuery UI **Datepicker** tool, to create two nice, JavaScript date selectors for the **datetime.php** script.

Example— Message Board

The functionality of a message board (aka a forum) is really rather simple: a post can either start a new topic or be in response to an existing one; posts are added to a database and then displayed on a page. That's really about it. Of course, sometimes implementing simple concepts can be quite hard!

To make this example even more exciting and useful, it's not going to be just a message board but rather a *multilingual* message board. Each language will have its own forum, and the key elements— navigation, prompts, introductory text, etc.—will be language-specific.

In order to focus on the most important aspects of this Web application, this chapter omits some others. The three glaring omissions will be: user management, error handling, and administration. This shouldn't be a problem for you, though, as the next chapter goes over user management and error handling in great detail. As for the administration, you'll find some recommendations at the chapter's end.

In This Chapter

Making the Database

The first step, naturally, is to create the database. A sample message board database **A** is developed in Chapter 6, "Database Design." Although that database is perfectly fine, a variation on it will be used here instead **B**. I'll compare and contrast the two to better explain the changes.

To start, the *forums* table is replaced with a *languages* table. Both serve the same purpose: allowing for multiple forums. In this new database, the topic—*PHP and MySQL for Dynamic Web Sites*—will be the same in every forum, but each forum will use a different language. The posts will differ in each forum (this won't be a translation of the same forum in multiple languages). The *languages* table stores the name of a language in its own alphabet and in English, for the administrator's benefit (this assumes, of course, that English is the administrator's primary language).

The *threads* table in the new database acts like the *messages* table in the old one, with one major difference. Just as the old *messages* table relates to *forums*, *threads* relates to the *languages* and *users* tables (each message can only be in one forum and by one user; each forum can have multiple messages, and each user can post multiple messages). However, this *threads* table will only store the subject, not the message itself. There are a couple of

A The model for the *forum* database developed in Chapter 6.

B The revised model for the forum database to be used in this chapter.

reasons for this change. First, having a subject repeat multiple times with each reply (replies, in my experience, almost always have the same subject anyway) is unnecessary. Second, the same goes for the *lang_id* association (it doesn't need to be in each reply as long as each reply is associated with a single thread). Third, I'm changing the way a thread's hierarchy will be indicated in this database (you'll see how in the next paragraph), and changing the table structures helps in that regard. Finally, the *threads* table will be used every time a user looks at the posts in a forum. Removing the message bodies from that table will improve the performance of those queries.

Moving on to the *posts* table, its sole purpose is to store the actual bodies of the messages associated with a thread. In Chapter 6's database, the *messages* table had a *parent_id* column, used to indicate the message to which a new message was a response. It was hierarchical: message 3 might be the starting post; message 18 might be a response to 3, message 20 a response to 18, and so on . That version of the database more directly indicated the responses; this version will only store the thread that a message goes under: messages 18 and 20 both use a *thread_id* of 3. This alteration will make showing a thread much more efficient (in terms of the PHP and MySQL required), and the date/time that each message was posted can be used to order them.

Those three tables provide the bulk of the forum functionality. The database also needs a *users* table. In this version of the forum, only registered users can post messages, which I think is a really, really, really good policy (it cuts way down on spam and hack attempts). Registered users can also have their default language (from the *languages* table) and time zone recorded along with their account information, in order to give them a more personalized experience. A combination of their username and password would be used to log in.

The final table, *words*, is necessary to make the site multilingual. This table will store translations of common elements: navigation links, form prompts, headers, and so forth. Each language in the site will have one record in this table. It'll be a nice and surprisingly easy feature to use. Arguably, the words listed in this table could also go in the *languages* table, but then the implication would be that the words are also related to the *threads* table, which would not be the case.

That's the thinking behind this new database design. You'll learn more as you create the tables in the following steps. As with the other examples in this book, you can also download the SQL necessary for this chapter—the commands suggested in these steps, plus more—from the book's corresponding Web site (**www.LarryUllman.com**).

message_id	parent_id
3	0
4	0
18	3
19	4
20	18

 C How the relationship among messages was indicated using the older database schema.

To make the database:

1. Access your MySQL server and set the character set to be used for communicating **D**:

   CHARSET utf8;

   I'll be using the mysql client in the figures, but you can use whatever interface you'd like. The first step, though, has to be changing the character set to UTF-8 for the queries to come. If you don't do this, some of the characters in the queries will be stored as gibberish in the database (see the sidebar "Strange Characters"). Note that if you're using phpMyAdmin, you'll need to establish the character set in its configuration file.

Strange Characters

If, when you're implementing this chapter's example, you see strange characters—boxes, numeric codes, or question marks instead of actual language characters—there might be several reasons why. When this happens, the underlying issue is one of *mismatching encodings* (or, in database terms, *character sets*).

A computer's ability to display a character depends on both the file's encoding and the characters (i.e., fonts) supported by the operating system. This means that every PHP or HTML page must use the proper encoding. Secondarily, the database in MySQL must use the proper encoding (as indicated in the steps for creating the database). Third, and this can be a common cause of problems, the communication between PHP and MySQL must also use the proper encoding. I address this issue in the **mysqli_connect.php** script (see the first tip). Finally, if you use the mysql client, phpMyAdmin, or another tool to populate the database, that interaction must use the proper encoding, too.

```
C:\Windows\system32\cmd.exe - C:\xampp\mysql\bin\mysql  -u root -p

Welcome to the MySQL monitor.  Commands end with ; or \g.
Your MySQL connection id is 2
Server version: 5.5.8 MySQL Community Server (GPL)

Copyright (c) 2000, 2010, Oracle and/or its affiliates. All rights reserved.

Oracle is a registered trademark of Oracle Corporation and/or its
affiliates. Other names may be trademarks of their respective
owners.

Type 'help;' or '\h' for help. Type '\c' to clear the current input statement.

mysql> CHARSET utf8;
Charset changed
mysql>
```

D In order to use Unicode data in queries, you need to change the character set used to communicate with MySQL.

2. Create a new database **E**:

```
CREATE DATABASE forum2 CHARACTER
→ SET utf8;
USE forum2;
```

So as not to muddle things with the tables created in the original *forum* database (from Chapter 6), a new database will be created.

If you're using a hosted site and cannot create your own databases, use the database provided for you and select that. If your existing database has tables with these same names—*words*, *languages*, *threads*, *users*, and *posts*, rename the tables (either the existing or the new ones) and change the code in the rest of the chapter accordingly.

Whether you create this database from scratch or use a new one, it's very important that the tables use the UTF-8 encoding, in order to be able to support multiple languages (see Chapter 6 for more). If you're using an existing database and don't want to potentially cause problems by changing the character set for all of your tables, just add

the **CHARACTER SET utf8** clause to each table definition (Steps 3 through 7).

3. Create the *languages* table **F**:

```
CREATE TABLE languages (
lang_id TINYINT UNSIGNED NOT NULL
→ AUTO_INCREMENT,
lang VARCHAR(60) NOT NULL,
lang_eng VARCHAR(20) NOT NULL,
PRIMARY KEY (lang_id),
UNIQUE (lang)
);
```

This is the simplest table of the bunch. There won't be many languages represented, so the primary key (*lang_id*) can be a **TINYINT**. The *lang* column is defined a bit larger, as it'll store characters in other languages, which may require more space. This column must also be unique. Note that I don't call this column "language," as that's a reserved keyword in MySQL (actually, I *could* still call it that, and you'll see what would be required to do that in Step 7). The *lang_eng* column is the English equivalent of the language so that the administrator can easily see which languages are which.

continues on next page

E Creating and selecting the database for this example. This database uses the UTF-8 character set, so that it can support multiple languages.

F Creating the *languages* table.

4. Create the *threads* table **G**:

```
CREATE TABLE threads (
thread_id INT UNSIGNED NOT NULL
→ AUTO_INCREMENT,
lang_id TINYINT(3) UNSIGNED NOT
→ NULL,
user_id INT UNSIGNED NOT NULL,
subject VARCHAR(150) NOT NULL,
PRIMARY KEY  (thread_id),
INDEX (lang_id),
INDEX (user_id)
);
```

The *threads* table contains four columns and relates to both the *languages* and *users* tables (through the *lang_id* and *user_id* foreign keys, respectively). The *subject* here needs to be long enough to store subjects in multiple languages (characters take up more bytes in non-Western languages).

The columns that will be used in joins and **WHERE** clauses—*lang_id* and *user_id*—are indexed, as is *thread_id* (as a primary key, it'll be indexed).

5. Create the *posts* table **H**:

```
CREATE TABLE posts (
post_id INT UNSIGNED NOT NULL
→ AUTO_INCREMENT,
thread_id INT UNSIGNED NOT NULL,
user_id INT UNSIGNED NOT NULL,
message TEXT NOT NULL,
posted_on DATETIME NOT NULL,
PRIMARY KEY (post_id),
INDEX (thread_id),
INDEX (user_id)
);
```

The main column in this table is *message*, which stores each post's body. Two columns are foreign keys, tying into the *threads* and *users* tables. The

G Creating the *threads* table. This table stores the topic subjects and associates them with a language (i.e., a forum).

H Creating the *posts* table, which links to both threads and users.

posted_on column is of type **DATETIME**, but will use UTC (Coordinated Universal Time, see Chapter 6). Nothing special needs to be done here for that, though.

6. Create the *users* table **❶**:

```
CREATE TABLE users (
user_id MEDIUMINT UNSIGNED NOT
→ NULL AUTO_INCREMENT,
lang_id TINYINT UNSIGNED NOT NULL,
time_zone VARCHAR(30) NOT NULL,
username VARCHAR(30) NOT NULL,
pass CHAR(40) NOT NULL,
email VARCHAR(60) NOT NULL,
PRIMARY KEY (user_id),
UNIQUE (username),
UNIQUE (email),
INDEX login (username, pass)
);
```

For the sake of brevity, I'm omitting some of the other columns you'd put in this table, such as registration date, first name, and last name. For more on creating and using a table like this, see the next chapter.

In my thinking about this site, I expect users will select their preferred language and time zone when they register, so that they can have a more personalized experience. They can also have a username, which will be displayed in posts (instead of their email address). Both the username and the email address must be unique, which is something you'd need to address in the registration process.

continues on next page

❶ Creating a bare-bones version of the *users* table.

7. Create the *words* table **J**:

```
CREATE TABLE words (
word_id TINYINT UNSIGNED NOT NULL
→ AUTO_INCREMENT,
lang_id TINYINT UNSIGNED NOT NULL,
title VARCHAR(80) NOT NULL,
intro TINYTEXT NOT NULL,
home VARCHAR(30) NOT NULL,
forum_home VARCHAR(40) NOT NULL,
`language` VARCHAR(40) NOT NULL,
register VARCHAR(30) NOT NULL,
login VARCHAR(30) NOT NULL,
logout VARCHAR(30) NOT NULL,
new_thread VARCHAR(40) NOT NULL,
subject VARCHAR(30) NOT NULL,
body VARCHAR(30) NOT NULL,
submit VARCHAR(30) NOT NULL,
posted_on VARCHAR(30) NOT NULL,
posted_by VARCHAR(30) NOT NULL,
replies VARCHAR(30) NOT NULL,
latest_reply VARCHAR(40) NOT NULL,
post_a_reply VARCHAR(40) NOT NULL,
PRIMARY KEY (word_id),
UNIQUE (lang_id)
);
```

This table will store different translations of common elements used on the site. Some elements—*home, forum_home, language, register, login, logout,* and *new_thread*—will be the names of links. Other elements—*subject, body, submit*—are used on the page for posting messages. Another category of elements are those used on the forum's main page: *posted_on, posted_by, replies,* and *latest_reply*.

Some of these will be used multiple times in the site, and yet, this is still an incomplete list. As you implement the site yourself, you'll see other places where word definitions could be added.

Each column is of **VARCHAR** type, except for *intro*, which is a body of text to be used on the main page. Most of the columns have a limit of 30, allowing for characters in other languages that require more bytes, except for a handful of columns that might need to be bigger.

For each column, its name implies the value to be stored in that column. For one—*language*—I've used a MySQL

J Creating the *words* table, which stores representations of key words in different languages.

keyword, simply to demonstrate how that can be done. The fix is to surround the column's name in backticks so that MySQL doesn't confuse this column's name with the keyword "language."

8. Populate the *languages* table:

```
INSERT INTO languages (lang,
→ lang_eng) VALUES
('English', 'English'),
('Português', 'Portuguese'),
('Français', 'French'),
('Norsk', 'Norwegian'),
('Romanian', 'Romanian'),
('Ελληνικά', 'Greek'),
('Deutsch', 'German'),
('Srpski', 'Serbian'),
('日本語', 'Japanese'),
('Nederlands', 'Dutch');
```

This is just a handful of the languages the site will represent thanks to some assistance provided me (see the sidebar "A Note on Translations").

For each, the native and English word for that language is stored **K**.

9. Populate the *users* table **L**:

```
INSERT INTO users (lang_id,
→ time_zone, username, pass,
→ email) VALUES
(1, 'America/New_York',
→ 'troutster', SHA1('password'),
→ 'email@example.com'),
(7, 'Europe/Berlin', 'Ute',
→ SHA1('pa24word'),
→ 'email1@example.com'),
(4, 'Europe/Oslo', 'Silje',
→ SHA1('2kll13'),
→ 'email2@example.com'),
(2, 'America/Sao_Paulo', 'João',
→ SHA1('fJDLN34'),
→ 'email3@example.com'),
(1, 'Pacific/Auckland', 'kiwi',
→ SHA1('conchord'),
→ 'kiwi@example.org');
```

continues on next page

```
mysql> SELECT * FROM languages;
+---------+------------+-----------+
| lang_id | lang       | lang_eng  |
+---------+------------+-----------+
|       1 | English    | English   |
|       2 | Português  | Portuguese|
|       3 | Français   | French    |
|       4 | Norsk      | Norwegian |
|       5 | Romanian   | Romanian  |
|       6 | Ελληνικά   | Greek     |
|       7 | Deutsch    | German    |
|       8 | Srpski     | Serbian   |
|       9 | 日本語      | Japanese  |
|      10 | Nederlands | Dutch     |
+---------+------------+-----------+
10 rows in set (0.00 sec)

mysql>
```

K The populated *languages* table, with each language written in its own alphabet.

```
mysql> INSERT INTO users (lang_id, time_zone, username, pass, email) VALUES
    -> (1, 'America/New_York', 'troutster', SHA1('password'), 'email@example.com'),
    -> (7, 'Europe/Berlin', 'Ute', SHA1('pa24word'), 'email1@example.com'),
    -> (4, 'Europe/Oslo', 'Silje', SHA1('2kll13'), 'email2@example.com'),
    -> (2, 'America/Sao_Paulo', 'João', SHA('fJDLN34'), 'email3@example.com'),
    -> (1, 'Pacific/Auckland', 'kiwi', SHA1('conchord'), 'kiwi@example.org');
Query OK, 5 rows affected (0.00 sec)
Records: 5  Duplicates: 0  Warnings: 0

mysql>
```

L A few users are added manually, as there is no registration process in this site (but see Chapter 18, "Example—User Registration," for that).

Because the PHP scripts will show the users associated with posts, a couple of users are necessary. A language and a time zone are associated with each (see Chapter 6 for more on time zones in MySQL). Each user's password will be encrypted with the **SHA1( )** function.

10. Populate the *words* table:

```
INSERT INTO words VALUES
(NULL, 1, 'PHP and MySQL for
→ Dynamic Web Sites: The Forum!',
→ '<p>Welcome to our site....
→ please use the links above...
→ blah, blah, blah.</p>\r\n
→ <p>Welcome to our site....please
→ use the links above...blah,
→ blah, blah.</p>', 'Home',
→ 'Forum Home', 'Language',
→ 'Register', 'Login', 'Logout',
→ 'New Thread', 'Subject', 'Body',
→ 'Submit', 'Posted on', 'Posted
→ by', 'Replies', 'Latest Reply',
→ 'Post a Reply');
```

These are the words associated with each term in English. The record has a *lang_id* of 1, which matches the *lang_id* for English in the *languages* table. The SQL to insert words for other languages into this table is available from the book's supporting Web site.

TIP This chapter doesn't go through the steps for creating the `mysqli_connect.php` page, which connects to the database. Instead, just copy the one from Chapter 9, "Using PHP with MySQL." Then change the parameters in the script to use a valid username/password/hostname combination to connect to the *forum2* database.

TIP As a reminder, the foreign key in one table should be of the exact same type and size as the matching primary key in another table.

A Note on Translations

Several readers around the world were kind enough to provide me with translations of key words, names, message subjects, and message bodies. For their help, I'd like to extend my sincerest thanks to (in no particular order): Angelo (Portuguese); Iris (German); Johan (Norwegian); Gabi (Romanian); Darko (Serbian); Emmanuel and Jean-François (French); Andreas and Simeon (Greek); Darius (Filipino/Tagalog); Olaf (Dutch); and Tsutomu (Japanese).

If you know one of these languages, you may see linguistic mistakes made in this text or in the corresponding images. If so, it's almost certainly my fault, having miscommunicated the words I needed translated or improperly entered the responses into the database. I apologize in advance for any such mistakes but hope you'll focus more on the database, the code, and the functionality. My thanks, again, to those who helped!

Writing the Templates

This example, like any site containing lots of pages, will make use of a template to separate out the bulk of the presentation from the logic. Following the instructions laid out in Chapter 3, "Creating Dynamic Web Sites," a header file and a footer file will store most of the HTML code. Each PHP script will then include these files to make a complete HTML page **A**. But this example is a little more complicated.

One of the goals of this site is to serve users in many different languages. Accomplishing that involves not just letting them *post messages* in their native language but making sure they can use the *whole site* in their native language as well. This means that the page title, the navigation links, the captions, the prompts, and even the menus need to appear in their language **B**.

The instructions for making the database show how this is accomplished: by storing translations of all key words in a table. The header file, therefore, needs to pull out all these key words so that they can be used as needed. Secondarily, this header file will also show different links based upon whether the user is logged in or not. Adding just one more little twist: if the user is on the forum page, viewing all the threads in a language, the user will also be given the option to post a new thread **C**.

The template itself uses CSS for some formatting (there's not much to it, really). You can download all these files from the book's supporting Web site (**www. LarryUllman.com**).

A The basic layout and appearance of the site.

B The home page viewed in French (compare with **A**).

C The same home page as in **A**, but with an added link allowing the user to start a new thread.

To make the template:

1. Begin a new document in your text editor or IDE, to be named **header.html** (Script 17.1):

```
<?php # Script 17.1 - header.html
header ('Content-Type: text/html;
→ charset=UTF-8');
```

As this script will need to do a fair amount of data validation and retrieval, it starts with a PHP block. The script also indicates to the Web browser its encoding—UTF-8, using the **header( )** function. The idea of setting the encoding via a **header( )** function call was mentioned in a tip in Chapter 11, "Web Application Development."

2. Start a session:

```
$_SESSION['user_id'] = 1;
$_SESSION['user_tz'] = 'America/
→ New_York';
// $_SESSION = array( );
```

To track users after they log in, the site will use sessions. Since the site doesn't have registration and login functionality in this chapter, two lines can virtually log in the user. Ordinarily, both values would come from a database, but they'll be set here for testing purposes. To virtually log the user out, uncomment the third line.

3. Include the database connection:

```
require ('../mysqli_connect.php');
```

As with many other examples in this book, the assumption is that the **mysqli_connect.php** script is stored in the directory above the current one, outside of the Web root. If that won't be the case for you, change this code accordingly.

Script 17.1 The **header.html** file begins the template. It also sets the page's encoding, starts the session, and retrieves the language-specific key words from the database.

```
1    <?php # Script 17.1 - header.html
2    /* This script...
3     * - starts the HTML template.
4     * - indicates the encoding using header( ).
5     * - starts the session.
6     * - gets the language-specific words
         from the database.
7     * - lists the available languages.
8     */
9
10   // Indicate the encoding:
11   header ('Content-Type: text/html;
         charset=UTF-8');
12
13   // Start the session:
14   session_start( );
15
16   // For testing purposes:
17   $_SESSION['user_id'] = 1;
18   $_SESSION['user_tz'] = 'America/New_York';
19   // For logging out:
20   //$_SESSION = array( );
21
22   // Need the database connection:
23   require ('../mysqli_connect.php');
24
25   // Check for a new language ID...
26   // Then store the language ID in the
         session:
27   if ( isset($_GET['lid']) &&
28       filter_var($_GET['lid'], FILTER_
           VALIDATE_INT, array('min_range' => 1))
29       ) {
30       $_SESSION['lid'] = $_GET['lid'];
31   } elseif (!isset($_SESSION['lid'])) {
32       $_SESSION['lid'] = 1; // Default.
33   }
34
35   // Get the words for this language:
36   $q = "SELECT * FROM words WHERE lang_id
         = {$_SESSION['lid']}";
37   $r = mysqli_query($dbc, $q);
38   if (mysqli_num_rows($r) == 0) { //
         Invalid language ID!
39
40       // Use the default language:
41       $_SESSION['lid'] = 1; // Default.
```

code continues on next page

Script 17.1 *continued*

```
42    $q = "SELECT * FROM words WHERE
      lang_id = {$_SESSION['lid']}";
43    $r = mysqli_query($dbc, $q);
44
45    }
46
47    // Fetch the results into a variable:
48    $words = mysqli_fetch_array($r,
      MYSQLI_ASSOC);
49
50    // Free the results:
51    mysqli_free_result($r);
52    ?>
53    <!DOCTYPE html PUBLIC "-//W3C//DTD XHTML
      1.0 Transitional//EN"
54          "http://www.w3.org/TR/xhtml1/DTD/
            xhtml1-transitional.dtd">
55    <html xmlns="http://www.w3.org/1999/xhtml"
      xml:lang="en" lang="en">
56    <head>
57        <meta http-equiv="content-type"
          content="text/html; charset=utf-8" />
58        <title><?php echo $words['title']; ?>
          </title>
59        <style type="text/css" media="screen">
60        body { background-color: #ffffff; }
61
62        .content {
63            background-color: #f5f5f5;
64            padding-top: 10px; padding-right:
              10px; padding-bottom: 10px;
              padding-left: 10px;
65            margin-top: 10px; margin-right:
              10px; margin-bottom: 10px;
              margin-left: 10px;
66        }
67
68        a.navlink:link { color: #003366;
          text-decoration: none; }
69        a.navlink:visited { color: #003366;
          text-decoration: none; }
70        a.navlink:hover { color: #cccccc;
          text-decoration: none; }
71
72        .title {
73            font-size: 24px; font-weight:
              normal; color: #ffffff;
74            margin-top: 5px; margin-bottom:
              5px; margin-left: 20px;
```

code continues on next page

4. Determine the language ID:

```
if ( isset($_GET['lid']) &&
   filter_var($_GET['lid'],
   → FILTER_VALIDATE_INT,
   → array('min_range' => 1))
   ) {
   $_SESSION['lid'] = $_GET['lid'];
} elseif (!isset($_SESSION['lid'])) {
   $_SESSION['lid'] = 1; // Default.
}
```

Next, the language ID value (abbreviated *lid*) needs to be established. The language ID controls what language is used for all of the site elements, and it also dictates the forum to be viewed. The language ID could be found in the session, after retrieving that information upon a successful login (because the user's language ID is stored in the *users* table). Alternatively, any user can change the displayed language on the fly by submitting the language form in the navigation links (see Ⓐ). In that case, the submitted language ID needs to be validated as an integer greater than 1: easily accomplished using the Filter extension (see Chapter 13, "Security Approaches"). If you're not using a version of PHP that supports the Filter extension, you'll need to use typecasting here instead (again, see Chapter 13).

The second clause applies if the page did not receive a language ID in the URL and the language ID has not already been established in the session. In that case, a default language is selected. This value corresponds to English in the *languages* table in the database. You can change it to any ID that matches the default language you'd like to use.

continues on next page

5. Get the keywords for this language:

```
$q = "SELECT * FROM words WHERE
→ lang_id = {$_SESSION['lid']}";
$r = mysqli_query($dbc, $q);
```

The next step in the header file is to retrieve from the database all of the key words for the given language.

6. If the query returned no records, get the default words:

```
if (mysqli_num_rows($r) == 0) {
  $_SESSION['lid'] = 1;
  $q = "SELECT * FROM words WHERE
  → lang_id = {$_SESSION['lid']}";
  $r = mysqli_query($dbc, $q);
}
```

It's possible, albeit unlikely, that **$_SESSION['lid']** does not equate to a record from the *words* table. In that case the query would return no records (but run without error). Consequently, the default language words must now be retrieved. Notice that neither this block of code, nor that in Step 5, actually fetches the returned record. That will happen, for both potential queries, in Step 7.

7. Fetch the retrieved words into an array, free the resources, and close the PHP section:

```
$words = mysqli_fetch_array($r,
→ MYSQL_ASSOC);
mysqli_free_result($r);
?>
```

After this point, the **$words** array represents all of the navigation and common elements in the user's selected language (or the default language).

Calling **mysqli_free_result( )** isn't necessary, but makes for tidy programming.

Script 17.1 *continued*

```
75        padding-top: 5px; padding-bottom:
          5px; padding-left: 20px;
76      }
77    </style>
78  </head>
79  <body>
80
81  <table width="90%" border="0"
    cellspacing="10" cellpadding="0"
    align="center">
82
83    <tr>
84      <td colspan="2" bgcolor="#003366"
        align="center"><p class="title"><?php
        echo $words['title']; ?></p></td>
85    </tr>
86
87    <tr>
88      <td valign="top" nowrap="nowrap"
        width="10%"><b>
89  <?php // Display links:
90
91  // Default links:
92  echo '<a href="index.php"
    class="navlink">' . $words['home'] .
    '</a><br />
93  <a href="forum.php" class="navlink">' .
    $words['forum_home'] . '</a><br />';
94
95  // Display links based upon login status:
96  if (isset($_SESSION['user_id'])) {
97
98    // If this is the forum page, add a
    link for posting new threads:
99    if (basename($_SERVER['PHP_SELF']) ==
      'forum.php') {
100       echo '<a href="post.php"
          class="navlink">' . $words['new_
          thread'] . '</a><br />';
101   }
102
103   // Add the logout link:
104   echo '<a href="logout.php"
      class="navlink">' . $words['logout'] .
      '</a><br />';
105
106 } else {
107
```

code continues on next page

```
108    // Register and login links:
109    echo '<a href="register.php"
       class="navlink">' . $words['register']
       . '</a><br />
110    <a href="login.php" class="navlink">'
       . $words['login'] . '</a><br />';
111
112  }
113
114  // For choosing a forum/language:
115  echo '</b><p><form action="forum.php"
     method="get">
116  <select name="lid">
117  <option value="0">' . $words['language']
     . '</option>
118  ';
119
120  // Retrieve all the languages...
121  $q = "SELECT lang_id, lang FROM
     languages ORDER BY lang_eng ASC";
122  $r = mysqli_query($dbc, $q);
123  if (mysqli_num_rows($r) > 0) {
124    while ($menu_row = mysqli_fetch_
       array($r, MYSQLI_NUM)) {
125      echo "<option value=\"$menu_row
         [0]\">$menu_row[1]</option>\n";
126    }
127  }
128  mysqli_free_result($r);
129
130  echo '</select><br />
131  <input name="submit" type="submit"
     value="' . $words['submit'] . '" />
132  </form></p>
133    </td>
134
135    <td valign="top" class="content">';
136  ?>
```

8. Start the HTML page:

```
<!DOCTYPE html PUBLIC "-//W3C//DTD
→XHTML 1.0 Transitional//EN"
"http://www.w3.org/TR/xhtml1/DTD/
→xhtml1-transitional.dtd">
<html xmlns="http://www.w3.org/
→1999/xhtml" xml:lang="en"
→lang="en">
<head>
  <meta http-equiv="content-type"
  → content="text/html;
  → charset=utf-8" />
  <title><?php echo
$words['title']; ?></title>
```

Note that the encoding is also indicated in a **META** tag, even though the PHP **header( )** call already identifies the encoding. This is just a matter of being thorough.

The header file as written uses as the title of every page a value in the **$words** array (i.e., the page title will always be the same for every page in a chosen language). You could easily modify this code so that the page's title is a combination of the language word and a page-specific variable, such as **$page_title** used in Chapter 3 and subsequent examples.

9. Add the CSS:

```
<style type="text/css"
media="screen">
body { background-color: #ffffff; }
.content {
  background-color: #f5f5f5;
  padding-top: 10px; padding-right:
  →10px; padding-bottom: 10px;
  →padding-left: 10px;
  margin-top: 10px; margin-right:
  →10px; margin-bottom: 10px;
  →margin-left: 10px;
}
```

continues on next page

```
a.navlink:link { color: #003366;
→ text-decoration: none; }
a.navlink:visited { color:
→ #003366; text-decoration:
→ none; }
a.navlink:hover { color: #cccccc;
→ text-decoration: none; }
.title {
  font-size: 24px; font-weight:
  → normal; color: #ffffff;
  margin-top: 5px; margin-bottom:
  → 5px; margin-left: 20px;
  padding-top: 5px; padding-bottom:
  → 5px; padding-left: 20px;
}
</style>
```

This is all taken from a template I found somewhere some time ago. It adds a little decoration to the site.

10. Complete the HTML head and begin the page:

```
</head>
<body>
<table width="90%" border="0"
→ cellspacing="10" cellpadding="0"
→ align="center">
```

```
<tr>
  <td colspan="2" bgcolor=
  → "#003366" align="center">
  → <p class="title"><?php echo
  → $words['title']; ?></p></td>
</tr>
<tr>
  <td valign="top" nowrap=
  → "nowrap" width="10%"><b>
```

The page itself uses a table for the layout, with one row showing the page title, the next row containing the navigation links on the left and the page-specific content on the right, and the final row containing the copyright . You'll see in this code that the page title will also be language-specific.

11. Start displaying the links:

```
<?php
echo '<a href="index.php"
→ class="navlink">' .
→ $words['home'] . '</a><br />
<a href="forum.php"
→ class="navlink">' .
→ $words['forum_home'] .
→ '</a><br />';
```

D The page layout showing the rows and columns of the main HTML table.

The first two links will always appear, whether the user is logged in or not, and regardless of the page they're currently viewing. For each link, the text of the link itself will be language-specific.

12. If the user is logged in, show "new thread" and logout links:

```
if (isset($_SESSION['user_id'])) {
   if (basename($_SERVER['PHP_
   → SELF']) == 'forum.php') {
      echo '<a href="post.php"
      → class="navlink">' .
      → $words['new_thread'] .
      → '</a><br />';
   }
   echo '<a href="logout.php"
   → class="navlink">' .
   → $words['logout'] . '</a><br />';
```

Confirmation of the user's logged-in status is achieved by checking for the presence of a **$_SESSION['user_id']** variable. If it's set, then the logout link can be created. Before that, a check is made to see if this is the **forum.php** page. If so, then a link to start a new thread is created (users can only create new threads if they're on the forum page; you wouldn't want them to create a new thread on some of the other pages, like the home page, because it wouldn't be clear to which forum the thread should

be posted). The code for checking what page it is, using the **basename( )** function, was first introduced in Chapter 12, "Cookies and Sessions."

13. Display the links for users not logged in:

```
} else {
   echo '<a href="register.php"
   → class="navlink">' .
   → $words['register'] . '</a><br />
   <a href="login.php" class=
   → "navlink">' . $words['login'] .
   → '</a><br />';
}
```

If the user isn't logged in, links are provided for registering and logging in.

14. Start a form for choosing a language:

```
echo '</b><p><form action=
   → "forum.php" method="get">
<select name="lid">
<option value="0">' . $words
→ ['language'] . '</option>
';
```

The user can choose a language (which is also a forum), via a pull-down menu **E**. The first value in the menu will be the word "language," in the user's default language. The select menu's **name** is *lid*, short for *language ID*, and its **action** attribute points to **forum.php**. When the user submits this simple form, they'll be taken to the forum of their choice.

continues on next page

E The language pull-down menu, with each option in its native language.

15. Retrieve every language from the database, and add each to the menu:

```
$q = "SELECT lang_id, lang FROM
→ languages ORDER BY lang_eng ASC";
$r = mysqli_query($dbc, $q);
if (mysqli_num_rows($r) > 0) {
  while ($menu_row = mysqli_
  → fetch_array($r, MYSQLI_NUM)) {
    echo "<option value=\"$menu_
    → row[0]\">$menu_row[1]
    → </option>\n";
  }
}
mysqli_free_result($r);
```

This query retrieves the languages and the language ID from the *languages* table. Each is added as an option to the select menu.

Again, calling `mysqli_free_result()` isn't required, but doing so can help limit bugs and improve performance. In particular, when you have pages that run multiple **SELECT** queries, `mysqli_free_result()` can help avoid confusion issues between PHP and MySQL.

16. Complete the form and the PHP page:

```
echo '</select><br />
<input name="submit" type="submit"
→ value="' . $words['submit'] . '" />
</form></p>
    </td>
    <td valign="top"
    → class="content">';
?>
```

17. Save the file as **header.html**.

Even though it contains a fair amount of PHP, this script will still use the **.html** extension (which I prefer to use for template files). Make sure that the file is saved using UTF-8 encoding.

18. Create a new document in your text editor or IDE, to be named **footer.html** (Script 17.2):

```
<!-- Script 17.2 - footer.html -->
```

19. Complete the HTML page:

```
      </td>
    </tr>
    <tr>
      <td colspan="2"
align="center">&copy; 2011 Larry
→ Ullman</td>
    </tr>
  </table>
</body>
</html>
```

20. Save the file as **footer.html**.

Again, make sure that the file is saved using UTF-8 encoding.

21. Place both files in your Web directory, within a folder named *includes*.

Script 17.2 The footer file completes the HTML page.

```
1   <!-- Script 17.2 - footer.html -->
2       </td>
3     </tr>
4
5     <tr>
6       <td colspan="2" align="center">&copy;
        2011 Larry Ullman</td>
7     </tr>
8
9   </table>
10  </body>
11  </html>
```

Creating the Index Page

The index page in this example won't do that much. It'll provide some introductory text and the links for the user to register, log in, choose the preferred language/forum, and so forth. From a programming perspective, it'll show how the template files are to be used.

To make the home page:

1. Begin a new PHP document in your text editor or IDE, to be named **index.php** (**Script 17.3**):

   ```
   <?php # Script 17.3 - index.php
   ```

   Because all of the HTML is in the included files, this page can begin with the opening PHP tags.

2. Include the HTML header:

   ```
   include ('includes/header.html');
   ```

   The included file uses the **header( )** and **session_start( )** functions, so you have to make sure that nothing is sent to the Web browser prior to this line. That shouldn't be a problem as long as there are no spaces before the opening PHP tag.

3. Print the language-specific content:

   ```
   echo $words['intro'];
   ```

   The **$words** array is defined within the header file. It can be referred to here, since the header file was just included. The value indexed at *intro* is a bit of welcoming text in the selected or default language.

4. Complete the page:

   ```
   include ('includes/footer.html');
   ?>
   ```

   That's it for the home page!

5. Save the file as **index.php**, place it in your Web directory, and test it in your Web browser (see Ⓐ and Ⓑ in the previous section).

   Once again, make sure that the file is saved using UTF-8 encoding. This will be the last time I remind you!

Script 17.3 The home page includes the header and footer files to make a complete HTML document. It also prints some introductory text in the chosen language.

```
1    <?php # Script 17.3 - index.php
2    // This is the main page for the site.
3
4    // Include the HTML header:
5    include ('includes/header.html');
6
7    // The content on this page is introductory text
8    // pulled from the database, based upon the
9    // selected language:
10   echo $words['intro'];
11
12   // Include the HTML footer file:
13   include ('includes/footer.html');
14   ?>
```

Creating the Forum Page

The next page in the Web site is the forum page, which displays the threads in a forum (each language being its own forum). The page will use the language ID, passed to this page in a URL and/or stored in a session, to know what threads to display.

The basic functionality of this page—running a query, displaying the results—is simple **A**. The query this page uses is perhaps the most complex one in the book. It's complicated for three reasons:

1. It performs a **JOIN** across three tables.

2. It uses three aggregate functions and a **GROUP BY** clause.

3. It converts the dates to the user's time zone, but only if the person viewing the page is logged in.

So, again, the query is intricate, but I'll go through it in detail in the following steps.

To write the forum page:

1. Begin a new PHP document in your text editor or IDE, to be named **forum.php** (**Script 17.4**):

```php
<?php # Script 17.4 - forum.php
include ('includes/header.html');
```

continues on page 540

Script 17.4 This script performs one rather complicated query to display five pieces of information—the subject, the original poster, the date the thread was started, the number of replies, and the date of the latest reply—for each thread in a forum.

```php
1    <?php # Script 17.4 - forum.php
2    // This page shows the threads in a
     forum.
3    include ('includes/header.html');
4
5    // Retrieve all the messages in this
     forum...
6
7    // If the user is logged in and has
     chosen a time zone,
8    // use that to convert the dates and
     times:
9    if (isset($_SESSION['user_tz'])) {
10       $first = "CONVERT_TZ(p.posted_on,
         'UTC', '{$_SESSION['user_tz']}')";
11       $last = "CONVERT_TZ(p.posted_on,
         'UTC', '{$_SESSION['user_tz']}')";
12   } else {
13       $first = 'p.posted_on';
14       $last = 'p.posted_on';
15   }
16
```

code continues on next page

A The forum page, which lists information about the threads in a given language. The threads are linked to a page where they can be read.

```
17   // The query for retrieving all the threads in this forum, along with the original user,
18   // when the thread was first posted, when it was last replied to, and how many replies it's had:
19   $q = "SELECT t.thread_id, t.subject, username, COUNT(post_id) - 1 AS responses, MAX(DATE_FORMAT
     ($last, '%e-%b-%y %l:%i %p')) AS last, MIN(DATE_FORMAT($first, '%e-%b-%y %l:%i %p')) AS first
     FROM threads AS t INNER JOIN posts AS p USING (thread_id) INNER JOIN users AS u ON t.user_id =
     u.user_id WHERE t.lang_id = {$_SESSION['lid']} GROUP BY (p.thread_id) ORDER BY last DESC";
20   $r = mysqli_query($dbc, $q);
21   if (mysqli_num_rows($r) > 0) {
22
23       // Create a table:
24       echo '<table width="100%" border="0" cellspacing="2" cellpadding="2" align="center">
25           <tr>
26               <td align="left" width="50%"><em>' . $words['subject'] . '</em>:</td>
27               <td align="left" width="20%"><em>' . $words['posted_by'] . '</em>:</td>
28               <td align="center" width="10%"><em>' . $words['posted_on'] . '</em>:</td>
29               <td align="center" width="10%"><em>' . $words['replies'] . '</em>:</td>
30               <td align="center" width="10%"><em>' . $words['latest_reply'] . '</em>:</td>
31           </tr>';
32
33       // Fetch each thread:
34       while ($row = mysqli_fetch_array($r, MYSQLI_ASSOC)) {
35
36           echo '<tr>
37               <td align="left"><a href="read.php?tid=' . $row['thread_id'] . '">' . $row['subject']
                   . '</a></td>
38               <td align="left">' . $row['username'] . '</td>
39               <td align="center">' . $row['first'] . '</td>
40               <td align="center">' . $row['responses'] . '</td>
41               <td align="center">' . $row['last'] . '</td>
42           </tr>';
43
44       }
45
46       echo '</table>'; // Complete the table.
47
48   } else {
49       echo '<p>There are currently no messages in this forum.</p>';
50   }
51
52   // Include the HTML footer file:
53   include ('includes/footer.html');
54   ?>
```

2. Determine what dates and times to use:

```
if (isset($_SESSION['user_tz'])) {
  $first = "CONVERT_TZ
  →(p.posted_on, 'UTC',
  →'{$_SESSION['user_tz']}')";
  $last = "CONVERT_TZ(p.posted_on,
  →'UTC', '{$_SESSION['user_tz']}')";
} else {
  $first = 'p.posted_on';
  $last = 'p.posted_on';
}
```

As already stated, the query will format the date and time to the user's time zone (presumably selected during the registration process), but only if the viewer is logged in. Presumably, this information would be retrieved from the database and stored in the session upon login.

To make the query dynamic, what exact date/time value should be selected will be stored in a variable to be used in the query later in the script. If the user *is not* logged in, which means that **$_SESSION['user_tz']** is not set, the two dates—when a thread was started and when the most recent reply was posted—will be unadulterated values from the table. In both cases, the table column being referenced is *posted_on* in the *posts* table (*p* will be an alias to *posts* in the query).

If the user *is* logged in, the **CONVERT_TZ( )** function will be used to convert the value stored in *posted_on* from UTC to the user's chosen time zone. See Chapter 6 for more on this function. Note that using this function requires that your MySQL installation includes the list of time zones (see Chapter 6 for more).

3. Define and execute the query:

```
$q = "SELECT t.thread_id,
→t.subject, username, COUNT
→(post_id) - 1 AS responses,
→MAX(DATE_FORMAT($last,
→'%e-%b-%y %l:%i %p')) AS last,
→MIN(DATE_FORMAT($first, '%e-%b-%y
→%l:%i %p')) AS first FROM
→threads AS t INNER JOIN posts
→AS p USING (thread_id) INNER
→JOIN users AS u ON t.user_id =
→u.user_id WHERE t.lang_id =
→{$_SESSION['lid']} GROUP BY
→(p.thread_id) ORDER BY last DESC";
$r = mysqli_query($dbc, $q);
if (mysqli_num_rows($r) > 0) {
```

The query needs to return six things: the ID and subject of each thread (which comes from the *threads* table), the name of the user who posted the thread in the first place (from *users*), the number of replies to each thread, the date the thread was started, and the date the thread last had a reply (all from *posts*).

The overarching structure of this query is a join between *threads* and *posts* using the *thread_id* column (which is the same in both tables). This result is then joined with the *users* table using the *user_id* column.

As for the selected values, three aggregate functions are used (see Chapter 7): **COUNT( )**, **MIN( )**, and **MAX( )**. Each is applied to a column in the *posts* table, so the query has a **GROUP BY (p.thread_id)** clause. **MIN( )** and **MAX( )** are used to return the earliest (for the original post) and latest dates.

Both will be shown on the forum page (see **A**). The latest date is also used to order the results so that the most recent activity always gets returned first. The **COUNT( )** function is used to count the number of posts in a given thread. Because the original post is also in the *posts* table, it'll be factored into **COUNT( )** as well, so 1 is subtracted from that value.

Finally, aliases are used to make the query shorter to write and to make it easier to use the results in the PHP script. If you're confused by what this query returns, execute it using the mysql client **B** or phpMyAdmin.

4. Create a table for the results:

```
echo '<table width="100%"
→ border="0" cellspacing="2"
→ cellpadding="2" align="center">
```

```
<tr>
  <td align="left" width="50%">
  → <em>' . $words['subject'] .
  → '</em>:</td>
  <td align="left" width=
  "20%"><em>' . $words
  → ['posted_by'] . '</em>:</td>
  <td align="center" width=
  → "10%"><em>' . $words['posted_
  → on'] . '</em>:</td>
  <td align="center" width=
  → "10%"><em>' . $words['replies']
  → . '</em>:</td>
  <td align="center" width="10%">
  → <em>' . $words['latest_
  → reply'] . '</em>:</td>
</tr>';
```

As with some items in the header file, the captions for the columns in this HTML page will use language-specific terminology.

continues on next page

```
PHP and MySQL for Dynamic Web Sites: Visual QuickPro Guide
mysql> SELECT t.thread_id, t.subject, username, COUNT(post_id) - 1 AS re
sponses, MAX(DATE_FORMAT(CONVERT_TZ(p.posted_on, 'UTC', 'America/New_Yor
k'), '%e-%b-%y %l:%i %p')) AS last, MIN(DATE_FORMAT(CONVERT_TZ(p.posted_
on, 'UTC', 'America/New_York'), '%e-%b-%y %l:%i %p')) AS first FROM thre
ads AS t INNER JOIN posts AS p USING (thread_id) INNER JOIN users AS u O
N t.user_id = u.user_id WHERE t.lang_id = 4 GROUP BY (p.thread_id) ORDER
 BY last DESC\G
*************************** 1. row ***************************
thread_id: 1
  subject: Byttet til PHP 5.0 fra PHP 4.0 - variabler utilgjengelige
 username: troutster
responses: 4
     last: 30-Oct-11 2:16 AM
    first: 29-Oct-11 12:15 AM
*************************** 2. row ***************************
thread_id: 2
  subject: Automatisk bildekontroll
 username: Ute
responses: 0
     last: 29-Oct-11 6:45 PM
    first: 29-Oct-11 6:45 PM
2 rows in set (0.00 sec)

mysql>
```

B The results of running the complex query in the mysql client.

5. Fetch and print each returned record:

```
while ($row = mysqli_fetch_array
→ ($r, MYSQLI_ASSOC)) {
  echo '<tr>
      <td align="left"><a href=
      → "read.php?tid=' . $row
      → ['thread_id'] . '">' .
      → $row['subject'] . '</a></td>
      <td align="left">' .
      → $row['username'] . '</td>
      <td align="center">' .
      → $row['first'] . '</td>
      <td align="center">' .
      → $row['responses'] . '</td>
      <td align="center">' .
      → $row['last'] . '</td>
    </tr>';
}
```

This code is fairly simple, and there are similar examples many times over in the book. The thread's subject is linked to **read.php**, passing that page the thread ID in the URL.

6. Complete the page:

```
    echo '</table>';
  } else {
    echo '<p>There are currently no
    → messages in this forum.</p>';
  }
  include ('includes/footer.html');
?>
```

This **else** clause applies if the query returned no results. In actuality, this message should also be in the user's chosen language. I've omitted that for the sake of brevity. To fully implement this feature, create another column in the *words* table and store for each language the translated version of this text.

7. Save the file as **forum.php**, place it in your Web directory, and test it in your Web browser **C**.

TIP If you see no values for the dates and times when you run this script, it is probably because your MySQL installation hasn't been updated with the full list of time zones.

TIP As noted in the chapter's introduction, I've omitted all error handling in this example. If you have problems with the queries, apply the debugging techniques outlined in Chapter 8, "Error Handling and Debugging."

		Sites internet dynamiques avec PHP et MySQL : le forum!			

Sites internet dynamiques avec PHP et MySQL : le forum!

Accueil
Page d'accueil du forum
Nouvelle discussion
Déconnexion

[Langue ▼]
[Soumettez]

Sujet:	Posté par:	Posté le:	Réponses:	La Plus défunte Réponse:
Ajouter des adresses a PHP List depuis un formulaire	João	29-Oct-11 12:43 AM	1	31-Oct-11 8:06 AM
Lancer une Page HTML en PHP	kiwi	29-Oct-11 12:42 AM	1	29-Oct-11 1:17 AM

© 2011 Larry Ullman

C The **forum.php** page, viewed in another language (compare with **A**).

Creating the Thread Page

Next up is the page for viewing all of the messages in a thread **A**. This page is accessed by clicking a link in **forum.php B**. Thanks to a simplified database structure, the query used by this script is not that complicated (with the database design from Chapter 6, this page would have been much more complex). All this page has to do then is make sure it receives a valid thread ID, display every message, and display the form for users to add their own replies.

A The **read.php** page shows every message in a thread.

```
<td align="left"><a href="read.php?tid=1">Byttet til PHP 5.0
<td align="left">troutster</td>
<td align="center">29-Oct-11 12:15 AM</td>
<td align="center">4</td>
<td align="center">30-Oct-11 2:16 AM</td>
:>
<td align="left"><a href="read.php?tid=2">Automatisk bildeko
<td align="left">Ute</td>
<td align="center">29-Oct-11 6:45 PM</td>
<td align="center">0</td>
<td align="center">29-Oct-11 6:45 PM</td>
```

B Part of the source code from **forum.php** shows how the thread ID is passed to **read.php** in the URL.

To make read.php:

1. Begin a new PHP document in your text editor or IDE, to be named **read.php** (**Script 17.5**):

   ```
   <?php # Script 17.5 - read.php
   include ('includes/header.html');
   ```

2. Begin validating the thread ID:

   ```
   $tid = FALSE;
   if (isset($_GET['tid']) &&
   ➝ filter_var($_GET['tid'],
   ➝ FILTER_VALIDATE_INT,
   ➝ array('min_range' => 1)) ) {
     $tid = $_GET['tid'];
   ```

To start, a flag variable is defined as FALSE, a way of saying: prove that the thread ID is valid, which is the most important aspect of this script. Next, a check confirms that the thread ID was passed in the URL and that it is an integer greater than 1. This is done using the Filter extension (see Chapter 13). Finally, the value passed to the page is assigned to the **$tid** variable, so that it no longer has a FALSE value.

If your version of PHP does not support the Filter extension, you'll need to typecast **$_GET['tid']** to an integer and then confirm that it has a value greater than 1 (as shown in Chapter 13).

Script 17.5 The **read.php** page shows all of the messages in a thread, in order of ascending posted date. The page also shows the thread's subject at the top and includes a form for adding a reply at the bottom.

```
1    <?php # Script 17.5 - read.php
2    // This page shows the messages in a thread.
3    include ('includes/header.html');
4
5    // Check for a thread ID...
6    $tid = FALSE;
7    if (isset($_GET['tid']) && filter_var($_GET['tid'], FILTER_VALIDATE_INT, array('min_range' => 1)) ) {
8
9        // Create a shorthand version of the thread ID:
10       $tid = $_GET['tid'];
11
12       // Convert the date if the user is logged in:
13       if (isset($_SESSION['user_tz'])) {
14           $posted = "CONVERT_TZ(p.posted_on, 'UTC', '{$_SESSION['user_tz']}')";
15       } else {
16           $posted = 'p.posted_on';
17       }
18
19       // Run the query:
20       $q = "SELECT t.subject, p.message, username, DATE_FORMAT($posted, '%e-%b-%y %l:%i %p') AS
             posted FROM threads AS t LEFT JOIN posts AS p USING (thread_id) INNER JOIN users AS u ON
             p.user_id = u.user_id WHERE t.thread_id = $tid ORDER BY p.posted_on ASC";
21       $r = mysqli_query($dbc, $q);
22       if (!(mysqli_num_rows($r) > 0)) {
23           $tid = FALSE; // Invalid thread ID!
24       }
25
26   } // End of isset($_GET['tid']) IF.
```

code continues on next page

3. Determine if the dates and times should be adjusted:

```
if (isset($_SESSION['user_tz'])) {
  $posted = "CONVERT_TZ
  → (p.posted_on, 'UTC',
  → '{$_SESSION['user_tz']}')";
} else {
  $posted = 'p.posted_on';
}
```

As in the **forum.php** page (Script 17.4), the query will format all of the dates and times in the user's time zone, if the user is logged in. To be able to adjust the query accordingly, this variable stores either the column's name (*posted_on*, from the *posts* table) or the invocation of MySQL's **CONVERT_TZ( )** function.

4. Run the query:

```
$q = "SELECT t.subject, p.message,
→ username, DATE_FORMAT($posted,
→ '%e-%b-%y %l:%i %p') AS posted
→ FROM threads AS t LEFT JOIN
→ posts AS p USING (thread_id)
→ INNER JOIN users AS u ON
→ p.user_id = u.user_id WHERE
→ t.thread_id = $tid ORDER BY
→ p.posted_on ASC";
$r = mysqli_query($dbc, $q);
if (!(mysqli_num_rows($r) > 0)) {
  $tid = FALSE;
}
```

continues on next page

Script 17.5 *continued*

```
27
28   if ($tid) { // Get the messages in this thread...
29
30       $printed = FALSE; // Flag variable.
31
32       // Fetch each:
33       while ($messages = mysqli_fetch_array($r, MYSQLI_ASSOC)) {
34
35           // Only need to print the subject once!
36           if (!$printed) {
37               echo "<h2>{$messages['subject']}</h2>\n";
38               $printed = TRUE;
39           }
40
41           // Print the message:
42           echo "<p>{$messages['username']} ({$messages['posted']})<br />{$messages['message']}</p><br />\n";
43
44       } // End of WHILE loop.
45
46       // Show the form to post a message:
47       include ('includes/post_form.php');
48
49   } else { // Invalid thread ID!
50       echo '<p>This page has been accessed in error.</p>';
51   }
52
53   include ('includes/footer.html');
54   ?>
```

This query is like the query on the forum page, but it's been simplified in two ways. First, it doesn't use any of the aggregate functions or a **GROUP BY** clause. Second, it only returns one date and time. The query is still a **JOIN** across three tables, in order to get the subject, message bodies, and usernames. The records are ordered by their posted dates in ascending order (i.e., from the first post to the most recent).

If the query doesn't return any rows, then the thread ID isn't valid and the flag variable is made false again.

5. Complete the **$_GET['tid']** conditional and check, again, for a valid thread ID:

```
} // End of isset($_GET['tid']) IF.
if ($tid) {
```

Before printing the messages in the thread, one last conditional is used. This conditional would be false if:

- No **$_GET['tid']** value was passed to this page.

- A **$_GET['tid']** value was passed to the page, but it was not an integer greater than 0.

- A **$_GET['tid']** value was passed to the page and it was an integer greater than 0, but it matched no thread records in the database.

6. Print each message:

```
$printed = FALSE;
while ($messages = mysqli_fetch_
→ array($r, MYSQLI_ASSOC)) {
  if (!$printed) {
    echo
"<h2>{$messages['subject']}</h2>\n";
    $printed = TRUE;
  }
  echo "<p>{$messages['username']}
  → ({$messages['posted']})<br />
  → {$messages['message']}</p>
  → <br />\n";
} // End of WHILE loop.
```

As you can see in Ⓐ, the thread subject needs to be printed only once. However, the query will return the subject for each returned message Ⓒ.

```
●○○        PHP and MySQL for Dynamic Web Sites: Visual QuickPro Guide
*************************** 1. row ***************************
 subject: Byttet til PHP 5.0 fra PHP 4.0 - variabler utilgjengelige
 message: Jeg har nettopp gått over til PHP 5.0 og forsøkte å benytte meg av mine
gamle scripts. Dette viste seg å være noe vanskelig ettersom de bare generer feil.
 Hovedproblemet virker å være at jeg ikke får tilgang til variabler som tidligere
var tilgjengelige. Noen som har noen forslag?
username: Silje
   posted: 29-Oct-11 12:15 AM
*************************** 2. row ***************************
 subject: Byttet til PHP 5.0 fra PHP 4.0 - variabler utilgjengelige
 message: Har du sjekket om variablene du prøver å få tilgang på er superglobals?
Dette forandret seg fra 4.2 og utover, tror jeg...
username: troutster
   posted: 29-Oct-11 12:20 AM
*************************** 3. row ***************************
 subject: Byttet til PHP 5.0 fra PHP 4.0 - variabler utilgjengelige
 message: Hva er superglobals?
username: João
   posted: 29-Oct-11 12:30 AM
*************************** 4. row ***************************
 subject: Byttet til PHP 5.0 fra PHP 4.0 - variabler utilgjengelige
 message: Linken Terje ga er manualsiden, men du kan også ta en titt på http://www
.linuxjournal.com/article/6559 for en grundig innføring og forklaring. Lykke til!
username: kiwi
   posted: 29-Oct-11 6:26 AM
*************************** 5. row ***************************
 subject: Byttet til PHP 5.0 fra PHP 4.0 - variabler utilgjengelige
 message: http://no.php.net/variables.predefined
username: troutster
   posted: 30-Oct-11 2:16 AM
5 rows in set (0.00 sec)

mysql> █
```

Ⓒ The results of the **read.php** query when run in the mysql client. This version of the query converts the dates to the logged-in user's preferred time zone.

To achieve this effect, a flag variable is created. If **$printed** is FALSE, then the subject needs to be printed. This would be the case for the first row fetched from the database. Once that's been displayed, **$printed** is set to TRUE so that the subject is not printed again. Then the username, posted date, and message are displayed.

7. Include the form for posting a message:

```
include ('includes/post_form.php');
```

As users could post messages in two ways—as a reply to an existing thread and as the first post in a new thread, the form for posting messages is defined within a separate file (to be created next), stored within the **includes** directory.

8. Complete the page:

```
} else { // Invalid thread ID!
  echo '<p>This page has been
→ accessed in error.</p>';
}
include ('includes/footer.html');
?>
```

Again, in a complete site, this error message would also be stored in the *words* table in each language. Then you would write here:

```
echo "<p>{$words['access_error']}
→ </p>";
```

9. Save the file as **read.php**, place it in your Web directory, and test it in your Web browser **D**.

D The **read.php** page, viewed in Japanese.

Posting Messages

The final two pages in this application are the most important, because you won't have threads to read without them. Two files for posting messages are required: One will *make* the form, and the other will *handle* the form.

Creating the form

The first page required for posting messages is **post_form.php**. It has some contingencies:

1. It can only be included by other files, never accessed directly.

2. It should only be displayed if the user is logged in (which is to say only logged-in users can post messages).

3. If it's being used to add a reply to an existing message, it only needs a message body input **A**.

4. If it's being used to create a new thread, it needs both subject and body inputs **B**.

5. It needs to be sticky **C**.

Still, all of this can be accomplished in 60 lines of code and some smart conditionals.

To create post_form.php:

1. Begin a new PHP document in your text editor or IDE, to be named **post_form.php** (Script 17.6):

   ```
   <?php # Script 17.6 - post_form.php
   ```

2. Redirect the Web browser if this page has been accessed directly:

   ```
   if (!isset($words)) {
     header ("Location: http://www.
     → example.com/index.php");
     exit( );
   }
   ```

A The form for posting a message, as shown on the thread-viewing page.

B The same form for posting a message, if being used to create a new thread.

C The form will recall entered values when not completed correctly.

Script 17.6 This script will be included by other pages (notably, **read.php** and **post.php**). It displays a form for posting messages that is also sticky.

```
1   <?php # Script 17.6 - post_form.php
2   // This page shows the form for posting
    messages.
3   // It's included by other pages, never
    called directly.
4
5   // Redirect if this page is called
    directly:
6   if (!isset($words)) {
7       header ("Location: http://www.example.
        com/index.php");
8       exit();
9   }
10
11  // Only display this form if the user is
    logged in:
12  if (isset($_SESSION['user_id'])) {
13
14      // Display the form:
15      echo '<form action="post.php"
        method="post" accept-charset="utf-8">';
16
17      // If on read.php...
18      if (isset($tid) && $tid) {
19
20          // Print a caption:
21          echo '<h3>' . $words['post_a_reply']
            . '</h3>';
22
23          // Add the thread ID as a hidden
            input:
24          echo '<input name="tid" type=
            "hidden" value="' . $tid . '" />';
25
26      } else { // New thread
27
28          // Print a caption:
29          echo '<h3>' . $words['new_thread']
            . '</h3>';
30
31          // Create subject input:
32          echo '<p><em>' . $words['subject']
            . '</em>: <input name="subject"
            type="text" size="60"
            maxlength="100" ';
33
```

code continues on next page

This script does not include the header and footer and therefore won't make a complete HTML page. Consequently, the script must be included by a script that does all that. PHP has no **been_ included( )** function that will indicate if this page was included or loaded directly. Instead, since I know that the header file creates a **$words** variable, if that variable isn't set, then **header.html** hasn't been included prior to this script and the browser should be redirected.

Change the URL in the **header( )** call to match your site.

3. Confirm that the user is logged in and begin the form:

```
if (isset($_SESSION['user_id'])) {
  echo '<form action="post.php"
  → method="post"
  accept-charset="utf-8">';
```

Because only registered users can post, the script checks for the presence of **$_SESSION['user_id']** before displaying the form. The form itself will be submitted to **post.php**, to be written next. The **accept-charset** attribute is added to the form to make it clear that UTF-8 text is acceptable (although this isn't technically required, as each page uses the UTF-8 encoding already).

4. Check for a thread ID:

```
if (isset($tid) && $tid) {
  echo '<h3>' . $words['post_a_
  → reply'] . '</h3>';
  echo '<input name="tid"
  → type="hidden" value="' .
  → $tid . '" />';
```

continues on next page

This is where things get a little bit tricky. As mentioned earlier, and as shown in **Ⓐ** and **Ⓑ**, the form will differ slightly depending upon how it's being used. When included on **read.php**, the form will be used to provide a reply to an existing thread. To check for this scenario, the script sees if **$tid** (short for *thread ID*) is set and if it has a TRUE value. That will be the case when this page is included by **read.php**. When this script is included by **post.php**, **$tid** will be set but have a FALSE value.

If this conditional is true, the language-specific version of "Post a Reply" will be printed and the thread ID will be stored in a hidden form input.

5. Complete the conditional begun in Step 4:

```
} else { // New thread
  echo '<h3>' . $words['new_
  → thread'] . '</h3>';
  echo '<p><em>' . $words['subject']
  → . '</em>: <input name="subject"
  → type="text" size="60"
  → maxlength="100" ';
  if (isset($subject)) {
    echo "value=\"$subject\" ";
  }
  echo '/></p>';
} // End of $tid IF.
```

If this is not a reply, then the caption should be the language-specific version of "New Thread" and a subject input should be created. That input needs to be sticky. To check for that, look for the existence of a **$subject** variable. This variable will be created in **post.php**, and that file will then include this page.

Script 17.6 *continued*

```
34        // Check for existing value:
35        if (isset($subject)) {
36            echo "value=\"$subject\" ";
37        }
38
39        echo '/></p>';
40
41    } // End of $tid IF.
42
43        // Create the body textarea:
44        echo '<p><em>' . $words['body'] .
          '</em>: <textarea name="body"
          rows="10" cols="60">';
45
46        if (isset($body)) {
47            echo $body;
48        }
49
50        echo '</textarea></p>';
51
52        // Finish the form:
53        echo '<input name="submit" type="submit"
          value="' . $words['submit'] . '" />
54        </form>';
55
56    } else {
57        echo '<p>You must be logged in to
          post messages.</p>';
58    }
59
60    ?>
```

Nouvelle discussion

Sujet: [_____]

Corps:

[   ]
[   ]
[   ]
[   ]

(Soumettez)

D The form prompts and even the submit button will be in the user's chosen language (compare with the other figures in this section of the chapter).

Sample Thread

troutster (29-Oct-11 5:12 AM)
This is the body of the sample thread. This is the body of the sample thread. This is the body of the sample thread.

troutster (29-Oct-11 5:44 AM)
I like your thread. It's simple and sweet.

You must be logged in to post messages.

E The result of the **post_form.php** page if the user is not logged in (remember that you can emulate not being logged in by using the **$_SESSION = array( );** line in the header file).

6. Create the textarea for the message body:

```
echo '<p><em>' . $words['body'] .
→'</em>: <textarea name="body"
→rows="10" cols="60">';
if (isset($body)) {
   echo $body;
}
echo '</textarea></p>';
```

Both uses of this page will have this textarea. Like the subject, it will be made sticky if a **$body** variable (defined in **post.php**) exists. For both inputs, the prompts will be language-specific.

7. Complete the form:

```
echo '<input name="submit"
→type="submit" value="' .
→$words['submit'] . '" />
</form>';
```

All that's left is a language-specific submit button **D**.

8. Complete the page:

```
} else {
   echo '<p>You must be logged in
   →to post messages.</p>';
}
?>
```

Once again, you could store this message in the *words* table and use the translated version here. I didn't only for the sake of simplicity.

9. Save the file as **post_form.php**, place it in the **includes** folder of your Web directory, and test it in your Web browser by accessing **read.php E**.

Handling the form

This file, **post.php**, will primarily be used to handle the form submission from **post_form.php**. That sounds simple enough, but there's a bit more to it. This page will actually be called in three different ways:

1. To handle the form for a thread reply
2. To display the form for a new thread submission
3. To handle the form for a new thread submission

This means that the page will be accessed using either POST (modes 1 and 3) or GET (mode 2). Also, the data that will be sent to the page, and therefore needs to be validated, will differ between modes 1 and 3 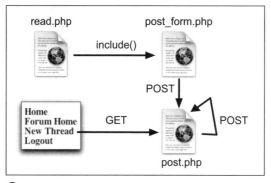.

Adding to the complications, if a new thread is being created, two queries must be run: one to add the thread to the *threads* table and a second to add the new thread body to the *posts* table. If the submission is a reply to an existing thread, then only one query is required, inserting a record into *posts*.

Of course, successfully pulling this off is just a matter of using the right conditionals, as you'll see. In terms of validation, the subject and body, as text types, will just be checked for a non-empty value. All tags will be stripped from the subject (because why should it have any?) and turned into entities in the body. This will allow for HTML, JavaScript, and PHP code to be *written* in a post but still not be *executed* when the thread is shown (because in a forum about Web development, you'll need to show some code).

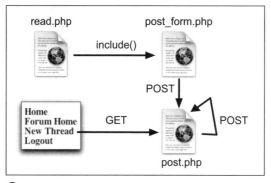

F The various uses of the **post.php** page.

Script 17.7 The **post.php** page will process the form submissions when a message is posted. This page will be used to both create new threads and handle replies to existing threads.

```
1    <?php # Script 17.7 - post.php
2    // This page handles the message post.
3    // It also displays the form if creating
     a new thread.
4    include ('includes/header.html');
5
6    if ($_SERVER['REQUEST_METHOD'] == 'POST')
     { // Handle the form.
7
8        // Language ID is in the session.
9        // Validate thread ID ($tid), which
         may not be present:
10       if (isset($_POST['tid']) && filter_var
         ($_POST['tid'], FILTER_VALIDATE_INT,
         array('min_range' => 1)) ) {
11           $tid = $_POST['tid'];
12       } else {
13           $tid = FALSE;
14       }
15
16       // If there's no thread ID, a subject
         must be provided:
17       if (!$tid && empty($_POST['subject'])) {
18           $subject = FALSE;
19           echo '<p>Please enter a subject
             for this post.</p>';
20       } elseif (!$tid && !empty($_POST
         ['subject'])) {
21           $subject = htmlspecialchars(strip_
             tags($_POST['subject']));
22       } else { // Thread ID, no need for
         subject.
23           $subject = TRUE;
24       }
25
26       // Validate the body:
27       if (!empty($_POST['body'])) {
28           $body = htmlentities($_POST['body']);
29       } else {
30           $body = FALSE;
```

code continues on next page

To create post.php:

1. Begin a new PHP document in your text editor or IDE, to be named **post.php** (Script 17.7):

```
<?php # Script 17.7 - post.php
include ('includes/header.html');
```

This page will use the header and footer files, unlike **post_form.php**.

2. Check for the form submission and validate the thread ID:

```
if ($_SERVER['REQUEST_METHOD'] ==
→'POST') {
  if (isset($_POST['tid']) &&
  →filter_var($_POST['tid'],
  →FILTER_VALIDATE_INT, array
  →('min_range' => 1)) ) {
    $tid = $_POST['tid'];
  } else {
    $tid = FALSE;
  }
```

The thread ID will be present if the form was submitted as a reply to an existing thread (the thread ID is stored as a hidden input **G**). The validation process is fairly routine, thanks to the Filter extension.

continues on next page

```
<form action="post.php" method="post" accept-charset="utf-8"><h3>Post a
Reply</h3><input name="tid" type="hidden" value="7" /><p><em>Body</em>:
<textarea name="body" rows="10" cols="60"></textarea></p><input
name="submit" type="submit" value="Submit" />
```

G The source code of **read.php** shows how the thread ID is stored in the form. This indicates to **post.php** that the submission is a reply, not a new thread.

3. Validate the message subject:

```
if (!$tid && empty($_POST
→['subject'])) {
  $subject = FALSE;
  echo '<p>Please enter a subject
  →for this post.</p>';
```

```
} elseif (!$tid && !empty($_POST
→['subject'])) {
  $subject = htmlspecialchars
  →(strip_tags($_POST['subject']));
} else { // Thread ID, no need
→for subject.
  $subject = TRUE;
}
```

Script 17.7 *continued*

```
31          echo '<p>Please enter a body for this post.</p>';
32      }
33
34      if ($subject && $body) { // OK!
35
36          // Add the message to the database...
37
38          if (!$tid) { // Create a new thread.
39              $q = "INSERT INTO threads (lang_id, user_id, subject) VALUES ({$_SESSION['lid']},
                {$_SESSION['user_id']}, '" . mysqli_real_escape_string($dbc, $subject) . "')";
40              $r = mysqli_query($dbc, $q);
41              if (mysqli_affected_rows($dbc) == 1) {
42                  $tid = mysqli_insert_id($dbc);
43              } else {
44                  echo '<p>Your post could not be handled due to a system error.</p>';
45              }
46          } // No $tid.
47
48          if ($tid) { // Add this to the replies table:
49              $q = "INSERT INTO posts (thread_id, user_id, message, posted_on) VALUES ($tid,
                {$_SESSION['user_id']}, '" . mysqli_real_escape_string($dbc, $body) . "', UTC_TIMESTAMP())";
50              $r = mysqli_query($dbc, $q);
51              if (mysqli_affected_rows($dbc) == 1) {
52                  echo '<p>Your post has been entered.</p>';
53              } else {
54                  echo '<p>Your post could not be handled due to a system error.</p>';
55              }
56          } // Valid $tid.
57
58      } else { // Include the form:
59          include ('includes/post_form.php');
60      }
61
62  } else { // Display the form:
63
64      include ('includes/post_form.php');
65
66  }
67
68  include ('includes/footer.html');
69  ?>
```

The tricky part about validating the subject is that three scenarios exist. First, if there's no valid thread ID, then this should be a new thread and the subject can't be empty. If the subject element *is* empty, then an error occurred and a message is printed.

In the second scenario, there's no valid thread ID and the subject *isn't* empty, meaning this is a new thread and the subject was entered, so it should be handled. In this case, any tags are removed, using the **strip_tags( )** function, and **htmlspecialchars( )** will turn any remaining quotation marks into their entity format. Calling this second function will prevent problems should the form be displayed again and the subject placed in the input to make it sticky. To be more explicit, if the submitted subject contains a double quotation mark but the body wasn't completed, the form will be shown again with the subject placed within **value=""**, and the double quotation mark in the subject will cause problems.

The third scenario is when the form has been submitted as a reply to an existing thread. In that case, **$tid** will be valid and no subject is required.

4. Validate the body:

```
if (!empty($_POST['body'])) {
  $body = htmlentities($_POST
  → ['body']);
} else {
  $body = FALSE;
  echo '<p>Please enter a body
  → for this post.</p>';
}
```

This is a much easier validation, as the body is always required. If present, it'll be run through **htmlentities( )**.

5. Check if the form was properly filled out:

```
if ($subject && $body) {
```

6. Create a new thread, when appropriate:

```
if (!$tid) {
  $q = "INSERT INTO threads
  → (lang_id, user_id, subject)
  → VALUES ({$_SESSION['lid']},
  → {$_SESSION['user_id']}, '" .
  → mysqli_real_escape_string
  → ($dbc, $subject) . "')";
  $r = mysqli_query($dbc, $q);
  if (mysqli_affected_rows($dbc)
  → == 1) {
    $tid = mysqli_insert_id
    → ($dbc);
  } else {
    echo '<p>Your post could
    → not be handled due to a
    → system error.</p>';
  }
}
```

If there's no thread ID, then this is a new thread and a query must be run on the *threads* table. That query is simple, populating the three columns. Two of these values come from the session (after the user has logged in). The other is the subject, which is run through **mysqli_real_escape_string( )**. Because the subject already had **strip_tags( )** and **htmlspecialchars( )** applied to it, you could probably get away with not using this function, but there's no need to take that risk.

If the query worked, meaning it affected one row, then the new thread ID is retrieved.

continues on next page

7. Add the record to the *posts* table:

```
if ($tid) {
    $q = "INSERT INTO posts
    ⇥ (thread_id, user_id,
    ⇥ message, posted_on) VALUES
    ⇥ ($tid, {$_SESSION['user_
    ⇥ id']}, '" . mysqli_real_
    ⇥ escape_string($dbc, $body) .
    ⇥ "', UTC_TIMESTAMP( ))";
    $r = mysqli_query($dbc, $q);
    if (mysqli_affected_rows
    ⇥ ($dbc) == 1) {
        echo '<p>Your post has
        been entered.</p>';
    } else {
        echo '<p>Your post could
        ⇥ not be handled due to a
        ⇥ system error.</p>';
    }
}
```

This query should only be run if the thread ID exists. That will be the case if this is a reply to an existing thread or if the new thread was just created in the database (Step 6). If that query failed, then this query won't be run.

The query populates four columns in the table, using the thread ID, the user ID (from the session), the message body, run through **mysqli_real_escape_string( )** for security, and the posted date. For this last value, the **UTC_TIMESTAMP( )** column is used so that it's not tied to any one time zone (see Chapter 6).

Note that for all of the printed messages in this page, I've just used hard-coded English. To finish rounding out the examples, each of these messages should be stored in the *words* table and printed here instead.

How This Example Is Complicated

In the introduction to this chapter, I state that the example is fundamentally simple, but that sometimes the simple things take some extra effort to do. So how is this example complicated, in my opinion?

First, supporting multiple languages does add a couple of issues. If the encoding isn't handled properly everywhere—when creating the pages in your text editor or IDE, in communicating with MySQL, in the Web browser, etc.—things can go awry. Also, you have to have the proper translations for every language for every bit of text that the site might need. This includes error messages (ones the user should actually see), the bodies of emails, and so forth.

How the PHP files are organized and what they do also complicates things. In particular, some variables are created in one file but used in another. Doing this can lead to confusion at best and bugs at the worst. To overcome those problems, I recommend adding lots of comments indicating where variables come from or where else they might be used. Also, try to use unique variable names within pages so that they are less likely to conflict with variables in included files.

Finally, this example was complicated by the way only one page is used to display the posting form and only one page is used to handle it, despite the fact that messages can be posted in two different ways, with different expectations.

Please enter a subject for this post.

New Thread

Subject:

This is the body with HTML and some PHP code:
<?php // Blah!

Body:

Submit

H The result if no subject was provided while attempting to post a new thread.

PHP and MySQL for Dynamic Web Sites: The Forum!

PHP and MySQL for Dynamic Web Sites: The Forum!

Home
Forum Home
Logout

Your post has been entered.

Language
Submit

© 2011 Larry Ullman

I The reply has been successfully added to the thread.

8. Complete the page:

```
} else { // Include the form:
   include ('includes/
   → post_form.php');
}
} else { // Display the form:
   include ('includes/post_form.php');
}
include ('includes/footer.html');
?>
```

The first **else** clause applies if the form was submitted but not completed. In that case, the form will be included again and can be sticky, as it'll have access to the **$subject** and **$body** variables created by this script. The second **else** clause applies if this page was accessed directly (by clicking a link in the navigation), thereby creating a GET request (i.e., without a form submission).

9. Save the file as **post.php**, place it in your Web directory, and test it in your Web browser (**H** and **I**).

Administering the Forum

Much of the administration of the forum would involve user management, discussed in the next chapter. Depending upon who is administering the forum, you might also create forms for managing the languages and lists of translated words.

Administrators would also likely have the authority to edit and delete posts or threads. To accomplish this, store a user level in the session as well (the next chapter shows you how). If the logged-in user is an administrator, add links to edit and delete threads on **forum.php**. Each link would pass the thread ID to a new page (like **edit_user.php** and **delete_user.php** from Chapter 10, "Common Programming Techniques"). When deleting a thread, you have to make sure you delete all the records in the *posts* table that also have that thread ID. A foreign key constraint (see Chapter 6) can help in this regard.

Finally, an administrator could edit or delete individual posts (the replies to a thread). Again, check for the user level and then add links to **read.php** (a pair of links after each message). The links would pass the post ID to edit and delete pages (different ones than are used on threads).

Review and Pursue

If you have any problems with the review questions or the pursue prompts, turn to the book's supporting forum (**www.LarryUllman.com/forums/**).

Note: Most of these questions and some of the prompts rehash information covered in earlier chapters, in order to reinforce some of the most important points.

Review

- What impact does a database's *character set*, or a PHP or HTML page's *encoding*, have?

- Why does the encoding and character set have to be the same everywhere? What happens if there are differences?

- What is a *primary key*? What is a *foreign key*?

- What is the benefit of using *UTC* for stored dates and times?

- Why is the *pass* column in the *users* table set as a **CHAR** instead of a **VARCHAR**, when each user's password could be of a variable length?

- How do you begin a session in PHP? How do you store a value in a session? How do you retrieve a previously stored value?

- How do you create an *alias* in a SQL command? What are the benefits of using an alias?

Pursue

- Review Chapter 6 if you need a refresher on database design.

- Review Chapter 6 to remind yourself as to what kinds of columns in a table should be indexed.

- Review Chapter 6's section on time zones if your MySQL installation is not properly converting the dates and times from the UTC time zone to another (i.e., if the returned converted date value is **NULL**).

- Review Chapter 7, "Advanced SQL and MySQL," for a refresher on joins and the aggregating functions.

- Modify the header and other files so that each page's title uses both the default language page title and a subtitle based upon the page being viewed (e.g., the name of the thread currently shown).

- Add pagination—see Chapter 10—to the **forum.php** script.

- If you want, add the necessary columns to the *words* table, and the appropriate code to the PHP scripts, so that every navigational, error, and other element is language-specific. Use a Web site such as Yahoo! Babel Fish (**http://babelfish.yahoo.com**) for the translations.

- Apply the **redirect_user( )** function from Chapter 12 to **post_form.php** here.

- Create a search page for this forum. If you need some help, see the **search.php** basic example available in the downloadable code.

Example—
User Registration

The second example in the book—a user registration system—has already been touched upon in several other chapters, as the registration, login, and logout processes make for good examples of many concepts. But this chapter will place all of those ideas within the same context, using a consistent programming approach.

Users will be able to register, log in, log out, and change their password. This chapter includes three features not shown elsewhere: the ability to *reset a password*, should it be forgotten; the requirement that users *activate their account* before they can log in; and support for *different user levels*, allowing you to control the available content according to the type of user logged in.

As in the preceding chapter, the focus here will be on the public side of things, but along the way you'll see recommendations as to how this application could easily be expanded or modified, including how to add administrative features.

In This Chapter

Creating the Templates

The application in this chapter will use a new template design . This template makes extensive use of Cascading Style Sheets (CSS), creating a clean look without the need for images. It has tested well on all current browsers and will appear as unformatted text on browsers that don't support CSS2. The layout for this site is derived from one freely provided by BlueRobot (**www.bluerobot.com**).

Creating this chapter's example begins with two template files: **header.html** and **footer.html**. As in the Chapter 12, "Cookies and Sessions," examples, the footer file will display certain links depending upon whether or not the user is logged in, determined by checking for the existence of a session variable. Taking this concept one step further, additional links will be displayed if the logged-in user is also an administrator (a session value will indicate such).

The header file will begin sessions and *output buffering*, while the footer file will terminate output buffering. Output buffering hasn't been formally covered in the book, but it's introduced sufficiently in the sidebar.

To make header.html:

1. Begin a new document in your text editor or IDE, to be named **header.html** (Script 18.1):

   ```
   <?php # Script 18.1 - header.html
   ```

A The basic appearance of this Web application.

Script 18.1 The header file begins the HTML, starts the session, and turns on output buffering.

```
1   <?php # Script 18.1 - header.html
2   // This page begins the HTML header for
    the site.
3
4   // Start output buffering:
5   ob_start();
6
7   // Initialize a session:
8   session_start();
9
10  // Check for a $page_title value:
11  if (!isset($page_title)) {
12      $page_title = 'User Registration';
13  }
14  ?>
15  <!DOCTYPE html PUBLIC "-//W3C//DTD XHTML
    1.0 Transitional//EN"
16          "http://www.w3.org/TR/xhtml1/DTD/
        xhtml1-transitional.dtd">
17  <html xmlns="http://www.w3.org/1999/
    xhtml" xml:lang="en" lang="en">
18  <head>
19      <meta http-equiv="content-type"
        content="text/html; charset=utf-8" />
20      <title><?php echo $page_title; ?></
        title>
21      <style type="text/css"
        media="screen">@import "includes/
        layout.css";</style>
22  </head>
23  <body>
24  <div id="Header">User Registration</div>
25      <div id="Content">
26  <!-- End of Header -->
```

2. Begin output buffering and start a session:

```
ob_start( );
session_start( );
```

This Web site will use output buffering, eliminating any error messages that could occur when using HTTP headers, redirecting the user, or sending cookies. Every page will make use of sessions as well. It's safe to place the **session_start( )** call after **ob_start( )**, since nothing has been sent to the Web browser yet.

Since every public page will use both output buffering and sessions, placing these lines in the **header.html** file saves the hassle of placing them in every single page. Secondarily, if you later want to change the session settings (for example), you only need to edit this one file.

3. Check for a **$page_title** variable and close the PHP section:

```
if (!isset($page_title)) {
  $page_title = 'User
  ⮞ Registration';
}
?>
```

As in the other times this book has used a template system, the page's title—which appears at the top of the browser window—will be set on a page-by-page basis. This conditional checks if the **$page_title** variable has a value and, if it doesn't, sets it to a default string. This is a nice, but optional, check to include in the header.

continues on next page

Using Output Buffering

By default, anything that a PHP script prints or any HTML outside of the PHP tags (even in included files) is immediately sent to the Web browser. *Output buffering* (or *output control*, as the PHP manual calls it) is a PHP feature that overrides this behavior. Instead of immediately sending HTML to the Web browser, that output will be placed in a buffer—temporary memory. Then, when the buffer is *flushed*, it's sent to the Web browser. There can be a performance improvement with output buffering, but the main benefit is that it eradicates those pesky *headers already sent* error messages. Some functions—**header( )**, **setcookie( )**, and **session_start( )**—can only be called if nothing has been sent to the Web browser. With output buffering, nothing will be sent to the Web browser until the end of the page, so you are free to call these functions at any point in a script.

To begin output buffering, invoke the **ob_start( )** function. Once you call it, the output from every **echo**, **print**, and similar function call will be sent to a memory buffer rather than the Web browser. Conversely, HTTP calls (like **header( )** and **setcookie( )**) will not be buffered and will operate as usual.

At the conclusion of the script, call the **ob_end_flush( )** function to send the accumulated buffer to the Web browser. Or, use the **ob_end_clean( )** function to delete the buffered data without sending it. Both functions have the secondary effect of turning off output buffering.

4. Create the HTML head:

```
<!DOCTYPE html PUBLIC "-//W3C//DTD
→ XHTML 1.0 Transitional//EN"
"http://www.w3.org/TR/xhtml1/DTD/
→ xhtml1-transitional.dtd">
<html xmlns="http://www.
→ w3.org/1999/xhtml" xml:lang="en"
→ lang="en">
<head>
  <meta http-equiv="content-type"
  → content="text/html;
  → charset=utf-8" />
  <title><?php echo $page_title;
  → ?></title>
<style type="text/css"
→ media="screen">@import
→ "includes/layout.css";</style>
</head>
```

The PHP **$page_title** variable is printed out between the **title** tags here. Then, the CSS document is included. It will be called **layout.css** and stored in a folder called **includes**. You can find the CSS file in the downloadable code found at the book's supporting Web site (**www.LarryUllman.com**).

5. Begin the HTML body:

```
<body>
<div id="Header">User
→ Registration</div>
<div id="Content">
```

The body creates the banner across the top of the page and then starts the content part of the Web page (up until *Welcome!* in Ⓐ).

6. Save the file as **header.html**.

Script 18.2 The footer file concludes the HTML, displaying links based upon the user status (logged in or not, administrator or not), and flushes the output to the Web browser.

```
1    <!-- Start of Footer -->
2    </div><!-- Content -->
3
4    <div id="Menu">
5        <a href="index.php" title="Home
         Page">Home</a><br />
6        <?php # Script 18.2 - footer.html
7        // This page completes the HTML
         template.
8
9        // Display links based upon the login
         status:
10       if (isset($_SESSION['user_id'])) {
11
12           echo '<a href="logout.php"
             title="Logout">Logout</a><br />
13       <a href="change_password.php"
         title="Change Your Password">Change
         Password</a><br />
14       ';
15
16           // Add links if the user is an
             administrator:
17           if ($_SESSION['user_level'] == 1) {
18               echo '<a href="view_users.php"
                 title="View All Users">View
                 Users</a><br />
19           <a href="#">Some Admin Page</a><br
             />
20           ';
21           }
22
23       } else { //  Not logged in.
24           echo '<a href="register.
             php" title="Register for the
             Site">Register</a><br />
25       <a href="login.php"
         title="Login">Login</a><br />
26       <a href="forgot_password.php"
         title="Password Retrieval">Retrieve
         Password</a><br />
27       ';
28       }
29       ?>
30       <a href="#">Some Page</a><br />
```

code continues on next page

Script 18.2 *continued*

```
31       <a href="#">Another Page</a><br />
32    </div><!-- Menu -->
33
34    </body>
35    </html>
36    <?php // Flush the buffered output.
37    ob_end_flush();
38    ?>paste code here
```

Home
Logout
Change Password
Some Page
Another Page

B The user will see these navigation links while she or he is logged in.

Home
Logout
Change Password
View Users
Some Admin Page
Some Page
Another Page

C A logged-in administrator will see extra links (compare with **B**).

To make footer.html:

1. Begin a new document in your text editor or IDE, to be named **footer.html** (Script **18.2**):

```
</div>
<div id="Menu">
<a href="index.php" title="Home
→ Page">Home</a><br />
<?php # Script 18.2 - footer.html
```

2. If the user is logged in, show logout and change password links:

```
if (isset($_SESSION['user_id'])) {
    echo '<a href="logout.php"
    → title="Logout">Logout</a><br />
<a href="change_password.php"
→ title="Change Your Password"
→ >Change Password</a><br />
';
```

If the user is logged in (which means that **$_SESSION['user_id']** is set), the user will see links to log out and to change their password **B**.

3. If the user is also an administrator, show some other links:

```
if ($_SESSION['user_level'] == 1) {
    echo '<a href="view_users.php"
    → title="View All Users">View
    → Users</a><br />
<a href="#">Some Admin Page</a><br
→ />
';
}
```

If the logged-in user also happens to be an administrator, then she or he should see some extra links **C**. To test for this, check the user's access level, which will also be stored in a session. A level value of 1 will indicate that the user is an administrator (non-administrators will have a level of 0).

continues on next page

4. Show the links for non-logged-in users and complete the PHP block:

```
} else { //  Not logged in.
  echo '<a href="register.php"
   → title="Register for the
   → Site">Register</a><br />
<a href="login.php" title=
   → "Login">Login</a><br />
<a href="forgot_password.php"
   → title="Password Retrieval"
   → >Retrieve Password</a><br />
';
}
?>
```

If the user isn't logged in, they will see links to register, log in, and reset a forgotten password 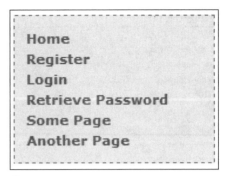.

5. Complete the HTML:

```
<a href="#">Some Page</a><br />
<a href="#">Another Page</a><br />
</div>
</body>
</html>
```

Two dummy links are included for other pages you could add.

6. Flush the buffer:

```
<?php
ob_end_flush( );
?>
```

The footer file will send the accumulated buffer to the Web browser, completing the output buffering begun in the header script (again, see the sidebar).

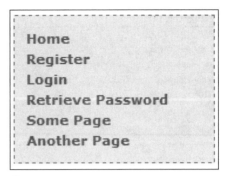

D The user will see these links if she or he is not logged in.

7. Save the file as **footer.html** and place it, along with **header.html** and **layout.css** (from the book's supporting Web site), in your Web directory, putting all three in an **includes** folder **E**.

TIP If this site has any page that does not make use of the header file but does need to work with sessions, that script must call **session_start( )** on its own. If you fail to do so, that page won't be able to access the session data.

TIP In more recent versions of PHP, output buffering is enabled by default. The buffer size—the maximum number of bytes stored in memory—is 4,096, but this can be changed in PHP's configuration file.

TIP The ob_get_contents( ) function will return the current buffer so that it may be assigned to a variable, should the need arise.

TIP The ob_flush( ) function will send the current contents of the buffer to the Web browser and then discard them, allowing a new buffer to be started. This function allows your scripts to maintain more moderate buffer sizes. Conversely, ob_end_flush( ) turns off output buffering after sending the buffer to the Web browser.

TIP The ob_clean( ) function deletes the current contents of the buffer without stopping the buffer process.

TIP PHP will automatically run ob_end_flush( ) at the conclusion of a script if it is not otherwise done.

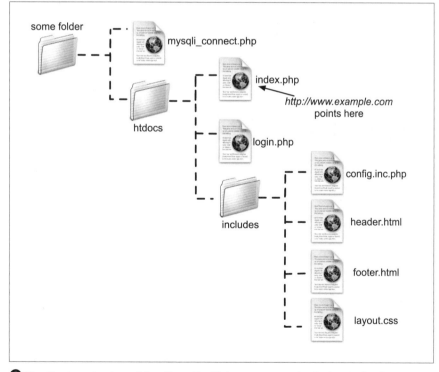

E The directory structure of the site on the Web server, assuming **htdocs** is the document root (where **www.example.com** points).

Writing the Configuration Scripts

This Web site will make use of two configuration-type scripts. One, **config. inc.php**, will really be the most important script in the entire application. It will

- Have comments about the site as a whole
- Define constants
- Establish site settings
- Dictate how errors are handled
- Define any necessary functions

Because it does all this, the configuration script will be included by every other page in the application.

The second configuration-type script, **mysqli_connect.php**, will store all of the database-related information. It will be included only by those pages that need to interact with the database.

Making a configuration file

The configuration file is going to serve many important purposes. It'll be like a cross between the site's owner's manual and its preferences file. The first purpose of this file will be to document the site overall: who created it, when, why, for whom, etc., etc. The version in the book will omit all that, but you should put it in your script. The second role will be to define all sorts of constants and settings that the various pages will use.

Third, the configuration file will establish the error-management policy for the site. The technique involved—creating your own error-handling function—was covered in Chapter 8, "Error Handling and Debugging." As in that chapter, during the development stages, every error will be reported in the most detailed way **A**.

User Registration

An error occurred in script 'C:\xampp\htdocs\change_password.php' on line 18: Use of undefined constant MYSQLS - assumed 'MYSQLS'
Date/Time: 5-20-2011 13:54:28

```
Array
(
    [GLOBALS] => Array
 *RECURSION*
    [_POST] => Array
        (
            [password1] =>
            [password2] =>
            [submit] => Change My Password
        )

    [_GET] => Array
        (
        )

    [_COOKIE] => Array
        (
            [PHPSESSID] => 5bs9e4afejm8sb18a4cq5im874
        )
```

A During the development stages of the Web site, all errors should be as obvious and as informative as possible.

User Registration

A system error occurred. We apologize for the inconvenience.

B If errors occur when the site is live, the user will only see a message like this (but a detailed error message will be emailed to the administrator).

Script 18.3 This configuration script dictates how errors are handled, defines site-wide settings and constants, and could (but doesn't) declare any necessary functions.

```
1    <?php # Script 18.3 - config.inc.php
2    /* This script:
3     * - define constants and settings
4     * - dictates how errors are handled
5     * - defines useful functions
6     */
7
8    // Document who created this site, when,
     why, etc.
9
10
11   // ******************************** //
12   // *********** SETTINGS *********** //
13
14   // Flag variable for site status:
15   define('LIVE', FALSE);
16
17   // Admin contact address:
18   define('EMAIL', 'InsertRealAddressHere');
19
20   // Site URL (base for all redirections):
21   define ('BASE_URL', 'http://www.example.
     com/');
22
23   // Location of the MySQL connection
     script:
24   define ('MYSQL', '/path/to/mysqli_connect.
     php');
25
26   // Adjust the time zone for PHP 5.1 and
     greater:
27   date_default_timezone_set ('US/Eastern');
28
29   // *********** SETTINGS *********** //
30   // ******************************** //
```

code continues on next page

Along with the specific error message, all of the existing variables will be shown, as will the current date and time. The error reporting will be formatted so that it fits within the site's template. During the production, or live, stage of the site, errors will be handled more gracefully **B**. At that time, the detailed error messages will not be printed in the Web browser, but instead sent to an email address.

Finally, this script could define any functions that might be used multiple times in the site. This site won't have any, but that would be another logical use of such a file.

To write the configuration file:

1. Begin a new PHP document in your text editor or IDE, to be named **config.inc.php** (Script 18.3):

   **<?php # Script 18.3 - config.inc.
   ⇥ php**

2. Establish two constants for error reporting:

   **define('LIVE', FALSE);
   define('EMAIL', 'InsertRealAddress
   ⇥ Here');**

   The **LIVE** constant will be used as it was in Chapter 8. If it is FALSE, detailed error messages are sent to the Web browser **A**. Once the site goes live, this constant should be set to TRUE so that detailed error messages are never revealed to the Web user **B**. The **EMAIL** constant is where the error messages will be sent when the site is live. You would obviously use your own email address for this value.

   continues on next page

3. Establish two constants for site-wide settings:

```
define ('BASE_URL', 'http://www.
→ example.com/');
define ('MYSQL', '/path/to/mysqli_
→ connect.php');
```

These two constants are defined just to make it easier to do certain things in the other scripts. The first, **BASE_URL**, refers to the root domain (*http://www. example.com/*), with an ending slash. If developing on your own computer, this might be *http://localhost/* or *http://localhost/ch18/*. When a script redirects the browser, the code can simply be something like

```
header('Location: ' . BASE_URL .
→ 'page.php');
```

The second constant, **MYSQL**, is an absolute path to the MySQL connection script (to be written next). By setting this as an absolute path, any file can include the connection script by referring to this constant:

```
require (MYSQL);
```

Change both of these values to correspond to your environment. When using XAMPP on Windows, for example, the proper value for the **MYSQL** constant may be **C:\\xampp\mysqli_connect.php**.

If you move the site from one server or domain to another, just change these two constants and the application will still work.

Script 18.3 *continued*

```
31
32
33    // ************************************
      **** //
34    // *********** ERROR MANAGEMENT
      ************ //
35
36    // Create the error handler:
37    function my_error_handler ($e_number,
      $e_message, $e_file, $e_line, $e_vars) {
38
39        // Build the error message:
40        $message = "An error occurred in
          script '$e_file' on line $e_line:
          $e_message\n";
41
42        // Add the date and time:
43        $message .= "Date/Time: " . date('n-
          j-Y H:i:s') . "\n";
44
45        if (!LIVE) { // Development (print the
          error).
46
47            // Show the error message:
48            echo '<div class="error">' .
              nl2br($message);
49
50            // Add the variables and a
              backtrace:
51            echo '<pre>' . print_r ($e_vars, 1)
              . "\n";
52            debug_print_backtrace( );
53            echo '</pre></div>';
54
55        } else { // Don't show the error:
56
57            // Send an email to the admin:
58            $body = $message . "\n" . print_r
              ($e_vars, 1);
59            mail(EMAIL, 'Site Error!', $body,
              'From: email@example.com');
60
61            // Only print an error message if
              the error isn't a notice:
62            if ($e_number != E_NOTICE) {
63                echo '<div class="error">A
                  system error occurred.
                  We apologize for the
                  inconvenience.</div><br />';
```

code continues on next page

Script 18.3 *continued*

```
64        }
65      } // End of !LIVE IF.
66
67    } // End of my_error_handler( )
      definition.
68
69    // Use my error handler:
70    set_error_handler ('my_error_handler');
71
72    // *********** ERROR MANAGEMENT
      *********** //
73    // ***********************************
      **** //
```

4. Establish any other site-wide settings:

   **date_default_timezone_set ('US/
   → Eastern');**

   As mentioned in Chapter 11, "Web Application Development," any use of a PHP date or time function (as of PHP 5.1) requires that the time zone be set. Change this value to match your time zone (see the PHP manual for the list of zones).

5. Begin defining the error-handling function:

   **function my_error_handler ($e_
   → number, $e_message, $e_file,
   → $e_line, $e_vars) {
     $message = "An error occurred
     → in script '$e_file' on line
     → $e_line: $e_message\n";**

   The function definition will be very similar to the one explained in Chapter 8. The function expects to receive five arguments: the error number, the error message, the script in which the error occurred, the line number on which PHP thinks the error occurred, and an array of variables that existed at the time of the error. Then the function begins defining the **$message** variable, starting with the information provided to this function.

6. Add the current date and time:

   **$message .= "Date/Time: " .
   → date('n-j-Y H:i:s') . "\n";**

   To make the error reporting more useful, it will include the current date and time in the message. A newline character terminates the string to make the resulting display more legible.

continues on next page

7. If the site is not live, show the error message in detail:

```
if (!LIVE) {
    echo '<div class="error">' .
    ⇥ nl2br($message);
    echo '<pre>' . print_r
    ⇥ ($e_vars, 1) . "\n";
    debug_print_backtrace( );
    echo '</pre></div>';
```

As mentioned earlier, if the site *isn't* live, the entire error message is printed, for any type of error. The message is placed within **<div class="error">**, which will format the message per the rules defined in the site's CSS file. The first part of the error message is the string already defined, with the added touch of converting newlines to HTML break tags. Then, within preformatted tags, all of the variables that exist at the time of the error are shown, along with a *backtrace* (a history of function calls and such). See Chapter 8 for more of an explanation on any of this.

8. If the site is live, email the details to the administrator and print a generic message for the visitor:

```
} else { // Don't show the error:
    $body = $message . "\n" .
    ⇥ print_r ($e_vars, 1);
    mail(EMAIL, 'Site Error!', $body,
    ⇥ 'From: email@example.com');
    if ($e_number != E_NOTICE) {
        echo '<div class="error">A
        ⇥ system error occurred. We
        ⇥ apologize for the
        ⇥ inconvenience.</div><br />';
    }
} // End of !LIVE IF.
```

If the site *is* live, the detailed message should be sent in an email and the Web user should only see a generic message. To take this one step further,

the generic message will not be printed if the error is of a specific type: **E_NOTICE**. Such errors occur for things like referring to a variable that does not exist, which may or may not be a problem. To avoid potentially inundating the user with error messages, only print the error message if **$e_number** is not equal to **E_NOTICE**, which is a constant defined in PHP (see the PHP manual).

9. Complete the function definition and tell PHP to use your error handler:

```
}
set_error_handler
⇥ ('my_error_handler');
```

You have to use the **set_error_handler( )** function to tell PHP to use your own function for errors.

10. Save the file as **config.inc.php**, and place it in your Web directory, within the **includes** folder.

Note that in keeping with many other examples in this book, as this script will be included by other PHP scripts, it omits the terminating PHP tag.

Making the database script

The second configuration-type script will be **mysqli_connect.php**, the database connection file used multiple times in the book already. Its purpose is to connect to MySQL, select the database, and establish the character set in use. If a problem occurs, this script will make use of the error-handling tools established in **config. inc.php**. To do so, this script will call the **trigger_error( )** function when appropriate. The **trigger_error( )** function lets you tell PHP that an error occurred. Of course PHP will handle that error using the **my_error_handler( )** function, as established in the configuration script.

Script 18.4 This script connects to the *ch18* database. If it can't, then the error handler will be triggered, passing it the MySQL connection error.

```
1   <?php # Script 18.4 - mysqli_connect.php
2   // This file contains the database
    access information.
3   // This file also establishes a
    connection to MySQL
4   // and selects the database.
5
6   // Set the database access information
    as constants:
7   DEFINE ('DB_USER', 'username');
8   DEFINE ('DB_PASSWORD', 'password');
9   DEFINE ('DB_HOST', 'localhost');
10  DEFINE ('DB_NAME', 'ch18');
11
12  // Make the connection:
13  $dbc = @mysqli_connect (DB_HOST, DB_
    USER, DB_PASSWORD, DB_NAME);
14
15  // If no connection could be made,
    trigger an error:
16  if (!$dbc) {
17      trigger_error ('Could not connect to
        MySQL: ' . mysqli_connect_error() );
18  } else { // Otherwise, set the encoding:
19      mysqli_set_charset($dbc, 'utf8');
20  }
```

To connect to the database:

1. Begin a new PHP document in your text editor or IDE, to be named **mysqli_connect.php** (Script 18.4):

   ```
   <?php # Script 18.4 - mysqli_
   → connect.php
   ```

2. Set the database access information:

   ```
   DEFINE ('DB_USER', 'username');
   DEFINE ('DB_PASSWORD', 'password');
   DEFINE ('DB_HOST', 'localhost');
   DEFINE ('DB_NAME', 'ch18');
   ```

   As always, change these values to those that will work for your MySQL installation.

3. Attempt to connect to MySQL and select the database:

   ```
   $dbc = @mysqli_connect (DB_HOST,
   → DB_USER, DB_PASSWORD, DB_NAME);
   ```

   In previous scripts, if this function didn't return the proper result, the **die( )** function was called, terminating the execution of the script. Since this site will be using a custom error-handling function instead, I'll rewrite the connection process.

   Any errors raised by this function call will be suppressed (thanks to the **@**) and handled using the code in the next step.

4. Handle any errors if the database connection was not made:

   ```
   if (!$dbc) {
     trigger_error ('Could not
     → connect to MySQL: ' .
     → mysqli_connect_error() );
   ```

   continues on next page

If the script could not connect to the database, the error message should be sent to the `my_error_handler()` function. By doing so, the error will be handled according to the currently set management technique (live stage versus development). Instead of calling `my_error_handler()` directly, use `trigger_error()`, whose first argument is the error message **C**.

5. Establish the encoding:

```
} else {
    mysqli_set_charset($dbc, 'utf8');
}
```

If a database connection could be made, the encoding used to communicate with the database is then established. See Chapter 9, "Using PHP with MySQL," for details.

6. Save the file as `mysqli_connect.php`, and place it in the directory above the Web document root.

This script, as an includable file, also omits the terminating PHP tag. As with other examples in this book, ideally the file should not be within the Web directory, but wherever you put it, make sure the value of the `MYSQL` constant (in `config.inc.php`) matches.

7. Create the database **D**.

See the sidebar "Database Scheme" for a discussion of the database and the command required to make the one table. If you cannot create your own database, just add the table to whatever database you have access to. Also make sure that you edit the `mysqli_connect.php` file so that it uses the proper username/password/hostname combination to connect to this database.

User Registration

An error occurred in script 'C:\xampp\mysqli_connect.php' on line 14: mysqli_connect()
[function.mysqli-connect]: (42000/1049): Unknown database 'chs18'
Date/Time: 5-27-2011 09:49:09

```
Array
(
    [GLOBALS] => Array
 *RECURSION*
    [_POST] => Array
        (
            [email] => larry@example.com
            [pass] => password
            [submit] => Login
        )

    [_GET] => Array
        (
        )

    [_COOKIE] => Array
        (
            [PHPSESSID] => i3gfkdj50g34qfs4eqa9f571e4
        )
```

C A database connection error occurring during the development of the site.

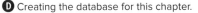

```
                PHP and MySQL for Dynamic Web Sites: Visual QuickPr...
mysql> CREATE DATABASE ch18;
Query OK, 1 row affected (0.00 sec)

mysql> USE ch18;
Database changed
mysql> CREATE TABLE users (
    -> user_id INT UNSIGNED NOT NULL AUTO_INCREMENT,
    -> first_name VARCHAR(20) NOT NULL,
    -> last_name VARCHAR(40) NOT NULL,
    -> email VARCHAR(60) NOT NULL,
    -> pass CHAR(40) NOT NULL,
    -> user_level TINYINT(1) UNSIGNED NOT NULL DEFAULT 0,
    -> active CHAR(32),
    -> registration_date DATETIME NOT NULL,
    -> PRIMARY KEY (user_id),
    -> UNIQUE KEY (email),
    -> INDEX login (email, pass)
    -> );
Query OK, 0 rows affected (0.05 sec)

mysql>
```

D Creating the database for this chapter.

TIP On the one hand, it might make sense to place the contents of both configuration files in one script for ease of reference. Unfortunately, doing so would add unnecessary overhead (namely, connecting to and selecting the database) to scripts that don't require a database connection (e.g., index.php).

TIP In general, define common functions in the configuration file or a separate functions file. One exception would be any function that requires a database connection. If you know that a function will only be used on pages that also connect to MySQL, then defining that function within the mysqli_connect.php script is only logical.

Database Scheme

The database being used by this application is called *ch18*. The database currently consists of only one table, *users*. To create the table, use this SQL command:

```
CREATE TABLE users (
user_id INT UNSIGNED NOT NULL AUTO_INCREMENT,
first_name VARCHAR(20) NOT NULL,
last_name VARCHAR(40) NOT NULL,
email VARCHAR(60) NOT NULL,
pass CHAR(40) NOT NULL,
user_level TINYINT(1) UNSIGNED NOT NULL DEFAULT 0,
active CHAR(32),
registration_date DATETIME NOT NULL,
PRIMARY KEY (user_id),
UNIQUE KEY (email),
INDEX login (email, pass)
);
```

Most of the table's structure should be familiar to you by now; it's quite similar to the *users* table in the *sitename* database, used in several examples in this book. One new addition is the *active* column, which will indicate whether a user has activated their account (by clicking a link in the registration email) or not. This column will either store the 32-character-long activation code or have a **NULL** value. Because the *active* column may have a **NULL** value, it cannot be defined as **NOT NULL**. If you do define *active* as **NOT NULL**, no one will ever be able to log in (you'll see why later in the chapter). The other new addition is the *user_level* column, which will differentiate the kinds of users the site has.

A unique index is placed on the *email* field, and another index is placed on the combination of the *email* and *pass* fields. These two fields will be used together during the login query, so indexing them as one, creating an index called *login*, makes sense.

Creating the Home Page

The home page for the site, called **index. php**, will be a model for the other pages on the public side. It will require the configuration file (for error management) and the header and footer files to create the HTML design. This page will also welcome the user by name, assuming the user is logged in **Ⓐ**.

To write index.php:

1. Begin a new PHP document in your text editor or IDE, to be named **index.php** (**Script 18.5**):

```
<?php # Script 18.5 - index.php
```

2. Include the configuration file, set the page title, and include the HTML header:

```
require ('includes/config.inc.
→ php');
$page_title = 'Welcome to this
→ Site!';
include ('includes/header.html');
```

The script includes the configuration file first so that everything that happens afterward will be handled using the error-management processes established therein. Then the **header.html** file is included, which will start output buffering, begin the session, and create the initial part of the HTML layout.

Script 18.5 The script for the site's home page, which will greet a logged-in user by name.

```
1    <?php # Script 18.5 - index.php
2    // This is the main page for the site.
3
4    // Include the configuration file:
5    require ('includes/config.inc.php');
6
7    // Set the page title and include the
     HTML header:
8    $page_title = 'Welcome to this Site!';
9    include ('includes/header.html');
10
11   // Welcome the user (by name if they are
     logged in):
12   echo '<h1>Welcome';
13   if (isset($_SESSION['first_name'])) {
14       echo ", {$_SESSION['first_name']}";
15   }
16   echo '!</h1>';
17   ?>
18   <p>Spam spam spam spam spam spam
19   spam spam spam spam spam spam
20   spam spam spam spam spam spam
21   spam spam spam spam spam spam.</p>
22   <p>Spam spam spam spam spam spam
23   spam spam spam spam spam spam
24   spam spam spam spam spam spam
25   spam spam spam spam spam spam.</p>
26
27   <?php include ('includes/footer.html');
     ?>
```

A If the user is logged in, the index page will greet them by name.

B If the user is not logged in, this is the home page they will see.

3. Greet the user and complete the PHP code:

```php
echo '<h1>Welcome';
if (isset($_SESSION['first_name']))
{
  echo ",
{$_SESSION['first_name']}";
}
echo '!</h1>';
?>
```

The *Welcome* message will be printed to all users. If a **$_SESSION['first_name']** variable is set, the user's first name will also be printed. So the end result will be either just *Welcome!* **B** or *Welcome, <Your Name>!* **A**.

4. Create the content for the page:

```html
<p>Spam spam…</p>
```

You might want to consider putting something more useful on the home page of a real site. Just a suggestion....

5. Include the HTML footer:

```php
<?php include ('includes/footer.
→ html'); ?>
```

The footer file will complete the HTML layout (primarily the menu bar on the right side of the page) and conclude the output buffering.

6. Save the file as **index.php**, place it in your Web directory, and test it in a Web browser.

Registration

The registration script was first started in Chapter 9. It has since been improved upon in many ways. This version of **register.php** will do the following:

- Both display and handle the form
- Validate the submitted data using regular expressions and the Filter extension
- Redisplay the form with the values remembered if a problem occurs (the form will be *sticky*)
- Process the submitted data using the **mysqli_real_escape_string( )** function for security
- Ensure a unique email address
- Send an email containing an activation link (users will have to activate their account prior to logging in—see the "Activation Process" sidebar)

To write register.php:

1. Begin a new PHP document in your text editor or IDE, to be named **register. php** (Script 18.6):

   ```
   <?php # Script 18.6 - register.php
   ```

2. Include the configuration file and the HTML header:

   ```
   require ('includes/config.inc.
   → php');
   $page_title = 'Register';
   include ('includes/header.html');
   ```

continues on page 579

Script 18.6 The registration script uses regular expressions for security and a sticky form for user convenience. It sends an email to the user upon a successful registration.

```
1   <?php # Script 18.6 - register.php
2   // This is the registration page for the
    site.
3   require ('includes/config.inc.php');
4   $page_title = 'Register';
5   include ('includes/header.html');
6
7   if ($_SERVER['REQUEST_METHOD'] == 'POST')
    { // Handle the form.
8
9       // Need the database connection:
10      require (MYSQL);
11
12      // Trim all the incoming data:
13      $trimmed = array_map('trim', $_POST);
14
15      // Assume invalid values:
16      $fn = $ln = $e = $p = FALSE;
17
18      // Check for a first name:
19      if (preg_match ('/^[A-Z \'.-]{2,20}$/i',
        $trimmed['first_name'])) {
20          $fn = mysqli_real_escape_string
            ($dbc, $trimmed['first_name']);
21      } else {
22          echo '<p class="error">Please enter
            your first name!</p>';
23      }
24
25      // Check for a last name:
26      if (preg_match ('/^[A-Z \'.-]{2,40}$/i',
        $trimmed['last_name'])) {
27          $ln = mysqli_real_escape_string
            ($dbc, $trimmed['last_name']);
28      } else {
29          echo '<p class="error">Please enter
            your last name!</p>';
30      }
31
32      // Check for an email address:
33      if (filter_var($trimmed['email'],
        FILTER_VALIDATE_EMAIL)) {
34          $e = mysqli_real_escape_string
            ($dbc, $trimmed['email']);
35      } else {
36          echo '<p class="error">Please enter
            a valid email address!</p>';
```

code continues on next page

```
37        }
38
39        // Check for a password and match against the confirmed password:
40        if (preg_match ('/^\w{4,20}$/', $trimmed['password1']) ) {
41            if ($trimmed['password1'] == $trimmed['password2']) {
42                $p = mysqli_real_escape_string ($dbc, $trimmed['password1']);
43            } else {
44                echo '<p class="error">Your password did not match the confirmed password!</p>';
45            }
46        } else {
47            echo '<p class="error">Please enter a valid password!</p>';
48        }
49
50        if ($fn && $ln && $e && $p) { // If everything's OK...
51
52            // Make sure the email address is available:
53            $q = "SELECT user_id FROM users WHERE email='$e'";
54            $r = mysqli_query ($dbc, $q) or trigger_error("Query: $q\n<br />MySQL Error: " .
                 mysqli_error($dbc));
55
56            if (mysqli_num_rows($r) == 0) { // Available.
57
58                // Create the activation code:
59                $a = md5(uniqid(rand( ), true));
60
61                // Add the user to the database:
62                $q = "INSERT INTO users (email, pass, first_name, last_name, active, registration_
                     date) VALUES ('$e', SHA1('$p'), '$fn', '$ln', '$a', NOW( ) )";
63                $r = mysqli_query ($dbc, $q) or trigger_error("Query: $q\n<br />MySQL Error: " .
                     mysqli_error($dbc));
64
65                if (mysqli_affected_rows($dbc) == 1) { // If it ran OK.
66
67                    // Send the email:
68                    $body = "Thank you for registering at <whatever site>. To activate your account,
                         please click on this link:\n\n";
69                    $body .= BASE_URL . 'activate.php?x=' . urlencode($e) . "&y=$a";
70                    mail($trimmed['email'], 'Registration Confirmation', $body, 'From: admin@sitename.
                         com');
71
72                    // Finish the page:
73                    echo '<h3>Thank you for registering! A confirmation email has been sent to
                         your address. Please click on the link in that email in order to activate your
                         account.</h3>';
74                    include ('includes/footer.html'); // Include the HTML footer.
75                    exit( ); // Stop the page.
76
77                } else { // If it did not run OK.
```

code continues on next page

```
78              echo '<p class="error">You could not be registered due to a system error. We
                apologize for any inconvenience.</p>';
79          }
80
81      } else { // The email address is not available.
82          echo '<p class="error">That email address has already been registered. If you have
                forgotten your password, use the link at right to have your password sent to you.
                </p>';
83      }
84
85  } else { // If one of the data tests failed.
86      echo '<p class="error">Please try again.</p>';
87  }
88
89  mysqli_close($dbc);
90
91  } // End of the main Submit conditional.
92  ?>
93
94  <h1>Register</h1>
95  <form action="register.php" method="post">
96      <fieldset>
97
98      <p><b>First Name:</b> <input type="text" name="first_name" size="20" maxlength="20"
          value="<?php if (isset($trimmed['first_name'])) echo $trimmed['first_name']; ?>" /></p>
99
100     <p><b>Last Name:</b> <input type="text" name="last_name" size="20" maxlength="40" value="<?php
          if (isset($trimmed['last_name'])) echo $trimmed['last_name']; ?>" /></p>
101
102     <p><b>Email Address:</b> <input type="text" name="email" size="30" maxlength="60" value="<?php
          if (isset($trimmed['email'])) echo $trimmed['email']; ?>" /> </p>
103
104     <p><b>Password:</b> <input type="password" name="password1" size="20" maxlength="20"
          value="<?php if (isset($trimmed['password1'])) echo $trimmed['password1']; ?>" /> <small>Use
          only letters, numbers, and the underscore. Must be between 4 and 20 characters long.
          </small></p>
105
106     <p><b>Confirm Password:</b> <input type="password" name="password2" size="20" maxlength="20"
          value="<?php if (isset($trimmed['password2'])) echo $trimmed['password2']; ?>" /></p>
107     </fieldset>
108
109     <div align="center"><input type="submit" name="submit" value="Register" /></div>
110
111 </form>
112
113 <?php include ('includes/footer.html'); ?>
```

3. Create the conditional that checks for the form submission and then include the database connection script:

```
if ($_SERVER['REQUEST_METHOD'] ==
→ 'POST') {
  require (MYSQL);
```

As the full path to the `mysqli_connect.php` script is defined as a constant in the configuration file, the constant can be used as the argument to `require( )`. The benefit to this approach is that any file stored anywhere in the site, even within a subdirectory, can use this same code to successfully include the connection script.

4. Trim the incoming data and establish some flag variables:

```
$trimmed = array_map('trim',
→ $_POST);
$fn = $ln = $e = $p = FALSE;
```

The first line runs every element in `$_POST` through the `trim( )` function, assigning the returned result to the new `$trimmed` array. The explanation for this line can be found in Chapter 13, "Security Methods," when `array_map( )` was used with data to be sent in an email. In short, the `trim( )` function will be applied to every value in `$_POST`, saving the hassle of applying `trim( )` to each individually.

The second line initializes four variables as FALSE. This one line is just a shortcut in lieu of

```
$fn = FALSE;
$ln = FALSE;
$e = FALSE;
$p = FALSE;
```

5. Validate the first and last names:

```
if (preg_match ('/^[A-Z \'.-]{2,20}
→ $/i', $trimmed['first_name'])) {
  $fn = mysqli_real_escape_string
  → ($dbc, $trimmed['first_name']);
} else {
  echo '<p class="error">Please
  → enter your first name!</p>';
}
if (preg_match ('/^[A-Z \'.-]
→ {2,40}$/i', $trimmed['last_
→ name'])) {
  $ln = mysqli_real_escape_string
  → ($dbc, $trimmed['last_name']);
} else {
  echo '<p class="error">Please
  → enter your last name!</p>';
}
```

Much of the form will be validated using regular expressions, covered in Chapter 14, "Perl-Compatible Regular Expressions." For the first name value, the assumption is that it will contain only letters, a period (as in an initial), an apostrophe, a space, and the dash. Further, the value should be within the range of 2 to 20 characters long. To guarantee that the value contains only these characters, the caret and the dollar sign are used to match both the beginning and end of the string. While using Perl-Compatible Regular Expressions, the entire pattern must be placed within delimiters (the forward slashes).

continues on next page

If this condition is met, the **$fn** variable is assigned the value of the **mysqli_ real_escape_string( )** version of the submitted value; otherwise, **$fn** will still be FALSE and an error message is printed .

The same process is used to validate the last name, although that regular expression allows for a longer length. Both patterns are also case-insensitive, thanks to the *i* modifier.

6. Validate the email address :

```
if (filter_var($trimmed['email'],
→ FILTER_VALIDATE_EMAIL)) {
    $e = mysqli_real_escape_string
    → ($dbc, $trimmed['email']);
} else {
    echo '<p class="error">Please
    → enter a valid email address!
    → </p>';
}
```

An email address can easily be validated using the Filter extension, discussed in Chapter 13. If your version of PHP does not support the Filter extension, you'll need to use a regular expression here instead (the pattern for an email address was described in Chapter 14).

7. Validate the passwords:

```
if (preg_match ('/^\w{4,20}$/',
→ $trimmed['password1']) ) {
    if ($trimmed['password1'] ==
    → $trimmed['password2']) {
        $p = mysqli_real_escape_
        → string ($dbc, $trimmed
        → ['password1']);
    } else {
        echo '<p class="error">Your
        → password did not match the
        → confirmed password!</p>';
    }
```

A If the first name value does not pass the regular expression test, an error message is printed.

User Registration

Please enter a valid email address!
Please try again.

Register

First Name: Larry

Last Name: Ullman

Email Address: Larry

B The submitted email address must be of the proper format.

C The passwords are checked for the proper format, length, and...

User Registration

Your password did not match the confirmed password!

Please try again.

Register

First Name: Larry

Last Name: Ullman

Email Address: Larry@LarryUllman.com

Password: ●●●●   Use only letters, numbers, and the underscore. Must be between 4 and 20 characters long.

Confirm Password: ●●●●●●●●

D ...that the password value matches the confirmed password value.

User Registration

An error occurred in script 'C:\xampp\htdocs\register.php' on line 54: Query: SELECT user_id FROM userss WHERE email='Larry@LarryUllman.com'

MySQL Error: Table 'ch18.userss' doesn't exist Date/Time: 5-27-2011 11:00:36

```
Array
(
    [GLOBALS] => Array
 *RECURSION*
    [_POST] => Array
        (
            [first_name] => Larry
            [last_name] => Ullman
            [email] => Larry@LarryUllman.com
            [password1] => password
            [password2] => password
            [submit] => Register
        )
```

E If a MySQL query error occurs, it should be easier to debug thanks to this informative error message.

```
} else {
  echo '<p class="error">Please
→ enter a valid password!</p>';
}
```

The password must be between 4 and 20 characters long and contain only letters, numbers, and the underscore **C**. That exact combination is represented by **\w** in Perl-Compatible Regular Expressions. Furthermore, the first password (*password1*) must match the confirmed password (*password2*) **D**.

8. If every test was passed, check for a unique email address:

```
if ($fn && $ln && $e && $p) {
  $q = "SELECT user_id FROM users
→ WHERE email='$e'";
  $r = mysqli_query ($dbc, $q)
→ or trigger_error("Query: $q\
n<br />MySQL Error: " .
→ mysqli_error($dbc));
```

If the form passed every test, this conditional will be TRUE. Then the script must search the database to see if the submitted email address is currently being used, since that column's value must be unique across each record. As with the MySQL connection script, if a query doesn't run, call the **trigger_error( )** function to invoke the self-defined error reporting function. The specific error message will include both the query being run and the MySQL error **E**, so that the problem can easily be debugged.

continues on next page

9. If the email address is unused, register the user:

```
if (mysqli_num_rows($r) == 0) {
    $a = md5(uniqid(rand( ), true));
    $q = "INSERT INTO users (email,
    → pass, first_name, last_name,
    → active, registration_date)
    → VALUES ('$e', SHA1('$p'), '$fn',
    → '$ln', '$a', NOW( ) )";
    $r = mysqli_query ($dbc, $q)
    → or trigger_error("Query:
    → $q\n<br />MySQL Error: " .
    → mysqli_error($dbc));
```

The query itself is rather simple, but it does require the creation of a unique activation code. Generating that requires the **rand( )**, **uniqid( )**, and **md5( )** functions. Of these, **uniqid( )** is the most important; it creates a unique identifier. It's fed the **rand( )** function to help generate a more random value. Finally, the returned result is *hashed* using **md5( )**, which creates a string exactly 32 characters long (a hash is a mathematically calculated representation of a piece of data). You do not need to fully comprehend these three functions, just note that the result will be a unique 32-character string.

As for the query itself, it should be familiar enough to you. Most of the values come from variables in the PHP script, after applying **trim( )** and **mysqli_real_escape_string( )** to them. The MySQL **SHA1( )** function is used to encrypt the password and **NOW( )** is used to set the registration date as the current moment. Because the *user_level* column has a default value of 0 (i.e., not an administrator), that column does not have to be provided a value in this query. Presumably the site's main administrator would edit a user's record to give him or her administrative power after the user has registered.

10. Send an email if the query worked:

```
if (mysqli_affected_rows($dbc) ==
→ 1) {
    $body = "Thank you for
    → registering at <whatever
    → site>. To activate your
    → account, please click on this
    → link:\n\n";
    $body .= BASE_URL . 'activate.
    → php?x=' . urlencode($e) .
    → "&y=$a";
    mail($trimmed['email'],
    → 'Registration Confirmation',
    → $body, 'From: admin@sitename.
    → com');
```

With this registration process, the important thing is that the confirmation mail gets sent to the user, because they will not be able to log in until after they've activated their account. This email should contain a link to the activation page, **activate.php**. The link to that page starts with **BASE_URL**, which is defined in **config.inc.php**. The link also passes two values along in the URL. The first, generically called *x*, will be the user's email address, encoded so that it's safe to have in a URL. The second, *y*, is the activation code. The URL, then, will be something like *http://www.example.com/activate. php?x=email%40example.com&y= 901e09ef25bf6e3ef95c93088450b008*.

```
User Registration

Thank you for registering! A          Home
confirmation email has been sent      Register
to your address. Please click on      Login
the link in that email in order to    Retrieve Password
activate your account.                 Some Page
                                       Another Page
```

F The resulting page after a user has successfully registered.

Activation Process

New in this chapter is an activation process, where users have to click a link in an email to confirm their accounts, prior to being able to log in. Using a system like this prevents bogus registrations from being usable. If an invalid email address is entered, that account can never be activated. And if someone registered another person's address, hopefully the maligned person would not activate this undesired account.

From a programming perspective, this process requires the creation of a unique activation code for each registered user, to be stored in the *users* table. The code is then sent in a confirmation email to the user (as part of a link). When the user clicks the link, he or she will be taken to a page on the site that activates the account (by removing that code from their record). The end result is that no one can register and activate an account without receiving the confirmation email (i.e., without having a valid email address that the registrant controls).

11. Tell the user what to expect and complete the page:

```
echo '<h3>Thank you for
→ registering! A confirmation
→ email has been sent to your
→ address. Please click on the
→ link in that email in order to
→ activate your account.</h3>';
include ('includes/footer.html');
exit( );
```

A thank-you message is printed out upon successful registration, along with the activation instructions **F**. Then the footer is included and the page is terminated.

12. Print errors if the query failed:

```
} else { // If it did not run OK.
  echo '<p class="error">You could
  → not be registered due to a
  → system error. We apologize
  → for any inconvenience.</p>';
}
```

If the query failed for some reason, meaning that `mysqli_affected_rows( )` did not return 1, an error message is printed to the browser. Because of the security methods implemented in this script, the live version of the site should never have a problem at this juncture.

continues on next page

13. Complete the conditionals and the PHP code:

```
    } else {
        echo '<p class="error">That
        ⇥email address has already
        ⇥been registered. If you
        ⇥have forgotten your
        ⇥password, use the link
        ⇥at right to have your
        ⇥password sent to you.
        ⇥</p>';
    }
  } else {
    echo '<p class="error">Please
    ⇥try again.</p>';
  }
  mysqli_close($dbc);
}
?>
```

The first **else** is executed if a person attempts to register with an email address that has already been used **G**. The second **else** applies when the submitted data fails one of the validation routines (see **A** through **D**).

User Registration

That email address has already been registered. If you have forgotten your password, use the link at right to have your password sent to you.

Register

G If an email address has already been registered, the user is told as much.

User Registration

Register

First Name:

Last Name:

Email Address:

Password: Use only letters, numbers, and the underscore. Must be between 4 and 20 characters long.

Confirm Password:

[Register]

Home
Register
Login
Retrieve Password
Some Page
Another Page

H The registration form as it looks when the user first arrives.

14. Begin the HTML form **ⓗ**:

```
<h1>Register</h1>
<form action="register.php"
→ method="post">
  <fieldset>
  <p><b>First Name:</b> <input
  → type="text" name="first_name"
  → size="20" maxlength="20"
  → value="<?php if (isset
  → ($trimmed['first_name']))
  →  echo $trimmed['first_name'];
  → ?>" /></p>
```

The HTML form has text inputs for all of the values. Each input has a name and a maximum length that match the corresponding column definition in the *users* table. The form will be sticky, using the trimmed values.

15. Add inputs for the last name and email address:

```
<p><b>Last Name:</b> <input
→ type="text" name="last_name"
→ size="20" maxlength="40" value="
→ <?php if (isset($trimmed['last_
→ name'])) echo $trimmed['last_
→ name']; ?>" /></p>
<p><b>Email Address:</b> <input
→ type="text" name="email" size=
→ "30" maxlength="60" value="<?php
→ if (isset($trimmed['email']))
→ echo $trimmed['email']; ?>" />
→ </p>
```

16. Add inputs for the password and the confirmation of the password:

```
<p><b>Password:</b> <input type=
→ "password" name="password1"
→ size="20" maxlength="20" value="
→ <?php if (isset($trimmed
→ ['password1'])) echo $trimmed
→ ['password1']; ?>" /> <small>Use
→ only letters, numbers, and the
```

```
→ underscore. Must be between 4
→ and 20 characters long.</small>
→ </p>
<p><b>Confirm Password:
→ </b> <input type="password"
→ name="password2" size="20"
→ maxlength="20" value="<?php if
→ (isset($trimmed['password2']))
→ echo $trimmed['password2'];
→ ?>" /></p>
```

When using regular expressions to limit what data can be provided, including that data's length, it's best to indicate those requirements to the user in the form itself. By doing so, the site won't report an error to the user for doing something the user didn't know she or he couldn't do.

17. Complete the HTML form:

```
  </fieldset>
  <div align="center"><input
  → type="submit" name="submit"
  → value="Register" /></div>
</form>
```

18. Include the HTML footer:

```
<?php include ('includes/footer.
→ html'); ?>
```

19. Save the file as **register.php**, place it in your Web directory, and test it in your Web browser.

> **TIP** Because every column in the *users* table cannot be NULL (except for *active*), each input must be correctly filled out. If a table has an optional field, you should still confirm that it is of the right type if submitted, but not require it.

> **TIP** Except for encrypted fields (such as the password), the maximum length of the form inputs and regular expressions should correspond to the maximum length of the column in the database.

Activating an Account

As described in the "Activation Process" sidebar earlier in the chapter, each user will have to activate her or his account prior to being able to log in. Upon successfully registering, the user will receive an email containing a link to **activate.php** . This link also passes two values to this page: the user's registered email address and a unique activation code. To complete the registration process—to activate the account, the user will need to click that link, taking her or him to the **activate.php** script on the Web site.

The **activate.php** script needs to first confirm that those two values were received in the URL. Then, if the received two values match those stored in the database, the activation code will be removed from the record, indicating an active account.

To create the activation page:

1. Begin a new PHP script in your text editor or IDE, to be named **activate.php** (Script 18.7):

    ```php
    <?php # Script 18.7 - activate.php
    require ('includes/config.inc.php');
    $page_title = 'Activate Your
    → Account';
    include ('includes/header.html');
    ```

2. Validate the values that should be received by the page:

    ```php
    if (isset($_GET['x'], $_GET['y'])
        && filter_var($trimmed['email'],
        → FILTER_VALIDATE_EMAIL)
        && (strlen($_GET['y']) == 32 )
        ) {
    ```

A The registration confirmation email.

Script 18.7 To activate an account, the user must come to this page, passing it her or his email address and activation code (all part of the link sent in an email upon registering).

```php
1   <?php # Script 18.7 - activate.php
2   // This page activates the user's
    account.
3   require ('includes/config.inc.php');
4   $page_title = 'Activate Your Account';
5   include ('includes/header.html');
6
7   // If $x and $y don't exist or aren't of
    the proper format, redirect the user:
8   if (isset($_GET['x'], $_GET['y'])
9       && filter_var($_GET['x'],
        FILTER_VALIDATE_EMAIL)
10      && (strlen($_GET['y']) == 32 )
11      ) {
12
13      // Update the database...
14      require (MYSQL);
15      $q = "UPDATE users SET active=NULL
        WHERE (email='" . mysqli_real_
        escape_string($dbc, $_GET['x']) . "'
        AND active='" . mysqli_real_escape_
        string($dbc, $_GET['y']) . "') LIMIT
        1";
16      $r = mysqli_query ($dbc, $q) or
        trigger_error("Query: $q\n<br />MySQL
        Error: " . mysqli_error($dbc));
17
18      // Print a customized message:
19      if (mysqli_affected_rows($dbc) == 1) {
20          echo "<h3>Your account is now
            active. You may now log in.</h3>";
21      } else {
```

code continues on next page

As already mentioned, when the user clicks the link in the registration confirmation email, two values will be passed to this page: the email address and the activation code. Both values must be present and validated, before attempting to use them in a query activating the user's account.

The first step is to ensure that both values are set. Since the `isset()` function can simultaneously check for the presence of multiple variables, the first part of the validation condition is `isset($_GET['x'], $_GET['y'])`.

Second, `$_GET['x']` must be in the format of a valid email address. The same code as in the registration script can be used for that purpose (either the Filter extension or a regular expression).

Third, for *y* (the activation code), the last clause in the conditional checks that this string's length (how many characters are in it) is exactly 32. The

`md5()` function, which created the activation code, always returns a string 32 characters long.

3. Attempt to activate the user's account:

```
require (MYSQL);
$q = "UPDATE users SET active=NULL
→ WHERE (email='" . mysqli_real_
→ escape_string($dbc, $_GET['x'])
→ . "' AND active='" . mysqli_
→ real_escape_string($dbc, $_
→ GET['y']) . "') LIMIT 1";
$r = mysqli_query ($dbc, $q)
→ or trigger_error("Query:
→ $q\n<br />MySQL Error: " .
→ mysqli_error($dbc));
```

If all three conditions (in Step 2) are TRUE, an **UPDATE** query is run. This query removes the activation code from the user's record by setting the *active* column to **NULL**. Before using the values in the query, both are run through `mysqli_real_escape_string()` for extra security.

4. Report upon the success of the query:

```
if (mysqli_affected_rows($dbc) ==
→ 1) {
   echo "<h3>Your account is now
   → active. You may now log in.</
   → h3>";
} else {
   echo '<p class="error">Your
   → account could not be
   → activated.  Please re-check
   → the link or  contact the
   → system administrator.</p>';
}
```

continues on next page

Script 18.7 *continued*

```
22          echo '<p class="error">Your account
            could not be activated. Please
            re-check the link or contact the
            system administrator.</p>';
23      }
24
25      mysqli_close($dbc);
26
27  } else { // Redirect.
28
29      $url = BASE_URL . 'index.php'; //
        Define the URL.
30      ob_end_clean(); // Delete the buffer.
31      header("Location: $url");
32      exit(); // Quit the script.
33
34  } // End of main IF-ELSE.
35
36  include ('includes/footer.html');
37  ?>
```

If one row was affected by the query, then the user's account is now active and a message says as much **B**. If no rows are affected, the user is notified of the problem **C**. This would most likely happen if someone tried to fake the *x* and *y* values or if there's a problem in following the link from the email to the Web browser.

5. Complete the main conditional:

```
    mysqli_close($dbc);
} else { // Redirect.
    $url = BASE_URL . 'index.php';
    ob_end_clean();
    header("Location: $url");
    exit();
} // End of main IF-ELSE.
```

The **else** clause takes effect if **$_GET['x']** and **$_GET['y']** are not of the proper value and length. In such a case, the user is just redirected to the index page. The **ob_end_clean()** line here deletes the buffer (whatever was to be sent to the Web browser up to this point, stored in memory), as it won't be used.

6. Complete the page:

```
    include ('includes/footer.html');
?>
```

7. Save the file as **activate.php**, place it in your Web directory, and test it by clicking the link in the registration email.

TIP If you wanted to be a little more forgiving, you could have this page print an error message if the correct values are not received, rather than redirect them to the index page (as if they were attempting to hack the site).

TIP I specifically use the vague *x* and *y* as the names in the URL for security purposes. While someone may figure out that the one is an email address and the other is a code, it's sometimes best not to be explicit about such things.

TIP An alternative method, which I used in the second edition of this book, was to place the activation code and the user's ID (from the database) in the link. That also works, but from a security perspective, it's really best that users never see, or are even aware of, a user ID that's otherwise not meant to be public.

B If the database *could be* updated using the provided email address and activation code, the user is notified that their account is now active.

C If an account is not activated by the query, the user is told of the problem.

```
1    <?php # Script 18.8 - login.php
2    // This is the login page for the site.
3    require ('includes/config.inc.php');
4    $page_title = 'Login';
5    include ('includes/header.html');
6
7    if ($_SERVER['REQUEST_METHOD'] == 'POST')
     {
8        require (MYSQL);
9
10       // Validate the email address:
11       if (!empty($_POST['email'])) {
12           $e = mysqli_real_escape_string
             ($dbc, $_POST['email']);
13       } else {
14           $e = FALSE;
15           echo '<p class="error">You forgot
             to enter your email address!</p>';
16       }
17
18       // Validate the password:
19       if (!empty($_POST['pass'])) {
20           $p = mysqli_real_escape_string
             ($dbc, $_POST['pass']);
21       } else {
22           $p = FALSE;
23           echo '<p class="error">You forgot
             to enter your password!</p>';
24       }
25
26       if ($e && $p) { // If everything's OK.
27
28           // Query the database:
29           $q = "SELECT user_id, first_name,
             user_level FROM users WHERE
             (email='$e' AND pass=SHA1('$p')) AND
             active IS NULL";
30           $r = mysqli_query ($dbc, $q)
             or trigger_error("Query: $q\
             n<br />MySQL Error: " .
             mysqli_error($dbc));
31
32           if (@mysqli_num_rows($r) == 1) {
             // A match was made.
33
34               // Register the values:
```

code continues on next page

Logging In and Logging Out

Chapter 12 created many versions of **login.php** and **logout.php** scripts, using variations on cookies and sessions. Here both scripts will be created once again, this time adhering to the same practices as the rest of this chapter's Web application. The login query itself is slightly different in this example in that it must also check that the *active* column has a **NULL** value, which is the indication that the user has activated his or her account.

To write login.php:

1. Begin a new PHP document in your text editor or IDE, to be named **login.php** (Script 18.8):

   ```
   <?php # Script 18.8 - login.php
   require ('includes/config.inc.php');
   $page_title = 'Login';
   include ('includes/header.html');
   ```

2. Check if the form has been submitted and require the database connection:

   ```
   if ($_SERVER['REQUEST_METHOD'] ==
   → 'POST') {
       require (MYSQL);
   ```

   continues on next page

3. Validate the submitted data:

```
if (!empty($_POST['email'])) {
    $e = mysqli_real_escape_string
    → ($dbc, $_POST['email']);
} else {
    $e = FALSE;
    echo '<p class="error">You
    → forgot to enter your email
    → address!</p>';
}
if (!empty($_POST['pass'])) {
    $p = mysqli_real_escape_string
    → ($dbc, $_POST['pass']);
} else {
    $p = FALSE;
    echo '<p class="error">You forgot
    → to enter your password!</p>';
}
```

There are two ways of thinking about the validation. On the one hand, you could use regular expressions and the Filter extension, copying the same code from **register.php**, to validate these values. On the other hand, the true test of the values will be whether the login query returns a record or not, so one could arguably skip more stringent PHP validation. This script uses the latter thinking.

If the user does not enter any values into the form, error messages will be printed **A**.

User Registration

You forgot to enter your email address!
You forgot to enter your password!
Please try again.

Login

A The login form checks only if values were entered, without using regular expressions.

Script 18.8 *continued*

```
35          $_SESSION = mysqli_fetch_array
            ($r, MYSQLI_ASSOC);
36          mysqli_free_result($r);
37          mysqli_close($dbc);
38
39          // Redirect the user:
40          $url = BASE_URL . 'index.php';
            // Define the URL.
41          ob_end_clean(); // Delete the
            buffer.
42          header("Location: $url");
43          exit(); // Quit the script.
44
45      } else { // No match was made.
46          echo '<p class="error">Either
            the email address and password
            entered do not match those
            on file or you have not yet
            activated your account.</p>';
47      }
48
49  } else { // If everything wasn't OK.
50      echo '<p class="error">Please try
        again.</p>';
51  }
52
53  mysqli_close($dbc);
54
55  } // End of SUBMIT conditional.
56  ?>
57
58  <h1>Login</h1>
59  <p>Your browser must allow cookies in
    order to log in.</p>
60  <form action="login.php" method="post">
61      <fieldset>
62          <p><b>Email Address:</b> <input
            type="text" name="email" size="20"
            maxlength="60" /></p>
63          <p><b>Password:</b> <input
            type="password" name="pass" size="20"
            maxlength="20" /></p>
64          <div align="center"><input
            type="submit" name="submit"
            value="Login" /></div>
65      </fieldset>
66  </form>
67
68  <?php include ('includes/footer.html');
    ?>
```

4. If both validation routines were passed, retrieve the user information:

```
if ($e && $p) {
    $q = "SELECT user_id, first_
    → name, user_level FROM users
    → WHERE (email='$e' AND pass=SHA1
    → ('$p')) AND active IS NULL";
    $r = mysqli_query ($dbc, $q)
    → or trigger_error("Query:
    → $q\n<br />MySQL Error: " .
    → mysqli_error($dbc));
```

The query will attempt to retrieve the user ID, first name, and user level for the record whose email address and password match those submitted. The MySQL query uses the **SHA1( )** function on the *pass* column, as the password is encrypted using that function in during the registration process. The query also checks that the *active* column has a **NULL** value, meaning that the user has successfully accessed the **activate. php** page.

If you know an account has been activated but you still can't log in using the proper values, it's likely because your *active* column was erroneously defined as **NOT NULL**.

5. If a match was made in the database, log the user in:

```
if (@mysqli_num_rows($r) == 1) {
    $_SESSION = mysqli_fetch_array
    → ($r, MYSQLI_ASSOC);
    mysqli_free_result($r);
    mysqli_close($dbc);
```

The login process consists of storing the retrieved values in the session (which was already started in **header. html**) and then redirecting the user to the home page. Because the query will return an array with three elements— one indexed at *user_id*, one at *first_name*, and the third at *user_level*, all three can be fetched right into **$_ SESSION**, resulting in **$_SESSION['user_ id']**, **$_SESSION['first_name']**, and **$_SESSION['user_level']**. If **$_SESSION** had other values in it already, you would not want to take this shortcut, as you'd wipe out those other elements.

6. Redirect the user:

```
$url = BASE_URL . 'index.php';
→ ob_end_clean( );
header("Location: $url");
exit( );
```

The **ob_end_clean( )** function will delete the existing buffer (the output buffering is also begun in **header.html**), since it will not be used.

7. Complete the conditionals and close the database connection:

```
        } else {
            echo '<p class="error">
            → Either the email address
            → and password entered do
            → not match those on file
            → or you have not yet
            → activated your account.
            → </p>';
        }
    } else {
        echo '<p class="error">Please
        → try again.</p>';
    }
    mysqli_close($dbc);
} // End of SUBMIT conditional.
?>
```

continues on next page

The error message **B** indicates that the login process could fail for two possible reasons. One is that the submitted email address and password do not match those on file. The other reason is that the user has not yet activated their account.

8. Display the HTML login form **C**:

```
<h1>Login</h1>
<p>Your browser must allow cook-
ies in order to log in.</p>
<form action="login.php"
method="post">
  <fieldset>
  <p><b>Email Address:</b> <input
type="text" name="email" size="20"
maxlength="60" /></p>
  <p><b>Password:</b> <input
type="password" name="pass"
size="20" maxlength="20" /></p>
  <div align="center"><input
type="submit" name="submit"
value="Login" /></div>
  </fieldset>
</form>
```

The login form, like the registration form, will submit the data back to itself. This one is not sticky, though, but you could add that functionality.

Notice that the page includes a message informing the user that cookies must be enabled to use the site (if a user does not allow cookies, she or he will never get access to the logged-in user pages).

9. Include the HTML footer:

```
<?php include ('includes/footer.
html'); ?>
```

10. Save the file as **login.php**, place it in your Web directory, and test it in your Web browser **D**.

B An error message is displayed if the login query does not return a single record.

C The login form.

D Upon successfully logging in, the user will be redirected to the home page, where they will be greeted by name.

User Registration

You are now logged out.

Home
Register
Login
Retrieve Password
Some Page
Another Page

E The results of successfully logging out.

To write logout.php:

1. Begin a new PHP document in your text editor or IDE, to be named **logout.php** (Script 18.9):

```
<?php # Script 18.9 - logout.php
require ('includes/config.inc.php');
$page_title = 'Logout';
include ('includes/header.html');
```

Script 18.9 The logout page destroys all of the session information, including the cookie.

```
1    <?php # Script 18.9 - logout.php
2    // This is the logout page for the site.
3    require ('includes/config.inc.php');
4    $page_title = 'Logout';
5    include ('includes/header.html');
6
7    // If no first_name session variable
     exists, redirect the user:
8    if (!isset($_SESSION['first_name'])) {
9
10       $url = BASE_URL . 'index.php'; //
         Define the URL.
11       ob_end_clean(); // Delete the buffer.
12       header("Location: $url");
13       exit(); // Quit the script.
14
15   } else { // Log out the user.
16
17       $_SESSION = array(); // Destroy the
         variables.
18       session_destroy(); // Destroy the
         session itself.
19       setcookie (session_name(), '',
         time()-3600); // Destroy the cookie.
20
21   }
22
23   // Print a customized message:
24   echo '<h3>You are now logged out.</h3>';
25
26   include ('includes/footer.html');
27   ?>
```

2. Redirect the user if she or he is not logged in:

```
if (!isset($_SESSION['first_name']))
→ {
  $url = BASE_URL . 'index.php';
  ob_end_clean();
  header("Location: $url");
  exit();
```

If the user is not currently logged in (determined by checking for a $_SESSION['first_name'] variable), the user will be redirected to the home page (because there's no point in trying to log the user out).

3. Log out the user if they are currently logged in:

```
} else { // Log out the user.
  $_SESSION = array();
  session_destroy();
  setcookie (session_name(), '',
  → time()-3600);
}
```

To log the user out, the session values will be reset, the session data will be destroyed on the server, and the session cookie will be deleted. These lines of code were first used and described in Chapter 12. The cookie name will be the value returned by the **session_name()** function. If you decide to change the session name later, this code will still be accurate.

4. Print a logged-out message and complete the PHP page:

```
echo '<h3>You are now logged
out.</h3>';
include ('includes/footer.html');
?>
```

5. Save the file as **logout.php**, place it in your Web directory, and test it in your Web browser **E** (on the previous page).

Password Management

The final aspect of the public side of this site is the management of passwords. There are two processes to consider: resetting a forgotten password and changing an existing one.

Resetting a password

It inevitably happens that people forget their login passwords for Web sites, so having a contingency plan for these occasions is important. One option would be to have the user email the administrator when this occurs, but administering a site is difficult enough without that extra hassle. Instead, this site will have a script whose purpose is to reset a forgotten password.

Because the passwords stored in the database are encrypted using MySQL's **SHA1( )** function, there's no way to retrieve an unencrypted version (the database actually stores a *hashed* version of the password, not an *encrypted* version). The alternative is to create a new, random password and change the existing password to this value. Rather than just display the new password in the Web browser (that would be terribly insecure), the new password will be emailed to the address with which the user registered.

To write forgot_password.php:

1. Begin a new PHP document in your text editor or IDE, to be named **forgot_password.php** (Script 18.10):

```
<?php # Script 18.10 - forgot_
→ password.php
require ('includes/config.inc.php');
$page_title = 'Forgot Your
→ Password';
include ('includes/header.html');
```

2. Check if the form has been submitted, include the database connection, and create a flag variable:

```
if ($_SERVER['REQUEST_METHOD'] ==
→ 'POST') {
  require (MYSQL);
  $uid = FALSE;
```

This form will take an email address input and change the password for that record. To do that, the script first needs to retrieve the user ID value that matches the submitted email address. To begin that process, a flag variable is assigned a FALSE value as an assumption of no valid user ID.

3. Validate the submitted email address:

```
if (!empty($_POST['email'])) {
  $q = 'SELECT user_id FROM
→ users WHERE email="'. mysqli_
→ real_escape_string ($dbc, $_
→ POST['email']) . '"';
  $r = mysqli_query ($dbc, $q) or
→ trigger_error("Query:
→ $q\n<br />MySQL Error: " .
→ mysqli_error($dbc));
```

This is a simple validation for a submitted email address (without using a regular expression or the Filter extension). If the submitted value is not empty, an attempt is made to retrieve the user ID for that email address in the database. You could, of course, add more stringent validation if you'd prefer.

continues on page 596

Script 18.10 The `forgot_password.php` script allows users to reset their password without administrative assistance.

```php
1   <?php # Script 18.10 - forgot_password.
    php
2   // This page allows a user to reset
    their password, if forgotten.
3   require ('includes/config.inc.php');
4   $page_title = 'Forgot Your Password';
5   include ('includes/header.html');
6
7   if ($_SERVER['REQUEST_METHOD'] == 'POST') {
8       require (MYSQL);
9
10      // Assume nothing:
11      $uid = FALSE;
12
13      // Validate the email address...
14      if (!empty($_POST['email'])) {
15
16          // Check for the existence of that
            email address...
17          $q = 'SELECT user_id FROM
            users WHERE email="'. mysqli_
            real_escape_string ($dbc, $_
            POST['email']) . '"';
18          $r = mysqli_query ($dbc, $q)
            or trigger_error("Query: $q\
            n<br />MySQL Error: " .
            mysqli_error($dbc));
19
20          if (mysqli_num_rows($r) == 1) { //
            Retrieve the user ID:
21              list($uid) = mysqli_fetch_array
                ($r, MYSQLI_NUM);
22          } else { // No database match
            made.
23              echo '<p class="error">The
                submitted email address does
                not match those on file!</p>';
24          }
25
26      } else { // No email!
27          echo '<p class="error">You forgot
            to enter your email address!</p>';
28      } // End of empty($_POST['email']) IF.
29
30      if ($uid) { // If everything's OK.
31
32          // Create a new, random password:
```

Script 18.10 *continued*

```php
33          $p = substr ( md5(uniqid(rand( ),
            true)), 3, 10);
34
35          // Update the database:
36          $q = "UPDATE users SET pass=SHA1
            ('$p') WHERE user_id=$uid LIMIT 1";
37          $r = mysqli_query ($dbc, $q) or
            trigger_error("Query: $q\
            n<br />MySQL Error: " .
            mysqli_error($dbc));
38
39          if (mysqli_affected_rows($dbc) ==
            1) { // If it ran OK.
40
41              // Send an email:
42              $body = "Your password to
                log into <whatever site> has
                been temporarily changed
                to '$p'. Please log in using
                this password and this email
                address. Then you may change
                your password to something
                more familiar.";
43              mail ($_POST['email'], 'Your
                temporary password.', $body,
                'From: admin@sitename.com');
44
45              // Print a message and wrap up:
46              echo '<h3>Your password has
                been changed. You will receive
                the new, temporary password at
                the email address with which
                you registered. Once you have
                logged in with this password,
                you may change it by clicking
                on the "Change Password"
                link.</h3>';
47              mysqli_close($dbc);
48              include ('includes/footer.html');
49              exit(); // Stop the script.
50
51          } else { // If it did not run OK.
52              echo '<p class="error">Your
                password could not be
                changed due to a system
                error. We apologize for any
                inconvenience.</p>';
53          }
54
```

code continues

code continues on next page

4. Retrieve the selected user ID:

```
if (mysqli_num_rows($r) == 1) {
   list($uid) = mysqli_fetch_array
   → ($r, MYSQLI_NUM);
} else { // No database match made.
   echo '<p class="error">The
   → submitted email address does
   → not match those on file!</p>';
}
```

If the query returns one row, it'll be fetched and assigned to **$uid** (short for *user ID*). This value will be needed to update the database with the new password, and it'll also be used as a flag variable.

The **list( )** function has not been formally discussed in the book, but you may have run across it. It's a shortcut function that allows you to assign array elements to other variables. Since **mysqli_fetch_array( )** will always return an array, even if it's an array of just one element, using **list( )** can save having to write:

```
$row = mysqli_fetch_array($r,
MYSQLI_NUM);
$uid = $row[0];
```

If no matching record could be found for the submitted email address, an error message is displayed **Ⓐ**.

5. Report upon no submitted email address:

```
} else { // No email!
   echo '<p class="error">You
   → forgot to enter your email
   → address!</p>';
} // End of empty($_POST['email'])
→ IF.
```

If no email address was provided, that is also reported **Ⓑ**.

Script 18.10 *continued*

```
55      } else { // Failed the validation
        test.
56          echo '<p class="error">Please try
            again.</p>';
57      }
58
59      mysqli_close($dbc);
60
61  } // End of the main Submit conditional.
62  ?>
63
64  <h1>Reset Your Password</h1>
65  <p>Enter your email address below and
    your password will be reset.</p>
66  <form action="forgot_password.php"
    method="post">
67      <fieldset>
68      <p><b>Email Address:</b> <input
        type="text" name="email" size="20"
        maxlength="60" value="<?php if
        (isset($_POST['email'])) echo $_
        POST['email']; ?>" /></p>
69      </fieldset>
70      <div align="center"><input
        type="submit" name="submit"
        value="Reset My Password" /></div>
71  </form>
72
73  <?php include ('includes/footer.html');
    ?>
```

User Registration

The submitted email address does not match those on file! Please try again.

Reset Your Password

Ⓐ If the user entered an email address that is not found in the database, an error message is shown.

User Registration

You forgot to enter your email address! Please try again.

Reset Your Password

Ⓑ Failure to provide an email address also results in an error.

6. Create a new, random password:

```
if ($uid) {
  $p = substr ( md5(uniqid(rand( ),
  ➝ true)), 3, 10);
```

Creating a new, random password will make use of four PHP functions. The first is **uniqid( )**, which will return a unique identifier. It is fed the arguments **rand( )** and **true**, which makes the returned string more random. This returned value is then sent through the **md5( )** function, which calculates the MD5 hash of a string. At this stage, a hashed version of the unique ID is returned, which ends up being a string 32 characters long. This part of the code is similar to that used to create the activation code in **activate.php** (Script 18.7).

From this string, the password is created by pulling out ten characters starting with the third one, using the **substr( )** function. All in all, this code will return a very random and meaningless ten-character string (containing both letters and numbers) to be used as the temporary password.

Note that the creation of a new, random password is only necessary if **$uid** has a TRUE value by this point.

7. Update the password in the database:

```
$q = "UPDATE users SET
➝ pass=SHA1('$p') WHERE user_
➝ id=$uid LIMIT 1";
$r = mysqli_query ($dbc, $q)
➝ or trigger_error("Query: $q\n<br
/>MySQL Error: " .
➝ mysqli_error($dbc));
if (mysqli_affected_rows($dbc) ==
➝ 1) {
```

Using the user ID (the primary key for the table) that was retrieved earlier, the password for this particular user is updated to the **SHA1( )** version of **$p**, the random password.

8. Email the password to the user:

```
$body = "Your password to log
➝ into <whatever site> has been
➝ temporarily changed to '$p'.
➝ Please log in using this
➝ password and this email address.
➝ Then you may change your password
➝ to something more familiar.";
mail ($_POST['email'], 'Your
➝ temporary password.', $body,
➝ 'From: admin@sitename.com');
```

Next, the user needs to be emailed the new password so that she or he may log in ⓒ. It's safe to use **$_POST['email']** in the **mail( )** code, because to get to this point, **$_POST['email']** must match an address already stored in the database. That address would have already been validated via the Filter extension (or a regular expression), in the registration script.

continues on next page

Your password to log into <whatever site> has been temporarily changed to '75338167d4'. Please log in using this password and this email address. Then you may change your password to something more familiar.

ⓒ The email message received after resetting a password.

9. Complete the page:

```
echo '<h3>Your password has been
→ changed. You will receive the
→ new, temporary password at the
→ email address with which you
→ registered. Once you have logged
→ in with this password, you may
→ change it by clicking on the
→ "Change Password" link.</h3>';
mysqli_close($dbc);
include ('includes/footer.html');
exit( );
```

Next, a message is printed and the page is completed so as not to show the form again **D**.

10. Complete the conditionals and the PHP code:

```
    } else {
        echo '<p class="error">Your
→ password could not be
→ changed due to a system
→ error. We apologize for
→ any inconvenience.</p>';
    }
  } else {
    echo '<p class="error">Please
→ try again.</p>';
  }
  mysqli_close($dbc);
} // End of the main Submit
→ conditional.
?>
```

The first **else** clause applies only if the **UPDATE** query did not work, which hopefully shouldn't happen on a live site. The second **else** applies if the user didn't submit an email address or if the submitted email address didn't match any in the database.

11. Make the HTML form **E**:

```
<h1>Reset Your Password</h1>
<p>Enter your email address
→ below and your password will
→ be reset.</p>
<form action="forgot_password.
→ php" method="post">
  <fieldset>
  <p><b>Email Address:</b> <input
→ type="text" name="email"
→ size="20" maxlength="60"
→ value="<?php if (isset($_
→ POST['email'])) echo $_
→ POST['email']; ?>" /></p>
  </fieldset>
  <div align="center"><input
→ type="submit" name="submit"
→ value="Reset My Password" /></
→ div>
</form>
```

The form takes only one input, the email address. If there is a problem when the form has been submitted, the submitted email address value will be shown again (i.e., the form is sticky).

User Registration

Your password has been changed. You will receive the new, temporary password at the email address with which you registered. Once you have logged in with this password, you may change it by clicking on the "Change Password" link.

D The resulting page after successfully resetting a password.

User Registration

Login

Your browser must allow cookies in order to log in.

Email Address:

Password:

Login

E The simple form for resetting a password.

Script 18.11 With this page, users can change an existing password (if they are logged in).

```
1    <?php # Script 18.11 - change_password.php
2    // This page allows a logged-in user to
     change their password.
3    require ('includes/config.inc.php');
4    $page_title = 'Change Your Password';
5    include ('includes/header.html');
6
7    // If no first_name session variable
     exists, redirect the user:
8    if (!isset($_SESSION['user_id'])) {
9
10       $url = BASE_URL . 'index.php';
         // Define the URL.
11       ob_end_clean(); // Delete the buffer.
12       header("Location: $url");
13       exit(); // Quit the script.
14
15   }
16
17   if ($_SERVER['REQUEST_METHOD'] == 'POST') {
18       require (MYSQL);
19
20       // Check for a new password and match
         against the confirmed password:
21       $p = FALSE;
22       if (preg_match ('/^(\w){4,20}$/',
         $_POST['password1']) ) {
23           if ($_POST['password1'] ==
             $_POST['password2']) {
24               $p = mysqli_real_escape_string
                 ($dbc, $_POST['password1']);
25           } else {
26               echo '<p class="error">Your
                 password did not match the
                 confirmed password!</p>';
27           }
28       } else {
29           echo '<p class="error">Please enter
             a valid password!</p>';
30       }
31
32       if ($p) { // If everything's OK.
33
34           // Make the query:
35           $q = "UPDATE users SET
             pass=SHA1('$p') WHERE user_id={$_
             SESSION['user_id']} LIMIT 1";
```

code continues on next page

12. Include the HTML footer:

```
<?php include ('includes/footer.
→ html'); ?>
```

13. Save the file as **forgot_password.php**, place it in your Web directory, and test it in your Web browser.

14. Check your email to see the resulting message after a successful password reset Ⓒ.

Changing a password

The **change_password.php** script was initially written in Chapter 9 (called just **password.php**), as an example of an **UDPATE** query. The one developed here will be very similar in functionality but will differ in that only users who are logged in will be able to access it. Therefore, the form will only need to accept the new password and a confirmation of it (the user's existing password and email address will have already been confirmed by the login page).

To write change_password.php:

1. Begin a new PHP document in your text editor or IDE, to be named **change_password.php** (Script 18.11):

```
<?php # Script 18.11 - change_
→ password.php
require ('includes/config.inc.php');
$page_title = 'Change Your
→ Password';
include ('includes/header.html');
```

continues on next page

2. Redirect the user if she or he is not logged in:

```php
if (!isset($_SESSION['user_id'])) {
    $url = BASE_URL . 'index.php';
    ob_end_clean( );
    header("Location: $url");
    exit( );
}
```

The assumption is that this page is only to be accessed by logged-in users. To enforce this idea, the script checks for the existence of the **$_SESSION['user_id']** variable (which would be required by the **UPDATE** query). If this variable is not set, then the user will be redirected.

3. Check if the form has been submitted and include the MySQL connection:

```php
if ($_SERVER['REQUEST_METHOD'] ==
→'POST') {
    require (MYSQL);
```

The key to understanding how this script performs is remembering that there are three possible scenarios: the user is not logged in (and therefore redirected), the user is logged in and viewing the form, and the user is logged in and has submitted the form.

The user will only get to this point in the script if she or he is logged in. Otherwise, the user would have been redirected by now. So the script just needs to determine if the form has been submitted or not.

Script 18.11 *continued*

```
36       $r = mysqli_query ($dbc, $q)
         or trigger_error("Query: $q\
         n<br />MySQL Error: " .
         mysqli_error($dbc));
37       if (mysqli_affected_rows($dbc) ==
         1) { // If it ran OK.
38
39           // Send an email, if desired.
40           echo '<h3>Your password has
             been changed.</h3>';
41           mysqli_close($dbc); // Close
             the database connection.
42           include ('includes/footer.
             html'); // Include the HTML
             footer.
43           exit( );
44
45       } else { // If it did not run OK.
46
47           echo '<p class="error">Your
             password was not changed.
             Make sure your new password
             is different than the current
             password. Contact the system
             administrator if you think an
             error occurred.</p>';
48
49       }
50
51   } else { // Failed the validation
     test.
52       echo '<p class="error">Please try
         again.</p>';
53   }
54
55   mysqli_close($dbc); // Close the
     database connection.
56
57   } // End of the main Submit conditional.
58   ?>
59
60   <h1>Change Your Password</h1>
61   <form action="change_password.php"
     method="post">
62       <fieldset>
```

code continues on next page

Script 18.11 *continued*

```
63       <p><b>New Password:</b> <input
         type="password" name="password1"
         size="20" maxlength="20" /> <small>Use
         only letters, numbers, and the
         underscore. Must be between 4 and 20
         characters long.</small></p>
64       <p><b>Confirm New Password:</b> <input
         type="password" name="password2"
         size="20" maxlength="20" /></p>
65       </fieldset>
66       <div align="center"><input
         type="submit" name="submit"
         value="Change My Password" /></div>
67  </form>
68
69  <?php include ('includes/footer.html');
    ?>
```

User Registration

Please enter a valid password!
Please try again.

Change Your Password

F As in the registration process, the user's new password must pass the validation routines; otherwise, they will see error messages.

4. Validate the submitted password:

```
$p = FALSE;
if (preg_match ('/^(\w){4,20}$/',
→ $_POST['password1']) ) {
  if ($_POST['password1'] == $_
  → POST['password2']) {
    $p = mysqli_real_escape_
    → string ($dbc,
$_POST['password1']);
  } else {
    echo '<p class="error">Your
    → password did not match the
    → confirmed password!</p>';
  }
} else {
  echo '<p class="error">Please
  → enter a valid password!</p>';
}
```

The new password should be validated using the same tests as those in the registration process. Error messages will be displayed if problems are found **F**.

5. Update the password in the database:

```
if ($p) {
  $q = "UPDATE users SET
  → pass=SHA1('$p') WHERE user_
  → id={$_SESSION['user_id']}
  → LIMIT 1";
  $r = mysqli_query ($dbc,
  → $q) or trigger_error("Query:
  → $q\n<br />MySQL Error: " .
mysqli_error($dbc));
```

Using the user's ID—stored in the session when the user logged in—the password field can be updated in the database. The **LIMIT 1** clause isn't strictly necessary but adds extra insurance.

continues on next page

6. If the query worked, complete the page:

```php
if (mysqli_affected_rows($dbc) ==
→ 1) {
  echo '<h3>Your password has been
  → changed.</h3>';
  mysqli_close($dbc);
  include ('includes/footer.html');
  → exit( );
```

If the update worked, a confirmation message is printed to the Web browser **G**.

7. Complete the conditionals and the PHP code:

```php
  } else {
    echo '<p class="error">Your
    → password was not changed.
    → Make sure your new
    → password is different
    → than the current
    → password. Contact the
    → system administrator if
    → you think an error
    → occurred.</p>';
  }
} else {
  echo '<p class="error">Please
  → try again.</p>';
}
mysqli_close($dbc);
} // End of the main Submit
→ conditional.
?>
```

The first **else** clause applies if the **mysqli_affected_rows( )** function did not return a value of 1. This could occur for two reasons. The first is that a query or database error happened. Hopefully, that's not likely on a live site, after you've already worked out all the bugs. The second reason is that the user tried to "change" their password but entered the same password again. In that case,

---

> **User Registration**
>
> **Your password has been changed.**

G The script has successfully changed the user's password.

Site Administration

For this application, how the site administration works depends upon what you want it to do. One additional page you would probably want for an administrator would be a **view_users. php** script, like the one created in Chapter 9 and modified in Chapter 10, "Common Programming Techniques." It's already listed in the administrator's links. You could use such a script to link to an **edit_user.php** page, which would allow the administrator to manually activate an account, declare that a user is an administrator, or change a person's password. An administrator could also delete a user using such a page.

While the footer file creates links to administrative pages only if the logged-in user is an administrator, every admin-istration page should also include such a check.

the **UPDATE** query wouldn't affect any rows because the password column in the database wouldn't be changed. A message implying such is printed.

8. Create the HTML form **H**:

```
<h1>Change Your Password</h1>
<form action="change_password.
→ php" method="post">
  <fieldset>
  <p><b>New Password:</b> <input
  → type="password" name=
  → "password1" size="20"
  → maxlength="20" /> <small>Use
  → only letters, numbers, and
  → the underscore. Must be
  → between 4 and 20 characters
  → long.</small></p>
  <p><b>Confirm New Password:</
  → b> <input type="password"
  → name="password2" size="20"
  → maxlength="20" /></p>
  </fieldset>
  <div align="center"><input
  → type="submit" name="submit"
  → value="Change My Password"
  → /></div>
</form>
```

This form takes two inputs: the new password and a confirmation of it. A description of the proper format is given as well. Because the form is so simple it's not sticky, but that's a feature you could add.

9. Complete the HTML page:

```
<?php include ('includes/footer.
→ html'); ?>
```

10. Save the file as `change_password.php`, place it in your Web directory, and test it in your Web browser.

TIP Once this script has been completed, users can reset their password with the previous script and then log in using the temporary, random password. After logging in, users can change their password back to something more memorable with this page.

TIP Because the site's authentication does not rely upon the user's password from page to page (in other words, the password is not checked on each subsequent page after logging in), changing a password will not require the user to log back in.

H The Change Your Password form.

Review and Pursue

If you have any problems with the review questions or the pursue prompts, turn to the book's supporting forum (**www.LarryUllman.com/forums/**).

Note: Most of these questions and some of the prompts rehash information covered in earlier chapters, in order to reinforce some of the most important points.

Review

- What is *output buffering*? What are the benefits of using it?

- Why shouldn't detailed error information be displayed on live sites?

- Why must the *active* column in the *users* table allow for **NULL** values? What is the result if *active* is defined as **NOT NULL**?

- What are the three steps in terminating a session?

- What does the **session_name( )** function do?

- What are the differences between truly *encrypting* data and creating a *hash* representation of some data?

Pursue

- Check out the PHP manual's pages for output buffering (or output control).

- Check out the PHP manual's pages for the **rand( )**, **uniqid( )**, and **md5( )** functions.

- Check out the PHP manual's page for the **trigger_error( )** function.

- Apply the same validation techniques to **login.php** as used in **register.php**.

- Make the login form sticky.

- Add a *last_login* **DATETIME** field to the *users* table and update its value when a user logs in. Use this information to indicate to the user how long it has been since the last time she or he accessed the site.

- If you've added the *last_login* field, use it to print a message on the home page as to how many users have logged in in the past, say, hour or day.

- Validate the submitted email address in **forgot_password.php** using the Filter extension or a regular expression.

- Check out the PHP manual's page for the **list( )** function.

- Create **view_users.php** and **edit_user.php** scripts as recommended in the final sidebar. Restrict access to these scripts to administrators (those users whose access level is 1).

Example—
E-Commerce

In this, the final chapter of the book, you'll develop one last Web application: an e-commerce site that sells prints of art. Unfortunately, to write and explain a complete application would require a book in itself, and some aspects of e-commerce—like how you handle the money—are particular to each individual site. With these limitations in mind, the focus in this chapter is on the core e-commerce functionality: designing the database, populating a catalog as an administrator, displaying products to the public, creating a shopping cart, and storing orders in a database.

This example includes many concepts that have already been covered: using PHP with MySQL (of course), handling file uploads, using PHP to send images to the Web browser, prepared statements, sessions, etc. This chapter also has one new topic: how to perform MySQL transactions from a PHP script. Along the way you'll find *tons* of suggestions for extending the project.

In This Chapter

Creating the Database

The e-commerce site in this example will use the simply named *ecommerce* database. I'll explain each table's role prior to creating the database in MySQL.

With any type of e-commerce application there are three kinds of data to be stored: the *product* information (what is being sold), the *customer* information (who is making purchases), and the *order* information (what was purchased and by whom). Going through the normalization process (see Chapter 6, "Database Design"), I've come up with five tables **A**.

The first two tables store all of the products being sold. As already stated, the site will be selling artistic prints. The *artists* table (**Table 19.1**) stores the information for the artists whose work is being sold. This table contains just a minimum of information (the artists' first, middle, and last names), but you could easily add the artists' birth and death dates, other biographical data, and so forth. The *prints* table (**Table 19.2**) is the main products table for the site. It stores

TABLE 19.1 The artists Table

Column	Type
artist_id	INT UNSIGNED NOT NULL
first_name	VARCHAR(20) DEFAULT NULL
middle_name	VARCHAR(20) DEFAULT NULL
last_name	VARCHAR(40) NOT NULL

TABLE 19.2 The prints Table

Column	Type
print_id	INT UNSIGNED NOT NULL
artist_id	INT UNSIGNED NOT NULL
print_name	VARCHAR(60) NOT NULL
price	DECIMAL(6,2) UNSIGNED NOT NULL
size	VARCHAR(60) DEFAULT NULL
description	VARCHAR(255) DEFAULT NULL
image_name	VARCHAR(60) NOT NULL

A This entity-relationship diagram (ERD) shows how the five tables in the *ecommerce* database relate to one another.

TABLE 19.3 The customers Table

Column	Type
customer_id	INT UNSIGNED NOT NULL
email	VARCHAR(60) NOT NULL
pass	CHAR(40) NOT NULL

TABLE 19.4 The orders Table

Column	Type
order_id	INT UNSIGNED NOT NULL
customer_id	INT UNSIGNED NOT NULL
total	DECIMAL(10,2) UNSIGNED NOT NULL
order_date	TIMESTAMP

TABLE 19.5 The order_contents Table

Column	Type
oc_id	INT UNSIGNED NOT NULL
order_id	INT UNSIGNED NOT NULL
print_id	INT UNSIGNED NOT NULL
quantity	TINYINT UNSIGNED NOT NULL DEFAULT 1
price	DECIMAL(6,2) UNSIGNED NOT NULL
ship_date	DATETIME DEFAULT NULL

the print names, prices, and other relevant details. It is linked to the *artists* table using the *artist_id*. The *prints* table is arguably the most important, as it provides a unique identifier for each product being sold. That concept is key to any e-commerce site (without unique identifiers, how would you know what a person bought?).

The *customers* table (**Table 19.3**) does exactly what you'd expect: it records the personal information for each client. At the least, it reflects the customer's first name, last name, email address, password, and shipping address, as well as the date they registered. Presumably the combination of the email address and password would allow the user to log in, shop, and access their account. Since it's fairly obvious what information this table would store, I'll define it with only the three essential columns for now.

The final two tables store all of the order information. There are any number of ways you could do this, but I've chosen to store general order information—the total, the date, and the customer's ID—in an *orders* table (**Table 19.4**). This table could also have separate columns reflecting the shipping cost, the amount of sales tax, any discounts that applied, and so on. The *order_contents* table (**Table 19.5**) will store the actual items that were sold, including the quantity and price. The *order_contents* table is essentially a middleman, used to intercept the many-to-many relationship between *prints* and *orders* (each print can be in multiple orders, and each order can have multiple prints).

In order to be able to use *transactions* (in the final script), the two order tables will use the InnoDB storage engine. The others will use MyISAM. See Chapter 6 for more information on the available storage engines (i.e., table types).

To create the database:

1. Log in to the mysql client and create the *ecommerce* database, if it doesn't already exist.

   CREATE DATABASE ecommerce;
   USE ecommerce;

   For these steps, you can use either the mysql client or another tool like phpMyAdmin. Depending upon your situation, you may also need to establish the character set at this point, in terms of the communications with the database application. You can also establish the default character set and encoding when creating the database (again, see Chapter 6).

   If you're using a hosted site, the hosting company will likely provide a database for you already.

2. Create the *artists* table **B**:

   CREATE TABLE artists (
   artist_id INT UNSIGNED NOT NULL
   → AUTO_INCREMENT,
   first_name VARCHAR(20) DEFAULT NULL,
   middle_name VARCHAR(20) DEFAULT
   → NULL,
   last_name VARCHAR(40) NOT NULL,
   PRIMARY KEY (artist_id),
   UNIQUE full_name (last_name,
   → first_name, middle_name)
) ENGINE=MyISAM;

This table stores just four pieces of information for each artist. Of these, only *last_name* is required (is defined as **NOT NULL**), as there are artists who go by a single name (e.g., Christo). I've added definitions for the indexes as well. The primary key is the *artist_id*, and an index is placed on the combination of the last name, first name, and middle name, which may be used in an **ORDER BY** clause. This index is more specifically a *unique* index, so that the same artist's name is not entered multiple times.

3. Create the *prints* table **C**:

   CREATE TABLE prints (
   print_id INT UNSIGNED NOT NULL
   → AUTO_INCREMENT,
   artist_id INT UNSIGNED NOT NULL,
   print_name VARCHAR(60) NOT NULL,
   price DECIMAL(6,2) UNSIGNED NOT
   → NULL,
   size VARCHAR(60) DEFAULT NULL,
   description VARCHAR(255) DEFAULT
   → NULL,
   image_name VARCHAR(60) NOT NULL,
   PRIMARY KEY (print_id),
   INDEX (artist_id),
   INDEX (print_name),
   INDEX (price)
) ENGINE=MyISAM;

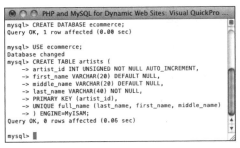

B Making the first table.

C Making the second table.

All of the columns in the *prints* table are required except for the *size* and *description*. There are indexes on the *artist_id*, *print_name*, and *price* fields, each of which may be used in queries.

Each print will be associated with one image. The image will be stored on the server using the same name as the *print_id*. When displaying the image in the Web browser, its original name will be used, so that needs to be stored in this table.

You could add to this table an *in_stock* or *qty_on_hand* field, to indicate the availability of products.

4. Create the *customers* table **D**:

```
CREATE TABLE customers (
customer_id INT UNSIGNED NOT NULL
→ AUTO_INCREMENT,
email VARCHAR(60) NOT NULL,
pass CHAR(40) NOT NULL,
PRIMARY KEY (customer_id),
UNIQUE (email),
INDEX login (email, pass)
) ENGINE=MyISAM;
```

This is the code used to create the *customers* table. You could throw in the other appropriate fields (name, address, phone number, the registration date, etc.). As this chapter won't be using those values—or user management at all—they are being omitted.

5. Create the *orders* table **E**:

```
CREATE TABLE orders (
order_id INT UNSIGNED NOT NULL
→ AUTO_INCREMENT,
customer_id INT UNSIGNED NOT NULL,
total DECIMAL(10,2) UNSIGNED NOT
→ NULL,
order_date TIMESTAMP,
PRIMARY KEY (order_id),
INDEX (customer_id),
INDEX (order_date)
) ENGINE=InnoDB;
```

All of the *orders* fields are required, and three indexes have been created. Notice that a foreign key column here, like *customer_id*, is of the same exact type as its corresponding primary key (*customer_id* in the *customers* table). The *order_date* field will store the date and time an order was entered. Being defined as a **TIMESTAMP**, it will automatically be given the current value when a record is inserted (for this reason it does not formally need to be declared as **NOT NULL**).

Finally, because transactions will be used with the *orders* and *order_contents* tables, both must use the InnoDB storage engine.

continues on next page

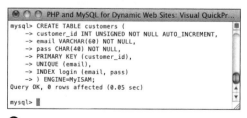

D Creating a basic version of the *customers* table. In a real e-commerce site, you'd need to expand this table to store more information.

E Making the *orders* table.

6. Create the *order_contents* table 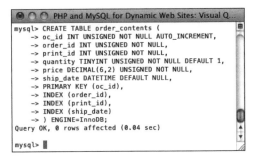:

```
CREATE TABLE order_contents (
oc_id INT UNSIGNED NOT NULL
→ AUTO_INCREMENT,
order_id INT UNSIGNED NOT NULL,
print_id INT UNSIGNED NOT NULL,
quantity TINYINT UNSIGNED NOT NULL
→ DEFAULT 1,
price DECIMAL(6,2) UNSIGNED NOT
→ NULL,
ship_date DATETIME DEFAULT NULL,
PRIMARY KEY (oc_id),
INDEX (order_id),
INDEX (print_id),
INDEX (ship_date)
) ENGINE=InnoDB;
```

In order to have a normalized database structure, each order is separated into its general information—the customer, the order date, and the total amount—and its specific information—the actual items ordered and in what quantity. This table has foreign keys to the *orders* and *prints* tables. The *quantity* has a set default value of 1. The *ship_date* is defined as a **DATETIME**, so that it can have a **NULL** value, indicating that the item has not yet shipped. Again, this table must use the InnoDB storage engine in order to be part of a transaction.

You may be curious why this table stores the price of an item when that information is already present in the *prints* table. The reason is simply this: the price of a product may change. The *prints* table indicates the current price of an item; the *order_contents* table indicates the price at which an item was purchased.

F Making the final table for the *ecommerce* database.

TIP Depending upon what a site is selling, the underlying database would have different tables in place of *artists* and *prints*. The most important attribute of any e-commerce database is that there is a "products" table that lists the individual items being sold with a product ID associated with each. So a large, red polo shirt would have one ID, which is different than a large, blue polo shirt's ID, which is different than a medium, blue polo shirt's ID. Without unique, individual product identifiers, it would be impossible to track orders and product quantities.

TIP If you wanted to store multiple addresses for users—home, billing, friends, etc.—create a separate addresses table. In this table store all of that information, including the address type, and link those records back to the *customers* table using the customer ID as a primary-foreign key.

Security

With respect to an e-commerce site, there are four broad security considerations. The first is how the data is stored on the server. You need to protect the MySQL database itself (by setting appropriate access permissions) and the directory where session information is stored (see Chapter 12, "Cookies and Sessions," for what settings could be changed). With respect to these issues, using a non-shared hosting would definitely improve the security of your site.

The second security consideration has to do with protecting access to sensitive information. The administrative side of the site, which would have the ability to view orders and customer records, must be safeguarded to the highest level. This means requiring authentication to access it, limiting who knows the access information, using a secure connection, and so forth.

The third factor is protecting the data during transmission. By the time the customer gets to the checkout process (where credit card and shipping information comes in), secure transactions *must* be used. To do so entails establishing a Secure Sockets Layer (SSL) on your server with a valid certificate and then changing to an *https://* URL. Also be aware of what information is being sent via email, since those messages are normally not transmitted through secure avenues.

The fourth issue has to do with the handling of the payment information. You really, really, really, really (*really!*) don't want to keep this information in any way. Ideally, let a third-party resource handle the payment and keep your site's figurative hands clean. I discuss this a little bit in a sidebar titled "The Checkout Process," found at the end of the chapter.

This broad topic of e-commerce, with lots of specific details and tons of real-world code, is thoroughly covered in my book *Effortless E-Commerce with PHP and MySQL* (New Riders, 2011).

The Administrative Side

The administration side of an e-commerce application is primarily for the management of the three main components:

- Products (the items being sold)
- Customers
- Orders

In this chapter, you'll create two scripts for adding products to the catalog. As the products being sold are works of art, one script will be for populating the *artists* table and a second will be for populating the *prints* table (which has a foreign key to *artists*).

Due to space constraints, and the fact that without a payment system, this will not be a complete e-commerce example anyway, the customers and orders aspects cannot be detailed in this chapter. However, customer management is just the same as user management, covered in the previous chapter, and you'll see many recommendations for administration of the orders.

The first two scripts—and pretty much every script in this chapter—will require a connection to the MySQL database. Instead of writing a new one from scratch, just copy `mysqli_connect.php` (Script 9.2) from Chapter 9, "Using PHP with MySQL," to the appropriate directory for this site's files. Then edit the information so that it connects to a database called *ecommerce*, using a username/password/hostname combination that has the proper privileges.

Also, the two administration scripts will use *prepared statements*, introduced in Chapter 13, "Security Methods," in order to provide you with more experience using them. If you're confused about the prepared statements syntax or functions, review that chapter.

Adding Artists

The first script to be written simply adds artist records to the *artists* table. The script presents a form with three inputs **A**; upon submission, the inputs are validated—but two are optional—and the record is added to the database.

A The HTML form for adding artists to the catalog.

```
1    <!DOCTYPE html PUBLIC "-//W3C//DTD XHTML
     1.0 Transitional//EN"
2        "http://www.w3.org/TR/xhtml1/DTD/
         xhtml1-transitional.dtd">
3    <html xmlns="http://www.w3.org/1999/
     xhtml" xml:lang="en" lang="en">
4    <head>
5      <meta http-equiv="content-type"
       content="text/html; charset=utf-8" />
6      <title>Add an Artist</title>
7    </head>
8    <body>
9    <?php # Script 19.1 - add_artist.php
10   // This page allows the administrator to
     add an artist.
11
12   if ($_SERVER['REQUEST_METHOD'] == 'POST')
     { // Handle the form.
13
14     // Validate the first and middle
       names (neither required):
15     $fn = (!empty($_POST['first_name'])) ?
       trim($_POST['first_name']) : NULL;
16     $mn = (!empty($_POST['middle_name'])) ?
       trim($_POST['middle_name']) : NULL;
17
18     // Check for a last_name...
19     if (!empty($_POST['last_name'])) {
20
21       $ln = trim($_POST['last_name']);
22
23       // Add the artist to the database:
24       require ('../../mysqli_connect.
         php');
25       $q = 'INSERT INTO artists (first_
         name, middle_name, last_name)
         VALUES (?, ?, ?)';
26       $stmt = mysqli_prepare($dbc, $q);
27       mysqli_stmt_bind_param($stmt,
         'sss', $fn, $mn, $ln);
28       mysqli_stmt_execute($stmt);
29
30       // Check the results....
31       if (mysqli_stmt_affected_
         rows($stmt) == 1) {
32         echo '<p>The artist has been
           added.</p>';
33         $_POST = array( );
```

code continues on next page

To create add_artist.php:

1. Begin a new PHP document, starting with the HTML head, to be named **add_artist.php** (Script 19.1):

   ```
   <!DOCTYPE html PUBLIC "-//W3C//
   → DTD XHTML 1.0 Transitional//EN"
   → "http://www.w3.org/TR/xhtml1/DTD/
   → xhtml1-transitional.dtd">
   <html xmlns="http://www.w3.org/
   → 1999/xhtml" xml:lang="en"
   → lang="en">
   <head>
     <meta http-equiv="content-type"
   → content="text/html;
   charset=utf-8" />
     <title>Add an Artist</title>
   </head>
   <body>
   <?php # Script 19.1 - add_artist.
   → php
   ```

   Normally, the administrative side of a site would use a template system (perhaps a different template than the public side), but since this chapter only has two administrative scripts, no template will be developed.

2. Check if the form has been submitted:

   ```
   if ($_SERVER['REQUEST_METHOD'] ==
   → 'POST') {
   ```

3. Validate the artist's first and middle names:

   ```
   $fn = (!empty($_POST['first_
   → name'])) ? trim($_POST['first_
   → name']) : NULL;
   $mn = (!empty($_POST['middle_
   → name'])) ? trim($_POST['middle_
   → name']) : NULL;
   ```

continues on page 615

```
34      } else { // Error!
35          $error = 'The new artist could not be added to the database!';
36      }
37
38      // Close this prepared statement:
39      mysqli_stmt_close($stmt);
40      mysqli_close($dbc); // Close the database connection.
41
42  } else { // No last name value.
43      $error = 'Please enter the artist\'s name!';
44  }
45
46  } // End of the submission IF.
47
48  // Check for an error and print it:
49  if (isset($error)) {
50      echo '<h1>Error!</h1>
51      <p style="font-weight: bold; color: #C00">' . $error . ' Please try again.</p>';
52  }
53
54  // Display the form...
55  ?>
56  <h1>Add a Print</h1>
57  <form action="add_artist.php" method="post">
58
59      <fieldset><legend>Fill out the form to add an artist:</legend>
60
61      <p><b>First Name:</b> <input type="text" name="first_name" size="10" maxlength="20"
        value="<?php if (isset($_POST['first_name'])) echo $_POST['first_name']; ?>" /></p>
62      <p><b>Middle Name:</b> <input type="text" name="middle_name" size="10" maxlength="20"
        value="<?php if (isset($_POST['middle_name'])) echo $_POST['middle_name']; ?>" /></p>
63      <p><b>Last Name:</b> <input type="text" name="last_name" size="10" maxlength="40" value="<?php
        if (isset($_POST['last_name'])) echo $_POST['last_name']; ?>" /></p>
64
65      </fieldset>
66
67      <div align="center"><input type="submit" name="submit" value="Submit" /></div>
68
69  </form>
70
71  </body>
72  </html>
```

The artist's first and middle names are optional fields, whereas the last name is not (since there are artists referred to by only one name). To validate the first two name inputs, I've reduced the amount of code by using the *ternary* operator (introduced in Chapter 10, "Common Programming Techniques"). The code here is the same as

```
if (!empty($_POST['first_name'])) {
$fn = trim($_POST['first_name']);
} else {
    $fn = NULL;
}
```

Because this script will rely upon prepared statements, the values to be used in the query don't need to be run through `mysqli_real_escape_string()`. See Chapter 13 for more on this subject.

4. Validate the artist's last name:

```
if (!empty($_POST['last_name'])) {
$ln = trim($_POST['last_name']);
```

The last name value is required. For more stringent validation, you could use regular expressions. For added security, you could apply the **strip_tags()** function.

5. Include the database connection:

```
require ('../../mysqli_connect.php');
```

The administration folder will be located inside of the main (**htdocs**) folder and is therefore two directories above the connection script. Keep your directory structure **B** in mind when including files.

continues on next page

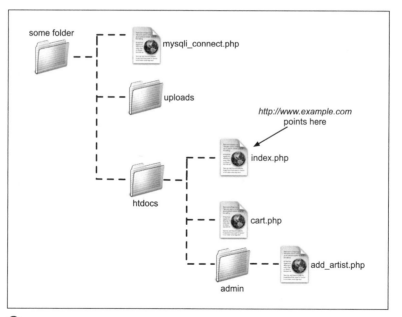

some folder

mysqli_connect.php

uploads

http://www.example.com points here

index.php

htdocs

cart.php

add_artist.php

admin

B The site structure for this Web application. The MySQL connection script and the **uploads** directory (where images will be stored) are not within the Web directory (they aren't available via *http://*).

6. Add the artist to the database:

```
$q = 'INSERT INTO artists (first_
→ name, middle_name, last_name)
→ VALUES (?, ?, ?)';
$stmt = mysqli_prepare($dbc, $q);
mysqli_stmt_bind_param($stmt,
→ 'sss', $fn, $mn, $ln);
mysqli_stmt_execute($stmt);
```

To add the artist to the database, the query will be something like **INSERT INTO artists (first_name, middle_name, last_name) VALUES ('John', 'Singer', 'Sargent')** or **INSERT INTO artists (first_name, middle_name, last_name) VALUES (NULL, NULL, 'Christo')**. The query is run using prepared statements, covered in Chapter 13.

The **mysqli_stmt_bind_param( )** function indicates that the query needs three inputs (one for each question mark) of the type: string, string, and string. For questions on any of this, see Chapter 13.

7. Report on the results:

```
if (mysqli_stmt_affected_
→ rows($stmt) == 1) {
  echo '<p>The artist has been
→ added.</p>';
  $_POST = array( );
} else {
  $error = 'The new artist could
→ not be added to the database!';
}
```

If executing the prepared statement affected one row, which is to say one row was created, a positive message is displayed **C**. In this case, the **$_POST** array is also reset, so that the sticky form does not redisplay the artist's information.

If the prepared statement failed, a message is added to the **$error** variable, to be outputted later in the script. For debugging purposes, you could add other details here, such as the MySQL error.

8. Close the prepared statement and the database connection:

```
mysqli_stmt_close($stmt);
mysqli_close($dbc);
```

9. Complete the artist's last name and submission conditionals:

```
    } else { // No last name value.
      $error = 'Please enter the
→ artist\'s name!';
    }
} // End of the submission IF.
```

If no last name value was submitted, then an error message is assigned to the **$error** variable.

C An artist has successfully been added to the database.

10. Print the error, if one occurred, and close the PHP block:

```php
if (isset($error)) {
  echo '<h1>Error!</h1>
  <p style="font-weight: bold;
  → color: #C00">' . $error . '
  → Please try again.</p>';
}
?>
```

Either of the two errors that could have occurred would be represented by the **$error** variable. If this variable is set, it can be printed out at this point **D**. The error will be written within some CSS to make it bold and red.

11. Begin creating the HTML form:

```html
<h1>Add a Print</h1>
<form action="add_artist.php"
→ method="post">
  <fieldset><legend>Fill out the
  → form to add an artist:</
  → legend>
```

D If the artist's last name is not provided, an error message is displayed. The form is sticky, however, remembering values entered into the other two form inputs.

12. Create the inputs for adding a new artist:

```html
<p><b>First Name:</b> <input
→ type="text" name="first_name"
→ size="10" maxlength="20" value=
→ "<?php if (isset($_POST['first_
→ name'])) echo $_POST['first_
→ name']; ?>" /></p>
<p><b>Middle Name:</b> <input
→ type="text" name="middle_name"
→ size="10" maxlength="20" value=
→ "<?php if (isset($_POST['middle_
→ name'])) echo $_POST['middle_
→ name']; ?>" /></p>
<p><b>Last Name:</b> <input
→ type="text" name="last_
→ name" size="10" maxlength="40"
→ value="<?php if (isset($_
→ POST['last_name'])) echo $_
→ POST['last_name']; ?>" /></p>
```

Each form element is made sticky, in case the form is being displayed again.

13. Complete the HTML form:

```html
    </fieldset>
    <div align="center"><input
    → type="submit" name="submit"
    → value="Submit" /></div>
</form>
```

14. Complete the HTML page:

```html
</body>
</html>
```

15. Save the file as **add_artist.php**.

16. Place **add_artist.php** in your Web directory (in the administration folder) and test it in your Web browser **A** and **C**.

Don't forget that you'll also need to place a **mysqli_connect.php** script, edited to connect to the *ecommerce* database, in the correct directory as well.

continues on next page

TIP Although I did not do so here for the sake of brevity, I would recommend that separate MySQL users be created for the administrative and the public sides. The admin user would need SELECT, INSERT, UPDATE, and DELETE privileges, while the public one would need only SELECT, INSERT and UPDATE.

TIP The administrative pages should be protected in the most secure way possible. This could entail HTTP authentication using Apache, a login system using sessions or cookies, or even placing the admin pages on another, possibly offline, server (so the site could be managed from just one location).

Adding Prints

The second script to be written is for adding a new product (specifically a print) to the database. The page will allow the administrator to select the artist from the database, upload an image, and enter the details for the print **E**. The image will be stored on the server and the print's record inserted into the database. This will be one of the more complicated scripts in this chapter, but all of the technology involved has already been covered elsewhere in the book.

To create add_print.php:

1. Begin a new PHP document, starting with the HTML head, to be named add_print.php (Script 19.2):

```
<!DOCTYPE html PUBLIC "-//W3C//
→ DTD XHTML 1.0 Transitional//EN"
→ "http://www.w3.org/TR/xhtml1/DTD/
→ xhtml1-transitional.dtd">
<html xmlns="http://www.w3.org/
→ 1999/xhtml" xml:lang="en"
→ lang="en">
<head>
```

continues on page 622

E The HTML form for adding prints to the catalog.

Script 19.2 This administration page adds products to the database. It handles a file upload and inserts the new print into the *prints* table.

```
1    <!DOCTYPE html PUBLIC "-//W3C//DTD XHTML
     1.0 Transitional//EN"
2         "http://www.w3.org/TR/xhtml1/DTD/
          xhtml1-transitional.dtd">
3    <html xmlns="http://www.w3.org/1999/
     xhtml" xml:lang="en" lang="en">
4    <head>
5        <meta http-equiv="content-type"
         content="text/html; charset=utf-8" />
6        <title>Add a Print</title>
7    </head>
8    <body>
9    <?php # Script 19.2 - add_print.php
10   // This page allows the administrator to
     add a print (product).
11
12   require ('../../mysqli_connect.php');
13
14   if ($_SERVER['REQUEST_METHOD'] == 'POST')
     { // Handle the form.
15
16       // Validate the incoming data...
17       $errors = array();
18
19       // Check for a print name:
20       if (!empty($_POST['print_name'])) {
21           $pn = trim($_POST['print_name']);
```

code continues on next page

```
22       } else {
23          $errors[] = 'Please enter the print\'s name!';
24       }
25
26       // Check for an image:
27       if (is_uploaded_file ($_FILES['image']['tmp_name'])) {
28
29          // Create a temporary file name:
30          $temp = '../../uploads/' . md5($_FILES['image']['name']);
31
32          // Move the file over:
33          if (move_uploaded_file($_FILES['image']['tmp_name'], $temp)) {
34
35             echo '<p>The file has been uploaded!</p>';
36
37             // Set the $i variable to the image's name:
38             $i = $_FILES['image']['name'];
39
40          } else { // Couldn't move the file over.
41             $errors[] = 'The file could not be moved.';
42             $temp = $_FILES['image']['tmp_name'];
43          }
44
45       } else { // No uploaded file.
46          $errors[] = 'No file was uploaded.';
47          $temp = NULL;
48       }
49
50       // Check for a size (not required):
51       $s = (!empty($_POST['size'])) ? trim($_POST['size']) : NULL;
52
53       // Check for a price:
54       if (is_numeric($_POST['price']) && ($_POST['price'] > 0)) {
55          $p = (float) $_POST['price'];
56       } else {
57          $errors[] = 'Please enter the print\'s price!';
58       }
59
60       // Check for a description (not required):
61       $d = (!empty($_POST['description'])) ? trim($_POST['description']) : NULL;
62
63       // Validate the artist...
64       if ( isset($_POST['artist']) && filter_var($_POST['artist'], FILTER_VALIDATE_INT, array('min_
         range' => 1)) ) {
65          $a = $_POST['artist'];
66       } else { // No artist selected.
67          $errors[] = 'Please select the print\'s artist!';
68       }
69
70       if (empty($errors)) { // If everything's OK.
```

code continues on next page

```
71
72          // Add the print to the database:
73          $q = 'INSERT INTO prints (artist_id, print_name, price, size, description, image_name)
            VALUES (?, ?, ?, ?, ?, ?)';
74          $stmt = mysqli_prepare($dbc, $q);
75          mysqli_stmt_bind_param($stmt, 'isdsss', $a, $pn, $p, $s, $d, $i);
76          mysqli_stmt_execute($stmt);
77
78          // Check the results...
79          if (mysqli_stmt_affected_rows($stmt) == 1) {
80
81              // Print a message:
82              echo '<p>The print has been added.</p>';
83
84              // Rename the image:
85              $id = mysqli_stmt_insert_id($stmt); // Get the print ID.
86              rename ($temp, "../../uploads/$id");
87
88              // Clear $_POST:
89              $_POST = array( );
90
91          } else { // Error!
92              echo '<p style="font-weight: bold; color: #C00">Your submission could not be processed
                due to a system error.</p>';
93          }
94
95          mysqli_stmt_close($stmt);
96
97      } // End of $errors IF.
98
99      // Delete the uploaded file if it still exists:
100     if ( isset($temp) && file_exists ($temp) && is_file($temp) ) {
101         unlink ($temp);
102     }
103
104 } // End of the submission IF.
105
106 // Check for any errors and print them:
107 if ( !empty($errors) && is_array($errors) ) {
108     echo '<h1>Error!</h1>
109     <p style="font-weight: bold; color: #C00">The following error(s) occurred:<br />';
110     foreach ($errors as $msg) {
111         echo " - $msg<br />\n";
112     }
113     echo 'Please reselect the print image and try again.</p>';
114 }
115
116 // Display the form...
117 ?>
118 <h1>Add a Print</h1>
```

code continues on next page

Script 19.2 *continued*

```
119   <form enctype="multipart/form-data" action="add_print.php" method="post">
120
121      <input type="hidden" name="MAX_FILE_SIZE" value="524288" />
122
123      <fieldset><legend>Fill out the form to add a print to the catalog:</legend>
124
125      <p><b>Print Name:</b> <input type="text" name="print_name" size="30" maxlength="60"
         value="<?php if (isset($_POST['print_name'])) echo htmlspecialchars($_POST['print_name']); ?>"
         /></p>
126
127      <p><b>Image:</b> <input type="file" name="image" /></p>
128
129      <p><b>Artist:</b>
130      <select name="artist"><option>Select One</option>
131      <?php // Retrieve all the artists and add to the pull-down menu.
132      $q = "SELECT artist_id, CONCAT_WS(' ', first_name, middle_name, last_name) FROM artists ORDER
         BY last_name, first_name ASC";
133      $r = mysqli_query ($dbc, $q);
134      if (mysqli_num_rows($r) > 0) {
135          while ($row = mysqli_fetch_array ($r, MYSQLI_NUM)) {
136              echo "<option value=\"$row[0]\"";
137              // Check for stickyness:
138              if (isset($_POST['existing']) && ($_POST['existing'] == $row[0]) ) echo '
                 selected="selected"';
139              echo ">$row[1]</option>\n";
140          }
141      } else {
142          echo '<option>Please add a new artist first.</option>';
143      }
144      mysqli_close($dbc); // Close the database connection.
145      ?>
146      </select></p>
147
148      <p><b>Price:</b> <input type="text" name="price" size="10" maxlength="10" value="<?php if
         (isset($_POST['price'])) echo $_POST['price']; ?>" /> <small>Do not include the dollar sign or
         commas.</small></p>
149
150      <p><b>Size:</b> <input type="text" name="size" size="30" maxlength="60" value="<?php if
         (isset($_POST['size'])) echo htmlspecialchars($_POST['size']); ?>" /> (optional)</p>
151
152      <p><b>Description:</b> <textarea name="description" cols="40" rows="5"><?php if (isset($_
         POST['description'])) echo $_POST['description']; ?></textarea> (optional)</p>
153
154      </fieldset>
155
156      <div align="center"><input type="submit" name="submit" value="Submit" /></div>
157
158   </form>
159
160   </body>
161   </html>
```

```
      <meta http-equiv="content-type"
      → content="text/html;
      → charset=utf-8" />
      <title>Add a Print</title>
</head>
<body>
<?php # Script 19.2 - add_print.php
```

2. Include the database connection
   script and check if the form has been
   submitted:

```
require ('../../mysqli_connect.php');
if ($_SERVER['REQUEST_METHOD'] ==
→ 'POST') {
   $errors = array();
```

Any form validation problems will be
added to the **$errors** array, which is
initiated here. (Because this script could
have multiple errors, an array is being
used; in **add_artist.php**, only a single
error at a time could occur.)

3. Validate the print's name:

```
if (!empty($_POST['print_name'])) {
   $pn = trim($_POST['print_name']);
} else {
   $errors[] = 'Please enter the
   → print\'s name!';
}
```

This is one of the required fields in the
prints table and should be checked
for a value. Again, because this
script will use prepared statements,
the values to be used in the query
don't need to be run through
mysqli_real_escape_string( ).

If you wanted to be extra careful,
you could apply **strip_tags( )** here
(although if a malicious user has gotten
into the administrative area, you've got
bigger problems).

If no value is entered, an error message
is added to the **$errors** array.

4. Create a temporary name for the
   uploaded image, if one was selected:

```
if (is_uploaded_file ($_
→ FILES['image']['tmp_name'])) {
   $temp = '../../uploads/' . md5($_
   → FILES['image']['name']);
```

When the techniques for handling
file uploads with PHP were covered
(in Chapter 11, "Web Application
Development"), the **is_uploaded_
file( )** function was mentioned. It
returns TRUE if a file was uploaded and
FALSE if not. If a file was uploaded, the
script will attempt to move the file over
to the **uploads** directory (in Step 5).

There is one other thing happening
here: the images will not be stored
on the server using their given names
(which can be a security concern).
Instead, the images will be stored using
their associated print ID. However, since
that value isn't yet known (because
the print's record hasn't been added
to the database), a temporary name
for this file has to be generated. To do
so, the **md5( )** function, which returns
a 32-character hash, is applied to the
image's original name. That temporary
name, along with a relative path to the
image's final destination (relative to this
script), are assigned to **$temp**.

There are improvements you could
make in this one area. You could also
validate that the image is of the right
size and type. To keep an already busy
script more manageable, I've omitted
that here, but see Chapter 11 for the
exact code to apply.

5. Move the file to its more permanent destination:

```
if (move_uploaded_file($_
→FILES['image']['tmp_name'],
→$temp)) {
  echo '<p>The file has been
→uploaded!</p>';
  $i = $_FILES['image']['name'];
```

At this point in the script, the print image will have been moved to its permanent location (the **uploads** directory) but given a temporary name (to be renamed later). A message is printed **F** indicating the success in doing so. Finally, the **$i** variable will be assigned the original name of the file (for use later on in the script).

The file has been uploaded!

The print has been added.

Add a Print

┌─Fill out the form to add a print to the catalog:─

F The result if a file was selected for the print's image and it was successfully uploaded.

Warning: move_uploaded_file(../../uploads/a0f60ad4ed629053d0bb7813e3beb127) [function.move-uploaded-file]: failed to open stream: No such file or directory in **/Users/larryullman/Sites/phpmysql4/ch19/admin/add_print.php** on line 33

Warning: move_uploaded_file() [function.move-uploaded-file]: Unable to move '/Applications/MAMP/tmp/php/phpnxNBhU' to '../../uploads/a0f60ad4ed629053d0bb7813e3beb127' in **/Users/larryullman/Sites/phpmysql4/ch19/admin/add_print.php** on line 33

Error!

The following error(s) occurred:
- The file could not be moved.
Please reselect the print image and try again.

G If the **uploads** directory is not writable by PHP, you'll see errors like these.

6. Complete the image-handling section:

```
} else {
  $errors[] = 'The file could
→not be moved.';
  $temp = $_FILES['image']
→['tmp_name'];
}
} else {
  $errors[] = 'No file was
→uploaded.';
  $temp = NULL;
}
```

The first **else** clause applies if the file could not be moved to the destination directory. This should only happen if the path to that directory is not correct or if the proper permissions haven't been set on the directory **G**. In either case, the **$temp** variable is assigned the value of the original upload, which is still residing in its temporary location. This is necessary, as unused files will be removed later in the script.

The second **else** clause applies if no file was uploaded. As the purpose of this site is to sell prints, it's rather important to actually display what's being sold. If you wanted, you could add to this error message more details or recommendations as to what type and size of file should be uploaded.

continues on next page

7. Validate the size, price, and description inputs:

```
$s = (!empty($_POST['size'])) ?
→ trim($_POST['size']) : NULL;
if (is_numeric($_POST['price']) &&
→ ($_POST['price'] > 0)) {
    $p = (float) $_POST['price'];
} else {
    $errors[] = 'Please enter the
    → print\'s price!';
}
$d = (!empty($_
→ POST['description'])) ? trim($_
→ POST['description']) : NULL;
```

The size and description values are optional, but the price is not. As a basic validity test, ensure that the submitted price is a number (it should be a decimal) using the **is_numeric( )** function, and that the price is greater than 0 (it'd be bad to sell products at negative prices). If the value is appropriate, it's typecast as a floating-point number just to be safe. An error message will be added to the array if no price or an invalid price is entered.

8. Validate the artist:

```
if ( isset($_POST['artist']) &&
→ filter_var($_POST['artist'],
→ FILTER_VALIDATE_INT, array('min_
→ range' => 1)) ) {
    $a = $_POST['artist'];
} else { // No artist selected.
    $errors[] = 'Please select the
    → print\'s artist!';
}
```

To enter the print's artist, the administrator will use a pull-down menu . The result will be a **$_POST['artist']** value that's a positive integer. Remember that if you're using an older version of PHP, that does not support the Filter extension, you'll need to use the **is_numeric( )** function, typecasting, and a conditional that checks for a value greater than 0 instead. See Chapter 13 for details.

9. Insert the record into the database:

```
if (empty($errors)) {
    $q = 'INSERT INTO prints
    → (artist_id, print_name, price,
    → size, description, image_
    → name) VALUES (?, ?, ?, ?, ?,
    → ?)';
    $stmt = mysqli_prepare($dbc, $q);
    mysqli_stmt_bind_param($stmt,
    → 'isdsss', $a, $pn, $p, $s, $d,
    → $i);
    mysqli_stmt_execute($stmt);
```

H The administrator can select an existing artist using this drop-down menu.

If the **$errors** array is still empty, then all of the validation tests were passed and the print can be added. Using prepared statements again, the query is something like **INSERT INTO prints (artist_id, print_name, price, size, description, image_name) VALUES (34, 'The Scream', 25.99, NULL, 'This classic…', 'scream.jpg')**.

The **mysqli_stmt_bind_param( )** function indicates that the query needs six inputs (one for each question mark) of the type: integer, string, double (aka float), string, string, and string. For questions on any of this, see Chapter 13.

10. Confirm the results of the query:

```
if (mysqli_stmt_affected_
→ rows($stmt) == 1) {
  echo '<p>The print has been
  → added.</p>';
  $id = mysqli_stmt_insert_
  → id($stmt);
  rename ($temp, "../../
  → uploads/$id");
  $_POST = array( );
} else {
  echo '<p style="font-weight:
  → bold; color: #C00">Your
  → submission could not be
  → processed due to a system
  → error.</p>';
}
```

If the query affected one row, then a message of success is printed in the Web browser ⒡. Next, the print ID has to be retrieved so that the associated image can be renamed (it currently

is in the **uploads** folder but under a temporary name), using the **rename( )** function. That function takes the file's current name as its first argument and the file's new name as its second. The value for the first argument was previously assigned to **$temp**. The value for the second argument is the path to the **uploads** directory, plus the print's ID value, just determined. Note that the file's new name will not contain a file extension. This may look strange when viewing the actual files on the server, but is not a problem when the files—the images—are served by the public side of the site, as you'll soon see.

Finally, the **$_POST** array is cleared so that its values are displayed in the sticky form.

If the query did not affect one row, there's probably some MySQL error happening and you'll need to apply the standard debugging techniques to figure out why.

11. Complete the conditionals:

```
    mysqli_stmt_close($stmt);
  } // End of $errors IF.
  if ( isset($temp) && file_exists
  → ($temp) && is_file($temp) ) {
    unlink ($temp);
  }
} // End of the submission IF.
```

The first closing brace terminates the check for **$errors** being empty. In this case, the file on the server should be deleted because it hasn't been permanently moved and renamed.

continues on next page

12. Print any errors:

```php
if ( !empty($errors) && is_
→ array($errors) ) {
  echo '<h1>Error!</h1>
  <p style="font-weight: bold;
  → color: #C00">The following
  → error(s) occurred:<br />';
  foreach ($errors as $msg) {
    echo " - $msg<br />\n";
  }
  echo 'Please reselect the print
  → image and try again.</p>';
}
?>
```

All of the errors that occurred would be in the **$errors** array. These can be printed using a **foreach** loop ❶. The errors are printed within some CSS to make them bold and red. Also, since a sticky form cannot recall a selected file, the user is reminded to reselect the print image. (My book *Effortless E-Commerce with PHP and MySQL* has an example script that does recall a previously uploaded file, but the code is somewhat tricky.)

13. Begin creating the HTML form:

```html
<h1>Add a Print</h1>
<form enctype="multipart/
→ form-data" action="add_print.
→ php" method="post">
  <input type="hidden" name="MAX_
  → FILE_SIZE" value="524288" />
  <fieldset><legend>Fill out
  → the form to add a print to
  → the catalog:</legend>
  <p><b>Print Name:</b> <input
  → type="text" name="print_
  → name" size="30" maxlength="60"
  → value="<?php if (isset($_
  → POST['print_name'])) echo
  → htmlspecialchars($_
  → POST['print_name']); ?>" /></p>
  <p><b>Image:</b> <input
  → type="file" name="image" /></
p>
```

Because this form will allow a user to upload a file, it must include the **enctype** in the **form** tag and the **MAX_FILE_SIZE** hidden input. The form will be sticky, thanks to the code in the **value** attribute of its inputs. Note that you cannot make a **file** input type sticky.

Error!

The following error(s) occurred:
- Please enter the print's name!
- No file was uploaded.
- Please enter the print's price!
- Please select the print's artist!
Please reselect the print image and try again.

Add a Print

┌─Fill out the form to add a print to the catalog:─

❶ An incompletely filled out form will generate several errors.

In case the print's name, size, or description uses potentially problematic characters, each is run through **htmlspecialchars( )**, so as not to mess up the value (e.g., the use of quotation marks in the print's size and description in ⓔ).

14. Begin the artist pull-down menu:

```
<p><b>Artist:</b>
<select
name="artist"><option>Select One</
→ option>
```

The artist pull-down menu will be dynamically generated from the records stored in the *artists* table using this PHP code ⓗ.

15. Retrieve every artist:

```
<?php
$q = "SELECT artist_id, CONCAT_
→ WS(' ', first_name, middle_name,
→ last_name) FROM artists ORDER BY
→ last_name, first_name ASC";
$r = mysqli_query ($dbc, $q);
if (mysqli_num_rows($r) > 0) {
  while ($row = mysqli_fetch_
→ array ($r, MYSQLI_NUM)) {
    echo "<option
→ value=\"$row[0]\"";
    // Check for stickyness:
    if (isset($_POST['existing'])
→ && ($_POST['existing'] ==
→ $row[0]) ) echo '
→ selected="selected"';
    echo ">$row[1]</option>\n";
  }
} else {
  echo '<option>Please add a new
→ artist first.</option>';
}
mysqli_close($dbc); // Close the
→ database connection.
?>
</select></p>
```

This query retrieves every artist's name and ID from the database (it doesn't use prepared statements, as there's really no need). The MySQL **CONCAT_WS( )** function—short for *concatenate with separator*—is used to retrieve the artist's entire name as one value. If you are confused by the query's syntax, run it in the mysql client or other interface to see the results.

If there are no existing artists in the database, there won't be any options for this pull-down menu, so an indication to add an artist would be made instead.

This otherwise-basic code is complicated by the desire to make the pull-down menu sticky. To make any **select** menu sticky, you have to add **selected="selected"** to the proper option. So the code in the **while** loop checks if **$_POST['existing']** is set and, if so, if its value is the same as the current artist ID being added to the menu.

16. Complete the HTML form:

```
<p><b>Price:</b> <input
→ type="text" name="price"
→ size="10" maxlength="10"
→ value="<?php if (isset($_
→ POST['price'])) echo $_
→ POST['price']; ?>" /> <small>Do
→ not include the dollar sign
→ or commas.</small></p>
<p><b>Size:</b> <input
→ type="text" name="size"
→ size="30" maxlength="60"
→ value="<?php if (isset($_
→ POST['size'])) echo
→ htmlspecialchars($_
→ POST['size']); ?>" />
→ (optional)</p>
```

continues on next page

```
<p><b>Description:</b>
→ <textarea name="description"
→ cols="40" rows="5"><?php if
→ (isset($_POST['description']))
→ echo $_POST['description'];
→ ?></textarea> (optional)</p>
</fieldset>
<div align="center"><input
→ type="submit" name="submit"
→ value="Submit" /></div>
</form>
```

Particulars about each form element, such as the description being optional or that the price should not contain a dollar sign **E**, help the administrator complete the form correctly.

17. Complete the HTML page:

```
</body>
</html>
```

18. Save the file as **add_print.php**.

19. Create the necessary directories on your server, if you have not already.

This administrative page will require the creation of two new directories. One, which I'll call **admin** (see **B**), will house the administrative files themselves. On a real site, it'd be better to name your administrative directory something less obvious.

The second, **uploads**, should be placed below the Web document directory and have its privileges changed so that PHP can move files into it. See Chapter 10 for more information on this.

20. Place **add_print.php** in your Web directory (in the administration folder) and test it in your Web browser.

```
1    <?php # Script 19.3 - header.html
2    // This page begins the session, the
     HTML page, and the layout table.
3
4    session_start(); // Start a session.
5    ?><!DOCTYPE html PUBLIC "-//W3C//DTD XHTML
     1.0 Transitional//EN"
6         "http://www.w3.org/TR/xhtml1/DTD/
          xhtml1-transitional.dtd">
7    <html xmlns="http://www.w3.org/1999/
     xhtml" xml:lang="en" lang="en">
8    <head>
9         <meta http-equiv="content-type"
          content="text/html; charset=utf-8" />
10        <title><?php echo (isset($page_title))
          ? $page_title : 'Welcome!'; ?></title>
11   </head>
12   <body>
13   <table cellspacing="0" cellpadding="0"
     border="0" align="center" width="600">
14        <tr>
15             <td align="center" colspan="3"><img
               src="images/title.jpg" width="600"
               height="61" border="0" alt="title"
               /></td>
16        </tr>
17        <tr>
18             <td><a href="index.php"><img
               src="images/home.jpg" width="200"
               height="39" border="0" alt="home
               page" /></a></td>
19             <td><a href="browse_prints.
               php"><img src="images/prints.jpg"
               width="200" height="39" border="0"
               alt="view the prints" /></a></td>
20             <td><a href="view_cart.php"><img
               src="images/cart.jpg" width="200"
               height="39" border="0" alt="view
               your cart" /></a></td>
21        </tr>
22        <tr>
23             <td align="left" colspan="3"
               bgcolor="#ffffcc"><br />
```

Creating the Public Template

Before getting to the heart of the public side, the requisite HTML header and footer files should be created. I'll whip through these quickly, since the techniques involved should be familiar territory by this point in the book.

To make header.html:

1. Begin a new PHP document in your text editor or IDE, to be named **header.html** (**Script 19.3**):

   `<?php # Script 19.3 - header.html`

2. Start the session:

   `session_start( );`

   It's very important that the user's session be maintained across every page, so the session will be started in the header file. If the session was lost on a single page, then a new session would begin on subsequent pages, and the user's history—the contents of the shopping cart—would be gone.

3. Create the HTML head:

   ```
   ?><!DOCTYPE html PUBLIC "-//W3C//
   → DTD XHTML 1.0 Transitional//EN"
   "http://www.w3.org/TR/xhtml1/DTD/
   → xhtml1-transitional.dtd">
   <html xmlns="http://www.w3.org/
   → 1999/xhtml" xml:lang="en"
   → lang="en">
   <head>
     <meta http-equiv="content-type"
   → content="text/html;
   charset=utf-8" />
     <title><?php echo (isset($page_
   → title)) ? $page_title :
   → 'Welcome!'; ?></title>
   </head>
   ```

   continues on next page

As with all the other versions of this script, the page's title will be set as a PHP variable and printed out within the **title** tags. In case it's not set before this page is included, a default title is also provided.

4. Create the top row of the table:

```
<body>
<table cellspacing="0"
→ cellpadding="0" border="0"
→ align="center" width="600">
  <tr>
    <td align="center"
    → colspan="3"><img src="images/
    → title.jpg" width="600"
    → height="61" border="0"
    → alt="title" /></td>
  </tr>
  <tr>
    <td><a href="index.php"><img
    → src="images/home.jpg"
width="200" height="39" border="0"
→ alt="home page" /></a></td>
    <td><a href="browse_prints.
    → php"><img src="images/
prints.jpg" width="200" height="39"
→ border="0" alt="view the prints"
→ /></a></td>
    <td><a href="view_cart.php">
    → <img src="images/cart.jpg"
    → width="200" height="39"
    → border="0" alt="view your
    → cart" /></a></td>
  </tr>
```

This layout will use images to create the links for the public pages **Ⓐ**.

5. Start the middle row:

```
<tr>
  <td align="left" colspan="3"
  → bgcolor="#ffffcc"><br />
```

All of each individual page's content will go in the middle row; the header file begins this row and the footer file will close it.

6. Save the file as **header.html** and place it in your Web directory (create an **includes** folder in which to store it).

Ⓐ The banner created by the header file.

Script 19.5 A minimal script for the site's home page.

```
1    <?php # Script 19.5 - index.php
2    // This is the main page for the site.
3
4    // Set the page title and include the
     HTML header:
5    $page_title = 'Make an Impression!';
6    include ('includes/header.html');
7    ?>
8
9    <p>Welcome to our site....please use the
     links above...blah, blah, blah.</p>
10   <p>Welcome to our site....please use the
     links above...blah, blah, blah.</p>
11
12   <?php include ('includes/footer.html');
     ?>
```

Script 19.4 The footer file closes the HTML, creating a copyright message in the process.

```
1    <!-- Script 19.4 - footer.html -->
2         <br /></td>
3       </tr>
4       <tr>
5         <td align="center" colspan="3"
     → bgcolor="#669966"><font
     → color="#ffffff">&copy;
     → Copyright...</font></td>
6       </tr>
7    </table>
8    </body>
9    </html>
```

To make footer.html:

1. Create a new HTML document in your text editor or IDE, to be named **footer. html** (Script 19.4):

   `<!-- Script 19.4 - footer.html -->`

2. Complete the middle row:

   ```
   <br /></td>
   </tr>
   ```

   This completes the table row begun in the header file.

3. Create the bottom row, complete the table, and complete the HTML **B**:

   ```
   <tr>
       <td align="center"
   → colspan="3" bgcolor=
   → "#669966"><font color=
   → "#ffffff">&copy;
   → Copyright...</font></td>
   </tr>
   </table>
   </body>
   </html>
   ```

4. Save the file as **footer.html** and place it in your Web directory (also in the **includes** folder).

To make index.php:

1. Begin a new PHP document in your text editor or IDE, to be named **index.php** (Script 19.5).

   ```
   <?php # Script 19.5 - index.php
   $page_title = 'Make an
   → Impression!';
   include ('includes/header.html');
   ?>
   ```

continues on next page

● Copyright...

B The copyright row created by the footer file.

2. Add the page's content:

```
<p>Welcome to our site....please
→use the links above...blah,
→blah, blah.</p>
<p>Welcome to our site....please
→use the links above...blah,
→blah, blah.</p>
```

Obviously a real e-commerce site would have some actual content on the main page. For example, you could easily display the most recently added prints here (see the second tip).

3. Complete the HTML page:

```
<?php include ('includes/footer.
→html'); ?>
```

4. Save the file as **index.php**, place it in your Web directory, and test it in your Web browser **C**.

TIP The images used in this example are available for download through the book's companion Web site (**www.LarryUllman. com**). You'll find them among all of the files in the complete set of downloadable scripts and SQL commands.

TIP You could easily show recently added items on the index page by adding a *date_ entered* column to the *prints* table and then retrieving a handful of products in descending order of *date_entered*.

C The public home page for the e-commerce site.

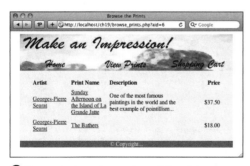

The Product Catalog

For customers to be able to purchase products, they'll need to view them first. To this end, two scripts will present the product catalog. The first, **browse_prints.php**, will display a list of the available prints **Ⓐ**. If a particular artist has been selected, only that artist's work will be shown **Ⓑ**; otherwise, every print will be listed.

The second script, **view_print.php**, will be used to display the information for a single print, including the image **Ⓒ**. On this page customers will find an *Add to Cart* link, so that the print may be added to the shopping cart. Because the print's image is stored outside of the Web root directory, **view_print.php** will use a separate script—nearly identical to **show_image. php** from Chapter 11—for the purpose of displaying the image.

Ⓐ The current product listing, created by **browse_prints.php**.

Ⓑ If a particular artist is selected (by clicking on the artist's name), the page displays works only by that artist.

Ⓒ The page that displays an individual product.

To make browse_prints.php:

1. Begin a new PHP document in your text editor or IDE, to be named **browse_prints.php** (Script 19.6):

   ```php
   <?php # Script 19.6 - browse_
   → prints.php
   $page_title = 'Browse the Prints';
   include ('includes/header.html');
   require ('../mysqli_connect.php');
   ```

2. Define the query for selecting every print:

   ```php
   $q = "SELECT artists.artist_id,
   → CONCAT_WS(' ', first_name,
   ```

→ middle_name, last_name) AS
→ artist, print_name, price,
→ description, print_id FROM
→ artists, prints WHERE artists.
→ artist_id = prints.artist_id
→ ORDER BY artists.last_name ASC,
→ prints.print_name ASC";

The query is a standard join across the *artists* and *prints* tables (to retrieve the artist name information with each print's information). The first time the page is viewed, every print by every artist will be returned **D**.

continues on page 636

D The results after running the main **browse_prints.php** query in the mysql client.

Script 19.6 The `browse_prints.php` script displays every print in the catalog or every print for a particular artist, depending upon the presence of `$_GET['aid']`.

```php
1   <?php # Script 19.6 - browse_prints.php
2   // This page displays the available prints (products).
3
4   // Set the page title and include the HTML header:
5   $page_title = 'Browse the Prints';
6   include ('includes/header.html');
7
8   require ('../mysqli_connect.php');
9
10  // Default query for this page:
11  $q = "SELECT artists.artist_id, CONCAT_WS(' ', first_name, middle_name, last_name) AS artist,
    print_name, price, description, print_id FROM artists, prints WHERE artists.artist_id = prints.
    artist_id ORDER BY artists.last_name ASC, prints.print_name ASC";
12
13  // Are we looking at a particular artist?
14  if (isset($_GET['aid']) && filter_var($_GET['aid'], FILTER_VALIDATE_INT, array('min_range' => 1))  ) {
15      // Overwrite the query:
16      $q = "SELECT artists.artist_id, CONCAT_WS(' ', first_name, middle_name, last_name) AS
        artist, print_name, price, description, print_id FROM artists, prints WHERE artists.artist_
        id=prints.artist_id AND prints.artist_id={$_GET['aid']} ORDER BY prints.print_name";
17  }
18
19  // Create the table head:
20  echo '<table border="0" width="90%" cellspacing="3" cellpadding="3" align="center">
21      <tr>
22          <td align="left" width="20%"><b>Artist</b></td>
23          <td align="left" width="20%"><b>Print Name</b></td>
24          <td align="left" width="40%"><b>Description</b></td>
25          <td align="right" width="20%"><b>Price</b></td>
26      </tr>';
27
28  // Display all the prints, linked to URLs:
29  $r = mysqli_query ($dbc, $q);
30  while ($row = mysqli_fetch_array ($r, MYSQLI_ASSOC)) {
31
32      // Display each record:
33      echo "\t<tr>
34          <td align=\"left\"><a href=\"browse_prints.php?aid={$row['artist_id']}\">{$row['artist']}
          </a></td>
35          <td align=\"left\"><a href=\"view_print.php?pid={$row['print_id']}\">{$row['print_name']}</td>
36          <td align=\"left\">{$row['description']}</td>
37          <td align=\"right\">\${$row['price']}</td>
38      </tr>\n";
39
40  } // End of while loop.
41
42  echo '</table>';
43  mysqli_close($dbc);
44  include ('includes/footer.html');
45  ?>
```

3. Overwrite the query if an artist ID was passed in the URL:

```php
if (isset($_GET['aid']) && filter_
→ var($_GET['aid'], FILTER_VALIDATE_
→ INT, array('min_range' => 1))  ) {
  $q = "SELECT artists.artist_id,
  → CONCAT_WS(' ', first_name,
  → middle_name, last_name) AS
  → artist, print_name, price,
  → description, print_id FROM
  → artists, prints WHERE artists.
  → artist_id=prints.artist_id
  → AND prints.artist_id={$_
  → GET['aid']} ORDER BY prints.
  → print_name";
}
```

If a user clicks an artist's name in the online catalog, the user will be returned back to this page, but now the URL will be, for example, *browse_prints. php?aid=6* Ⓑ. In that case, the query is redefined, adding the clause **AND prints.artist_id=X**, so just that artist's works are displayed (and the **ORDER BY** is slightly modified). Hence, the two different roles of this script—showing every print or just those for an individual artist—are handled by variations on the same query, while the rest of the script works the same in either case.

For security purposes, the Filter extension is used to validate the artist ID. If your version of PHP does not support the Filter extension, you'll need to use typecasting and make sure that the value is a positive integer prior to using it in a query.

4. Create the table head:

```php
echo '<table border="0"
→ width="90%" cellspacing="3"
→ cellpadding="3" align="center">
  <tr>
    <td align="left" width="20%">
    → <b>Artist</b></td>
    <td align="left" width="20%">
    → <b>Print Name</b></td>
    <td align="left" width="40%">
    → <b>Description</b></td>
    <td align="right" width="20%">
    → <b>Price</b></td>
  </tr>';
```

5. Display every returned record:

```php
$r = mysqli_query ($dbc, $q);
while ($row = mysqli_fetch_array
→ ($r, MYSQLI_ASSOC)) {
  echo "\t<tr>
    <td align=\"left\"><a href=\
    → "browse_prints.
php?aid={$row['artist_id']}\">
→ {$row['artist']}</a></td>
    <td align=\"left\"><a href=\
    → "view_print.php?pid={$row
    → ['print_id']}\">{$row['print_
    → name']}</td>
    <td align=\"left\">{$row
    → ['description']}</td>
    <td align=\"right\">\${$row
    → ['price']}</td>
  </tr>\n";
} // End of while loop.
```

The page should display the artist's full name, the print name, the description, and the price for each returned record. Further, the artist's name should be linked back to this page (with the artist's ID appended to the URL), and the print name should be linked to **view_print.php** (with the print ID appended to the URL **E**).

This code doesn't include a call to **mysqli_num_rows( )**, to confirm that some results were returned prior to fetching them, but you could add that in a live version, just to be safe.

6. Close the table, the database connection, and the HTML page:

```
echo '</table>';
mysqli_close($dbc);
include ('includes/footer.html');
?>
```

7. Save the file as **browse_prints.php**, place it in your Web directory, and test it in your Web browser (**A** and **B**).

TIP See the "Review and Pursue" section at the end of the chapter for many ways you could expand this particular script.

```
</tr>    <tr>
        <td align="left"><a href="browse_prints.php?aid=6">Georges-Pierre Seurat</a></td>
        <td align="left"><a href="view_print.php?pid=6">Sunday Afternoon on the Island of La Grande Jatte</td>
        <td align="left">One of the most famous paintings in the world and the best example of pointillism...</td>
        <td align="right">$37.50</td>
</tr>
<tr>
        <td align="left"><a href="browse_prints.php?aid=6">Georges-Pierre Seurat</a></td>
        <td align="left"><a href="view_print.php?pid=7">The Bathers</td>
        <td align="left"></td>
        <td align="right">$18.00</td>
</tr>
```

E The source code for the page reveals how the artist and print IDs are appended to the links.

To make view_print.php:

1. Begin a new PHP document in your text editor or IDE, to be named **view_print. php** (Script 19.7):

   ```php
   <?php # Script 19.7 - view_print.
   → php
   ```

2. Establish a flag variable:

   ```php
   $row = FALSE;
   ```

   The **$row** variable will be used to track whether or not a problem occurred on this page. This variable, if everything went right, will store the print information from the database. If a problem occurred, then, at the end of the script, **$row** will still be FALSE, and the page should indicate an error.

3. Validate that a print ID has been passed to this page:

   ```php
   if (isset($_GET['pid']) && filter_
   → var($_GET['pid'], FILTER_VALIDATE_
   → INT, array('min_range' => 1)) ) {
       $pid = $_GET['pid'];
   ```

   This script won't work if it does not receive a valid print ID. This conditional first checks that the page receives a print ID and then checks that the print ID is an integer greater than or equal to 1.

   For ease of reference later in the script, the value of **$_GET['pid']** is then assigned to **$pid**.

4. Retrieve the corresponding information from the database:

   ```php
   require ('../mysqli_connect.php');
   $q = "SELECT CONCAT_WS(' ', first_
   → name, middle_name, last_name)
   → AS artist, print_name, price,
   → description, size, image_name
   → FROM artists, prints WHERE
   → artists.artist_id=prints.artist_
   → id AND prints.print_id=$pid";
   $r = mysqli_query ($dbc, $q);
   ```

Script 19.7 The **view_print.php** script shows the details for a particular print. It also includes a link to add the product to the customer's shopping cart.

```php
1   <?php # Script 19.7 - view_print.php
2   // This page displays the details for a
    particular print.
3
4   $row = FALSE; // Assume nothing!
5
6   if (isset($_GET['pid']) && filter_
    var($_GET['pid'], FILTER_VALIDATE_INT,
    array('min_range' => 1)) ) { // Make
    |sure there's a print ID!
7
8       $pid = $_GET['pid'];
9
10      // Get the print info:
11      require ('../mysqli_connect.php'); //
        Connect to the database.
12      $q = "SELECT CONCAT_WS(' ', first_
        name, middle_name, last_name)
        AS artist, print_name, price,
        description, size, image_name FROM
        artists, prints WHERE artists.artist_
        id=prints.artist_id AND prints.
        print_id=$pid";
13      $r = mysqli_query ($dbc, $q);
14      if (mysqli_num_rows($r) == 1) { //
        Good to go!
15
16          // Fetch the information:
17          $row = mysqli_fetch_array ($r,
            MYSQLI_ASSOC);
18
19          // Start the HTML page:
20          $page_title = $row['print_name'];
21          include ('includes/header.html');
22
23          // Display a header:
24          echo "<div align=\"center\">
25          <b>{$row['print_name']}</b> by
26          {$row['artist']}<br />";
27
28          // Print the size or a default
            message:
29          echo (is_null($row['size'])) ? '(No
            size information available)' :
            $row['size'];
30
31          echo "<br />\${$row['price']}
```

code continues on next page

The query is a join like the one in **browse_prints.php**, but it selects only the information for a particular print **🅕**.

continues on next page

```
● ● ●          PHP and MySQL for Dynamic Web Sites: Visual QuickPro Guide
mysql> SELECT CONCAT_WS(' ', first_name, middle_name, last_name) AS artist, print_name, price, des
cription, size, image_name FROM artists, prints WHERE artists.artist_id=prints.artist_id AND print
s.print_id=6\G
*************************** 1. row ***************************
      artist: Georges-Pierre Seurat
  print_name: Sunday Afternoon on the Island of La Grande Jatte
       price: 37.50
 description: One of the most famous paintings in the world and the best example of pointillism...
        size: 40" x 30"
  image_name: C50741big.jpg
1 row in set (0.00 sec)

mysql> █
```

🅕 The result of running the **view_print.php** query in the mysql client.

Script 19.7 *continued*

```
32              <a href=\"add_cart.php?pid=$pid\">Add to Cart</a>
33              </div><br />";
34
35              // Get the image information and display the image:
36              if ($image = @getimagesize ("../uploads/$pid")) {
37                  echo "<div align=\"center\"><img src=\"show_image.php?image=$pid&name=" . urlencode
                    ($row['image_name']) . "\" $image[3] alt=\"{$row['print_name']}\" /></div>\n";
38              } else {
39                  echo "<div align=\"center\">No image available.</div>\n";
40              }
41
42              // Add the description or a default message:
43              echo '<p align="center">' . ((is_null($row['description'])) ? '(No description available)' :
                $row['description']) . '</p>';
44
45          } // End of the mysqli_num_rows() IF.
46
47          mysqli_close($dbc);
48
49      } // End of $_GET['pid'] IF.
50
51      if (!$row) { // Show an error message.
52          $page_title = 'Error';
53          include ('includes/header.html');
54          echo '<div align="center">This page has been accessed in error!</div>';
55      }
56
57      // Complete the page:
58      include ('includes/footer.html');
59      ?>
```

5. If a record was returned, retrieve the information, set the page title, and include the HTML header:

```php
if (mysqli_num_rows($r) == 1) {
    $row = mysqli_fetch_array ($r,
    → MYSQLI_ASSOC);
    $page_title = $row['print_name'];
    include ('includes/header.html');
```

The browser window's title will be the name of the print **G**.

6. Begin displaying the print information:

```php
echo "<div align=\"center\">
<b>{$row['print_name']}</b> by
{$row['artist']}<br />";
echo (is_null($row['size'])) ? '(No
→ size information available)' :
→ $row['size'];
echo "<br />\${$row['price']}
<a href=\"add_cart.php?pid=
→ $pid\">Add to Cart</a>
</div><br />";
```

The header for the print will be the print's name (in bold), followed by the artist's name, the size of the print, and its price. Finally, a link is displayed giving the customer the option of adding this print to the shopping cart **G**. The shopping cart link is to the **add_cart. php** script, passing it the print ID.

The Birth Of Venus by Sandro Botticelli
36" x 24"
$29.95 Add to Cart

G The print information and a link to buy it are displayed at the top of the page.

Because the print's size can have a **NULL** value, the ternary operator is used to print out either the size or a default message.

7. Display the image:

```php
if ($image = @getimagesize ("../
→ uploads/$pid")) {
    echo "<div align=\"center\"><img
    → src=\"show_image.php?image=
    → $pid&name=" . urlencode($row
    → ['image_name']) . "\" $image[3]
    → alt=\"{$row['print_name']}\" />
    → </div>\n";
} else {
    echo "<div align=\"center\">No
    → image available.</div>\n";
}
```

Because the images are being safely stored outside of the Web root directory, another PHP script is required to provide the image to the browser (the **show_image.php** script is being used as a *proxy script*). The name of the image itself is just the print ID, which was already passed to this page in the URL.

This section of the script will first attempt to retrieve the image's dimensions by using the **getimagesize( )** function. If it is successful in doing so, the image itself will be displayed. That process is a little unusual in that the source for the image calls the **show_ image.php** page **H**. The **show_image. php** script, to be written next, expects the print ID to be passed in the URL,

```
<b>The Birth Of Venus</b> by
Sandro Botticelli<br />36" x 24"<br />$29.95
<a href="add_cart.php?pid=1">Add to Cart</a>
</div><br /><div align="center"><img src="show_image.php?image=1&name=BirthOfVenus.jpeg" width="366" height="240" alt="The Birth
·">A nice print of Botticelli's classic "The Birth Of Venus." Blah, blah, blah.</p><!-- Script 19.4 - footer.html -->
```

H The HTML source of the **view_print.php** page shows how the **src** attribute of the **img** tag calls the **show_image.php** script, passing it the values it needs.

along with the image's filename (stored in the database when the print is added). This use of a PHP script to display an image is exactly like the use of **show_image.php** in Chapter 11, only now it's occurring within another page, not in its own window.

If the script could not retrieve the image information (because the image is not on the server or no image was uploaded), a message is displayed instead.

8. Display the description:

```
echo '<p align="center">' .
→ ((is_null($row['description']))
→ ? '(No description available)' :
→ $row['description']) . '</p>';
```

Finally, the print's description is added **I**. A default message will be created if no print description was stored in the database.

9. Complete the two main conditionals:

```
} // End of the mysqli_num_
→ rows( ) IF.
mysqli_close($dbc);
} // End of $_GET['pid'] IF.
```

10. If a problem occurred, display an error message:

```
if (!$row) {
  $page_title = 'Error';
  include ('includes/header.html');
  echo '<div align="center">This
  → page has been accessed in
  → error!</div>';
}
```

If the print's information could not be retrieved from the database for whatever reason, then **$row** is still false and an error should be displayed **J**. Because the HTML header would not have already been included if a problem occurred, it must be included here first.

11. Complete the page:

```
include ('includes/footer.html');
?>
```

12. Save the file as **view_print.php** and place it in your Web directory.

If you were to run this page in the browser at this point, no print image would be displayed as **show_image.php** has not yet been written.

continues on next page

A nice print of Botticelli's classic "The Birth Of Venus." Blah, blah, blah.

I The print's image followed by its description.

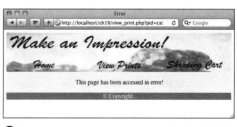

J The **view_print.php** page, should it not receive a valid print ID in the URL.

TIP Many e-commerce sites use an image for the *Add to Cart* link. To do so in this example, replace the text *Add to Cart* (within the `<a>` link tag) with the code for the image to be used. The important consideration is that the `add_cart.php` page still gets passed the product ID number.

TIP If you wanted to add *Add to Cart* links on a page that displays multiple products (like `browse_prints.php`), do exactly what's done here for individual products. Just make sure that each link passes the right print ID to the `add_cart.php` page.

TIP If you want to show the availability of a product, add an *in_stock* field to the *prints* table. Then display an *Add to Cart* link or *Product Currently Out of Stock* message according to the value from this column for that print.

To write show_image.php:

1. Begin a new PHP document in your text editor or IDE, to be named **show_image. php** (Script 19.8):

```
<?php # Script 19.8 - show_image.
→ php
$image = FALSE;
$name = (!empty($_GET['name'])) ?
→ $_GET['name'] : 'print image';
```

This script will do the same thing as **show_image.php** from Chapter 11, except that there are two values being passed to this page. The actual image's filename on the server will be a number, corresponding to the print ID. The original image's filename was stored in the database and will be used when sending the image to the Web browser. This page will not contain any HTML, and nothing can be sent to the Web browser prior to this opening PHP tag.

Two flag variables are initialized here. The first, **$image**, will refer to the physical image on the server. It's assumed to be false and needs to be

Script 19.8 This script is called by **view_print. php** (Script 19.7) and displays the image stored in the **uploads** directory.

```
1    <?php # Script 19.8 - show_image.php
2    // This pages retrieves and shows an
      image.
3
4    // Flag variables:
5    $image = FALSE;
6    $name = (!empty($_GET['name'])) ? $_
      GET['name'] : 'print image';
7
8    // Check for an image value in the URL:
9    if (isset($_GET['image']) && filter_
      var($_GET['image'], FILTER_VALIDATE_INT,
      array('min_range' => 1))  ) {
10
11       // Full image path:
12       $image = '../uploads/' . $_GET['image'];
13
14       // Check that the image exists and is
         a file:
15       if (!file_exists ($image) || (!is_
         file($image))) {
16          $image = FALSE;
17       }
18
19   } // End of $_GET['image'] IF.
20
21   // If there was a problem, use the
     default image:
22   if (!$image) {
23       $image = 'images/unavailable.png';
24       $name = 'unavailable.png';
25   }
26
27   // Get the image information:
28   $info = getimagesize($image);
29   $fs = filesize($image);
30
31   // Send the content information:
32   header ("Content-Type: {$info['mime']}\n");
33   header ("Content-Disposition: inline;
     filename=\"$name\"\n");
34   header ("Content-Length: $fs\n");
35
36   // Send the file:
37   readfile ($image);
```

proven otherwise. The **$name** variable, which will be the name of the file provided to the Web browser, should come from the URL. If not, a default value is assigned.

2. Check for an image value in the URL:

```
if (isset($_GET['image']) &&
→ filter_var($_GET['image'], FILTER_
→ VALIDATE_INT, array('min_range'
→ => 1))  ) {
```

Before continuing, ensure that the script received an image value, which should be part of the HTML **src** attribute for each print in **view_print.php** Ⓗ.

3. Check that the image exists as a file on the server:

```
$image = '../uploads/' .
→ $_GET['image'];
if (!file_exists ($image) ||
→ (!is_file($image))) {
    $image = FALSE;
}
```

As a security measure, the image's full path is hard-coded as a combination of *../uploads* and the received image name. You could also validate the MIME type (*image/jpg*, *image/gif*) of the file here, for extra security.

Next, the script checks that the image exists on the server and that it is a file (as opposed to a directory). If either condition is FALSE, then **$image** is set to FALSE, indicating a problem.

4. Complete the validation conditional and check for a problem:

```
} // End of $_GET['image'] IF.
if (!$image) {
    $image = 'images/unavailable.
    → png';
    $name = 'unavailable.png';
}
```

If the image doesn't exist, isn't a file, or if no image name was passed to this script, this condition will be TRUE. In such cases, a default image will be used. For that to happen, however, a fair amount of hacking on the user's part will have had to take place: the **view_print.php** script does some preliminary verification of the image, only calling **show_image.php** if it can access the image.

5. Retrieve the image information:

```
$info = getimagesize($image);
$fs = filesize($image);
```

To send the file to the Web browser, the script needs to know the file's type and size. This code is the same as in Chapter 11.

6. Send the file:

```
header ("Content-Type:
→ {$info['mime']}\n");
header ("Content-Disposition:
→ inline; filename=\"$name\"\n");
header ("Content-Length: $fs\n");
readfile ($image);
```

These **header( )** calls will send to the Web browser information about the file to follow, exactly as in Chapter 11. To revisit the overall syntax, the first line prepares the browser to receive the file, based upon the MIME type. The second line sets the name of the file being sent.

The last **header( )** function indicates how much data is to be expected. The file data itself is sent using the **readfile( )** function, which reads in a file and immediately sends the content to the Web browser.

continues on next page

7. Save the file as **show_image.php**, place it in your Web directory, and test it in your Web browser by viewing any print.

Notice that this page contains no HTML. It only sends an image file to the Web browser. As in Chapter 11, the closing PHP tag is omitted, to avoid potential problems.

TIP If the `view_print.php` page does not show the image for some reason, you'll need to debug the problem by running the `show_image.php` directly in your Web browser. View the HTML source of `view_print.php` and find the value of the `img` tag's `src` attribute. Then use this as your URL (in other words, go to `http://www.example.com/show_image.php?image=23&name=BirthOfVenus.jpeg`). If an error occurred, running `show_image.php` directly is the best way to find it.

Searching the Product Catalog

The structure of this database makes for a fairly easy search capability, should you desire to add it. As it stands, there are only three logical fields to use for search purposes: the print's name, its description, and the artist's last name. A **LIKE** query could be run on these fields using the following syntax:

```
SELECT…WHERE prints.description
→ LIKE'%keyword%' OR prints.print_
→ name LIKE '%keyword%' …
```

Another option would be to create an advanced search, wherein the user selects whether to search the artist's name or the print's name (similar to what the Internet Movie Database, **www.imdb.com**, does with people versus movie titles).

(index)	Quantity	Price
2	1	54.00
568	2	22.95
37	1	33.50

Script 19.9 This script adds products to the shopping cart by referencing the product (or print) ID and manipulating the session data.

```
1    <?php # Script 19.9 - add_cart.php
2    // This page adds prints to the shopping
     cart.
3
4    // Set the page title and include the
     HTML header:
5    $page_title = 'Add to Cart';
6    include ('includes/header.html');
7
8    if (isset ($_GET['pid']) && filter_
     var($_GET['pid'], FILTER_VALIDATE_INT,
     array('min_range' => 1))  ) { // Check
     for a print ID.
9        $pid = $_GET['pid'];
10
11       // Check if the cart already contains
         one of these prints;
12       // If so, increment the quantity:
13       if (isset($_SESSION['cart'][$pid])) {
14
15           $_SESSION['cart'][$pid]
             ['quantity']++; // Add another.
16
17           // Display a message:
18           echo '<p>Another copy of the print
             has been added to your shopping
             cart.</p>';
19
20       } else { // New product to the cart.
21
22           // Get the print's price from the
             database:
23           require ('../mysqli_connect.php');
             // Connect to the database.
24           $q = "SELECT price FROM prints
             WHERE print_id=$pid";
25           $r = mysqli_query ($dbc, $q);
```

code continues on next page

The Shopping Cart

Once you have created a product catalog, as the preceding pages do, the actual shopping cart itself can be surprisingly simple. The method I've chosen to use in this site is to record the product IDs, prices, and quantities in a session. Knowing these three things will allow scripts to calculate totals and do everything else required.

These next two examples will provide all the necessary functionality for the shopping cart. The first script, **add_cart. php**, is used to add items to the shopping cart. The second, **view_cart.php**, both displays the contents of the cart and allows the customer to update the cart.

Adding items

The **add_cart.php** script will take one argument—the ID of the print being purchased—and will use this information to update the cart. The cart itself is stored in a session, accessed through the **$_SESSION['cart']** variable. The cart will be a multidimensional array whose keys will be product IDs. The values of the array elements will themselves be arrays: one element for the quantity and another for the price (**Table 19.6**).

To create add_cart.php:

1. Begin a new PHP document in your text editor or IDE, to be named **add_cart. php** (Script 19.9):

   ```
   <?php # Script 19.9 - add_cart.php
   $page_title = 'Add to Cart';
   include ('includes/header.html');
   ```

   continues on next page

2. Check that a print ID was passed to this script:

```
if (isset ($_GET['pid']) &&
→ filter_var($_GET['pid'], FILTER_
→ VALIDATE_INT, array('min_range'
→ => 1))  ) {
  $pid = $_GET['pid'];
```

As with the **view_print.php** script, the script should not proceed if no, or a non-numeric, print ID has been received. If one has been received, then its value is assigned to **$pid**, to be used later in the script.

3. Determine if a copy of this print had already been added to the cart:

```
if (isset($_SESSION['cart'][$pid])) {
  $_SESSION['cart'][$pid]
  → ['quantity']++;
  echo '<p>Another copy of the
  → print has been added to your
  → shopping cart.</p>';
```

Before adding the current print to the shopping cart (by setting its quantity to 1), check if a copy is already in the cart. For example, if the customer selected print #519 and then decided to add another, the cart should now contain two copies of the print. The script therefore first checks if the cart has a value for the current print ID. If so, the quantity is incremented. The code **$_SESSION['cart'][$pid] ['quantity']++** is the same as

$_SESSION['cart'][$pid]['quantity'] → = $_SESSION['cart'][$pid] → ['quantity'] + 1.

Finally, a message is displayed Ⓐ.

Script 19.9 *continued*

```
26        if (mysqli_num_rows($r) == 1) { //
          Valid print ID.
27
28            // Fetch the information.
29            list($price) = mysqli_fetch_
              array ($r, MYSQLI_NUM);
30
31            // Add to the cart:
32            $_SESSION['cart'][$pid] = array
              ('quantity' => 1, 'price' =>
              $price);
33
34            // Display a message:
35            echo '<p>The print has been
              added to your shopping cart.</
              p>';
36
37        } else { // Not a valid print ID.
38            echo '<div align="center">This
              page has been accessed in
              error!</div>';
39        }
40
41        mysqli_close($dbc);
42
43    } // End of isset($_SESSION['cart']
      [$pid] conditional.
44
45 } else { // No print ID.
46    echo '<div align="center">This page
      has been accessed in error!</div>';
47 }
48
49 include ('includes/footer.html');
50 ?>
```

Ⓐ The result after clicking an *Add to Cart* link for an item that was already present in the shopping cart.

4. If the product is not already in the cart, retrieve its price from the database:

```
} else { // New product to the
→ cart.
  require ('../mysqli_connect.php');
  $q = "SELECT price FROM prints
→ WHERE print_id=$pid";
  $r = mysqli_query ($dbc, $q);
  if (mysqli_num_rows($r) == 1) {
    list($price) = mysqli_fetch_
→ array ($r, MYSQLI_NUM);
```

If the product is not currently in the cart, this **else** clause comes into play. Here, the print's price is retrieved from the database using the print ID.

5. Add the new product to the cart:

```
$_SESSION['cart'][$pid] = array
→ ('quantity' => 1, 'price' =>
→ $price);
echo '<p>The print has been added
→ to your shopping cart.</p>';
```

After retrieving the item's price, a new element is added to the **$_SESSION['cart']** multidimensional array. Since each element in **$_SESSION['cart']** is itself an array, use the **array( )** function to set the quantity and price. A simple message is then displayed **B**.

6. Complete the conditionals:

```
  } else { // Not a valid print
→ ID.
    echo '<div align="center">
→ This page has been
→ accessed in error!</div>';
  }
  mysqli_close($dbc);
} // End of isset($_SESSION
→ ['cart'][$pid] conditional.
} else { // No print ID.
  echo '<div align="center">This
→ page has been accessed in
→ error!</div>';
}
```

The first **else** applies if no price could be retrieved from the database, meaning that the submitted print ID is invalid. The second **else** applies if no print ID, or a non-numeric one, is received by this page. In both cases, an error message will be displayed **C**.

7. Include the HTML footer and complete the PHP page:

```
include ('includes/footer.html');
?>
```

8. Save the file as **add_cart.php**, place it in your Web directory, and test it in your Web browser (by clicking an *Add to Cart* link).

continues on next page

B The result after adding a new item to the shopping cart.

C The **add_cart.php** page will only add an item to the shopping cart if the page received a valid print ID in the URL.

Viewing the shopping cart

The **view_cart.php** script will be more complicated than **add_cart.php** because it serves two purposes. First, it will display the contents of the cart in detail **D**. Second, it will give the customer the option of updating the cart by changing the quantities of the items therein (or deleting an item by making its quantity 0). To fulfill both roles, the cart's contents will be displayed in a form that gets submitted back to this same page.

Finally, this page will link to a **checkout.php** script, intended as the first step in the checkout process.

To create view_cart.php:

1. Begin a new PHP document in your text editor or IDE, to be named **view_cart.php** (Script 19.10):

```php
<?php # Script 19.10 - view_cart.
→ php
$page_title = 'View Your Shopping
→ Cart';
include ('includes/header.html');
```

continues on page 650

D The shopping cart displayed as a form where the specific quantities can be changed.

Script 19.10 The **view_cart.php** script both displays the contents of the shopping cart and allows the user to update the cart's contents.

```php
1   <?php # Script 19.10 - view_cart.php
2   // This page displays the contents of
    the shopping cart.
3   // This page also lets the user update
    the contents of the cart.
4
5   // Set the page title and include the
    HTML header:
6   $page_title = 'View Your Shopping Cart';
7   include ('includes/header.html');
8
9   // Check if the form has been submitted
    (to update the cart):
10  if ($_SERVER['REQUEST_METHOD'] == 'POST')
    {
11
12      // Change any quantities:
13      foreach ($_POST['qty'] as $k => $v) {
14
15          // Must be integers!
16          $pid = (int) $k;
17          $qty = (int) $v;
18
19          if ( $qty == 0 ) { // Delete.
20              unset ($_SESSION['cart'][$pid]);
21          } elseif ( $qty > 0 ) { // Change
            quantity.
22              $_SESSION['cart'][$pid]
                ['quantity'] = $qty;
```

code continues on next page

```
23          }
24
25      } // End of FOREACH.
26
27  } // End of SUBMITTED IF.
28
29  // Display the cart if it's not empty...
30  if (!empty($_SESSION['cart'])) {
31
32      // Retrieve all of the information for the prints in the cart:
33      require ('../mysqli_connect.php'); // Connect to the database.
34      $q = "SELECT print_id, CONCAT_WS(' ', first_name, middle_name, last_name) AS artist, print_name
          FROM artists, prints WHERE artists.artist_id = prints.artist_id AND prints.print_id IN (";
35      foreach ($_SESSION['cart'] as $pid => $value) {
36          $q .= $pid . ',';
37      }
38      $q = substr($q, 0, -1) . ') ORDER BY artists.last_name ASC';
39      $r = mysqli_query ($dbc, $q);
40
41      // Create a form and a table:
42      echo '<form action="view_cart.php" method="post">
43      <table border="0" width="90%" cellspacing="3" cellpadding="3" align="center">
44      <tr>
45          <td align="left" width="30%"><b>Artist</b></td>
46          <td align="left" width="30%"><b>Print Name</b></td>
47          <td align="right" width="10%"><b>Price</b></td>
48          <td align="center" width="10%"><b>Qty</b></td>
49          <td align="right" width="10%"><b>Total Price</b></td>
50      </tr>
51      ';
52
53      // Print each item...
54      $total = 0; // Total cost of the order.
55      while ($row = mysqli_fetch_array ($r, MYSQLI_ASSOC)) {
56
57          // Calculate the total and sub-totals.
58          $subtotal = $_SESSION['cart'][$row['print_id']]['quantity'] * $_SESSION['cart'][$row['print_
          id']]['price'];
59          $total += $subtotal;
60
61          // Print the row:
62          echo "\t<tr>
63          <td align=\"left\">{$row['artist']}</td>
64          <td align=\"left\">{$row['print_name']}</td>
65          <td align=\"right\">\${$_SESSION['cart'][$row['print_id']]['price']}</td>
66          <td align=\"center\"><input type=\"text\" size=\"3\" name=\"qty[{$row['print_id']}]\"
          value=\"{$_SESSION['cart'][$row['print_id']]['quantity']}\" /></td>
67          <td align=\"right\">$" . number_format ($subtotal, 2) . "</td>
68          </tr>\n";
```

code continues on next page

2. Update the cart if the form has been submitted:

```php
if ($_SERVER['REQUEST_METHOD'] ==
→'POST') {
  foreach ($_POST['qty'] as $k =>
  →$v) {
    $pid = (int) $k;
    $qty = (int) $v;
    if ( $qty == 0 ) {
      unset ($_SESSION['cart']
      →[$pid]);
    } elseif ( $qty > 0 ) {
  $_SESSION['cart'][$pid]
  →['quantity'] = $qty;
    }
  } // End of FOREACH.
} // End of SUBMITTED IF.
```

If the form has been submitted, then the script needs to update the shopping cart to reflect the entered quantities. These quantities will come in the $_POST['qty'] array, whose index is the print ID and whose value is the new quantity (see **Ⓔ** for the HTML source code of the form). If the new quantity is 0, then that item should be removed

Script 19.10 *continued*

```php
69
70      } // End of the WHILE loop.
71
72      mysqli_close($dbc); // Close the
        database connection.
73
74      // Print the total, close the table,
        and the form:
75      echo '<tr>
76          <td colspan="4" align="right">
            <b>Total:</b></td>
77          <td align="right">$' . number_
            format ($total, 2) . '</td>
78      </tr>
79      </table>
80      <div align="center"><input
        type="submit" name="submit"
        value="Update My Cart" /></div>
81      </form><p align="center">Enter a
        quantity of 0 to remove an item.
82      <br /><br /><a href="checkout.
        php">Checkout</a></p>';
83
84      } else {
85      echo '<p>Your cart is currently
        empty.</p>';
86      }
87
88      include ('includes/footer.html');
89      ?>
```

```html
<tr>
<td align="left">Sandro Botticelli</td>
<td align="left">The Birth Of Venus</td>
<td align="right">$29.95</td>
<td align="center"><input type="text" size="3" name="qty[1]" value="1" /></td>
<td align="right">$29.95</td>
</tr>

<td align="left">Claude Monet</td>
<td align="left">Rouen Cathedral: Full Sunlight</td>
<td align="right">$39.50</td>
<td align="center"><input type="text" size="3" name="qty[4]" value="2" /></td>
<td align="right">$79.00</td>
</tr>

<td align="left">Georges-Pierre Seurat</td>
<td align="left">Sunday Afternoon on the Island of La Grande Jatte</td>
<td align="right">$37.50</td>
<td align="center"><input type="text" size="3" name="qty[6]" value="1" /></td>
<td align="right">$37.50</td>
</tr>
```

Ⓔ The HTML source code of the view shopping cart form shows how the quantity fields reflect both the product ID and the quantity of that print in the cart.

from the cart by unsetting it. If the new quantity is not 0 but is a positive number, then the cart is updated to reflect this.

If the quantity is not a number greater than or equal to 0, then no change will be made to the cart. This will prevent a user from entering a negative number, creating a negative balance due, and getting a refund!

Alternatively, you could use the Filter extension to validate the print ID and the quantity.

3. If the cart is not empty, create the query to display its contents:

```
if (!empty($_SESSION['cart'])) {
  require ('../mysqli_connect.php');
  $q = "SELECT print_id, CONCAT_
→WS(' ', first_name, middle_
→name, last_name) AS artist,
→print_name FROM artists,
→prints WHERE artists.artist_
→id = prints.artist_id AND
→prints.print_id IN (";
  foreach ($_SESSION['cart'] as
→$pid => $value) {
    $q .= $pid . ',';
  }
  $q = substr($q, 0, -1) . ')
→ORDER BY artists.last_name
→ASC';
  $r = mysqli_query ($dbc, $q);
```

The query is a **JOIN** similar to one used already in this chapter. It retrieves all the artist and print information for each print in the cart. One addition is the use of the **IN** SQL clause. Instead of just retrieving the information for one print (as in the **view_print.php** example), retrieve all the information for every print in the shopping cart. To do so, use

a list of print IDs in a query like **SELECT… print_id IN (519,42,427)…**. You can also use **SELECT… WHERE print_id=519 OR print_id=42 or print_id=427…**, but that's unnecessarily long-winded.

To generate the **IN (519,42,427)** part of the query, a **for** loop adds each print ID plus a comma to **$q**. To remove the last comma, the **substr( )** function is applied, chopping off the last character.

4. Begin the HTML form and create a table:

```
echo '<form action="view_cart.php"
→ method="post">
<table border="0" width="90%"
→cellspacing="3" cellpadding="3"
→align="center">
<tr>
  <td align="left" width="30%">
→ <b>Artist</b></td>
  <td align="left" width="30%">
→ <b>Print Name</b></td>
  <td align="right" width="10%">
→ <b>Price</b></td>
  <td align="center" width="10%">
→ <b>Qty</b></td>
  <td align="right" width="10%">
→ <b>Total Price</b></td>
</tr>
';
```

5. Retrieve the returned records:

```
$total = 0;
while ($row = mysqli_fetch_array
→($r, MYSQLI_ASSOC)) {
  $subtotal = $_SESSION['cart']
→[$row['print_id']]['quantity'] *
→ $_SESSION['cart'][$row['print_
→id']]['price'];
  $total += $subtotal;
```

continues on next page

When displaying the cart, the page should also calculate the order total, so a **$total** variable is initialized at 0 first. Then for each returned row (which represents one print), the price of that item is multiplied by the quantity to determine the subtotal (the syntax of this is a bit complex because of the multidimensional **$_SESSION['cart']** array). This subtotal is added to the **$total** variable.

6. Print the returned records:

```
echo "\t<tr>
<td align=\"left\">{$row['artist']}
→ </td>
<td align=\"left\">{$row['print_
→ name']}</td>
<td align=\"right\">\${$_SESSION
→ ['cart'][$row['print_id']]
→ ['price']}</td>
<td align=\"center\"><input type=\
→ "text\" size=\"3\" name=\"qty
→ [{$row['print_id']}]\" value=\"{$_
→ SESSION['cart'][$row['print_id']]
→ ['quantity']}\" /></td>
<td align=\"right\">$" . number_
→ format ($subtotal, 2) . "</td>
</tr>\n";
```

Each record is printed out as a row in the table, with the quantity displayed as a text input type whose value is preset (based upon the quantity value in the session). The subtotal amount (the quantity times the price) for each item is also formatted and printed.

7. Complete the **while** loop and close the database connection:

```
} // End of the WHILE loop.
mysqli_close($dbc);
```

8. Complete the table and the form:

```
echo '<tr>
  <td colspan="4" align="right">
  → <b>Total:</b></td>
  <td align="right">$' . number_
  → format ($total, 2) . '</td>
</tr>
</table>
<div align="center"><input
→ type="submit" name="submit"
→ value="Update My Cart" /></div>
</form><p align="center">Enter a
→ quantity of 0 to remove an item.
<br /><br /><a href="checkout.
→ php">Checkout</a></p>';
```

The order total is displayed in the final row of the table, using the **number_format( )** function for formatting. The form also provides instructions to the user on how to remove an item, and a link to the checkout page is included.

9. Finish the main conditional and the PHP page:

```
} else {
  echo '<p>Your cart is currently
  → empty.</p>';
}
include ('includes/footer.html');
?>
```

This **else** clause completes the **if (!empty($_SESSION['cart'])) {** conditional.

10. Save the file as **view_cart.php**, place it in your Web directory, and test it in your Web browser (**F** and **G**).

> **TIP** On more complex Web applications, I would be inclined to write a PHP page strictly for the purpose of displaying a cart's contents. Since several pages might want to display that, having that functionality in an includable file would make sense.

> **TIP** One aspect of a secure e-commerce application is watching how data is being sent and used. For example, it would be far less secure to place a product's price in the URL, where it could easily be changed.

F Changes made to any quantities update the shopping cart and order total after clicking *Update My Cart* (compare with **D**).

G Remove everything in the shopping cart by setting the quantities to 0.

Recording the Orders

After displaying all the products as a catalog, and after the user has filled the shopping cart, there are three final steps:

- Checking the user out
- Recording the order in the database
- Fulfilling the order

Ironically, the most important part—checking out (i.e., taking the customer's money)—could not be adequately demonstrated in a book, as it's so particular to each individual site. So what I've done instead is given an overview of that process in the sidebar. My book *Effortless E-Commerce with PHP and MySQL*, by contrast, specifically shows how to use two different payment gateways, but doing so requires two full chapters on their own.

Similarly, the act of fulfilling the order is beyond the scope of the book. For physical products, this means that the order will need to be packaged and shipped. Then the order in the database would be marked as shipped by indicating the shipping date. This concept shouldn't be too hard for you to implement, but you do also have to pay attention to managing the store's inventory. For virtual products, order fulfillment is a matter of providing the user with the digital content.

So those are some of the issues that cannot be well covered in this chapter; what I *can* properly demonstrate in this chapter is how the order information would be stored in the database. To ensure that the order is completely and correctly entered into both the *orders* and *order_contents* tables, the script will use *transactions*. This subject was introduced in Chapter 7, "Advanced MySQL," using the mysql client. Here the transactions will be

The Checkout Process

The checkout process involves three steps:

1. Confirmation of the order.
2. Confirmation and submission of the billing and shipping information.
3. Processing of the billing information.

Steps 1 and 2 should be easy enough for intermediate programmers to complete on their own by now. In all likelihood, most of the data in Step 2 would come from the *customers* table, after the user has registered and logged in.

Step 3 is the trickiest one and could not be adequately addressed in this book. The particulars of this step vary greatly, depending upon how the billing is being handled and by whom. To make it more complex, the laws are different depending upon whether the product being sold is to be shipped later or is immediately delivered (like access to a Web site or a downloadable file).

Most small- to medium-sized e-commerce sites use a third party to handle the financial transactions. Normally this involves sending the billing information, the order total, and a store number (a reference to the e-commerce site itself) to another Web site. That site will handle the actual billing process, debiting the customer and crediting the store. Then a result code will be sent back to the e-commerce site, which would be programmed to react accordingly. In such cases, the third party handling the billing will provide the developer with the appropriate code and instructions to interface with their system.

For more information, or assistance with, any of this, see my book *Effortless E-Commerce with PHP and MySQL* or turn to the supporting forums (**www.LarryUllman.com/forums/**).

```
1    <?php # Script 19.11 - checkout.php
2    // This page inserts the order
     information into the table.
3    // This page would come after the
     billing process.
4    // This page assumes that the billing
     process worked (the money has been
     taken).
5
6    // Set the page title and include the
     HTML header:
7    $page_title = 'Order Confirmation';
8    include ('includes/header.html');
9
10   // Assume that the customer is logged
     in and that this page has access to the
     customer's ID:
11   $cid = 1; // Temporary.
12
13   // Assume that this page receives the
     order total:
14   $total = 178.93; // Temporary.
15
16   require ('../mysqli_connect.php'); //
     Connect to the database.
17
18   // Turn autocommit off:
19   mysqli_autocommit($dbc, FALSE);
20
21   // Add the order to the orders table...
22   $q = "INSERT INTO orders (customer_id,
     total) VALUES ($cid, $total)";
23   $r = mysqli_query($dbc, $q);
24   if (mysqli_affected_rows($dbc) == 1) {
25
26       // Need the order ID:
27       $oid = mysqli_insert_id($dbc);
28
29       // Insert the specific order contents
         into the database...
30
31       // Prepare the query:
32       $q = "INSERT INTO order_contents
         (order_id, print_id, quantity, price)
         VALUES (?, ?, ?, ?)";
```

code continues on next page

performed through a PHP script. For added security and performance, this script will also make use of prepared statements, discussed in Chapter 13.

This script, **checkout.php**, represents the final step the customer would see in the e-commerce process. Because the steps that would precede this script have been skipped in this book, a little doctoring of the process is required.

To create checkout.php:

1. Begin a new PHP document in your text editor or IDE, to be named **checkout. php** (Script 19.11):

   ```
   <?php # Script 19.11 - checkout.php
   $page_title = 'Order Confirmation';
   include ('includes/header.html');
   ```

2. Create two temporary variables:

   ```
   $cid = 1;
   $total = 178.93;
   ```

   To enter the orders into the database, this page needs two additional pieces of information: the customer's identification number (which is the *customer_id* from the *customers* table) and the total of the order. The first would presumably be determined when the customer logged in (it would be stored in the session). The second value may also be stored in a session (after tax and shipping are factored in) or may be received by this page from the billing process. But as the script as written in this chapter does not have immediate access to either value (having skipped those steps), let's create these two variables to fake it.

   continues on next page

3. Include the database connection and turn off MySQL's autocommit mode:

```
require ('../mysqli_connect.php');
mysqli_autocommit($dbc, FALSE);
```

The `mysqli_autocommit( )` function can turn MySQL's *autocommit* feature on or off. Since *transactions* will be used to ensure that the entire order is entered properly, the autocommit behavior should be disabled first. If you have any questions about transactions, see Chapter 7 or the MySQL manual.

4. Add the order to the *orders* table:

```
$q = "INSERT INTO orders
→ (customer_id, total) VALUES
($cid, $total)";
$r = mysqli_query($dbc, $q);
if (mysqli_affected_rows($dbc) ==
→ 1) {
```

This query is very simple, entering only the customer's ID number and the total amount of the order into the *orders* table. The *order_date* field in the table will automatically be set to the current date and time, as it's a **TIMESTAMP** column.

5. Retrieve the order ID:

```
$oid = mysqli_insert_id($dbc);
```

The *order_id* value from the *orders* table is needed in the *order_contents* table to relate the two.

6. Prepare the query that inserts the order contents into the database:

```
$q = "INSERT INTO order_contents
→ (order_id, print_id, quantity,
→ price) VALUES (?, ?, ?, ?)";
$stmt = mysqli_prepare($dbc, $q);
mysqli_stmt_bind_param($stmt,
→ 'iiid', $oid, $pid, $qty, $price);
```

The query itself inserts four values into the *order_contents* table, where

Script 19.11 *continued*

```
33    $stmt = mysqli_prepare($dbc, $q);
34    mysqli_stmt_bind_param($stmt, 'iiid',
      $oid, $pid, $qty, $price);
35
36    // Execute each query; count the
      total affected:
37    $affected = 0;
38    foreach ($_SESSION['cart'] as $pid =>
      $item) {
39        $qty = $item['quantity'];
40        $price = $item['price'];
41        mysqli_stmt_execute($stmt);
42        $affected += $mysqli_stmt_
          affected_rows($stmt);
43    }
44
45    // Close this prepared statement:
46    mysqli_stmt_close($stmt);
47
48    // Report on the success....
49    if ($affected == count($_
      SESSION['cart'])) { // Whohoo!
50
51        // Commit the transaction:
52        mysqli_commit($dbc);
53
54        // Clear the cart:
55        unset($_SESSION['cart']);
56
57        // Message to the customer:
58        echo '<p>Thank you for your order.
          You will be notified when the
          items ship.</p>';
59
60        // Send emails and do whatever
      else.
61
62    } else { // Rollback and report the
      problem.
63
64        mysqli_rollback($dbc);
65
66        echo '<p>Your order could not be
          processed due to a system error.
          You will be contacted in order
          to have the problem fixed. We
          apologize for the inconvenience.</
          p>';
67        // Send the order information to
```

code continues on next page

there will be one record for each print purchased in this order. The query is defined, using placeholders for the values, and prepared. The **mysqli_stmt_bind_param( )** function associates four variables to the placeholders. Their types, in order, are: integer, integer, integer, double (aka float).

7. Run through the cart, inserting each print into the database:

```
$affected = 0;
foreach ($_SESSION['cart'] as $pid
→ => $item) {
  $qty = $item['quantity'];
  $price = $item['price'];
  mysqli_stmt_execute($stmt);
  $affected += mysqli_stmt_
  → affected_rows($stmt);
}
mysqli_stmt_close($stmt);
```

Script 19.11 *continued*

```
the administrator.
68
69     }
70
71   } else { // Rollback and report the
     problem.
72
73     mysqli_rollback($dbc);
74
75     echo '<p>Your order could not be
     processed due to a system error. You
     will be contacted in order to have
     the problem fixed. We apologize for
     the inconvenience.</p>';
76
77     // Send the order information to the
     administrator.
78
79   }
80
81   mysqli_close($dbc);
82
83   include ('includes/footer.html');
84   ?>
```

By looping through the shopping cart, as done in **view_cart.php**, the script can access each item, one at a time. To be clear about what's happening in this step: the query has already been *prepared*—sent to MySQL and parsed—and variables have been assigned to the placeholders. Within the loop, two new variables are assigned values that come from the session. Then, the **mysqli_stmt_execute( )** function is called, which executes the prepared statement, using the variable values at that moment. The **$oid** value will not change from iteration to iteration, but **$pid**, **$qty**, and **$price** will.

To confirm the success of all the queries, the number of affected rows must be tracked. A variable, **$affected**, is initialized to 0 outside of the loop. Within the loop, the number of affected rows is added to this variable after each execution of the prepared statement.

8. Report on the success of the transaction:

```
if ($affected == count($_SESSION
→ ['cart'])) {
  mysqli_commit($dbc);
  unset($_SESSION['cart']);
  echo '<p>Thank you for your
  → order. You will be notified
  → when the items ship.</p>';
```

The conditional checks to see if as many records were entered into the database as exist in the shopping cart. In short: did each product get inserted into the *order_contents* table? If so, then the transaction is complete and can be committed. Next, the shopping cart is emptied and the user is thanked. Logically you'd want to send a confirmation email to the customer here as well.

continues on next page

9. Handle any MySQL problems:

```
   } else {
     mysqli_rollback($dbc);
     echo '<p>Your order could
     → not be processed due to a
     → system error. You will be
     → contacted in order to have
     → the problem fixed. We
     → apologize for the
     → inconvenience.</p>';
   }
} else {
   mysqli_rollback($dbc);
   echo '<p>Your order could not be
   →  processed due to a
   → system error. You will be
   → contacted in order to have
   → the problem fixed. We
   → apologize for the
   → inconvenience.</p>';
}
```

The first **else** clause applies if the correct number of records were not inserted into the *order_contents* table. The second **else** clause applies if the original *orders* table query fails. In either case, the entire transaction should be undone, so the **mysqli_ rollback( )** function is called.

If a problem occurs at this point of the process, it's rather serious because the customer has been charged but no record of the order has made it into the database. This shouldn't happen, but just in case, you should write all the data to a text file and/or email all of it to the site's administrator or do *something* that will create a record of this order. If you don't, you'll have some very irate customers on your hands.

10. Complete the page:

```
mysqli_close($dbc);
include ('includes/footer.html');
?>
```

11. Save the file as **checkout.php**, place it in your Web directory, and test it in your Web browser **A**.

    You can access this page by clicking the link in **view_cart.php**.

12. Confirm that the order was properly stored by looking at the database using another interface **B**.

TIP On a live, working site, you should assign the $customer and $total variables real values for this script to work. You would also likely want to make sure that the cart isn't empty prior to trying to store the order in the database.

TIP If you'd like to learn more about e-commerce or see variations on this process, a quick search on the Web will turn up various examples and tutorials for making e-commerce applications with PHP, or check out my book *Effortless E-Commerce with PHP and MySQL*.

A The customer's order is now complete, after entering all of the data into the database.

B The order in the MySQL database, as viewed using the mysql client.

Review and Pursue

If you have any problems with the review questions or the pursue prompts, turn to the book's supporting forum (**www. LarryUllman.com/forums/**).

Note: Some of these questions and prompts rehash information covered earlier in the book, in order to reinforce some of the most important points.

Review

- What kind of storage engine in MySQL supports transactions?

- What types of indexes does MySQL support? What criteria go into deciding what columns should be indexed and what type of index is most appropriate?

- What is a Secure Sockets Layer (SSL)? Why is it important for e-commerce sites? Do you have SSL enabled for *your* Web site?

- Why isn't it problematic that the images for the prints are stored without file extensions?

- What steps should you take to debug problems in PHP scripts that interact with a MySQL database?

- What is a *multidimensional array*?

- What is meant by MySQL's *autocommit* feature?

- What does the `mysqli_insert_id()` function do?

- What does it mean to *commit* or *rollback* a transaction?

Pursue

- Expand the definition of the *artists* table to record other information about each artist. Also display this other information on the public side of the site.

- Add a *quantity_on_hand* column to the *prints* table. Add a form element to **add_print.php** so that the administrator can indicate how many copies of the product are initially in stock. On the public side, only offer an "Add to Cart" option for products that are available. When an item is sold (i.e., in **checkout. php**), reduce each product's quantity on hand by the number of copies sold.

- Expand the definition of the *customers* table to include other pertinent information.

- Create registration, login, and logout functionality for customers, using the information from Chapter 18, "Example—User Registration," as your basis.

- Create the ability for customers to view their accounts, change their passwords, view previous orders, etc.

- Create and use a template for the administrative side of the site.

- Using sessions, restrict access to the administrative side of the site to verified users.

- Apply the code from Chapter 11 to improve the security of **add_print. php**, so that it properly validates the uploaded file's type and size.

- Take the dynamically generated artists pull-down menu from **add_print.php** and use it as a navigational tool on the public side. To do so, set the form's **action** attribute to **browse_print.php**, change the **name** of the pull-down menu

continues on next page

to *aid*, use the GET method, and when users select an artist and click Submit, he or she will be taken to, for example, **browse_print.php?aid=5**.

- Apply *pagination* to **browse_prints. php**. See Chapter 10 for more on pagination.

- On **browse_prints.php**, add the option to affect how the prints are displayed by adding links to the column headings (e.g., to **browse_prints. php?order=price**). Then change the **ORDER BY** in the queries based upon the presence, and value, of **$_GET['order']**. Again, this idea was demonstrated in Chapter 9.

- Combine some of the functionality of **view_print.php** and **add_cart.php** so that the details of the print just added to the cart are also shown on **add_cart.php**.

- To show the contents of the cart on **add_cart.php**, add the applicable code from **view_cart.php** to the end of **add_cart.php**.

- Create the ability for the administrator to view the list of orders. Hint: the first page would function like **browse_prints. php**, except that it would perform a join across *orders* and *customers*. This page could display the order total, the order ID, the order date, and the customer's name. You could link the order ID to a **view_order.php** script, passing the order ID in the URL. That script would use the order ID to retrieve the details of the order from the *order_contents* table (joining *prints* and *artists* in the process).

- Add the ability to calculate tax and shipping for orders. Store these values in the *orders* table, too.

Index

Numbers

1NF (First Normal Form), 169–171
2NF (Second Normal Form), 172–174
3NF (Third Normal Form), 175–176
8-bit Unicode Transformation Format, 2

Symbols

-- operator, 23, 45
– operator, 23
! operator, 45
!= operator, 140
\\$ escape sequence, 29
% operator, 23
* operator, 23
. operator, 21, 26–27
/ operator, 23
@ error suppression operator, 250, 270
\\' escape sequence, 29
\\\\ escape sequence, 29
\\" escape sequence, 29
| operator, 140
|| operator, 45, 48, 140
+ operator, 23
++ operator, 23
‹ operator, 45
‹- operator, 45
< operator, 140
<= operator, 140
<> operator, 140
= operator, 14, 22, 25, 140
> operator, 45, 140
>- operator, 45
>= operator, 140
!- operator, 45
&& (and) operator, 45, 48, 56, 140
* (asterisk), using with **SELECT** queries, 138
`(backticks), use in SQL commands, 137
{ } (curly braces)
    using with arrays, 55, 57
    using with conditionals, 45, 48

$ (dollar sign), using with variables, 14
== (double equals sign) vs. = (equals sign), 47
" (double) quotation marks, using, 29–31
\\ (escape), using, 6
( ) (parentheses)
    using with clauses, 25
    using with functions, 8
(pound) symbol, using in comments, 10–11
; (semicolon)
    avoiding, 280
    using with statements, 6
' (single) quotation marks, using, 29–31
// (slashes), using in comments, 10–11
[] (square brackets)
    using with databases, 114
    using with functions, 104
_ (underscore), using with variables, 17

A

ABS( ) function, 157
absolute vs. relative paths, 76
access problems, debugging, 263
addition operator, symbol for, 23
AES_DECRYPT( ) function, 237
AES_ENCRYPT( ) function, 237, 239
Ajax. *See also* jQuery
    creating JavaScript, 485
    form, 481–482
    handling request, 484
    login_ajax.php script, 484
    login.php script, 481–482
    overview, 479–480
    performing request, 486–491
    server-side script, 483
aliases, 153, 155
ALTER command, 230
ALTER TABLE clauses, 222
ANALYZE command, 230
and (**&&**) operator, 45, 48, 56
and not (**XOR**) logical operator, 45, 48
AND operator, 45, 48, 156, 140

argument values, setting defaults, 101–104
arguments
empty strings, 104
FALSE value, 104
$name, 103
NULL value, 104
using with user-defined functions, 97–100
values, 104
arithmetic, precedence issue, 25
arithmetic operators
addition, 23
decrement, 23
division, 23
increment, 23
modulus, 23
multiplication, 23
subtraction, 23
array() function, using, 58
array values, printing during debugging, 261
array_map() function, 408
arrays
&& (and) operator, 56
{ } (curly braces), 55, 57
accessing, 58–59
arsort() function, 65, 68
$artists, 54
asort() function, 65, 68
associative, 54, 62
calendar.php document, 59–61
combining, 63
and conditionals, 56–57
$_COOKIE superglobal, 55
creating, 58
creating and accessing, 59–60
defined, 54
$_ENV superglobal, 55
examples, 54
foreach loop, 58–61, 63–64
$_GET superglobal, 55
$GLOBALS, 109
HTML table for sorting, 66
indexed, 54
indexing, 58
keys, 54, 57
key-value pairs, 54
ksort() function, 65, 67
of Mexican states, 62–64
multidimensional, 61–64
naming rules, 54
natsort() function, 68
$_POST superglobal, 55–56

printing, 55
printing after sorting, 67
randomizing order of, 68
referring to values in, 54
$_REQUEST superglobal, 55–56
returning from functions, 108
$_SERVER superglobal, 55
$_SESSION superglobal, 55
shuffle() function, 68
sort() function, 65
sorting, 65–68
of sphenic numbers, 61
$states, 54
and strings, 65
superglobals, 55–56
using, 56–57
using for pull-down menus, 59–60
using with loops, 70
usort() function, 68
arsort() function, using with arrays, 65, 68
asort() function, using with arrays, 65, 68
assignment operator (=), 140
example, 25
using for concatenation, 22
using with variables, 14
asterisk (*), using with **SELECT** queries, 138
AUTO_INCREMENT example, 135
autocommit nature, altering, 236
AVG() grouping function, 214–215, 217

B

backslash code, 29
backticks (`), use in SQL commands, 137
banking database
accounts table, 198
average account balance, 214
customers table, 197
transactions table, 199
BETWEEN operator, 140
blacklist validation, 409
blank page
displaying in error, 8
error, 258
books database, 176
Boolean **FULLTEXT** searches, performing, 227–229
Boolean mode operators, 227
boundaries, using with regular expressions, 444
browser
sending data to, 7–9
sending HTML to, 12
brute force attacks, preventing, 431

C

calculator.html page
  DOM manipulation, 474–478
  saving, 468
calculator.js page, saving, 472
calculator.php document
  changing echo statement, 107
  create_gallon_radio() function, 98
  creating, 86
  default argument values, 101–104
  Filter extension, 422–424
  formatting costs, 107
  $name argument, 103
  radio buttons, 98–103
  return statement, 108
  returning costs, 107
  rewriting for sticky form, 90–94
  saving, 90, 100
  saving for sticky form, 94
  script, 87, 92–93
  typecasting, 410–413
  user-defined function, 98–100
calendar.php document
  creating, 59
  loop examples, 70–71
  saving, 61
call to undefined function error, 97, 258
cannot redeclare function error, 258
CAPTCHA test, 408
carriage return code, 29
CASCADE action, using with foreign key
  constraints, 196
Cascading Style Sheets (CSS). See CSS
  (Cascading Style Sheets)
CASE() function, 219
ceil() function, 319
CEILING() function, 157
CHAR() function, 135
CHAR vs. VARCHAR, 117
character classes, using with regular expressions,
  443–445
character codes, replacing with values, 29
character sets
  assigning, 186–188
  collations, 184
  establishing for columns, 186
  explained, 184
  UTF-8, 188
  UTF-8 encoding, 185
characters, printing, 31
CHARSET command, 186

@charset "utf-8", using with CSS files, 5
cinema database, 172
clauses, grouping in parentheses, 25
COALESCE() function, 218
Codd, E.F., 166
collations
  assigning, 186–188
  establishing for columns, 186
  explained, 184
  specifying in queries, 188
  viewing, 185
column types, choosing for databases, 114–117
column values, applying functions to, 153
columns, using indexes on, 179
comma, concatenating to variables, 21
comments
  avoiding nesting, 13
  example, 15
  guidelines for, 13
  HTML, 10
  keeping up to date, 13
  multiline, 10, 12
  PHP, 10
  using at end of line, 13
  using to debug scripts, 259
  writing, 10–13
comments.php document
  creating, 11
  saving, 12
COMMIT command, using with queries, 233, 236
comparative operators
  -- (is equal to), 45
  < (less than), 45
  <- (less than or equal to), 45
  > (greater than), 45
  >- (greater than or equal to), 45
  !- (is not equal to), 45
comparison functions, 218
CONCAT() functions, 154–156
concatenating values, 22
concatenation
  assignment operator (=), 22
  defined, 21
  operator (.), 21
  using, 21–22
  using with numbers, 21
  using with strings, 21
concatenation operator (.)
  using, 21
  using with constants, 26–27
concat.php file, saving, 22

e-commerce *(continued)*
   order_contents table, 607, 610
   orders table, 607, 609
   prints table, 606, 608–609
   product catalog, 633–644
   public template, 629–632
   recording orders, 654–658
   security, 611
   shopping cart, 645–653
   show_image.php document, 642–644
   view_cart.php script, 648–653
   view_print.php document, 638–642, 644
edit_user.php script, 309–311
else conditional, 45
elseif conditional, 45
email, sending, 330–335
email.php script, 332–333
   array_map( ) function, 408
   preventing spam, 404
empty( ) function, using with forms, 49
empty variable value error, 258
encoding
   declaring for external CSS file, 5
   explained, 2
   indicating to Web browser, 2
   listing, 184
encrypting databases, 237–239. *See also* security methods
enctype, including with **form** tag, 342, 347
ENUM types, sorting on, 146
equals sign (=) vs. double equals sign (==), 47
ERD (entity-relationship diagram)
   example, 178
   explained, 169
error CSS class, defining, 51
error handlers, customizing, 253–257
error management
   die( ) function, 261
   exit( ) function, 261
error messages. *See also* debugging
   access-denied, 263
   call to undefined function error, 97
   column values in MySQL, 137
   deleting parent records, 195
   SHOW WARNINGS command, 137
   trusting, 33
   Undefined variable: variablename, 44
error reporting
   adjusting in PHP, 250–252
   levels, 250
   notices, 250
   warnings, 250

errors
   in book, 247
   display_errors, 248–249
   PHP, 248–249
   suppressing with @, 250
   syntactical, 242
   types of, 242–243
escape (\), 6
escape sequences, 29
exit( ) function, using in debugging, 261
EXPLAIN command, 231, 233
extensions, 4
external files. *See also* Web sites
   absolute paths, 76
   include( ) function, 76–77, 82
   referencing, 76
   relative paths, 76
   require( ) function, 76–77
   using, 78

F

fetch_object( ) method, 507
file extensions, 4
file not found error, receiving, 5
file uploads
   allowing for, 336–337
   configurations, 336
   $_FILES array, 342
   with PHP, 342–347
   preparing server, 338–341
   secure folder permissions, 337
   Unix **chmod** command, 341
Fileinfo extension, 415–416
files
   including multiple, 76–84
   validating by type, 414–417
$_FILES array, using with uploads, 342
filters, 421–424
   sanitation, 421
   validation, 421
Firefox, using for debugging, 246
First Normal Form (1NF), 169–171
first.php document
   creating, 3
   running in browser, 4
   saving, 4
   sending data to Web browser, 7
FLOOR( ) function, 157
FLUSH PRIVILEGES, using in debugging, 263
folder permissions, securing, 337
footer file, including in HTML form, 90

H

handle_form.php document
- for arrays, 56–57
- conditionals example, 46–48
- creating, 42
- saving, 43, 53
- using stripslashes() function in, 44
- validating form data, 49–53

HAVING clause, explained, 217

header() function, 356–361

header.html file
- for logout link, 386
- modifying, 266–267
- saving, 81, 266
- for session variables, 392

headers already sent error, 258

hidden form inputs, 304–308

home page, creating for message board, 537

HOUR() function, 159

.htaccess file, 337

HTML
- printing with PHP, 31
- resource for, 5
- sending to Web browser, 12

HTML attributes, double quoting, 94

HTML code, sending, 8

HTML errors, debugging, 246–247

.html extension, 3, 78

HTML for Web page script, 80

HTML forms. *See also* dynamic Web sites; forms; sticky forms
- age element, 42
- beginning, 89
- comments element, 42
- completing, 89
- creating, 37–40
- CSS (Cascading Style Sheets), 37
- echo statement, 43
- email element, 42
- encoding for form tag, 39
- footer file, 90
- form data variables, 42
- form tag, 36, 38
- gender element, 42
- gender radio button, 46
- GET method, 36
- GET request, 85
- handling, 42–44, 86–90
- .html extension, 39
- input types, 44
- method attribute, 36
- multidimensional arrays from, 64
- name element, 42

number_format() function, 88
performing calculations, 88
POST method, 36, 85
printing, 42
printing results, 88
printing values in, 42
pull-down menu, 39, 59–60
radio buttons, 39, 90
$_REQUEST[] variables, 42–43
sample script, 37–38
starting, 38
submit element, 42
submitting back to itself, 90
testing, 43
testing submission of, 85–86
text box for comments, 39
text inputs, 38
textarea element, 39
validating, 88
variables for form elements, 42

HTML source code
- altering spacing of, 9
- checking, 33

HTML table, creating to sort arrays, 66

HTML template script, 79

HTML5, development of, 3

HTML-embedded language, PHP as, 2

htmlentities() function, 418–420

.html extension, 39

htmlspecialchars() function, 418, 420

HTTP headers, 355–357

I

if conditional, 45

if-else conditional, 52

if-elseif-else conditional, 47

IFNULL() function, 221

images.php document. *See also* show_image.php script
- creating, 352
- date and time functions, 363–365
- script, 353–355

IN operator, 140

.inc file extension, 78

include() function
- vs. require() function, 84
- using, 76–77, 82

increment operator, symbol for, 23

index page, creating for message board, 537

indexes
- creating, 179–181
- FULLTEXT, 180
- PRIMARY KEY, 180

SET, 114–115
SHOW ENGINES command, 183
SMALLINT, 115
TEXT, 115
TIME, 115
TIMESTAMP, 115, 117
TINYBLOB, 117
TINYINT, 115, 117
TINYTEXT, 115
UPDATE, 117
VARBINARY, 117
VARCHAR, 115, 117
MySQL functions, support for, 267. *See also* functions
MySQL Workbench program, 169
`mysqli_connect.php` document
    creating, 268
    saving, 270
    script, 269
    security, 271
`mysqli_fetch_array()` constants, 281
`mysqli_num_rows()` function, 290–291
`mysqli_real_escape_string()` function, 286–289, 425

N

\n (newline) character
    escape sequence, meaning, 29, 31
    printing, 9
namespaces, support for, 496
`natsort()` function, using with arrays, 68
newline (\n) character, printing, 9
newline code, 29, 31
`nl2br()` function, 420
normalization
    1NF (First Normal Form), 169–171
    2NF (Second Normal Form), 172–174
    3NF (Third Normal Form), 175–176
    defined, 165
    development, 166
    forms, 169
    overruling, 176
    process, 166, 169
not (!) operator, 45
NOT BETWEEN operator, 140
NOT IN operator, 140
NOT LIKE keyword
    literal underscore, 144
    percentage, 144
    using, 143–144
NOT operator, 140
Notepad, avoiding use of, 3–4
notices, error reporting, 250

NOW() function, 135, 159
NULL type, explained, 45
NULL values vs. empty strings, 141
`number_format()` function, 23, 25, 88
numbers
    arithmetic operators, 23
    functions for, 23
    quoting, 23
    sphenic, 61
    using, 24–25
    using typecasting with, 413
    using variables with, 24
`numbers.php` document
    creating, 24
    quotation marks examples, 29–31
    saving, 25
number-type variables, examples, 23
numeric functions, 157–158

O

one-to-many relationship, 168
one-to-one relationship, 168
OOP (Object-Oriented Programming). *See also* programming techniques
    classes, 496
    DateTime class, 511–517
    executing queries, 501–504
    `fetch_object()` method, 507
    fetching results, 505–507
    fundamentals, 494–495
    MySQL connection, 497–500
    outbound parameters, 510
    prepared statements, 508–510
    vs. procedural, 494
    syntax in PHP, 495–496
operating system (OS) constant, 26
operators
    comparative, 45
    exclusive or, 48
    logical, 45
    ternary, 317
OPTIMIZE command, 230
or (||) operator, 45, 48
OR operator, 45, 48, 140
ORDER BY clause
    alias in, 155
    using with indexes, 180
ORDER BY clause, using with queries, 145–146
OS (operating system) constant, 26
outbound parameters, 510
outer joins, 208–211
output buffering, 561

P

pagination, explained, 316
parameters. *See* arguments
parentheses (( ))
    using with clauses, 25
    using with functions, 8
parse error, 258
    for arrays, 55
    receiving, 8
password, validating, 277
password.php script, 292–297
paths, absolute vs. relative, 76
patterns
    back references, 455
    defining for regular expressions, 438–440
    matching, 452–455
    meta-characters, 438
    modifiers, 450
    replacing, 452–455
pcre.php script
    character classes, 444–445
    matching patterns, 435
    quantifiers, 441–442
    reporting matches, 446–449
    using patterns, 439–440
PHP
    adjusting error reporting, 250–252
    debugging technique, 258–261
    namespaces, 496
    OOP syntax in, 495–496
    updating records with, 292–297
PHP and JavaScript, 348
PHP code
    executing, 5
    objects in, 500
    placing in PHP tags, 3
PHP errors
    blank page, 258
    call to undefined function, 258
    cannot redeclare function, 258
    displaying, 248–249
    empty variable value, 258
    headers already sent, 258
    logging, 257
    parse error, 258
    undefined variable, 258
.php extension
    using, 3, 78
    using with connection scripts, 271
PHP files, including extensions with, 3
PHP functions, using with MySQL, 267. *See also* functions
PHP **mail()** dependencies, 330

PHP manual, accessing, 22
PHP pages, storing data sent to, 44
PHP scripts. *See also* scripts
    debugging, 5, 8, 33, 259–261
    for JavaScript, 352–354
    making, 3–5
    running through URLs, 7, 33
    sending values to, 300–303
    writing, 3
PHP tags, 4
PHP_OS constant
    explained, 26
    using, 27
PHP_VERSION constant
    explained, 26
    using, 27, 33
phpinfo() function
    using, 33
    using for debugging, 245
php.ini configuration file, **include_path**
    setting, 84
phpMyAdmin
    INSERT form, 137
    INSERT tab, 137
    SELECT queries, 139
    sitename database, 132
    updating records, 150
    using, 124–127
"Plain and Simple" template, 78
POST method, using with HTML forms, 85
$_POST variable vs. variable scope, 109
post_message.php script, 427–431, 508–510
pound (#) symbol, using in comments, 10–11
POW() function, 157
precedence, explained, 25
predefined.php document
    creating, 15
    saving, 17
preg_match() function, using with regular
    expressions, 446–447
preg_replace() function, 452–454
prepared statements
    in OOP, 508–510
    performance, 425
    using, 427–431
primary key, assigning, 167
PRIMARY KEY index, adding, 180–181
print language construct
    sending HTML code to browser, 8
    using, 6–7
    using over multiple lines, 9
    using to debug scripts, 260
print_r() function, 500

T

\t escape sequence, meaning, 29
tab code, 29
table types
 confirming, 223
 establishing, 183
 finding, 183
 MyISAM, 182
 storage engine, 182
 using, 182
tables. *See* database tables
template system
 creating, 77–78
 header file, 266–267
 `index.php` page, 83
ternary operator, structure of, 317
text
 converting, 188
 formatting, 155–156
text box for comments, adding to HTML form, 39
text editor, 3
text functions, 154–156
textarea element
 adding to HTML form, 39
 presetting value in sticky forms, 91
Third Normal Form (3NF), 175–176
thread page, creating for message board,
 543–547
`Thumbs.db` file, 354
time. *See* date and time
time zones, changing, 190
transactions
 creating savepoints in, 236
 performing, 234–236
triggers vs. constraints, 201
`TRIM( )` function, 154
`TRUNCATE` command, 297
`TRUNCATE TABLE` command, 151
`.txt` extension, avoiding use of, 4
type validation functions, 409
typecasting, 410–413

U

`ucfirst( )` function, 22
`ucwords( )` function, 22
undefined variable error, 258
Undefined variable: variablename error, 44
underscore (_), using with variables, 17
`UNIQUE` indexes, adding, 180
Unix `chmod` command, using for file uploads, 341
`UNIX_TIMESTAMP( )` functions, 159
`UPDATE` query, running, 292–297

`UPDATE` syntax, 149–150
`upload_image.php` document, 343–345
`upload_rtf.php` script, 415–417
`UPPER( )` function, 153–154
URLs
 appending variables to, 303
 using with PHP scripts, 5, 7, 33
user information, printing, 16
user registration
 account activation, 586–588
 activation page, 586–588
 activation process, 583
 `change_password.php` script, 599–603
 configuration scripts, 566–573
 database connection, 571–573
 database scheme, 573
 database script, 570
 `footer.html` file, 563–565
 `forgot_password.php` script, 594–599
 `header.html` file, 560–562
 home page, 574–575
 `index.php` script, 574–575
 `login.php` script, 589–592
 `logout.php` script, 593
 output buffering, 561
 password management, 594–603
 `register.php` script, 576–585
 site administration, 602
 templates, 560–565
user-defined functions. *See also* functions
 calculation script, 105–107
 calling after creating, 97
 case insensitivity, 95
 `create_ad( )`, 97
 creating, 95–97
 default argument values, 101–104
 memory usage, 97
 naming, 95
 `return` statement, 105
 returning values from, 105–108
 taking arguments, 97–100
 variable scope, 109
users table
 creating, 187
 finding records in, 319
`usort( )` function, using with arrays, 68
UTC (Coordinated Universal Time)
 explained, 189
 using, 191–194
UTC Offsets table, 189
`UTC_TIMESTAMP( )` functions, 159
UTF-8 characters, increasing column size for, 188
UTF-8 encoding, 2, 185, 191

V

validating files by type, 414–417
validation
  blacklist, 409
  typecasting, 410–413
  whitelist, 409
validation errors, reporting forms, 279
validation filters, 421
validation tools, using for debugging, 246
$var, removing backslashes from, 44
VARCHAR vs. **CHAR**, 117
variable names, replacing, 29
variable scope
  altering, 109
  circumventing, 109
  global statement, 109
  superglobal alternative, 109
variables. *See also* strings
  adding to function definitions, 97
  appending to URLs, 303
  arrays, 14
  assigning values to, 14, 20
  assignment operator (=), 14
  Boolean, 14
  case sensitivity, 14
  confirming values of, 44
  vs. constants, 26
  defined, 14
  floating point, 14
  including underscore, 17
  integer, 14
  naming, 14, 17
  nonscalar, 14
  NULL, 14
  objects, 14
  omitting spaces, 17
  preceding with **$** (dollar sign), 14
  predefined, 14
  printing, 14–15
  printing values of, 31
  scalar, 14
  shorthand version, 16
  strings, 14
  superglobal, 44
  syntactical rules, 14
  tracking during debugging, 260
  treatment of, 17
  typecasting, 410
  using, 15–17
  using with numbers, 24
  using with strings, 19
version of PHP constant, 26, 33

view_users.php script, 282–283, 300–302
  modifying, 290–291
  OOP example, 506–507
  paginating, 316–322
  sortable displays, 323–325

W

warnings, error reporting, 250
Web applications
  date and time functions, 362–365
  file uploads, 336–338
  file uploads with PHP, 342–347
  HTTP headers, 355–361
  PHP and JavaScript, 348–354
  preparing servers for uploads, 338–341
  sending email, 330–335
Web browser
  sending data to, 7–9
  sending HTML to, 12
Web pages, altering spacing in, 9
Web sites, dynamic vs. static, 75. *See also*
  dynamic Web sites
WHEN...THEN clauses, 219
WHERE clause, 140–141
  using with indexes, 180
  using with **UPDATE**, 150
while loop. *See also* loops
  example, 69
  functionality, 70
white space, areas of, 9
whitelist validation, 409
wildcards, using with **LIKE** and **NOT LIKE**, 144
WITH QUERY EXPANSION modifier, 229
wordwrap( ) function, 333
www.query.com, loading, 461

X

XHTML, resource for, 5
XHTML 1.0 Transitional document, 2
XML-style tags, 4
XOR (and not) operator, 45, 48, 140
XSS attacks, preventing, 418–420
xss.php script, 419

Y

YEAR( ) function, 159

Z

Z (Zulu) time
  explained, 189
  using, 191–194